Fourth Workshop on Neural Generation and Translation 2020

Online
5 - 10 July 2020

ISBN: 978-1-7138-1381-1

ACL 2020

Neural Generation and Translation

Proceedings of the Fourth Workshop

July 5 - 10, 2020 Online (due to COVID-19 pandemic)

Introduction

Welcome to the Fourth Workshop on Neural Generation and Translation. This workshop aims to cultivate research on the leading edge in neural machine translation and other aspects of machine translation, generation, and multilinguality that utilize neural models. We received a total of 28 submissions in total. From the 21 long papers we accepted 16. There were two cross-submissions, three extended abstracts. All research papers were reviewed twice through a double blind review process, and avoiding conflicts of interest. The topics of the papers were split equally between the natural language generation and machine translation themes. We would like to thank all authors for their submissions, and the program committee members for their valuable efforts in reviewing the papers for the workshop.

Organizers:

Alexandra Birch, (Edinburgh)
Andrew Finch, (Apple)
Hiroaki Hayashi (CMU)
Kenneth Heafield (Edinburgh)
Marcin Junczys-Dowmunt (Microsoft)
Ioannis Konstas (Heriot Watt University)
Xian Li (Facebook)
Graham Neubig, (CMU)
Yusuke Oda, (Google)

Program Committee:

Roee Aharoni	Martin Andrews
Duygu Ataman	Joost Bastings
Alexandre Berard	Klinton Bicknell
Nikolay Bogoychev	Chris Brockett
Chris Brust	Daniel Cer
Boxing Chen	David Chiang
Nathan Dalal	Michael Denkowski
Li Dong	Kevin Duh
Ondřej Dušek	Marc Dymetman
Elozino Egonmwan	Andrew Finch
Markus Freitag	Claire Gardent
Kevin Gimpel	Isao Goto
Roman Grundkiewicz	Jiatao Gu
Felix Hieber	Hieu Hoang
Sébastien Jean	Mihir Kale
Yuta Kikuchi	Philipp Koehn
Ioannis Konstas	Shumpei Kubosawa
Sneha Kudugunta	Lemao Liu
Hongyin Luo	Benjamin Marie
Bill McDowell	Hideya Mino
Will Monroe	Makoto Morishita
Vivek Natarajan	Yusuke Oda
Vinay Rao	Andrew Runge
Chinnadhurai Sankar	Jean Senellart
Rico Sennrich	Alessandro Suglia
Simeng Sun	Alexey Tikonov
Yulia Tsvetkov	Ivan Vulić
Rui Wang	Xiaolin Wang
Taro Watanabe	Ruiyi Zhang
Biao Zhang	

Invited Speakers:

He He
Jiatao Gu
Shashi Narayan
Claire Gardent

Table of Contents

Workshop Program

Findings of the Fourth Workshop on Neural Generation and Translation

Kenneth Heafield♠, Hiroaki Hayashi♢, Yusuke Oda♣, Ioannis Konstas△,
Andrew Finch♡, Graham Neubig♢, Xian Li⋆, Alexandra Birch♠

♢Carnegie Mellon University, ♣Google Research, ♠University of Edinburgh
△Heriot-Watt University, ♡Apple, ⋆Facebook

Abstract

We describe the finding of the Fourth Workshop on Neural Generation and Translation, held in concert with the annual conference of the Association for Computational Linguistics (ACL 2020). First, we summarize the research trends of papers presented in the proceedings. Second, we describe the results of the three shared tasks 1) efficient neural machine translation (NMT) where participants were tasked with creating NMT systems that are both accurate and efficient, and 2) document-level generation and translation (DGT) where participants were tasked with developing systems that generate summaries from structured data, potentially with assistance from text in another language and 3) STAPLE task: creation of as many possible translations of a given input text. This last shared task was organised by Duolingo.

1 Introduction

Neural sequence to sequence models (Kalchbrenner and Blunsom, 2013; Sutskever et al., 2014; Bahdanau et al., 2015) are the workhorse behind a wide variety of different natural language processing tasks such as machine translation, generation, summarization and simplification. The 4th Workshop on Neural Machine Translation and Generation (WNGT 2020) provided a forum for research in applications of neural models to machine translation and other language generation tasks (including summarization, NLG from structured data, dialog response generation, among others). Overall, the workshop was held with two goals. First, it aimed to synthesize the current state of knowledge in neural machine translation and generation: this year we continued to encourage submissions that not only advance the state of the art through algorithmic advances, but also analyze and understand the current state of the art, pointing to future research directions. Towards this goal, we received a number of high-quality research contributions on the workshop topics, as summarized in Section 2. Second, the workshop aimed to expand the research horizons in NMT: we continued to organize the Efficient NMT task which encouraged participants to develop not only accurate but computationally efficient systems. This task had three participants each with a number of individual systems. We organized the second shared task on "Document-level Generation and Translation", which aims to push forward document-level generation technology and contrast the methods for different types of inputs. Unfortunately this task only had one participant. Finally, we introduced a new shared task, organised by Duolingo, which encouraged models to produce as many correct translations as possible for a given input. This task generated a lot of interest and there were 11 participants. The results of the shared task are summarized in Sections 3, 4 and 5.

2 Summary of Research Contributions

Similar to last year we invited the MT and NLG community to contribute to the workshop with long papers, extended abstracts for preliminary work, and cross-submissions of papers that have appeared in other venues. Keeping up with with the main vision of the workshop, we were aiming for a variety of works at the intersection of Machine Translation and Language Generation tasks.

We received a total of 28 submissions, from which we accepted 16. There were 2 cross-submissions, 3 extended abstracts and 11 full papers. There were also 15 system submission papers. We elicted two double-blind reviews for each submission, avoiding conflicts of interest.

With regards to thematology there were 8 papers with a focus on Natural Language Generation and 8 with the application of Machine Translation

1

Proceedings of the 4th Workshop on Neural Generation and Translation (WNGT 2020), pages 1–9
Online, July 10, 2020. ©2020 Association for Computational Linguistics
www.aclweb.org/anthology/D19-56%2d

in mind. The underlying emphasis across submissions was placed this year on capitalizing on the use of pre-training models (e.g., BERT; (Devlin et al., 2019) especially for low-resource datasets. The quality of the accepted publications was very high; there was a significant drop in numbers though in comparison to last year (36 accepted papers from 68 submissions) which is most likely due to the extra overhead on conducting research under lockdown policies sanctioned globally due to COVID-19 pandemic.

3 Efficiency Task

The efficiency task complements machine translation quality evaluation campaigns by also measuring and optimizing the computational cost of inference. This is the third edition of the task, updating and building upon the second edition of the task (Hayashi et al., 2019).

We asked participants to build English→German machine translation systems following the data condition of the 2019 Workshop on Machine Translation (Barrault et al., 2019) and submit them as Docker containers. Docker contains enabled consistent measurement of computational cost on several dimensions: time, memory, and disk space. These are measured under three hardware conditions: a GPU, a single CPU core, and multi-core CPU on all cores. Participants were free to choose what metrics and hardware platforms to optimize for.

Three teams submitted to the shared task: Niu-Trans, OpenNMT, and UEdin. All teams submitted to the GPU and multi-core CPU tracks; Open-NMT and UEdin submitted to the single-CPU track. Some CPU submissions from UEdin had a memory leak; their post-deadline fix is shown as "UEdin Fix."

Common techniques across teams were variations on the transformer architecture, model distillation, 16-bit floating point inference on GPUs (except OpenNMT), and 8-bit integer inference on CPUs (except NiuTrans). Curiously, all submissions used autoregressive models despite the existence of non-autoregressive models motivated by speed.

3.1 Hardware

The GPU track used a `g4dn.xlarge` instance with one NVIDIA T4 GPU, 16 GB GPU RAM, 16 GB host RAM, and 2 physical cores of an Intel Xeon Platinum 8259CL CPU. The NVIDIA T4

GPU is relatively small compared to the NVIDIA V100 GPU, but the newer Turing architecture introduces support for 4-bit and 8-bit integer operations in Tensor Cores. In practice, however, participants used floating-point operations on the GPU even though both OpenNMT and UEdin used 8-bit integers in their CPU submissions. This was primarily due to code readiness. Timing was run on a non-exclusive virtual machine because the instance is not yet available without virtualization.

The CPU tracks used a `c5.metal` instance which has two sockets of the Intel Xeon Platinum 8275CL CPU, 48 physical cores, hyperthreading enabled, and 192 GB RAM. As a Cascade Lake processor, it supports the Vector Neural Network Instructions (VNNI) that OpenNMT and UEdin used for 8-bit integer matrix multiplication. For the single core track, we reserved the entire machine then ran Docker with `--cpuset-cpus=0`. For the multi-core track, participants were free to configure their own CPU sets and affinities. The `c5.metal` instance runs directly on the full hardware; it is not a virtual machine.

Teams were offered AWS time to tune their submissions on the test hardware. All participants experimented on the test hardware using provided time or their own funds.

3.2 Measurement

Previous editions of the task specified the test set, but last year's organizers removed a team for generating the test outputs even with empty input. Moreover, translation time for some submissions was approaching one second and often lower than loading time. Hence we updated the task to make it more robust to adversarial participants while also increasing reliability of speed measurements. We told participants the test set would have one million lines, lines would have at most 100 space-separated words, source sentences from an unspecified quality evaluation corpus would be hidden in their input, and quality would be evaluated with BLEU.

After the submission deadline, we announced the main quality score is the unweighted average SacreBLEU[1] (Post, 2018) on WMT test sets from 2010–2019, excluding 2012.[2] The 2012 test set

---

[2]Participants are likely to have used these test sets in development. The WMT 2020 test set was not yet available and others were out of the domain the systems were trained for.

Corpus	Lines	Words	Characters
EMEA	759876	13152485	86584513
Tatoeba	214943	1398154	7303297
Federal	785	13458	87724
WMT10	2489	54021	328648
WMT11	3003	65829	396884
WMT13	3000	56089	332972
WMT14	2737	54268	329121
WMT15	2169	40771	241016
WMT16	2999	56789	337711
WMT17	3004	56435	336817
WMT18	2998	58628	351779
WMT19	1997	42034	249742
Total	1000000	15048961	96880224

Table 1: Size of corpora in the efficiency task input.

was excluded because it has lines longer than 100 words. We refer to this score as WMT1* while also reporting the usual WMT19 scores for the translation task.

Shown in Table 1, the test set consisted of the aforementioned WMT input sentences and filler. For filler, we used parallel corpora outside the WMT data condition to verify that the system was still translating reasonably. Specifically, we used a recent crawl of the European Medicines Agency (EMEA),[3] the Tatoeba project,[4] and a crawl of the German Federal Foreign Office Berlin[5] all gathered by the European Language Resource Consortium. We do not consider the filler corpora clean or in-domain enough to be official evaluations of quality; results appear in supplementary material. To meet our promise to participants that lines would not be longer than 100 words (space-separated tokens), we excluded WMT12 and removed any English sentences longer than 100 words from the filler. We then truncated the German Federal Foreign Office Berlin corpus to obtain a total of 1 million lines. The input sentences were randomly shuffled and mixed across corpora, retaining a separate file to enable reconstruction. The final corpus and evaluation tools are available at `http://data.statmt.org/heafield/wngt20/test/`.

Time was measured with wall (real) time reported by `time` and CPU time reported by the kernel for the process group. We no longer measure loading time because it is small compared to

---

[3] `https://edin.ac/2TSPnC7`
[4] `https://edin.ac/2ywYp01`
[5] `https://edin.ac/3bWrBes`

the cost of translating 1 million sentences, is easy to game with busywork, and some toolkits do lazy initialization which makes loading time difficult to measure.

Peak RAM consumption was measured using `memory.max_usage_in_bytes` from the kernel for the CPU and by polling `nvidia-smi` for the GPU. Swap was disabled.

Participants were told to separate their Docker images into model and code files so that models could be measured separately from the relatively noisy size of code and libraries. A model was defined as "everything derived from data: all model parameters, vocabulary files, BPE configuration if applicable, quantization parameters or lookup tables where applicable, and hyperparameters like embedding sizes." Code could include "simple rule-based tokenizer scripts and hard-coded model structure that could plausibly be used for another language pair." They were also permitted to use standard compression tools such as `xz` to compress models; decompression time was included in results but small relative to the cost of translation. We report size of the model directory and Docker image size, both captured before the model ran.

Each evaluation started from a fresh boot of a constant Ubuntu 18.04 LTS disk image (one for CPU and one for GPU). Internet access was blocked at the cloud provider level except for the evaluation controller. This also prevented automatic upgrades.

3.3 Results

Measurements are reported in Table 2. The trade-offs between quality, model size, speed, and RAM are shown in Figure 1. We compare the cost-effectiveness of GPU and multi-core CPU hardware at the prices charged by Amazon Web Services in Figure 2.

Every team had a Pareto optimal submission for speed. This is largely due to teams focusing on different parts of the Pareto curve. OpenNMT focused on fast, small, and lower-quality systems plus one higher-quality submission. UEdin focused on higher-quality systems that were slower. Two of NiuTrans's four GPU submissions were Pareto optimal on speed, lying between OpenNMT and UEdin; their multi-core CPU submission performed poorly on all metrics.

Regarding model size, OpenNMT and UEdin made a range of Pareto-optimal submissions,

		BLEU		Seconds		Disk MB		RAM MB	
Team	**Variant**	**WMT19**	**WMT1***	**Wall**	**CPU**	**Model**	**Docker**	**CPU**	**GPU**
UEdin	large	42.9	35.3	5441	5462	422	933	5463	4992
UEdin	base	42.7	34.5	2385	2406	157	668	3793	3196
OpenNMT	base	42.9	34.0	2328	2377	104	308	488	1528
UEdin	tiny.untied	41.9	33.3	1971	1994	73	584	3146	2514
UEdin	tiny.push.i6	41.1	32.4	1536	1558	64	579	1000	1228
NiuTrans	35_6	40.9	32.2	3166	3450	291	887	2115	7748
NiuTrans	35_1	40.7	32.0	2023	2318	251	847	2115	5700
NiuTrans	18_1	40.2	31.4	1355	1646	149	745	2117	5700
NiuTrans	9_1	40.0	31.1	978	1260	95	691	2117	5444
OpenNMT	4-3-256-2ffn	40.0	30.9	762	812	32	235	388	1256
OpenNMT	6-3-256	39.9	30.7	731	782	30	233	393	892
OpenNMT	4-3-256	38.9	30.0	706	758	28	232	402	1064

		BLEU		Seconds		Disk MB		RAM MB
Team	**Variant**	**WMT19**	**WMT1***	**Wall**	**CPU**	**Model**	**Docker**	**CPU**
UEdin	base32	42.6	34.5	18649	18648	160	659	1728
UEdin Fix	base8	42.5	34.3	9128	9127	54	751	2001
OpenNMT	base	42.2	33.6	15978	15977	104	198	378
UEdin	tiny	41.6	32.9	14634	14634	41	737	164686
UEdin Fix	tiny	41.6	32.9	4799	4799	34	559	1549
UEdin	tiny.steady.i12	40.8	32.0	14553	14553	49	578	163388
UEdin	tiny.pushy.i6	40.5	32.0	14399	14399	49	578	164427
UEdin Fix	tiny.steady.i12	40.8	32.0	4577	4577	49	587	674
UEdin Fix	tiny.pushy.i6	40.5	32.0	4554	4554	49	587	675
OpenNMT	4-3-256-2ffn	39.8	30.8	3922	3922	32	125	238
OpenNMT	6-3-256	39.5	30.5	3717	3717	30	123	233
OpenNMT	4-3-256	38.7	29.8	3348	3348	28	122	220
UEdin	micro.voc8k	37.5	29.0	7184	7184	27	723	77158
UEdin Fix	micro.voc8k	37.5	29.0	4660	4660	19	716	2540

		BLEU		Seconds		Disk MB		RAM MB
Team	**Variant**	**WMT19**	**WMT1***	**Wall**	**CPU**	**Model**	**Docker**	**CPU**
OpenNMT	base	42.0	33.5	795	38300	104	198	1552
UEdin	tiny	41.5	32.9	215	10014	41	737	108124
UEdin Fix	tiny	41.5	32.9	210	9840	34	737	28890
OpenNMT	4-3-256-2ffn	39.7	30.7	181	8735	32	125	1283
OpenNMT	6-3-256	39.4	30.5	155	7471	30	123	904
OpenNMT	4-3-256	38.6	29.7	144	6959	28	122	958
UEdin	micro.voc8k	37.4	29.0	188	8711	27	723	77157
UEdin Fix	micro.voc8k	37.4	29.0	190	8768	19	723	35051
NiuTrans	cpu	33.8	27.0	811	36198	64	432	19732

Table 2: Submissions to the efficiency shared task sorted in decreasing order of WMT1* BLEU. Systems translated 1,000,000 lines with 15,048,961 space-separated words.

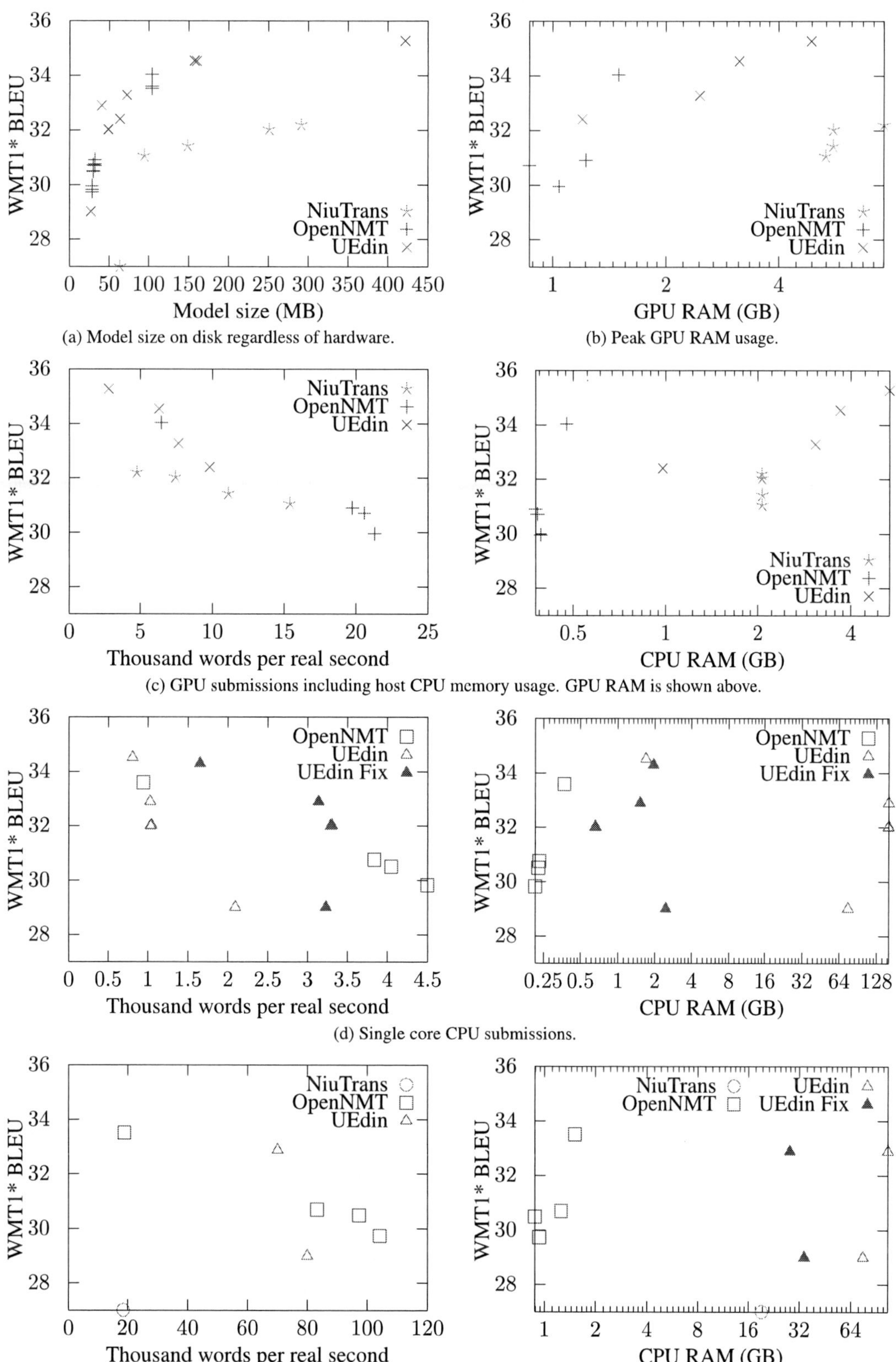

(a) Model size on disk regardless of hardware.

(b) Peak GPU RAM usage.

(c) GPU submissions including host CPU memory usage. GPU RAM is shown above.

(d) Single core CPU submissions.

(e) Multi-core CPU submissions; UEdin's fixed submissions had similar speed.

Figure 1: Performance of Efficiency Task Submissions.

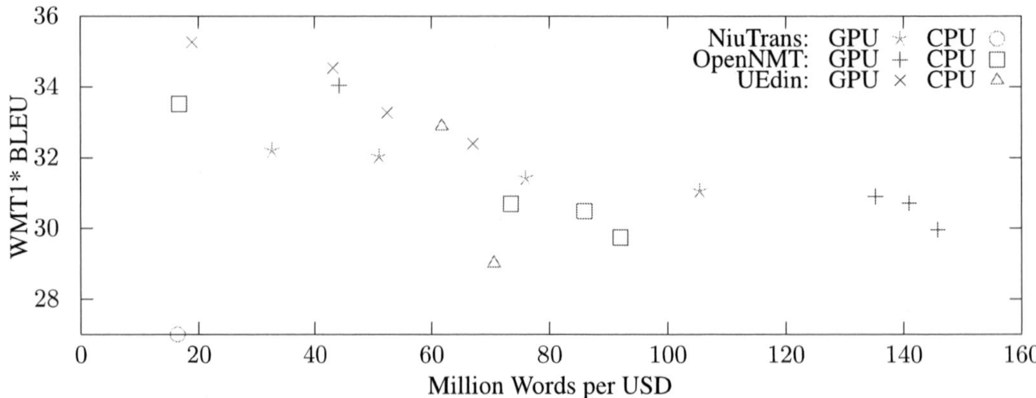

Figure 2: Price comparison of GPU and multi-core CPU submissions based on Amazon Web Services pricing of $4.08/hr for the `c5.metal` CPU instance and $0.526/hr for a `g4dn.xlarge` GPU instance. A single CPU core does not have a well-defined price.

mostly driven by the number of parameters and 8-bit quantization.

OpenNMT's small lower-quality models have low CPU RAM and Docker image size; UEdin is Pareto-optimal for higher-quality models. Open-NMT was the only team to optimize for these metrics in their system description. In their multi-core CPU submission, OpenNMT shared memory amongst processes while other participants simply used multiple processes with copies of the model.

4 Document Generation and Translation Task

Following the previous workshop, we continued with the shared task of document-level generation and translation. This task is motivated as the central evaluation testbed for document-level generation systems with different types of inputs by providing parallel dataset consisting of structured tables and text in two languages. We host various tracks within the testbed based on input and output constraints and investigate and contrast the system differences.

In particular, we conducted the following six tracks:

- **NLG (Data → En, Data → De):** Generate a document summary in the target language given only structured tables (*i.e.*, data-to-text).

- **MT (De ↔ En):** Translate a document in the source language to the target language (*i.e.*, document-level translation).

- **MT+NLG (Data+En → De, Data+De → En):** Generate a document summary given the structured tables and the summary in another language.

4.1 Evaluation Measures

We employ standard evaluation metrics for the tasks above along two axes following (Hayashi et al., 2019):

Textual Accuracy: BLEU (Papineni et al., 2002) and ROUGE (Lin, 2004) as measures for surface-level texual accuracy compared to reference summaries.

Content Accuracy: Relation generation (RG), content selection (CS), and content ordering (CO) metrics (Wiseman et al., 2017) to assess the fidelity of the *content* to the input data.

An information extraction model is employed for content accuracy measures for each target language. We followed (Wiseman et al., 2017) and ensembled six information extraction models (three CNN-based, three LSTM-based) with different random seeds.

4.2 Data

We re-use Rotowire English-German dataset (Hayashi et al., 2019), which consists of a subset of the Rotowire dataset (Wiseman et al., 2017) with professional German translations. Each instance corresponds to an NBA game and consists of a box-score table for the match, base information about the teams (*e.g.* team name, city), English game summary, and the same game summary translated to German. Final evaluation was performed on the test split of the Rotowire English-German dataset.

We followed the same setting in terms of additional resources participants could adopt.

Systems conforming to the data requirements are marked constrained, otherwise unconstrained. Results are indicated by the initials (C/U).

4.3 Baselines

We prepared two baselines for different tracks:

FairSeq-19 We use FairSeq (Ng et al., 2019) (WMT'19 single model[6]) for MT and MT+NLG tracks.

NCP+CC: We use a two-stage model from (Puduppully et al., 2019) for NLG tracks. English model was with the pretrained weights by the author and German model was trained only on Rotowire English-German dataset.

4.4 Submitted Systems

One team participated in the task, who focused on the German-English MT track of the task.

Team FJWU developed a system around Transformer-based sequence-to-sequence model. Additionally, the model employed hierarchical attention following (Miculicich et al., 2018) for both encoder and decoder to account for the document-level context. The system was trained in a two-stage process, where a base (sentence-level) NMT model was trained followed by the training of hierarchcal attention networks component. To handle the scarcity of in-domain translation data, they experimented with upsizing the in-domain data up to three times to construct training data. Their ablation experiments showed that this upsizing of in-domain data is effective at increasing the BLEU score.

4.5 Results

We show the MT track results in Table 3. We confirm that the use of both document-level models and in-domain data helps achieve better BLEU score, which has also been shown from the last workshop (Hayashi et al., 2019).

System	BLEU	Type
FJWU	45.04	C
FairSeq-19	42.91	C

Table 3: DGT results on the MT track (De $\rightarrow$ En).

5 STAPLE Task

Machine translation systems are typically trained to produce a single output, but in certain cases, it is desirable to have many possible translations of a given input text. At Duolingo, the world's largest online language-learning platform,[7] we grade translation-based challenges with sets of human-curated acceptable translation options. Given the many ways of expressing a piece of text, these sets are slow to create, and may be incomplete. This process is ripe for improvement with the aid of rich multi-output translation and paraphrase systems. To this end, we introduce a shared task called STAPLE: Simultaneous Translation and Paraphrasing for Language Education (Mayhew et al., 2020).

5.1 Task Description

In this shared task, participants are given a training set consisting of 2500 to 4000 English sentences (or *prompts*), each of which is paired with a list of comprehensive translations in the target language, weighted and ordered by normalized learner response frequency. At test time, participants are given 500 English prompts, and are required to produce the set of comprehensive translations for each prompt. We also provide a high-quality automatic reference translation for each prompt, in the event that a participant wants to work on paraphrase-only approaches. The target languages were Hungarian, Japanese, Korean, Portuguese, and Vietnamese.

5.2 Submitted Systems

There were 20 participants who submitted to the development phase, 14 participants who submitted to the test phase, and 11 participants who submitted system description papers. Submission models largely consisted of high-quality machine translation systems fine-tuned on in-domain shared task data from Duolingo, with different tricks for training, ensembling, and output filtering.

In the test phase, three teams submitted to all 5 language tracks, and one team submitted to two

---

[6]Model identifier: `transformer.wmt19.en-de`, `transformer.wmt19.de-en`.

[7]`www.duolingo.com`

tracks (Portuguese, and Hungarian). Of the remaining single-language submissions, Portuguese and Japanese were the most popular. In these single language submissions, teams did not tend to take language-specific approaches.

5.3 Results

Submission performance varied widely, but nearly all submissions improved significantly over organizer-provided baselines. The top submissions have comparable scores to taking the top 5 translations from each gold translation set.

Techniques popular among the more successful teams included weighting of training data according to learner response frequency, and classifier-based output filtering. Interestingly, techniques such as diverse beam search and beam reranking did not appear to improve results, despite their close relevance to the task. For more details and analysis, see Mayhew et al. (2020).

6 Conclusion

This paper summarized the results of the Fourth Workshop on Neural Generation and Translation, where we saw a number of research advances. Particularly, this year introduced a more rigorous efficiency task, and a new STAPLE task.

7 Acknowledgements

The efficiency shared task was partly funded from European Union's Horizon 2020 research and innovation programme under grant agreement No 825303 (Bergamot) and by the Connecting Europe Facility (CEF) - Telecommunications from the project No 2019-EU-IA-0045 (User-focused Marian). This work represents the authors' opinions, not necessarily those of the European Union.

We thank Amazon Web Services for its gift of credits to support the efficiency shared task evaluation.

References

Dzmitry Bahdanau, Kyunghyun Cho, and Yoshua Bengio. 2015. Neural machine translation by jointly learning to align and translate. In *3rd International Conference on Learning Representations, ICLR 2015*.

Loïc Barrault, Ondřej Bojar, Marta R. Costa-jussà, Christian Federmann, Mark Fishel, Yvette Graham, Barry Haddow, Matthias Huck, Philipp Koehn, Shervin Malmasi, Christof Monz, Mathias Müller, Santanu Pal, Matt Post, and Marcos Zampieri. 2019. Findings of the 2019 conference on machine translation (wmt19). In *Proceedings of the Fourth Conference on Machine Translation (Volume 2: Shared Task Papers, Day 1)*, pages 1–61, Florence, Italy. Association for Computational Linguistics.

Jacob Devlin, Ming-Wei Chang, Kenton Lee, and Kristina Toutanova. 2019. BERT: Pre-training of Deep Bidirectional Transformers for Language Understanding. In *Proceedings of the 2019 Conference of the North American Chapter of the Association for Computational Linguistics: Human Language Technologies, Volume 1 (Long and Short Papers)*, pages 4171–4186, Minneapolis, Minnesota. Association for Computational Linguistics.

Hiroaki Hayashi, Yusuke Oda, Alexandra Birch, Ioannis Konstas, Andrew Finch, Minh-Thang Luong, Graham Neubig, and Katsuhito Sudoh. 2019. Findings of the third workshop on neural generation and translation. In *Proceedings of the 3rd Workshop on Neural Generation and Translation*, pages 1–14, Hong Kong. Association for Computational Linguistics.

Nal Kalchbrenner and Phil Blunsom. 2013. Recurrent continuous translation models. In *Proceedings of EMNLP*.

Chin-Yew Lin. 2004. ROUGE: A Package for Automatic Evaluation of Summaries. In *Text Summarization Branches Out*, pages 74–81, Barcelona, Spain. Association for Computational Linguistics.

Stephen Mayhew, Klinton Bicknell, Chris Brust, Bill McDowell, Will Monroe, and Burr Settles. 2020. Simultaneous translation and paraphrase for language education. In *Proceedings of the ACL Workshop on Neural Generation and Translation (WNGT)*. ACL.

Lesly Miculicich, Dhananjay Ram, Nikolaos Pappas, and James Henderson. 2018. Document-level neural machine translation with hierarchical attention networks. In *Proceedings of the 2018 Conference on Empirical Methods in Natural Language Processing*, pages 2947–2954, Brussels, Belgium. Association for Computational Linguistics.

Nathan Ng, Kyra Yee, Alexei Baevski, Myle Ott, Michael Auli, and Sergey Edunov. 2019. Facebook FAIR's WMT19 news translation task submission. In *Proceedings of the Fourth Conference on Machine Translation (Volume 2: Shared Task Papers, Day 1)*, pages 314–319, Florence, Italy. Association for Computational Linguistics.

Kishore Papineni, Salim Roukos, Todd Ward, and Wei-Jing Zhu. 2002. Bleu: a method for automatic evaluation of machine translation. In *Proceedings of the 40th Annual Meeting of the Association for Computational Linguistics*, pages 311–318, Philadelphia, Pennsylvania, USA. Association for Computational Linguistics.

Matt Post. 2018. A call for clarity in reporting BLEU scores. In *Proceedings of the Third Conference on Machine Translation: Research Papers*, pages 186–191, Belgium, Brussels. Association for Computational Linguistics.

Ratish Puduppully, Li Dong, and Mirella Lapata. 2019. Data-to-text generation with content selection and planning. In *Proceedings of the AAAI Conference on Artificial Intelligence*, volume 33, pages 6908–6915.

Ilya Sutskever, Oriol Vinyals, and Quoc V Le. 2014. Sequence to sequence learning with neural networks. In *Advances in neural information processing systems*, pages 3104–3112.

Sam Wiseman, Stuart Shieber, and Alexander Rush. 2017. Challenges in Data-to-Document Generation. In *Proceedings of the 2017 Conference on Empirical Methods in Natural Language Processing*, pages 2253–2263.

Learning to Generate Multiple Style Transfer Outputs for an Input Sentence

Kevin Lin♣, Ming-Yu Liu♦, Ming-Ting Sun♣, Jan Kautz♦

♣University of Washington ♦NVIDIA Research

`{kvlin,mts}@uw.edu`, `{mingyul,jkautz}@nvidia.com`

Abstract

Text style transfer refers to the task of rephrasing a given text in a different style. While various methods have been proposed to advance the state of the art, they often assume the transfer output follows a delta distribution, and thus their models cannot generate different style transfer results for a given input text. To address the limitation, we propose a one-to-many text style transfer framework. In contrast to prior works that learn a one-to-one mapping that converts an input sentence to one output sentence, our approach learns a one-to-many mapping that can convert an input sentence to multiple different output sentences, while preserving the input content. This is achieved by applying adversarial training with a latent decomposition scheme. Specifically, we decompose the latent representation of the input sentence to a style code that captures the language style variation and a content code that encodes the language style-independent content. We then combine the content code with the style code for generating a style transfer output. By combining the same content code with a different style code, we generate a different style transfer output. Extensive experimental results with comparisons to several text style transfer approaches on multiple public datasets using a diverse set of performance metrics validate effectiveness of the proposed approach.

1 Introduction

Text style transfer aims at changing the language style of an input sentence to a target style with the constraint that the style-independent content should remain the same across the transfer. While several methods are proposed for the task (John et al., 2019; Smith et al., 2019; Jhamtani et al., 2017; Kerpedjiev, 1992; Xu et al., 2012; Shen et al., 2017; Subramanian et al., 2018; Xu et al., 2018), they commonly model the distribution of the transfer outputs as a delta distribution, which implies a one-to-one mapping mechanism that converts an input sentence in one language style to a *single* corresponding sentence in the target language style.

We argue a multimodal mapping is better suited for the text style transfer task. For examples, the following two reviews:

1. *"This lightweight vacuum is simply effective."*,
2. *"This easy-to-carry vacuum picks up dust and trash amazingly well."*

would both be considered correct negative-to-positive transfer results for the input sentence, *"This heavy vacuum sucks"*. Furthermore, a one-to-many mapping allows a user to pick the preferred text style transfer outputs in the inference time.

In this paper, we propose a one-to-many text style transfer framework that can be trained using non-parallel text. That is, we assume the training data consists of two corpora of different styles, and no paired input and output sentences are available. The core of our framework is a latent decomposition scheme learned via adversarial training. We decompose the latent representation of a sentence into two parts where one encodes the style of a sentence, while the other encodes the style-independent content of the sentence. In the test time, for changing the style of an input sentence, we first extract its content code. We then sample a sentence from the training dataset of the target style corpus and extract its style code. The two codes are combined to generate an output sentence, which would carry the same content but in the target style. As sampling a different style sentence, we have a different style code and have a different style transfer output. We conduct experiments with comparison to several state-of-the-art approaches on multiple public datasets, including Yelp (yel) and Amazon (He and McAuley, 2016). The results, evaluated using various performance metrics, including content preservation, style accuracy, output diversity, and user preference, show that the model trained with our framework performs consistently better than the competing approaches.

Proceedings of the 4th Workshop on Neural Generation and Translation (WNGT 2020), pages 10–23
Online, July 10, 2020. ©2020 Association for Computational Linguistics
www.aclweb.org/anthology/D19-56%2d

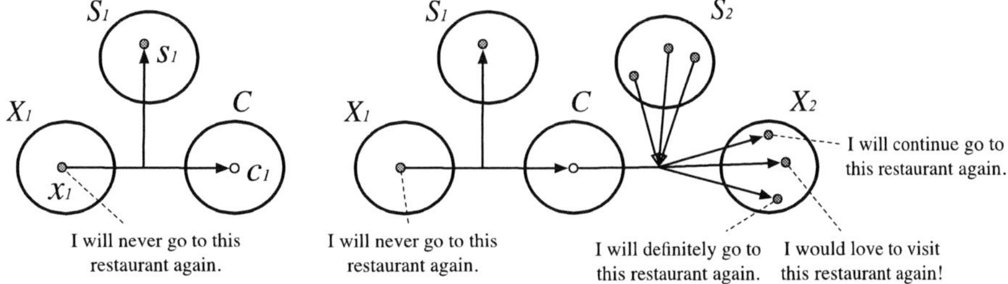

Figure 1: We formulate text style transfer as a one-to-many mapping function. Left: We decompose the sentence x_1 to a content code c_1 that controls the sentence meaning, and a style code s_1 that captures the stylistic properties of the input x_1. Right: One-to-many style transfer is achieved by fusing the content code c_1 and a style code s_2 randomly sampled from the target style space S_2.

2 Methodology

Let X_1 and X_2 be two spaces of sentences of two different language styles. Let Z_1 and Z_2 be their corresponding latent spaces. We further assume Z_1 and Z_2 can be decomposed into two latent spaces $Z_1 = S_1 \times C_1$ and $Z_2 = S_2 \times C_2$ where S_1 and S_2 are the latent spaces that control the style variations in X_1 and X_2 and C_1 and C_2 are the latent spaces that control the style-independent content information. Since C_1 and C_2 are style-independent content representation, we have $C \equiv C_1 \equiv C_2$. For example, X_1 and X_2 may denote the spaces of negative and positive product reviews where the elements in C encode the product and its features reviewed in a sentence, the elements in S_1 represent variations in negative styles such as the degree of preferences and the exact phrasing, and the elements in S_2 represent the corresponding variations in positive styles. The above modeling implies

1. A sentence $x_1 \in X_1$ can be decomposed to a content code $c_1 \in C$ and a style code $s_1 \in S_1$.
2. A sentence $x_1 \in X_1$ can be reconstructed by fusing its content code c_1 and its style code s_1.
3. To transfer a sentence in X_1 to a corresponding sentence in X_2, one can simply fuse the content code c_1 with a style code s_2 where $s_2 \in S_2$.

Figure 1 provides a visualization of the modeling.

Under this formulation, the text style transfer mechanism is given by a conditional distribution $p(x_{1\to2}|x_1)$, where $x_{1\to2}$ is the sentence generated by transferring sentence x_1 to the target domain X_2. Note that existing works (Fu et al., 2018; Shen et al., 2017) formulate the text style transfer mechanism to be a one-to-one mapping that converts an input sentence to only a single corresponding output sentence. That is $p(x_{1\to2}|x_1) = \delta(x_1)$ where δ is the Dirac delta function. As a results, they

Figure 2: Overview of the proposed one-to-many style transfer approach. We show an example of transferring a negative restaurant review sentence x_1 to multiple different positive ones $y_{1\to2}$. To transfer the sentence, we first randomly sample a sentence x_2 from the space of positive reviews X_2 and extract its style code s_2 using E_2^s. We then compute $z_{1\to2}$ by combining c_1 with s_2 and convert it to the transfer output $y_{1\to2}$ using G_2. We note that by sampling a different x_2 and hence a different s_2, we have a different style transfer output $y_{1\to2}$.

can not be used to generate multiple style transfer outputs for an input sentence.

One-to-Many Style Transfer. To model the transfer function, we use a framework consists of a set of networks as visualized in Figure 2. It has a content encoder E_i^c, a style encoder E_i^s, and a decoder G_i for each domain X_i. In the following, we will explain the framework in details using the task of transferring from X_1 to X_2. The task of transferring from X_2 to X_1 follows the same pattern.

The content encoder E_1^c takes the sequence $x_1 = \{x_1^1, x_1^2, \ldots, x_1^{m_1(x_1)}\}$ of $m_1(x_1)$ elements as input and computes a content code $c_1 \equiv \{c_1^1, c_1^2, \ldots, c_1^{m_1(x_1)}\} = E_1^c(x_1)$, which is a sequence of vectors describing the sentence's style-independent content. The style encoder E_2^S converts x_2 to a style code $s_2 \equiv (s_{2,\mu}, s_{2,\sigma}) = E_2^s(x_2)$, which is a pair of vectors. Note that we will use $s_{2,\mu}$ and $s_{2,\sigma}$ as the new mean and standard deviation of the feature activation of the input x_1 for the style transfer task of converting a sentence in X_1 to a corresponding sentence in X_2. Specifically, we combine the content code c_1 and the style code s_2 using a composition function F, which will be discussed momentarily, to obtain $z_{1\to2} = \{z_{1\to2}^1, z_{1\to2}^2, \ldots, z_{1\to2}^{m_1(x_1)}\}$. Then, we use the decoder G_2 to map the representation $z_{1\to2}$ to the output sequence $y_{1\to2}$. Note that s_2 is extracted from a randomly sampled $x_2 \in X_2$, and by sampling a different sentence, say $x_2' \in X_2$ where $x_2' \neq x_2$, we have $s_2' \neq s_2$ and hence a different style transfer output. By treating style variations as sample-able quantities, we achieve one-to-many style transfer output capability.

The combination function is given by

$$F(c_i^k, s_j) = s_{j,\sigma} \otimes (c_i^k - \mu(c_i)) \oslash \sigma(c_i) + s_{j,\mu}, \quad (1)$$

where $\otimes$ denotes element-wise product, $\oslash$ denotes element-wise division, $\mu(\cdot)$ and $\sigma(\cdot)$ indicate the operation of computing mean and standard derivation for the content latent code by treating each vector in c_i as an independent realization of a random variable. In other words, the latent representation $z_{i\to j}^k = F(c_i^k, s_j)$ is constructed by first normalizing the content code c_i in the latent space and then applying the non-linear transformation whose parameters are provided from a sentence of target style. Since F contains no learnable parameters, we consider F as part of the decoder. This design draws inspirations from image style transfer works (Huang and Belongie, 2017; Dumoulin et al., 2016), which show that image style transfer can be achieved by controlling the mean and variance of the feature activations in the neural networks. We hypothesize this is the same case for the text style transfer task and apply it to achieve the one-to-many style transfer capability.

Network Design. We realize the content encoder E_i^c using a convolutional network. To ensure the length of the output sequence c is equal to the length of the input sentence, we pad the input by $m - 1$ zero vectors on both left and right side, where m is the length of the input sequence as discussed in (Gehring et al., 2017). For the convolution operation, we do not include any stride

convolution. We also realize the style encoder E_i^s using a convolutional network. To extract the style code, after several convolution layers, we apply global average pooling and then project the results to $s_{i,\mu}$ and $s_{i,\sigma}$ using a two-layer multi-layer perceptron. We apply the log-exponential nonlinearity to compute $s_{i,\sigma}$ to ensure the outputs are strictly positive, required for modeling the deviations. The decoder G_i is realized using a convolutional network with an attention mechanism followed by a convolutional sequence-to-sequence network (ConvS2S) (Gehring et al., 2017). We realized our method based on ConvS2S, but it can be extended to work with transformer models (Vaswani et al., 2017; Devlin et al., 2018; Radford et al., 2019). Further details are given in the supplementary materials.

2.1 Learning Objective

We train our one-to-many text style transfer model by minimizing multiple loss terms.

Reconstruction loss. We use reconstruction loss to regularize the text style transfer learning. Specifically, we assume the pair of content encoder E_i^c and style encoder E_i^s and the decoder G_i form an auto-encoder. We train them by minimizing the negative log likelihood of the training corpus:

$$\mathcal{L}_{rec}^i = \mathbb{E}_{x_i}[-\log P(y_i^k | x_i^k; \theta_{E_i^c}, \theta_{E_i^s}, \theta_{G_i})] \quad (2)$$

where $\theta_{E_i^c}$, $\theta_{E_i^s}$ and θ_{G_i} denote the parameters of E_i^c, E_i^s, and G_i respectively.

For each training sentence, G_i synthesizes the output sequence by predicting the most possible token y^t based on the latent representation $z_i \equiv \{z_i^1, z_i^2, \ldots, z_i^m\}$ and the previous output predictions $\{y^1, y^2, \ldots, y^{t-1}\}$, so that the probability of a sentence can be calculated by

$$P(y|x; \theta_{E_i^c}, \theta_{E_i^s}, \theta_{G_i}) =$$
$$\prod_{t=1}^{T} p(y^t | z_i, y^1, y^2, \ldots, y^{t-1}; \theta_{G_i}), \quad (3)$$

where t denotes the token index and T is the sentence length. Following (Gehring et al., 2017), the probability of a token is computed by the linear projection of the decoder output using softmax.

Back-translation loss. Inspired by recent studies (Prabhumoye et al., 2018; Sennrich et al., 2015; Brislin, 1970) that show that back-translation loss, which is closely related to the cycle-consistency

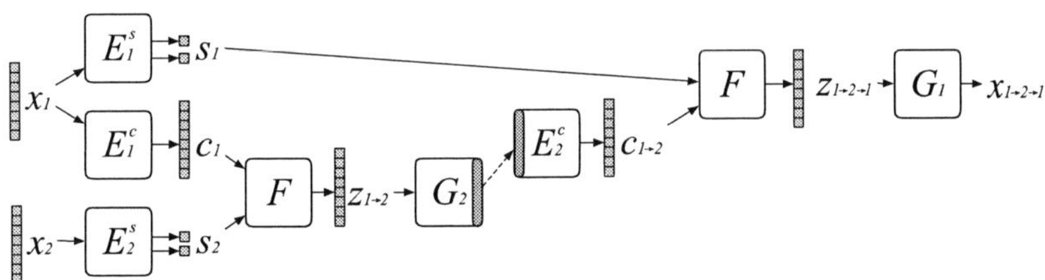

Figure 3: Illustration of the back-translation loss. We transfer x_1 to the domain of X_2 and then transfer it back to the domain of X_1 using its original style code s_1. The resultant sentence $x_{1\to2\to1}$ should be as similar as possible to x_1 if the content code is preserved across transfer. To tackle the non-differentiable of the sentence decoding mechanism (beam search), we replace the hard decoding of $x_{1\to2}$ by a learned non-linear projections between the decoder G_2 and the content encoder E_2^c.

loss (Zhu et al., 2017a) used in computer vision, is helpful for preserving the content of the input, we adopt a back-translation loss to regularize the learning. To achieve the goal, as shown in Figure 3, we transfer the input x_1 to the other style domain X_2. We then transfer it back to the original domain X_1 by using its original style code s_1. By doing so, the resulting sentence $x_{1\to2\to1}$ should be as similar as possible to the original input x_1. In other words, we minimize the discrepancy between x_1 and $x_{1\to2\to1}$ given by

$$\mathcal{L}_{back}^1 = \mathbb{E}_{x_1,x_2}[-\log P(y_1^k|x_{1\to2\to1}^k;\underline{\theta})] \quad (4)$$

where $\underline{\theta} = \{\theta_{E_1^c}, \theta_{E_1^s}, \theta_{G_1}, \theta_{E_2}, \theta_{E_2^s}, \theta_{G_2}\}$. We also define $\mathcal{L}_{back}^2$ in a similar way.

To avoid the non-differentiability of the beam search (Och and Ney, 2004; Sutskever et al., 2014), we substitute the hard decoding of $x_{1\to2}$ by using a set of differentiable non-linear transformations between the decoder G_2 and the content encoder E_1^c when minimizing the back-translation loss. The non-linear transformations project the feature activation of the second last layer of the decoder G_2 to the second layer of the content encoder E_1^c. These non-linear projections are learned by the multilayer perceptron (MLP), which are trained jointly with the text style transfer task. We also apply the same mechanism to compute $x_{2\to1}$. This way, our model can be trained purely using back-propagation.

To ensure the MLP correctly project the feature activation to the second layer of E_2^c, we enforce the output of the MLP to be as similar as possible to the feature activation of the second layer of E_1^c. This is based on the idea that x_1 and $x_{1\to2}$ should have the same content code across transfer, and their feature activation in the content encoder should also be the same. Accordingly, we apply Mean Square Error

(MSE) loss function to achieve this objective:

$$\mathcal{L}_{mse}^1 = \mathbb{E}_{x_1,x_2}[||E_2^{c,h}(x_{1\to2}) - E_1^{c,h}(x_1)||_2^2]$$
$$(5)$$

where $E_1^{c,h}$ and $E_2^{c,h}$ denote the function for computing feature activation of the second layer of E_1^c and E_2^c, respectively. The loss $\mathcal{L}_{mse}^2$ for the other domain is defined in a similar way.

Style classification loss. During learning, we enforce a style classification loss on the style code $s_i = E_i^s(x_i)$ with the standard cross-entropy loss $\mathcal{L}_{cls}^i$. This encourages the style code s_i to capture the stylistic properties of the input sentences.

Adversarial loss. We use GANs (Goodfellow et al., 2014) for matching the distribution of the input latent code to the decoder from the reconstruction streams to the distribution of the input latent code to the decoder from the translation stream. That is (1) we match the distribution of $z_{1\to2}$ to the distribution of z_2, and (2) we match the distribution of $z_{2\to1}$ to the distribution of z_1. This way we ensure distribution of the transfer outputs matches distribution of the target style sentences since they use the same decoder. As we apply adversarial training to the latent representation, we also avoid dealing with the non-differentiability of beam search. The adversarial loss for the second domain is given by

$$\mathcal{L}_{adv}^2 = \mathbb{E}_{x_1,x_2}[\log(1 - D_2(z_{1\to2}))]$$
$$+ \mathbb{E}_{x_2}[\log(D_2(z_2))], \quad (6)$$

where D_2 is the discriminator which aims at distinguishing the latent representation of the sentence $z_{1\to2}$ from $z_2 = \mathcal{C}_z(c_2, s_2)$. The adversarial loss $\mathcal{L}_{adv}^1$ is defined in a similar manner.

Overall learning objective. We then learn a one-to-many text style transfer model by solving

$$\min_{E_1,E_2,G_1,G_2} \max_{D_1,D_2} \sum_{i=1}^{2} \left(\mathcal{L}_{rec}^i + \mathcal{L}_{back}^i \right. \tag{7}$$
$$\left. + \mathcal{L}_{mse}^i + \mathcal{L}_{cls}^i + \mathcal{L}_{adv}^i \right).$$

3 Experiments

In the following, we first introduce the datasets and evaluation metrics and then present the experiment results with comparison to the competing methods.
Datasets. We use the following datasets.

- **Amazon product reviews (Amazon)** (He and McAuley, 2016) contains $277,228$ positive and $277,769$ negative review sentences for training, and 500 positive and 500 negative review sentences for testing. The length of a sentence ranges from 8 to 25 words. We use this dataset for converting a negative product review to a positive one, and vice versa. Our evaluation follows the protocol described in Li et al. (2018).
- **Yelp restaurant reviews (Yelp)** (yel) contains a training set of $267,314$ positive and $176,787$ negative sentences, and a test set of $76,392$ positive and $50,278$ negative testing sentences. The length of a sentence ranges from 1 to 15 words. We use this dataset for converting a negative restaurant review to a positive one, and vice versa. We use two evaluation settings: Yelp500 and Yelp25000. Yelp500 is proposed by (Li et al., 2018), which includes randomly sampled 500 positive and 500 negative sentences from the test set, while Yelp25000 includes randomly sampled 25000 positive and 25000 negative sentences from the test set.

Evaluation metrics. We evaluate a text style transfer model on several aspects. Firstly, the transfer output should carry the target style (style score). Secondly, the style-independent content should be preserved (content preservation score). We also measure the diversity of the style transfer outputs for an input sentence (diversity score).

- **Style score.** We use a classifier to evaluate the fidelity of the style transfer results(Fu et al., 2018; Shen et al., 2017). Specifically, we apply the Byte-mLSTM (Radford et al., 2017) to classify the output sentence generated by a text style transfer model. As transferring a negative sentence to a positive one, we expect a good transfer model should be able to generate a sentence that is classified positive by the classifier. The overall style transfer performance of a model is then given by the average accuracy on the test set measured by the classifier.
- **Content score.** We build a style-independent distance metric that can quantify content similarity between two sentences, by comparing embeddings of the sentences after removing their style words. Specifically, we compute embedding of each non-style word in the sentence using the word2vec (Mikolov et al., 2013). Next, we compute the average embedding, which serves as the content representation of the sentence. The content similarity between two sentences is given by the cosine distance of their average embeddings. We compute the relative n-gram frequency to determine which word is a style word based on the observation that the language style is largely encoded in the n-gram distribution (Xu et al., 2012). This is in spirit similar to the term frequency-inverse document frequency analysis (Sparck Jones, 1972). Let D_1 and D_2 be the n-gram frequencies of two corpora of different styles. The style magnitude of an n-gram u in style domain i is given by

$$s_i(u) = \frac{D_i(u) + \lambda}{\sum_{j \neq i} D_j(u) + \lambda} \tag{8}$$

where λ is a small constant. We use 1-gram. A word is considered a style word if $\min_{k \in \{i,j\}} s_k(u)$ is greater than a threshold.
- **Diversity score.** To quantify the diversity of the style transfer outputs, we resort to the self-BLEU score proposed by Zhu et al. (2018). Given an input sentence, we apply the style transfer model 5 times to obtain 5 outputs. We then compute self-BLEU scores between any two generated sentences (10 pairs). We apply this procedure to all the sentences in the test set and compute the average self-BLEU score v. After that, we define the diversity score as $100 - v$. A model with a higher diversity score means that the model is better in generating diverse outputs. In the experiments, we denote Diversity-K as the diversity score computed by using self-BLEU-K.

Implementation. We use the convolutional sequence-to-sequence model (Gehring et al., 2017). Our content and style encoder consist of 3 convolution layers, respectively. The decoder has 4 convolution layers. The content and style codes are 256 dimensional. We use the `pytorch` (Paszke et al., 2017) and `fairseq` (Ott et al., 2019) libraries and train our model using a single GeForce

GTX 1080 Ti GPU. We use the SGD algorithm with the learning rate set to 0.1. Once the content and style scores converge, we reduce the learning rate by an order of magnitude after every epoch until it reaches 0.0001. Detail model parameters are given in the appendix.

Baselines. We compare the proposed approach to the following competing methods.

- **CAE** (Shen et al., 2017) is based on auto-encoder and is trained using a GAN framework. It assumes a shared content latent space between different domains and computes the content code by using a content encoder. The output is generated with a pre-defined binary style code.
- **MD** (Fu et al., 2018) extends the CAE to work with multiple style-specific decoders. It learns style-independent representation by adversarial training and generates output sentences by using style-specific decoders.
- **BTS** (Prabhumoye et al., 2018) learns style-independent representations by using back-translation techniques. BTS assumes the latent representation of the sentence preserves the meaning after machine translation.
- **DR** (Li et al., 2018) employs retrieval techniques to find similar sentences with desired style. They use neural networks to fuse the input and the retrieved sentences for generating the output.
- **CopyPast** simply uses the input as the output, which serves as a reference for evaluation.

3.1 Results on One-to-Many Style Transfer

Our model can generate different text style transfer outputs for an input sentence. To generate multiple outputs for an input, we randomly sample a style code from the target style training dataset during testing. Since the **CAE** (Shen et al., 2017) and **BTS** (Prabhumoye et al., 2018) are not designed for the one-to-many style transfer, we extend their methods to achieve this capability by injecting random noise, termed **CAE+noise** and **BTS+noise**. Specifically, we add random Gaussian noise to the latent code of their models during training, which is based on the intuition that the randomness would result in different activations in the networks, leading to different outputs. Table 1 shows the average diversity scores achieved by the competing methods over 5 runs. We find that our method performs favorably against others.

User Study. We conduct a user study to evaluate one-to-many style transfer performance using the

Amazon	Diversity-4	Diversity-3	Diversity-2
CAE	2.60	2.15	1.64
CAE+noise	33.01	29.33	24.66
BTS+noise	39.22	35.46	30.48
Ours	**46.31**	**41.69**	**36.01**

Yelp	Diversity-4	Diversity-3	Diversity-2
CAE	1.03	0.80	0.60
CAE+noise	16.91	14.63	11.73
BTS+noise	48.36	43.69	37.38
Ours	**58.29**	**50.90**	**42.34**

Table 1: One-to-many text style transfer results.

Method	Diversity	Fluency	Overall
CAE+noise	13.13	11.62	12.12
No Pref.	35.35	16.16	36.87
Ours	**51.52**	**72.22**	**51.01**
BTS+noise	13.13	11.11	16.16
No Pref.	42.93	22.22	40.40
Ours	**43.94**	**66.67**	**43.43**

Table 2: User study results on one-to-many text style transfer. The numbers are the user preference score of competing methods.

Amazon Mechanical Turk (AMT) platform. We set up the pairwise comparison following Prabhumoye et al. (2018). Given an input sentence and two sets of model-generated sentences (5 sentences per set), the workers are asked to choose which set has more diverse sentences with the same meaning, and which set provides more desirable sentences considering both content preservation and style transfer. These are denoted as *Diversity*, and *Overall* in Table 2. The workers are also asked to compare the transfer quality in terms of grammatically and fluency, which is denoted as *Fluency*. For each comparison, a third option *No Preference* is given for cases that both are equally good or bad.

We randomly sampled 250 sentences from Yelp500 test set for the user study. Each comparison is evaluated by at least three different workers. We received more than 3, 600 responses from the AMT, and the results are summarized in Table 2. Our method outperforms the competing methods by a large margin in terms of diversity, fluency, and overall quality. In the appendix, we present further details of the comparisons with different variants of **CAE+noise** and **BTS+noise**. Our method achieves significantly better performance. Table 3 shows the qualitative results of the proposed method. Our

| Input: I will never go to this restaurant again. |
| Output A: I will definitely go to this restaurant again. |
| Output B: I will continue go to this restaurant again. |
| Output C: I will definitely go to this place again. |
| Input: It was just a crappy experience over all. |
| Output A: It was just a wonderful experience at all. |
| Output B: Great place just a full experience over all. |
| Output C: It was such a good experience as all. |
| Input: This place just keeps getting worse and worse. |
| Output A: This place just worth everything and good. |
| Output B: Fantastic place just top notch prices and service. |
| Output C: This place goes out pretty fast and fresh. |

Table 3: One-to-many style transfer results computed by the proposed algorithm.

3.2 More Results and Ablation Study

In addition to generating multiple style transfer outputs, our model can also generate high-quality style transfer outputs. In Figure 4, we compare the quality of our style transfer outputs with those from the competing methods. We show the performance of our model using the style–content curve where each point in the curve is the achieved style score and the content score at different training iterations. In Figure 4a, given a fixed content preservation score, our method achieves a better style score on Amazon dataset. Similarly, given a fixed style score, our model achieves a better content preservation score. The results on Yelp500 and Yelp25000 datasets also demonstrate a similar trend as shown in Figure 4b and Figure 4c, respectively.

The style–content curve also depicts the behavior of the proposed model during the entire learning process. As visualized in Figure 5, we find that our model achieves a high style score but a low content score in the early training stage. With more iterations, our model improves the content score with the expense of a reduced style score. To strike a balance between the two scores, we decrease the learning rate when the model reaches a similar number for the two scores.

User Study. We also conduct a user study on the transfer output quality. Given an input sentence with two generated style transferred sentences from two different models[1], workers are asked to compare the transferred quality of the two generated sentences in terms of content preservation, style

---

[1]The sentences generated by other methods have been made publicly available by (Li et al., 2018).

Method	Style	Content	Fluency	Overall
CAE	30.56	36.81	23.26	30.56
No Pref.	31.60	**39.93**	**51.74**	**37.50**
Ours	**37.85**	23.26	25.00	31.94
MD	29.26	27.56	27.35	28.41
No Pref.	21.88	**52.84**	**47.01**	29.83
Ours	**48.86**	19.60	25.64	**41.76**
BTS	30.66	**40.88**	16.79	30.29
No Pref.	31.75	22.99	**56.93**	32.12
Ours	**37.59**	36.13	26.28	**37.59**
DR	26.30	18.09	22.61	24.96
No Pref.	11.89	**69.01**	**57.96**	21.61
Ours	**61.81**	12.90	19.43	**53.43**

Table 4: User study results. The numbers are the user preference scores of the competing methods.

Model	Style Score	Content Score
sharing-decoder	63.75	42.54
sharing-encoders	81.41	81.48
full	**82.64**	**83.11**

Table 5: Comparison of different design choices of the proposed framework.

transfer, fluency, and overall performance, respectively. We received more than 2500 responses from AMT platform, and the results are summarized in Table 4. We observe *No Preference* was chosen more often than others, which shows exiting methods may not fully satisfy human expectation. However, our method achieves comparable or better performance than the prior works.

Ablation Study. We conduct a study where we consider three different designs of the proposed models. (1) *full*: This is the full version of the proposed model; (2) *sharing-encoders*: In this case, we have a content encoder and a style encoder that are shared by the two domains; (3) *sharing-decoder*: In this case, we have a decoder that is shared by the two domains. Through this study, we aim for studying if regularization via weight-sharing is beneficial to our approach.

Table 5 shows the comparison of our method using different designs. The *sharing-encoders* baseline performs much better than the *sharing-decoder* baseline, and our *full* method performs the best. The results show that the style-specific decoder is more effective for generating target-style outputs. On the other hand, the style-specific encoder extracts more domain-specific style codes from the inputs. Weight-sharing schemes do not lead to a better performance.

Impact of the loss terms. In the appendix, we

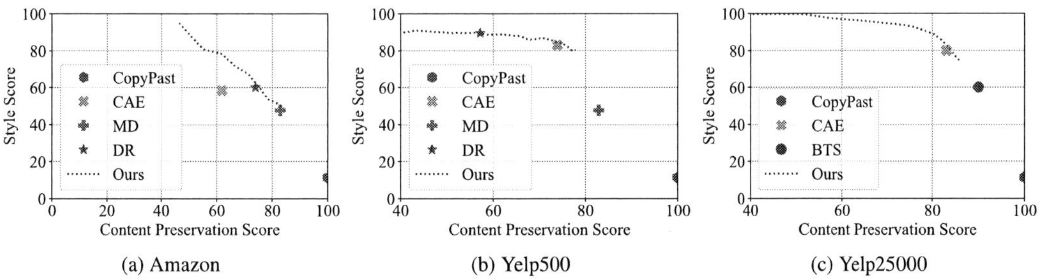

Figure 4: Comparison to different style transfer algorithms on output quality.

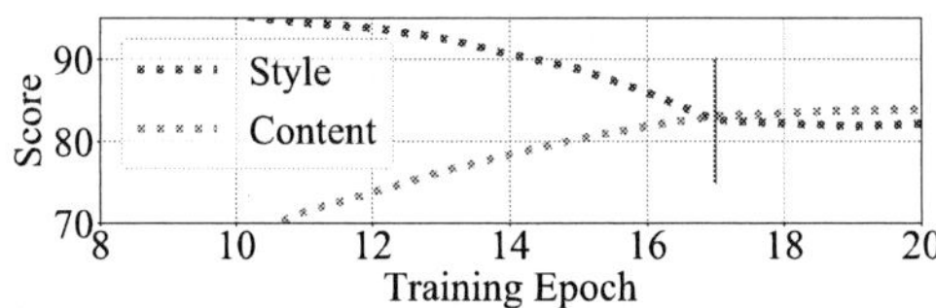

Figure 5: Style–content trade-off curves. The vertical line indicates the iteration at which the learning rate is decreased.

present an ablation study on the loss terms, which shows that all the terms in our objective function are important.

4   Related Works

Language modeling is a core problem in natural language processing. It has a wide range of applications including machine translation (Johnson et al., 2017; Wu et al., 2016), image captioning (Vinyals et al., 2015), and dialogue systems (Li et al., 2016a,b). Recent studies (Devlin et al., 2018; Gehring et al., 2017; Graves, 2013; Johnson et al., 2017; Radford et al., 2019; Wu et al., 2016) proposed to train deep neural networks using maximum-likelihood estimation (MLE) for computing the lexical translation probabilities in parallel corpus. Though effective, acquiring parallel corpus is difficult for many language tasks.

Text style transfer has a longstanding history (Kerpedjiev, 1992). Early studies utilize strongly supervision on parallel corpus (Rao and Tetreault, 2018; Xu, 2017; Xu et al., 2012). However, the lack of parallel training data renders existing methods non-applicable to many text style transfer tasks. Instead of training with paired sentences, recent studies (Fu et al., 2018; Hu et al., 2017; Prabhumoye et al., 2018; Shen et al., 2017) addressed this problem by using adversarial learning techniques. Recent studies further improve the

performance by leveraging domain adaptation (Li et al., 2019) or contextual information (Cheng et al., 2020). In this paper, we argue while the existing methods address the parallel data acquisition difficulty, they do not address the diversity problem in the translated outputs. We address the issue by formulating text style transfer as a one-to-many mapping problem and demonstrate one-to-many style transfer results.

Generative adversarial network (GANs) (Arjovsky et al., 2017; Goodfellow et al., 2014; Salimans et al., 2016; Zhu et al., 2017a) have achieved great success on image generation (Huang et al., 2018; Zhu et al., 2017b). Several attempts are made to applying GAN for the text generation task (Guo et al., 2018; Lin et al., 2017; Yu et al., 2017; Zhang et al., 2017). However, these methods are based on unconditional GANs and tend to generate context-free sentences. Our method is different in that our model is conditioned on the content and style codes, and our method allows a more controllable style transfer.

5   Conclusion

We have presented a novel framework for generating different style transfer outputs for an input sentence. This was achieved by modeling the style transfer as a one-to-many mapping problem with a novel latent decomposition scheme. Experimental results showed that the proposed method achieves better performance than the baselines in terms of the diversity and the overall quality.

Acknowledgement

We would like to thank the anonymous reviewers for their constructive comments. We thank NVIDIA for the donation of the GPU used for this research. We thank Dianqi Li for the helpful discussion.

References

Yelp Dataset Challenge. `https://www.yelp.com/dataset/challenge`.

Martin Arjovsky, Soumith Chintala, and Léon Bottou. 2017. Wasserstein gan. *arXiv preprint arXiv:1701.07875*.

Richard W Brislin. 1970. Back-translation for cross-cultural research. *Journal of cross-cultural psychology*, 1(3):185–216.

Cheng Kuan Chen, Zhu Feng Pan, Min Sun, and Ming-Yu Liu. 2019. Unsupervised stylish image description generation via domain layer norm. In *Proc. AAAI*.

Yu Cheng, Zhe Gan, Yizhe Zhang, Oussama Elachqar, Dianqi Li, and Jingjing Liu. 2020. Contextual text style transfer. *arXiv preprint arXiv:2005.00136*.

Jacob Devlin, Ming-Wei Chang, Kenton Lee, and Kristina Toutanova. 2018. Bert: Pre-training of deep bidirectional transformers for language understanding. *arXiv preprint arXiv:1810.04805*.

Vincent Dumoulin, Jonathon Shlens, and Manjunath Kudlur. 2016. A learned representation for artistic style. In *Proc. ICLR*.

Zhenxin Fu, Xiaoye Tan, Nanyun Peng, Dongyan Zhao, and Rui Yan. 2018. Style transfer in text: Exploration and evaluation. In *Proc. AAAI*.

Jonas Gehring, Michael Auli, David Grangier, Denis Yarats, and Yann N Dauphin. 2017. Convolutional sequence to sequence learning. In *Proc. ICML*.

Ian Goodfellow, Jean Pouget-Abadie, Mehdi Mirza, Bing Xu, David Warde-Farley, Sherjil Ozair, Aaron Courville, and Yoshua Bengio. 2014. Generative adversarial nets. In *Proc. NeurIPS*.

Alex Graves. 2013. Generating sequences with recurrent neural networks. *arXiv preprint arXiv:1308.0850*.

Jiaxian Guo, Sidi Lu, Han Cai, Weinan Zhang, Yong Yu, and Jun Wang. 2018. Long text generation via adversarial training with leaked information. In *Prof. AAAI*.

Ruining He and Julian McAuley. 2016. Ups and downs: Modeling the visual evolution of fashion trends with one-class collaborative filtering. In *Proc. WWW*.

Zhiting Hu, Zichao Yang, Xiaodan Liang, Ruslan Salakhutdinov, and Eric P Xing. 2017. Toward controlled generation of text. In *Proc. ICML*.

Xun Huang and Serge Belongie. 2017. Arbitrary style transfer in real-time with adaptive instance normalization. In *Proc. ICCV*.

Xun Huang, Ming-Yu Liu, Serge Belongie, and Jan Kautz. 2018. Multimodal unsupervised image-to-image translation. In *Proc. ECCV*.

Harsh Jhamtani, Varun Gangal, Eduard Hovy, and Eric Nyberg. 2017. Shakespearizing modern language using copy-enriched sequence to sequence models. In *Proc. EMNLP Workshop on Stylistic Variation*.

Vineet John, Lili Mou, Hareesh Bahuleyan, and Olga Vechtomova. 2019. Disentangled representation learning for non-parallel text style transfer. In *Proc. ACL*.

Melvin Johnson, Mike Schuster, Quoc V Le, Maxim Krikun, Yonghui Wu, Zhifeng Chen, Nikhil Thorat, Fernanda Viégas, Martin Wattenberg, Greg Corrado, et al. 2017. Googles multilingual neural machine translation system: Enabling zero-shot translation. *TACL*.

Stephan M. Kerpedjiev. 1992. Generation of informative texts with style. In *Proc. COLING*.

Dianqi Li, Yizhe Zhang, Zhe Gan, Yu Cheng, Chris Brockett, Bill Dolan, and Ming-Ting Sun. 2019. Domain adaptive text style transfer. In *Proc. EMNLP-IJCNLP*.

Jiwei Li, Michel Galley, Chris Brockett, Georgios Spithourakis, Jianfeng Gao, and Bill Dolan. 2016a. A persona-based neural conversation model. In *Proc. ACL*.

Jiwei Li, Will Monroe, Alan Ritter, Michel Galley, Jianfeng Gao, and Dan Jurafsky. 2016b. Deep reinforcement learning for dialogue generation. *arXiv preprint arXiv:1606.01541*.

Juncen Li, Robin Jia, He He, and Percy Liang. 2018. Delete, retrieve, generate: a simple approach to sentiment and style transfer. In *Proc. NAACL*.

Kevin Lin, Dianqi Li, Xiaodong He, Zhengyou Zhang, and Ming-Ting Sun. 2017. Adversarial ranking for language generation. In *Proc. NeurIPS*.

Tomas Mikolov, Ilya Sutskever, Kai Chen, Greg S Corrado, and Jeff Dean. 2013. Distributed representations of words and phrases and their compositionality. In *Proc. NeurIPS*.

Franz Josef Och and Hermann Ney. 2004. The alignment template approach to statistical machine translation. *Computational linguistics*.

Myle Ott, Sergey Edunov, Alexei Baevski, Angela Fan, Sam Gross, Nathan Ng, David Grangier, and Michael Auli. 2019. fairseq: A fast, extensible toolkit for sequence modeling. In *Proc. NAACL Demonstrations*.

Kishore Papineni, Salim Roukos, Todd Ward, and Wei-Jing Zhu. 2002. Bleu: a method for automatic evaluation of machine translation. In *Proc. ACL*.

Adam Paszke, Sam Gross, Soumith Chintala, Gregory Chanan, Edward Yang, Zachary DeVito, Zeming Lin, Alban Desmaison, Luca Antiga, and Adam Lerer. 2017. Automatic differentiation in PyTorch. In *Proc. NeurIPS Autodiff Workshop*.

Shrimai Prabhumoye, Yulia Tsvetkov, Ruslan Salakhutdinov, and Alan W Black. 2018. Style transfer through back-translation. In *Proc. ACL*.

Alec Radford, Rafal Jozefowicz, and Ilya Sutskever. 2017. Learning to generate reviews and discovering sentiment. *arXiv preprint arXiv:1704.01444*.

Alec Radford, Jeffrey Wu, Rewon Child, David Luan, Dario Amodei, and Ilya Sutskever. 2019. Language models are unsupervised multitask learners. *OpenAI Tech Report*.

Sudha Rao and Joel Tetreault. 2018. Dear sir or madam, may i introduce the yafc corpus: Corpus, benchmarks and metrics for formality style transfer. In *Proc. NAACL*.

Tim Salimans, Ian Goodfellow, Wojciech Zaremba, Vicki Cheung, Alec Radford, and Xi Chen. 2016. Improved techniques for training gans. In *Proc. NeurIPS*.

Rico Sennrich, Barry Haddow, and Alexandra Birch. 2015. Improving neural machine translation models with monolingual data. *arXiv preprint arXiv:1511.06709*.

Tianxiao Shen, Tao Lei, Regina Barzilay, and Tommi Jaakkola. 2017. Style transfer from non-parallel text by cross-alignment. In *Proc. NeruIPS*.

Eric Michael Smith, Diana Gonzalez-Rico, Emily Dinan, and Y-Lan Boureau. 2019. Zero-shot fine-grained style transfer: Leveraging distributed continuous style representations to transfer to unseen styles. *arXiv preprint arXiv:1911.03914*.

Karen Sparck Jones. 1972. A statistical interpretation of term specificity and its application in retrieval. *Journal of documentation*.

Sandeep Subramanian, Guillaume Lample, Eric Michael Smith, Ludovic Denoyer, Marc'Aurelio Ranzato, and Y-Lan Boureau. 2018. Multiple-attribute text style transfer. *arXiv preprint arXiv:1811.00552*.

Ilya Sutskever, Oriol Vinyals, and Quoc V Le. 2014. Sequence to sequence learning with neural networks. In *Proc. NeurIPS*.

Ashish Vaswani, Noam Shazeer, Niki Parmar, Jakob Uszkoreit, Llion Jones, Aidan N Gomez, Łukasz Kaiser, and Illia Polosukhin. 2017. Attention is all you need. In *Proc. NeurIPS*.

Oriol Vinyals, Alexander Toshev, Samy Bengio, and Dumitru Erhan. 2015. Show and tell: A neural image caption generator. In *Proc. CVPR*.

Yonghui Wu, Mike Schuster, Zhifeng Chen, Quoc V Le, Mohammad Norouzi, Wolfgang Macherey, Maxim Krikun, Yuan Cao, Qin Gao, Klaus Macherey, et al. 2016. Google's neural machine translation system: Bridging the gap between human and machine translation. *arXiv preprint arXiv:1609.08144*.

Jingjing Xu, SUN Xu, Qi Zeng, Xiaodong Zhang, Xuancheng Ren, Houfeng Wang, and Wenjie Li. 2018. Unpaired sentiment-to-sentiment translation: A cycled reinforcement learning approach. In *Proc. ACL*.

Wei Xu. 2017. From shakespeare to twitter: What are language styles all about? In *Proc. EMNLP Workshop on Stylistic Variation*.

Wei Xu, Alan Ritter, Bill Dolan, Ralph Grishman, and Colin Cherry. 2012. Paraphrasing for style. *Proc. COLING*.

L Yu, W Zhang, J Wang, and Y Yu. 2017. Seqgan: sequence generative adversarial nets with policy gradient. In *Proc. AAAI*.

Yizhe Zhang, Zhe Gan, Kai Fan, Zhi Chen, Ricardo Henao, Dinghan Shen, and Lawrence Carin. 2017. Adversarial feature matching for text generation. *arXiv preprint arXiv:1706.03850*.

Jun-Yan Zhu, Taesung Park, Phillip Isola, and Alexei A Efros. 2017a. Unpaired image-to-image translation using cycle-consistent adversarial networks. In *Proc. ICCV*.

Jun-Yan Zhu, Richard Zhang, Deepak Pathak, Trevor Darrell, Alexei A Efros, Oliver Wang, and Eli Shechtman. 2017b. Toward multimodal image-to-image translation. In *Proc. NeurIPS*.

Yaoming Zhu, Sidi Lu, Lei Zheng, Jiaxian Guo, Weinan Zhang, Jun Wang, and Yong Yu. 2018. Texygen: A benchmarking platform for text generation models. *Proc. SIGIR*.

A User Study Design

To control the quality of human evaluation, we conduct pilot study to design and improve our evaluation questionnaire. We invite 23 participants who are native or proficient English speakers to evaluate the sentences generated by different methods. For each participant, we randomly present 10 sentences from Yelp500 test set, and the corresponding style transferred sentences generated by different models. We ask the participants to vote the transferred sentence which they think the sentence meaning is closely related to the original sentence with an opposite sentiment. However, we find that it may be difficult to interpret the evaluation results in terms of transfer quality in details.

Therefore, instead of asking the participants to directly vote one sentence, we switch the task to evaluating the sentences in terms of four different aspects including style transfer, content preservation, fluency and grammatically, and overall performance. Following the literature (Prabhumoye et al.,

Method	Style	Content	Fluency	Diversity	Overall
Ours	36.36	42.42	**51.52**	**72.22**	**51.01**
No Pref.	28.79	**43.43**	35.35	16.16	36.87
$CAE_{\sigma=0.001}$	**34.85**	14.14	13.13	11.62	12.12
Ours	30.30	42.93	41.41	**72.73**	**51.01**
No Pref.	**35.35**	**43.94**	**44.95**	14.65	33.84
$CAE_{\sigma=0.01}$	34.34	13.13	13.64	12.63	15.15
Ours	34.34	**43.94**	**48.48**	**60.10**	**47.47**
No Pref.	29.29	42.93	42.42	28.79	39.39
$CAE_{\sigma=0.1}$	**36.36**	13.13	9.09	11.11	13.13
Ours	24.24	**48.48**	**41.41**	**56.57**	**50.00**
No Pref.	36.87	35.86	37.88	28.28	33.33
$CAE_{\sigma=1}$	**38.89**	15.66	20.71	15.15	16.67
Ours	30.81	**44.95**	37.88	**48.99**	**44.44**
No Pref.	**35.86**	41.41	**41.41**	39.39	34.34
$CAE_{\sigma=10}$	33.33	13.64	20.71	11.62	21.21
Ours	33.84	42.42	**46.97**	**68.18**	**43.94**
No Pref.	29.80	**48.80**	37.88	17.17	41.92
$CAE_{k=\{1\}}$	**36.36**	9.09	15.15	14.65	14.14
Ours	**36.87**	43.43	**45.96**	**76.77**	**48.48**
No Pref.	26.26	**45.96**	40.91	11.11	37.88
$CAE_{k=\{1,5\}}$	**36.87**	10.61	13.13	12.12	13.64
Ours	32.32	41.92	**44.44**	**71.72**	**46.46**
No Pref.	26.77	**46.46**	41.41	15.15	38.38
$CAE_{k=\{1,5,10\}}$	**40.91**	11.62	14.14	13.13	15.15
Ours	31.31	**43.94**	**50.51**	**73.74**	**47.47**
No Pref.	33.33	43.43	36.87	12.63	13.64
$CAE_{k=\{1,5,10,15\}}$	**35.35**	12.63	12.63	13.64	15.66

Table 6: Human preference comparison with the **CAE** on one-to-many style transfer results. The numbers are the user preference score of competing methods.

Method	Style	Content	Fluency	Diversity	Overall
Ours	34.34	37.88	**43.94**	**66.67**	**43.43**
No Pref.	30.30	**47.47**	42.93	22.22	40.40
$BTS_{\sigma=0.001}$	**35.35**	14.65	13.13	11.11	16.16
Ours	37.88	38.38	**44.95**	**54.55**	**46.46**
No Pref.	22.73	**45.45**	34.85	32.32	34.34
$BTS_{\sigma=0.01}$	**39.39**	16.16	20.20	13.13	19.19
Ours	29.80	**42.42**	**45.96**	**50.51**	**50.51**
No Pref.	29.29	41.92	36.36	35.86	35.35
$BTS_{\sigma=0.1}$	**40.91**	15.66	17.68	13.64	14.14
Ours	33.33	**42.93**	**46.97**	38.89	**52.53**
No Pref.	31.31	40.40	33.33	**46.97**	24.24
$BTS_{\sigma=1}$	**35.35**	16.67	19.70	14.14	23.23
Ours	34.34	**50.51**	**55.56**	**63.64**	**59.60**
No Pref.	30.30	33.84	25.25	25.25	18.69
$BTS_{\sigma=10}$	**35.35**	15.66	19.19	11.11	21.72
Ours	31.31	**45.96**	41.41	**72.22**	**56.06**
No Pref.	28.28	44.44	**42.93**	15.15	32.83
$BTS_{k=\{1\}}$	**40.40**	9.6	15.66	12.63	11.11
Ours	37.88	39.39	**48.48**	**71.72**	**48.99**
No Pref.	19.70	**48.99**	37.37	14.14	35.86
$BTS_{k=\{1,5\}}$	**42.42**	11.62	14.14	14.14	15.15
Ours	**37.88**	36.87	**44.95**	**71.72**	**47.47**
No Pref.	25.25	**47.47**	38.89	13.64	35.35
$BTS_{k=\{1,5,10\}}$	36.87	15.66	16.16	14.65	17.17
Ours	**36.36**	44.95	41.92	**72.73**	**56.57**
No Pref.	27.78	**46.46**	**45.96**	11.62	31.31
$BTS_{k=\{1,5,10,15\}}$	35.86	8.59	12.12	15.66	12.12

Table 7: Human preference comparison with the **BTS** on one-to-many style transfer results. The numbers are the user preference score of competing methods.

2018), for each pairwise comparison, a third option *No Preference* is given for cases that both are equally good or bad. Figure 8 and Figure 9 show the instructions and the guidelines of our questionnaire for human evaluation on Amazon Mechanical Turk platform. We refer the reader to Sec 3. in the submitted manuscript for the details of the human evaluation results.

To evaluate the performance of one-to-many style transfer, we extend the pair-wise comparison to set-wise comparison. Given an input sentence and two sets of model-generated sentences (5 sentences per set), the workers are asked to choose which set has more diverse sentences with the same meaning, and which set provides more desirable sentences considering both content preservation and style transfer. We also ask the workers to compare the transfer quality in terms of content preservation, style transfer, grammatically and fluency.

B Diversity Baselines

We report further comparisons with different variants of **CAE** and **BTS**. We added random Gaussian noise to the style code of **CAE** and **BTS**, respec-tively. Specifically, we randomly sample the noise from the Gaussian distribution with $\mu = 0$ and $\sigma \in \{0.001, 0.01, 0.1, 1, 10\}$, respectively. We empirically found that the generations will be of poor quality when $\sigma > 10$. Thus, we evaluated the baselines with $\sigma \leq 10$ in the experiments. On the other hand, we also explored different extensions to enhance the diversity of sequence generation of the baselines. For example, we expanded the generations by randomly select a beam search size $k \in \{1, 5, 10, 15\}$ per generation.

C Additional One-to-Many Style Transfer User Study Results

We report the human evaluation with comparisons to different variants of the **CAE** and **BTS**. Similar to the human study presented in the submitted manuscript, we conduct evaluation using Amazon Mechanical Turk. We randomly sampled 200 sentences from Yelp test set for user study. Each comparison is evaluated by at least three experts whose HIT Approval Rate is greater than 90%. We received more than 3600 responses, and the results are summarized in Table 6 and Table 7. We ob-

Recon. Loss	Back-Trans. Loss	Style Cls. Loss	Style Score	Content Preservation Score	BLEU
✗	✓	✗	31.20	45.89	0.00 (66.2/0.2/0.0/0.0)
✗	✗	✓	75.30	20.65	0.00 (0.0/0.0/0.0/0.0)
✗	✓	✓	100.00	42.46	0.00 (35.8/0.1/0.1/0.0)
✓	✗	✗	57.40	90.10	41.28 (69.7/48.2/34.8/25.2)
✓	✓	✗	61.38	90.14	39.72 (70.6/46.5/32.9/23.3)
✓	✗	✓	90.05	74.84	13.87 (48.0/20.4/9.6/4.1)
✓	✓	✓	82.64	83.11	24.5 (59.0/31.8/18.7/10.7)

Table 8: Empiricial analysis of the impact of each term in the proposed objective function for the proposed one-to-many style transfer task.

served previous models achieve higher style scores, but their output sentences are often in a generic format and may not preserve the content with correct grammar. In contrast, our method achieves significantly better performance than the baselines in terms of diversity, fluency, and overall quality.

D Ablation Study on Objective Function

The proposed objective function consists of five different learning objectives. We conduct ablation study to understand which loss function contributes to the performance. Since adversarial loss is essential for domain alignment, we evaluate loss functions by iterating different combination of the reconstruction loss, the back-translation loss (together with the mean square loss), and the style loss.

We report the style score and the content preservation score in this experiment. We additionally present the BLEU score (Papineni et al., 2002), which is a common metric for evaluating the performance of machine translation. A model with a higher BLEU score means that the model is better in translating reasonable sentences. As shown in Table 8, we find that training without reconstruction loss may not produce reasonable sentences according to the BLEU score. Training with reconstruction loss works well for content preservation yet it performs less favorably for style transfer. Back-translation loss is able to improve style and content preservation scores since it encourage content and style representations to be disentangle. When training with the style loss, our model improves the style accuracy, yet performs worse on content preservation. Overall, we observe that training with all the objective terms achieves a balanced performance in terms of different evaluation scores. The results show that the reconstruction loss, the back-translation loss, and the style loss are important for style transfer.

E Style Code Sampling Scheme

We design a sampling scheme that can lead to a more accurate style transfer. During inference, our network takes the input sentence as a query, and retrieves a pool of target style sentences whose content information is similar to the query. We measure the similarity by estimating the cosine similarity between the sentence embeddings. Next, we randomly sample a target style code from the retrieved pool, and generate the output sentence. The test-time sampling scheme improves the content preservation score from 83.11 to 83.41, and achieves similar style score from 82.64 to 82.66 on Yelp25000 test set. The results show that it is possible to improve the content preservation by using the top ranked target style sentences.

We provide further analysis on the sampling scheme for the training phase. Specifically, during training, we sample the target style code from the pool of top ranked sentences in the target style domain. Figure 6 shows the content preservation scores of our method using different sampling schemes. The results suggest we can improve the content preservation by learning with the style codes extracted from the top ranked sentences in the target style domain. However, we noticed that this sampling scheme actually reduces the number of training data. It becomes more challenging for the model to learn the style transfer function as shown in Figure 7. The results suggest that it is more suitable to apply the sampling scheme in the inference phase.

F Additional Implementation Details

We use 256 hidden units for the content encoder, the style encoder, and the decoder. All embeddings in our model have dimensionality 256. We use the same dimensionalities for linear layers mapping between the hidden and embedding sizes. Addi-

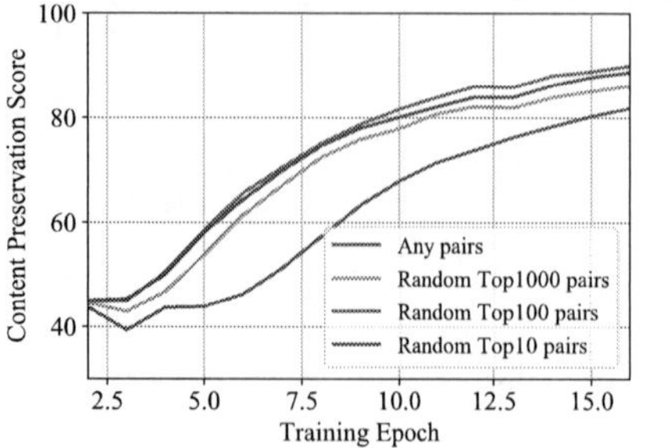

Figure 6: Performance comparison of our model using different sampling schemes.

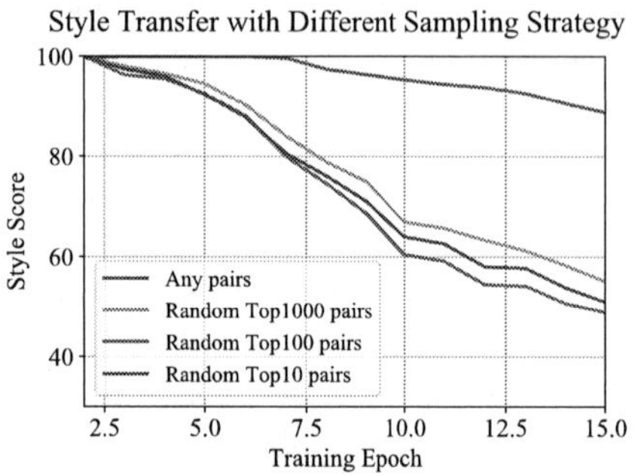

Figure 7: Performance comparison of our model using different sampling schemes.

tionally, we modify the convolution block in the style encoder E_i^s to have max pooling layers for capturing the activation of the style words. On the other hand, we also modify the convolution block of the content encoder E_i^c to have average pooling layers for computing the average activation of the input. During inference, the decoder generates the output sentence with the multi-step attention mechanism (Gehring et al., 2017).

G Application to Other Styles

Our approach is general and can be applied to other sentences that are different from restaurant reviews. We have studied this capability by implementing our method on the Stylish descriptions dataset (Chen et al., 2019), which has the country song lyrics and romance novel collections. Table 9 shows the example results of the proposed method.

H Failure Cases

Although our approach performs more favorably against the previous methods, our model still fails in a couple of situations. Table 10 shows the common failure example generated by our model. We

Lyrics input: My friends they told me you change like the weather; From one love to another you would go; But when I first met you your love was like the summer; Love I never dreamed of turning cold
Romantic style: My friends they told me you change like the light; From one love to another you would go; But when I first met you your love was like the sun; Love I never dreamed of turning cold
Romantic style: My lips they told me you change like the light; From one love to find you would go; But when I am you your love was like the mountain; Love I never wanted of me before

Table 9: One-to-many style transfer results computed by the proposed algorithm.

Input: I stayed here but was disappointed as its air conditioner does not work properly.
Output: I love here but was but as well feel's me work too.

Input: I might as well been at a street fest it was so crowded everywhere.
Output: I well as well a at a reasonable price it was so pleasant.

Input: Free cheese puff - but had rye in it (I hate rye!).
Output: It's not gourmet but it definitely satisfies my taste for good Mexican food.

Table 10: Example failure cases generated by the proposed method.

observe that it is challenging to preserve the content when the inputs are the lengthy sentences. It is also challenging to transfer the style if the sentence contains novel symbols or complicated structure.

Instruction

The goal of this evaluation is to investigate the performance of different models on the text style transfer task.

During the evaluation, you are given a reference sentence that **either has positive sentiment or negative sentiment**. Meanwhile, two model-generated sentences, **which should be written in an opposite sentiment style**, are also presented to you. Your task is to **compare the transferred quality of the two generated sentences in terms of the following aspects:**

- Opposite Sentiment:

  When compared to the reference sentence, choose one of the generated sentences has better **opposite** sentiment information. If you have no preference, choose "No preference".

- Content Preservation:

  When compared to the reference sentence, choose one of the generated sentences has better content preservation quality **by ignoring the sentiment information.** If you have no preference, choose "No preference".

- Grammaticality & Fluency:

  Choose one of the generated sentences has less grammatical errors and reads more fluently to you. If you have no preference, choose "No preference".

- Over performance (Content Preservation & Opposite Sentiment):

  Choose one of the generated sentences which you think the sentence meaning is closely related to the reference sentence with an **opposite** sentiment. If you have no preference, choose "No preference".

Figure 8: Instruction of our questionnaire on Amazon Mechanical Turk platform.

Give the reference sentence:

  "This is a great movie!"

- Opposite Sentiment:

  You should choose these sentences that have the **opposite** sentiment:

  "This is not a good movie.";
  "This is a bad actor";
  "This pizza is disgusting!"

  You should not choose these sentences that have the same sentiment:

  "This is a good movie.";
  "This is a fantastic journey!";
  "I love this restaurant."

- Content Preservation (by ignoring the sentiment information):

  You should choose these sentences that have similar content:

  "This is a good movie.";
  "This is very terrible movie";

  You should not choose these sentences that have a completely different content:

  "I did not like the salad";
  "This pizza is tasty";
  "What a terrible experience!"

- Overall Performance (Content Preservation & Opposite Sentiment):

  You should choose these sentences that have similar content with the **opposite** sentiment:

  "This is not a good movie.";
  "This is very terrible movie";
  "I don't like this movie";

  You should not choose these sentences that have unrelated content or don't have opposite sentiment:

  "This is an awesome movie.";
  "This pizza is tasty";
  "What a terrible experience!"

Figure 9: Example and guideline of our questionnaire on Amazon Mechanical Turk platform.

Balancing Cost and Benefit with Tied-Multi Transformers

Raj Dabre   **Raphael Rubino**   **Atsushi Fujita**
National Institute of Information and Communications Technology
3-5 Hikaridai, Seika-cho, Soraku-gun, Kyoto, 619-0289, Japan
`firstname.lastname@nict.go.jp`

Abstract

We propose a novel procedure for training multiple Transformers with tied parameters which compresses multiple models into one enabling the dynamic choice of the number of encoder and decoder layers during decoding. In training an encoder-decoder model, typically, the output of the last layer of the N-layer encoder is fed to the M-layer decoder, and the output of the last decoder layer is used to compute loss. Instead, our method computes a single loss consisting of $N \times M$ losses, where each loss is computed from the output of one of the M decoder layers connected to one of the N encoder layers. Such a model subsumes $N \times M$ models with different number of encoder and decoder layers, and can be used for decoding with fewer than the maximum number of encoder and decoder layers. Given our flexible tied model, we also address to a-priori selection of the number of encoder and decoder layers for faster decoding, and explore recurrent stacking of layers and knowledge distillation for model compression. We present a cost-benefit analysis of applying the proposed approaches for neural machine translation and show that they reduce decoding costs while preserving translation quality.

1   Introduction

Neural networks for sequence-to-sequence modeling typically consist of an encoder and a decoder coupled via an attention mechanism. Whereas the very first deep models used stacked recurrent neural networks (RNN) (Sutskever et al., 2014; Cho et al., 2014; Bahdanau et al., 2015) in the encoder and decoder, the recent Transformer model (Vaswani et al., 2017) constitutes the current state-of-the-art approach, owing to its better context modeling via multi-head self- and cross-attentions.

Given an encoder-decoder architecture and its hyper-parameters, such as the number of encoder and decoder layers, vocabulary sizes (in the case of models for texts), and hidden layers, the parameters of the model, i.e., matrices and biases for non-linear transformations, are optimized by iteratively updating them so that the loss for the training data is minimized. The hyper-parameters can also be tuned, for instance, through maximizing the automatic evaluation score on the development data. However, in general, it is highly unlikely (or impossible) that a single optimized model suffices diverse cost-benefit demands at the same time. For instance, in practical low-latency scenarios, one may accept some performance drop for speed. However, a model used with a subset of optimized parameters might perform badly. Also, a single optimized model cannot guarantee the best performance for each individual input. An existing solution for these problems is to train multiple models and host them simultaneously. However, this approach is not very practical, because it requires a large number of resources. We also lack a well-established method for selecting appropriate models for each individual input prior to decoding.

As a more effective solution, we consider training a single model that subsumes multiple models which can be used for decoding with different hyper-parameter settings depending on the input or on the latency requirements. In this paper, we focus on the number of layers as an important hyper-parameter that impacts both speed and quality of decoding, and propose a *multi-layer softmaxing* method, which uses the outputs of all layers during training. Conceptually, as illustrated in Figure 1, this is the same as tying (sharing) the parameters of multiple models with different number of layers and is not specific to particular types of multi-layer neural models.

Despite the generality of our proposed method, in this paper, we focus on encoder-decoder models with N encoder and M decoder layers, and

Proceedings of the 4th Workshop on Neural Generation and Translation (WNGT 2020), pages 24–34
Online, July 10, 2020. ©2020 Association for Computational Linguistics
www.aclweb.org/anthology/D19-56%2d

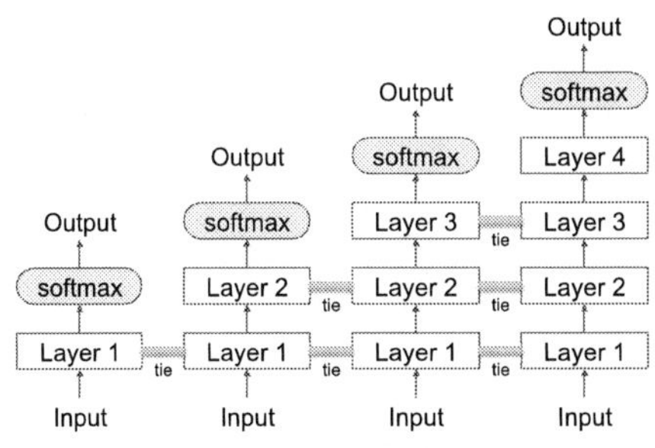

(a) Multiple tied-layer vanilla models.

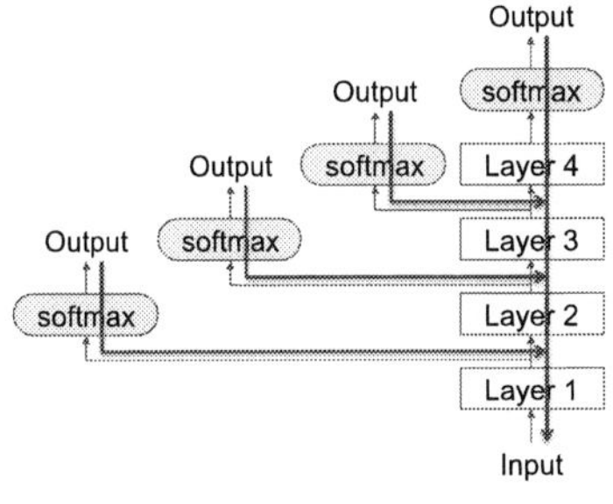

(b) Collapsing tied layers into one.

Figure 1: The general concept of multi-layer softmaxing for training multi-layer neural models with an example of a 4-layer model. Figure 1a is a depiction of our idea in the form of multiple vanilla models whose layers are tied together. Figure 1b shows the result of collapsing all tied layers into a single layer. The red lines indicate the flow of gradients and hence the shallowest layer in the stack receives the largest number of updates.

compress $N \times M$ models[1] by updating the model with a total of $N \times M$ losses computed by softmaxing the output of each of the M decoder layers, where it attends to the output of each of the N encoder layers. The number of parameters of the resultant encoder-decoder model is equivalent to that of the most complex subsumed model with N encoder and M decoder layers. Yet, we can now perform faster decoding using a fewer number of layers, given that shallower layers are also directly trained.

To evaluate our proposed method, we take the case study of neural machine translation (NMT) (Cho et al., 2014; Bahdanau et al., 2015), using the Transformer model (Vaswani et al., 2017), and demonstrate that a single model with N encoder and M decoder layers trained by our method can be used for flexibly decoding with fewer than N and M layers without appreciable quality loss. We evaluate our proposed method on WMT18 English-to-German translation task, and give a cost-benefit analysis for translation quality vs. decoding speed.

Given a flexible tied model, for saving decoding time, we then design mechanisms to choose, prior to decoding, the appropriate number of encoder and decoder layers depending on the input. We also focus on compact modeling, where we leverage other orthogonal types of parameter tying approaches. Compact models are faster to decode and will be useful in cases where a-priori layer prediction might be infeasible.

The rest of the paper is organized as follows. Section 2 briefly reviews related work for compressing neural models. Section 3 covers our

method that ties multiple models by softmaxing all encoder-decoder layer combinations. Section 4 describes our efforts towards designing and evaluating a mechanism for dynamically selecting encoder-decoder layer combinations prior to decoding. Section 5 describes two orthogonal extensions to our model aiming at further model compression and speeding-up of decoding. The paper ends with Section 6 containing conclusion and future work.

2 Related Work

There are studies that exploit multiple layers simultaneously. Wang et al. (2018) fused hidden representations of multiple layers in order to improve the translation quality. Belinkov et al. (2017) and Dou et al. (2018) attempted to identify which layer can generate useful representations for different natural language processing tasks. Unlike them, we make all layers of the encoder and decoder usable for decoding with any encoder-decoder layer combination. In practical scenarios, we can save significant amounts of time by choosing shallower encoder and decoder layers for inference.

Our method ties the parameters of multiple models, which is orthogonal to the work that ties parameters between layers (Dabre and Fujita, 2019) and/or between the encoder and decoder within a single model (Xia et al., 2019; Dabre and Fujita, 2019). Parameter tying leads to compact models, but they usually suffer from drops in inference quality. In this paper, we counter such drops with knowledge distillation (Hinton et al., 2015; Kim and Rush, 2016; Freitag et al., 2017). This approach utilizes smoothed data or smoothed training signals instead of the actual training data. A model with a large number of parameters and high per-

---

[1]Rather than casting the encoder-decoder model into a single column model with $(N + M)$ layers.

formance provides smoothed distributions that are then used as labels for training small models instead of one-hot vectors.

As one of the aims in this work is model size reduction, it is related to a growing body of work that addresses the computational requirement reduction. Pruning of pre-trained models (See et al., 2016) makes it possible to discard around 80% of the smallest weights of a model without deterioration in inference quality, given it is re-trained with appropriate hyper-parameters after pruning. Currently, most deep learning implementations use 32-bit floating point representations, but 16-bit floating point representations (Gupta et al., 2015; Ott et al., 2018) or aggressive binarization (Courbariaux et al., 2017) can be alternatives. Compact models are usually faster to decode; studies on quantization (Lin et al., 2016) and average attention networks (Xiong et al., 2018) address this topic.

None of the above work has attempted to combine multi-model parameter tying, knowledge distillation, and dynamic layer selection for obtaining and exploiting highly-compressed and flexible deep neural models.

3 Multi-Layer Softmaxing

3.1 Proposed Method

Consider an N-layer encoder and M-layer decoder model. Let X be the embedded input to the encoder, Y the expected output of the decoder as well as the input to the decoder (for training), and $\hat{Y}$ the output predicted by the decoder. Algorithm 1 shows the pseudo-code for our proposed method. Line 3 represents the process done by the i-th encoder layer, L_i^{enc}, and line 5 does the same for the j-th decoder layer, L_j^{dec}, given the embedded decoder input, dec_0. In simple words, we compute a loss using the output of each of the M decoder layers which in turn is computed using the output of each of the N encoder layers. In line 8, the $N \times M$ losses are aggregated[2] before back-propagation. Henceforth, we will refer to this as the *Tied-Multi model*.

For a comparison, the vanilla model is formulated as follows: $dec_j = L_j^{dec}(dec_{j-1}, enc_N)$, $\hat{Y} = softmax(dec_M)$, and $overall\_loss = cross\_entropy(\hat{Y}, Y)$.

Algorithm 1: Training a tied-multi model

1   $enc_0 = X$;
2   **for** i *in 1 to N* **do**
3      $enc_i = L_i^{enc}(enc_{i-1})$;
4   **for** j *in 1 to M* **do**
5          $dec_j = L_j^{dec}(dec_{j-1}, enc_i)$;
6          $\hat{Y} = softmax(dec_j)$;
7          $loss_{i,j} = cross\_entropy(\hat{Y}, Y)$;
8   $overall\_loss = aggregate(loss_{1,1}, \ldots, loss_{N,M})$;
9   Back-propagate using $overall\_loss$;

3.2 Experimental Setup

We evaluated the utility of our multi-layer softmaxing method on a neural machine translation task. We experimented with the WMT18 English-to-German (En→De) translation task. We used all the parallel corpora available for WMT18, except ParaCrawl corpus,[3] consisting of 5.58M sentence pairs, as the training data and 2,998 sentences in newstest2018 as test data. The English and German sentences were pre-processed using the `tokenizer.perl` and `truecase.perl` in `Moses`.[4] The true-case models for English and German were trained on 10M sentences randomly extracted from the monolingual data made available for the WMT18 translation task, using the `train-truecaser.perl` in `Moses`.

We evaluated the following two types of models on both translation quality and decoding speed.

Vanilla models: 36 vanilla models with 1 to 6 encoder and 1 to 6 decoder layers, each trained referring only to the last layer for computing loss.

Tied-Multi model: A single tied-multi model with $N = 6$ encoder and $M = 6$ decoder layers, trained by our multi-layer softmaxing.

Our multi-layer softmaxing method was implemented on top of an open-source toolkit of the Transformer model (Vaswani et al., 2017) in the version 1.6 branch of `tensor2tensor`.[5] For training, we used the default model settings corresponding to `transformer_base_single_gpu` in the implementation, except what follows. We used a shared sub-word vocabulary of 32k determined using the internal sub-word segmenter of tensor2tensor. To ensure that each model sees roughly

---

[2] We averaged multiple losses in our experiment, but there are a number of options, such as weighted averaging.

[3] http://www.statmt.org/wmt18/translation-task.html
We excluded ParaCrawl following the instruction on the WMT18 website: "BLEU score dropped by 1.0" for this task.

[4] https://github.com/moses-smt/mosesdecoder

[5] https://github.com/tensorflow/tensor2tensor

| | BLEU score | | | | | | | | | | | | Decoding time (sec) | | | | | |
| | 36 vanilla models | | | | | | Single tied-multi model | | | | | | | | | | | |
$n \backslash m$	1	2	3	4	5	6	1	2	3	4	5	6	1	2	3	4	5	6
1	26.3	30.3	31.9	32.2	32.4	32.9	23.2	28.6	30.5	30.8	31.2	31.5	94.7	101.9	143.4	174.7	215.5	244.5
2	28.6	32.5	33.1	33.3	33.5	33.2	26.5	31.5	33.0	33.6	33.8	34.0	100.5	110.8	153.7	185.6	227.8	253.6
3	29.2	32.6	33.6	34.4	34.3	34.1	27.8	32.5	33.9	34.6	34.7	34.7	102.5	114.2	168.5	194.8	234.0	259.8
4	29.8	33.6	34.3	34.7	34.4	34.5	28.3	33.0	34.3	34.8	34.9	34.9	104.1	105.6	143.9	197.0	219.1	264.6
5	30.7	33.9	34.6	35.5	34.4	35.0	28.6	33.1	34.5	34.8	35.0	35.1	105.1	111.5	156.4	186.0	236.1	268.8
6	30.8	34.0	34.4	**35.7**	35.0	35.0	28.7	33.1	34.6	34.7	34.9	35.0	107.4	113.6	168.1	190.1	229.5	257.9

Table 1: BLEU scores of 36 separately trained vanilla models and our single tied-multi model used with n ($1 \leq n \leq N$) encoder and m ($1 \leq m \leq M$) decoder layers. One set of decoding times is also shown given the fact that vanilla and our tied-multi models have identical shapes when n and m for encoder and decoder layers are specified.

the same number of examples during training,[6] we trained the models for 300k iterations, with 1 GPU for the vanilla models and 2 GPUs with batch size halved for our tied-multi model. We averaged the last 10 checkpoints saved every after 1k updates, decoded the test sentences, fixing a beam size[7] of 4 and length penalty of 0.6, and post-processed the decoded results using the `detokenizer.perl` and `detruecase.perl` in `Moses`.

We evaluated our models using the BLEU metric (Papineni et al., 2002) implemented in sacreBLEU (Post, 2018).[8] We also present the time consumed to translate the test data, which includes times for the model instantiation, loading the checkpoints, sub-word splitting and indexing, decoding, and sub-word de-indexing and merging, whereas times for detokenization are not taken into account.

Note that we did not use any development data for two reasons. First, we train all models for the same number of iterations. Second, we use checkpoint averaging before decoding, which does not require development data unlike early stopping.

3.3 Results

Table 1 summarizes the BLEU scores and the average decoding times[9] over 3 runs of all the models, exhibiting the cost-benefit property of our tied-multi model in comparison with the results of the corresponding 36 vanilla models.

Even though the objective function for the tied-multi model is substantially more complex than the one for the vanilla model, when performing decoding with the 6 encoder and 6 decoder layers, it achieved a BLEU score of 35.0, which is approaching to the best BLEU score of 35.7 given by the vanilla model with 6 encoder and 4 decoder layers. Note that when using a single encoder layer and/or a single decoder layer, the vanilla models gave significantly higher BLEU score than the tied-multi model. However, when the number of layers is increased, there is no significant difference between the two types of models.

Regarding the cost-benefit property of our tied-multi model, two points must be noted:

- BLEU score and decoding time increase only slightly, when we use more encoder layers.

- The bulk of the decoding time is consumed by the decoder, since it works in an auto-regressive manner. We can substantially cut down decoding time by using fewer decoder layers which does lead to sub-optimal translation quality.

One may argue that training a single vanilla model with optimal number of encoder and decoder layers is enough. However, as discussed in Section 1, it is impossible to know a priori which combination is the best for different input sentences. More importantly, a single vanilla model cannot suffice diverse cost-benefit demands and cannot guarantee the best translation for any input (see Section 3.4). Recall that we aim at a flexible model and that all the results in Table 1 have been obtained using a single tied-multi model, albeit using different number of encoder and decoder layers for decoding.

3.4 Analysis and Discussion

We conducted an analysis from the perspective of training time, model size, and decoding behavior, in comparison with vanilla models.

---

[6]This might lead to sub-optimal models, such as immature or over-fit ones, so we will examine the convergence in future.

[7]One can realize faster decoding by narrowing down the beam width. This approach is orthogonal to ours and in this paper we do not insist which is superior to the other.

[8]https://github.com/mjpost/sacreBLEU signature: BLEU+case.mixed+lang.en-de+numrefs.1 +smooth.exp+test.wmt18+tok.13a+version.1.3.7

[9]These numbers will vary depending on machine, model architecture, concurrent processes, implementation, hyperparameters, etc. For instance, decoding with a larger length penalty produces longer sentences consuming a longer time.

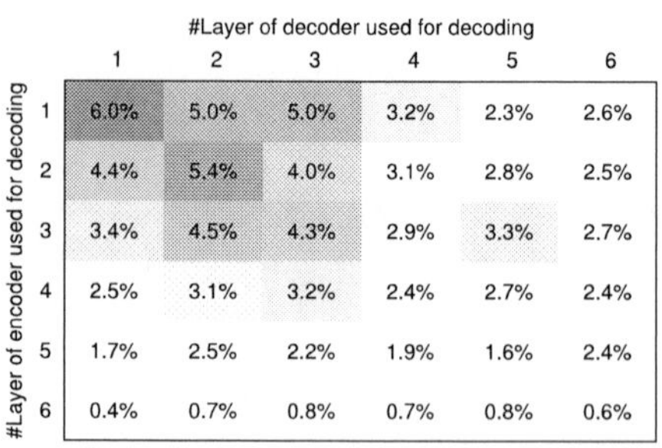

(a) 36 vanilla models.   (b) Single tied-multi model.

Figure 2: Distribution of oracle translations determined by chrF scores between reference and each of the hypotheses derived from the 36 combinations of encoder and decoder layers (newstest2018, 2,998 sentences).

Training Time: Given that all our models were trained for the same number of iterations, we compared the training times between vanilla and tied-multi models. As a reference, we use the vanilla model with 6 encoder and 6 decoder layers. The total training time for all the 36 vanilla models was 25.5 times[10] that of the reference model. In contrast, the training time for our tied-multi model was about 9.5 times that of the same reference model. This is because training of a tied-multi model can aggressively leverage GPU parallellism for its vast number of computations.

Model Size: The number of parameters of our tied-multi model is exactly the same as the vanilla model with N encoder and M decoder layers. If we train a set of vanilla models with different numbers of encoder and decoder layers, we end up with significantly more parameters. For instance, in case of $N = M = 6$ in our experiment, we have 25.2 times more parameters: a total of 4,607M for the 36 vanilla models against 183M for our tied-multi model. In Section 5, we discuss the possibility of further model compression.

Decoding Behavior: To better understand the nature of our proposed method, we analyzed the distribution of oracle translations within 36 translations generated by each of the vanilla and our tied-multi models. Let (n, m) be an encoder-decoder layer combination of a given model with n encoder and m decoder layers. The oracle layer combination for an input sentence was determined by measuring the quality of the translation derived from each layer combination. We used a reference-based metric,

chrF (Popović, 2016), since it has been particularity designed for sentence-level translation evaluation and was shown to have relatively high correlation with human judgment of translation quality at sentence level for the English–German pair (Ma et al., 2018). In cases where multiple combinations have the highest score, we chose the fastest one following the overall trend of decoding time (Table 1). Formally, we considered a combination (n_1, m_1) is faster than another combination (n_2, m_2) if the following holds.

$$(n_1, m_1) < (n_2, m_2)$$
$$\equiv m_1 < m_2 \vee (m_1 = m_2 \wedge n_1 < n_2). \tag{1}$$

Figure 2 compares the distributions of oracle layer combinations for the vanilla and our tied-multi models, revealing that the shallower layer combinations in our tied-multi model often generates better translations than deeper ones unlike the vanilla models, despite the lower corpus-level BLEU scores. This sharp bias towards shallower layer combinations suggests the potential reduction of decoding time by dynamically selecting the layer combination per input sentence prior to decoding, ideally without performance drop. We address this task in Section 4.

4 Dynamic Layer Selection

Motivated by the results shown in Figure 2, we tackled an advanced problem: dynamic selection of one layer combination prior to decoding.[11]

4.1 Method

We formalize the encoder-decoder layer combination selection with a supervised learning approach

---

[10]We measured the collapsed time for a fair comparison, assuming that all vanilla models were trained on a single GPU one after another, even though one may be able to use multiple GPUs to train the 36 vanilla models in parallel.

[11]This is the crucial difference from two post-decoding processes: translation quality estimation (Specia et al., 2010) and n-best-list re-ranking (Kumar and Byrne, 2004).

where the objective is to minimize the following loss function (2).

$$\arg\min_\theta \frac{1}{|S|} \sum_{s^i \in S} \mathcal{L}(f(s^i; \theta), t_k^i), \qquad (2)$$

where s^i is the i-th input sentence ($1 \leq i \leq |S|$), t_k^i is the translation for s^i derived from the k-th layer combination ($1 \leq k \leq K$) among K possible combinations, where $K = N \times M$ in our case, f is the model with parameters θ, and $\mathcal{L}$ is a loss function. Assuming that the independence of target labels (layer combinations) for a given input sentence allows for ties, the model is able to predict multiple layer combinations for the same input sentence.

We implemented the model f with a multi-head self-attention neural network inspired by Vaswani et al. (2017). The number of layers and attention heads are optimized during a hyper-parameter search, while the feed-forward layer dimensionality is fixed to 2,048. Input sequences of tokens are mapped to their corresponding embeddings, initialized by the embedding table of the tied-multi NMT model. Similarly to BERT (Devlin et al., 2019), a specific token is prepended to input sequence before being fed to the classifier. This token is finally fed during the forward pass to the output linear layer for sentence classification. The output linear layer has K dimensions, allowing to output as many logits as the number of layer combinations in the tied-multi NMT model. Finally, a sigmoid function outputs probabilities for each layer combination among the K possible combinations.

The parameters θ of the model f are learned using mini-batch stochastic gradient descent with Nesterov momentum (Sutskever et al., 2013) and the loss function $\mathcal{L}$, implemented as a weighted binary cross-entropy (BCE) function (3).

$$
\begin{aligned}
&\mathcal{L}_{\mathrm{BCE}_k^i} \\
&= -w_k^i \left[\delta_k y_k^i \cdot \log \hat{y}_k^i + (1 - y_k^i) \cdot \log(1 - \hat{y}_k^i) \right],
\end{aligned} \qquad (3)
$$

where y_k^i is the reference class of the i-th input sentence s^i, $\hat{y}_k^i$ is the output of the network after the sigmoid layer given s^i, and $\delta_k = (1 - p(t_k))^\alpha$ is the weight given to the k-th class based on class distribution prior. During our experiment, we have found that the classifier tends to favor recall in detriment to precision. To tackle this issue, we introduce another loss using an approximation of the macro F_β implemented following (4).

$$\mathcal{L}_{F_\beta}^i = 1 - \left[(1 + \beta^2) \cdot \frac{P \cdot R}{(\beta^2 \cdot P) + R} \right], \qquad (4)$$

where $P = \mu / \sum_k \hat{y}_k^i$, $R = \mu / \sum_k y_k^i$, and $\mu = \sum_k (\hat{y}_k^i \cdot y_k^i)$.

The final loss function is the linear interpolation of $\mathcal{L}_{\mathrm{BCE}}$ averaged over the K classes and $\mathcal{L}_{F_\beta}$ with parameter λ, both averaged over the batch: $\lambda \times \mathcal{L}_{\mathrm{BCE}} + (1 - \lambda) \times \mathcal{L}_{F_\beta}$. We tune α, β, and λ during the classifier hyper-parameter search based on the validation loss.

4.2 Experiment

The layer combination classifier was trained on a subset of the training data for NMT models (Section 3.2) containing 5.00M sentences, whereas the remaining sentences compose a development and a test sets each containing approximately 200k sentences. The two latter subsets were used for hyper-parameter search and evaluation of the classifier, respectively. To allow for comparison and reproducibility, the final evaluation of the proposed approach in terms of translation quality and decoding speed were conducted on the official WMT development (newstest2017, 3,004 sentences) and test (newstest2018, 2,998 sentences) sets; the latter is the one also used in Section 3.2.

The training, development, and test sets were translated by each layer combination of the tied-multi NMT model. Each source sentence was thus aligned with 36 translations whose quality were measured by the chrF metric. Because several combinations can lead to the best score, the obtained dataset was labeled with multiple classes (36 layer combinations) and multiple labels (ties with regard to the metric). During inference, the ties were broken by selecting the layer combination with the highest value given by the sigmoid function, or backing-off to the deepest layer combination (6, 6) if no output value reaches 0.5. This tie breaking method differs from the oracle layer selection presented in Equation (1) and in Figure 2 which prioritizes shallowest layer combinations. In this experiment, decoding time was measured by processing one sentence at a time instead of batch decoding, the former being slower compared to the latter, but leads to precise results. The decoding times were 954s and 2,773s when using (1,1) and (6,6) layer combinations, respectively. By selecting the fastest encoder-decoder layer combinations

Classifier	Fine-tuning	Time (s)	BLEU
Baseline (tied (6,6))		2,773	35.0
Oracle (tied)		1,812	42.1
(#1) 8 layers, 8 heads	✓	2,736	35.0
(#2) 2 layers, 4 heads	✓	2,686	34.8
(#3) 2 layers, 4 heads		2,645	34.7
(#4) 4 layers, 2 heads		2,563	34.3

Table 2: Dynamic layer combination selection results in decoding time (in seconds, batch size of 1) and BLEU, including the baseline and oracle for the WMT newstest2018 using the tied-multi model architecture.

according to an oracle, the decoding times went down to 1,918s and 1,812s for the individual and tied-multi models, respectively. However, our objective is to be faster than default setting, that is, where one would choose (6,6) combination.

Several classifiers were trained and evaluated on the WMT test set, with or without fine-tuning on the WMT development set. Table 2 presents the results in terms of corpus-level BLEU and decoding speed.[12] Some classifiers maintain the translation quality (middle rows), whereas others show quality degradation but further gain in decoding speed (bottom rows). The classification results show that gains in decoding speed are possible with an a-priori decision for which encoder-decoder combination to select, based on the information contained in the source sentence only. However, no BLEU gain has so far been observed, demonstrating a trade-off between decoding speed and translation quality. Our best configuration for decoding speed (#4) reduced 210s but leads to a 0.7 point BLEU degradation. On the other hand, when preserving the translation quality compared to the baseline configuration (#1) we saved only 37s. The oracle layer combination can achieve substantial gains both in terms of BLEU (7.1 points) and decoding speed (961s). These oracle results motivate possible future work in layer combination prediction for the tied-multi NMT model.

5 Further Model Compression

We examined the combination of our multi-layer softmaxing approach with another parameter-tying method in neural networks, called *recurrent stacking* (RS) (Dabre and Fujita, 2019), complemented by *sequence-level knowledge distillation* (Kim and Rush, 2016), a specific type of knowledge distillation (Hinton et al., 2015). We demonstrate that

these existing techniques help reduce the number of parameters in our model even further.

5.1 Distillation into a Recurrently Stacked Model

In Section 2, we have discussed several model compression methods orthogonal to multi-layer softmaxing. Having already compressed $N \times M$ models with our approach, we consider further compressing it using RS. However, models that use RS layers tend to suffer from performance drops due to the large reduction in the number of parameters. As a way of compensating the performance drop, we apply sequence-level knowledge distillation.

First, we decode all source sentences in the training data to generate a pseudo-parallel corpus containing distillation target sentences, i.e., soft-targets for the child model which makes learning easier and hence is able to mimic the behavior of the parent model. Then, an RS child model is trained with multi-layer softmaxing on the generated pseudo-parallel corpus. Among a variety of distillation techniques, we chose the simplest one to show the impact that distillation can have in our setting, leaving an extensive exploration of more complex methods for the future.

5.2 Experiment

We conducted an experiment to show that RS and sequence distillation can lead to an extremely compressed tied-multi model which no longer suffers from performance drops. We compared the following four variations of our tied-multi model trained with multi-layer softmaxing.

Tied-multi model: A model that does not share the parameters across layers, trained on the original parallel corpus.

Distilled tied-multi model: The same model as above but trained on the pseudo-parallel corpus.

Tied-multi RS model: A tied-multi model that uses RS layers, trained on the original parallel corpus.

Distilled tied-multi RS model: The same model as above but trained on the pseudo-parallel corpus.

First, we trained 5 vanilla models with 6 encoder and 6 decoder layers, because the performance of

---

[12]Decoding time does not include the time spent for layer selection, which took up to 1.0 second for the entire test set.

	$n \backslash m$	Tied-multi model						Tied-multi RS model					
		1	2	3	4	5	6	1	2	3	4	5	6
	1	23.2	28.6	30.5	30.8	31.2	31.5	25.7	29.8	30.6	30.8	30.7	30.9
	2	26.5	31.5	33.0	33.6	33.8	34.0	28.5	32.3	32.9	33.0	33.1	33.2
without	3	27.8	32.5	33.9	34.6	34.7	34.7	29.2	32.9	33.6	33.8	33.6	33.5
distillation	4	28.3	33.0	34.3	34.8	34.9	34.9	29.3	33.2	33.7	33.9	33.6	33.7
	5	28.6	33.1	34.5	34.8	35.0	35.1	29.4	33.2	33.7	33.9	33.9	34.0
	6	28.7	33.1	34.6	34.7	34.9	35.0	29.2	33.2	33.7	33.9	34.0	33.8
	1	30.1	34.0	35.1	35.3	35.6	35.7	31.2	33.5	34.1	34.2	34.3	34.3
	2	33.4	35.8	36.6	36.8	37.1	37.3	33.7	35.5	35.7	35.7	35.8	35.8
with	3	34.7	36.5	37.0	37.4	37.4	37.5	34.1	35.8	36.1	36.1	36.2	36.2
distillation	4	35.2	36.8	37.2	37.4	37.5	37.5	34.3	36.0	36.2	36.2	36.3	36.3
	5	35.5	36.9	37.1	37.4	37.5	37.6	34.5	36.1	36.2	36.3	36.3	36.3
	6	35.5	37.0	37.2	37.5	37.6	37.6	34.6	36.1	36.2	36.2	36.3	36.2

Table 3: BLEU scores of the tied-multi models with (left block) and without (center and right blocks) RS layers, each trained with (bottom block) and without (top block) sequence distillation. n and m respectively denote the number of layers in the encoder and the decoder. The top-left block is identical to the middle block in Table 1.

distilled models is affected by the quality of parent models, and NMT models vary vastly in performance (around 2.0 BLEU points) depending on parameter initialization. We then decode the source side (English side) of the entire training data (5.58M sentences) with the one[13] with the highest BLEU score on the newstest2017 (used in Section 4.2) in order to generate pseudo-parallel corpus for sequence distillation.

Table 3 gives the BLEU scores for all models. Comparing top-left and top-right blocks of the table, we can see that the BLEU scores for RS models are higher than their non-RS counterparts when using fewer than 3 decoder layers. This shows the benefit of RS layers despite the large parameter reduction. However, the reduction in parameters negatively affects (up to 1.3 BLEU points) when decoding with more decoder layers, confirming the limitation of RS as expected.

Comparing the scores of the top and bottom halves of the table, we can see that distillation dramatically boosts the performance of the shallower encoder and decoder layers. For instance, without distillation, the tied-multi model gave a BLEU of 23.2 when decoding with 1 encoder and 1 decoder layers, but the same layer combination reaches 30.1 BLEU through distillation. Given that RS further improves performance using lower layers, the BLEU score increases to 31.2. As such, distillation enables decoding using fewer layers without substantial drops in performance. Furthermore, the BLEU scores did not vary significantly when the layers deeper than 3 were used, meaning that we might as well train shallower models using distil-

---

[13]Ensemble of multiple models (Freitag et al., 2017) is commonly used for distillation, but we used a single model to save decoding time.

Model(s)	Parameters	Relative size
36 vanilla models	4,608M	25.16
Single tied-multi model	183M	1.00
36 RS models	2,623M	14.33
Single tied-multi RS model	73M	0.40

Table 4: Total model sizes for covering all 36 encoder-decoder layer combinations. The relative size is calculated regarding the tied-multi model as a standard. Similarly to "36 vanilla models," "36 RS models" represents the total number of parameters of all models.

lation. The performance of our final model, i.e., the distilled tied-multi RS model (bottom-right), was significantly lower than the non-RS model (up to 1.5 BLEU points) similarly to its non-distilled counterpart. However, given that it outperforms our original tied-multi model (top-left) in all the encoder-decoder layer combinations, we conclude that we can obtain a highly compact model with better performance.

We now analyze the effect of RS and knowledge distillation on model size and decoding speed.

Model Size: Table 4 gives the sizes of several models and their ratio with respect to the tied-multi model. Training vanilla and RS models with 36 different encoder-decoder layer combinations required 25.2 and 14.3 times the number of parameters of a single tied-multi model, respectively. Although RS led to some parameter reduction, combining RS with our tied-multi model resulted in a further compressed single model. This model has 63.2 times and 36.0 times fewer parameters than all the individual vanilla and RS models, respectively.

Decoding Speed: Table 5 compares results obtained by beam and greedy search using our distilled tied-multi RS model. In general, greedy

	$n\backslash m$	BLEU score						Decoding time (sec)					
		1	2	3	4	5	6	1	2	3	4	5	6
Beam search	1	31.2	33.5	34.1	34.2	34.3	34.3	94.7	101.9	143.4	174.7	215.5	244.5
	2	33.7	35.5	35.7	35.7	35.8	35.8	100.5	110.8	153.7	185.6	227.8	253.6
	3	34.1	35.8	36.1	36.1	36.2	36.2	102.5	114.2	168.5	194.8	234.0	259.8
	4	34.3	36.0	36.2	36.2	36.3	36.3	104.1	105.6	143.9	197.0	219.1	264.6
	5	34.5	36.1	36.2	36.3	36.3	36.3	105.1	111.5	156.4	186.0	236.1	268.8
	6	34.6	36.1	36.2	36.2	36.3	36.2	107.4	113.6	168.1	190.1	229.5	257.9
Greedy search	1	30.4	33.1	33.8	34.0	33.8	33.9	58.8	69.1	78.4	94.6	110.7	124.3
	2	33.2	35.0	35.3	35.5	35.4	35.5	62.7	68.0	78.8	94.1	112.8	125.8
	3	33.8	35.5	35.7	35.7	35.8	35.8	71.8	70.3	79.3	99.9	114.9	128.4
	4	34.0	35.8	35.8	35.8	35.8	35.8	72.1	70.7	82.3	98.8	115.2	127.5
	5	34.0	35.7	35.8	35.8	35.8	35.9	76.2	68.6	80.9	99.4	120.9	136.7
	6	34.1	35.6	35.8	35.8	35.8	35.9	76.6	69.3	81.5	99.2	120.7	131.5

Table 5: BLEU scores and decoding times of our distilled tied-multi RS model by beam and greedy search. The top-left block is identical to the bottom-right block in Table 3. The top-right block is identical to the right-most block in Table 1.

decoding is faster than beam decoding, but suffers from reduced performance. By using our distilled model, however, greedy decoding reduced the BLEU scores only by 0.5 points compared to beam decoding. For instance, whereas beam decoding with our tied-multi model without RS and distillation (top-left block in Table 3) achieved the highest BLEU score of 35.1 with 5 encoder and 6 decoder layers consuming 268.8s, greedy decoding with our distilled tied-multi RS model with 2 encoder and 2 decoder layers resulted in a comparable BLEU score of 35.0 in 68.0s, i.e., with a factor of 4.0 in decoding time thanks to RS and distillation. This happens because we have used translations generated by beam decoding as target sentences for knowledge distillation, which has the ability to loosely distill beam search behavior into greedy decoding behavior (Kim and Rush, 2016).

6 Conclusion

In this paper, we have proposed a novel procedure for training encoder-decoder models, where the softmax function is applied to the output of each of the M decoder layers derived using the output of each of the N encoder layers. This compresses $N \times M$ models into a single model that can be used for decoding with a variable number of encoder ($1 \leq n \leq N$) and decoder ($1 \leq m \leq M$) layers. This model can be used in different latency scenarios and hence is highly versatile. We have made a cost-benefit analysis of our method, taking NMT as a case study of encoder-decoder models. We have proposed and evaluated two orthogonal extensions and show that we can (a) dynamically choose layer combinations for slightly faster decoding and (b) further compress models using recurrent stacking with knowledge distillation leading to models that also enable faster decoding.

For further speed up in decoding as well as model compression, we plan to combine our approach with other techniques, such as those mentioned in Section 2. Although we have only tested our idea for NMT, it should be applicable to other tasks based on deep neural networks.

Acknowledgments

We would like to thank all the reviewers for their insightful comments and suggestions. A part of this work was conducted under the program "Research and Development of Enhanced Multilingual and Multipurpose Speech Translation System" of the Ministry of Internal Affairs and Communications (MIC), Japan. Atsushi Fujita was partly supported by JSPS KAKENHI Grant Number 19H05660.

References

Dzmitry Bahdanau, Kyunghyun Cho, and Yoshua Bengio. 2015. Neural machine translation by jointly learning to align and translate. In *Proceedings of the 3rd International Conference on Learning Representations*, San Diego, USA.

Yonatan Belinkov, Lluís Màrquez, Hassan Sajjad, Nadir Durrani, Fahim Dalvi, and James Glass. 2017. Evaluating layers of representation in neural machine translation on part-of-speech and semantic tagging tasks. In *Proceedings of the Eighth International Joint Conference on Natural Language Processing (Volume 1: Long Papers)*, pages 1–10, Taipei, Taiwan.

Kyunghyun Cho, Bart van Merriënboer, Çaglar Gülçehre, Dzmitry Bahdanau, Fethi Bougares, Holger Schwenk, and Yoshua Bengio. 2014. Learning phrase representations using RNN encoder–decoder for statistical machine translation. In *Proceedings of the 2014 Conference on Empirical Methods in Natural Language Processing*, pages 1724–1734, Doha, Qatar.

Matthieu Courbariaux, Itay Hubara, Daniel Soudry, Ran El-Yaniv, and Yoshua Bengio. 2017. Binarized neural networks: Training deep neural networks with weights and activations constrained to +1 or -1. *CoRR*, abs/1602.02830.

Raj Dabre and Atsushi Fujita. 2019. Recurrent stacking of layers for compact neural machine translation models. In *Proceedings of the AAAI Conference on Artificial Intelligence*, pages 6292–6299, Honolulu, USA.

Jacob Devlin, Ming-Wei Chang, Kenton Lee, and Kristina Toutanova. 2019. BERT: Pre-training of deep bidirectional Transformers for language understanding. In *Proceedings of the 2019 Conference of the North American Chapter of the Association for Computational Linguistics: Human Language Technologies, Volume 1 (Long and Short Papers)*, pages 4171–4186, Minneapolis, USA.

Zi-Yi Dou, Zhaopeng Tu, Xing Wang, Shuming Shi, and Tong Zhang. 2018. Exploiting deep representations for neural machine translation. In *Proceedings of the 2018 Conference on Empirical Methods in Natural Language Processing*, pages 4253–4262, Brussels, Belgium.

Markus Freitag, Yaser Al-Onaizan, and Baskaran Sankaran. 2017. Ensemble distillation for neural machine translation. *CoRR*, abs/1702.01802.

Suyog Gupta, Ankur Agrawal, Kailash Gopalakrishnan, and Pritish Narayanan. 2015. Deep learning with limited numerical precision. In *Proceedings of the 32nd International Conference on Machine Learning*, pages 1737–1746, Lille, France.

Geoffrey Hinton, Oriol Vinyals, and Jeffrey Dean. 2015. Distilling the knowledge in a neural network. *CoRR*, abs/1503.02531.

Yoon Kim and Alexander M. Rush. 2016. Sequence-level knowledge distillation. In *Proceedings of the 2016 Conference on Empirical Methods in Natural Language Processing*, pages 1317–1327, Austin, USA.

Shankar Kumar and William Byrne. 2004. Minimum Bayes-risk decoding for statistical machine translation. In *Proceedings of the Human Language Technology Conference of the North American Chapter of the Association for Computational Linguistics: HLT-NAACL 2004*, pages 169–176, Boston, USA.

Darryl D. Lin, Sachin S. Talathi, and V. Sreekanth Annapureddy. 2016. Fixed point quantization of deep convolutional networks. In *Proceedings of the 33rd International Conference on International Conference on Machine Learning*, pages 2849–2858, New York, USA.

Qingsong Ma, Ondřej Bojar, and Yvette Graham. 2018. Results of the WMT18 metrics shared task. In *Proceedings of the Third Conference on Machine Translation, Volume 2: Shared Task Papers*, pages 682–701, Brussels, Belgium.

Myle Ott, Sergey Edunov, David Grangier, and Michael Auli. 2018. Scaling neural machine translation. In *Proceedings of the Third Conference on Machine Translation: Research Papers*, pages 1–9, Brussels, Belgium.

Kishore Papineni, Salim Roukos, Todd Ward, and Wei-Jing Zhu. 2002. BLEU: A method for automatic evaluation of machine translation. In *Proceedings of the 40th Annual Meeting on Association for Computational Linguistics*, pages 311–318, Philadelphia, USA.

Maja Popović. 2016. chrF deconstructed: β parameters and n-gram weights. In *Proceedings of the First Conference on Machine Translation: Volume 2, Shared Task Papers*, pages 499–504, Berlin, Germany.

Matt Post. 2018. A call for clarity in reporting BLEU scores. In *Proceedings of the Third Conference on Machine Translation: Research Papers*, pages 186–191, Brussels, Belgium.

Abigail See, Minh-Thang Luong, and Christopher D. Manning. 2016. Compression of neural machine translation models via pruning. In *Proceedings of the 20th SIGNLL Conference on Computational Natural Language Learning*, pages 291–301, Berlin, Germany.

Lucia Specia, Dhwaj Raj, and Marco Turchi. 2010. Machine translation evaluation versus quality estimation. *Machine Translation*, 24(1):39–50.

Ilya Sutskever, James Martens, George Dahl, and Geoffrey Hinton. 2013. On the importance of initialization and momentum in deep learning. In *Proceedings of the International Conference on Machine Learning*, pages 1139–1147, Atlanta, USA.

Ilya Sutskever, Oriol Vinyals, and Quoc V. Le. 2014. Sequence to sequence learning with neural networks. In *Proceedings of the 27th Neural Information Processing Systems Conference*, pages 3104–3112, Montréal, Canada.

Ashish Vaswani, Noam Shazeer, Niki Parmar, Jakob Uszkoreit, Llion Jones, Aidan N. Gomez, Łukasz Kaiser, and Illia Polosukhin. 2017. Attention is all you need. In *Proceedings of the 30th Neural Information Processing Systems Conference*, pages 5998–6008, Long Beach, USA.

Qiang Wang, Fuxue Li, Tong Xiao, Yanyang Li, Yinqiao Li, and Jingbo Zhu. 2018. Multi-layer representation fusion for neural machine translation. In *Proceedings of the 27th International Conference on Computational Linguistics*, pages 3015–3026, Santa Fe, USA.

Yingce Xia, Tianyu He, Xu Tan, Fei Tian, Di He, and Tao Qin. 2019. Tied Transformers: Neural machine translation with shared encoder and decoder. In *Proceedings of the AAAI Conference on Artificial Intelligence*, pages 5466–5473, Honolulu, USA.

Deyi Xiong, Biao Zhang, and Jinsong Su. 2018. Accelerating neural Transformer via an average attention network. In *Proceedings of the 56th Annual Meeting of the Association for Computational Linguistics, Long Papers*, pages 1789–1798, Melbourne, Australia.

Compressing Neural Machine Translation Models with 4-bit Precision

Alham Fikri Aji and **Kenneth Heafield**
School of Informatics, University of Edinburgh
10 Crichton Street
Edinburgh EH8 9AB
Scotland
`a.fikri@ed.ac.uk, kheafiel@inf.ed.ac.uk`

Abstract

Quantization is one way to compress Neural Machine Translation (NMT) models, especially for edge devices. This paper pushes quantization from 8 bits, seen in current work on machine translation, to 4 bits. Instead of fixed-point quantization, we use logarithmic quantization since parameters are skewed towards zero. We then observe that quantizing the bias terms in this way damages quality, so we leave them uncompressed. Bias terms are a tiny fraction of the model so the impact on compression rate is minimal. Retraining is necessary to preserve quality, for which we propose to use an error-feedback mechanism that treats compression errors like noisy gradients. We empirically show that NMT models based on the Transformer or RNN architectures can be compressed up to 4-bit precision without any noticeable quality degradation. Models can be compressed up to binary precision, albeit with lower quality. The RNN architecture appears more robust towards compression, compared to the Transformer.

1 Introduction

Neural Machine Translation (NMT) is resource-demanding. Current state-of-the-art architectures, such as the Transformer (Vaswani et al., 2017) or deep RNN (Barone et al., 2017) are typically hundreds of megabytes in size. In a client-based translation system, these large models must be deployed locally, thus consuming network bandwidth for distributing the model, and disk space for storing the model.

Model quantisation has been widely studied as a way to compress model size and increase the inference speed. However, most of this work has focused on convolution neural networks for computer vision tasks (Miyashita et al., 2016; Lin et al., 2016; Hubara et al., 2016, 2017; Jacob et al., 2018).

As such, research on model quantisation for NMT tasks remains limited.

We find that the model can be compressed at up to 4-bit precision without sacrificing quality. We first explore the use of logarithmic-based quantisation over fixed-point quantisation (Miyashita et al., 2016) based on the empirical findings that parameter distribution is not uniform, but instead concentrated near zero (Lin et al., 2016; See et al., 2016). The magnitude of a parameter also varies across layers; therefore, we propose an improved method of scaling the quantization centres. We also notice that biases do not quantise very well. However, since biases do not consume a noticeable amount of memory, they can be left unquantised. Lastly, we explore the significance of re-training in the model compression scenario. We adopt an error feedback mechanism (Seide et al., 2014) to preserve the quantisation error rather than discarding it at every update during re-training.

2 Related Work

A considerable amount of research on model quantisation has been performed in the area of computer vision with convolutional neural networks; however, research on model quantisation in the field of neural machine translation is far more limited. Therefore, we will also refer to work on neural models for image processing in this section, where appropriate.

Hubara et al. (2016) quantised the model and activation to binary on a CNN network for various image classification tasks. The binary network achieved near state-of-the-art quality on several easier tasks such as MNIST and CIFAR-10 but achieved sub-par performance on the more challenging ImageNet dataset (losing over 20% accuracy with quantised GoogleNet). Hubara et al. (2017) later reported that with 6-bit fixed-point

35

Proceedings of the 4th Workshop on Neural Generation and Translation (WNGT 2020), pages 35–42
Online, July 10, 2020. ©2020 Association for Computational Linguistics
www.aclweb.org/anthology/D19-56%2d

quantisation, GoogleNet "only" lost 5% accuracy. (Lin et al., 2016) used different bit precisions on various CNN layers, achieving over 20% compression on the CIFAR-10 task.

Since the model's parameters are highly concentrated near zero, Miyashita et al. (2016) opted for logarithmic quantisation. They report an improvement in preserving model accuracy over linear quantisation while achieving the same model compression rate. They also reported negligible accuracy degradation when compressing VGG16 with 3-bit logarithmic quantisation, whereas 3-bit fixed-point quantisation suffered a 6% accuracy drop.

Hubara et al. (2017) compress an LSTM-based architecture for language modelling to 4-bits without any quality degradation but had to scale the hidden layer size by 3. See et al. (2016) pruned an NMT model by removing any weight values lower than a certain threshold. They achieve 80% model sparsity without any quality degradation.

A relevant work with respect to our purposes is the submission of Junczys-Dowmunt et al. (2018) to the Shared Task on Efficient Neural Machine Translation in 2018. This submission applied an 8-bit linear quantisation for NMT models without any noticeable deterioration in translation quality. Similarly, Quinn and Ballesteros (2018) proposed the use of 8-bit matrix multiplication to increase the CPU inference speed of an NMT system.

3 Low-precision Neural Machine Translation

3.1 Log-based Compression

Parameters in deep learning models are normally distributed (Lin et al., 2016; See et al., 2016). Therefore, a uniformly distributed fixed-point quantisation may not fit the parameter distribution. To improve resolution for small values, we adopt logarithmic quantisation following Miyashita et al. (2016) where parameter density is the highest. Figure 1 illustrates the weight distribution and our log-based quantisation.

We use the same quantisation centres for positive and negative values. When compressing to B bits, a single bit represents the sign while the remaining $B-1$ bits represent the log magnitude. The centres are tuned based on the absolute value of the data.

For efficient implementation and because the impact on quality was minimal after re-training, we use log base 2. Log base 2 means that ex-

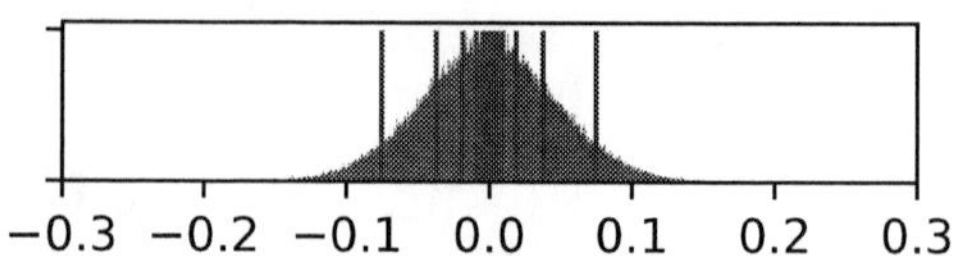

(a) First layer encoder self attention weight histogram

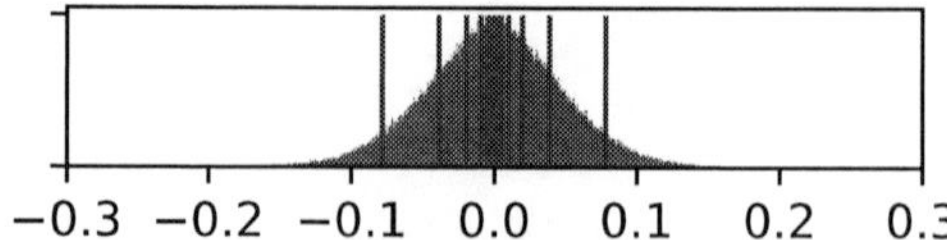

(b) First layer decoder self attention weight histogram

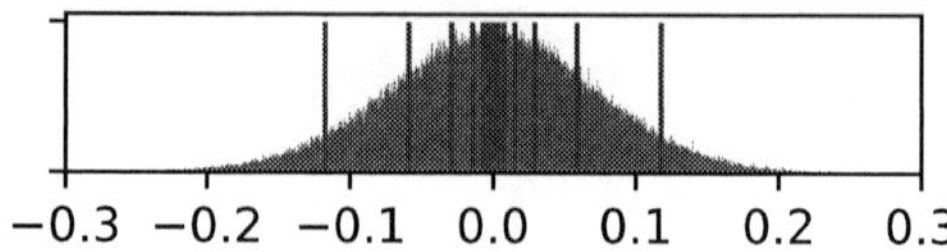

(c) First layer decoder context attention weight

Figure 1: Histograms of the first layer's attention key weights. Parameters follow a normal distribution. Vertical lines illustrate the log-based quantisation centres.

ponentiation amounts to a bit-shift while taking a rounded log (which will be used to quantise a value) amounts to addition followed by finding the leftmost 1 in binary.

We find that tensors might not have the same parameter magnitude. Therefore we also scale the quantisation centres to approximate each tensor better. This approach is different from that of Miyashita et al. (2016), where quantisation centres are not scaled, thus letting every tensor to have the same set of centres. Formally, each quantisation centre takes the form $\pm S2^q$ where S is a scaling factor, and q is an integer in the range $(-2^{B-1}, 0]$. The scaling factor S is selected separately for each tensor in the model.

To minimise the mean squared encoding error, values should be quantised to the nearest centre. Miyashita et al. (2016) find the nearest centre in logarithmic space by taking the log and then rounding to the nearest integer, which is not the same as finding the nearest centre in normal space. For example, their approach will quantise 5.8 to 2^3 instead of 2^2 because $\log_2(5.8) \approx 2.536$, which rounds to 3. In normal space, 5.8 is closer to 2^2 instead of 2^3.

We can implement rounding to the nearest centre in normal space efficiently by multiplying by $\frac{2}{3}$, taking the log and rounding up to the next integer. Let $x \in [2^q, 2^{q+1}]$. Thus:

$$x \text{ rounds up to } 2^{q+1} \iff x > \frac{2^q + 2^{q+1}}{2}$$
$$\iff x > \frac{2^q(1+2)}{2}$$
$$\iff \frac{2}{3}x > 2^q \quad (1)$$
$$\iff \log_2 \frac{2}{3}x > q$$

Therefore, given a positive x, we can find the quantised magnitude of q with respect to rounding scheme in normal space by:

$$q = \lceil \log_2(\frac{2}{3}t) \rceil \quad (2)$$

Ultimately, given a value v that will be quantised a B-bit logarithmic quantisation. We encode v as $(sign, q)$, where $sign$ represents the sign (1-bit), and q represents the magnitude ($B - 1$ bits). Our quantisation functions as follows:

$$sign = sign(v)$$
$$t = clip(|v|/S, [1, 2^{1-2^{B-1}}]) \quad (3)$$
$$q = \lceil \log_2(\frac{2}{3}t) \rceil$$

where t is a temporary variable. We first scale the value to the desired range based on scaling factor S. We will discuss more on computing S later. Then, we clip the value into the given range since we have limited quantisation centres. This then decodes to $v' \approx v$ as $v' = \text{sign}S2^q$. In practice, the sign is stored with q.

3.2 Selecting the Scaling Factor

There are a few heuristics to choose a scaling factor of S. Junczys-Dowmunt et al. (2018) and Jacob et al. (2018) scale the model based on its maximum value, which can be very unstable–especially during re-training. Alternatively, Lin et al. (2016) and Hubara et al. (2016) use a pre-defined step size for fixed-point quantization. Our objective is to select a scaling factor S such that the quantised parameters are as close to the original as possible. Therefore, we optimise S such that it minimises the squared error between the original and the compressed parameters.

We propose a method to fit S by minimising the SME. We start with an initial scale S based on the

parameters' maximum value. For a given S, we apply our quantisation routine described in Equation 3 to a tensor v, resulting in an approximation of v'. For a given assignment v', we fit a new scale S such that:

$$S = \arg \min_S \sum_i (v'_i - v_i)^2 \quad (4)$$

Substituting v'_i within Eq. 4, we have:

$$S = \arg \min_S \sum_i (sign(v_i)S2^{q_i} - v_i)^2 \quad (5)$$

To simplify the equation, let a temporary variable a_i to substitute $sign(v_i)2^{q_i}$. Hence we have:

$$S = \arg \min_S \sum_i (a_iS - v_i)^2 \quad (6)$$

To optimise the given objective, we take the first derivative of Equation 6 such that:

$$\frac{d}{dS} \sum_i (a_iS - v_i)^2 = 0$$
$$2\sum_i (a_i(a_iS - v_i)) = 0$$
$$\sum_i (a_i^2 S) - \sum_i (a_iv_i) = 0$$
$$S \sum_i a_i^2 = \sum_i (a_iv_i)$$
$$S = \frac{\sum_i (a_iv_i)}{\sum_i a_i^2}$$
$$S = \frac{\sum_i (sign(v_i)2^{q_i}v_i)}{\sum_i (sign(v_i)2^{q_i})^2}$$
$$S = \frac{\sum_i (2^{q_i}|v_i|)}{\sum_i 4^{q_i}}$$

$$(7)$$

We optimise S for each tensor independently.

3.3 Re-training

We observe later in Section 4.2 that quantisation damages the model. Therefore, we re-train the model after initial quantisation to allow it to recover some of the quality loss. In the re-training phase, we compute the gradients normally with full precision. We then re-quantise the model after

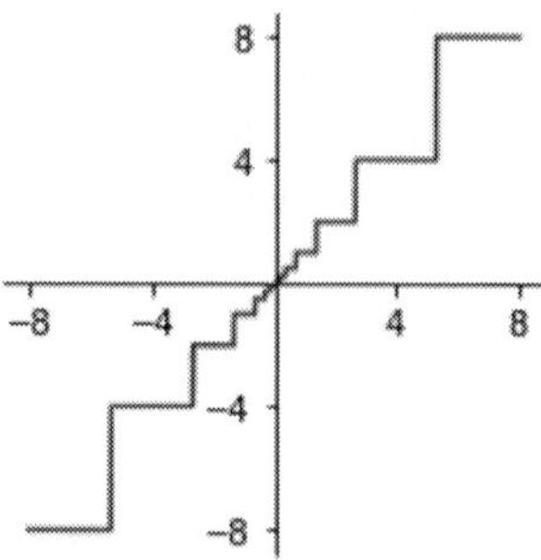

Figure 2: Log-quantization step function.

every update to the parameters, including fitting scaling factors.

Re-quantising the model after every update introduces quantisation errors. The re-quantisation error is preserved in a residual variable and added to the next step's parameter (Seide et al., 2014) before quantisation. We find that re-training fails to work without this mechanism (Section 4.2).

3.4 Handling Biases

We do not quantise bias values in the model. We find that biases are not as highly concentrated near zero when compared to other parameters. Empirically, in our pre-trained Transformer architecture, bias has a higher standard deviation of 0.17 (compared to 0.07 for other parameters). Attempting to log-quantise them used only a fraction of the available quantisation points. In any case, bias values do not consume a lot of memory relative to other parameters. In our Transformer architecture, they account for only $\sim$0.2% of the parameter values.

3.5 Low-precision Dot Products

To improve the CPU inference speed, we explore training and computing dot products in low precision. Activations coming into a matrix multiplication are quantised on the fly, while intermediate activations (such as tanh) are not quantised.

We use the same log-based quantisation procedure described in Section 3.1 when training the model. However, we only attempt a fixed predetermined scale. Running the slower EM approach to optimise the scale before every dot product would not be fast enough for inference applications.

Training with Quantised Dot Products

Our log-quantised activation is a step function, as illustrated in in Figure 2. Therefore, the deriva-

tive of this function is 0 almost everywhere, or undefined in the quantization centres. Thus, we cannot back-propagate through this function normally. Inspired by (Hubara et al., 2017), we utilise a straight-through estimator (Bengio et al., 2013) to set the derivative of the the function to 1, thus enabling training.

Computing Dot Products in Log-space

A dot product operation consists of two sub-operations: element-wise multiplication and sum. In our case, we now have two vectors a and b, both in the form of:

$$a = S_a * [(sign_{j1} * 2^{j_1}), \ldots, (sign_{jn} * 2^{j_n})]$$
$$b = S_b * [(sign_{k1} * 2^{k_1}), \ldots, (sign_{kn} * 2^{k_n})]$$

Multiplication is performed by adding the powers. We then add the resulting multiplications together normally, as follows:

$$a \cdot b = S_a * S_b \sum_i (sign_{ji} * sign_{ki} * 2^{j_i + k_i}) \quad (8)$$

Computing power is obtained by using a bit-shift, while computing $sign_{ji} * sign_{ki}$ can be performed using bitwise xor, therefore avoiding expensive multiplication instructions (Miyashita et al., 2016).

4 Experiments

4.1 Experiment Setup

We use systems for the WMT 2017 English-to-German news translation task for our experiment, which differs from the WNGT shared task setting previously reported. We use back-translated monolingual corpora (Sennrich et al., 2016a) and byte pair encoding (Sennrich et al., 2016b) to preprocess the corpus. Quality is measured based on BLEU (Papineni et al., 2002) score using sacreBLEU script (Post, 2018).

We first pre-train baseline models with both Transformer and RNN architectures. Our Transformer model consists of six encoder and six decoder layers with tied embedding. Our deep RNN model consists of eight layers of bidirectional LSTM. Models were trained synchronously with a dynamic batch size of 40 GB per batch using the Marian toolkit (Junczys-Dowmunt et al., 2018). The models are trained until we observe no improvement in 10 consecutive validations. Models are optimised with the Adam optimiser (Kingma and Ba, 2014). The rest of the hyperparameter settings on both models follow the suggested configurations (Vaswani et al., 2017; Sennrich et al., 2017). We use wmt2016 as the test set.

4.2 4-bit Transformer Model

In this experiment subsection, we explore different ways to scale the quantisation centres, the significance of quantising biases and the significance of re-training. We use a pre-trained Transformer model as our baseline and apply our quantisation algorithm on top of that. This experiment focuses solely on the compression ratio. Therefore, models are decompressed back into a 32-bit floating-point value for inference.

Table 1 summarises the results. Using a simple (albeit unstable) max-based scaling has shown to perform better than not using the scale factor. However, fitting the scaling factor to minimise the quantisation squared error produces the best quality. The BLEU score differences between methods of choosing the scaling factor are diminished after re-training.

We can also see improvements by not quantising biases, especially without re-training. Without any re-training involved, we reached the highest BLEU score of 35.47 by using an optimised scale in addition to uncompressed biases. Without bias quantisation, we obtained a $\sim$7.9x compression ratio (instead of 8x) with a 4-bit quantisation. Based on this trade-off, we argue that it is more beneficial to keep the biases in full precision.

Re-training has shown to generally improve quality. After re-training, the quality differences between various scaling and biases quantisation configurations are minimal. These results suggest that re-training helps the model to fine-tune under a new quantised parameter space.

Training Routine

We prepare our 4-bit quantisation model by re-training from a full precision model. We also store the quantisation errors to be considered for the next update. In this subsection, we answer the question of whether it is necessary to perform these steps. We explore the preparation of the 4-bit model if trained from scratch. Similarly, we explore 4-bit model preparation without an error feedback mechanism. For this experiment, we use optimised scaling and 32-bit bias when applying 4-bit log quantisation. Based on the previous result, we left biases unquantised.

The results in Table 2 indicate that fine-tuning from a pre-trained model and error feedback are necessary to produce a high-quality 4-bit model. Removing either of them degrades the quality. BLEU score is dramatically reduced if we train the model from scratch. Likewise, the quantised model is practically unable to learn without the error feedback mechanism. As shown in Table 1, the quantised model achieved a 34.31 BLEU score without re-training. Re-training said model barely improves the BLEU to 34.45 without the error feedback mechanism.

Size Comparison

To demonstrate the improvement of our method, we compare several compression approaches to our 4-bit logarithmic quantisation method with re-training and without bias quantisation. One of the arguably naive methods used to reduce model size is the use of smaller unit size. For Transformer, we set the feed-forward dimension to 512 (from 2048) and the embedding size to 128 (from 512). For RNN, we set the dimension to 320 (from 1024) and the embedding size to 160 (from 512). Using this method, the model size is $\sim$8x smaller and similar to 4-bit quantisation in terms of the model compression rate.

We also introduce the 4-bit fixed-point quantisation approach as a comparison, which is based on Junczys-Dowmunt et al. (2018). However, we made a few modifications to the original approach. Firstly, we apply re-training, which is absent in their implementation. Moreover, we skip bias quantisation. Finally, we optimise the scaling factor instead of the suggested max-based scale.

Table 3 summarises the results, which indicate that reducing the model size by simply reducing the dimension resulted in the worst performance. Our result is in line with (Huang et al., 2019), who show that reducing the model size by using fewer layers degrades quality. Logarithmic-based quantisation has been shown to perform better when compared to fixed-point quantisation using both architectures.

The RNN model seems to be more robust towards the compression. RNN models exhibit reduced quality degradation in all compression scenarios. We hypothesise that the gradients computed with a highly compressed model are very noisy, thus resulting in noisy parameter updates. Our finding is in line with prior research (Chen et al., 2018; Aji and Heafield, 2019), which state Transformer is more sensitive towards noisy training conditions.

Method	Compression	Scaling		
		Unscaled	Max	Optimized
32-bit FP model (Baseline)	-	35.66	-	-
4-bit log model	8x	25.20	28.08	33.33
4-bit log model + 32-bit FP bias	7.88x	34.16	34.29	34.31
4-bit log model + re-training	8x	34.92	34.81	35.26
4-bit log model + 32-bit FP bias + re-training	7.88x	35.09	35.25	35.47

Table 1: 4-bit Transformer quantisation performance for English-to-German translation, measured in BLEU score. We explore different methods of determining the scaling factor as well as skipping bias quantisation and re-training.

Method	FT	EF	Transformer	RNN
Baseline	-	-	35.66	34.28
4-bit	✓	✓	35.47 (-0.19)	34.22 (-0.06)
4-bit	✓	✗	34.45 (-1.21)	33.32 (-0.96)
4-bit	✗	✓	28.54 (-7.12)	28.45 (-5.83)
4-bit	✗	✗	0.05(-35.61)	0.00(-34.48)

Table 2: The model performance (based on BLEU score) of various training scenarios using both Transformer and RNN architectures. FT = Fine-Tuning, EF = Error-Feedback.

Method	Transformer	RNN
Baseline	35.66	34.28
Reduced Dimension	29.03 (-6.63)	30.88 (-3.40)
4-bit fixed point	34.61 (-1.05)	34.05 (-0.23)
4-bit log (Ours)	35.47 (-0.19)	34.22 (-0.06)

Table 3: The model performance (based on BLEU score) of various quantisation approaches using both Transformer and RNN architecture.

Method	Transformer	RNN
Baseline	35.66	34.28
+ 4-bit model	35.47 (-0.19)	34.22 (-0.06)
+ 4-bit dot-product	35.05 (-0.61)	33.12 (-1.16)

Table 4: Model performance (in BLEU) of model quantisation with dot product quantisation using both Transformer and RNN architecture.

Dot-Product Method	time (ns)
32-bit float	8.45699
8-bit integer	2.08390
4-bit log (16-bit Shift)	3.89595
4-bit log (8-bit Lookup table)	2.51924

Table 5: Time measurement of dot products of 128 elements with different value representations. We use a Cascade Lake processor.

4.3 Quantised Dot-Product

Quality Benchmark

We now apply logarithmic quantisation for all matrix multiplication inputs. We use the same quantisation procedure as the parameter. However, we do not fit the scaling factor since it is very inefficient. Hence, we do not scale the quantization centres for the activation. For the parameter quantisation, we use an optimised scale with uncompressed biases based on the previous experiment. Table 4 presents the quality results of the experiment. Generally, we observe quality degradation compared to a full-precision dot product.

Speed Benchmark

Unfortunately, current hardware does not support a 4-bit instruction, thus our dot-product must be emulated using instructions with wider bit widths.[1]

Since there is no 4-bit or 8-bit shift instruction, we emulate 2^q in 16-bit instead. Alternatively, we can choose a lower base, for example $256^{\frac{1}{14}}$ instead of 2 so that the resulting power fits in 8-bit precision. In this case, we can use the 8-bit lookup table instruction vpshufb instead.

We benchmark our result with an 8-bit integer dot product based on the vpdpbusds instruction (which was introduced in the Cascade Lake to optimise 8-bit matrix multiplication) and a basic 32-bit float dot product using fused multiplication and addition.

Table 5 reports the time required to perform a dot product under different quantisation schemes. 8-bit lookup table is faster than 16-bit. Unfortunately, our 4-bit dot product is inefficient, resulting in it being much slower than an 8-bit dot product. With current hardware, the main advantage over 8-bit quantization is smaller model size, which is

Bit	Transformer		RNN	
	Size (rate)	**BLEU(Δ)**	**Size (rate)**	**BLEU(Δ)**
32	251 MB	35.66	361 MB	34.28
4	32 MB (7.88x)	35.47 (-0.19)	46 MB (7.90x)	34.22 (-0.06)
3	24 MB (10.45x)	34.95 (-0.71)	34 MB (10.49x)	34.11 (-0.17)
2	16 MB (15.50x)	33.40 (-2.26)	23 MB (15.59x)	32.78 (-1.50)
1	8 MB (30.00x)	29.43 (-6.23)	12 MB (30.35x)	31.71 (-2.51)

Table 6: Compression rate and performance of both Transformer and RNN with various bit widths. The compression rate between Transformer and RNN is not equal since they have different biases to parameter size ratio.

of interest for local deployment on mobile devices. Should future hardware also support 4-bit instructions natively, 4-bit models could also improve decoding efficiency.

4.4 Beyond 4-bit precision

With 4-bit quantisation and uncompressed biases, we obtain a 7.9x compression rate. Bit width can be set below 4 bit to achieve an even better compression rate, albeit introducing more compression error. To explore this, we sweep several bit widths. Moreover, we skip bias quantisation and optimise the scaling factor.

Training an NMT system below 4-bit precision remains a challenge. As shown in Table 6, model performance degrades with fewer bits being used. While this result might be acceptable, we argue that the result can be improved. One worthwhile idea would be to increase the unit size in an extremely low-precision setting. We have shown that 4-bit precision performs better compared to the full-precision model with (near) 8x compression rate. Moreover, Han et al. (2015) demonstrated that 2-bit precision image classification can be achieved by scaling the parameter size. An alternative approach is to have different bit widths for each layer (Hwang and Sung, 2014; Anwar et al., 2015).

We also observe the robustness of RNN over Transformer in this experiment since RNN models degrade less compared to the Transformer counterpart. The RNN model outperforms Transformer when compressing at binary precision.

5 Conclusion

We compress the model size in neural machine translation to approximately 7.9x smaller than 32-bit floats by using a 4-bit logarithmic quantisation. Bias terms can be left uncompressed without significantly affecting the compression rate. We also find that re-training after quantisation is necessary to restore the model's performance.

Matrix multiplication can further be quantised, although quality is sacrificed. Unfortunately, 4-bit dot products found in matrix multiplication are slow because current hardware does not natively support the necessary 4-bit instructions.

Acknowledgements

This work was conducted within the scope of the Horizon 2020 Research and Innovation Action *Bergamot*, which has received funding from the European Union's Horizon 2020 research and innovation programme under grant agreement No 825303. Additional support was provided by Intel Corporation. This work was performed using resources provided by the Cambridge Service for Data Driven Discovery (CSD3) operated by the University of Cambridge Research Computing Service (`http://www.csd3.cam.ac.uk/`), provided by Dell EMC and Intel using Tier-2 funding from the Engineering and Physical Sciences Research Council (capital grant EP/P020259/1), and DiRAC funding from the Science and Technology Facilities Council (`http://www.dirac.ac.uk`).

References

Alham Fikri Aji and Kenneth Heafield. 2019. Making asynchronous stochastic gradient descent work for transformers. *EMNLP-IJCNLP 2019*, page 80.

Sajid Anwar, Kyuyeon Hwang, and Wonyong Sung. 2015. Fixed point optimization of deep convolutional neural networks for object recognition. In *2015 IEEE International Conference on Acoustics, Speech and Signal Processing (ICASSP)*, pages 1131–1135. IEEE.

Antonio Valerio Miceli Barone, Jindřich Helcl, Rico Sennrich, Barry Haddow, and Alexandra Birch. 2017. Deep architectures for neural machine translation. In *Proceedings of the Second Conference on Machine Translation*, pages 99–107.

Yoshua Bengio, Nicholas Léonard, and Aaron Courville. 2013. Estimating or propagating gradients through stochastic neurons for conditional computation. *arXiv preprint arXiv:1308.3432*.

Mia Xu Chen, Orhan Firat, Ankur Bapna, Melvin Johnson, Wolfgang Macherey, George Foster, Llion Jones, Mike Schuster, Noam Shazeer, Niki Parmar, et al. 2018. The best of both worlds: Combining recent advances in neural machine translation. In *Proceedings of the 56th Annual Meeting of the Association for Computational Linguistics (Volume 1: Long Papers)*, pages 76–86.

Song Han, Huizi Mao, and William J Dally. 2015. Deep compression: Compressing deep neural networks with pruning, trained quantization and huffman coding. *arXiv preprint arXiv:1510.00149*.

Yanping Huang, Youlong Cheng, Ankur Bapna, Orhan Firat, Dehao Chen, Mia Chen, HyoukJoong Lee, Jiquan Ngiam, Quoc V Le, Yonghui Wu, et al. 2019. Gpipe: Efficient training of giant neural networks using pipeline parallelism. In *Advances in Neural Information Processing Systems*, pages 103–112.

Itay Hubara, Matthieu Courbariaux, Daniel Soudry, Ran El-Yaniv, and Yoshua Bengio. 2016. Binarized neural networks. In *Advances in neural information processing systems*, pages 4107–4115.

Itay Hubara, Matthieu Courbariaux, Daniel Soudry, Ran El-Yaniv, and Yoshua Bengio. 2017. Quantized neural networks: Training neural networks with low precision weights and activations. *The Journal of Machine Learning Research*, 18(1):6869–6898.

Kyuyeon Hwang and Wonyong Sung. 2014. Fixed-point feedforward deep neural network design using weights+ 1, 0, and- 1. In *2014 IEEE Workshop on Signal Processing Systems (SiPS)*, pages 1–6. IEEE.

Benoit Jacob, Skirmantas Kligys, Bo Chen, Menglong Zhu, Matthew Tang, Andrew Howard, Hartwig Adam, and Dmitry Kalenichenko. 2018. Quantization and training of neural networks for efficient integer-arithmetic-only inference. In *Proceedings of the IEEE Conference on Computer Vision and Pattern Recognition*, pages 2704–2713.

Marcin Junczys-Dowmunt, Kenneth Heafield, Hieu Hoang, Roman Grundkiewicz, and Anthony Aue. 2018. Marian: Cost-effective high-quality neural machine translation in c++. In *Proceedings of the 2nd Workshop on Neural Machine Translation and Generation*, pages 129–135.

Diederik P Kingma and Jimmy Ba. 2014. Adam: A method for stochastic optimization. *arXiv preprint arXiv:1412.6980*.

Darryl Lin, Sachin Talathi, and Sreekanth Annapureddy. 2016. Fixed point quantization of deep convolutional networks. In *International Conference on Machine Learning*, pages 2849–2858.

Daisuke Miyashita, Edward H Lee, and Boris Murmann. 2016. Convolutional neural networks using logarithmic data representation. *arXiv preprint arXiv:1603.01025*.

Kishore Papineni, Salim Roukos, Todd Ward, and Wei-Jing Zhu. 2002. Bleu: a method for automatic evaluation of machine translation. In *Proceedings of the 40th annual meeting on association for computational linguistics*, pages 311–318. Association for Computational Linguistics.

Matt Post. 2018. A call for clarity in reporting bleu scores. In *Proceedings of the Third Conference on Machine Translation: Research Papers*, pages 186–191.

Jerry Quinn and Miguel Ballesteros. 2018. Pieces of eight: 8-bit neural machine translation. In *Proceedings of the 2018 Conference of the North American Chapter of the Association for Computational Linguistics: Human Language Technologies, Volume 3 (Industry Papers)*, pages 114–120.

Abigail See, Minh-Thang Luong, and Christopher D Manning. 2016. Compression of neural machine translation models via pruning. *arXiv preprint arXiv:1606.09274*.

Frank Seide, Hao Fu, Jasha Droppo, Gang Li, and Dong Yu. 2014. 1-bit stochastic gradient descent and application to data-parallel distributed training of speech DNNs. In *Interspeech*.

Rico Sennrich, Alexandra Birch, Anna Currey, Ulrich Germann, Barry Haddow, Kenneth Heafield, Antonio Valerio Miceli Barone, and Philip Williams. 2017. The University of Edinburgh's neural mt systems for WMT17. In *Proceedings of the Second Conference on Machine Translation*, pages 389–399.

Rico Sennrich, Barry Haddow, and Alexandra Birch. 2016a. Improving neural machine translation models with monolingual data. In *Proceedings of the 54th Annual Meeting of the Association for Computational Linguistics (Volume 1: Long Papers)*, pages 86–96, Berlin, Germany. Association for Computational Linguistics.

Rico Sennrich, Barry Haddow, and Alexandra Birch. 2016b. Neural machine translation of rare words with subword units. In *Proceedings of the 54th Annual Meeting of the Association for Computational Linguistics*, pages 1715–1725.

Ashish Vaswani, Noam Shazeer, Niki Parmar, Jakob Uszkoreit, Llion Jones, Aidan N Gomez, Łukasz Kaiser, and Illia Polosukhin. 2017. Attention is all you need. In *Advances in Neural Information Processing Systems*, pages 5998–6008.

Meta-Learning for Few-Shot NMT Adaptation

Amr Sharaf
University of Maryland
amr@cs.umd.edu

Hany Hassan
Microsoft
hanyh@microsoft.com

Hal Daumé III
Microsoft Research &
University of Maryland
me@hal3.name

Abstract

We present META-MT, a meta-learning approach to adapt Neural Machine Translation (NMT) systems in a few-shot setting. META-MT provides a new approach to make NMT models easily adaptable to many target domains with the minimal amount of in-domain data. We frame the adaptation of NMT systems as a meta-learning problem, where we learn to adapt to new unseen domains based on simulated offline meta-training domain adaptation tasks. We evaluate the proposed meta-learning strategy on ten domains with general large scale NMT systems. We show that META-MT significantly outperforms classical domain adaptation when very few in-domain examples are available. Our experiments shows that META-MT can outperform classical fine-tuning by up to 2.5 BLEU points after seeing only $4,000$ translated words (300 parallel sentences).

1 Introduction

Neural Machine Translation (NMT) systems (Bahdanau et al., 2016; Sutskever et al., 2014) are usually trained on large general-domain parallel corpora to achieve state-of-the-art results (Barrault et al., 2019). Unfortunately, these generic corpora are often qualitatively different from the target domain of the translation system. Moreover, NMT models trained on one domain tend to perform poorly when translating sentences in a significantly different domain (Koehn and Knowles, 2017; Chu and Wang, 2018). A widely used approach for adapting NMT is *domain adaptation by fine-tuning* (Luong and Manning, 2015; Freitag and Al-Onaizan, 2016; Sennrich et al., 2016), where a model is first trained on general-domain data and then adapted by continuing the training on a smaller amount of in-domain data. This approach often leads to empirical improvements in the targeted

domain; however, it falls short when the amount of in-domain training data is insufficient, leading to model over-fitting and catastrophic forgetting, where adapting to a new domain leads to degradation on the general-domain (Thompson et al., 2019). Ideally, we would like to have a model that is easily adaptable to many target domains with minimal amount of in-domain data.

We present a meta-learning approach that *learns* to adapt neural machine translation systems to new domains given only a small amount of training data in that domain. To achieve this, we simulate many domain adaptation tasks, on which we use a *meta-learning* strategy to learn how to adapt. Specifically, based on these simulations, our proposed approach, META-MT (Meta-learning for Machine Translation), learns model parameters that should generalize to future (real) adaptation tasks (§ 3.1).

At training time (§ 3.2), META-MT simulates many small-data domain adaptation tasks from a large pool of data. Using these tasks, META-MT simulates what would happen after fine-tuning the model parameters to each such task. It then uses this information to compute parameter updates that will lead to efficient adaptation during deployment. We optimize this using the Model Agnostic Meta-Learning algorithm (MAML) (Finn et al., 2017).

The contribution of this paper is as follows: first, we propose a new approach that enables NMT systems to effectively adapt to a new domain using few-shots learning. Second, we show what models and conditions enable meta-learning to be useful for NMT adaptation. Finally, We evaluate META-MT on ten different domains, showing the efficacy of our approach. To the best of our knowledge, this is the first work on adapting large scale NMT systems in a few-shot learning setup [1].

---

[1] **Code Release:** We make the code publicly available online: https://www.dropbox.com/s/jguxb75utg1dmxl/meta-mt.zip?dl=0

Proceedings of the 4th Workshop on Neural Generation and Translation (WNGT 2020), pages 43–53
Online, July 10, 2020. ©2020 Association for Computational Linguistics
www.aclweb.org/anthology/D19-56%2d

2   Related Work

Our goal for few-shot NMT adaptation is to adapt a pre-trained NMT model (e.g. trained on general domain data) to new domains (e.g. medical domain) with a small amount of training examples. Chu et al. (2018) surveyed several recent approaches that address the shortcomings of traditional fine-tuning when applied to domain adaptation. Our work distinguishes itself from prior work by learning to fine-tune with tiny amounts of training examples.

Most recently, Bapna et al. (2019) proposed a simple approach for adaptation in NMT. The approach consists of injecting task specific adapter layers into a pre-trained model. These adapters enable the model to adapt to new tasks as it introduces a bottleneck in the architecture that makes it easier to adapt. Our approach uses a similar model architecture, however, instead of injecting a new adapter for each task separately, META-MT uses a single adapter layer, and meta-learns a better initialization for this layer that can easily be fine-tuned to new domains with very few training examples.

Similar to our goal, Michel and Neubig (2018) proposed a space efficient approach to adaptation that learns domain specific biases to the output vocabulary. This enables large-scale personalization for NMT models when small amounts of data are available for a lot of different domains. However, this approach assumes that these domains are static and known at training time, while META-MT can dynamically generalize to totally new domains, previously unseen at meta-training time.

Several approaches have been proposed for lightweight adaptation of NMT systems. Vilar (2018) introduced domain specific gates to control the contribution of hidden units feeding into the next layer. However, Bapna et al. (2019) showed that this introduced a limited amount of per-domain capacity; in addition, the learned gates are not guaranteed to be easily adaptable to unseen domains. Khayrallah et al. (2017) proposed a lattice search algorithm for NMT adaptation, however, this algorithm assumes access to lattices generated from a phrase based machine translation system.

Our meta-learning strategy mirrors that of Gu et al. (2018) in the low resource translation setting, as well as Wu et al. (2019) for cross-lingual named entity recognition with minimal resources, Mi et al. (2019) for low-resource natural language generation in task-oriented dialogue systems, and Dou et al. (2019) for low-resource natural language understanding tasks. To the best of our knowledge, this is the first work using meta-learning for few-shot NMT adaptation.

3   Approach: Meta-Learning for Few-Shot NMT Adaptation

Neural Machine Translation systems are not robust to domain shifts (Chu and Wang, 2018). It is a highly desirable characteristic of the system to be adaptive to any domain shift using weak supervision without degrading the performance on the general domain. This dynamic adaptation task can be viewed naturally as a learning-to-learn (meta-learning) problem: how can we train a global model that is capable of using its previous experience in adaptation to learn to adapt faster to unseen domains? A particularly simple and effective strategy for adaptation is fine-tuning: the global model is adapted by training on in-domain data. One would hope to improve on such a strategy by decreasing the amount of required in-domain data. META-MT takes into account information from previous adaptation tasks, and aims at learning how to update the global model parameters, so that the resulting learned parameters after meta-learning can be adapted faster and better to previously unseen domains via a weakly supervised fine-tuning approach on a tiny amount of data.

Our goal in this paper is to learn how to adapt a neural machine translation system from experience. The training procedure for META-MT uses offline simulated adaptation problems to learn model parameters θ which can adapt faster to previously unseen domains. In this section, we describe META-MT, first by describing how it operates at test time when applied to a new domain adaptation task (§3.1), and then by describing how to train it using offline simulated adaptation tasks (§3.2).

3.1   Test Time Behavior of META-MT

At test time, META-MT adapts a pre-trained NMT model to a new given domain. The adaptation is done using a small in-domain data that we call the *support set* and then tested on the new domain using a *query set*. More formally, the model parametrized by θ takes as input a new adaptation task T. This is illustrated in Figure 1: the adaptation task T consists of a standard domain adaptation problem: T includes a support set $T_{support}$ used for training the fine-tuned model, and a query set T_{query} used for evaluation. We're particularly

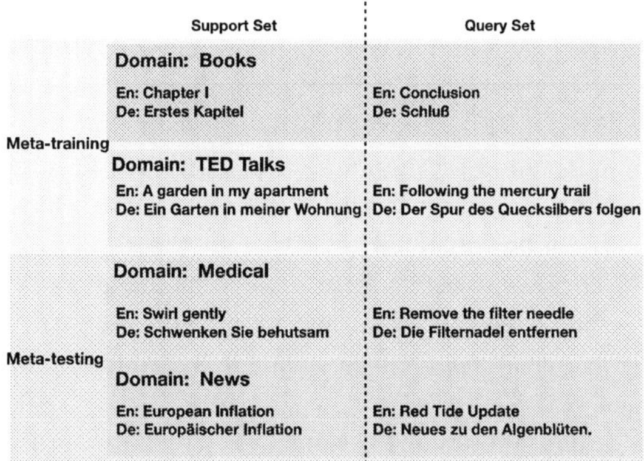

Figure 1: Example meta-learning set-up for few-shot NMT adaptation. The top represents the meta-training set $\mathcal{D}_{\text{meta-train}}$, where inside each box is a separate dataset T that consists of the support set T_{support} (left side of dashed line) and the query set T_{query} (right side of dashed line). In this illustration, we are considering the books and TED talks domains for meta-training. The meta-test set $\mathcal{D}_{\text{meta-test}}$ is defined in the same way, but with a different set of domains not present in any of the datasets in $\mathcal{D}_{\text{meta-train}}$: Medical and News.

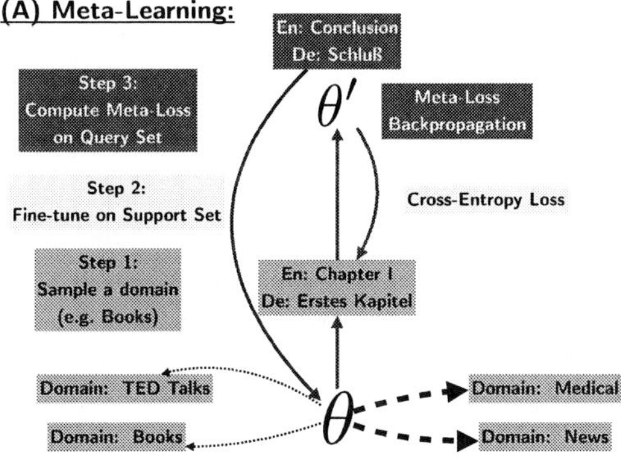

Figure 2: **[Top-A]** a training step of META-MT. **[Bottom-B]** Differences between meta-learning and Traditional fine-tuning. Wide lines represent high resource domains (Medical, News), while thin lines represent low-resource domains (TED, Books). Traditional fine-tuning may favor high-resource domains over low-resource ones while meta-learning aims at learning a good initialization that can be adapted to any domain with minimal training samples. [2]

interested in the distribution of tasks $P(\mathcal{T})$ where the support and query sets are very small. In our experiments, we restrict the size of these sets to only few hundred parallel training sentences. We consider support sets of sizes: 4k to 64k source words (i.e. ~ 200 to 3200 sentences). At test time, the meta-learned model θ interacts with the world as follows (Figure 2):

1. **Step 1:** The world draws an adaptation task T from a distribution P, $T \sim P(\mathcal{T})$;
2. **Step 2:** The model adapts from θ to θ' by fine-tuning on the task's support set T_{support};
3. **Step 3:** The fine-tuned model θ' is evaluated on the query set T_{query}.

Intuitively, meta-training should optimize for a representation θ that can quickly adapt to new tasks, rather than a single individual task.

3.2 Training META-MT via Meta-learning

The meta-learning challenge is: how do we learn a good representation θ? We initialize θ by training an NMT model on global-domain data. In addition, we assume access to meta-training tasks on which we can train θ; these tasks must include support/query pairs, where we can simulate a domain adaptation setting by fine-tuning on the support set and then evaluating on the query. This is a weak assumption: in practice, we use purely simulated data as this meta-training data. We construct this data as follows: given a parallel corpus for the desired language pair, we randomly sample training example to form a few-shot adaptation task. We build tasks of 4k, 8k, 16k, 32k, and 64k training words. Under this formulation, it's natural to think of θ's learning process as a process to learn a good parameter initialization for fast adaptation, for which a class of learning algorithms to consider are Model-agnostic Meta-Learning (MAML) and it's first order approximations like First-order MAML (FoMAML) (Finn et al., 2017) and Reptile (Nichol et al., 2018).

Informally, at training time, META-MT will treat one of these simulated domains T as if it were a domain adaptation dataset. At each time step, it will update the current model representation from θ to θ' by fine-tuning on T_{support} and then ask: what is the meta-learning loss estimate given θ, θ', and T_{query}? The model representation θ is then updated to minimize this meta-learning loss. More formally, in meta-learning, we assume access to a

---

[2] colorblind friendly palette was selected from Neuwirth and Brewer (2014).

Algorithm 1 META-MT (trained model f_θ, meta-training dataset $\mathcal{D}_{\text{meta-train}}$, learning rates α, β)

1: **while** not done **do**
2:     Sample a batch of domain adaptation tasks $\text{T} \sim \mathcal{D}_{\text{meta-train}}$
3:     **for all** $\text{T}_i \in \text{T}$ **do**
4:         Evaluate $\nabla_\theta L_{\text{T}_i}(f_\theta)$ on the support set $\text{T}_{i,\text{support}}$
5:         Compute adapted parameters with gradient descent: $\theta'_i = \theta - \alpha \nabla_\theta L_{\text{T}_i}(f_\theta)$
6:     **end for**
7:     Update $\theta \leftarrow \theta - \beta \nabla_\theta \Sigma_{\text{T}_i \in \text{T}} L_{\text{T}_i}(f_{\theta'_i})$ on the query set $\text{T}_{i,\text{query}} \forall \text{T}_i \in \text{T}$
8: **end while**

---

distribution P over different tasks $\mathcal{T}$. From this, we can sample a meta-training dataset $\mathcal{D}_{\text{meta-train}}$. The meta-learning problem is then to estimate θ to minimize the meta-learning loss on $\mathcal{D}_{\text{meta-train}}$.

The meta-learning algorithm we use is MAML by Finn et al. (2017), and is instantiated for the meta-learning to adapt NMT systems in Alg 1. MAML considers a model represented by a parametrized function f_θ with parameters θ. When adapting to a new task T, the model's parameters θ become θ'. The updated vector θ' is computed using one or more gradient descent updates on the task T. For example, when using one gradient update:

$$\theta' = \theta - \alpha \nabla_\theta L_{\text{T}}(f_\theta) \tag{1}$$

where α is the learning rate and L is the task loss function. The model parameters are trained by optimizing for the performance of $f_{\theta'}$ with respect to θ across tasks sampled from $\text{P}(\mathcal{T})$. More concretely, the meta-learning objective is:

$$\min_\theta \Sigma_{\text{T} \sim \text{P}(\mathcal{T})} L_{\text{T}}(f_{\theta'}),$$
$$L_{\text{T}}(f_{\theta'}) = L_{\text{T}}(f_{\theta - \alpha \nabla_\theta L_{\text{T}}(f_\theta)}) \tag{2}$$

Following the MAML template, META-MT operates in an iterative fashion, starting with a trained NMT model f_θ and improving it through optimizing the meta-learning loss from Eq 2 on the meta-training dataset $\mathcal{D}_{\text{meta-train}}$. Over learning rounds, META-MT selects a random batch of training tasks from the meta-training dataset and simulates the test-time behavior on these tasks (Line 2). The core functionality is to observe how the current model representation θ is adapted for each task in the batch, and to use this information to improve θ by optimizing the meta-learning loss (Line 7). META-MT achieves this by simulating a domain adaptation setting by fine-tuning on the task specific support set (Line 4). This yields, for each task T_i, a new adapted set of parameters θ'_i (Line 5). These parameters are evaluated on the query sets for each task $\text{T}_{i,\text{query}}$, and a meta-gradient w.r.t the original model representation θ is used to improve θ (Line 7).

Our pre-trained baseline NMT model f_θ is a sequence to sequence model that parametrizes the conditional probability of the source and target sequences as an encoder-decoder architecture using self-attention Transformer models (Vaswani et al., 2017)).

4 Experimental Setup and Results

We seek to answer the following questions experimentally:

1. How does META-MT compare empirically to alternative adaptation strategies? (§4.4)
2. What is the impact of the support and the query sizes used for meta-learning? (§4.5)
3. What is the effect of the NMT model architecture on performance? (§4.6)

In our experiments, we train META-MT only on simulated data, where we simulate a few-shot domain adaptation setting as described in §3.2. This is possible because META-MT learns model parameters θ that can generalize to future adaptation tasks by optimizing the meta-objective function in Eq 2.

We train and evaluate META-MT on a collection of ten different datasets. All of these datasets are collected from the Open Parallel Corpus (OPUS) (Tiedemann, 2012), and are publicly available online. The datasets cover a variety of diverse domains that should enable us to evaluate our proposed approach. The datasets we consider are:

1. Bible: a parallel corpus created from translations of the Bible (Christodouloupoulos and Steedman, 2015).
2. European Central Bank: website and documentations from the European Central Bank.
3. KDE: a corpus of KDE4 localization files.
4. Quran: a collection of Quran translations compiled by the Tanzil project.
5. WMT news test sets: a parallel corpus of

News Test Sets provided by WMT.

6. Books: a collection of copyright free books.

7. European Medicines Agency (EMEA): a parallel corpus made out of PDF documents from the European Medicines Agency.

8. Global Voices: parallel news stories from the Global Voices web site.

9. Medical (ufal-Med): the UFAL medical domain dataset from Yepes et al. (2017).

10. TED talks: talk subtitles from Duh (2018).

We simulate the few-shot NMT adaptation scenarios by randomly sub-sampling these datasets with different sizes. We sample different data sets with sizes ranging from 4k to 64k training words (i.e. $\sim$ 200 to 3200 sentences). This data is the only data used for any given domain across all adaptation setups. It is worth noting that different datasets have a wide range of sentence lengths. We opted to sample using number of words instead of number of sentences to avoid introducing any advantages for domains with longer sentences.

4.1 Domain Adaptation Approaches

Our experiments aim to determine how META-MT compares to standard domain adaptation strategies. In particular, we compare to:

(A) **No fine-tuning:** The non-adaptive baseline. Here, the pre-trained model is evaluated on the meta-test and meta-validation datasets (see Figure 1) without any kind of adaptation.

(B) **Fine-tuning on a single task:** The domain adaptation by fine-tuning baseline. For a single adaptation task T, this approach performs domain adaptation by fine-tuning only on the support set $T_{support}$. For instance, if $|T_{support}| = K$ words, we fine tune the pre-trained model f_θ only on K training words to show how classical fine-tuning behaves in few-shot settings.

(C) **Fine-tuning on meta-train:** Similar to (B), however, this approach fine-tunes on much more data. This approach fine-tunes on all the support sets used for meta-training: $\{T_{support}, \forall T \in \mathcal{D}_{meta\text{-}train}\}$. The goal of this baseline is to ensure that META-MT doesn't get an additional advantage by training on more data during the meta-training phase. For instance, if we are using N adaptation tasks each with a support set of size K, this will be using $N * K$ words for classical fine-tuning. This establishes a fair baseline to evaluate how classical fine-tuning would perform using the same data albeit in a different configuration.

(D) **META-MT:** Our proposed approach from Alg 1. In this setup, we use N adaptation tasks T in $\mathcal{D}_{meta\text{-}train}$, each with a support set of size K words to perform Meta-Learning. Second order meta-gradients are ignored to decrease the computational complexity.

4.2 Model Architecture and Implementation Details

We use the Transformer Model (Vaswani et al., 2017) implemented in fairseq (Ott et al., 2019). In this work, we use a transformer model with a modified architecture that can facilitate better adaptation. We use *"Adapter Modules"* (Houlsby et al., 2019; Bapna et al., 2019) which introduce an extra layer after each transformer block that can enable more efficient tuning of the models. Following Bapna et al. (2019), we augment the Transformer model with feed-forward adapters: simple single hidden-layer feed-forward networks, with a nonlinear activation function between the two projection layers. These adapter modules are introduced after the Layer Norm and before the residual connection layers. It is composed of a down projection layer, followed by a ReLU, followed by an up projection layer. This bottle-necked module with fewer parameters is very attractive for domain adaptation as we will discuss in §4.6. These modules are introduced after every layer in both the encoder and the decoder. All experiments are based on the "base" transformer model with six blocks in the encoder and decoder networks. Each encoder block contains a self-attention layer, followed by two fully connected feed-forward layers with a ReLU non-linearity between them. Each decoder block contains self-attention, followed by encoder-decoder attention, followed by two fully connected feed-forward layers with a ReLU non-linearity between them.

We use word representations of size 512, feed-forward layers with inner dimensions $2,048$, multi-head attention with 8 attention heads, and adapter modules with 32 hidden units. We apply dropout (Srivastava et al., 2014) with probability 0.1. The model is optimized with Adam (Kingma and Ba, 2014) using $\beta_1 = 0.9, \beta_2 = 0.98$, and a learning rate $\alpha = 7e-4$. We use the same learning rate schedule as Vaswani et al. (2017) where the learning rate increases linearly for $4,000$ steps to $7e - 4$, after which it is decayed proportionally to the inverse square root of the number of steps. For meta-learning, we used a meta-batch size of 1. We optimized the meta-learning loss function using Adam with a learning rate of $1e - 5$ and default parameters for β_1, β_2.

All data is pre-processed with joint sentence-pieces (Kudo and Richardson, 2018) of size 40k. In all cases, the baseline machine translation system is a neural English to German (En-De) transformer model (Vaswani et al., 2017), initially trained on 5.2M sentences filtered from the the standard parallel data (Europarl-v9, CommonCrawl, NewsCommentary-v14, wikititles-v1 and Rapid-2019) from the WMT-19 shared task (Barrault et al., 2019). We use WMT14 and WMT19 newtests as validation and test sets respectively. The baseline system scores 37.99 BLEU on the full WMT19 newstest which compares favorably with strong single system baselines at WMT19 shared task (Ng et al., 2019; Junczys-Dowmunt, 2019).

For meta-learning, we use the MAML algorithm as described in Alg 1. To minimize memory consumption, we ignored the second order gradient terms from Eq 2. We implement the First-Order MAML approximation (FoMAML) as described in Finn et al. (2017). We also experimented with the first-order meta-learning algorithm Reptile (Nichol et al., 2018). We found that since Reptile doesn't directly account for the performance on the task query set, along with the large model capacity of the Transformer architecture, it can easily over-fit to the support set, thus achieving almost perfect performance on the support, while the performance on the query degrades significantly. Even after performing early stopping on the query set, Reptile didn't account correctly for learning rate scheduling, and finding suitable learning rates for optimizing the meta-learner and the task adaptation was difficult. In our experiments, we found it essential to match the behavior of the dropout layers when computing the meta-objective function in Eq 2 with the test-time behavior described in §3.1. In particular, the model has to run in *"evaluation mode"* when computing the loss on the task query set to match the test-time behavior during evaluation.

4.3 Evaluation Tasks and Metrics

Our experimental setup operates as follows: using a collection of simulated machine translation adaptation tasks, we train an NMT model f_θ using META-MT (Alg 1). This model learns to adapt faster to new domains, by fine-tuning on a tiny support set. Once f_θ is learned and fixed, we follow the test-time behavior described in §3.1. We evaluate META-MT on the collection of ten different domains described in §4. We simulate domain adaptation problems by sub-sampling tasks with 4k English tokens for the support set, and 32k tokens for the query set. We study the effect of varying the size of the query and the support sets in §4.5. We use $N = 160$ tasks for the meta-training dataset $\mathcal{D}_{\text{meta-train}}$, where we sample 16 tasks from each of the ten different domains. We use a meta-validation $\mathcal{D}_{\text{meta-test}}$ and meta-test $\mathcal{D}_{\text{meta-test}}$ sets of size 10, where we sample a single task from each domain. We report the mean and standard-deviation over three different meta-test sets. For evaluation, we use BLEU (Papineni et al., 2002). We measure case-sensitive de-tokenized BLEU with SacreBLEU (Post, 2018). All results use beam search with a beam of size five.

4.4 Experimental Results

Here, we describe our experimental results comparing the several algorithms from §4.1. The overall results are shown in Table 1 and Figure 3. Table 1 shows the BLEU scores on the meta-test dataset for all the different approaches across the ten domains. From these results we draw the following conclusions:

1. The pre-trained En-De NMT model performs well on general domains. For instance, BLEU for WMT-News [3], GlobalVoices, and ECB is at least 26 points. However, performance degrades on closed domains like Books, Quran, and Bible. [Column A].

2. Domain adaptation by fine-tuning on a single task doesn't improve the BLEU score. This is expected, since we're only fine-tuning on 4k tokens (i.e. $\sim 200 - 300$ sentences) [A vs B].

3. Significant leverage is gained by increasing the amount of fine-tuning data. Fine-tuning on all the available data used for meta-learning improves the BLEU score significantly across all domains. [B vs C]. To put this into perspective, this setup is tuned on all data aggregated from all tasks: $160 * 4k$ words which is approximately $40K$ sentences.

---

[3]This is subset of the full test set to match the sizes of query sets from other domains

Domain	A. No fine-tuning	B. Fine-tuning on task	C. Fine-tuning on meta-train	D. META-MT
Books	11.338 ± 0.25	11.34 ± 0.24	$\underline{12.49 \pm 0.15}$	$\mathbf{12.92 \pm 0.94}$
Tanzil	11.25 ± 0.04	11.33 ± 0.04	$\underline{13.62 \pm 0.05}$	$\mathbf{15.16 \pm 0.94}$
Bible	12.93 ± 0.93	12.95 ± 0.94	$\underline{17.19 \pm 0.54}$	$\mathbf{24.70 \pm 0.61}$
KDE4	20.53 ± 0.34	20.54 ± 0.32	$\underline{26.61 \pm 0.16}$	$\mathbf{27.26 \pm 0.36}$
Med	19.30 ± 0.24	19.53 ± 0.28	28.31 ± 0.04	$\mathbf{29.59 \pm 0.05}$
GlobalVoices	25.10 ± 0.11	25.17 ± 0.23	25.83 ± 0.25	$\mathbf{26.03 \pm 0.13}$
WMT-News	26.93 ± 0.36	26.92 ± 0.48	$\mathbf{27.26 \pm 0.55}$	$\underline{27.23 \pm 0.12}$
TED	27.69 ± 0.05	27.85 ± 0.06	28.78 ± 0.03	$\mathbf{29.37 \pm 0.03}$
EMEA	27.81 ± 0.01	27.79 ± 0.05	29.77 ± 0.59	$\mathbf{32.38 \pm 0.01}$
ECB	29.18 ± 0.03	29.21 ± 0.04	31.18 ± 0.01	$\mathbf{33.23 \pm 0.40}$

Table 1: BLEU scores on meta-test split for different approaches evaluated across ten domains. Best results are highlighted in bold, results with-in two standard-deviations of the best value are underlined.

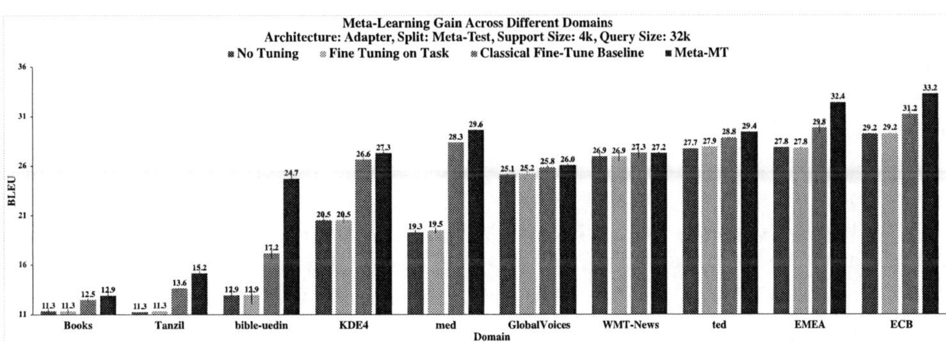

Figure 3: BLEU scores on meta-test split for different approaches evaluated across ten domains.

4. META-MT outperforms alternative domain adaptation approaches on all domains with negligible degradation on the baseline domain. META-MT is better than the non-adaptive baseline [A vs D], and succeeds in learning to adapt faster given the same amount of fine-tuning data [B vs D, C vs D]. Both **Fine-tuning on meta-train** [C] and **META-MT** [D] have access to exactly the same amount of training data, and both use the same model architecture. The difference however is in the learning algorithm. META-MT uses MAML (Alg 1) to optimize the meta-objective function in Eq 2. This ensures that the learned model initialization can easily be fine-tuned to new domains with very few examples.

4.5 Impact of Adaptation Task Size

To evaluate the effectiveness of META-MT when adapting with small in-domain corpora, we further compare the performance of META-MT with classical fine-tuning on varying amounts of training data per adaptation task. In Figure 4 we plot the overall adaptation performance on the ten domains when using different data sizes for the support set. In this experiment, the only parameter that

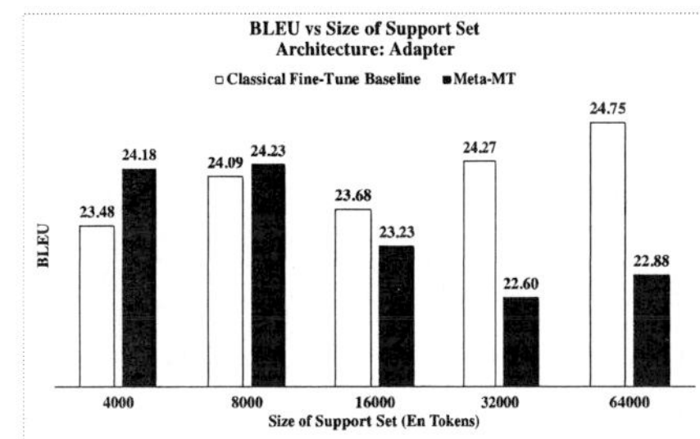

Figure 4: META-MT and fine-tuning adaptation performance on the meta-test set $\mathcal{D}_{\text{meta-test}}$ vs different support set sizes per adaptation task.

varies is the size of the task support set T_{support}. We fix the size of the query set per task to $16k$ tokens, and we vary the size of the support set from $4k$ to $64k$. To ensure that the total amount of meta-training data $\mathcal{D}_{\text{meta-train}}$ is the same, we use $N = 160$ tasks for meta-training when the support size T_{support} is $4k$, $N = 80$ tasks when the support size is $8k$, $N = 40$ tasks for support size of $16k$, $N = 20$ tasks when the support size is $32k$, and finally $N = 10$ meta-training tasks when the support size is $64k$. This controlled setup ensures that no setting has any advantage by getting access to additional amounts of training data. We notice

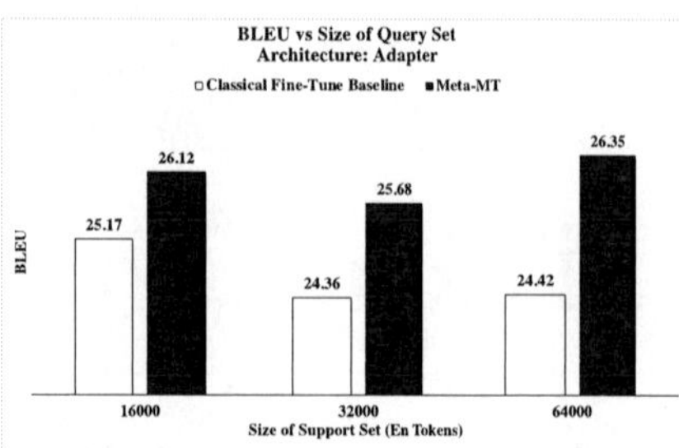

Figure 5: META-MT and fine-tuning adaptation performance on the meta-test set $\mathcal{D}_{\text{meta-test}}$ vs different query set sizes per adaptation task.

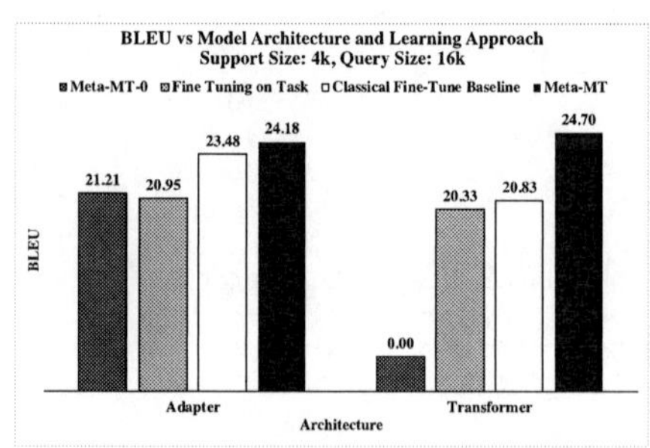

Figure 6: BLEU scores reported for two different model architectures: Adapter Transformer (Bapna et al., 2019) (Left), and the Transformer base architecture (Vaswani et al., 2012) (Right).

that for reasonably small size of the support set ($4k$ and $8k$), META-MT outperforms the classical fine-tuning baseline. However, when the data size increase ($16k$ to 64), META-MT is outperformed by the fine-tuning baseline. This happens because for a larger support size, e.g. $64k$, we only have access to 10 meta-training tasks in $\mathcal{D}_{\text{meta-train}}$, this is not enough to generalize to new unseen adaptation tasks, and META-MT over-fits to the training tasks from $\mathcal{D}_{\text{meta-train}}$, however, the performance degrades and doesn't generalize to $\mathcal{D}_{\text{meta-test}}$.

To understand more directly the impact of the query set on META-MT's performance, in Figure 5 we show META-MT and fine-tuning adaptation performance on the meta-test set $\mathcal{D}_{\text{meta-test}}$ on varying sizes for the query set. We fix the support size to $4k$ and vary the query set size from $16k$ to $64k$. We observe that the edge of improvement of META-MT over fine-tuning adaptation increases as we increase the size of the query set. For instance, when we use a query set of size $64k$, META-MT outperforms fine-tuning by 1.93 BLEU points, while the improvement is only 0.95 points when the query set is $16k$.

4.6 Impact of Model Architecture

In our experiments, we used the Adapter Transformer architecture (Bapna et al., 2019). This architecture fixes the parameters of the pre-trained Transformer model, and only adapts the feed-forward adapter module. Our model included $\sim 66M$ parameters, out of which we adapt only $405K$ (only 0.6%). We found this adaptation strategy to be more robust to meta-learning. To better understand this, Figure 6 shows the BLEU scores for the two different model architectures. We find that while the meta-learned Transformer architecture (Right) slightly outperforms the Adapter model (Left), it

suffers from catastrophic forgetting: **META-MT-0** shows the zero-shot BLEU score before fine-tuning the task on the support set. For the Transformer model, the score drops to zero and then quickly improves once the parameters are tuned on the support set. This is undesirable, since it hurts the performance of the pre-trained model, even on the general domain data. We notice that the Adapter model doesn't suffer from this problem.

5 Conclusion

We presented META-MT, a meta-learning approach for few shot NMT adaptation. We formulated few shot NMT adaptation as a meta-learning problem, and presented a strategy that learns better parameters for NMT systems that can be easily adapted to new domains. We validated the superiority of META-MT to alternative domain adaptation approaches. META-MT outperforms alternative strategies in most domains using only a small fraction of fine-tuning data.

Acknowledgements

The authors would like to thank members of the Microsoft Machine Translation Team as well as members of the Computational Linguistics and Information Processing (CLIP) lab for reviewing earlier versions of this work. Part of this work was conducted when the first author was on a summer internship with Microsoft Research. This material is based upon work supported by the National Science Foundation under Grant No. 1618193. Any opinions, findings, and conclusions or recommendations expressed in this material are those of the author(s) and do not necessarily reflect the views of the National Science Foundation.

References

Dzmitry Bahdanau, Kyunghyun Cho, and Yoshua Bengio. 2016. Neural machine translation by jointly learning to align and translate. *arXiv preprint arXiv:1409.0473*.

Ankur Bapna, Naveen Arivazhagan, and Orhan Firat. 2019. Simple, scalable adaptation for neural machine translation. *arXiv preprint arXiv:1909.08478*.

Loïc Barrault, Ondřej Bojar, Marta R Costa-jussà, Christian Federmann, Mark Fishel, Yvette Graham, Barry Haddow, Matthias Huck, Philipp Koehn, Shervin Malmasi, et al. 2019. Findings of the 2019 conference on machine translation (wmt19). In *Proceedings of the Fourth Conference on Machine Translation (Volume 2: Shared Task Papers, Day 1)*, pages 1–61.

Christos Christodouloupoulos and Mark Steedman. 2015. A massively parallel corpus: the bible in 100 languages. *Language resources and evaluation*, 49(2):375–395.

Chenhui Chu, Raj Dabre, and Sadao Kurohashi. 2018. A comprehensive empirical comparison of domain adaptation methods for neural machine translation. *Journal of Information Processing*, 26:529–538.

Chenhui Chu and Rui Wang. 2018. A survey of domain adaptation for neural machine translation. In *Proceedings of the 27th International Conference on Computational Linguistics*, pages 1304–1319, Santa Fe, New Mexico, USA. Association for Computational Linguistics.

Zi-Yi Dou, Keyi Yu, and Antonios Anastasopoulos. 2019. Investigating meta-learning algorithms for low-resource natural language understanding tasks. In *Proceedings of the 2019 Conference on Empirical Methods in Natural Language Processing and the 9th International Joint Conference on Natural Language Processing (EMNLP-IJCNLP)*, pages 1192–1197, Hong Kong, China. Association for Computational Linguistics.

Kevin Duh. 2018. The multitarget ted talks task. `http://www.cs.jhu.edu/~kevinduh/a/multitarget-tedtalks/`.

Chelsea Finn, Pieter Abbeel, and Sergey Levine. 2017. Model-agnostic meta-learning for fast adaptation of deep networks. In *Proceedings of the 34th International Conference on Machine Learning*, volume 70 of *Proceedings of Machine Learning Research*, pages 1126–1135, International Convention Centre, Sydney, Australia. PMLR.

Markus Freitag and Yaser Al-Onaizan. 2016. Fast domain adaptation for neural machine translation. *ArXiv*, abs/1612.06897.

Jiatao Gu, Yong Wang, Yun Chen, Victor O. K. Li, and Kyunghyun Cho. 2018. Meta-learning for low-resource neural machine translation. In *Proceedings of the 2018 Conference on Empirical Methods in Natural Language Processing*, pages 3622–3631, Brussels, Belgium. Association for Computational Linguistics.

Neil Houlsby, Andrei Giurgiu, Stanislaw Jastrzkebski, Bruna Morrone, Quentin de Laroussilhe, Andrea Gesmundo, Mona Attariyan, and Sylvain Gelly. 2019. Parameter-efficient transfer learning for NLP. *CoRR*, abs/1902.00751.

Marcin Junczys-Dowmunt. 2019. Microsoft translator at wmt 2019: Towards large-scale document-level neural machine translation. In *WMT*.

Huda Khayrallah, Gaurav Kumar, Kevin Duh, Matt Post, and Philipp Koehn. 2017. Neural lattice search for domain adaptation in machine translation. In *Proceedings of the Eighth International Joint Conference on Natural Language Processing (Volume 2: Short Papers)*, pages 20–25, Taipei, Taiwan. Asian Federation of Natural Language Processing.

Diederik P Kingma and Jimmy Ba. 2014. Adam: A method for stochastic optimization. *arXiv preprint arXiv:1412.6980*.

Philipp Koehn and Rebecca Knowles. 2017. Six challenges for neural machine translation. In *Proceedings of the First Workshop on Neural Machine Translation*, pages 28–39, Vancouver. Association for Computational Linguistics.

Taku Kudo and John Richardson. 2018. SentencePiece: A simple and language independent subword tokenizer and detokenizer for neural text processing. In *Proceedings of the 2018 Conference on Empirical Methods in Natural Language Processing: System Demonstrations*, pages 66–71, Brussels, Belgium. Association for Computational Linguistics.

Minh-Thang Luong and Christopher D. Manning. 2015. Stanford neural machine translation systems for spoken language domain. In *International Workshop on Spoken Language Translation*.

Fei Mi, Minlie Huang, Jiyong Zhang, and Boi Faltings. 2019. Meta-learning for low-resource natural language generation in task-oriented dialogue systems. In *Proceedings of the 28th International Joint Conference on Artificial Intelligence*, IJCAI'19, pages 3151–3157. AAAI Press.

Paul Michel and Graham Neubig. 2018. Extreme adaptation for personalized neural machine translation. In *Proceedings of the 56th Annual Meeting of the Association for Computational Linguistics (Volume 2: Short Papers)*, pages 312–318, Melbourne, Australia. Association for Computational Linguistics.

Erich Neuwirth and R Color Brewer. 2014. Colorbrewer palettes. *R package version*, pages 1–1.

Nathan Ng, Kyra Yee, Alexei Baevski, Myle Ott, Michael Auli, and Sergey Edunov. 2019. Facebook FAIR's WMT19 news translation task submission.

In *Proceedings of the Fourth Conference on Machine Translation (Volume 2: Shared Task Papers, Day 1)*, pages 314–319, Florence, Italy. Association for Computational Linguistics.

Alex Nichol, Joshua Achiam, and John Schulman. 2018. On first-order meta-learning algorithms. *arXiv preprint arXiv:1803.02999*.

Myle Ott, Sergey Edunov, Alexei Baevski, Angela Fan, Sam Gross, Nathan Ng, David Grangier, and Michael Auli. 2019. fairseq: A fast, extensible toolkit for sequence modeling. In *Proceedings of NAACL-HLT 2019: Demonstrations*.

Kishore Papineni, Salim Roukos, Todd Ward, and Wei-Jing Zhu. 2002. Bleu: a method for automatic evaluation of machine translation. In *Proceedings of the 40th annual meeting on association for computational linguistics*, pages 311–318. Association for Computational Linguistics.

Matt Post. 2018. A call for clarity in reporting bleu scores. *arXiv preprint arXiv:1804.08771*.

Rico Sennrich, Barry Haddow, and Alexandra Birch. 2016. Improving neural machine translation models with monolingual data. In *Proceedings of the 54th Annual Meeting of the Association for Computational Linguistics (Volume 1: Long Papers)*, pages 86–96, Berlin, Germany. Association for Computational Linguistics.

Nitish Srivastava, Geoffrey Hinton, Alex Krizhevsky, Ilya Sutskever, and Ruslan Salakhutdinov. 2014. Dropout: a simple way to prevent neural networks from overfitting. *The journal of machine learning research*, 15(1):1929–1958.

Ilya Sutskever, Oriol Vinyals, and Quoc V Le. 2014. Sequence to sequence learning with neural networks. In Z. Ghahramani, M. Welling, C. Cortes, N. D. Lawrence, and K. Q. Weinberger, editors, *Advances in Neural Information Processing Systems 27*, pages 3104–3112. Curran Associates, Inc.

Brian Thompson, Jeremy Gwinnup, Huda Khayrallah, Kevin Duh, and Philipp Koehn. 2019. Overcoming catastrophic forgetting during domain adaptation of neural machine translation. In *Proceedings of the 2019 Conference of the North American Chapter of the Association for Computational Linguistics: Human Language Technologies, Volume 1 (Long and Short Papers)*, pages 2062–2068, Minneapolis, Minnesota. Association for Computational Linguistics.

Jorg Tiedemann. 2012. Parallel data, tools and interfaces in opus. In *Proceedings of the Eight International Conference on Language Resources and Evaluation (LREC'12)*, Istanbul, Turkey. European Language Resources Association (ELRA).

Ashish Vaswani, Liang Huang, and David Chiang. 2012. Smaller alignment models for better translations: Unsupervised word alignment with the l0-norm. In *Proceedings of the 50th Annual Meeting of the Association for Computational Linguistics (Volume 1: Long Papers)*, pages 311–319, Jeju Island, Korea. Association for Computational Linguistics.

Ashish Vaswani, Noam Shazeer, Niki Parmar, Jakob Uszkoreit, Llion Jones, Aidan N Gomez, Łukasz Kaiser, and Illia Polosukhin. 2017. Attention is all you need. In *Advances in neural information processing systems*, pages 5998–6008.

David Vilar. 2018. Learning hidden unit contribution for adapting neural machine translation models. In *Proceedings of the 2018 Conference of the North American Chapter of the Association for Computational Linguistics: Human Language Technologies, Volume 2 (Short Papers)*, pages 500–505, New Orleans, Louisiana. Association for Computational Linguistics.

Qianhui Wu, Zijia Lin, Guoxin Wang, Hui Chen, Börje F Karlsson, Biqing Huang, and Chin-Yew Lin. 2019. Enhanced meta-learning for cross-lingual named entity recognition with minimal resources. *arXiv preprint arXiv:1911.06161*.

Antonio Jimeno Yepes, Aurélie Névéol, Mariana Neves, Karin Verspoor, Ondrej Bojar, Arthur Boyer, Cristian Grozea, Barry Haddow, Madeleine Kittner, Yvonne Lichtblau, et al. 2017. Findings of the wmt 2017 biomedical translation shared task. In *Proceedings of the Second Conference on Machine Translation*, pages 234–247.

Supplementary Material For:
Meta-Learning for Few-Shot NMT
Adaptation

A Background

A.1 Neural Machine Translation

Neural Machine Translation (NMT) is a sequence to sequence model that parametrizes the conditional probability of the source and target sequences as a neural network following encoder-decoder architecture (Bahdanau et al., 2016; Sutskever et al., 2014). Initially, the encode-decoder architecture was represented by recurrent networks. Currently, this has been replaced by self-attention models aka Transformer models (Vaswani et al., 2017)). Currently, Transformer models achieves state-of-the-art performance in NMT as well as many other language modeling tasks. While transformers models are performing quite well on large scale NMT tasks, the models have huge number of parameters and require large amount of training data which is really prohibitive for adaptation tasks especially in few-shot setup like ours.

A.2 Few Shots Domain Adaptation

Traditional domain adaptation for NMT models assumes the availability of relatively large amount of in domain data. For instances most of the related work utilizing traditional fine-tuning experiment with hundred-thousand sentences in-domain. This setup in quite prohibitive, since practically the domain can be defined by few examples. In this work we focus on few-shot adaptation scenario where we can adapt to a new domain not seen during training time using just couple of hundreds of in-domain sentences. This introduces a new challenge where the models have to be quickly responsive to adaptation as well as robust to domain shift. Since we focus on the setting in which very few in-domain data is available, this renders many traditional domain adaptation approaches inappropriate.

A.3 Meta-Learning

Meta-learning or Learn-to-Learn is widely used for few-shot learning in many applications where a model trained for a particular task can learn another task with a few examples. A number of approaches are used in Meta-learning, namely: Model-agnostic Meta-Learning (MAML) and its first order approximations like First-order MAML (FoMAML) (Finn et al., 2017) and Reptile (Nichol et al., 2018). In

Domain	# sentences	# En Tokens
bible-uedin	62195	1550431
ECB	113174	3061513
KDE4	224035	1746216
Tanzil	537128	9489824
WMT-News	912212	5462820
Books	51467	1054718
EMEA	1108752	12322425
GlobalVoices	66650	1239921
ufal-Med	140600	5527010
TED	51368	1060765

Table 2: Dataset statistics for different domains.

this work, we focus on using MAML to enable few-shots adaptation of NMT transformer models.

B Statistics of in-domain data sets

Table 2 lists the sizes of various in-domain datasets from which we sample our in-domain data to simulate the few-shot adaptation setup.

Automatically Ranked Russian Paraphrase Corpus for Text Generation

Vadim Gudkov[1], Olga Mitrofanova[2], Elizaveta Filippskikh[3]

Saint Petersburg State University[1,2]
st071220@student.spbu.ru[1], o.mitrofanova@spbu.ru[2]
CraftTalk[3]
efilippskikh@crafttalk.ru[3]

Abstract

The article is focused on automatic development and ranking of a large corpus for Russian paraphrase generation which proves to be the first corpus of such type in Russian computational linguistics. Existing manually annotated paraphrase datasets for Russian are limited to small-sized ParaPhraser corpus and ParaPlag which are suitable for a set of NLP tasks, such as paraphrase and plagiarism detection, sentence similarity and relatedness estimation, etc. Due to size restrictions, these datasets can hardly be applied in end-to-end text generation solutions. Meanwhile, paraphrase generation requires a large amount of training data. In our study we propose a solution to the problem: we collect, rank and evaluate a new publicly available headline paraphrase corpus (ParaPhraser Plus), and then perform text generation experiments with manual evaluation on automatically ranked corpora using the Universal Transformer architecture.

1 Introduction

A large amount of work is dedicated for a clear understanding of the nature of a paraphrase. On the one hand, traditional theories of language allow to trace the notion of paraphrase back to the ancient rhetorical tradition (cf. Greek παράφρασις 'retelling') and treat it quite broadly in case of different types of prose, verse, musical pieces, etc. On the other hand, the generative trend in linguistic research encouraged description of transformations involved in the transition from deep to surface structures and at the same time responsible for the emergence of a wide range of paraphrases, cf. Chomskian generative grammar giving account of various lexical transformations, Melchuk's Sense-Text theory postulating the process of paraphrasing as synonymic conversion, etc. In recent works paraphrases are treated as "alternative expressions of the same (or similar) meaning" (Agirre et al., 2015). Ranking paraphrases as regards their similarity in form and meaning is reflected in a set of paraphrase classifications, where precise paraphrases are distinguished from quasi-paraphrases and non-paraphrases (Andrew and Gao, 2007). At the same time, paraphrase corpora development required deep analysis of paraphrase transformations types (e.g. morphosyntactic, lexical and semantic shifts).

Paraphrasing plays an important role in a broad range of NLP tasks, including but not limited to question answering, summarization, information retrieval, sentence simplification, machine translation and dialogue systems. However, in order to be able to train a good paraphrasing system, large parallel corpora are required, which can be a problem in underdeveloped languages from a data resources standpoint. In order to bridge this gap, we propose a methodology to collect enough data for proper deep learning.

2 Motivation and Related Work

Paraphrase identification inspired a set of NLP competitions within SemEval conferences in 2012, 2013, 2015 and 2016, so that baseline decisions and their improvements were worked out for English. There also exist several well-known manually annotated paraphrase datasets for English: Microsoft Paraphrase (Dolan and Brockett, 2005), Quora Question Pairs and MS COCO (Lin et al., 2014).

However, Russian is less represented in paraphrase research both in case of resource development and algorithm evaluation, a few exceptions being AINL Paraphrase detection competition in 2016 based on Paraphraser corpus and Dialogue Paraphrased plagiarism detection competition in 2017 based on ParaPlag corpus. Alongside with Paraphraser and ParaPlag, there are some para-

Proceedings of the 4th Workshop on Neural Generation and Translation (WNGT 2020), pages 54–59
Online, July 10, 2020. ©2020 Association for Computational Linguistics
www.aclweb.org/anthology/D19-56%2d

phrase resources which include Russian language, for instance by Opusparcus (Creutz, 2018) and PPDB (Ganitkevitch et al., 2013).

In our study we mainly focus on the collection, evaluation and generation of the, so called, sentential paraphrases. This approach is different from the collection of PPDB, where sub-sentential paraphrases, such as individual word-pairs, were also included and ParaPlag with main focus on text-level rephrasing.

Recent work (Gupta et al., 2018; Fu et al., 2019; Egonmwan and Chali, 2019) provides solid evidence in favour of paraphrase generation by means of seq-2-seq architectures. The main problem, however, is that such systems require significant expansion of existing datasets for proper machine learning (Roy and Grangier, 2019). The lack of data still remains the greatest obstacle to the development of a stable generation system which could be lexically rich and insensitive to rare words. E.g., the largest datasets supplied with proper annotation seldom exceed 100K samples in size. The authors of the aforementioned articles claim that any user generated content is valuable even though noisy to a certain extent. We propose a solution which overcomes the given problem, and it is based on the denoising procedure which has recently attracted growing attention. We argue that automatically matched and ranked datasets can be used for paraphrase generation task, especially in low-resource languages, by providing experimental results obtained on the Russian Opusparcus subcorpus and on the novel ParaPhraser Plus corpus.

3   Source Data

The ParaPhraser Plus corpus [1] is distilled from a database of news headlines, that was kindly provided by the Russian Internet monitoring service, "Webground". Although, the contents of the resources are pretty similar, the data itself in the original ParaPhraser corpus and the ParaPhraser Plus corpus as well as the methodology used to collect the headlines are not the same by any means. It is important to note, however, that ranking model which will be described in the corresponding section was based on the original corpus. The headlines in "Webground" were initially clustered by events over a ten year span, beginning from the year 2009. Following the hypothesis that within such theme-based user-generated clusters the chance of seeing a paraphrase is particularly high, we formed sets of pairs of all possible combinations within each of them. After weeding out pairs, consisting of the same tokens, we were left with just over 56 million pairs of potential paraphrases. We have also discarded over 200 thousand headlines where it was not possible to verify the authorship.

4   Ranking methodology

There are several known approaches to paraphrase ranking, including heuristic scoring (Pavlick et al., 2015) and supervised modelling (Creutz, 2018). Heuristic scoring can be effectively conducted in resources with cross-linguistic support, such as PPDB and Opuspracus. However, ParaPhraser, as well as our addition, is monolingual, therefore this approach was not possible. On the other hand, supervised modelling techniques can be adopted: there is a significant amount of labeled data in the original ParaPhraser corpus and several approaches to paraphrase identification in Russian headlines have been thoroughly researched and summarized in (Pivovarova et al., 2017). The methods included shallow neural networks, linguistic features based classifier and a combination of machine translation with semantic similarity.

However, recent research conducted in (Kuratov and Arkhipov, 2019) shows that deep bidirectional pretrained monolingual transformers improve paraphrase detection in Russian by a large margin. It was shown that finetuning a monolingual BERT based model (RuBERT) on the ParaPhraser corpus yields results far better than all of the aforementioned approaches (see Table 1).

The training set in ParaPhraser includes 7,227 pairs of sentences, which are classified by humans into three classes: 2,582 non-paraphrases, 2,957 near-paraphrases, and 1,688 precise-paraphrases. The aforementioned RuBERT model was fine-tuned to a binary classification task: both near-paraphrases and paraphrases were considered to be a single class. Such approach helps in automatic ranking: it is possible to sort the items in accordance to the probability of the paraphrase class in descending order. The fine-tuned RuBERT model is available as part of the DeepPavlov library (Burtsev et al., 2018), which enabled us to adopt this approach in our corpus construction study.

---

[1] Available at:
`http://paraphraser.ru/download/`

Model	F1	Accuracy
Shallow Neural Networks (Pivovarova et al., 2017)	79.82	76.65
Linguistic Features Classifier (Pivovarova et al., 2017)	81.10	77.39
Machine Translation Based Semantic Similarity (Kravchenko, 2018)	78.51	81.41
RuBERT (Kuratov and Arkhipov, 2019)	87.73	84.99

Table 1: Paraphrase detection algorithms evaluation.

5 Ranking evaluation

In order to evaluate our supervised automatic ranking approach we randomly select a subsample of 500 pairs for manual annotation. To provide a more thorough comparison analysis we step aside from the original 3-way annotation scheme utilized in ParaPhraser and adopt the approach provided in (Creutz, 2018) with more similarity degrees.

The annotation scheme from the original paper is provided in Table 2.

To measure The inter-annotator agreement we use Fleiss Kappa, which is a Cohen's Kappa generalization to more than two annotators (in our case - 5); expected agreement is calculated on the basis of the assumption that random assignment of categories to items, by any annotator, is governed by the distribution of items among categories in the actual world. The annotators reach a fair agreement (Kappa 0.267, p-value < 0.05).

The cosine similarity baseline solution of Word2Vec embeddings achieves a manual annotation Pearson's correlation coefficient of 0.535. Our supervised model rankings for ParaPhraser Plus dramatically improve correlation with human judgments (p = 0.734).

6 Paraphrase generation

To test our initial hypothesis we conduct a paraphrase generation experiment on two datasets: Opusparcus and our ParaPhraser Plus.

There exist several methods to generate paraphrases. The following techniques are known: rule-based (McKeown, 1983), Seq-2-Seq (Gupta et al., 2018; Fu et al., 2019; Egonmwan and Chali, 2019; Roy and Grangier, 2019), reinforcement learning (Li et al., 2017), deep generative models (Iyyer et al., 2018) and a varied combination (Gupta et al., 2018; Mallinson et al., 2017) of the later three.

We show the results that can be achieved on large automatically ranked corpora using a Sequence-to-Sequence model based on the Universal Transformer architecture as it has demonstrated superior performance over the past year in multiple generative tasks, such as abstractive summarization, machine translation and, of course, paraphrase generation. (Gupta et al., 2018; Mallinson et al., 2017; Gupta et al., 2018; Fu et al., 2019; Egonmwan and Chali, 2019; Roy and Grangier, 2019).

As pointed out in (Vaswani et al., 2017), the attention heads in the transformer model can be found very useful in learning grammatical, syntactical, morphological and semantic behavior in the language, which is essential in paraphrase generation. Such results are being achieved thanks to the fact that input vectors are connected to every other via the attention mechanism, thus allowing the network to learn complex rephrasing dependencies. Moreover, contrary to recurrent neural networks, a transformer can be trained in parallel.

For both datasets, Opusparcus and ParaPhraser Plus, we used the same set of model hyperparameters: 4 layers in the encoder and decoder with 8 heads of attention. In addition, we added a Dropout of p = 0.3. The models were trained until convergence with the Adam optimizer using a scaled learning rate, as proposed by the authors of the original Transformer

We also adopt byte-pair encoding (BPE), a data compression technique where often occuring pairs of bytes are replaced by additional extra-alphabet symbols. Thanks to this approach, the most frequent parts of words are kept in the vocabulary, while rarely occuring words are replaced by a sequence of several tokens. Languages with rich morphology benefit the most as the word endings could be separated since each word form is definitely less frequent than its stem. BPE encoding allows us to represent all words, including the ones unseen during training (e.g. first and last names, which are common in headlines), with a fixed vocabular.

Category	Description	Examples
Good (4)	The two sentences can be used in the same situation and essentially "mean the same thing"	It was a last minute thing <-> This wasn't planned; I have goose flesh <-> The hair's standing upon my arms
Mostly Good (3)	It is acceptable to think that the two sentences refer to the same thing, although one sentence might be more specific than the other one, or there are differences in style.	Go to your bedroom <-> Just go to sleep; Next man, move it <-> Next, please; Calvin, now what? <-> What are we doing?
Mostly Bad (2)	There is some connection between the sentences that explains why they occur together, but one would not really consider them to mean the same thing.	Did you ask him <-> Have you asked her?; Hello, operator? <-> Yes, operator, I'm trying to get to the police
Bad (1)	There is no obvious connection. The sentences mean different things.	She's over there <-> Take me to him; All the cons <-> Nice and comfy

Table 2: Paraphrase annotation scheme as provided in (Creutz, 2018). A pair can also be ranked "in-between" categories (e.g. 2.5 or 3.5).

	Metric	250k	500k	1m	2m
Opusparcus	BLEU	5.04	6.54	6.58	6.46
	METEOR	28.36	30.02	31.25	33.19
ParaPhraser Plus	BLEU	7.54	7.76	8.73	9.81
	METEOR	34.35	35.58	37.46	38.09

Table 3: Generation scores on the test set of each dataset for different train sizes.

7 Results

We perform experiments on the above mentioned datasets, and report, both qualitative and quantitative results of our approach. As can be seen in Table 3 which demonstrates the quantitative results, there is a strong correlation between the size of the training set, selected from top N samples, and the final score of the model. We also perform a qualitative analysis by sampling 100 examples of the original phrase, reference and our 2m model generated phrase for human evaluation. We asked 3 annotators to choose their paraphrase preference over three possible options: original paraphrase (Human), generated paraphrase (Machine), no preference (Tie). The results can be seen in Table 4.

	Human	Tie	Machine
Opusparcus	52.3	26.2	21.5
ParaPhraser Plus	60.6	23.9	14.5

Table 4: Human evaluation of generated paraphrases.

For the both corpora, we could see that our model is not reaching human parity yet, having 47.7 and 38.4 of (Machine + Tie) user preference for Opusparcus and ParaPhraser datasets respectively. Some examples of the produced paraphrases can be seen below (translated into English):

- **Original:** *"State Duma may prohibit doctors and teachers from accepting gifts other than flowers"*

Reference: *"Teachers and doctors in Russia may be prohibited from accepting gifts"*
Generated: *"The State Duma proposed to ban doctors and teachers from accepting gifts"*

- **Original:** *"The Bank of Russia revoked its license from the Yekaterinburg Plateau Bank"*
  Reference: *"Yekaterinburg Plateau Bank is left without its license"*
  Generated: *"Central Bank revoked the license from "plateau-bank""*

- **Original:** *"Stocks are ready to rise in the stock market."*
  Reference: *"Stocks are going to rise on the market"*
  Generated: *"Stock market ready to go up"*

Despite the fact that both of the training sets are noisy to a certain extent, the model is able to generalize and generate paraphrases of decent quality (from semantic and grammatical standpoint) for types of content it has never seen during the training phase.

8   Conclusion

This study confirms our initial hypothesis that data size restrictions can be effectively resolved with automatically ranked corpora, especially in low-resource languages where large manually annotated datasets are not available. We also present a newly gathered ParaPhraser Plus corpus and results achieved by a transformer model applied to it.

9   Future work

In the future we would like to extend our work to other generative tasks and create more diverse and large ranked corpora utilizing different approaches for supervised ranking. In addition to that, we are interested in investigating how a combination of ranking techniques could be used for better data sampling in generation oriented tasks. Also we would like to investigate what is the minimal amount of manually annotated data that is sufficient for successful automatic ranking in parallel corpora.

References

Eneko Agirre, Carmen Banea, Claire Cardie, Daniel Cer, Mona Diab, Aitor Gonzalez-Agirre, Weiwei Guo, Iñigo Lopez-Gazpio, Montse Maritxalar, Rada Mihalcea, German Rigau, Larraitz Uria, and Janyce Wiebe. 2015. SemEval-2015 task 2: Semantic textual similarity, English, Spanish and pilot on interpretability. pages 252–263.

Galen Andrew and Jianfeng Gao. 2007. Scalable training of L1-regularized log-linear models. pages 33–40.

Mikhail Burtsev, Alexander Seliverstov, Rafael Airapetyan, Mikhail Arkhipov, Dilyara Baymurzina, Nickolay Bushkov, Olga Gureenkova, Taras Khakhulin, Yurii Kuratov, Denis Kuznetsov, et al. 2018. Deeppavlov: Open-source library for dialogue systems. pages 122–127.

Mathias Creutz. 2018. Open subtitles paraphrase corpus for six languages. *arXiv preprint arXiv:1809.06142*.

William B Dolan and Chris Brockett. 2005. Automatically constructing a corpus of sentential paraphrases.

Elozino Egonmwan and Yllias Chali. 2019. Transformer and seq2seq model for paraphrase generation. pages 249–255.

Yao Fu, Yansong Feng, and John P Cunningham. 2019. Paraphrase generation with latent bag of words. pages 13623–13634.

Juri Ganitkevitch, Benjamin Van Durme, and Chris Callison-Burch. 2013. PPDB: The paraphrase database. pages 758–764.

Ankush Gupta, Arvind Agarwal, Prawaan Singh, and Piyush Rai. 2018. A deep generative framework for paraphrase generation.

Mohit Iyyer, John Wieting, Kevin Gimpel, and Luke Zettlemoyer. 2018. Adversarial example generation with syntactically controlled paraphrase networks. *arXiv preprint arXiv:1804.06059*.

Dmitry Kravchenko. 2018. Paraphrase detection using machine translation and textual similarity algorithms. pages 277–292.

Yuri Kuratov and Mikhail Arkhipov. 2019. Adaptation of deep bidirectional multilingual transformers for russian language. *arXiv preprint arXiv:1905.07213*.

Zichao Li, Xin Jiang, Lifeng Shang, and Hang Li. 2017. Paraphrase generation with deep reinforcement learning. *arXiv preprint arXiv:1711.00279*.

Tsung-Yi Lin, Michael Maire, Serge Belongie, James Hays, Pietro Perona, Deva Ramanan, Piotr Dollár, and C Lawrence Zitnick. 2014. Microsoft coco: Common objects in context. pages 740–755.

Jonathan Mallinson, Rico Sennrich, and Mirella Lapata. 2017. Paraphrasing revisited with neural machine translation. pages 881–893.

Kathleen McKeown. 1983. Focus constraints on language generation.

Ellie Pavlick, Pushpendre Rastogi, Juri Ganitkevitch, Benjamin Van Durme, and Chris Callison-Burch. 2015. Ppdb 2.0: Better paraphrase ranking, fine-grained entailment relations, word embeddings, and style classification. pages 425–430.

Lidia Pivovarova, Ekaterina Pronoza, Elena Yagunova, and Anton Pronoza. 2017. Paraphraser: Russian paraphrase corpus and shared task. pages 211–225.

Aurko Roy and David Grangier. 2019. Unsupervised paraphrasing without translation. pages 6033–6039.

Ashish Vaswani, Noam Shazeer, Niki Parmar, Jakob Uszkoreit, Llion Jones, Aidan N Gomez, Łukasz Kaiser, and Illia Polosukhin. 2017. Attention is all you need. pages 5998–6008.

A Deep Reinforced Model for Zero-Shot Cross-Lingual Summarization with Bilingual Semantic Similarity Rewards

Zi-Yi Dou   Sachin Kumar   Yulia Tsvetkov
Language Technologies Institute
Carnegie Mellon University
{zdou, sachink, ytsvetko}@cs.cmu.edu

Abstract

Cross-lingual text summarization aims at generating a document summary in one language given input in another language. It is a practically important but under-explored task, primarily due to the dearth of available data. Existing methods resort to machine translation to synthesize training data, but such pipeline approaches suffer from error propagation. In this work, we propose an end-to-end cross-lingual text summarization model. The model uses reinforcement learning to directly optimize a bilingual semantic similarity metric between the summaries generated in a target language and gold summaries in a source language. We also introduce techniques to pre-train the model leveraging monolingual summarization and machine translation objectives. Experimental results in both English–Chinese and English–German cross-lingual summarization settings demonstrate the effectiveness of our methods. In addition, we find that reinforcement learning models with bilingual semantic similarity as rewards generate more fluent sentences than strong baselines.[1]

1 Introduction

Cross-lingual text summarization (XLS) is the task of compressing a long article in one language into a summary in a different language. Due to the dearth of training corpora, standard sequence-to-sequence approaches to summarization cannot be applied to this task. Traditional approaches to XLS thus follow a pipeline, for example, summarizing the article in the source language followed by translating the summary into the target language or vice-versa (Wan et al., 2010; Wan, 2011). Both of these approaches require separately trained summarization and translation models, and suffer from error propagation (Zhu et al., 2019).

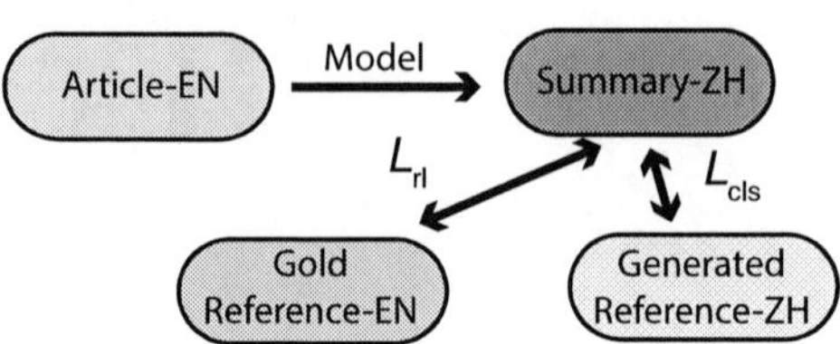

Figure 1: Along with minimizing the XLS cross-entropy loss L_{xls}, we also apply reinforcement learning to optimize the model by directly comparing the outputs with gold references in the source language.

Prior studies have attempted to train XLS models in an end-to-end fashion, through knowledge distillation from pre-trained machine translation (MT) or monolingual summarization models (Ayana et al., 2018; Duan et al., 2019), but these approaches have been only shown to work for short outputs. Alternatively, Zhu et al. (2019) proposed to automatically translate source-language summaries in the training set thereby generating pseudo-reference summaries in the target language. With this parallel dataset of source documents and target summaries , an end-to-end model is trained to simultaneously summarize and translate using a multi-task objective. Although the XLS model is trained end-to-end, it is trained on MT-generated reference translations and is still prone to compounding of translation and summarization errors.

In this work, we propose to train an end-to-end XLS model to directly generate target language summaries given the source articles by matching the semantics of the predictions with the semantics of the source language summaries. To achieve this, we use reinforcement learning (RL) with a bilingual semantic similarity metric as a reward (Wieting et al., 2019b). This metric is computed between the machine-generated summary in the target language and the gold summary in the source language. Additionally, to better initialize our XLS

---

[1] https://github.com/zdou0830/crosslingual_summarization_semantic.

Proceedings of the 4th Workshop on Neural Generation and Translation (WNGT 2020), pages 60–68
Online, July 10, 2020. ©2020 Association for Computational Linguistics
www.aclweb.org/anthology/D19-56%2d

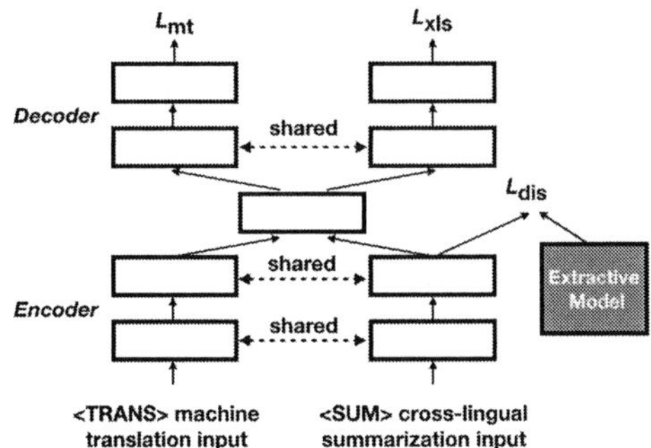

Figure 2: Illustration of the supervised pre-training stage. The model is trained with cross-lingual summarization, machine translation and distillation objectives. The parameters of bottom layers of the decoders are shared across tasks.

model for RL, we propose a new multi-task pre-training objective based on machine translation and monolingual summarization to encode common information available from the two tasks. To enable the model to still differentiate between the two tasks, we add task specific tags to the input (Wu et al., 2016).

We evaluate our proposed method on English–Chinese and English–German XLS test sets. These test corpora are constructed by first using an MT-system to translate source summaries to the target language, and then being post-edited by human annotators. Experimental results demonstrate that just using our proposed pre-training method without fine-tuning with RL improves the best-performing baseline by up to 0.8 ROUGE-L points. Applying reinforcement learning yields further improvements in performance by up to 0.5 ROUGE-L points. Through extensive analyses and human evaluation, we show that when the bilingual semantic similarity reward is used, our model generates summaries that are more accurate, longer, more fluent, and more relevant than summaries generated by baselines.

2 Model

In this section, we describe the details of the task and our proposed approach.

2.1 Problem Description

We first formalize our task setup. We are given N articles and their summaries in the source language $\{(x_{\text{src}}^{(1)}, y_{\text{src}}^{(1)}), \ldots, (x_{\text{src}}^{(N)}, y_{\text{src}}^{(N)})\}$ as a training set. Our goal is to train a summarization model $f(\cdot; \theta)$ which takes an article in the source language x_{src} as input and generates its summary in a pre-specified target language $\hat{y}_{\text{tgt}} = f(x_{\text{src}}; \theta)$. Here, θ are the learnable parameters of f. During training, no gold summary $y_{\text{tgt}}^{(i)}$ is available.

Our model consists of one encoder, denoted as E, which takes x_{src} as input and generates its vector representation $\mathbf{h}$. $\mathbf{h}$ is fed as input to two decoders. The first decoder D_1 predicts the summary in the target language ($\hat{y}_{\text{tgt}}$) one token at a time. The second decoder D_2 predicts the translation of the input text ($\hat{v}_{\text{tgt}}$). While both D_1 and D_2 are used during training, only D_1 is used for XLS at test time. Intuitively, we want the model to select parts of the input article which might be important for the summary and also translate them into the target language. To bias our model to encode this behavior, we propose the following algorithm for pre-training:

- Use a machine translation (MT) model to generate pseudo reference summaries ($\tilde{y}_{\text{tgt}}$) by translating y_{src} to the target language. Then, translate $\tilde{y}_{\text{tgt}}$ back to the source language using a target-to-source MT model and discard the examples with high reconstruction errors, which are measured with ROUGE (Lin, 2004) scores. The details of this step can be found in Zhu et al. (2019).

- Pre-train the model parameters θ using a multi-task objective based on MT and monolingual summarization objectives with some simple yet effective techniques as described in §2.2.

- Further fine-tune the model using reinforcement learning with bilingual semantic similarity metric (Wieting et al., 2019b) as reward, which is described in §2.3.

2.2 Supervised Pre-Training Stage

Here, we describe the second step of our algorithm (Figure 2). The pre-training loss we use is a weighted combination of three objectives. Similarly to Zhu et al. (2019), we use an XLS pre-training objective and an MT pre-training objective as described below with some simple but effective improvements. We also introduce an additional objective based on distilling knowledge from a monolingual summarization model.

XLS Pre-training Objective (L_{xls}) This objective computes the cross-entropy loss of the predictions from D_1, considering the machine-generated summaries in the target language, $\tilde{y}_{\text{tgt}}^{(i)}$ as references, given $x_{\text{src}}^{(i)}$ as inputs. Per sample, this loss can be formally written as:

$$L_{\text{xls}} = \sum_{j=1}^{M} \log p(\tilde{y}_{\text{tgt},j}^{(i)} | \tilde{y}_{\text{tgt},<j}^{(i)}, x_{\text{src}}^{(i)})$$

where M is the number of tokens in the summary i.

Joint Training with Machine Translation Zhu et al. (2019) argue that machine translation can be considered a special case of XLS with a compression ratio of 1:1. In line with Zhu et al. (2019), we train E and D_2 as the encoder and decoder of a translation model using an MT parallel corpus $\{(u_{\text{src}}^{(i)}, v_{\text{tgt}}^{(i)})\}$. The goal of this step is to make the encoder have an inductive bias towards encoding information specific to translation. Similar to L_{xls}, the machine translation objective per training sample L_{mt} is:

$$L_{\text{mt}} = \sum_{j=1}^{K} \log p(v_{\text{tgt},j}^{(i)} | v_{\text{tgt},<j}^{(i)}, u_{\text{src}}^{(i)})$$

where K is the number of tokens in $v_{\text{tgt}}^{(i)}$. The L_{xls} and L_{mt} objectives are inspired by Zhu et al. (2019). We propose the following two enhancements to the model to leverage better the two objectives:

1. We share the parameters of bottom layers of the two decoders, namely D_1 and D_2, to share common high-level representations while the parameters of the top layers more specialized to decoding are separately trained.

2. We append an artificial task tag ⟨SUM⟩ (during XLS training) and ⟨TRANS⟩ (during MT training) at the beginning of the input document to make the model aware of which kind of input it is dealing with.

We show in §4.1 that such simple modifications result in noticeable performance improvements.

Knowledge Distillation from Monolingual Summarization To bias the encoder to identify sentences which can be most relevant to the summary, first, we use an extractive monolingual summarization method to predict the probability q_i of each sentence or keyword in the input article being relevant to the summary. We then distill knowledge from this model into the encoder E by making it predict these probabilities. Concretely, we append

an additional output layer to the encoder of our model and it predicts the probability p_i of including the i-th sentence or word in the summary. The objective is to minimize the difference between p_i and q_i. We use the following loss (for each sample) for the model encoder:[2]

$$L_{\text{dis}} = \frac{1}{L} \sum_{j=1}^{L} (\log q_j - \log p_j)^2, \qquad (1)$$

where L is the number of sentences or keywords in each article.

Our final pre-training objective during the supervised pre-training stage is:

$$L_{\text{sup}} = L_{\text{xls}} + L_{\text{mt}} + \lambda L_{\text{dis}} \qquad (2)$$

where λ is a hyper-parameter and is set to 10 in our experiments. Training with L_{mt} requires an MT parallel corpus whereas the other two objectives utilize the cross-lingual summarization dataset. Pre-training algorithm alternates between the two parts of the objective using mini-batches from the two datasets as follows until convergence:

1. Sample a minibatch from the MT corpus $\{(u_{\text{src}}^{(i)}, v_{\text{tgt}}^{(i)})\}$ and train the parameters of E and D_2 with L_{mt}.

2. Sample a minibatch from the XLS corpus, $\{(x_{\text{src}}^{(i)}, \tilde{y}_{\text{tgt}}^{(i)})\}$ and train the parameters of E and D_1 with $L_{\text{xls}} + \lambda L_{\text{dis}}$.

2.3 Reinforcement Learning Stage

For XLS, the target language reference summaries ($\tilde{y}_{\text{tgt}}$) used during pre-training are automatically generated with MT models and thus they may contain errors. In this section, we describe how we further fine-tune the model using only human-generated source language summaries (y_{src}) with reinforcement learning (RL). Specifically, we first feed the article x_{src} as an input to the encoder E, and generate the target language summary $\hat{y}_{\text{tgt}}$ using D_1. We then compute a cross-lingual similarity metric between $\hat{y}_{\text{tgt}}$ and y_{src} and use it as a reward to fine-tune E and D_1.

Following Paulus et al. (2018), we adopt two different strategies to generate $\hat{y}_{\text{tgt}}$ at each training iteration, (a) $\hat{y}_{\text{tgt}}^{s}$ obtained by sampling from the softmax layer at each decoding step, and (b) $\hat{y}_{\text{tgt}}^{g}$

---

[2] We also experimented with a common distillation objective based on minimizing KL divergence, $\frac{1}{n} \sum_{i=1}^{n} q_i \log p_i$, but it did not perform as well.

obtained by greedy decoding. The RL objective per sample is given by:

$$L_{\text{rl}} = \left(r(\hat{y}_{\text{tgt}}^g) - r(\hat{y}_{\text{tgt}}^s) \right) \sum_{j=1}^{M} \log p(\hat{y}_{\text{tgt,i}}^s | \hat{y}_{\text{tgt,<j}}^s, x),$$

(3)

where $r(\cdot)$ is the reward function. To fine-tune the model, we use the following hybrid training objective: $\gamma L_{\text{rl}} + (1 - \gamma) L_{\text{xls}}$, where γ is a scaling factor.

We train a cross-lingual similarity model (XSIM) with the best performing model in Wieting et al. (2019b). This model is trained using an MT parallel corpus. Using XSIM, we obtain sentence representations for both $\hat{y}_{\text{tgt}}$ and y_{src} and treat the cosine similarity between the two representations as the reward $r(\cdot)$.

3 Experimental Setup

3.1 Datasets

We evaluate our models on English–Chinese and English–German article-summary datasets. The English–Chinese dataset is created by Zhu et al. (2019), constructed using the CNN/DailyMail monolingual summarization corpus (Hermann et al., 2015). The training, validation and test sets consist of about 364K, 3K and 3K samples, respectively. The English–German dataset is our contribution, constructed from the Gigaword dataset (Rush et al., 2015). We sample 2.48M training, 2K validation and 2K test samples from the dataset. Pseudo-parallel corpora for both language pairs are constructed by translating the summaries to the target language (and filtered after back-translation; see §2). This is done for training, validation as well as test sets. These two pseudo-parallel training sets are used for pre-training with L_{xls}. Translated Chinese and German summaries of the test articles are then post-edited by human annotators to construct the test set for evaluating XLS. We refer the readers to (Zhu et al., 2019) for more details. For the English–Chinese dataset, we use word-based segmentation for the source (articles in English) and character-based segmentation for the target (summaries in Chinese) as in (Zhu et al., 2019). For the English–German dataset, byte-pair encoding is used (Sennrich et al., 2016) with 60K merge operations. For machine translation and training the XSIM model, we sub-sample 5M sentences from the WMT2017 Chinese–English and WMT2014 German–English training dataset (Bojar et al., 2014, 2017).

3.2 Implementation Details

We use the Transformer-BASE model (Vaswani et al., 2017) as the underlying architecture for our model (E, D_1, D_2, extractive summarization model for distillation and baselines). We refer the reader to Vaswani et al. (2017) for hyperparameter details. In the input article, a special token ⟨SEP⟩ is added at the beginning of each sentence to mark sentence boundaries. For the CNN/DailyMail corpus, the monolingual extractive summarization used in the distillation objective has the same architecture as the encoder E and is trained the CNN/DailyMail corpus constructed by (Liu and Lapata, 2019). To train the encoder with L_{dis}, we take the final hidden representation of each ⟨SEP⟩ token and apply a 2-layer feed-forward network with ReLU activation in the middle layer and sigmoid at the final layer to get q_i for each sentence i (see §2.2).

For the Gigaword dataset, because the inputs and outputs are typically short, we choose keywords rather than sentences as the prediction unit. Specifically, we first use TextRank (Mihalcea and Tarau, 2004) to extract all the keywords from the source document. Then, for each keyword i that appears in the target summary, the gold label q_i in equation 1 is assigned to 1, and q_i is assigned to 0 for keywords that do not appear in the target side.

We share the parameters of the bottom four layers of the decoder in the multi-task setting. We use the TRIGRAM model in (Wieting et al., 2019b,a) to measure the cross-lingual sentence semantic similarities. As pointed out in §2, after the pre-training stage, we only use D_1 for XLS. The final results are obtained using only E and D_1. We use two metrics for evaluating the performance of models: ROUGE (1, 2 and L) (Lin, 2004) and XSIM (Wieting et al., 2019b).

Following Paulus et al. (2018), we select γ in equation 3 to 0.998 for the Gigaword Corpus and $\gamma = 0.9984$ for the CNN/DailyMail dataset.

3.3 Baselines

We compare our proposed method with the following baselines:

Pipeline Approaches We report results of summarize-then-translate (SUM-TRAN) and

Method	English–Chinese				English–German			
	ROUGE-1	ROUGE-2	ROUGE-L	XSIM	ROUGE-1	ROUGE-2	ROUGE-L	XSIM
Pipeline-Based Methods								
TRAN-SUM (Zhu et al., 2019)	28.19	11.40	25.77	-	-	-	-	-
SUM-TRAN (Zhu et al., 2019)	32.17	13.85	29.43	-	-	-	-	-
End-to-End Training Methods								
MLE-XLS	37.38	17.96	33.85	45.17	23.06	8.40	21.28	43.41
MLE-XLS+MT (Zhu et al., 2019)	40.23	22.32	36.59	-	-	-	-	-
MLE-XLS+MT (Reimplemented)	41.25	22.40	37.93	48.77	36.83	17.62	35.54	49.21
MLE-XLS+MT+DIS	42.19*	22.91*	38.74*	49.20*	37.74*	18.40*	36.34*	49.53*
RL-ROUGE	42.51*	22.96*	38.98*	49.65	38.32*	18.46	36.86*	49.66
RL-XSIM	**42.83***	**23.30***	**39.29***	**50.85***	**38.69***	**18.76***	**37.20***	**50.17***
RL-ROUGE+XSIM	42.49	23.29*	38.95	49.88*	38.19*	18.17	36.72*	49.64

Table 1: Performance of different models. The highest scores are in **bold** and statistical significance compared with the best baseline is indicated with * ($p <$0.05, computed using *compare-mt* (Neubig et al., 2019)). XSIM is computed between the target language system outputs and the source language reference summaries.

translate-then-summarize (TRAN-SUM) pipelines. These results are taken from Zhu et al. (2019).

MLE-XLS We pre-train E and D_1 with only L_{xls} without any fine-tuning.

MLE-XLS+MT We pre-train E, D_1 and D_2 with $L_{\mathrm{xls}} + L_{\mathrm{mt}}$ without using L_{dis}. This is the best performing model in (Zhu et al., 2019). We show their reported results as well as results from our re-implementation.

MLE-XLS+MT+DIS We pre-train the model using (2) without fine-tuning with RL. We also share the decoder layers and add task specific tags to the input as described in §2.2.

RL-ROUGE Using ROUGE score as a reward function has been shown to improve summarization quality for monolingual summarization models (Paulus et al., 2018). In this baseline, we fine-tune the pre-trained model in the above baseline using ROUGE-L as a reward instead of the proposed XSIM. The ROUGE-L score is computed between the output of D_1 and the machine-generated summary $\tilde{y}_{\mathrm{tgt}}$.

RL-ROUGE+XSIM Here, we use the average of ROUGE score and XSIM score as a reward function to fine-tune the pre-trained model (MLE-XLS+MT+DIS).

4   Results

The main results of our experiments are summarized in Table 1. Pipeline approaches, as expected, show the weakest performance, lagging behind even the weakest end-to-end approach by more than 5 ROUGE-L points. TRAN-SUM performs even worse than SUM-TRAN, likely because the

Method	ROUGE-1	ROUGE-2	ROUGE-L
MLE-XLS	37.38	17.96	33.85
+EXTRACT	39.19	19.58	35.68
+DIS	**40.46**	**20.47**	**36.93**
MLE-XLS+MT	41.25	22.40	37.93
+EXTRACT	40.04	21.58	36.74
+DIS	**41.68**	**22.48**	**38.29**

Table 2: Effect of using hard (EXTRACT) vs soft (DIS) extraction of summary sentences from the input article

translation model is trained on sentences and not long articles. First translating the article with many sentences introduces way more errors than translating a short summary with fewer sentences would. Using just our pre-training method as described in 2.2 (MLE-XLS+MT+DIS), our proposed model outperforms the strongest baseline (MLE-XLS+MT) in both ROUGE-L (by 0.8) and XSIM (by 0.5). Applying reinforcement learning to fine-tune the model with both ROUGE (RL-ROUGE), XSIM (RL-XSIM) or their mean (RL-ROUGE+XSIM) as rewards results in further improvements. Our proposed method, RL-XSIM performs the best overall, indicating the importance of using cross-lingual similarity as a reward function. RL-ROUGE uses a machine-generated reference to compute the rewards since target language summaries are unavailable, which might be a reason for its worse performance.

4.1   Analysis

In this section, we conduct experiments on the CNN/DailyMail dataset to establish the importance of every part of the proposed method and gain further insights into our model.

Soft Distillation vs. Hard Extraction The results in table 1 already show that adding the knowl-

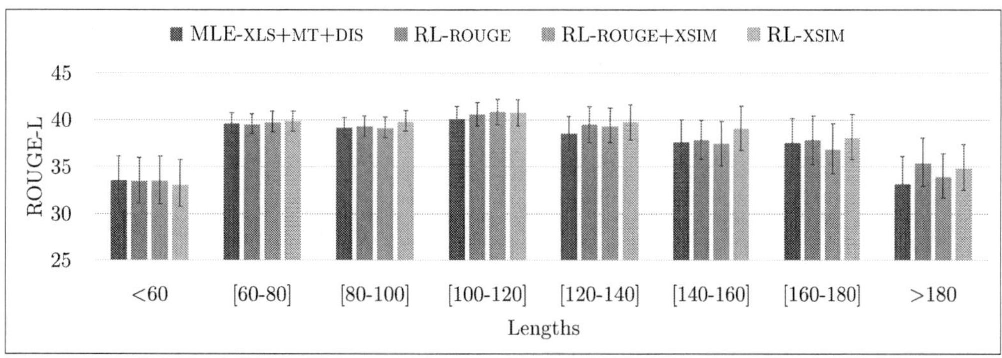

Figure 3: Reinforcement learning can make the model better at generating long summaries. We use the *compare-mt* tool (Neubig et al., 2019) to get these statistics.

Method	ROUGE-1	ROUGE-2	ROUGE-L
MLE+XLS+MT	41.25	22.40	37.93
+SHARE	41.36	22.43	37.95
+TAG	41.45	22.47	38.04

Table 3: Effect of sharing decoder layers and adding task-specific tags

edge distillation objective L_{dis} to the pre-training leads to an improvement in performance. The intuition behind using L_{dis} is to bias the model to (softly) select sentences in the input article that might be important for the summary. Here, we replace this soft selection with a hard selection. That is, using the monolingual extractive summarization model (as described in §3.2), we extract top 5 sentences from the input article and use them as the input to the encoder instead. We compare this method with L_{dis} as shown in Table 2. With just MLE-XLS as the pre-training objective, EXTRACT shows improvement (albeit with lower overall numbers) in performance but leads to a decrease in performance of MLE-XLS+MT. On the other hand, using the distillation objective helps in both cases.

Effect of the Sharing and Tagging Techniques In Table 3, we demonstrate that introducing simple enhancements like sharing the lower-layers of the decoder (share) and adding task-specific tags (tags) during multi-task pre-training also helps in improving the performance while at the same using fewer parameters and hence a smaller memory footprint.

Effect of Summary Lengths Next, we study how different baselines and our model performs with respect to generating summaries (in Chinese) of different lengths, in terms of number of characters. As shown in Figure 3, after fine-tuning the model with RL, our proposed model becomes

better at generating longer summaries than the one with only pre-training (referred to as MLE-XLS+MT+DIS in the figure) with RL-XSIM performing the best in most cases. We posit that this improvement is due to RL based fine-tuning reducing the problem of exposure bias introduced during teacher-forced pre-training, which especially helps longer generations.

Human Evaluation In addition to automatic evaluation, which can sometimes be misleading, we perform human evaluation of summaries generated by our models. We randomly sample 50 pairs of the model outputs from the test set and ask three human evaluators to compare the pre-trained supervised learning model and reinforcement learning models in terms of *relevance* and *fluency*. For each pair, the evaluators are asked to pick one out of: first model (MLE-XLS+MT+DIS; lose) , second model(RL models; win) or say that they prefer both or neither (tie). The results are summarized in table 4. We observe that the outputs of model trained with ROUGE-L rewards are more favored than the ones generated by only pre-trained model in terms of relevance but not fluency. This is likely because the RL-ROUGE model is trained using machine-generated summaries as references which might lack fluency. Figure 4 displays one such example. On the other hand, cross-lingual semantic similarity as a reward results in generations which are more favored both in terms of relevance and fluency.

5 Related Work

Most previous work on cross-lingual text summarization utilize either the summarize-then-translate or translate-then-summarize pipeline (Wan et al., 2010; Wan, 2011; Yao et al., 2015; Ouyang et al.,

	Output
Ref	市议会周三投票通过了一项提高购买香烟法定年龄的法案。纽约是美国最大的将购买年龄提高到18岁以上的城市。这项法律预计明年初生效。 A bill to raise the legal age to buy cigarettes was voted into law Wednesday by the City Council. New York is the largest US city to raise the purchase age above the federal limit of 18-years-old. The law is expected to go into effect early next year.
Sup	纽约成为美国最大的购买年龄。纽约不是第一个提高法定饮酒年龄的城市。 New York has become the largest purchase age in the United States. New York is not the first city to raise the legal drinking age.
RL-ROUGE	纽约成为美国最大的购买年龄，法律年龄从18岁提高到21岁。市议会周三批准了一项法案，将烟草购买年龄从18岁提高到21岁。纽约不是第一个提高法定饮酒年龄的城市。 New York has become the largest purchase age in the United States, and the legal age has increased from 18 to 21. The City Council approved a law on Wednesday to increase the age of tobacco purchases from 18 to 21. New York is not the first city to raise the legal drinking age.
RL-XSIM	纽约成为美国最大的购买香烟的城市。市议会周三批准了一项法案，将烟草购买年龄从18岁提高到21岁。纽约不是第一个提高法定饮酒年龄的城市。 New York has become the largest city in the United States for buying cigarettes. The City Council approved a law on Wednesday to increase the age of tobacco purchases from 18 to 21. New York is not the first city to raise the legal drinking age.

Figure 4: Example outputs. The bilingual semantic similarity rewards can make the output more fluent than using ROUGE-L as rewards. "Sup" refers to the MLE-XLS+MT+DIS baseline.

Metric	Model v. MLE	Win (%)	Lose (%)	Tie (%)
Relevance	RL-ROUGE	25.3	15.3	59.3
	RL-XSIM	36.0	31.3	32.7
Fluency	RL-ROUGE	13.3	17.3	69.3
	RL-XSIM	37.3	28.7	34.0

Table 4: Results showing preferences of human evaluators towards the summaries generated by the mentioned RL methods vs ones from the pre-trained model (MLE-XLS+MT+DIS referred in short as MLE)

2019). These methods suffer from error propagation and we have demonstrated their sub-optimal performance in our experiments. Recently, there has been some work on training models for this task in an end-to-end fashion (Ayana et al., 2018; Duan et al., 2019; Zhu et al., 2019), but these models are trained with cross-entropy using machine-generated summaries as references which have already lost some information in the translation step.

Prior work in monolingual summarization have explored hybrid extractive and abstractive summarization objectives which inspires our distillation objective (Gehrmann et al., 2018; Hsu et al., 2018; Chen and Bansal, 2018). This line of research mainly focus on either compressing sentences extracted by a pre-trained model or biasing the prediction towards certain words.

Language generation models trained with cross-entropy using teacher-forcing suffer from exposure bias and a mismatch between training and evaluation objective. To solve these issues, using reinforcement learning to fine-tune such models

have been explored for monolingual summarization where ROUGE rewards is typically used (Paulus et al., 2018; Liu et al., 2018; Pasunuru and Bansal, 2018). Other rewards such as BERT score (Zhang et al., 2019) have also been explored (Li et al., 2019). Computing such rewards requires access to the gold summaries which are typically unavailable for cross-lingual summarization. This work is the first to explore using cross-lingual similarity as a reward to work around this issue.

6 Conclusion

In this work, we propose to use reinforcement learning with a bilingual semantic similarity metric as rewards for cross-lingual document summarization. We demonstrate the effectiveness of the proposed approach in a resource-deficient setting, where target language gold summaries are not available. We also propose simple strategies to better initialize the model towards reinforcement learning by leveraging machine translation and monolingual summarization. In future work, we plan to explore methods for stabilizing reinforcement learning as well to extend our methods to other datasets and tasks, such as using the bilingual similarity metric as a reward to improve the quality of machine translation.

Acknowledgements

We are grateful to anonymous reviewers for their helpful suggestions and Chunting Zhou, Shuyan

Zhou for proofreading the paper. We also thank Ruihan Zhai, Zhi-Hao Zhou for the help with human evaluation and Anurag Katakkar for post-editing the dataset. This material is based upon work supported by NSF grants IIS1812327 and by Amazon MLRA award. We also thank Amazon for providing GPU credits.

References

Ayana, Shi-qi Shen, Yun Chen, Cheng Yang, Zhi-yuan Liu, and Mao-song Sun. 2018. Zero-shot cross-lingual neural headline generation. *IEEE/ACM Transactions on Audio, Speech and Language Processing*.

Ondřej Bojar, Christian Buck, Christian Federmann, Barry Haddow, Philipp Koehn, Johannes Leveling, Christof Monz, Pavel Pecina, Matt Post, Herve Saint-Amand, et al. 2014. Findings of the 2014 workshop on statistical machine translation. In *Proc. WMT*.

Ondřej Bojar, Rajen Chatterjee, Christian Federmann, Yvette Graham, Barry Haddow, Shujian Huang, Matthias Huck, Philipp Koehn, Qun Liu, Varvara Logacheva, et al. 2017. Findings of the 2017 conference on machine translation. In *Proc. WMT*.

Yen-Chun Chen and Mohit Bansal. 2018. Fast abstractive summarization with reinforce-selected sentence rewriting. In *Proc. ACL*.

Xiangyu Duan, Mingming Yin, Min Zhang, Boxing Chen, and Weihua Luo. 2019. Zero-shot cross-lingual abstractive sentence summarization through teaching generation and attention. In *Proc. ACL*.

Sebastian Gehrmann, Yuntian Deng, and Alexander Rush. 2018. Bottom-up abstractive summarization. In *Proc. EMNLP*.

Karl Moritz Hermann, Tomas Kocisky, Edward Grefenstette, Lasse Espeholt, Will Kay, Mustafa Suleyman, and Phil Blunsom. 2015. Teaching machines to read and comprehend. In *Proc. NeurIPS*.

Wan-Ting Hsu, Chieh-Kai Lin, Ming-Ying Lee, Kerui Min, Jing Tang, and Min Sun. 2018. A unified model for extractive and abstractive summarization using inconsistency loss. In *Proc. ACL*.

Siyao Li, Deren Lei, Pengda Qin, and William Yang Wang. 2019. Deep reinforcement learning with distributional semantic rewards for abstractive summarization. In *Proc. EMNLP*.

Chin-Yew Lin. 2004. ROUGE: A package for automatic evaluation of summaries. In *Text Summarization Branches Out*.

Linqing Liu, Yao Lu, Min Yang, Qiang Qu, Jia Zhu, and Hongyan Li. 2018. Generative adversarial network for abstractive text summarization. In *Proc. AAAI*.

Yang Liu and Mirella Lapata. 2019. Text summarization with pretrained encoders. In *Proc. EMNLP*.

Rada Mihalcea and Paul Tarau. 2004. Textrank: Bringing order into text. In *Proc. EMNLP*.

Graham Neubig, Zi-Yi Dou, Junjie Hu, Paul Michel, Danish Pruthi, and Xinyi Wang. 2019. compare-mt: A tool for holistic comparison of language generation systems. In *Proc. NAACL Demo*.

Jessica Ouyang, Boya Song, and Kathleen McKeown. 2019. A robust abstractive system for cross-lingual summarization. In *Proc. NAACL*.

Ramakanth Pasunuru and Mohit Bansal. 2018. Multi-reward reinforced summarization with saliency and entailment. In *Proc. NAACL*.

Romain Paulus, Caiming Xiong, and Richard Socher. 2018. A deep reinforced model for abstractive summarization. In *Proc. ICLR*.

Alexander M Rush, Sumit Chopra, and Jason Weston. 2015. A neural attention model for abstractive sentence summarization. In *Proc. EMNLP*.

Rico Sennrich, Barry Haddow, and Alexandra Birch. 2016. Neural machine translation of rare words with subword units. In *Proc. ACL*.

Ashish Vaswani, Noam Shazeer, Niki Parmar, Jakob Uszkoreit, Llion Jones, Aidan N Gomez, Łukasz Kaiser, and Illia Polosukhin. 2017. Attention is all you need. In *Proc. NeurIPS*.

Xiaojun Wan. 2011. Using bilingual information for cross-language document summarization. In *Proc. ACL*.

Xiaojun Wan, Huiying Li, and Jianguo Xiao. 2010. Cross-language document summarization based on machine translation quality prediction. In *Proc. ACL*.

John Wieting, Taylor Berg-Kirkpatrick, Kevin Gimpel, and Graham Neubig. 2019a. Beyond bleu: Training neural machine translation with semantic similarity. In *Proc. ACL*.

John Wieting, Kevin Gimpel, Graham Neubig, and Taylor Berg-Kirkpatrick. 2019b. Simple and effective paraphrastic similarity from parallel translations. In *Proc. ACL*.

Yonghui Wu, Mike Schuster, Zhifeng Chen, Quoc V Le, Mohammad Norouzi, Wolfgang Macherey, Maxim Krikun, Yuan Cao, Qin Gao, Klaus Macherey, et al. 2016. Google's neural machine translation system: Bridging the gap between human and machine translation. *arXiv preprint arXiv:1609.08144*.

Jin-ge Yao, Xiaojun Wan, and Jianguo Xiao. 2015. Phrase-based compressive cross-language summarization. In *Proc. EMNLP*.

Tianyi Zhang, Varsha Kishore, Felix Wu, Kilian Q Weinberger, and Yoav Artzi. 2019. Bertscore: Evaluating text generation with bert. *arXiv preprint arXiv:1904.09675*.

Junnan Zhu, Qian Wang, Yining Wang, Yu Zhou, Jiajun Zhang, Shaonan Wang1, and Chengqing Zong. 2019. NCLS: Neural cross-lingual summarization. In *Proc. EMNLP*.

A Question Type Driven and Copy Loss Enhanced Framework for Answer-Agnostic Neural Question Generation

Xiuyu Wu[1], Nan Jiang[2], Yunfang Wu[2]*

[1]School of Foreign Language, Peking University
[2]MOE Key Lab of Computational Linguistics, School of EECS, Peking University
textttxiuyu_wu@pku.edu.cn,jnhsyxxy@126.com,wuyf@pku.edu.cn

Abstract

The answer-agnostic question generation is a significant and challenging task, which aims to automatically generate questions for a given sentence but without an answer. In this paper, we propose two new strategies to deal with this task: question type prediction and copy loss mechanism. The question type module is to predict the types of questions that should be asked, which allows our model to generate multiple types of questions for the same source sentence. The new copy loss enhances the original copy mechanism to make sure that every important word in the source sentence has been copied when generating questions. Our integrated model outperforms the state-of-the-art approach in answer-agnostic question generation, achieving a BLEU-4 score of 13.9 on SQuAD. Human evaluation further validates the high quality of our generated questions. We will make our code public available for further research.

1 Introduction

Question Generation (QG) has been investigated for many years because of its huge potential benefits to various fields, especially for education (Mitkov et al., 2006; Rus and Arthur, 2009; Heilman and Smith, 2010). QG can also act as an essential component of other comprehensive task, such as dialogue systems (Piwek et al., 2007; Shum et al., 2018). Besides, it can supplement question answering task by automatically constructing a large question set (Duan et al., 2017; Tang et al., 2017).

Traditional methods for automatic question generation are mostly rule-based, which need a set of complex empirical rules (Beulen and Ney, 1998; Brown et al., 2005; Heilman and Smith, 2010; Mazidi and Nielsen, 2014). Recently, with the flourish of deep learning, especially the sequence-to-sequence (seq2seq) frame (Sutskever et al., 2014)

*Corresponding author.

Source sentence: the notion of style in the arts was not developed until the 16th century , with the writing of vasari : by the 18th century, his lives of the most excellent painters , sculptors, and architects had been translated into italian , french , spanish and english .
Groud-truth:
Q1: **when** were the *styles* of *arts* created ?
Q2: **who** wrote *lives* of the most *excellent painters , sculptors* , and *architects* ?
Q3: by the *18th century* **which** languages was *vasaris* book *translated* in ?
Q4: in **what** *century* did " *style* " as an artistic concept arise ?

Table 1: Different types of questions with respect to the same source sentence, where the italics words are keywords occurring both in the source sentence and reference questions.

with attention mechanism (Bahdanau et al., 2015), many neural models have been proposed to solve the QG task and achieve rapid progress (Du et al., 2017; Zhou et al., 2017; Tang et al., 2017; Tong et al., 2017; Zhao et al., 2018; Dong et al., 2019; Nema et al., 2019; Zhou et al., 2019).

However, most of the previous works are devoted to deal with answer-aware question generation. That is, given a text and also an answer span, the system is required to generate questions. But in a real application for educational purpose, people or machines are often required to generate questions for natural sentences without explicitly annotated answer. Comparing with the answer-aware QG, the answer-agnostic QG (AG-QG) task is more challenging and attractive. Unfortunately, AG-QG has been much less studied. Du's work (Du et al., 2017) is the first one to tackle this problem, and (Scialom et al., 2019) achieve the state-of-the-art by employing an extended transformer network.

For the AG-QG task, where the input is only a sentence but without any answer, multiple questions might be asked from various perspectives. According to our statistics on SQuAD (Rajpurkar

69

Proceedings of the 4th Workshop on Neural Generation and Translation (WNGT 2020), pages 69–78
Online, July 10, 2020. ©2020 Association for Computational Linguistics
www.aclweb.org/anthology/D19-56%2d

et al., 2016), nearly 34% of the source sentences are offered multiple gold reference questions, and nearly 20% of the source sentences are offered different types of questions. Table 1 gives an example, where one source sentence corresponds with four different types of questions. However, most existing approaches can only generate one question for one input sentence.

To enable the model to ask different types of questions given the same input sentence, we propose a question type driven framework for AG-QG task. Specially, our model firstly predicts the probability of different question types distribution on the input sentence, which allows us to choose the best K question types with higher possibility. Then these different question types will be embedded into different vectors, which will guide the decoder to pay attention to informative parts with respect to different questions.

Meanwhile, according to the statistics on SQuAD, on average there are 3.09 non-stop words copying from the source sentence for each reference question. Those non-stop words appearing in both questions and sentences are regarded as keywords, since they act as the connection of these two parts. To increase the probability of copying keywords from source sentences, we design a new copy loss to enhance the traditional copy mechanism. In our model, by minimizing the new copy loss, the model will be forced to copy these keywords at least once during decoding.

We conduct experiments on SQuAD. Both the question type module and the new copy loss improve performance over the baseline model, and our full model combining two modules obtains a new state-of-the-art performance with a BLEU-4 of 13.9. Moreover, our model can ask different types of questions for a given sentence.

We conclude the contributions as follows:

- We propose a question type driven framework for AG-QG, which enables the model to generate diverse questions with high quality.

- We design a new copy loss function to enhance the standard copy mechanism, which increases the probability of copying keywords from source sentences.

- Our model achieves a new state-of-the-art performance for the challenging AG-QG. The human evaluation further validates a high quality of our generated questions in fluency, relevance and answer-ability.

2 Related Work

Answer-Aware Question Generation. Most previous works on question generation focus on answer-aware QG task. Yuan (Yuan et al., 2017) proposes three parts of loss to enhance the performance of sequence-to-sequence attention model. Zhou (Zhou et al., 2017) leverage lexical features (part-of-speech and named entity tags) to help the model get better encoder representation. Zhao (Zhao et al., 2018) uses paragraph information to do answer-aware QG task. And to use answer information more efficiently, Song (Song et al., 2018) uses multi-perspective matching and Sun (Sun et al., 2018) proposes position-aware model to pay more attention to the surrounding context of answer span. (Nema et al., 2019) uses a answer encoder to encode answer and fusion it with paragraph representation. (Chen et al., 2019) applies reinforcement learning to increase the performance.

Answer-Agnostic Question Generation. AG-QG is more challenging than answer-aware QG. Du's work (Du et al., 2017) is the first one to tackle this problem, and they achieve better performance than rule-based approaches by employing a sequence-to-sequence attention model. (Du and Cardie, 2017) aim to automatically find question-worthy sentences from a paragraph and then generate questions. (Subramanian et al., 2017) treat QG as a two-stage task: answer phrase extraction and answer-aware question generation. (Wang et al., 2019) propose a multi-agent communication framework, using a local extraction agent to extract question-worthy phrases, and then taking extracted phrases as assistance to generate questions. (Scialom et al., 2019) employ the transformer network (Vaswani et al., 2017) and extend it with the placeholder strategy, copy mechanism and contextualized embedding.

Question Word Prediction. Question word is one of the most important components of a question. (Fan et al., 2018) study multi-types visual question generation, by feeding the encoded representation to a multi-layer perception to calculate the question words distribution. (Sun et al., 2018) propose an answer-focused and position-aware model to generate the first question word. (Kim et al., 2019) propose an answer-separated sequence-to-sequence model to identify the proper question word. They replace the answer span in the source sentence with a special token to make better use of the context information.

Multi-Types Question Generation. The multi-types QG has been much less researched. In Ma's work (Ma et al., 2018), in order to generate different types of questions, they use question type embedding at the first step of decoding. However, because of the difficulty in automatically predicting question types, their model fails to outperform the previous works. The question type driven framework has also been tried for visual question generation (Fan et al., 2018), where they concatenate the question type embedding with the encoded representation of input.

3 Proposed Framework

3.1 Framework Overview

For each sample in our dataset, we have a source sentence $S = (x_1, x_2, \ldots, x_l)$, which is a word sequence and l denotes the number of words. Let $Q = (y_1, y_2, \ldots, y_m)$ to represent the question, which is another word sequence and m is the length. The answer-agnostic QG task can be defined as finding the best $\overline{Q}$ that:

$$
\begin{aligned}
\overline{Q} &= \arg\max_{Q} \log P(Q \mid S) \\
&= \arg\max_{Q} \sum_{i=1}^{m} \log P(y_i \mid S, y_{<i})
\end{aligned}
$$

Figure 1 shows the framework of our full question type driven QG model. With the development of pointer network (Vinyals et al., 2015), the copy mechanism (Gu et al., 2016) has been increasingly more applied to natural language generation task. Thus, our model is based on the general sequence-to-sequence attention model with copy mechanism, which we regard as our baseline. In the next sections, we firstly describe the baseline model and then separately show our question type module and enhanced copy mechanism.

3.2 Baseline Model

Our baseline method is a sequence-to-sequence attention model with copy mechanism. Let x_t represent the $t - th$ word in the source sentence and $e(x_t)$ is its corresponding embedded vector. A bi-directional LSTM layer (Hochreiter et al., 1997) is used to encode the embedded vector sequence:

$$
\begin{aligned}
\overrightarrow{u_t} &= \overrightarrow{LSTM}(\overrightarrow{u_{t-1}}, e(x_t)) \\
\overleftarrow{u_t} &= \overleftarrow{LSTM}(\overleftarrow{u_{t+1}}, e(x_t)) \\
u_t &= [\overrightarrow{u_t}; \overleftarrow{u_t}]
\end{aligned}
\tag{1}
$$

The hidden state at time step t is the concatenation of the forward $\overrightarrow{u_t}$ and backward $\overleftarrow{u_t}$, which can be represented as $\mathbf{U} = [\overrightarrow{u_t}; \overleftarrow{u_t}]_{t=1}^{l}$, where l is the number of words in the source sequence.

The decoder is another LSTM network, which generates a new hidden state h_t, conditioned on the previous state h_{t-1} and previously embedded generated word $e(y_{t-1})$. At the first decoding step, it takes the last encoding hidden state u_l and a special token $[SOS]$, which stands for the start of sequence, as input:

$$
\begin{aligned}
h_t &= LSTM(h_{t-1}, e(y_{t-1})) \\
h_0 &= LSTM(u_l, e([SOS]))
\end{aligned}
\tag{2}
$$

Given the encoded state $\mathbf{U}$ and decoder state h_t, the baseline model calculates a generating distribution of words at each time step t, which is calculated as follow:

$$
\begin{aligned}
g_t &= softmax(\mathbf{W^o} tanh(\mathbf{W^t}[h_t; v_t])) \\
v_t &= \sum_{i=1}^{l} a_{it} u_i \\
a_{it} &= \frac{\exp(h_t^\top \mathbf{W^b} u_i)}{\sum_j \exp(h_t^\top \mathbf{W^b} u_j)}
\end{aligned}
\tag{3}
$$

where v_t is the weighted sum of the encoded representation $\mathbf{U}$, and the attention weight a_t is calculated by a bi-linear scoring function and a softmax normalization. $\mathbf{W^t}$ and $\mathbf{W^o}$ are both trainable parameters, which can be regarded as applying a multi-layer perceptron to the concatenation of hidden state h_t and global attention representation v_t. $\mathbf{W^b}$ is also trainable parameter that is applied to calculate attention weights.

Our baseline model also utilizes the copy mechanism. We use the attention score a_t obtained from the decoder attention as the copy distribution. The probability of generating a word, p_gen, is calculated as $p\_gen = sigmoid(\mathbf{W^g}[h_t; v_t])$. The final distribution is the weighted sum of generating distribution and copy distribution:

$$
\begin{aligned}
\hat{g}_t &= p\_gen \cdot g_t \\
c_t &= (1 - p\_gen) \cdot a_t
\end{aligned}
\tag{4}
$$

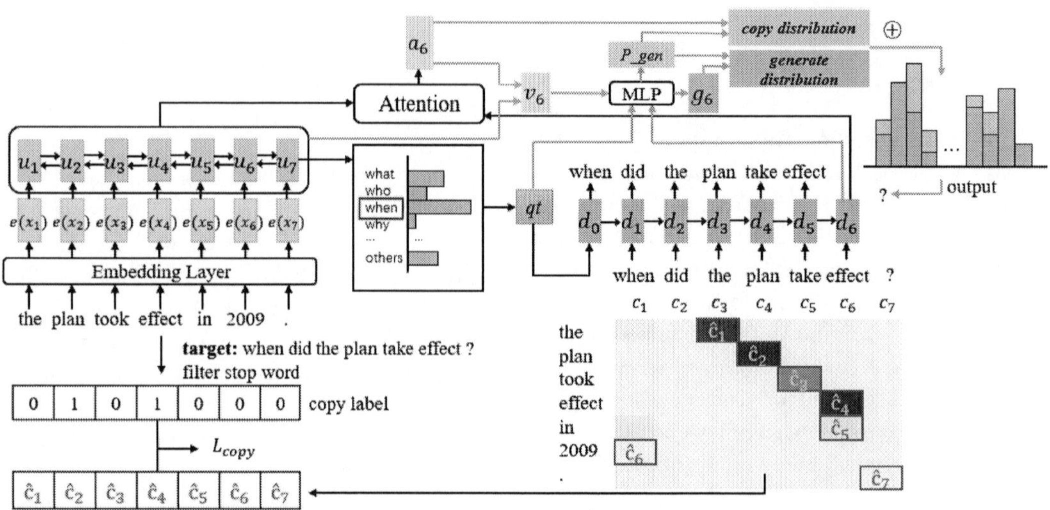

Figure 1: Our copy loss enhanced and question types driven framework

where $\hat{g}_t$, c_t are the weighted generate distribution and copy distribution, respectively. We use f_t to represent the final distribution and f_{ti} is the probability of decoding the $i-th$ word in the vocabulary. Let w_i represent the $i-th$ word in the vocabulary. The final distribution is calculated as follow:

$$f_{ti} = \begin{cases} \hat{g}_{ti} + \sum\limits_{k,where\ x_k=w_i} c_{tk} & w_i \in \mathbf{X} \\ \hat{g}_{ti} & otherwise \end{cases}$$

Given the training corpus D, in which each sample contains a source sentence S and a target question Q, the training objective is to minimize the negative log-likelihood of the target questions L:

$$L = -\sum_{<S,Q>\in D} \log P(Q|S;\theta) \qquad (5)$$

where θ represents all the parameters of our model.

3.3 Question Type Prediction

We propose the question type module for two goals. One is to enable our model to generate multiple types of questions for one source sentence, and the other is to improve the generating performance. Our question type module firstly predicts the most proper type and then uses the embedding of it to help the decoding process.

As for question types, we count the distribution of question types in SQuAD and finally category all the questions into 7 types: what, who, how, where, when, yes/no and others.

The question type prediction is a multi-layer perceptron, which takes the last hidden state of encoder as input to predict the probability distribution of question types, denoted by $\mathbf{T}$:

$$\mathbf{T} = softmax(MLP(u_l)) \qquad (6)$$

Please note that our model can generate multiple questions for one source sentence. When the number of questions need to be generated is set to K, our model will select K question types with the highest probability as output. Consequently, our decoder will decode K times.

$$ty_1, ty_2, \ldots, ty_K = TopK(\mathbf{T}) \qquad (7)$$

At every decoding time, for one of the best K question types, ty, we embed it into a question type vector qt:

$$qt = Embedding(ty)$$
$$ty \in ty_1, ty_2, \ldots, ty_K \qquad (8)$$

The embedded question type vector will be used in decoding, and in this way, the question type vector would guide the model to generate questions that follow the pattern of a specific question type. Specially, we use the question type vector qt instead of the embedding of $[SOS]$ token as the input of the decoder at the first decoding step:

$$h_0 = LSTM(u_l, qt) \qquad (9)$$

Besides, when calculating the generating distribution p_gen, we concatenate qt with the global

72

attention representation and the decoder hidden state:

$$g_t = softmax(\mathbf{W^o} tanh(\mathbf{W^t}[h_t; v_t; qt]))$$
$$p\_gen = sigmoid(\mathbf{W^g}[h_t; v_t; qt]) \qquad (10)$$

Finally, we train the question type prediction and question generating simultaneously in multi-task learning framework. For each sample $< S, Q >$, we calculate the ground-truth question type distribution TY and we add an additional factor to the loss function, which is the negative log-likelihood of the target questions' types:

$$L = - \sum_{<S,Q,TY>\in D} [\log P(Q|S; \theta) +$$
$$\lambda_1 \log P(TY|S; \theta)] \qquad (11)$$

where λ_1 is a hyper-parameter to balance two parts.

3.4 Enhanced Copy Mechanism

According to our observation on SQuAD, when creating questions people often (may have to) copy some keywords from the source sentence. So we consider non stop words appearing in both questions and source sentences as keywords, and we assume that these keywords should also occur in the generated sequence. In order to push the model to copy keywords from source sentences, we propose a copy loss to enhance the traditional copy mechanism. For a word x_l in the source sentence, we first define a function $cl(copylabel)$ as follow:

$$cl(x_i) = \begin{cases} 1 & x_i \in Q \text{ and } x_i \notin stopword \\ 0 & otherwise \end{cases}$$
$$(12)$$

We believe that at one decoding step, the copy probability of keywords ($cl(x_i) = 1$) should be close to 1. So we define the copy loss as:

$$\hat{c}_i = max(c_{1i}, c_{2i}, \ldots, c_{mi})$$
$$L_{copy} = \sum_{i=1}^{l} cl(x_i)(\hat{c}_i - 1)^2 \qquad (13)$$

where c_{ti} is the copy probability of the $i - th$ word in the source sentence at the $t - th$ decoding step, computed by Equation 4. Thus, $\hat{c}_i$ is the highest copy probability of the $i - th$ word in the source sentence among all the m decoding step. l denotes the number of words in the source sentence.

Finally, we add the copy loss into the total loss:

$$L = - \sum_{<S,Q,TY>\in D} [\log P(Q|S; \theta)$$
$$+ \lambda_1 \log P(TY|S; \theta) \qquad (14)$$
$$+ \frac{\lambda_2}{l} \sum_{i=1}^{l} cl(x_i)(\hat{c}_i - 1)^2]$$

where λ_2 is another hyper-parameter to control the impact of penalty loss.

4 Experimental Settings

4.1 Dataset and Pre-processing

We conduct experiments on the SQuAD dataset (Rajpurkar et al., 2016), which contains more than 70k training samples, 10k development samples and 11k test samples. In either training, development or test dataset, multiple samples might share the same source sentence but with different target questions. But a same source sentence will not appear in different datasets, which ensures the confidentiality of test data.

We adopt subword representations (Sennrich et al., 2015) rather than raw words, which can not only reduce the size of vocabulary, increase the training speed, address the problem of out of vocabulary words, but also improve the model performance. By using byte-pair encoding, our vocabulary size is reduced to less than 6k. Due to the vanishing gradient problem in recurrent neural networks (Pascanu et al., 2013; ?), we choose 256 for the maximum length of inputs and 50 for the maximum length of target questions.

4.2 Implementation Details

We adopt a 2-layers bi-directional LSTM for encoding and a 1-layer LSTM for decoding. The number of hidden units is 600, and the dimension of both word embedding and question type embedding is 300. We do not use pre-trained word embedding since we use subword representations rather than word-level representations. The drop rate (Krizhevsky et al., 2012) between each layer is 0.3. We firstly use Adam (Kingma and Ba, 2014) with learning rate of 0.001 for fast training, and after training 5 epochs, the stochastic gradient descent(SGD) with learning rate of 0.01 is used for fine-tuning. We train our model for 15 epochs with mini-batch size of 64. During training, hyper-parameter K is set to 1 and when decoding, we do beam search with a beam size of 4. For hyperparameters λ_1 and λ_2, we try different settings and choose the best one by observing the descending trend of total loss and ascending trend of BLEU-4 score on the valid set. Finally, both λ_1 and λ_2 are set to 0.1.

4.3 Evaluation Metrics

We adopt BLEU (Papineni et al., 2002), METEOR (Denkowski and Lavie, 2014) and ROUGE-L (Flick, 2004) for evaluation, and use the evaluation package released by Chen (Chen et al., 2015). BLEU measures the precision of n-grams on a set of references, with a penalty for over short generation. METEOR calculates the similarity between generations and references by considering synonyms, stemming and paraphrases. ROUGE measures the recall of n-grams on the set of references.

5 Results and Analysis

In this section, we report the automatic evaluation results of our proposed model and do ablation study to prove the effectiveness of different parts of the model. Then we conduct human evaluation and case study to test the quality of generated questions. Furthermore, we give a detailed analysis on multiple questions generation.

5.1 Main Results

We compare our model with the following previous works:

- **Seq2Seq Attention**: It is a traditional sequence-to-sequence attention model.

- **Seq2SeqAtt (Du)**: This is the first work in AG-QG task, which is a sequence-to-sequence attention model (Du et al., 2017).

- **Transformer (Scialom)**: This is the state-of-the-art result for the AG-QG task, which adopts a transformer network with some extension. (Scialom et al., 2019).

We do not take (Wang et al., 2019) into comparison because their evaluation is done on a different test set and is not accessible.

The experimental results are shown in Table 2. The full version of our model which uses both the question type module and copy loss mechanism obtains the best results on all of metrics, achieving a new state-of-the-art result of BLEU-4 13.90

for the challenging AG-QG task. It outperforms the baseline model with 0.73 points and beats the previous best result by 0.67 points.

5.2 Ablation Study

We conduct extensive experiments with different model modules, where k is set to 1 in decoding. The results are reported in Table 3.

- **Baseline**: Our baseline model is a general sequence-to-sequence attention model enhanced with copy mechanism.

- **Baseline+Type**: It adds the question type module to the baseline model.

- **Baseline+CopyLoss**: Based on the baseline model, it calculates and minimizes the additional copy loss.

- **Baseline+CopyLoss+Type**: This is the full version of our proposed model. That is, the question type module is applied to the baseline model and the extra copy loss is also calculated.

- **Upper Bound**: Since our full model incorporates the question type prediction part, the accuracy of question type prediction will undoubtedly affect the final quality of generation. If the right question type is given for every test sample, we get the upper bound of our model.

Effect of Question Type Module. Comparing with the baseline model, the question type module brings a slight performance gain. The upper bound shows if the right type is given for each test sample, the model will yield a much better performance with a BLEU-4 score of 15.27, which demonstrates the huge potential of our model. It proves that our model has successfully learned the patterns of different types of questions.

However, our question type predict module cannot achieve a 100% accuracy, and once a wrong question type is offered to the decoder, it will have negative influence on the generating quality. Actually, our question type predict part achieves an overall 69% accuracy, and the prediction results of different question types are shown in Table 4. It shows that without the answer as input, to predict the types of questions that should be asked for a given sentence is non-trivia.

model	BLEU-1	BLEU-2	BLEU-3	BLEU-4	METEOR	ROUGE-L
Seq2SeqAtt	42.90	25.97	17.68	12.49	16.85	39.59
Seq2SeqAtt (Du)	43.09	25.96	17.50	12.28	16.62	39.75
Transformer (Scialom)	43.33	26.27	18.32	13.23	-	40.22
Our model	**45.08**	**27.98**	**19.38**	**13.90**	**18.12**	**40.77**

Table 2: Experimental results comparing with previous works.

model	BLEU-1	BLEU-2	BLEU-3	BLEU-4	METEOR	ROUGE-L
Baseline	43.39	26.75	18.48	13.17	17.40	40.57
Baseline+Type	44.59	27.25	18.76	13.41	17.54	40.41
Baseline+CopyLoss	44.45	27.62	19.08	13.65	17.90	40.16
Baseline+CopyLoss+Type	**45.08**	**27.98**	**19.38**	**13.90**	**18.12**	**40.77**
Upper Bound	48.42	30.28	21.12	15.27	19.43	43.82

Table 3: Ablation study of our model.

Type	Total	Predict	Precision	Recall	Fscore
what	6707	8542	0.63	0.80	0.71
who	1421	1298	0.35	0.32	0.34
how	1476	1258	0.59	0.50	0.54
where	455	350	0.19	0.15	0.17
when	647	346	0.27	0.15	0.19
yes/no	868	65	0.09	0.01	0.01
others	303	18	< 0.01	< 0.01	< 0.01

Table 4: Prediction results of different question types.

	Key Words	Percentage
Baseline+Type	1.26	40.78%
Our model	**1.40**	**45.31%**
Golden	3.09	100%

Table 5: Performance of copying key words between two models with and without the enhanced copy mechanism.

	Fluency	Relevance	Answer-ability
Baseline	3.78	3.73	3.54
Our model	**4.23**	**4.23**	**4.20**
Golden	4.69	4.44	4.48
Spearman	0.59	0.67	0.65

Table 6: Human evaluation results of different models.

Effect of Enhanced Copy Mechanism Our designed copy loss aims to enhance the copy mechanism. Since it tries to make the model ensure that every key word is copied, it directly leads to a higher BLEU-1. To our delight, the experiment shows the copy loss mechanism also contributes to a stable 0.48 increment of BLEU-4.

To make an in-depth analysis on the new copy mechanism, we also conduct experiments with and without the copy loss, counting the average number of keywords in questions generated by different models. The results are shown in Table 5. Our copy loss brings an absolute 4.53% increment on copying words from source sentences, which helps the model generate higher quality questions.

5.3 Human Evaluation

We also conduct human evaluation to judge the quality of questions generated by our model and the baseline model, respectively. We take three metrics into consideration: 1) Fluency: it measures whether the question is grammatical; 2) Relevance: it measures whether the question is asked for and highly related to the source sentence; and 3) Answer-ability: it measures whether the generated question can be answered by the information of the source sentence. We randomly selected 100 sentence-question pairs generated by different models, and asked three annotators to score the questions on a 1–5 scale (5 for the best). We also exploit the Spearman correlation coefficient to measure the inter-annotator agreement. The results are shown in Table 6. It shows that the consistency among three annotators is satisfying, and our generated questions are better from different perspectives.

Besides, a further two-tailed t-test proves that our generated questions are better than that of the baseline model significantly, with $p < 0.001$ for every metric.

5.4 Case Study

In order to show the effectiveness of our model, we offer two real samples in the test set, as shown in Table 7. In both samples, the baseline model generates a wrong type of question while our model predicts the right type of question. At the same time, our model successfully copies more key words from the source sentence, which are shown in italics, while baseline model fails. In both samples,

Sample 1
Source sentence: the ex-president of def jam l.a. reid has described beyonc as the greatest entertainer alive .
Ground-truth: **who** has said that *beyonc* is the best entertainer alive ?
Baseline: what is the greatest entertainer alive ?
Our model(K=1): **who** described *beyonc* as the greatest entertainer alive ?

Sample 2
Source sentence: tibetan sources say deshin shekpa also persuaded the yongle emperor not to impose his military might on tibet as the mongols had previously done .
Ground-truth: **who** convinced the *yongle emperor* not to send *military* forces into *tibet* ?
Baseline: what did tibetan sources say deshin ?
Our model(K=1): **who** persuaded the *yongle emperor* not to impose his *military* might on *tibet* ?

Table 7: Examples of generated questions by different models.

Sample 1
Source sentence: by 1790 , new york had surpassed philadelphia as the largest city in the united states .
Groud-truth: by **which** year , did new york city become the largest city in the united states ? **what** was the second largest city in the united states in 1790 ?
Our Model (K=2): 1st: in **what** year did new york city surpassed philadelphia ? 2nd: **which** city had surpassed philadelphia in the us ?

Sample 2
Source sentence: buddhist architecture , in particular , showed great regional diversity .
Groud-truth: **which** cultures architecture showed a lot of diversity ? **what** type of architectural is especially known for its regional differences ?
Our Model (K=2): 1st: **which** buddhist architecture has showed great regional diversity? 2nd: **what** is buddhist architecture ?

Table 8: Different types of questions generated from the same input sentence.

our generated questions are more fluent and coherent.

5.5 Asking Different Types of Questions

For a given sentence, our question type driven framework offers the model the ability to generate different types of questions. In this case, the parameter K is set to more than 1, and the question type predictor will give K question types with the highest possibility. Then the model automatically decodes K times to generate the best K types of questions. We list a sample in Table 8 with $K = 2$ to show the generating diversity of our model, where two types of questions (what and

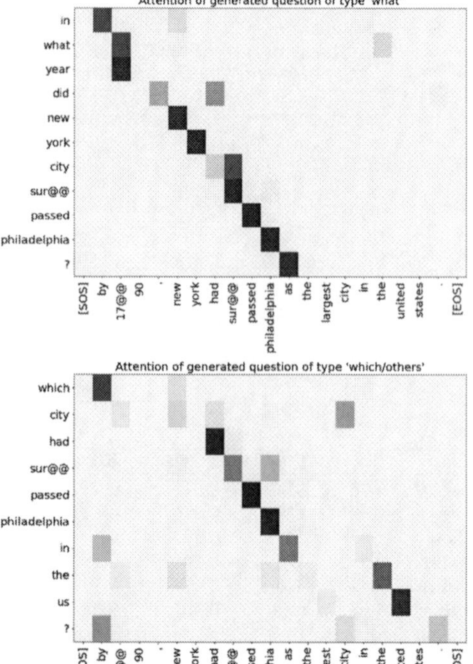

Figure 2: Heat map of attention for different types of generated questions.

which) are generated from the same input sentence.

Besides, to identify the effect of our model, we visualize the decoder attention, as shown in Figure 2. The two attention maps show the attention points when our model is generating different types (which and what) of questions with respect to the same input sentence, where x-axis is the source sentence and y-axis is the generated question. Differences between these attention maps prove that our model can attend on different information when generating different types of questions.

From the table, we prove that our model has the ability to generate multiple questions. However, the limitation is also obvious. First, if K is too large, the generated questions of some low probable types are of low quality. Second, since the probability distribution of question types are automatically calculated, the types of generated questions cannot be known beforehand.

6 Conclusion

In this paper, we propose two new strategies to deal with the answer-agnostic QG: question type module and copy loss mechanism. These proposed modules improve the performance over the baseline model, achieving the state-of-the-art. Moreover, our model has the ability and flexibility to generate multiple questions for one source sentence. Hopefully, the idea of question type module and copy loss mechanism can also be used to do answer-aware QG task or other similar text generation tasks.

Acknowledgments

This work is supported by the National Natural Science Foundation of China (61773026) and the Key Project of Natural Science Foundation of China (61936012).

References

Dzmitry Bahdanau, KyungHyun Cho, and Yoshua Bengio. 2015. Neural machine translation by jointly learning to alignand translate. In *3rd International Conference on Learning Representations, ICLR 2015*.

Klaus Beulen and Hermann Ney. 1998. Automatic question generation for decision tree based state tying. In *Proceedings of the 1998 IEEE International Conference on Acoustics, Speech and Signal Processing, ICASSP'98 (Cat. No. 98CH36181)*, volume 2, pages 805–808. IEEE.

Jonathan Brown, Gwen A. Frishkoff, and Maxine Eskenazi. 2005. Automatic question generation for vocabulary assessment. In *Proceedings of the conference on Human Language Technology and Empirical Methods in Natural Language Processing*.

Xinlei Chen, Hao Fang, Tsung Yi Lin, Ramakrishna Vedantam, Saurabh Gupta, Piotr Dollar, and C. Lawrence Zitnick. 2015. Microsoft coco captions: Data collection and evaluation server. *arXiv preprint arXiv:1504.00325*.

Yu Chen, Lingfei Wu, and Mohammed J. Zaki. 2019. Natural question generation with reinforcement learning based graph-to-sequence model. *arXiv preprint arXiv:1908.11813*.

Michael Denkowski and Alon Lavie. 2014. Meteor universal: Language specific translation evaluation for any target language. In *Proceedings of the ninth workshop on statistical machine translation*, pages 376–380.

Li Dong, Nan Yang, Wenhui Wang, Furu Wei, Xiaodong Liu, Yu Wang, Jianfeng Gao, Ming Zhou, and Hsiao-Wuen Hon. 2019. Unified language model pre-training for natural language understanding and generation. In *Advances in Neural Information Processing Systems*, pages 13042–13054.

Xinya Du and Claire Cardie. 2017. Identifying where to focus in reading comprehension for neural question generation. In *Proceedings of the 2017 Conference on Empirical Methods in Natural Language Processing*.

Xinya Du, Junru Shao, and Claire Cardie. 2017. Learning to ask: Neural question generation for reading comprehension. *arXiv preprint arXiv:1705.00106*.

Nan Duan, Duyu Tang, Peng Chen, and Ming Zhou. 2017. Question generation for question answering. In *Proceedings of the 2017 Conference on Empirical Methods in Natural Language Processing*, pages 866–874.

Zhihao Fan, Zhongyu Wei, Piji Li, Yanyan Lan, and Xuanjing Huang. 2018. A question type driven framework to diversify visual question generation. In *IJCAI*, pages 4048–4054.

Carlos Flick. 2004. Rouge: A package for automatic evaluation of summaries. In *Workshop on Text Summarization Branches Out*.

Jiatao Gu, Zhengdong Lu, Li Hang, and Victor O. K. Li. 2016. Incorporating copying mechanism in sequence-to-sequence learning. *arXiv preprint arXiv:1603.06393*.

Michael Heilman and Noah A. Smith. 2010. Good question! statistical ranking for question generation. In *Human Language Technologies: The 2010 Annual Conference of the North American Chapter of the Association for Computational Linguistics*.

S Hochreiter, Schmidhuber, and Jrgen. 1997. Long short-term memory. *Neural Computation*, 9(8):1735–1780.

Yanghoon Kim, Hwanhee Lee, Joongbo Shin, and Kyomin Jung. 2019. Improving neural question generation using answer separation. In *Proceedings of the AAAI Conference on Artificial Intelligence*, volume 33, pages 6602–6609.

Diederik P Kingma and Jimmy Ba. 2014. Adam: A method for stochastic optimization. *arXiv preprint arXiv:1412.6980*.

Alex Krizhevsky, Ilya Sutskever, and Geoffrey E Hinton. 2012. Imagenet classification with deep convolutional neural networks. In *Advances in neural information processing systems*, pages 1097–1105.

Jinwen Ma, Wenpeng Hu, Bing Liu, Dongyan Zhao, and Rui Yan. 2018. Aspect-based question generation. *International Conference on Learning Representations 2018*.

Karen Mazidi and Rodney Nielsen. 2014. Linguistic considerations in automatic question generation. In *Proceedings of the 52nd Annual Meeting of the Association for Computational Linguistics (Volume 2: Short Papers)*, pages 321–326.

Ruslan Mitkov, Le An Ha, and Nikiforos Karamanis. 2006. A computer-aided environment for generating multiple-choice test items. *Natural Language Engineering*, 12(2):177–194.

Preksha Nema, Akash Kumar Mohankumar, Mitesh M. Khapra, Balaji Vasan Srinivasan, and Balaraman Ravindran. 2019. Lets ask again: Refine network for automatic question generation. *arXiv preprint arXiv:1909.05355*.

Kishore Papineni, Salim Roukos, Todd Ward, and Wei-Jing Zhu. 2002. Bleu: a method for automatic evaluation of machine translation. In *Proceedings of the 40th annual meeting on association for computational linguistics*, pages 311–318. Association for Computational Linguistics.

Razvan Pascanu, Tomas Mikolov, and Yoshua Bengio. 2013. On the difficulty of training recurrent neural networks. In *International conference on machine learning*, pages 1310–1318.

Paul Piwek, Hugo Hernault, Helmut Prendinger, and Mitsuru Ishizuka. 2007. T2d: Generating dialogues between virtual agents automatically from text. In *International Conference on Intelligent Virtual Agents*.

Pranav Rajpurkar, Zhang Jian, Konstantin Lopyrev, and Percy Liang. 2016. Squad: 100,000+ questions for machine comprehension of text. In *Proceedings of the 2016 Conference on Empirical Methods in Natural Language Processing*.

Vasile Rus and C Graesser Arthur. 2009. The question generation shared task and evaluation challenge. In *The University of Memphis. National Science Foundation*. Citeseer.

Thomas Scialom, Benjamin Piwowarski, and Jacopo Staiano. 2019. Self-attention architectures for answer-agnostic neural question generation. In *Proceedings of the 57th Annual Meeting of the Association for Computational Linguistics*.

Rico Sennrich, Barry Haddow, and Alexandra Birch. 2015. Neural machine translation of rare words with subword units. *arXiv preprint arXiv:1508.07909*.

Heung-Yeung Shum, Xiao-dong He, and Di Li. 2018. From eliza to xiaoice: challenges and opportunities with social chatbots. *Frontiers of Information Technology & Electronic Engineering*, 19(1):10–26.

Linfeng Song, Zhiguo Wang, Wael Hamza, Yue Zhang, and Daniel Gildea. 2018. Leveraging context information for natural question generation. In *Proceedings of the 2018 Conference of the North American Chapter of the Association for Computational Linguistics: Human Language Technologies, Volume 2 (Short Papers)*, pages 569–574.

Sandeep Subramanian, Wang Tong, Xingdi Yuan, and Adam Trischler. 2017. Neural models for key phrase detection and question generation. *arXiv preprint arXiv:1706.04560*.

Xingwu Sun, Jing Liu, Yajuan Lyu, Wei He, Yanjun Ma, and Shi Wang. 2018. Answer-focused and position-aware neural question generation. In *Proceedings of the 2018 Conference on Empirical Methods in Natural Language Processing*, pages 3930–3939.

Ilya Sutskever, Oriol Vinyals, and Quoc V. Le. 2014. Sequence to sequence learning with neural networks.

Duyu Tang, Duan Nan, Qin Tao, and Zhou Ming. 2017. Question answering and question generation as dual tasks. *arXiv preprint arXiv:1706.02027*.

Wang Tong, Xingdi Yuan, and Adam Trischler. 2017. A joint model for question answering and question generation. *arXiv preprint arXiv:1706.01450*.

Ashish Vaswani, Noam Shazeer, Niki Parmar, Jakob Uszkoreit, Llion Jones, Aidan N Gomez, Łukasz Kaiser, and Illia Polosukhin. 2017. Attention is all you need. In *Advances in neural information processing systems*, pages 5998–6008.

Oriol Vinyals, Meire Fortunato, and Navdeep Jaitly. 2015. Pointer networks. In *Advances in neural information processing systems*, pages 2692–2700.

Siyuan Wang, Zhongyu Wei, Zhihao Fan, Yang Liu, and Xuanjing Huang. 2019. A multi-agent communication framework for question-worthy phrase extraction and question generation. In *Proceedings of the AAAI Conference on Artificial Intelligence*, volume 33, pages 7168–7175.

Xingdi Yuan, Wang Tong, Caglar Gulcehre, Alessandro Sordoni, Philip Bachman, Sandeep Subramanian, Saizheng Zhang, Adam Trischler, Xingdi Yuan, and Wang Tong. 2017. Machine comprehension by text-to-text neural question generation. *arXiv preprint arXiv:1705.02012*.

Yao Zhao, Xiaochuan Ni, Yuanyuan Ding, and Qifa Ke. 2018. Paragraph-level neural question generation with maxout pointer and gated self-attention networks. In *Proceedings of the 2018 Conference on Empirical Methods in Natural Language Processing*, pages 3901–3910.

Qingyu Zhou, Nan Yang, Furu Wei, Chuanqi Tan, Hangbo Bao, and Ming Zhou. 2017. Neural question generation from text: A preliminary study. In *National CCF Conference on Natural Language Processing and Chinese Computing*, pages 662–671. Springer.

Wenjie Zhou, Minghua Zhang, and Yunfang Wu. 2019. Multi-task learning with language modeling for question generation. In *Proceedings of the 2019 Conference on Empirical Methods in Natural Language Processing (EMNLP)*.

A Generative Approach to Titling and Clustering Wikipedia Sections

Anjalie Field
Carnegie Mellon University*
anjalief@cs.cmu.edu

Sascha Rothe
Google Research
rothe@google.com

Simon Baumgartner
Google Research
simonba@google.com

Cong Yu
Google Research
congyu@google.com

Abe Ittycheriah
Google Research
aittycheriah@google.com

Abstract

We evaluate the performance of transformer encoders with various decoders for information organization through a new task: generation of section headings for Wikipedia articles. Our analysis shows that decoders containing attention mechanisms over the encoder output achieve high-scoring results by generating extractive text. In contrast, a decoder without attention better facilitates semantic encoding and can be used to generate section embeddings. We additionally introduce a new loss function, which further encourages the decoder to generate high-quality embeddings.

1 Introduction

Automated information labeling and organization has become a desirable way to process the copious amounts of available text. We develop methods for producing text headings and section-level embeddings through a new task: generation of section titles for Wikipedia articles. This task is useful for improving Wikipedia, an active area of research due to the long tail of poor quality articles, including articles lacking section subdivisions or consistent headings (Lebret et al., 2016; Piccardi et al., 2018; Liu et al., 2018). Additionally, the types of labels used to denote sections can be useful for organizing other unstructured collections of text.

We approach this task in two ways: first we train a text generation model for producing section titles, and second, we leverage our model architecture to extract section embeddings, which offer a useful mechanism for comparing and clustering sections with similar information (Banerjee et al., 2007; Hu et al., 2009; Reimers et al., 2019). This approach provides a flexible framework for creating paragraph-level embeddings, in which the type of information encoded in the embedding can be controlled by changing the generation task.

Section title generation is similar to existing tasks, such as generating titles for newspaper articles (Rush et al., 2015; Nallapati et al., 2016). However, Wikipedia section titles contain a unique mix of short abstractive headings like "History" and longer extractive headings like song titles, where many of the words in the section title also appear in the section text. The variations in the type of headings makes this dataset useful for analyzing how models perform on different subsets of the data.

A common state-of-the-art model for many existing text generation tasks uses an encoder-decoder framework where the encoder is initialized with BERT and the decoder is also a transformer (Vaswani et al., 2017; Devlin et al., 2019; Zhang et al., 2019; Rothe et al., 2019). The entire output of the encoder is passed to the decoder, which allows the decoder to attend over the entire input sequence during each generation step.

In contrast, we explore using transformer encoders with RNN decoders and show that RNN decoders better generate short abstractive titles while transformer decoders perform better on longer extractive titles. Embeddings extracted from the RNN decoders also perform better in clustering evaluations, which suggests that the attention-based mechanisms in the transformer facilitate copying input text into the output, but the RNN architecture better facilitates encoding semantic meaning.

We additionally introduce a new loss function for the RNN decoder that encourages the start and end states of the RNN to be similar. This loss function encourages the model to encode meaningful information into a single state, which further improves the quality of the generated section-level embeddings.

We first describe our models (Section 2) and

---

*Work done while the first author was an intern at Google Research.

Proceedings of the 4th Workshop on Neural Generation and Translation (WNGT 2020), pages 79–87
Online, July 10, 2020. ©2020 Association for Computational Linguistics
www.aclweb.org/anthology/D19-56%2d

our data set (Section 3) and then present results, evaluating our models on a held-out test corpus (Section 5). Our main contributions include: (1) the introduction of a new short-text generation task that is useful for information labeling and organization; (2) an analysis of text generation models for this task; (3) the introduction of a novel loss function that results in high-quality section embeddings.

2 Models

Our primary task is to generate section titles, and our secondary task is to generate section-level embeddings. All models use an encoder-decoder architecture, where the encoder is initialized with BERT (Devlin et al., 2019). We use 4 decoder variants, including one trained with a novel loss function.

TRANS This model contains a (randomly initialized) transformer decoder, with hyperparameters identical to the BERT-base model. The hidden states generated by the encoder for the entire input sequence are passed to the decoder, thus allowing the decoder to attend over the entire input sequence during each decoding step. This model serves as our primary baseline, as it is identical to the BERT2RND model in Rothe et al. (2019). We use the same hyperparameters as Rothe et al. (2019), which were selected after extensive tuning.

RNN Instead of a transformer decoder, we use an RNN, specifically a gated recurrent neural network (GRU) (Cho et al., 2014), as the decoder. Unlike the transformer decoder, which computes attention over the full input sequence, we do not use any attention mechanisms over the input to the decoder. Instead, we only pass the last hidden layer for the first token ("CLS" token), forcing the model to encode all meaningful information about the input sequence into this single state. The RNN decoder, which consists of a single decoder layer, is substantially smaller than the transformer decoder used in the TRANS model.

RNN+SC Our third model uses the same architecture as the RNN model, but we add an additional component to the loss function that encourages the start state and the end state of the decoder to be similar, which we call a state constraint (SC). The primary intuition behind this loss function is that it encourages the decoder to stay "on topic" while generating text, as it discourages the RNN from wandering too far away from where it started. It further encourages the start state to encode all information needed to generate the entire output se-

quence, rather than allowing the start state to focus on information in the beginning of the sequence and the end state to encode information for the end of the sequence.

The general form for the state of an RNN decoder (Cho et al., 2014) is

$$h_t = f(h_{t-1}, y_{t-1}) \tag{1}$$

Here, f is a GRU, $t \in \{1, \ldots, T\}$ is the target token position, and h_0 is initialized to the CLS token of the BERT source encoder.

The formula for the state constraint function is given in Equation 2:

$$d = \frac{h_0}{||h_0||_2} - \frac{h_T}{||h_T||_2}$$
$$\mathcal{L}_{SC} = ||d||_2 \tag{2}$$

The normalization terms force the loss term to focus on embedding direction rather than magnitude; they are necessary to account for the arbitrary magnitude of model states. During training, we multiply the state constraint loss, $\mathcal{L}_{SC}$, by a fixed scalar (α) and add it to the standard cross-entropy (*CE*) loss function. The final loss function is then given by:

$$\mathcal{L} = \mathcal{L}_{CE} + \alpha \mathcal{L}_{SC}$$

RNN+ATTN Our final model also uses a transformer encoder and an RNN decoder. However, unlike the previous model, we pass the entire last layer of the encoder to the decoder and add an attention mechanism over this input sequence (Luong et al., 2015). This model and the TRANS model are attention-based decoders, while the RNN and the RNN+SC models do not use attention over the decoder input.

3 Data

Our primary data set consists of articles from English Language Wikipedia collected on June 25, 2019. We filter out articles that contain the word "redirect" and omit any section whose title has fewer than 2 characters. We extracted sections and section titles from each article and randomly divided the data into train, test, and development sets, using an 80/10/10 split (11.43M/1.43M/1.44M articles).

Wikipedia articles are often hierarchical, containing multiple subsections. However, we make no distinction between titles that are complete sections and titles that are subsections. This lack of distinction makes the generation task harder, as our models are not able to take advantage of hierarchical information and also allows our models and results to better generalize to other data sets that do not have this hierarchy.

More detailed statistics on the data set are shown in Table 1. For reference, we also show statistics for the commonly-used Gigaword Corpus (Rush et al., 2015), which we also use to evaluate our models in §5. The Gigaword corpus entails an abstractive short summary generation task: given the first sentence of a newspaper article, predict the article title. We use this task for comparison because it uses a well-studied data set that is more similar to the Wikipedia section heading generation task than other text generation tasks, such as summarization tasks, which typically involve much longer outputs (Narayan et al., 2018). However, as shown in Table 1, there are notable differences between these data sets.

	Wikipedia	Gigaword
Total size	14.3M	4.4M
Train size	11.43M	4.2M
Test size	1.43M	1.9K
Dev size	1.44M	210K
Distinct titles	45.25%	80.45%
Unique titles	41.82%	70.28%
Most common title	3.35%	0.17%
Avg. words per title	2.65	8.64

Table 1: Overview of the Wikipedia section title data, as compared with the Gigaword corpus. "Distinct titles" refers to the total number of titles with duplicates removed. "Unique titles" refers to the number of titles that occur exactly 1 time. In general, the Wikipedia titles are shorter and more repetitive than Gigaword titles.

In the Wikipedia corpus, across 14.3M data points, there are only 6.5M distinct headings (45.25% of all titles). Approximately 6M headings (41.82%) occur only 1 time in the data, meaning the other 0.5M headings are reused multiple times across 8.3M articles to constitute the remainder of the corpus. The most common heading, "History", occurs 480K times in the data set, making up 3.35% of the total corpus. Other common headings include "Career" (181K), "Biography" (151K), "Early Life" (111K), "Background" (102K) and "Plot" (96K).

In contrast, the titles in Gigaword are generally longer and more distinctive than the Wikipedia section titles, with 80.45% of all titles being unique. However, in the absence of generic abstract headings like "History", the Gigaword corpus tends to be more extractive, meaning there is high token-overlap between articles and their titles. The Wikipedia corpus is also much larger than Gigaword, which facilitates analyses.

4 Experimental Setup

For all encoders, we use the BERT-base uncased model. Thus, we lowercase all text and use word-piece tokenization from the public BERT word-piece vocabulary (Devlin et al., 2019). We use the same preprocessing pipeline, including word-piece tokenization, when computing target text length and extractive scores.

For all models, we limit the encoder input size to 128 tokens and the decoder output size to 32 tokens and use a batch size of 32. We generally use a learning rate of 0.05 with square root decay, 40K warm-up steps, and the Adam optimizer; however, for the RNN models with the Gigaword data, we use 100K warm-up steps, clip gradients to 20, and optimize with Adagrad, which we found to produce smoother training curves. For the state constraint models, we start by setting the scalar $\alpha = 0$, and linearly increase α to 1, between 100k and 200k training steps. We train the RNN models for 2M steps using v100 GPUs, and we train the transformer models for 500K steps using TPUs. In practice, we find that the RNN performance stops improving within 1M steps and the transformer performance stops within 50K steps.

5 Results and Analysis

5.1 Section Heading Generation

Our main task is to generate a Wikipedia section title given the section text. Table 2 reports results using standard summarization metrics: Rouge-1, Rouge-L, and exact match. Rouge-1 measures the unigram overlap between the generated text and the reference text; Rouge-L measures the longest subsequence that occurs in both the generated text and the reference; exact match measures if the generated text exactly matches the reference. The RNN+ATTN model performs the best overall. The TRANS and the RNN+SC models perform approximately the same, and both outperform the regular RNN model.

Because the Wikipedia dataset contains diverse types of headings, including short abstractive headings and long extractive headings, we subdivide our test data in order to better understand model performance. In Table 3, we examine how well these models generate outputs of different lengths by dividing the test set according to the number of tokens in the target headings.

All of the RNN decoders outperform the transformer decoder for short headings containing 1-5 tokens, and the RNN+SC model performs the best overall. Over these short headings, the attention mechanism provides little advantage. However, the two attention-based decoders, TRANS and RNN+ATTN outperform the RNNs without attention for mid-range-length headings containing 5-10 tokens, which is consistent with prior work suggesting that attention improves the modeling of long-term dependencies (Vaswani et al., 2017). Nevertheless, on headings with > 10 tokens, the Rouge-L scores for all decoders decline.

	Rouge-1	Rouge-L	Exact
TRANS	52.0	51.9	39.3
RNN	50.2	50.1	33.8
RNN+SC	52.6	52.4	36.5
RNN+ATTN	**54.4**	**54.3**	**40.5**

Table 2: Results on Wikipedia section heading generation over the full test set.

# Tokens	1-5	5-10	10-15	15+
Data Size	1M	300K	56K	9K
TRANS	52.5	53.8	36.3	20.8
RNN	54.0	39.6	35.1	25.3
RNN+SC	**55.8**	44.2	37.7	24.0
RNN+ATTN	54.4	**55.7**	**47.8**	**32.9**

Table 3: Rouge-L on Wikipedia section heading generation by length. The attention-based decoders outperform the decoders without attention on target texts containing 5-10 tokens, but not on shorter target sequences.

Prior work has also examined the trend of extractiveness in text generation models, specifically observing that models achieve high performance when they can copy input tokens directly into the output, rather than having to encode semantic information and produce new tokens (Nallapati et al., 2016; Cheng and Lapata, 2016; See et al., 2017; Nallapati et al., 2017; Narayan et al., 2018; Grusky et al., 2018; Pasunuru and Bansal, 2018). Because

we ultimately extract embeddings from our models, understanding to what extent they copy tokens or encode more abstract information offers insight into how useful we can expect embeddings to be. To examine this, we introduce a metric called *extractive score*, which measures what percentage of the output text can be directly copied from the input text: $\frac{|T_{target} \cap T_{input}|}{|T_{target}|}$, where T_{target} and T_{input} represent the tokens in the target text and the input text respectively.

Thus, for a section and title pair, an extractive score of 0 indicates that there is no token overlap between the title and the section text, while a score of 1 indicates that every token in the title is also in the section text. Because of the short length of our section titles, we focus on unigrams, rather than examining higher-order n-grams. When computing extractive scores, we use the same text preprocessing pipeline as used in our models, including wordpiece tokenization and lowercasing.

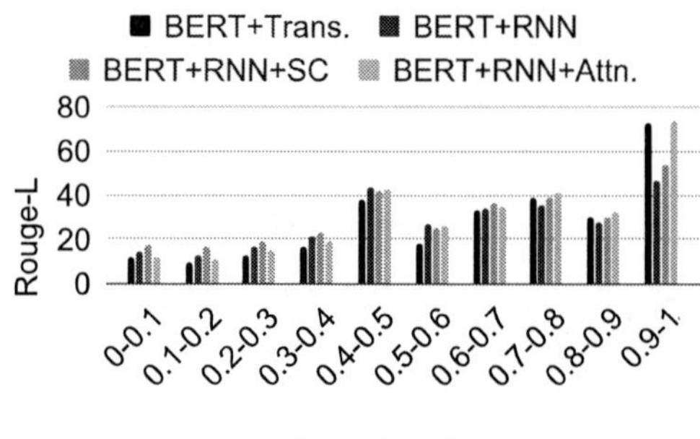

Figure 1: Rouge-L scores for each model over test data of length 5-10 tokens (300K test samples), segmented according to extractive score.

In Figure 1, we limit the test data to headings with 5-10 tokens and divide it into segments according to extractive score. The RNN and RNN+SC models outperform the attention-based models on data with low extractive scores (≤ 0.5). The higher performance of the TRANS and the RNN+ATTN models as compared to the RNN and RNN+SC models over this data segment (Table 3) is almost entirely on headings where the extractive score is ≥ 0.9. The attention-based models are not better at producing long titles *in general*, but rather their ability to copy from the input text allows them to generate long titles *when they are extractive*.

We can further examine this trend by computing correlations between Rouge-L and extractive score.

TRANS	RNN	RNN+SC	RNN+ATTN
0.215	0.115	0.136	0.205

Table 4: Partial correlations between Rouge-L and extractive score, controlled for length. All values are statistically significant.

However, as Table 3 shows, all decoders perform differently over texts of different lengths. Thus, in order to isolate the effect of extractiveness, we compute partial correlations (Rummel, 1976). The idea behind a partial correlation is to identify the relationship between two variables X and Y that is not explained by a confound Z. We first compute the residuals $e_{X,i}$ and $e_{Y,i}$, and then compute the correlation between these residuals:

$$e_{X,i} = x_i - \langle \mathbf{w}_X^*, \mathbf{z}_i \rangle$$

$$e_{Y,i} = y_i - \langle \mathbf{w}_Y^*, \mathbf{z}_i \rangle$$

$$\texttt{Partial Correlation} = \rho_{e_{X,i}, e_{Y,i}}$$

where w_X^* and w_Y^* are the coefficients learned by a linear regression between X and Z and between Y and Z. In our case, $X = $ Rouge-L, $Y = $ extractive score, and $Z = $ target length.

Table 4 reports results. For all models, the resulting correlations are positive, indicating that they generate extractive headings better than non-extractive headings. However, the correlations for the TRANS and RNN+ATTN models are highest. Overall, these results suggest that decoders with attention mechanisms achieve high performance on this task because they better copy tokens from the input into the output, rather than because they encode more semantics. Encoding semantic information is essential for generating section embeddings, which we extract and evaluate in Section 5.3.

	Rouge-1	R.-L	P. Corr
Song et al. (2019)	38.7	36.0	–
TRANS	**37.1**	**34.6**	0.647
RNN	35.6	32.6	0.619
RNN+SC	35.1	32.8	0.630
RNN+ATTN	36.3	33.8	0.667

Table 5: Results on Gigaword heading generation. The correlations between extractive score and model performance are stronger than for the Wikipedia corpus for all models. All correlations are statistically significant.

5.2 Gigaword Results

In order to compare our models against published benchmarks and to generalize our observations about extractiveness, we conduct the same experiments over the Gigaword corpus as the Wikipedia corpus, using the established train, test, and dev splits (Rush et al., 2015).

Table 5 reports the results of our models as well as a state-of-the-art model for reference (Song et al., 2019). Like TRANS, the MASS model from Song et al. (2019) uses a transformer encoder-decoder architecture but with generalizations that allow for additional pre-training. From our models, the transformer decoder performs the best overall. However, the attention-based decoders TRANS and RNN+ATTN also have the highest partial correlations, suggesting much of their performance stems from extractive titles. For all models the partial correlations between Rouge-L and extractive score are higher for the Gigaword corpus than for the Wikipedia corpus. This correlation is visually evident in Figure 2, which we constructed the same way as Figure 1.

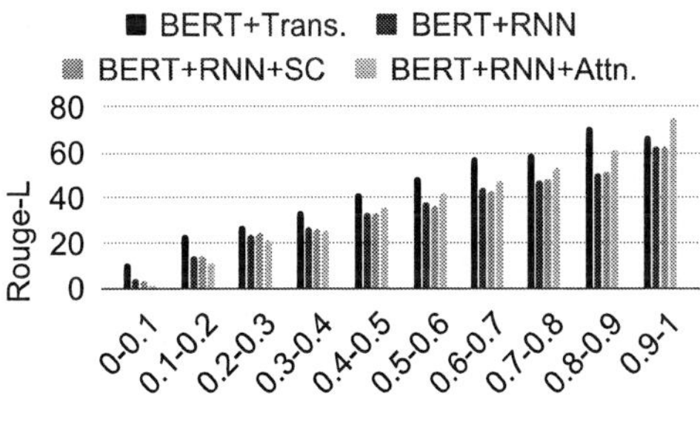

Figure 2: Rouge-L scores for each model over the Gigaword test data of length 5-10 tokens, segmented according to extractive score. Each data segment contains at least 35 samples.

Figure 2 mirrors the trend in the Wikipedia data (Figure 1). While the TRANS model performs well across all extractiveness levels, the RNNs with and without attention perform similarly for lower levels of extractiveness. However, the RNN+ATTN begins outperforming the RNNs without attention when the extractive score is ≥ 0.5, and especially when the extractive score is ≥ 0.9.

	Homogeneity	Completeness	V-measure	ARI
Doc2Vec	0.334	0.443	0.381	0.065
TF-IDF	0.428	0.361	0.392	0.044
TRANS	0.633	0.529	0.576	0.065
RNN	0.668	0.558	0.608	0.079
RNN+SC	**0.670**	**0.561**	**0.611**	**0.088**
RNN+ATTN	0.626	0.521	0.569	0.067

Table 6: Results on Wikipedia section clustering. The RNN+SC model performs the best on all metrics.

5.3 Section-embedding Generation and Clustering

While labeling sections can improve Wikipedia articles and identify the type of information contained in general paragraphs, embedding representations for paragraphs and documents can offer a more useful way to structure corpora, by facilitating information clustering and retrieval. Rather than creating generic all-purpose embeddings (Le and Mikolov, 2014), our generative models facilitate creating embeddings that target specific information, in our case, the title of the section.

We extract internal states from our models as section embeddings, and we evaluate them through a clustering task. Because many Wikipedia articles use the same generic headings, like "History" and "Plot", we can use these headings as gold cluster assignments by assuming that all sections with the same title constitute a cluster.

For all models, we use the final hidden layer for the first token in the input sequence (CLS token) as the embedding. In the case of the RNN decoder, this embedding is also the initial state of the RNN, and thus is the single state that the model is forced to encode the entire input sequence into.[1]

We cluster these embeddings using k-means clustering, where we set the number of clusters to the true number of clusters in the gold cluster assignments. We discard any section titles that occur fewer than 100 times, ensuring that the minimum size of any cluster is 100, resulting in 467,286 data points and 755 clusters. The large number of data points makes this task particularly difficult.

Table 6 reports results using standard metrics for evaluating a proposed cluster assignment against gold data (Hubert and Arabie, 1985; Rosenberg and Hirschberg, 2007). Homogeneity assesses to what extent each cluster contains only members of the same class (e.g. does each cluster contain only sections with the same title?); completeness assesses to what extent members of the same class are in the same cluster (e.g. are sections with the same title in the same cluster?); V-measure is the harmonic mean between homogeneity and completeness; and adjusted Rand index (ARI) counts how many pairs of data points are assigned to the same or different clusters in the predicted and gold clusterings. On all metrics, the RNN+SC model performs the best.

To show how our embeddings, which are tailored to this task, differ from off-the-shelf embeddings, we report results using embeddings constructed from two popular methods for generating document embeddings: distributed representations using Doc2Vec (Le and Mikolov, 2014; Lau and Baldwin, 2016; Vu and Iyyer, 2019) and sparse embeddings using TF-IDF weighting (Banerjee et al., 2007). We train a Doc2Vec model over the training set using a window size of 5 and embedding size of 768, to match the embedding size of our models, and then infer embeddings over the test set. For the TF-IDF vectors, we give this method an additional advantage by directly training the model over the test set with an embedding size of 1000. As expected, all of our models outperform these off-the-shelf models.

Unlike off-the-shelf models, our customizable models encourage the embeddings to encode information specific to our prediction task. In this case, we train them to encode section title information. However, by training our models on a different prediction task, such as predicting the name of a newspaper outlet or a comment on a newspaper article, we can encourage the model to generate document embeddings that encode different information. Thus, our model architecture offers a way to generate high-quality document embeddings that encode information specific to the task at hand.

---

[1]For TRANS and RNN+ATTN, preliminary experiments showed that using this hidden state as the embedding achieved strictly better performance than other pooling possibilities.

6   Related Work

While we introduce the task of Wikipedia section heading generation, the task of article headline generation using the Gigaword corpus has been well-studied, primarily using an encoder-decoder architecture with additional modules like attention or copy mechanisms (Rush et al., 2015; Nallapati et al., 2016). Zhang et al. (2019) further explore how to leverage the pretrained BERT model for abstractive summarization, primarily using the CNN/Daily Mail data set. Rothe et al. (2019) perform a comprehensive assessment of pretrained language models for text generation tasks, including the Gigaword task. Our TRANS model is identical to their BERT2RND model and achieves comparable results over the Gigaword corpus.

The high level of extraction in existing text generation tasks has motivated the use of mechanisms that explicitly copy input text into the output (See et al., 2017) or the introduction of new data sets (Narayan et al., 2018; Grusky et al., 2018). Furthermore, models trained for extractive summarization often outperform abstractive models on abstractive data sets (Cheng and Lapata, 2016; Nallapati et al., 2016, 2017). Our work extends these results by showing that even abstractive models are implicitly learning extraction, as they perform better on extractive text. Our metric for measuring extractiveness is similar to the 'novel n-gram percentage' proposed by See et al. (2017); however, we use the same input pipeline for computing this metric as for training our models, and we correlate extractive score with performance, rather than just using it as an extrinsic measure of abstraction (Pasunuru and Bansal, 2018).

In our Wikipedia section heading generation task, the prevalence of generic headings makes the task more abstractive than datasets like Gigaword (Rush et al., 2015), or even other short-text generation tasks, like email subject prediction (Zhang and Tetreault, 2019), which makes it a useful dataset for analyzing model performance. It is also extrinsically useful - most automated methods for improving Wikipedia focus on creating new content, such as through multi-document summarization (Liu et al., 2018) or generating text from structured data (Lebret et al., 2016). However, less than 1% of all English Wikipedia articles are considered to be of quality class good, suggesting there is a need for improving existing articles. Piccardi et al. (2018) show that many low quality articles consist of 0-1 sections and present a method for recommending new sections for an author to add to the article. Our approach offers a way to label existing paragraphs as distinct sections.

Our approach also results in document embeddings, which we show can be used to cluster sections. Document embeddings are useful for a variety of tasks including news clustering (Banerjee et al., 2007; Hu et al., 2009), argument clustering (Reimers et al., 2019), and as features for downstream tasks like text classification (Lau and Baldwin, 2016; Liu and Lapata, 2018). While TF-IDF vectors have historically been a popular construction method (Banerjee et al., 2007), more recent methods have focused on distributive representations, particularly Doc2Vec, a generalization of the Word2Vec algorithm (Le and Mikolov, 2014; Lau and Baldwin, 2016; Vu and Iyyer, 2019).

Finally, the growing popularity of pretrained language models like BERT has led to numerous investigations on what these models learn (Liu et al., 2019; Goldberg, 2019; Jawahar et al., 2019). Most investigations involve using targeted probing tasks. While our work shares similar goals, in that we investigate what type of information these models learn, we focus on data subsets and performance analysis.

7   Future Work

Our work offers several avenues for future exploration. We focus only on English Wikipedia. However, there are numerous language editions of Wikipedia, many of which have far fewer articles than the English edition and could benefit from tools for text generation.[2] Additionally, while we discard the hierarchical nature of Wikipedia sections, this information could offer a way to improve model performance (potentially at the cost of generalizability to other data sets). Furthermore, while we evaluate the performance of our generated section embeddings for clustering, more work is needed to assess their usefulness on other tasks, such as retrieving relevant sections from a query, measuring section similarities, or as features for text classification.

8   Conclusions

Overall, our work introduces the task of generating section titles for text. We also introduce the

---

[2]https://en.wikipedia.org/wiki/List_of_Wikipedias

RNN+SC model and demonstrate how RNN decoders can be utilized for short text generation and improved section embeddings. Specifically, our method for generating text embeddings, which involves leveraging internal states of models trained for generation, allows the embeddings to contain targeted information that maximizes their usefulness for specific tasks.

9 Acknowledgements

We would like to thank anonymous reviewers, Vidhisha Balakrishna, Keith Hall, Shan Jiang, Kevin Lin, Riley Matthews, and Yulia Tsvetkov for their helpful feedback and advice.

References

Somnath Banerjee, Krishnan Ramanathan, and Ajay Gupta. 2007. Clustering short texts using Wikipedia. In *Proc. of SIGIR*, pages 787–788.

Jianpeng Cheng and Mirella Lapata. 2016. Neural summarization by extracting sentences and words. In *Proc. of ACL*, pages 484–494.

Kyunghyun Cho, Bart Van Merriënboer, Caglar Gulcehre, Dzmitry Bahdanau, Fethi Bougares, Holger Schwenk, and Yoshua Bengio. 2014. Learning phrase representations using RNN encoder-decoder for statistical machine translation. In *Proc. of EMNLP*, pages 1724–1734.

Jacob Devlin, Ming-Wei Chang, Kenton Lee, and Kristina Toutanova. 2019. Bert: Pre-training of deep bidirectional transformers for language understanding. In *Proc. of NAACL*, pages 4171–4186.

Yoav Goldberg. 2019. Assessing BERT's syntactic abilities. *arXiv preprint arXiv:1901.05287*.

Max Grusky, Mor Naaman, and Yoav Artzi. 2018. Newsroom: A dataset of 1.3 million summaries with diverse extractive strategies. In *ACL*, pages 708–719.

Xiaohua Hu, Xiaodan Zhang, Caimei Lu, Eun K Park, and Xiaohua Zhou. 2009. Exploiting Wikipedia as external knowledge for document clustering. In *Proc. of SIGKDD*, pages 389–396.

Lawrence Hubert and Phipps Arabie. 1985. Comparing partitions. *Journal of classification*, 2(1):193–218.

Ganesh Jawahar, Benoît Sagot, Djamé Seddah, Samuel Unicomb, Gerardo Iñiguez, Márton Karsai, Yannick Léo, Márton Karsai, Carlos Sarraute, Éric Fleury, et al. 2019. What does BERT learn about the structure of language? In *Proc. of ACL*, pages 3651–3657.

Jey Han Lau and Timothy Baldwin. 2016. An empirical evaluation of doc2vec with practical insights into document embedding generation. In *Proc. of ACL Workshop on Representation Learning for NLP*, pages 78–86.

Quoc Le and Tomas Mikolov. 2014. Distributed representations of sentences and documents. In *Proc. of ICML*, pages II1188–II1196.

Rémi Lebret, David Grangier, and Michael Auli. 2016. Neural text generation from structured data with application to the biography domain. In *Proc. of EMNLP*, pages 1203–1213.

Nelson F Liu, Matt Gardner, Yonatan Belinkov, Matthew E Peters, and Noah A Smith. 2019. Linguistic knowledge and transferability of contextual representations. In *Proc. of NAACL*, pages 1073–1094.

Peter J Liu, Mohammad Saleh, Etienne Pot, Ben Goodrich, Ryan Sepassi, Lukasz Kaiser, and Noam Shazeer. 2018. Generating Wikipedia by summarizing long sequences. In *Proc. of ICLR*.

Yang Liu and Mirella Lapata. 2018. Learning structured text representations. *TACL*, 6:63–75.

Thang Luong, Hieu Pham, and Christopher D Manning. 2015. Effective approaches to attention-based neural machine translation. In *Proc. of EMNLP*, pages 1412–1421.

Ramesh Nallapati, Feifei Zhai, and Bowen Zhou. 2017. Summarunner: A recurrent neural network based sequence model for extractive summarization of documents. In *Proc. of AAAI*, pages 3075–3081.

Ramesh Nallapati, Bowen Zhou, Cicero dos Santos, Caglar Gulcehre, and Bing Xiang. 2016. Abstractive text summarization using sequence-to-sequence rnns and beyond. In *Proc. of CoNLL*, pages 280–290.

Shashi Narayan, Shay B Cohen, and Mirella Lapata. 2018. Dont give me the details, just the summary! topic-aware convolutional neural networks for extreme summarization. In *Proc. of EMNLP*, pages 1797–1807.

Ramakanth Pasunuru and Mohit Bansal. 2018. Multi-reward reinforced summarization with saliency and entailment. In *Proc. of NAACL*, pages 646–653.

Tiziano Piccardi, Michele Catasta, Leila Zia, and Robert West. 2018. Structuring wikipedia articles with section recommendations. In *Proc. of SIGIR*, pages 665–674.

Nils Reimers, Benjamin Schiller, Tilman Beck, Johannes Daxenberger, Christian Stab, and Iryna Gurevych. 2019. Classification and clustering of arguments with contextualized word embeddings. In *Proc. of ACL*, pages 567–578.

Andrew Rosenberg and Julia Hirschberg. 2007. V-measure: A conditional entropy-based external cluster evaluation measure. In *Proc. of EMNLP-CoNLL*, pages 410–420.

Sascha Rothe, Shashi Narayan, and Aliaksei Severyn. 2019. Leveraging pre-trained checkpoints for sequence generation tasks. *arXiv preprint arXiv:1907.12461*.

Rudolph J Rummel. 1976. Understanding correlation. *Honolulu: Department of Political Science, University of Hawaii*.

Alexander M Rush, Sumit Chopra, and Jason Weston. 2015. A neural attention model for abstractive sentence summarization. In *Proc. of EMNLP*, pages 379–389.

Abigail See, Peter J Liu, and Christopher D Manning. 2017. Get to the point: Summarization with pointer-generator networks. In *Proc. of ACL*, pages 1073–1083.

Kaitao Song, Xu Tan, Tao Qin, Jianfeng Lu, and Tie-Yan Liu. 2019. MASS: Masked sequence to sequence pre-training for language generation. In *Proc. of ICML*, pages 5926–5936.

Ashish Vaswani, Noam Shazeer, Niki Parmar, Jakob Uszkoreit, Llion Jones, Aidan N Gomez, Łukasz Kaiser, and Illia Polosukhin. 2017. Attention is all you need. In *Proc. of NeurIPS*, pages 5998–6008.

Tu Vu and Mohit Iyyer. 2019. Encouraging paragraph embeddings to remember sentence identity improves classification. In *Proc. of ACL*, pages 6331–6338.

Haoyu Zhang, Jingjing Cai, Jianjun Xu, and Ji Wang. 2019. Pretraining-based natural language generation for text summarization. In *Proc. of CoNLL*, pages 789–797.

Rui Zhang and Joel Tetreault. 2019. This email could save your life: Introducing the task of email subject line generation. *Proc. of ACL*, pages 446–456.

The Unreasonable Volatility of
Neural Machine Translation Models

Marzieh Fadaee[†]
Informatics Institute
University of Amsterdam
marzieh.f@gmail.com

Christof Monz
Informatics Institute
University of Amsterdam
c.monz@uva.nl

Abstract

Recent works have shown that while Neural Machine Translation (NMT) models achieve impressive performance, questions about understanding the behaviour of these models remain unanswered. We investigate the unexpected volatility of NMT models where the input is semantically and syntactically correct. We discover that with trivial modifications of source sentences, we can identify cases where *unexpected changes* happen in the translation and in the worst case lead to mistranslations. This volatile behaviour of translating extremely similar sentences in surprisingly different ways highlights the underlying generalization problem of current NMT models. We find that both RNN and Transformer models display volatile behaviour in 26% and 19% of sentence variations, respectively.

1 Introduction

The performance of Neural Machine Translation (NMT) models has dramatically improved in recent years, and with sufficient and clean data these models outperform more traditional models. Challenges when sufficient data is not available include translations of rare words (Pham et al., 2018) and idiomatic phrases (Fadaee et al., 2018) as well as domain mismatches between training and testing (Koehn and Knowles, 2017; Khayrallah and Koehn, 2018).

Recently, several approaches investigated NMT models when encountering noisy input and how *worst-case examples* of noisy input can 'break' state-of-the-art NMT models (Goodfellow et al., 2015; Michel and Neubig, 2018). Belinkov and Bisk (2018) show that character-level noise in the input leads to poor translation performance. Lee et al. (2018) randomly insert words in different positions in the source sentence and observe that in

Source: *Ich bin* ___[1] ***erleichtert*** *und* ___[2] *bescheiden.*

[1]	[2]	NMT output
ϕ	ϕ	I am <u>easier</u> and modest.
ϕ	*sehr* [‡]	I am **relieved** and very modest.
sehr	ϕ	I am very much <u>easier</u> and modest.
sehr	*sehr*	I am very <u>easy</u> and very modest.
		Reference
ϕ	ϕ	*I am relieved and humble.*
sehr	*sehr*	*I am very relieved and very humble.*

Table 1: Insertion of the German word *sehr* (English: *very*) in different positions in the source sentence results in substantially different translations. [‡] indicates the original sentence from WMT 2017.

some cases the translations are completely unrelated to the input. While it is to some extent expected that the performance of NMT models that are trained on predominantly clean but tested on noisy data deteriorates, other changes are more unexpected.

In this paper, we explore unexpected and erroneous changes in the output of NMT models. Consider the simple example in Table 1 where the Transformer model (Vaswani et al., 2017) is used to translate very similar sentences. Surprisingly, we observe that by simply altering one word in the source sentence—inserting the German word *sehr* (English: *very*)—an unrelated change occurs in the translation. In principle, an NMT model that generates the translation of the word *erleichtert* (English: *relieved*) in one context, should also be able to generalize and translate it correctly in a very similar context. Note that there are no infrequent words in the source sentence and after each modification, the input is still syntactically correct and semantically plausible. We call a model *volatile* if it displays inconsistent behaviour across similar input sentences during inference.

We investigate to what extent well-established

[†]Marzieh is now affiliated with Zeta Alpha Vector.

Proceedings of the 4th Workshop on Neural Generation and Translation (WNGT 2020), pages 88–96
Online, July 10, 2020. ©2020 Association for Computational Linguistics
www.aclweb.org/anthology/D19-56%2d

Modification	Sentence variations
DEL	Some 500 years after the Reformation, Rome [**now**\ϕ] has a Martin Luther Square.
SUBNUM	I'm very pleased for it to have happened at Newmarket because this is where I landed [**30****31**] years ago.
INS	I loved Amy and she is [ϕ**also**] the only person who ever loved me.
SUBGEN	[**He****She**] received considerable appreciation and praise for this.

Table 2: Examples of different variations from WMT. $[w_i \backslash w_j]$ indicates that w_i in the original sentence is replaced by w_j. ϕ is an empty string.

NMT models are volatile during inference. Specifically, we locally modify sentence pairs in the test set and identify examples where a trivial modification in the source sentence causes an 'unexpected change' in the translation. These modifications are generated conservatively to avoid insertion of any noise or rare words in the data (Section 2.2). Our goal is not to *fool* NMT models, but instead identify common cases where the models exhibit unexpected behaviour and in the worst cases result in incorrect translations.

We observe that our modifications expose volatilities of both RNN and Transformer translation models in 26% and 19% of sentence variations, respectively. Our findings show how vulnerable current NMT models are to trivial linguistic variations, putting into question the generalizability of these models.

2 Sentence Variations

2.1 Is this another noisy text translation problem?

Noisy input text can cause mistranslations in most MT systems, and there has been growing research interest in studying the behaviour of MT systems when encountering noisy input (Li et al., 2019).

Belinkov and Bisk (2018) propose to swap or randomize letters in a word in the input sentence. For instance, they change the word *noise* in the source sentence into *iones*. Lee et al. (2018) examine how the insertion of a random word in a random position in the source sentence leads to mistranslations. Michel and Neubig (2018) proposes a benchmark dataset for translation of noisy input sentences, consisting of noisy, user-generated comments on Reddit. The types of noisy input text they observe include spelling or typographical errors, word omission/insertion/repetition, and grammatical errors.

In these previous works, the focus of the research is on studying how the MT systems are not robust when handling noisy input text. In these approaches, the input sentences are semantically or syntactically incorrect which leads to mistranslations.

However, in this paper, our focus is on input text that does *not* contain any types of noise. We modify input sentences in a way that the outcomes are still syntactically and semantically correct. We investigate how the MT systems exhibit volatile behaviour in translating sentences that are extremely similar and only differ in one word without any noise injection.

2.2 Variation generation

While there are various ways to automatically modify sentences, we are interested in simple semantic and syntactic modifications. These trivial linguistic variations should have almost no effect on the translation of the rest of the sentence.

We define a set of rules to slightly modify the source and target sentences in the test data and keep the sentences syntactically correct and semantically plausible.

DEL   A conservative approach of modifying a sentence automatically without breaking the grammaticality of a sentence is to remove adverbs. We identify a list of the 50 most frequent adverbs in English and their translations in German*. For every sentence in the WMT test sets, if we find a sentence pair containing both a word and its translation from this list, we remove both words and create a new sentence pair.

SUBNUM   Another simple yet effective approach to safely modify sentences is to substitute numbers with other numbers. In this approach, we select every sentence pair from the test sets that contains a number and substitute the number i in both source and target sentences with $i + k$ where $1 \leqslant k \leqslant 5$. We choose a small range for change so that the sentences are still semantically correct

---

*dict.cc

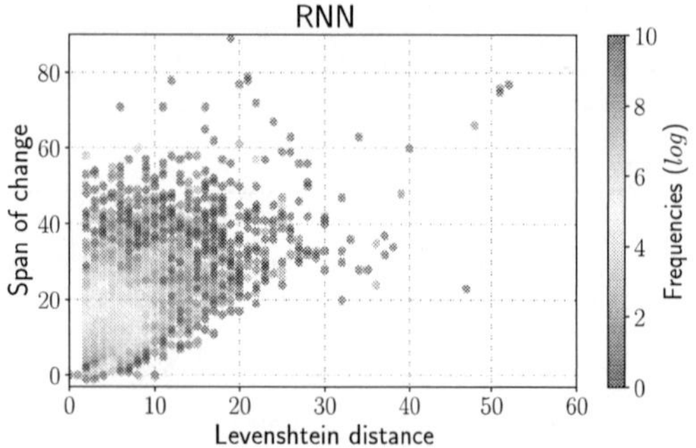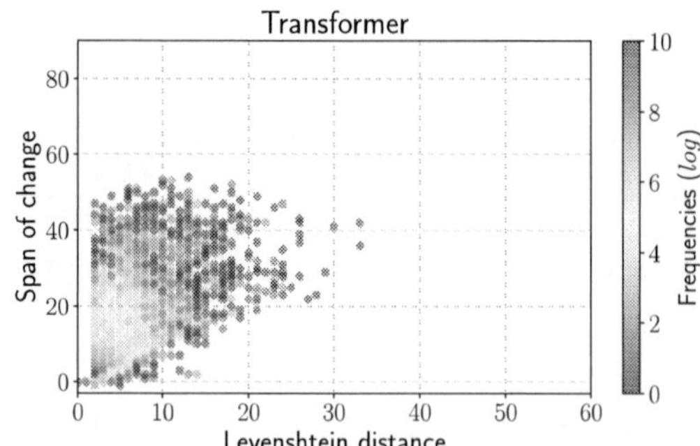

Figure 1: *Levenshtein distance* and *span of change* between translations of sentence variations for RNN and Transformer. The majority of sentence variations falls into the category of *minor* changes between translations (blue area). However, a surprising number of cases have significant changes (red area). RNN exhibits a slightly more unstable pattern i.e., sentence variations with large edit differences and large spans of change.

for the most part and result in few implausible sentences.

INS Randomly inserting words in a sentence has a high chance of producing a syntactically incorrect sentence. To ensure that sentences remain grammatical and semantically plausible after modification, we define a bidirectional n-gram probability for inserting new words as follows:

$$P(w_3|w_1w_2w_4w_5) = \frac{C(w_1w_2w_3w_4w_5)}{C(w_1w_2 \bullet w_4w_5)}$$

w_3 is inserted in the middle of the phrase $w_1w_2w_4w_5$, if the conditional probability is greater than a predefined threshold. The probabilities are computed on the WMT data. This simple approach, instead of using a more complex language model, serves our purposes since we are interested in inserting very common words that are already captured by the n-grams in the training data.

SUBGEN Finally, a local modification is changing the gender of the person in the sentences. The goal of this modification is to investigate the existence and severity of gender bias in our models. This is inspired by recent approaches that have shown that NMT models learn social stereotypes such as gender bias from training data (Escudé Font and Costa-jussà, 2019; Stanovsky et al., 2019).

Note that in a minority of cases these procedures can lead to semantically incorrect sentences, for instance, by substituting numbers we can potentially generate sentences such as *"She was*

born on October 34th". While this can cause problems for a reasoning task, it barely affects the translation task, as long as the modifications are consistent on the source and target side.

Table 2 shows examples of generated variations. We emphasize that only modifications with local consequences have been selected and we intentionally ignore cases such as *negation* which can result in wider structural changes in the translation of the sentence.

	DE-EN			EN-DE		
	2016	2017	2018	2016	2017	2018
RNN	32.5	28.2	35.2	28.1	22.4	34.6
Transformer	36.2	32.1	40.1	33.4	27.9	39.8

Table 3: BLEU scores for different models on the WMT data for translation DE↔EN.

We generate $10k$ sentence variations by applying these modifications to all sentence pairs in WMT test sets 2013–2018 (Bojar et al., 2018). We use RNN and Transformer models to translate sentences and their variations.

2.3   Experimental setup

In the translation experiments, we use the standard EN↔DE WMT-2017 training data (Bojar et al., 2018). We perform NMT experiments with two different architectures: RNN (Luong et al., 2015) and Transformer (Vaswani et al., 2017). We preprocess the training data with Byte-Pair Encoding (BPE) using 32K merge operations (Sennrich et al., 2016). During inference, we use beam search with a beam size of 5. Table 3 shows the case-sensitive BLEU scores as calculated by

Table 4: A random sample of sentences from the WMT test sets and our proposed variations shown with 'unexpected change' annotations ($\Delta Translation$). The cases where the unexpected change leads to a change in translation quality are marked in column $\Delta Quality$. [$w_i \backslash w_j$] indicates that w_i in the original sentence is replaced by w_j. S is the original and modified source sentence, R is the original and modified reference translation, T is the translation of the original sentence, and T_m is the translation of the modified sentence. Differences in translations related to annotations in the original and the modified translations are in **red** and orange, respectively. Note that we are interested in *unexpected* changes and do not highlight the changes that are a direct consequence of the modifications.

S	Coes letztes Buch "Chop Suey" handelte von der chinesischen Küche in den USA, während Ziegelman in ihrem Buch "[**97****101**] Orchard" über das Leben in einem Wohnhaus an der Lower East Side aus der Lebensmittelperspektive erzählt.
R	Mr. Coe's last book, "Chop Suey," was about Chinese cuisine in America, while Ms. Ziegelman told the story of life in a Lower East Side tenement through food in her book "[**97****101**] Orchard."
T	Coes's last book, "Chop Suey," was about Chinese cuisine in the US, while Ziegelman, **in her book "97 Orchard" talks about** living in a lower East Side.
T_m	Coes last book "Chop Suey" was about Chinese cuisine in the United States, while Ziegelman writes in her book "101 Orchard" about living in a lower East Side.

$\Delta Translation$: `[reordered] [paraphrased]`
$\Delta Quality$: `No`

S	Man hält [**bereits**\\ϕ] Ausschau nach Parkbank, Hund und Fußball spielenden Jungs und Mädels.
R	You are [**already**\\ϕ] on the lookout for a park bench, a dog, and boys and girls playing football.
T	**We are** already **looking** for Parkbank, dog and football playing boys and girls.
T_m	Look for Parkbank, dog and football playing boys and girls.

$\Delta Translation$: `[word form] [add/remove]`
$\Delta Quality$: `Yes`

S	Bei einem Unfall eines Reisebusses mit [**43****45**] Senioren als Fahrgästen sind am Donnerstag in Krummhörn (Landkreis Aurich) acht Menschen verletzt worden.
R	On Thursday, an accident involving a coach carrying [**43****45**] elderly people in Krummhörn (district of Aurich) led to eight people being injured.
T	In the event of an accident involving **a coach with 43 senior citizens as passengers**, eight people were injured on Thursday in **Krummaudin (County Aurich)**.
T_m	In the event of an accident involving a 45-year-old coach as a passenger, eight people were injured on Thursday in the district of Aurich.

$\Delta Translation$: `[word form] [add/remove] [other]`
$\Delta Quality$: `Yes`

S	Es ist ein anstrengendes Pensum, aber die Dorfmusiker helfen [**normalerweise**\\ϕ], das Team motiviert zu halten.
R	It's a backbreaking pace, but village musicians [**usually**\\ϕ] help keep the team motivated.
T	It's **a demanding child**, but the village **musicians** usually **help** keep the team motivated.
T_m	It is a hard-to-use, but the village musician helps to keep the team motivated.

$\Delta Translation$: `[word form] [other]`
$\Delta Quality$: `Yes`

`multi-bleu.perl.`

RNN As the first NMT system, we use a 2-layer bidirectional attention-based LSTM model implemented in OpenNMT (Klein et al., 2017) trained with an embedding size of 512, hidden dimension size of 1024, and batch size of 64 sentences. We use Adam (Kingma and Ba, 2015) for optimization.

Transformer We also experiment with the Transformer model (Vaswani et al., 2017) implemented in OpenNMT. We train a model with 6 layers, the hidden size is set to 512 and the fil-

ter size is set to 2048. The multi-head attention has 8 attention heads. We use Adam (Kingma and Ba, 2015) for optimization. All parameters are set based on the suggestions in Klein et al. (2017) to replicate the results of the original paper.

3   Evaluation of unexpected and erroneous changes

The modifications described above generate sentences that are extremely similar and hence are expected to have a very similar difficulty of translation. We evaluate the NMT models on how robust and consistent they are in translating these sen-

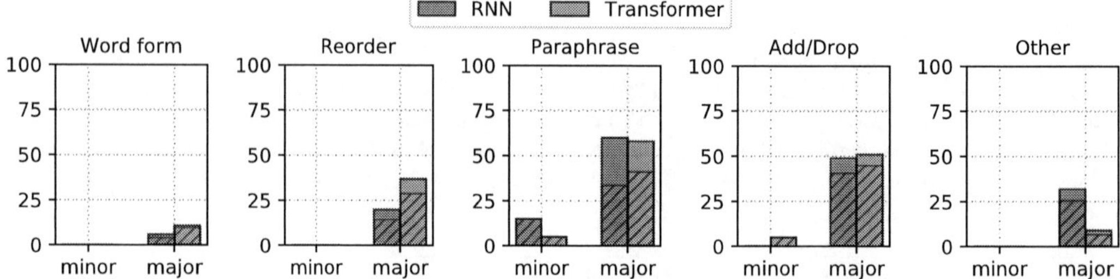

Figure 2: Categories of *unexpected changes* in the translation of sentence variations as provided by annotators. The percentage of sentence variations with *minor* and *major* edit differences, as defined in 3.1, are shown separately. The hatched pattern indicates the ratio of sentence variations for which the translation quality changes. Note that *expected changes* are not plotted here.

tence variations rather than their absolute quality.

3.1 Deviations from Original Translations

The variations are aimed to have minimal effect on changing the meaning of the sentences. Hence, major changes in the translations of these variations can be an indication of volatility in the model. To assess whether the proposed sentence variations result in major changes in the translations, we measure changes in the translations of sentence variations with Levenshtein distance (Levenshtein, 1966). Specifically, Levenshtein distance measures the edit distance between the two translations. We also use the first and last positions of change in the translations, which represents the span of changes.

Ideally, with our simple modifications, we expect a value of zero for the span of change and a value of at most 2 for the Levenshtein distance for a translation pair. This indicates that there is only one token difference between the translation of the original sentence and the modified sentence. We define two types of changes based on these measures: *minor* and *major*. We choose the threshold to distinguish between minor and major changes more conservatively to allow for more variations in the translations. The change in translations is empirically considered *major* if both metrics are greater than 10, and *minor* if both are less than 10. Note that edit distances and spans are based on BPE subword units.

With two very similar source sentences, we expect the Levenshtein distance and span of change between translations of these sentences to be small. Figure 1 shows the results for the RNN and Transformer model. While the majority of sentence variations have minor changes, a substan-

tial number of sentences, 18% of RNN and 13% of Transformer translations, result in translations with major differences. This is surprising and an indication of volatility since these trivial modifications, in principle, should only result in minor and local changes in the translations.

3.2 Oscillations of Variation in Translations

In this section, we look into various sentence-level metrics to further analyze the observed behaviour. In particular, we focus on the SUBNUM modification because with this modification we can generate numerous variations of the same sentence. Having a high number of variations for each sentence gives us the opportunity of observing oscillations of various string matching metrics.

We use sentence-level BLEU, METEOR (Denkowski and Lavie, 2011), TER (Snover et al., 2006), and LengthRatio to quantify changes in the translations. LengthRatio represents the translation length over reference length as a percentage. For a given source sentence, we define the oscillation range as changes in the sentence-level metric for the translations of variations of a given sentence.

While sentence-level metrics are not reliable indicators of translation quality, they do capture fluctuations in translations. With the variations we introduce, in theory there should be no fluctuations in the translations. Table 5 and Figure 3 provide the results. We observe that even though these sentence variations differ by only one number, there are many cases where an insignificant change in the sentence results in unexpectedly large oscillations. Both RNN and Transformer exhibit this behaviour to a certain extent.

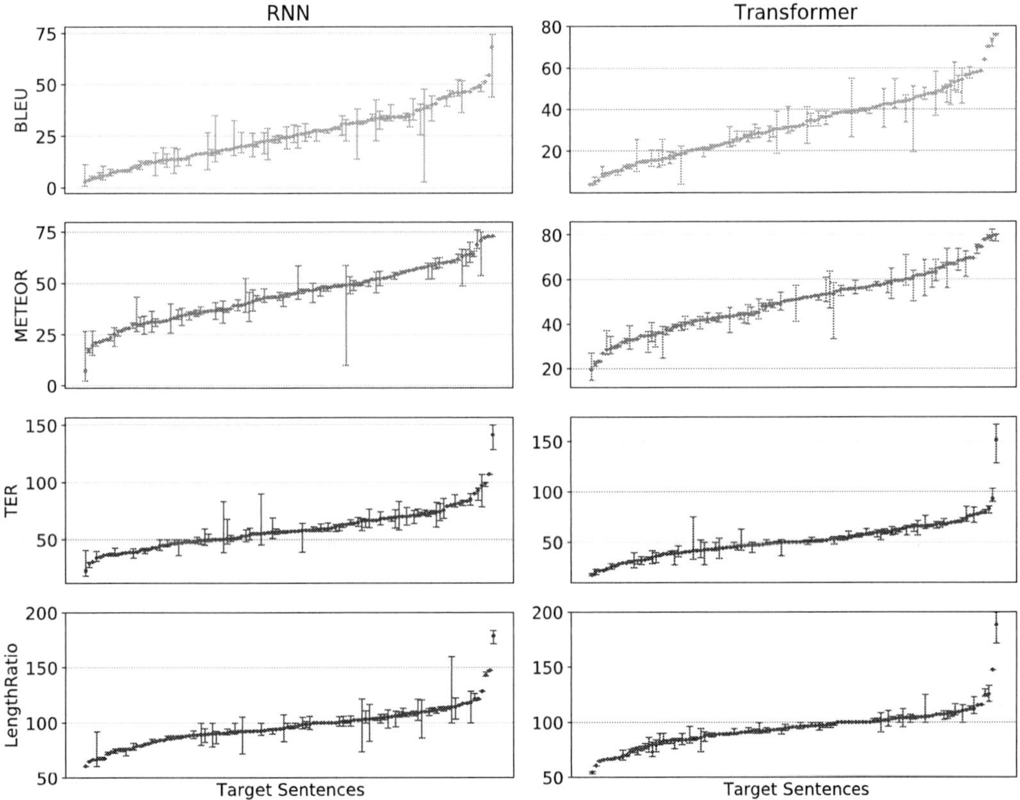

Figure 3: Oscillations of various sentence-level attributes for randomly sampled sentences from our test data and their SUBNUM variations. The data points are the mean values for all variations of each sentence, and the error bars indicate the range of oscillation of the metrics. The x-axis represents test sentence instances, sorted based on the corresponding metric. Ideally each data point should have zero oscillation.

Table 5: Mean oscillations for SUBNUM variations. In theory the variations should result in zero oscillations for every metric.

	BLEU	METEOR	TER	LengthRatio
RNN	4.0	3.8	5.2	5.3
Transformer	3.8	3.3	4.2	3.4

3.3 The Effect of Volatility on Translation Quality

While edit distances and spans of change provide some indication of volatility, they do not capture all aspects of this unexpected behaviour. It is also not entirely clear what effect these unexpected changes have on translation quality. To further investigate this, we also perform manual evaluations.

In the first evaluation, we provide annotators with a pair of sentence variations and their corresponding translations and ask them to identify the differences between the two sentence pairs. In the second evaluation, we additionally provide the source sentences and reference translations, and ask the annotators to rank the sentence variations based on the translation quality similar to Bojar et al. (2016). In total the annotators evaluated 400 randomly selected sentence quadruplets.

The annotators identified 71% and 68% of changes in the variation translation as *expected* for the RNN and Transformer model, respectively. The main types of *unexpected* changes identified by the annotators are a change of word form, e.g., verb tense,, reordering of phrases, paraphrasing parts of the sentence, and an 'other' category, e.g., preposition. A sentence pair can have multiple labels based on the types of changes. Table 4 provides examples from the test data.

Statistics for each category of unexpected change is shown in Figure 2. Our first observation is that, as to be expected, there are very few 'unexpected changes' when two variations lead to translations with *minor* differences. Interestingly, the vast majority of changes are due to paraphrasing and dropping of words. Comparing the performance of the RNN and Transformer model, we see that both RNN and Transformer display inconsistent translation behaviour. While Transformer has slightly fewer sentences with major changes, it has a higher number of sentence variations in the major category that result in a change in translation quality. From the annotators' assessments, we find that in 26% and 19% of sentence variations, the modification results in a change in *translation quality* for the RNN and Transformer model, respectively.

3.4 Generalization and Compositionality

Because of their ability to generalize beyond their training data, deep learning models achieve exceptional performances in numerous tasks. The generalization ability allows MT systems to generate long sentences not seen before. Recently there has been some interest in understanding whether this performance depends on recognizing shallow patterns, or whether the networks are indeed capturing and generalizing linguistic rules.

In simple terms, compositionality is the ability to construct larger linguistic expressions by combining simpler parts. For instance, if a model understands the correct compositional rules to understand *'John loves Mary'*, it must also understand *'Mary loves John'* (Fodor and LePore, 2002). Investigating the compositional behaviour of neural networks in real-world natural language problems is a challenging task. Recently, several works have studied deep learning models' understanding of compositionality in natural language by using synthetic and simplified languages (Andreas, 2019; Chevalier-Boisvert et al., 2019). Baroni (2019) shows that to a certain extent neural networks can be productive without being compositional.

Although we do not specifically look into the compositional potential of MT systems, we are inspired by compositionality in defining our modifications. We argue that the observed volatile behaviour of the MT systems in this paper is a side effect of current models not being compositional. If an MT system has a good 'understanding' of the underlying structures of the sentences *'Mary is 10 years old'* and *'Mary is 11 years old'*, it must also translate them very similarly regardless of the accuracy of the translation. While current evaluation metrics capture the accuracy of the NMT models, these volatilities go unnoticed.

Current neural models are successful in generalizing without learning any explicit compositional rules, however, our findings signal that they still lack robustness. We highlight this lack of robustness and suspect that it is associated with these models' lack of understanding of the compositional nature of language.

4 Conclusion

In this paper, we showed the unexpected volatility of NMT models by using a simple approach to modifying standard test sentences without introducing noise, i.e., by generating semantically and syntactically correct variations. We show that even with trivial linguistic modifications of source sentences we can effectively identify a surprising number of cases where the translations of extremely similar sentences are surprisingly different, see Figure 1. Our manual analyses show that both RNN and Transformer models exhibit volatile behaviour with changes in translation quality for 26% and 19% of sentence variations, respectively. This highlights the problem of generalizability of current NMT models and we hope that our insights will be useful for developing more robust NMT models.

Acknowledgments

We thank Arianna Bisazza for helpful discussions. This research was funded in part by the Netherlands Organization for Scientific Research (NWO) under project numbers 639.022.213 and 612.001.218. We also thank NVIDIA for their hardware support and the anonymous reviewers for their helpful comments.

References

Jacob Andreas. 2019. Measuring compositionality in representation learning. *CoRR*, abs/1902.07181.

Marco Baroni. 2019. Linguistic generalization and compositionality in modern artificial neural networks. *CoRR*, abs/1904.00157.

Yonatan Belinkov and Yonatan Bisk. 2018. Synthetic and natural noise both break neural machine translation. In *Proceedings of the International Conference on Learning Representations (ICLR)*.

Ondřej Bojar, Rajen Chatterjee, Christian Federmann, Yvette Graham, Barry Haddow, Matthias Huck, Antonio Jimeno Yepes, Philipp Koehn, Varvara Logacheva, Christof Monz, Matteo Negri, Aurelie Neveol, Mariana Neves, Martin Popel, Matt Post, Raphael Rubino, Carolina Scarton, Lucia Specia, Marco Turchi, Karin Verspoor, and Marcos Zampieri. 2016. Findings of the 2016 conference on machine translation. In *Proceedings of the First Conference on Machine Translation*, pages 131–198, Berlin, Germany. Association for Computational Linguistics.

Ondřej Bojar, Christian Federmann, Mark Fishel, Yvette Graham, Barry Haddow, Matthias Huck, Philipp Koehn, and Christof Monz. 2018. Findings of the 2018 conference on machine translation (wmt18). In *Proceedings of the Third Conference on Machine Translation, Volume 2: Shared Task Papers*, pages 272–307, Belgium, Brussels. Association for Computational Linguistics.

Maxime Chevalier-Boisvert, Dzmitry Bahdanau, Salem Lahlou, Lucas Willems, Chitwan Saharia, Thien Huu Nguyen, and Yoshua Bengio. 2019. BabyAI: First steps towards grounded language learning with a human in the loop. In *International Conference on Learning Representations*.

Michael Denkowski and Alon Lavie. 2011. Meteor 1.3: Automatic metric for reliable optimization and evaluation of machine translation systems. In *Proceedings of the Sixth Workshop on Statistical Machine Translation*, pages 85–91, Edinburgh, Scotland. Association for Computational Linguistics.

Joel Escudé Font and Marta R. Costa-jussà. 2019. Equalizing gender bias in neural machine translation with word embeddings techniques. In *Proceedings of the First Workshop on Gender Bias in Natural Language Processing*, pages 147–154, Florence, Italy. Association for Computational Linguistics.

Marzieh Fadaee, Arianna Bisazza, and Christof Monz. 2018. Examining the tip of the iceberg: A data set for idiom translation. In *Proceedings of the Eleventh International Conference on Language Resources and Evaluation (LREC-2018)*. European Language Resource Association.

J.A. Fodor and E. LePore. 2002. *The Compositionality Papers*. Clarendon Press.

G. Frege. 1892. "uber sinn und bedeutung. In Mark Textor, editor, *Funktion - Begriff - Bedeutung*, volume 4 of *Sammlung Philosophie*. Vandenhoeck & Ruprecht, G"ottingen.

Ian J Goodfellow, Jonathon Shlens, and Christian Szegedy. 2015. Explaining and harnessing adversarial examples. In *Proceedings of the International Conference on Learning Representations (ICLR)*.

Theo M. V. Janssen. 2001. Frege, contextuality and compositionality. *Journal of Logic, Language and Information*, 10(1):115–136.

Huda Khayrallah and Philipp Koehn. 2018. On the impact of various types of noise on neural machine translation. In *Proceedings of the 2nd Workshop on Neural Machine Translation and Generation*, pages 74–83. Association for Computational Linguistics.

Diederik P Kingma and Jimmy Lei Ba. 2015. Adam: A method for stochastic optimization. In *Proceedings of the International Conference on Learning Representations (ICLR)*.

Guillaume Klein, Yoon Kim, Yuntian Deng, Jean Senellart, and Alexander Rush. 2017. Opennmt: Open-source toolkit for neural machine translation. In *Proceedings of ACL 2017, System Demonstrations*, pages 67–72. Association for Computational Linguistics.

Philipp Koehn and Rebecca Knowles. 2017. Six challenges for neural machine translation. *arXiv preprint arXiv:1706.03872*.

Katherine Lee, Orhan Firat, Ashish Agarwal, Clara Fannjiang, and David Sussillo. 2018. Hallucinations in neural machine translation. In *Neural Information Processing Systems (NeurIPS) Workshop on Interpretability and Robustness for Audio, Speech, and Language*. NeurIPS.

Vladimir I Levenshtein. 1966. Binary codes capable of correcting deletions, insertions, and reversals. *Soviet physics doklady*, 10(8):707–710.

Xian Li, Paul Michel, Antonios Anastasopoulos, Yonatan Belinkov, Nadir Durrani, Orhan Firat, Philipp Koehn, Graham Neubig, Juan Pino, and Hassan Sajjad. 2019. Findings of the first shared task on machine translation robustness. In *Proceedings of the Fourth Conference on Machine Translation (Volume 2: Shared Task Papers, Day 1)*, pages 91–102, Florence, Italy. Association for Computational Linguistics.

Thang Luong, Hieu Pham, and Christopher D. Manning. 2015. Effective approaches to attention-based neural machine translation. In *Proceedings of the 2015 Conference on Empirical Methods in Natural Language Processing*, pages 1412–1421, Lisbon, Portugal. Association for Computational Linguistics.

Paul Michel and Graham Neubig. 2018. Mtnt: A testbed for machine translation of noisy text. In *Proceedings of the 2018 Conference on Empirical Methods in Natural Language Processing*, pages 543–553. Association for Computational Linguistics.

Richard Montague. 1974. Universal grammar. In *Formal Philosophy: Selected Papers of Richard Montague*, number 222–247 in Theoria, New Haven, London. Yale University Press.

Francis Jeffry Pelletier. 1994. The principle of semantic compositionality. *Topoi*, 13:11–24.

Ngoc-Quan Pham, Jan Niehues, and Alexander Waibel.
2018. Towards one-shot learning for rare-word
translation with external experts. In *Proceedings
of the 2nd Workshop on Neural Machine Translation and Generation*, pages 100–109. Association
for Computational Linguistics.

Rico Sennrich, Barry Haddow, and Alexandra Birch.
2016. Neural machine translation of rare words
with subword units. In *Proceedings of the 54th Annual Meeting of the Association for Computational
Linguistics (Volume 1: Long Papers)*, pages 1715–
1725, Berlin, Germany. Association for Computational Linguistics.

Matthew Snover, Bonnie Dorr, Richard Schwartz, Lin-
nea Micciulla, and John Makhoul. 2006. A study
of translation edit rate with targeted human annotation. In *In Proceedings of Association for Machine
Translation in the Americas*, pages 223–231.

Gabriel Stanovsky, Noah A. Smith, and Luke Zettlemoyer. 2019. Evaluating gender bias in machine
translation. In *Proceedings of the 57th Annual Meeting of the Association for Computational Linguistics*, pages 1679–1684, Florence, Italy. Association
for Computational Linguistics.

Ashish Vaswani, Noam Shazeer, Niki Parmar, Jakob
Uszkoreit, Llion Jones, Aidan N Gomez, Ł ukasz
Kaiser, and Illia Polosukhin. 2017. Attention is all
you need. In I. Guyon, U. V. Luxburg, S. Bengio,
H. Wallach, R. Fergus, S. Vishwanathan, and R. Garnett, editors, *Advances in Neural Information Processing Systems 30*, pages 5998–6008. Curran Associates, Inc.

Leveraging Sentence Similarity in Natural Language Generation: Improving Beam Search using Range Voting

Sebastian Borgeaud
DeepMind & University of Cambridge
sborgeaud@google.com

Guy Emerson
University of Cambridge
gete2@cam.ac.uk

Abstract

We propose a method for natural language generation, choosing the most representative output rather than the most likely output. By viewing the language generation process from the voting theory perspective, we define representativeness using range voting and a similarity measure. The proposed method can be applied when generating from any probabilistic language model, including n-gram models and neural network models. We evaluate different similarity measures on an image captioning task and a machine translation task, and show that our method generates longer and more diverse sentences, providing a solution to the common problem of short outputs being preferred over longer and more informative ones. The generated sentences obtain higher BLEU scores, particularly when the beam size is large. We also perform a human evaluation on both tasks and find that the outputs generated using our method are rated higher.

1 Introduction

A language model specifies a probability distribution over sequences of words: given a sequence $s = x_1 x_2 \cdots x_n$ of length n, the model assigns a probability $P(s)$ to the entire sequence. The probability distribution may be conditioned: for example in machine translation the distribution is conditioned on the source language sentence.

In many applications, it is desirable to output a single sequence, rather than a distribution. A common approach is to choose the most likely sequence. However, this is problematic when the most likely sequence is not *representative* of the whole distribution.

For example, in dialogue generation tasks, the most likely output can be "I don't know", even when most of the probability mass is assigned to long informative sequences. Cao and Clark (2017) call this the "boring output problem".

For a real-valued distribution, we can choose a representative output by taking the mean. However, for a discrete distribution (such as over sequences), the mean is not defined. In this paper, we choose a representative output using tools from voting theory, allowing us to avoid the boring output problem. The general idea is that, if the distribution assigns most of the probability mass to a group of similar sequences, we would like to generate one of them – even if they have low probability as individual sequences, they have high probability as a group. We can formulate this process as a range voting election, where the sentences vote for each other, with the strength of a vote being proportional to the similarity between the voter sequence and the candidate sequence.

Our approach can be used to mitigate problems commonly associated with language models. For example, a long-recognised problem is that shorter sequences are assigned higher probabilities and thus choosing the most likely sequence favours short sequences (Brown et al., 1995). Indeed, Stahlberg and Byrne (2019) show that the most likely output in machine translation is often the empty string. By designing the similarity function to be asymmetric such that more informative candidate sequences receive stronger votes, we can generate longer and more diverse outputs (see Fig. 1 for an example).

We focus on simple similarity metrics based on n-grams and generate the candidates and voters using beam search. We evaluate on two tasks: image captioning and machine translation. For both tasks, we find that our approach achieves higher BLEU scores, and performs better in a human evaluation. Our approach also generates longer and more diverse outputs, with the generated length and diversity more closely matching the length and diversity of the reference captions and reference translations.

Proceedings of the 4th Workshop on Neural Generation and Translation (WNGT 2020), pages 97–109
Online, July 10, 2020. ©2020 Association for Computational Linguistics
www.aclweb.org/anthology/D19-56%2d

Figure 1: Image from the MSCOCO validation dataset and beam search captions with their probabilities (beam size k=10). See §3.1 for beam search, §4.1 for the sequence model. Range voting with overlap_2 similarity (see §3.2) on this set of sequences selects "a black and white photo of a man sitting on a bench", which shares many bigrams with other sequences.

2 Related work

Much work has gone into analysing sources of errors in language generation, often focused on machine translation. Koehn and Knowles (2017) raise 6 challenges for machine translation, including degrading performance for longer sentences, and degrading performance for larger beam sizes. Stahlberg and Byrne (2019) distinguish *model errors* (high probabilities of bad sequences) and *search errors* (failing to find sequences preferred by the model). They show that the global optimal translations (according to likelihood) are considerably worse than translations found by beam search. This points to both serious model errors and serious search errors, which cancel out to some degree. This suggests there is much work to be done in improving both our models and our search objectives – the latter is the aim of this paper.

Ott et al. (2018) find that beam search typically covers only a small proportion of the model's probability mass,[1] and they show that the degradation for large beams is at least partly due to the training data containing target sentences that are exact copies of source sentences. They also suggest that beam search is an effective search strategy, for the maximum-likelihood search objective, finding hypotheses with higher model probabilities than the reference translations.

Cohen and Beck (2019) also find a performance degradation with larger beam sizes across different tasks (translation, image captioning and summarisation) and propose to add a search discrepancy

heuristic to beam search. For image captioning, Vinyals et al. (2017) show that larger beams not only decrease performance but also reduce the diversity of the captions. They claim this is an overfitting effect and propose the use of small beam sizes as further regularization.

In unconditional, open-ended language generation, Holtzman et al. (2020) find that using likelihood as the decoding objective leads to bland and repetitive text with unnaturally high probability and too little variance. They claim this is not due to a search error, but due to the maximum-likelihood decoding objective. They propose sampling, truncated the distribution to the top p percent of tokens.

2.1 Generation length and diversity

To increase the length and diversity of a model's outputs, some authors have proposed changes to the model architecture. In dialogue generation, Cao and Clark (2017) use a latent variable model to capture the possible "topics" of a response.

Others have proposed changing the objective function. In dialogue generation, Li et al. (2016a) optimise mutual information instead of probability. In machine translation, Tu et al. (2017) modify an encoder-decoder model by adding a "reconstructor" to predict the input based on the output.

However, modifying the model or the objective function depends on the particular task, and applying these techniques to an existing system requires retraining the model. In this paper, we focus on general methods which can be applied to any probabilistic model in any generation task. Length normalisation (Wu et al., 2016; Freitag and Al-Onaizan, 2017) explicitly penalises shorter sequences during the beam expansion phase by dividing the log-probability of a sequence by its length. Diverse decoding (Li et al., 2016b; Li and Jurafsky, 2016) penalises repeated expansions of the same beam node. Diverse beam search (Vijayakumar et al., 2018) penalises generation of similar beams using their Hamming diversity. These last two methods aim to increase the diversity within a beam, but not necessarily across the dataset.

Kool et al. (2019) propose a stochastic beam search based on the Gumbel-Top-k trick to sample without replacement. The proposed approach can trade-off BLEU score against translation diversity.

Finally, it is important to make sure that improvements to a model can be properly evaluated. After our paper was submitted, Freitag et al. (2020) re-

---

[1]Since our paper was submitted, this finding was replicated by Eikema and Aziz (2020), who further argue that the maximum-likelihood decoding objective is hard to justify when the maximum likelihood is so low.

port that the references used in machine translation often exhibit poor diversity, which can unfairly penalise models which exhibit good diversity. They propose to use paraphrased reference translations instead. These paraphrases yield higher correlation with human judgement when evaluated using BLEU, and could be used in future work to improve the evaluation of translation systems which aim to generate appropriately diverse outputs.

2.2 Minimum Bayes Risk Decoding

Kumar and Byrne (2004) introduce the Minimum Bayes Risk (MBR) decoder for machine translation. Like our proposed approach, this aims to use the whole distribution, rather than picking the most likely sequence. They frame the problem in terms of Bayes Risk: given the true distribution over outputs, and given a loss function between the system output and the target output, the Bayes Risk is defined as the expected loss. The best output is the one which minimises the Bayes Risk.

However, the true distribution over outputs is not known, so Kumar and Byrne approximate it using the model's distribution. The MBR decoder first uses beam search, and then re-ranks it according to the BLEU scores between sequences in the beam.

Tromble et al. (2008) apply MBR over translation lattices. Shimizu et al. (2012) use MBR with a smoothed BLEU loss function and propose to limit the possible translations to those that are similar to most-likely translation generated by beam search.

Blain et al. (2017) propose to re-rank the sentences generated by beam search using a similarity metric. Their approach is similar to ours but doesn't include the probability of the sentences given by the decoder, and thus would degrade completely in the limit of very large beam sizes. They find that using BLEU as a similarity metric reduces the quality of generated translations, according to both BLEU and a human evaluation.

3 Method

3.1 Beam search

When working with a distribution over sequences, it is not feasible to consider all possible sequences. Finding the most likely sequence can be computationally expensive – in fact, for an RNN it is undecidable in the general case (Chen et al., 2018). A common solution is to use **beam search**, which generates the sequence one token at a time, maintaining a list of the k most promising sequences at each time step (for example: Brown et al., 1995; Koehn, 2004a). **Greedy search** is the special case where $k = 1$.

Beam search introduces an extra hyperparameter, the beam size k. Increasing k covers more of the search space, but increases the computational cost. It is tempting to assume that increasing k will produce better results, but empirically, the quality of the most likely sequence starts to decrease after k exceeds a certain threshold (Koehn and Knowles, 2017; Cohen and Beck, 2019).

In the next section, we propose an alternative way to generate from a beam, which aims to avoid the drop in performance as beam size increases. Rather than choosing the most *likely* sequence, we choose the most *representative* sequence.

3.2 Range voting

To formalise representativeness, we propose to use a voting procedure. Although voting has been applied to ensembles of classifiers (for an overview, see: Kuncheva, 2004; Kuncheva and Rodríguez, 2014), we are not aware of work using voting to select from a distribution.

We can see each sequence as a candidate in an election, and the probability of a sequence as the proportion of votes for that candidate. From this perspective, the problem of probability mass being split across long sequences is the well-known problem of **vote splitting**. Suppose candidate i wins an election. Now suppose we run the election again, but add an additional candidate j, identical to i. A voting system is robust against vote splitting (and called **independent of clones**) if the winner must be i or j (Tideman, 1987).

A well-studied system which is independent of clones is **range voting** (Heckscher, 1892; Smith, 2000; Tideman, 2006; Lagerspetz, 2016). Each voter scores each candidate in the range $[0, 1]$, and the candidate with the highest total score wins.

In our setting, probability mass can be seen as the proportion of votes placing a candidate as first choice (see Fig. 1 for an example). For range voting, we need to augment the votes with scores for all other candidates. We propose to do this using a similarity measure. The final score for a sequence $\mathbf{c} \in \mathcal{C}$ (the set of candidates) is given in (1), for a set of voter sequences $\mathcal{V}$ and a similarity measure sim.

$$\text{score}(\mathbf{c}) = \sum_{\mathbf{v} \in \mathcal{V}} P(\mathbf{v}) \cdot \text{sim}(\mathbf{v}, \mathbf{c}) \qquad (1)$$

A sequence can act as both voter and candidate. Each voter sequence is weighted by its probability, and casts a vote for each candidate sequence, where the strength of the vote is the similarity between the voter and the candidate. The simplest way to apply this method is to use beam search to define both the set of candidates and the set of voters.

This can be seen as a generalisation of taking an average. In a Euclidean space, the mean is equivalent to voting with quadratic similarity $1 - k(x - y)^2$, and the median is equivalent to voting with linear similarity $1 - k|x - y|$, for some constant k.

Although the vote splitting problem may appear abstract, it can happen in practice, even without considering similarity. When using subword vocabularies (Sennrich et al., 2016), there are multiple ways of encoding any given sentence. The model's probability mass is split across sentences with identical surface form but different encodings.

Defining semantic similarity between sentences is recognised as a hard problem (Achananuparp et al., 2008; Cer et al., 2017; Pawar and Mago, 2019). In this work, we focus on simple, domain-agnostic similarity measures which do not require additional training.

First, we consider similarity based on n-grams. For a sequence $\mathbf{s}$, we write $\mathrm{set}_n(\mathbf{s})$ for its set of n-grams, and $\mathrm{bag}_n(\mathbf{s})$ for its bag (or multiset) of n-grams. We define two measures in (2–3). Both are asymmetric, to encourage informative sequences: if $\mathbf{c}$ contains $\mathbf{v}$ plus more information, $\mathrm{sim}(\mathbf{v}, \mathbf{c})$ should be high, but if $\mathbf{c}$ contains less information, then $\mathrm{sim}(\mathbf{v}, \mathbf{c})$ should be lower. This allows an informative candidate sequence to gather more votes.

$$\mathrm{precision}_n(\mathbf{v}, \mathbf{c}) = \frac{|\,\mathrm{bag}_n(\mathbf{v}) \cap \mathrm{bag}_n(\mathbf{c})\,|}{|\,\mathrm{bag}_n(\mathbf{v})\,|} \quad (2)$$

$$\mathrm{overlap}_n(\mathbf{v}, \mathbf{c}) = \frac{|\,\mathrm{set}_n(\mathbf{v}) \cap \mathrm{set}_n(\mathbf{c})\,|}{|\,\mathrm{set}_n(\mathbf{v})\,|} \quad (3)$$

Second, inspired by Mueller and Thyagarajan (2016), we consider a similarity measure based on the hidden states of the decoders (LSTM and Transformer) during generation (see §4.1). For each sequence, we find the average of the hidden states, and then compute the cosine similarity. We refer to this measure as lstm_states and transformer_states.

3.3　Comparison with MBR Decoding

The formulation used for range voting is reminiscent of MBR decoding (see §2.2). In fact, if the similarity measure in (1) is $\mathrm{sim}(\mathbf{v}, \mathbf{c}) = \mathrm{BLEU}(\mathbf{c}, \mathbf{v})$, range voting recovers MBR decoding. From a theoretical point of view, range voting provides an independent motivation for MBR decoding, and furthermore, one which does not require the assumption that we can approximate the true distribution by the model's distribution. We know that the model's distribution does not match the true distribution (or else we would have already solved the task), and so this is a strong assumption to make.

From a practical point of view, range voting suggests that any similarity measure could be used, and not necessarily the evaluation metric. Using BLEU has several disadvantages. Firstly, BLEU can be harsh: when there are no 3- or 4-gram matches, the score is 0. Secondly, BLEU is a corpus-level metric which does not decompose over sentences. Finally, BLEU is precision-based, penalising translations containing information that is not in the reference. In MBR, this means that candidate sequences are penalised for containing more information than voter sequences. Our proposed similarity measures are asymmetric in the opposite direction, to encourage generation of long and informative sequences.

Indeed, in our experiments, we have found that simple similarity measures produce longer and more diverse sentences than BLEU, and for translation better results, even though BLEU is used as the evaluation metric.

Furthermore, the voting theory perspective can yield analytical insights even when range voting is not used. For example, the performance degradation found by Cohen and Beck (2019) can be interpreted in terms of vote splitting. They argue for the need to filter out sequences which begin with a low-probability token that is followed by very-high-probability tokens, in favour of sequences where all tokens have fairly high probability. The sequences they want to filter out have *not* split the vote (later tokens have probability close to 1, so there are no similar sequences that have high probability), but the sequences they want to keep *have* split the vote (there are similar sequences with similar probability). Their method aims to remove these problematic sequences that don't split the vote, while our method aims to be robust against vote splitting.

| | BLEU-1 | | | | BLEU-4 | | | |
Beam size k	1	2	10	100	1	2	10	100
Beam search	66.66	67.97	67.22	66.18	25.39	26.83	27.16	26.31
Length normalisation	66.66	68.47	64.72	63.10	25.39	26.72	25.76	24.72
Diverse decoding	66.66	67.90	67.24	66.43	25.39	26.68	26.93	26.37
overlap$_1$	66.66	**68.55**	66.26	66.36	25.39	26.47	25.61	24.60
precision$_1$	66.66	68.54	66.31	66.46	25.39	26.47	25.62	24.58
overlap$_2$	66.66	68.20	67.36	67.19	25.39	26.82	27.22	27.13
precision$_2$	66.66	68.20	67.63	67.21	25.39	26.82	27.23	27.13
lstm_states	66.66	67.97	**68.42**	69.10	25.39	**26.83**	**27.96**	28.23
bleu$_4$ (MBR)	66.66	67.93	67.66	68.56	25.39	26.83	27.80	28.71
smoothed_bleu$_4$ (MBR)	66.66	67.98	67.87	**69.45**	25.39	26.84	27.89	**29.19**

Table 1: BLEU-1 and BLEU-4 scores obtained on the MSCOCO validation images.

4 Experiments

We evaluate our method on two tasks: image captioning and machine translation. For MBR, we use BLEU (bleu$_4$) and a smoothed version of BLEU (smoothed_bleu$_4$) which adds 1 to the n-gram counts for $n>1$ to mitigate the harshness of the metric (Shimizu et al., 2012).

We consider two baselines: length normalisation and diverse decoding, described in §2.1. For machine translation, we also consider diverse beam search as a further baseline. Other methods mentioned in §2 cannot be straightforwardly applied as they require modifying the model or the training objective.

4.1 Image captioning

We use the MSCOCO dataset (Lin et al., 2014), which consists of 82,783 training images and 40,504 validation images, each annotated with 5 captions from human annotators.

We use the "Show and Tell" encoder-decoder architecture of Vinyals et al. (2015). The encoder is a pretrained Inception V3 CNN (Szegedy et al., 2016) from which we extract a feature vector from the final pooling layer (Ioffe and Szegedy, 2015). The decoder is an LSTM (Hochreiter and Schmidhuber, 1997) with 512 hidden units, initialising the hidden state using the encoder. The vocabulary consists of the 5000 most common words in the training captions, for which embeddings of size 512 are learned from scratch.

4.1.1 BLEU scores

Table 1 shows BLEU scores (Papineni et al., 2002) on the MSCOCO validation set computed using NLTK (Bird et al., 2009). The bigram similarity measures and the lstm_states measure improve BLEU scores for almost all beam sizes. In contrast, diverse decoding has almost no effect on BLEU, while length normalisation performs worse than standard beam search. The best result with our similarity metrics is achieved by lstm_states at $k=100$. This is significantly better than the best result for standard beam search ($k=10$), with $p<0.001$ for a paired bootstrap test following Koehn (2004b). Using smoothed_bleu$_4$ and increasing the beam size to $k=100$ gives the overall best results.

Sampling methods proposed for open-ended generation perform poorly. Top-k sampling (Fan et al., 2018) achieves BLEU scores of 17.15 ($k=4$) and 13.79 ($k=10$), nucleus sampling (Holtzman et al., 2020) achieves a score of 13.62 (top_p=0.9)

Consistent with Ott et al. (2018) and Koehn and Knowles (2017), increasing k with beam search too much reduces BLEU. However, this drop does not occur for our voting method.

4.1.2 Caption length

To analyse differences between methods, we first look at caption length, shown in Table 3. Standard beam search produces slightly longer captions as k increases up to 10. All n-gram measures generate longer captions than standard beam search, and length continues to increase as k goes to 100. Length normalisation also increases caption length, but this is at the cost of BLEU score (see §4.1.1). Diverse decoding does not increase caption length. The lstm_states measure produces slightly shorter captions – as it is symmetric, it does not favour long sequences as the asymmetric n-gram measures do (see §3.2). As predicted by our range voting interpretation, MBR, for which the asymmetry is in the

	Distinct captions			Distinct unigrams			Distinct bigrams		
Beam size k	2	10	100	2	10	100	2	10	100
Beam search	9208	5488	4150	668	621	605	3395	2778	2479
Length normalisation	9978	6418	5039	681	627	587	3502	2863	2471
Diverse decoding	9942	6424	4403	672	646	612	3402	3023	2561
overlap$_1$	**10727**	**8916**	**10808**	**687**	**646**	628	**3576**	3232	3596
precision$_1$	**10727**	8902	10768	**687**	645	638	3572	**3238**	**3607**
overlap$_2$	9519	7598	9221	673	620	580	3446	2854	2887
precision$_2$	9522	7590	9248	673	620	581	3444	2848	2892
lstm_states	9208	7613	10133	668	629	**655**	3395	2891	3331
bleu$_4$ (MBR)	9159	6512	6763	667	612	570	3392	2666	2446
smoothed_bleu$_4$ (MBR)	9206	6522	7019	667	613	560	3396	2675	2415

Table 2: Number of distinct captions, unigrams and bigrams in the generated captions.

	Average caption length			
Beam size k	1	2	10	100
Beam search	8.41	8.79	9.18	9.11
Length norm.	8.41	9.19	10.24	10.43
Diverse decod.	8.41	8.71	9.12	9.15
overlap$_1$	8.41	**9.22**	**10.40**	**11.20**
precision$_1$	8.41	9.21	10.38	11.15
overlap$_2$	8.41	8.96	9.86	10.55
precision$_2$	8.41	8.96	9.86	10.55
lstm_states	8.41	8.79	9.17	8.82
bleu$_4$ (MBR)	8.41	8.77	9.27	9.32
smoothed_bleu$_4$	8.41	8.79	9.24	9.13

Table 3: Average length of the generated captions. The reference captions contain on average 10.59 words.

opposite direction, produces shorter captions than the simple n-gram similarity metrics.

4.1.3 Caption diversity

Following the approach of Li et al. (2016a), Dhingra et al. (2017), and Xu et al. (2017, 2018), we investigate the diversity of the generated captions by counting the number of distinct captions, unigrams, and bigrams (see Table 2).

For standard beam search, the number of distinct captions drops as k increases. Both baselines weaken this effect, but the drop is still present. In contrast, range voting maintains caption diversity as k increases, for all similarity measures.

Similarly, standard beam search sees a drop in the number of distinct unigrams and bigrams as k increases, and the baselines do not seem to mitigate this. In contrast, the unigram measures and the lstm_states measure maintain both unigram diversity and bigram diversity as k increases, while the

bigram measures partially maintain bigram diversity. As expected from our range voting perspective, MBR generates less diverse captions.

4.1.4 Human evaluation

BLEU is known to be imperfect, and does not always match human judgements (Callison-Burch et al., 2006; Blain et al., 2017). While the n-gram similarity measures produce similar BLEU scores to standard beam search, they also produce longer captions, which are potentially more informative. To investigate whether they are more informative in way that is not reflected by BLEU, we took 500 validation images for human evaluation, comparing the captions produced by standard beam search (k=10) against our best-performing n-gram measure (precision$_2$, k=100). Each pair of captions was presented in a random order, with the original image, and judged on a five-point scale (one caption much better, slightly better, or no difference).

The voted caption was rated better 106 times, and worse 73 times. This is statistically significant, with p=0.0165 for a two-tailed sign test, discarding ties (Emerson and Simon, 1979). However, for captions rated much better, the voted caption was better 27 times and worse 40 times. This is suggestive but not fully significant (p=0.142).

These results support the claim that a voted caption represents more of the information present in a model's distribution over captions – this often leads to a better caption, but where the model is wrong, adding wrong information can make the caption much worse. After all, our method is designed as a better way to select from a distribution, not as an improvement to the distribution itself.

Beam size k	1	2	4	10	30	100
Beam search	24.04	25.10	25.36	24.91	23.46	20.56
Length normalisation	24.04	25.19	**25.59**	25.55	24.40	21.78
Diverse decoding	24.04	24.88	25.17	24.71	23.49	20.82
Diverse beam search	24.04	24.55	24.70	23.93	22.14	18.38
Beam search (no copy)	23.96	25.10	25.43	25.23	24.38	22.59
overlap$_1$	23.96	25.17	25.48	25.55	24.97	24.20
precision$_1$	23.96	25.17	25.47	25.54	24.95	24.21
overlap$_2$	23.96	25.14	25.49	**25.70**	**25.08**	**24.62**
precision$_2$	23.96	**25.20**	25.53	25.39	24.69	23.96
transformer_states	23.96	25.10	25.44	25.51	24.67	23.36
bleu$_4$ (MBR)	23.96	25.09	25.42	25.51	24.79	23.53
smoothed_bleu$_4$ (MBR)	23.96	25.10	25.42	25.51	24.81	23.65

Table 4: BLEU scores on newstest2014, with range voting applied to the beams obtained with no-copy filtering.

4.2 Machine translation

For the translation task, we use the WMT'14 English-German dataset, consisting of 4.5M sentence pairs. We train a Transformer 'big' model (Vaswani et al., 2017), implemented in the Tensor2Tensor library (Vaswani et al., 2018). We use the joint source and target byte-pair encoding vocabulary (Sennrich et al., 2016) with 32,000 tokens available on Tensor2Tensor. All results reported are for the newstest2014 test set, containing 2737 sentence pairs (Bojar et al., 2014).[2] The BLEU scores were computed using SacreBleu (Post, 2018).

Ott et al. (2018) found that a common source of model error comes from outputting a copy of the input sentence, still in the source language. We also observe this phenomenon: with beam size 4, 0.4% of the outputs are exact copies of the input. This increases to 3.8% of the outputs for beam size 100. When counting the number of partial copies[3] the effect is even stronger: for beam sizes 4 and 100, respectively 1.3% and 12.4% of the generated translations are partial copies. Because of this, we add the method proposed by Ott et al.

(2018), which filters out partial copies during beam search, as an extra baseline.

4.2.1 BLEU scores

The BLEU scores obtained on the WMT'14 En-De newstest2014 test set are shown in Table 4.

For beam search and all considered baselines, the scores for the larger beam sizes drop considerably. Adding the copy pruning heuristic from Ott et al. (2018) does help mitigate this problem somewhat but does not solve it: there is almost a 3 BLEU point drop between $k{=}4$ and $k{=}100$.

To decouple a trivial source of model errors (input copies) from search errors, we apply our range voting method on the beams obtained with the filtering heuristic (Table 4, bottom half). Regardless of which similarity metric is used, re-ranking using range voting improves the BLEU score, and with the overlap$_2$ similarity, we achieve the best overall score of 25.70. Furthermore, the performance drop at large beam sizes is reduced when using range voting to about 1 BLEU point for overlap$_2$.

There are two possible reasons for lower performance at larger beams: (1) different candidates: the sentence selected for a small beam is not in the larger beam; or (2) different voter preferences: the sentence selected for a small beam size is still there, but range voting selects a different sentence. In fact, both phenomena occur. First, for beam search and all similarity metrics, about 10% and 5% of the sentences selected at $k{=}4$ and $k{=}10$ respectively are not in the beam of size 100. Second, 48% and 61% of the sentences chosen by standard beam search with $k{=}4$ and $k{=}10$ respectively are also chosen for $k{=}100$, but this drops to 32% and

---

[2] We are evaluating systems translating from English into German, but half of the newstest2014 sentences were originally in German and translated into English. Translation artifacts are known to have an impact on machine translation performance (for example: Kurokawa et al., 2009; Holmqvist et al., 2009; Lembersky et al., 2012). One reviewer asked whether there is a difference in performance for the two halves of the dataset, as found by Freitag et al. (2019). In terms of BLEU score, range voting appears more effective for forward-translation (original text in English), but in terms of manual evaluation, it appears more effective for backward-translation (original text in German). For reasons of space, we only report results for the whole dataset.

[3] A partial copy is defined to be a generated sentence containing at least 50% of the unigrams in the input sentence.

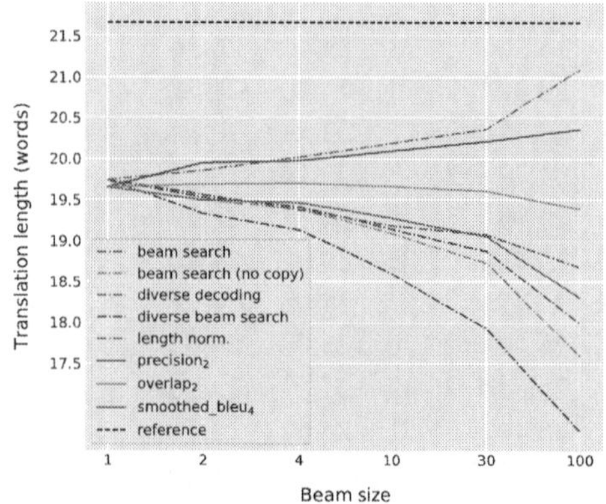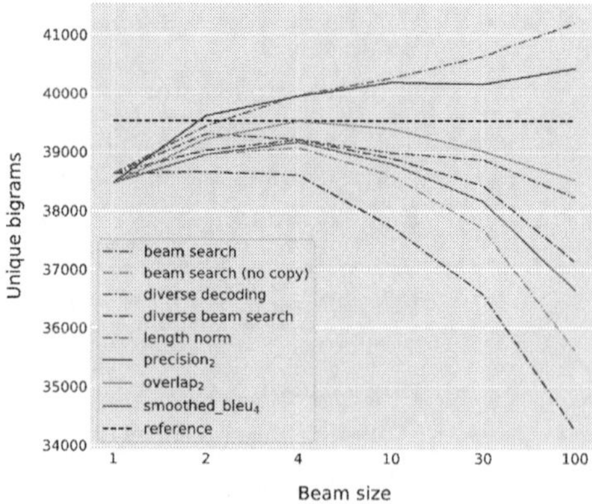

Figure 2: The lengths (left) and the number of unique bigrams in the generated translations (right). Baseline methods are shown as dashed lines, voting and MBR results as solid lines, and reference translations in black (the horizontal line). Full tables of results are given in Appendix A.

36% respectively when using range voting with overlap$_2$ similarity. This suggests that generating candidates and voters independently could lead to further improvements, which we explore in §4.2.5.

Sampling methods also perform poorly on this task. Top k sampling achieves BLEU scores of 17.39 (k=4) and 15.21 (k=10), nucleus sampling achieves a score of 10.10 (top_p=0.9)

4.2.2 Translation length

The average length of the generated translations are shown in Figure 2. All similarity metrics generate longer translations than standard beam search with and without filtering, but shorter than length normalisation. At beam size k=100, length normalised beam search generates almost an extra word per translation compared to k=30.

Just as for image captioning, the length of translations generated by standard beam search decreases as the beam size increases. We again note that the translations generated by range voting with asymmetric similarity metrics are on average longer, except for MBR where the asymmetry in the similarity metric penalises longer candidates. However, it is no longer the case that increasing the beam size also increases the length of the translations generated by range voting.

4.2.3 Translation diversity

The numbers of distinct bigrams generated are shown in Figure 2. Out of diverse decoding and diverse beam search, which aim to increase diversity within a beam, only diverse decoding increases the number of generated bigrams compared to beam search. Length normalisation generates the most unique bigrams, and this increases with beam size, also due to the translations being longer on average. On the other hand, the copy filtering heuristic decreases the number of distinct bigrams generated. Just as for image captioning, range voting increases the diversity of the generated translations. For all similarity metrics, more unique bigrams are generated than beam search with copy filtering (on top of which range voting was applied). Furthermore, the simple n-gram metrics generate more unique bigrams than standard beam search, recovering the drop occurring for the filtering heuristic.

4.2.4 Human evaluation

We used a human evaluation to investigate differences not reflected by BLEU. For 500 sentences, we compared the strongest baseline (length normalisation, k=4) with range voting (precision$_2$, k=10, as this performed well on BLEU, length, and diversity), following the procedure as in §4.1.4. The voted translation was rated better 69 times, and worse 44 times. This is statistically significant, with p=0.0235 for a two-tailed sign test. For translations rated much better, the difference is not significant (36 better, 28 worse).

4.2.5 Including more voters

The range voting formulation doesn't require the set of candidates $\mathcal{C}$ and voters $\mathcal{V}$ to be the same (see Equation 1). We can capture more knowledge from the underlying distribution by using a larger and more diverse set of voters (and could be acquired more efficiently by repeatedly sampling) whilst

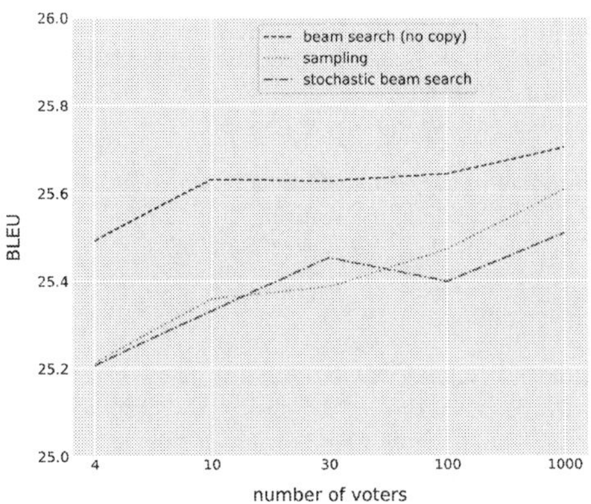

Figure 3: Performance of overlap$_2$ range voting, varying the number of voters for a fixed set of candidates.

constraining the set of candidates to avoid model errors. This was similarly done by Tromble et al. (2008), who refer to the sets of voters and candidates as the "evidence" and "hypothesis" spaces.

For the voters, we increase k from 4 to 1000 and apply 3 different search methods: sampling k times, stochastic beam search (Kool et al., 2019), and beam search with copy filtering. For the candidates we use beam search with copy filtering and $k{=}4$. We fix the similarity metric to overlap$_2$, which was the best performing metric for large $k{\geq}4$ (§4.2.1).

For all 3 generation methods, increasing the number of voters increases BLEU (Figure 3), suggesting that the previous drop in performance is due to worse candidates in larger beams, rather than worse voter preferences.

5 Conclusion

Instead of generating the most *likely* sequence, we propose a method to generate the most *representative* sequence, formalising representativeness using a similarity measure and range voting.

The evaluation on image captioning and machine translation shows that despite using simple similarity measures, we achieve an increase in BLEU score, an increase in caption length and diversity, and statistically significantly better human evaluation performance on both tasks.

For the image captioning task, performance of our method does not drop as beam size increases, removing the sensitivity of results to this hyperparameter. On the machine translation task, performance does drop for larger beam sizes, although by much less than with standard beam search or the baselines. Furthermore, performance increases as the number of voters increases, for a fixed set of candidates.

Using better similarity measures that capture semantics could further improve results and is a promising direction for further research.

Finally, our approach can be applied to any probabilistic language model, without any need for additional training. This opens up many other tasks, including summarisation, dialogue systems, and question answering. If multiple outputs can be used (e.g. offering options to a user), our method can be extended to use reweighted range voting (Smith, 2005), a procedure that elects multiple candidates.

Acknowledgements

We would like to thank Kris Cao for discussions about distributions over sequences, which prompted the initial idea for this project. We would like to thank Dr. Robert Harle and Prof. Ann Copestake for making this project possible, and for providing some early feedback. We would like to thank Andreas Vlachos, Guy Aglionby, James Thorne, Chris Davis, and the NLIP reading group in Cambridge, for feedback on earlier drafts of this paper. Finally, we would like to thank Chris Dyer for his insightful comments and suggestions.

References

Palakorn Achananuparp, Xiaohua Hu, and Xiajiong Shen. 2008. The evaluation of sentence similarity measures. In *Proceedings of the 10th International Conference on Data Warehousing and Knowledge Discovery*, pages 305–316. Springer.

Steven Bird, Ewan Klein, and Edward Loper. 2009. *Natural Language Processing with Python: Analyzing Text with the Natural Language Toolkit*. O'Reilly Media Inc.

Frédéric Blain, Lucia Specia, and Pranava Madhyastha. 2017. Exploring hypotheses spaces in neural machine translation. In *Proceedings of the 16th Machine Translation Summit (MT Summit XVI)*. Asia-Pacific Association for Machine Translation (AAMT).

Ondřej Bojar, Christian Buck, Christian Federmann, Barry Haddow, Philipp Koehn, Johannes Leveling, Christof Monz, Pavel Pecina, Matt Post, Herve Saint-Amand, et al. 2014. Findings of the 2014 Workshop on Statistical Machine Translation. In *Proceedings of the Ninth Workshop on Statistical Machine Translation*, pages 12–58.

Peter F Brown, John Cocke, Stephen A Della Pietra, Vincent J Della Pietra, Frederick Jelinek, Jennifer C Lai, and Robert L Mercer. 1995. Method and system for natural language translation. US Patent 5,477,451.

Chris Callison-Burch, Miles Osborne, and Philipp Koehn. 2006. Re-evaluation the role of BLEU in machine translation research. In *Proceedings of the 11th Conference of the European Chapter of the Association for Computational Linguistics (EACL)*.

Kris Cao and Stephen Clark. 2017. Latent variable dialogue models and their diversity. In *Proceedings of the 15th Conference of the European Chapter of the Association for Computational Linguistics (EACL)*.

Daniel Cer, Mona Diab, Eneko Agirre, Iñigo Lopez-Gazpio, and Lucia Specia. 2017. SemEval-2017 task 1: Semantic textual similarity multilingual and crosslingual focused evaluation. In *Proceedings of the 11th International Workshop on Semantic Evaluation (SemEval-2017)*, pages 1–14.

Yining Chen, Sorcha Gilroy, Kevin Knight, and Jonathan May. 2018. Recurrent neural networks as weighted language recognizers. In *Proceedings of the 2018 Conference of the North American Chapter of the Association for Computational Linguistics: Human Language Technologies (Volume 1: Long Papers)*, pages 2261–2271.

Eldan Cohen and Christopher Beck. 2019. Empirical analysis of beam search performance degradation in neural sequence models. In *Proceedings of the 36th International Conference on Machine Learning*, volume 97 of *Proceedings of Machine Learning Research*, pages 1290–1299. PMLR.

Bhuwan Dhingra, Lihong Li, Xiujun Li, Jianfeng Gao, Yun-Nung Chen, Faisal Ahmed, and Li Deng. 2017. Towards end-to-end reinforcement learning of dialogue agents for information access. In *Proceedings of the 55th Annual Meeting of the Association for Computational Linguistics (Volume 1: Long Papers)*, pages 484–495. Association for Computational Linguistics.

Bryan Eikema and Wilker Aziz. 2020. Is MAP decoding all you need? the inadequacy of the mode in neural machine translation. Unpublished manuscript, arXiv preprint 2005.10283v1.

John D Emerson and Gary A Simon. 1979. Another look at the sign test when ties are present: The problem of confidence intervals. *The American Statistician*, 33(3):140–142.

Angela Fan, Mike Lewis, and Yann Dauphin. 2018. Hierarchical neural story generation. In *Proceedings of the 56th Annual Meeting of the Association for Computational Linguistics (Volume 1: Long Papers)*, pages 889–898. Association for Computational Linguistics.

Markus Freitag and Yaser Al-Onaizan. 2017. Beam search strategies for neural machine translation. In *Proceedings of the First Workshop on Neural Machine Translation*, pages 56–60.

Markus Freitag, Isaac Caswell, and Scott Roy. 2019. APE at scale and its implications on MT evaluation biases. In *Proceedings of the Fourth Conference on Machine Translation (Volume 1: Research Papers)*, pages 34–44.

Markus Freitag, David Grangier, and Isaac Caswell. 2020. BLEU might be guilty but references are not innocent. Unpublished manuscript, arXiv preprint 2004.06063v1.

Albert Gottlieb Heckscher. 1892. *Bidrag til grundlæggelse af en afstemningslære. Om methoderne ved udfindelse af stemmerflerhed i parlamenter (afsteming over ændringforslag m.v.) ved valg og domstole*. Ph.D. thesis, University of Copenhagen.

Sepp Hochreiter and Jürgen Schmidhuber. 1997. Long Short-Term Memory. *Neural Computation*, 9(8):1735–1780.

Maria Holmqvist, Sara Stymne, Jody Foo, and Lars Ahrenberg. 2009. Improving alignment for smt by reordering and augmenting the training corpus. In *Proceedings of the Fourth Workshop on Statistical Machine Translation*, pages 120–124. Association for Computational Linguistics.

Ari Holtzman, Jan Buys, Maxwell Forbes, and Yejin Choi. 2020. The curious case of neural text degeneration. In *Proceedings of the 8th International Conference on Learning Representations (ICLR)*.

Sergey Ioffe and Christian Szegedy. 2015. Batch normalization: Accelerating deep network training by reducing internal covariate shift. In *Proceedings of the 32nd International Conference on Machine Learning*, volume 37 of *Proceedings of Machine Learning Research*, pages 448–456.

Philipp Koehn. 2004a. Pharaoh: a beam search decoder for phrase-based statistical machine translation models. In *Conference of the Association for Machine Translation in the Americas*, pages 115–124. Springer.

Philipp Koehn. 2004b. Statistical significance tests for machine translation evaluation. In *Proceedings of the 2004 conference on empirical methods in natural language processing (EMNLP)*, pages 388–395.

Philipp Koehn and Rebecca Knowles. 2017. Six challenges for neural machine translation. In *First Workshop on Neural Machine Translation*, pages 28–39. Association for Computational Linguistics.

Wouter Kool, Herke Van Hoof, and Max Welling. 2019. Stochastic beams and where to find them: The Gumbel-top-k trick for sampling sequences without replacement. In *Proceedings of the International Conference on Machine Learning*, pages 3499–3508.

Shankar Kumar and William Byrne. 2004. Minimum Bayes-Risk decoding for statistical machine translation. In *Proceedings of the Human Language Technology Conference of the North American Chapter of the Association for Computational Linguistics: HLT-NAACL 2004*, pages 169–176.

Ludmila I. Kuncheva. 2004. *Combining Pattern Classifiers: Methods and Algorithms*. John Wiley & Sons.

Ludmila I. Kuncheva and Juan J Rodríguez. 2014. A weighted voting framework for classifiers ensembles. *Knowledge and Information Systems*, 38(2):259–275.

David Kurokawa, Cyril Goutte, and Pierre Isabelle. 2009. Automatic detection of translated text and its impact on machine translation. In *Proceedings of the 12th Machine Translation Summit (MT Summit XII)*. Association for Machine Translation in the Americas.

Eerik Lagerspetz. 2016. *Social Choice and Democratic Values*. Springer.

Gennadi Lembersky, Noam Ordan, and Shuly Wintner. 2012. Language models for machine translation: Original vs. translated texts. *Computational Linguistics*, 38(4):799–825.

Jiwei Li, Michel Galley, Chris Brockett, Jianfeng Gao, and Bill Dolan. 2016a. A diversity-promoting objective function for neural conversation models. In *Proceedings of the 2016 Conference of the North American Chapter of the Association for Computational Linguistics: Human Language Technologies (Volume 1: Long Papers)*, pages 110–119.

Jiwei Li and Dan Jurafsky. 2016. Mutual information and diverse decoding improve neural machine translation. Unpublished manuscript, arXiv preprint 1601.00372v2.

Jiwei Li, Will Monroe, and Dan Jurafsky. 2016b. A simple, fast diverse decoding algorithm for neural generation. Unpublished manuscript, arXiv preprint 1611.08562v2.

Tsung-Yi Lin, Michael Maire, Serge Belongie, James Hays, Pietro Perona, Deva Ramanan, Piotr Dollár, and C Lawrence Zitnick. 2014. Microsoft COCO: Common objects in context. In *European Conference on Computer Vision*, pages 740–755. Springer.

Jonas Mueller and Aditya Thyagarajan. 2016. Siamese recurrent architectures for learning sentence similarity. In *Proceedings of the 30th AAAI Conference on Artificial Intelligence*.

Myle Ott, Michael Auli, David Grangier, and Marc'Aurelio Ranzato. 2018. Analyzing uncertainty in neural machine translation. In *Proceedings of the 35th International Conference on Machine Learning (ICML)*.

Kishore Papineni, Salim Roukos, Todd Ward, and Wei-Jing Zhu. 2002. BLEU: a method for automatic evaluation of machine translation. In *Proceedings of the 40th Annual Meeting of the Association for Computational Linguistics*, pages 311–318.

Atish Pawar and Vijay Mago. 2019. Challenging the boundaries of unsupervised learning for semantic similarity. *IEEE Access*, 7.

Matt Post. 2018. A call for clarity in reporting BLEU scores. In *Proceedings of the Third Conference on Machine Translation: Research Papers*, pages 186–191. Association for Computational Linguistics.

Rico Sennrich, Barry Haddow, and Alexandra Birch. 2016. Neural machine translation of rare words with subword units. In *Proceedings of the 54th Annual Meeting of the Association for Computational Linguistics (Volume 1: Long Papers)*, pages 1715–1725.

Hiroaki Shimizu, Masao Utiyama, Eiichiro Sumita, and Satoshi Nakamura. 2012. Minimum Bayes-Risk decoding extended with similar examples: NAIST-NICT at IWSLT 2012. In *International Workshop on Spoken Language Translation (IWSLT) 2012*.

Warren D. Smith. 2000. Range voting. Unpublished manuscript.

Warren D. Smith. 2005. Reweighted range voting – new multiwinner voting method. Unpublished manuscript.

Felix Stahlberg and Bill Byrne. 2019. On NMT search errors and model errors: Cat got your tongue? In *Proceedings of the 2019 Conference on Empirical Methods in Natural Language Processing and the 9th International Joint Conference on Natural Language Processing (EMNLP-IJCNLP)*, pages 3347–3353.

Christian Szegedy, Vincent Vanhoucke, Sergey Ioffe, Jon Shlens, and Zbigniew Wojna. 2016. Rethinking the inception architecture for computer vision. In *Proceedings of the IEEE Conference on Computer Vision and Pattern Recognition*, pages 2818–2826. Institute of Electrical and Electronics Engineers.

Nicolaus Tideman. 1987. Independence of clones as a criterion for voting rules. *Social Choice and Welfare*, 4(3):185–206.

Nicolaus Tideman. 2006. *Collective Decisions and Voting: The Potential for Public Choice*. Routledge.

Roy Tromble, Shankar Kumar, Franz Och, and Wolfgang Macherey. 2008. Lattice Minimum Bayes-Risk decoding for statistical machine translation. In *Proceedings of the 2008 Conference on Empirical Methods in Natural Language Processing*, pages 620–629. Association for Computational Linguistics.

Zhaopeng Tu, Yang Liu, Lifeng Shang, Xiaohua Liu, and Hang Li. 2017. Neural machine translation with reconstruction. In *Proceedings of the 31st AAAI Conference on Artificial Intelligence*.

Ashish Vaswani, Samy Bengio, Eugene Brevdo, Francois Chollet, Aidan Gomez, Stephan Gouws, Llion Jones, Łukasz Kaiser, Nal Kalchbrenner, Niki Parmar, Ryan Sepassi, Noam Shazeer, and Jakob Uszkoreit. 2018. Tensor2Tensor for neural machine translation. In *Proceedings of the 13th Conference of the Association for Machine Translation in the Americas (Volume 1: Research Papers)*, pages 193–199.

Ashish Vaswani, Noam Shazeer, Niki Parmar, Jakob Uszkoreit, Llion Jones, Aidan N Gomez, Łukasz Kaiser, and Illia Polosukhin. 2017. Attention is all you need. In *Advances in neural information processing systems*, pages 5998–6008.

Ashwin Vijayakumar, Michael Cogswell, Ramprasaath Selvaraju, Qing Sun, Stefan Lee, David Crandall, and Dhruv Batra. 2018. Diverse beam search for improved description of complex scenes.

Oriol Vinyals, Alexander Toshev, Samy Bengio, and Dumitru Erhan. 2015. Show and tell: A neural image caption generator. In *Proceedings of the 2015 IEEE Conference on Computer Vision and Pattern Recognition (CVPR)*, pages 3156–3164. Institute of Electrical and Electronics Engineers.

Oriol Vinyals, Alexander Toshev, Samy Bengio, and Dumitru Erhan. 2017. Show and tell: Lessons learned from the 2015 MSCOCO image captioning challenge. *IEEE Transactions on Pattern Analysis and Machine Intelligence*, 39(4):652–663.

Yonghui Wu, Mike Schuster, Zhifeng Chen, Quoc V Le, Mohammad Norouzi, Wolfgang Macherey, Maxim Krikun, Yuan Cao, Qin Gao, Klaus Macherey, Klingner Jeff, Shah Apurva, Johnson Melvin, Liu Xiaobing, Kaiser Łukasz, Gouws Stephan, Kato Yoshikiyo, Kudo Taku, Kazawa Hideto, Stevens Keith, Kurian George, Patil Nishant, Wang Wei, Young Cliff, Smith Jason, Riesa Jason, Rudnick Alex, Vinyals Oriol, Corrado Greg, Hughes Macduff, and Dean Jeffrey. 2016. Google's neural machine translation system: Bridging the gap between human and machine translation. Unpublished manuscript, arXiv preprint 1609.08144v2.

Xinnuo Xu, Ondřej Dušek, Ioannis Konstas, and Verena Rieser. 2018. Better conversations by modeling, filtering, and optimizing for coherence and diversity. In *Proceedings of the 2018 Conference on Empirical Methods in Natural Language Processing (EMNLP)*, pages 3981–3991.

Zhen Xu, Bingquan Liu, Baoxun Wang, SUN Chengjie, Xiaolong Wang, Zhuoran Wang, and Chao Qi. 2017. Neural response generation via GAN with an approximate embedding layer. In *Proceedings of the 2017 Conference on Empirical Methods in Natural Language Processing (EMNLP)*, pages 617–626.

A Translation length and diversity

	Average translation length					
Beam size k	1	2	4	10	30	100
Beam search	19.74	19.53	19.42	19.15	18.88	17.99
Length norm.	19.74	19.86	20.02	20.19	20.36	21.09
Diverse decoding	19.74	19.57	19.38	19.19	19.08	18.69
Diverse beam search	19.74	19.33	19.13	18.60	17.93	16.68
Beam search (no copy)	19.66	19.50	19.39	19.09	18.73	17.59
overlap$_1$	19.66	19.79	19.86	19.93	20.03	19.96
precision$_1$	19.66	19.79	19.86	19.93	20.03	19.96
overlap$_2$	19.66	19.69	19.70	19.67	19.61	19.39
precision$_2$	19.66	19.95	19.98	20.09	20.21	20.36
transformer_states	19.66	19.50	19.48	19.31	19.12	18.27
bleu$_4$ (MBR)	19.66	19.50	19.46	19.28	19.06	18.18
smoothed_bleu$_4$ (MBR)	19.66	19.50	19.46	19.28	19.06	18.30

Table 5: Average length of the generated translations on the newstest2014 dataset. The reference translations contain on average 21.66 words, more than for any of the above generation methods.

	Number of distinct bigrams					
Beam size k	1	2	4	10	30	100
Beam search	38629	39029	39205	38894	38424	37135
Length normalisation	38629	39445	39971	40263	40638	41195
Diverse decoding	38629	39307	39217	38989	38870	38227
Diverse beam search	38629	38661	38611	37740	36575	34266
Beam search (no copy)	38473	38956	39073	38593	37694	35609
overlap$_1$	38473	39353	39743	39775	39636	39334
precision$_1$	38473	39354	39739	39772	39634	39334
overlap$_2$	38473	39221	39528	39396	39015	38526
precision$_2$	38473	39617	39955	40195	40170	40426
transformer_states	38473	38956	39223	38930	38277	36787
bleu$_4$ (MBR)	38473	38957	39157	38792	38166	36564
smoothed_bleu$_4$ (MBR)	38473	38961	39169	38799	38166	36645

Table 6: Number of distinct bigrams in the generated translations for the newstest2014 dataset. The reference translations consist of 39,533 unique bigrams.

Distill, Adapt, Distill:
Training Small, In-Domain Models for Neural Machine Translation

Mitchell A. Gordon
Johns Hopkins University
mitchg@jhu.edu

Kevin Duh
Johns Hopkins University
kevinduh@cs.jhu.edu

Abstract

We explore best practices for training small, memory efficient machine translation models with sequence-level knowledge distillation in the domain adaptation setting. While both domain adaptation and knowledge distillation are widely-used, their interaction remains little understood. Our large-scale empirical results in machine translation (on three language pairs with three domains each) suggest distilling twice for best performance: once using general-domain data and again using in-domain data with an adapted teacher. The code for these experiments can be found here.[1]

1 Introduction

Machine translation systems rely on large amounts of data to deduce the rules underlying translation from one language to another. This presents challenges in some important niche domains, such as patent and medical literature translation, due to the high cost of hiring experts to generate suitable training data. A cost-effective alternative is *domain adaptation*, which leverages large amounts of parallel documents from less difficult and more readily-available domains, such as movie subtitles and news articles.

Domain adaptation works well in practice. However, these large datasets, which we call *general domain* datasets, introduce some scalability problems. Large datasets require large models; neural machine translation systems can take days or weeks to train. Some models require gigabytes of disk space, making deployment to edge computing devices challenging. They can also require excessive compute during inference, making them slow and costly to scale up in production environments (Gordon, 2019).

To alleviate these issues, *knowledge distillation* (aka Teacher-Student) (Hinton et al., 2015) is used

to compress models into a manageable form. But although knowledge distillation is the most commonly used form of model compression in practice, it is also one of the least understood.

In this work, we perform a **large-scale empirical analysis** to attempt to discover best practices when using knowledge distillation in combination with domain adaptation. Out of several common-sense configurations, we find that two stages of knowledge distillation give the best performance: one using general-domain data and another using in-domain data with an adapted teacher. We perform experiments on multiple language pairs (Russian-English, German-English, Chinese-English), domains (patents, subtitles, news, TED talks), and student sizes.

2 Background

Domain Adaptation helps overcome a lack of quality training data in niche domains by leveraging large amounts of data in a more accessible general-domain. Domain adaptation is usually accomplished by *continued training* (Luong and Manning, 2015; Zoph et al., 2016), which involves two steps:

1. A model is randomly initialized and trained until convergence on the general-domain data.

2. A new model is initialized with the parameters resulting from Step 1 and trained until convergence on the in-domain dataset.

We can consider domain adaptation as extracting a useful *inductive-bias* from the general-domain dataset, which is encoded and passed along to the in-domain model as a favorable weight initialization. While there are other methods of extracting inductive bias from general-domain datasets (including mixed fine-tuning (Chu et al., 2017) and

---

[1] https://git.io/Jf2t8

110

Proceedings of the 4th Workshop on Neural Generation and Translation (WNGT 2020), pages 110–118
Online, July 10, 2020. ©2020 Association for Computational Linguistics
www.aclweb.org/anthology/D19-56%2d

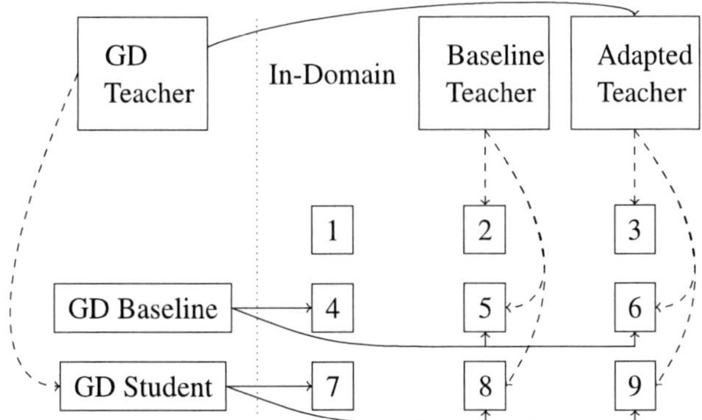

Figure 1: There are 9 possible configurations for training small, in-domain models with knowledge distillation and domain adaptation. Models trained on general-domain data are shown on the left, and in-domain models are shown on the right. Solid arrows represent domain adaptation via continued training. Dashed arrows represent improved optimization via sequence-level knowledge distillation. Configuration 1 is the model which is trained on in-domain data with random initializations and without the assistance of a teacher.

cost weighting (Chen et al., 2017)), continued training is most common and the focus of this paper.

Knowledge Distillation is a method for improving the performance of under-parameterized "Student" models by exploiting the probability distribution of a more computationally complex "Teacher" network. Kim and Rush (2016) presented an extension of knowledge distillation to machine translation in two flavors: word-level and sequence-level knowledge distillation.

Sequence-level knowledge distillation, which is more general, involves three steps:

1. A large Teacher network is randomly initialized and trained until convergence on the data.

2. The source-side of the training data is decoded using the Teacher to produce "distilled" target data.

3. A smaller Student model is randomly initialized and trained until convergence on the distilled source-target pairs (discarding the original target sequences in the data).

The goal of knowledge distillation is to train the student model to mimic the teacher's probability distribution over translations. Since the teacher and the student are trained on the same dataset, they should be capable of learning the same distribution in theory. In practice, however, pre-processing the training data with the teacher improves student test performance.[2] Explanations for this phenomenon

include dark knowledge (Furlanello et al., 2018), mode reduction (Zhou et al., 2019), and regularization (Gordon and Duh, 2019; Dong et al., 2019), but no definitive evidence has been given.

Sequence-level knowledge distillation is widely used in both industry (Xia et al., 2019) and research and is the second focus of this paper. [3]

3 Distilling and Adapting

How domain adaptation and knowledge distillation would interact when applied in combination was not previously clear. Specifically, our research questions are:

- Is a distilled model easier or harder to adapt to new domains?

- Should knowledge distillation be used on in-domain data? If so, how should the teacher be trained?

To answer these questions, we performed experiments on 9 possible configurations which are assigned configuration numbers in Figure 1. For ease of reference, we will primarily refer to small, in-domain models by their configuration number and encourage readers to consult Figure 1. Each configuration has two attributes of interest.

---

[2] Interestingly, this can be true even when the student has the same computational resources as the teacher (Furlanello et al., 2018)

[3] Sequence-level knowledge distillation is also commonly used to train non-autoregressive machine translation models (Zhou et al., 2019).

Distilling In-Domain Data How is in-domain data pre-processed using knowledge distillation? Some models are trained with no pre-processing (configurations 1, 4, and 7), while others use a teacher to pre-process the in-domain training data. This teacher might be a baseline trained on in-domain data only (configurations 2, 5, and 8) or it can be trained on general-domain data and then adapted to in-domain via continued training (configurations 3, 6, and 9).

Initialization How are models initialized? A model might be randomly initialized (configurations 1, 2, and 3), or it might be adapted from a model trained on general-domain data. This general-domain model might be a baseline trained directly on the general-domain data (configurations 4, 5, and 6) or it might be a student model trained on the output of a general-domain teacher (configurations 7, 8, 9).

4 Experiments

4.1 Data

General-Domain Data We train models in multiple settings: 3 language pairs (German-English, Russian-English, and Chinese-English) each with 1 general-domain dataset and 2 different in-domain datasets. The general-domain datasets for each language are a concatenation of data from Open-Subtitles2018 (Tiedemann, 2016; Lison and Tiedemann, 2016) (which contains translated movie subtitles) and the WMT 2017 datasets (Ondrej et al., 2017) (which includes a variety of sources, including news commentary, parliamentary proceedings, and web-crawled data).

In-Domain Data We use the World International Property Organization (WIPO) COPPA-V2 dataset (Junczys-Dowmunt et al., 2018) and the TED Talks dataset (Duh, 2019a) as our two in-domain datasets. The WIPO data contains parallel sentences from international patent abstracts, while the TED Talks dataset consists of translated transcripts of public speeches.

Data Statistics The size of each training dataset is presented in Table 1. General-domain datasets contain tens of millions of sentences, while in-domain datasets contain much less. German-English WIPO has an exceptional amount of training data (4.5 times more than the next biggest in-domain dataset) and helps qualify how our results

Language	General-Domain	WIPO	TED
De-En	28.3 M	821 k	152 k
Ru-En	51.1 M	29 k	180 k
Zh-En	35.9 M	154 k	169 k

Table 1: The number of training sentences in each dataset.

might change when more in-domain data is available.

Pre-processing All datasets are tokenized using the Moses[4] tokenizer. A BPE vocabulary (Sennrich et al., 2016) of 30,000 tokens is constructed for each language using the training set of the general-domain data. This BPE vocabulary is then applied to both in-domain and general-domain datasets. This mimics the typical scenario of a single, general-domain model being trained and then adapted to new domains as they are encountered. Note that re-training BPE on in-domain data to produce a different vocabulary would force us to re-build the model, making adaptation impossible.

Evaluation The general-domain development set for each language contains newstest2016 concatenated with the last 2500 lines of OpenSubtitles2018. We reserve 3000 lines of WIPO to use as the in-domain development set. TED talks development sets are provided by the authors and contain around 2000 lines each. Evaluations of each model are performed by decoding the appropriate development set with a beam-search size of 10 and comparing to the reference using multi-bleu.perl from the Moses toolkit. The tokenization used during multi-bleu.perl evaluation is the same as the one provided in (Duh, 2019a).

4.2 Architectures and Training

A list of architecture sizes is provided in Table 2. Teachers are trained using the Large hyperparameter settings, while we experiment with Medium, Small, and Tiny students for each configuration and language/domain setting.

All models are Transformers (Vaswani et al., 2017). We use the same hyper-parameters (which are based on a template from (Duh, 2019b)[5]) for every model, except those that affect the size of the model (Table 2). Models are trained either for 300,000 updates, 100 epochs, or until the

---

[4]statmt.org/moses
[5]https://git.io/JvL85

Size	Layers	FF Size	Hidden Size
Large	12	2048	512
Medium	6	2048	512
Small	6	1024	256
Tiny	2	1024	256

Table 2: Hyper-parameters of various model sizes used in this work. For example, the Large Transformer model architecture uses 6 encoder and 6 decoder layers, a feed-forward hidden dimension of 2048 at each layer, and a word-embedding / hidden dimension of 512.

Domain	Size	Init	de-en	ru-en	zh-en
ted	Lrg	Rand	29.25	19.38	14.79
		GD Lrg	37.64	26.57	20.45
wipo	Lrg	Rand	48.31	21.36	31.02
		GD Lrg	48.56	37.08	36.80

Table 3: BLEU development score of in-domain teachers when either randomly initialized or initialized from the weights of a large model trained on general-domain data. Adaptation drastically improves performance on every language pair and domain, except de-en WIPO.

model does not improve for 10 checkpoints (early-stopping), whichever comes first.

Continued Training Work by (Gordon and Duh, 2019) suggests that students may benefit from training on some combination of the distilled and un-distilled reference dataset. We experimented with this by continuing to train each in-domain student model on the original, un-distilled dataset, using similar stopping criterion to the first round of training. This improved some models by up to 1 BLEU. Because of this, we recommend that any distilled model continue training on the original dataset as long as development accuracy improves. When continued training improves performance of a student, we show that score instead of the score without continued training.

5 Recommendations

5.1 Adapt Teachers

In this section, we compare training in-domain models with no teacher (config 1), a teacher trained on in-domain data only (config 2), and a teacher adapted from the general domain (config 3). The performance of the two teachers in each language-pair and domain is listed in Table 3. It shows that adaptation greatly improves the performance of every in-domain teacher except German-English WIPO.[6]

Table 4 shows the results of using these teachers to distill the in-domain data before training student models in various settings. **We see that in almost every case, using an adapted teacher gives the best or close to the best results.** This is somewhat expected since models with better development scores tend to make better teachers (Zhang

et al., 2018). Although knowledge distillation is typically seen as "simplifying" data for students, in this case we suspect that the adapted teacher's knowledge about the general-domain is making its way to students via the distilled in-domain data.

5.2 Adapt the Best Student

We also train small models directly on the general-domain data and adapt them to in-domain data. The possible configurations are random initialization (config 1), initializing from a baseline model trained on general-domain data (config 4), or initializing from a student model distilled from a general-domain teacher (config 7). Table 5 shows the performance of the models trained on the general-domain datasets, and Table 6 shows their performance after being fine-tuned on in-domain data.

Training small models directly on the general-domain data and then fine-tuning on in-domain data gives much more substantial gains (5-10 BLEU) than providing indirect access to the general-domain data through an adapted teacher (config 3). We believe this is because a large amount of data is required to fully reveal the teacher's probability distribution over translations (Fang et al., 2019). While an adapted teacher might contain much information from the general-domain, it is unable to express that knowledge to students just by translating the smaller in-domain dataset. **To get the full benefit of general-domain data, the small models must be directly pre-trained on general-domain data.**[7] Indirect access to the general-domain data through a general-domain teacher is insufficient.

We also observe that Medium-sized models are not small enough to benefit from knowledge distillation in the general-domain, and so their general-domain scores do not improve with distillation.

---

[6]German WIPO is also the largest in-domain dataset we test, which might make adaptation unnecessary. Another explanation might be that the German-English general-domain is not similar enough to the patent domain in this case to improve performance.

[7]A reasonable alternative to this might include data-free KD (Yin et al., 2019), which explores the teacher's probability distribution without any dependence on data.

Domain	Size	Cfg #	de-en	ru-en	zh-en
ted	med	1	27.73	19.34	15.17
		2	29.11	20.31	15.71
		3	**29.54**	**20.56**	**15.90**
	small	1	27.89	18.42	14.87
		2	28.93	19.65	14.95
		3	**29.52**	**19.88**	**15.79**
	tiny	1	25.78	17.48	13.03
		2	27.20	17.87	13.39
		3	**27.58**	**19.27**	**13.74**
wipo	med	1	48.89	24.45	30.13
		2	**50.66**	**24.62**	32.13
		3	50.23	24.60	**33.16**
	small	1	47.94	21.91	30.66
		2	49.46	**23.70**	32.19
		3	**49.72**	23.50	**32.61**
	tiny	1	44.15	21.39	27.67
		2	48.03	**22.24**	28.18
		3	**48.51**	22.03	**29.88**

Table 4: BLEU development scores for in-domain students with no teacher (config 1), an in-domain only teacher (config 2), or an adapted teacher continued from the general-domain (config 3). In almost every case, using an adapted teacher gives the best or close to the best results.

Model	de-en	ru-en	zh-en
Teacher	41.08	32.25	47.17
Medium Baseline	39.86	30.81	45.40
Medium Student	39.40	30.65	45.11
Small Baseline	36.78	27.54	42.09
Small Student	38.51	28.88	42.73
Tiny Baseline	31.27	23.63	34.71
Tiny Student	34.58	25.86	36.09

Table 5: General-domain models, teachers and students. While knowledge distillation improves small and tiny models, it appears medium-sized models are not under-parameterized enough for knowledge distillation to improve performance.

These distilled Medium-sized models (config 7) also tend to do slightly worse than their baseline counter-parts (config 4) on in-domain data. Indeed, Figure 2 shows that in-domain performance is roughly linearly related to general-domain performance regardless of whether distillation is applied before adaptation.

This implies that **distillation does not interfere with the adaptability of a model**, so the model with the best general-domain performance should be adapted, regardless of whether distillation was applied. Adapting a distilled model can improve performance slightly over adapting the baseline model without distillation.

5.3 Distill, Adapt, Distill

Finally, we test whether these two ways of improving small, in-domain models are orthogonal. We might hypothesize that training small models directly on general-domain data eliminates the need to adapt teachers or use an in-domain teacher at all. To test this, we also train adapted student models using a baseline teacher (config 8) and an adapted teacher (config 9).

Table 7 shows that **distilling a second time us-**

Domain	Size	Cfg #	de-en	ru-en	zh-en
ted	med	1	27.73	19.34	15.17
		4	**36.94**	**25.82**	20.13
		7	35.93	25.43	**20.18**
	small	1	27.89	18.42	14.87
		4	34.78	24.10	18.84
		7	**35.33**	**24.30**	**19.32**
	tiny	1	25.78	17.48	13.03
		4	31.52	21.30	16.51
		7	**32.30**	**21.65**	**17.06**
wipo	med	1	**48.89**	24.45	30.13
		4	48.58	**35.98**	**35.33**
		7	48.53	35.55	35.27
	small	1	47.94	21.91	30.66
		4	48.13	**35.30**	**34.90**
		7	**48.31**	35.18	34.52
	tiny	1	44.15	21.39	27.67
		4	46.06	31.13	28.45
		7	**46.54**	**31.74**	**29.07**

Table 6: In-domain models that are initialized randomly (config 1), initialized from a baseline trained on general-domain data directly (config 4), or initialized from a general-domain student trained using a general-domain teacher (config 7).

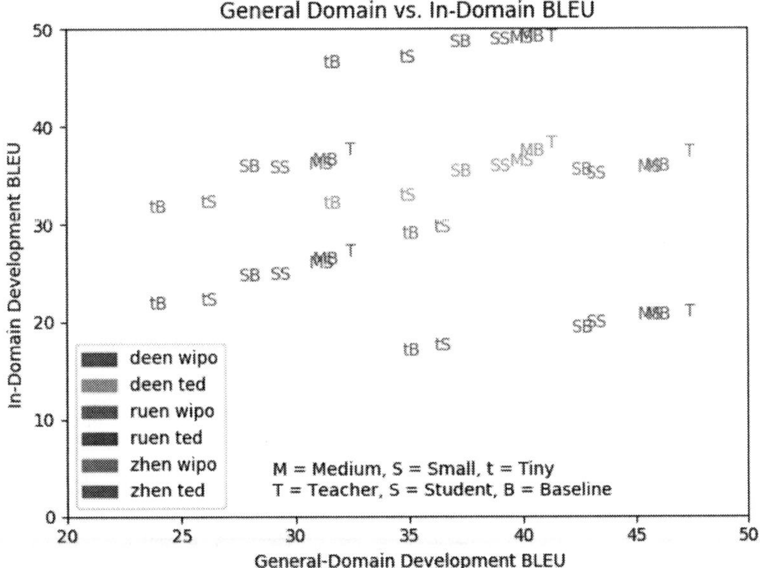

Figure 2: The BLEU of general-domain models vs. their corresponding in-domain scores when adapted to a different domain. We see that in-domain performance is roughly linearly related to general-domain performance regardless of whether distillation is applied before adaptation.

Domain	Size	Cfg #	de-en	ru-en	zh-en
ted	med	7	35.93	25.43	**20.18**
		8	35.23	25.18	19.96
		9	**36.65**	**25.91**	20.13
	small	7	35.33	24.30	19.32
		8	35.11	23.97	19.17
		9	**35.57**	**24.95**	**19.48**
	tiny	7	32.30	21.65	17.06
		8	32.21	21.45	16.72
		9	**33.12**	**22.49**	**17.54**
wipo	med	7	48.53	35.55	35.27
		8	49.07	34.71	35.09
		9	**49.82**	**35.83**	**36.48**
	small	7	48.31	**35.18**	34.52
		8	**48.79**	34.27	34.89
		9	48.35	35.10	**35.55**
	tiny	7	46.54	31.74	29.07
		8	**49.90**	31.12	30.05
		9	49.70	**31.75**	**31.82**

Table 7: In-domain models which are initialized from a general-domain student and trained on in-domain data which is pre-processed either with no teacher (config 7), an in-domain only teacher (config 8), or an adapted teacher continued from general-domain data (config 9).

ing in-domain data with an adapted teacher can further boost performance of an already distilled model, while using a teacher trained only on in-domain data can sometimes hurt performance.

These results lead us to a general recipe for training small, in-domain models using knowledge distillation and domain adaptation in combination:

1. Distill general-domain data to improve general-domain student performance.

2. Adapt the best model from Step 1 to in-domain data.
   (2-10 BLEU better than no adaptation)

3. Adapt the teacher and distill again in-domain.
   (0-2 BLEU better than no or non-adapted teacher)

Following this procedure will result in either configuration 6 or 9 as described in Figure 1. And indeed, configuration 9 performs the best or near best (within 0.1 BLEU) in almost every case, as shown in Table 9. For those Medium sized models which were not improved by distillation in the general-domain, configuration 6 performs the best.

Models trained on German-English WIPO are an exception, with adaptation from the general-domain not improving performance. This is in line

Domain	Size	Cfg #	de-en	ru-en	zh-en
ted	med	6	36.80	26.26	20.13
	small	6	35.50	24.68	19.31
	tiny	6	32.09	22.20	17.25
wipo	med	6	48.31	35.82	36.58
	small	6	49.04	35.30	35.40
	tiny	6	48.02	31.57	30.53

Table 8: Development scores for models initialized from a model trained on general-domain data. The in-domain data is pre-processed with a teacher adapted from the general-domain (config 6).

Domain	Size	de-en	ru-en	zh-en
ted	med	4/6	6	4/6/7/9
	small	6/9	9	9
	tiny	9	9	9
wipo	med	2	4/6/9	6
	small	3	4/6	9
	tiny	8	7/9	9

Table 9: Best configurations for each setting. Scores within 0.1 BLEU of the best are also listed. Configuration 9 generally performs best, while configuration 6 is best for those medium-sized models which were not improved by distillation in the general-domain.

with the results from Table 3 which shows adaptation does not improve teachers, either. We suspect this is because the German-English WIPO dataset is the biggest out of any in-domain dataset, making adaptation unnecessary. Future work might also benefit from a quantification of domain similarity between datasets (Britz et al., 2017), which would guide the use of domain adaptation in cases like these.

5.4 Training Times

The models trained in this work collectively required 10 months of single-GPU compute time. Table 10 breaks this down by model size and dataset.

While distilling twice might give the best performance, it also increases the amount of computation time required. Rather than training a single in-domain model, configuration 9 requires training a general-domain teacher, a general-domain student, and then adapting both. This can increase compute required to train models by 2-4x.

A huge portion of computation was also spent on decoding the general-domain data using a teacher model for sequence-level knowledge distillation, which could take up to 24 days of GPU time (using a beam size of 10 and a batch size of 10). This

Model	Gen-Domain	In-Domain	Adapting
Large	2-4 days	2-4 days	7-48 hrs
Med	2-4 days	2-4 days	1-48 hrs
Small	1-2 days	1-2 days	2-14 hrs
Tiny	1 days	1-24 hrs	2-24 hrs
Distill	10-24 days	1-2 days	

Table 10: Estimates of the computation time required for training randomly initialized models on just general-domain data or just in-domain data. We also show the time required for adapting general-domain models and distilling data using teachers.

can be arbitrarily sped up using multiple GPUs in parallel, but future work might explore how to distill teachers in a less expensive way.

6 Related Work

Our work is one the few that focuses specifically on training small, under-parameterized in-domain models. There is, however, similar work which is *not directly comparable* but uses knowledge distillation to adapt to new domains.

Knowledge Adaptation uses knowledge distillation to transfer knowledge from multiple, labeled source domains to un-labeled target domains. This is in contrast to our setting, which has labels for both general-domain and in-domain data. Ruder et al. (2017) introduced this idea as "Knowledge Adaptation," using multi-layer perceptrons to provide sentiment analysis labels for unlabeled in-domain data. Similar work includes Iterative Dual Domain Adaptation (Zeng et al., 2019) and Domain Transformation Networks (Wang et al., 2019). These ideas are not limited to machine translation; recent work by Meng et al. (2020) trains in-domain speech recognition systems with knowledge distillation, while Orbes-Arteaga et al. (2019) does similar work on segmentation of magnetic resonance imaging scans.

Compressing Pre-trained Language Models Domain adaptation via continued training in NMT is closely related to the idea of pre-training a language model and fine-tuning to different tasks, which might come from different data distributions than the pre-training data. Because language models tend to be extremely cumbersome to train and evaluate, more focus is given to the compression aspect of knowledge distillation. Sanh et al. (2019), Sun et al. (2019), and Liu et al. (2019) independently showed that knowledge distillation could be used to compress pre-trained models without affecting downstream tasks. Tang et al. (2019) showed that task-specific information could be distilled from a large Transformer into a much smaller Bi-directional RNN. These methods might reasonably be extended to domain adaptation for NMT.

7 Conclusion

In this work, we conducted a large-scale empirical investigation to determine best practices when using sequence-level knowledge distillation and domain adaptation in combination. We found that adapting models from the general-domain makes them better teachers and that distilling using general-domain data does not impact a model's adaptability. This leads us to recommend distilling twice for best results: once in the general-domain to possibly improve student performance, and again using an adapted in-domain teacher. The results are robust among multiple language pairs, student sizes, in-domain settings.

References

Denny Britz, Quoc Le, and Reid Pryzant. 2017. Effective domain mixing for neural machine translation. In *Proceedings of the Second Conference on Machine Translation*, pages 118–126.

Boxing Chen, Colin Cherry, George Foster, and Samuel Larkin. 2017. Cost weighting for neural machine translation domain adaptation. In *Proceedings of the First Workshop on Neural Machine Translation*, pages 40–46, Stroudsburg, PA, USA. Association for Computational Linguistics.

Chenhui Chu, Raj Dabre, and Sadao Kurohashi. 2017. An empirical comparison of domain adaptation methods for neural machine translation. In *Proceedings of the 55th Annual Meeting of the Association for Computational Linguistics (Volume 2: Short Papers)*, pages 385–391, Stroudsburg, PA, USA. Association for Computational Linguistics.

Bin Dong, Jikai Hou, Yiping Lu, and Zhihua Zhang. 2019. Distillation $\approx$ early stopping? harvesting dark knowledge utilizing anisotropic information retrieval for overparameterized neural network.

Kevin Duh. 2019a. The multitarget TED talks task (MTTT). http://www.cs.jhu.edu/~kevinduh/a/multitarget-tedtalks/.

Kevin Duh. 2019b. sockeye-recipes.

Gongfan Fang, Jie Song, Chengchao Shen, Xinchao Wang, Da Chen, and Mingli Song. 2019. Data-Free adversarial distillation.

Tommaso Furlanello, Zachary C Lipton, Michael Tschannen, Laurent Itti, and Anima Anandkumar. 2018. Born again neural networks.

Mitchell A. Gordon. 2019. All the ways you can compress bert.

Mitchell A Gordon and Kevin Duh. 2019. Explaining Sequence-Level knowledge distillation as Data-Augmentation for neural machine translation.

Geoffrey Hinton, Oriol Vinyals, and Jeff Dean. 2015. Distilling the knowledge in a neural network.

Marcin Junczys-Dowmunt, Bruno Pouliquen, and Christophe Mazenc. 2018. COPPA v2. 0: Corpus of parallel patent applications building large parallel corpora with GNU make.

Yoon Kim and Alexander M Rush. 2016. Sequence-Level knowledge distillation.

Pierre Lison and Jörg Tiedemann. 2016. Opensubtitles2016: Extracting large parallel corpora from movie and tv subtitles.

Linqing Liu, Huan Wang, Jimmy Lin, Richard Socher, and Caiming Xiong. 2019. Attentive student meets Multi-Task teacher: Improved knowledge distillation for pretrained models.

Minh-Thang Luong and Christopher D Manning. 2015. Stanford neural machine translation systems for spoken language domains. In *Proceedings of the International Workshop on Spoken Language Translation*, pages 76–79.

Zhong Meng, Jinyu Li, Yashesh Gaur, and Yifan Gong. 2020. Domain adaptation via Teacher-Student learning for End-to-End speech recognition.

Bojar Ondrej, Rajen Chatterjee, Federmann Christian, Graham Yvette, Haddow Barry, Huck Matthias, Koehn Philipp, Liu Qun, Logacheva Varvara, Monz Christof, and Others. 2017. Findings of the 2017 conference on machine translation (wmt17). In *Second Conference onMachine Translation*, pages 169–214.

Mauricio Orbes-Arteaga, Jorge Cardoso, Lauge Sørensen, Christian Igel, Sebastien Ourselin, Marc Modat, Mads Nielsen, and Akshay Pai. 2019. Knowledge distillation for semi-supervised domain adaptation.

Sebastian Ruder, Parsa Ghaffari, and John G Breslin. 2017. Knowledge adaptation: Teaching to adapt.

Victor Sanh, Lysandre Debut, Julien Chaumond, and Thomas Wolf. 2019. DistilBERT, a distilled version of BERT: smaller, faster, cheaper and lighter.

Rico Sennrich, Barry Haddow, and Alexandra Birch. 2016. Neural machine translation of rare words with subword units. In *Proceedings of the 54th Annual Meeting of the Association for Computational Linguistics (Volume 1: Long Papers)*, pages 1715–1725,

Stroudsburg, PA, USA. Association for Computational Linguistics.

Siqi Sun, Yu Cheng, Zhe Gan, and Jingjing Liu. 2019. Patient knowledge distillation for BERT model compression. In *Proceedings of the 2019 Conference on Empirical Methods in Natural Language Processing and the 9th International Joint Conference on Natural Language Processing (EMNLP-IJCNLP)*, pages 4314–4323, Stroudsburg, PA, USA. Association for Computational Linguistics.

Raphael Tang, Yao Lu, Linqing Liu, Lili Mou, Olga Vechtomova, and Jimmy Lin. 2019. Distilling Task-Specific knowledge from BERT into simple neural networks.

Jörg Tiedemann. 2016. Finding alternative translations in a large corpus of movie subtitle. In *Proceedings of the Tenth International Conference on Language Resources and Evaluation (LREC'16)*, pages 3518–3522.

Ashish Vaswani, Noam Shazeer, Niki Parmar, Jakob Uszkoreit, Llion Jones, Aidan N Gomez, Lukasz Kaiser, and Illia Polosukhin. 2017. Attention is all you need.

Yong Wang, Longyue Wang, Shuming Shi, Victor O K Li, and Zhaopeng Tu. 2019. Go from the general to the particular: Multi-Domain translation with domain transformation networks.

Yingce Xia, Xu Tan, Fei Tian, Fei Gao, Weicong Chen, Yang Fan, Linyuan Gong, Yichong Leng, Renqian Luo, Yiren Wang, and Others. 2019. Microsoft research asia's systems for WMT19. In *Proceedings of the Fourth Conference on Machine Translation (Volume 2: Shared Task Papers, Day 1)*, pages 424–433.

Hongxu Yin, Pavlo Molchanov, Zhizhong Li, Jose M Alvarez, Arun Mallya, Derek Hoiem, Niraj K Jha, and Jan Kautz. 2019. Dreaming to distill: Data-free knowledge transfer via DeepInversion.

Jiali Zeng, Yang Liu, Jinsong Su, Yubin Ge, Yaojie Lu, Yongjing Yin, and Jiebo Luo. 2019. Iterative dual domain adaptation for neural machine translation.

Dakun Zhang, Josep Crego, and Jean Senellart. 2018. Analyzing knowledge distillation in neural machine translation. In *2018 International Workshop on Spoken Language Translation, IWSLT 2005, Pittsburgh, PA, USA, October 24-25, 2005*, pages 68–75.

Chunting Zhou, Jiatao Gu, and Graham Neubig. 2019. Understanding knowledge distillation in non-autoregressive machine translation.

Barret Zoph, Deniz Yuret, Jonathan May, and Kevin Knight. 2016. Transfer learning for Low-Resource neural machine translation. In *Proceedings of the 2016 Conference on Empirical Methods in Natural Language Processing*, pages 1568–1575, Stroudsburg, PA, USA. Association for Computational Linguistics.

Training and Inference Methods for High-Coverage Neural Machine Translation

Michael Yang   **Yixin Liu**   **Rahul Mayuranath**

Language Technologies Institute, Carnegie Mellon University, Pittsburgh PA, U.S.A.
{myang2,yixinl2,rmayuran}@cs.cmu.edu

Abstract

In this paper, we introduce a system built for the Duolingo Simultaneous Translation And Paraphrase for Language Education (STAPLE) shared task at the 4th Workshop on Neural Generation and Translation (WNGT 2020). We participated in the English-to-Japanese track with a Transformer model pretrained on the JParaCrawl corpus and fine-tuned in two steps on the JESC corpus and then the (smaller) Duolingo training corpus. First, during training, we find it is essential to deliberately expose the model to higher-quality translations more often during training for optimal translation performance. For inference, encouraging a small amount of diversity with Diverse Beam Search to improve translation coverage yielded marginal improvement over regular Beam Search. Finally, using an auxiliary filtering model to filter out unlikely candidates from Beam Search improves performance further. We achieve a weighted F1 score of 27.56% on our own test set, outperforming the STAPLE AWS translations baseline score of 4.31%.

1   Introduction

Currently, state of the art machine translation systems generally produce a single output translation. However, human evaluators of translation tasks will often accept multiple translations as correct. We introduce a neural machine translation (NMT) system that generates high-coverage translation sets for a single given prompt in the source language.

Our system was prepared for the English-to-Japanese track[1] of the Duolingo Simultaneous Translation And Paraphrase for Language Education (STAPLE) shared task (Mayhew et al., 2020) at the 4th Workshop on Neural Generation and Translation (WNGT 2020). The shared task datasets consist of English prompts and a weighted set of target language translations for each prompt. The task requires systems to produce translation sets for given English prompts that are evaluated on weighted F1 score, defined in Appendix A. We have made our code publicly available.[2]

We experimented with models trained and fine-tuned on the provided Duolingo English-Japanese prompt-translation data (Mayhew et al., 2020), the JParaCrawl web-crawled corpus (Morishita et al., 2019), as well as the Japanese-English Subtitle Corpus (JESC) (Pryzant et al., 2018). The sizes of each dataset are summarized in Table 1.

Our system uses a Transformer-based (Vaswani et al., 2017) NMT model and we began with weights pretrained on the large JParaCrawl corpus (Morishita et al., 2019). Section 4 describes in detail how the model was pretrained. Our system's NMT model was then obtained by fine-tuning first on the Japanese-English Subtitle Corpus (JESC) (Pryzant et al., 2018) before further fine-tuning on the Duolingo training set (Mayhew et al., 2020). We outline these datasets in more detail in Section 2.

Given the small size of the Duolingo data, this multi-step fine-tuning helped the model generalize and outperformed single-step fine-tuning and no fine-tuning. High-coverage translation bitext data is not easy to mine or create, so we expect that in other settings, the size of such available training data will also be small. Therefore, it is very likely that adopting a multi-step fine-tuning method may be advantageous more generally. The fine-tuning procedure is described in Section 6.

Outputting the entire beam of candidates from 150-width Beam Search, scored on per token log likelihood, this two-step fine-tuned system produced the translations that we submitted to the

---

[1]There were five tracks of target languages in total, the others being Hungarian, Korean, Portuguese and Vietnamese.

[2]Our code can be found at https://github.com/michaelzyang/high-coverage-translation.

Proceedings of the 4th Workshop on Neural Generation and Translation (WNGT 2020), pages 119–128
Online, July 10, 2020. ©2020 Association for Computational Linguistics
www.aclweb.org/anthology/D19-56%2d

Dataset	English Sentences	Japanese Sentences
JParaCrawl	8,763,995	8,763,995
JESC	2,801,388	2,801,388
Duolingo	2,500	855,940

Table 1: Number of sentence-pairs in the datasets (Duolingo pairs have a one-to-many correspondence)

shared task leaderboard. It achieved 25.69 % weighted F1 score on the shared task blind development set and 26.0% on the blind test set.

After the leaderboard closed, we conducted further experiments and discovered several notable optimizations.

The most effective optimization was using the ground truth weights that indicate variations in translation quality during training. We find that it is essential to deliberately expose the model to higher-quality translations more often during training. Otherwise, overexposure to low-quality translations harms the model's translation performance.

Secondly, Diverse Beam Search with a very small penalty outperformed Beam Search. However, too much diversity begins to introduce minor semantic shifts that deviate from correct translations.

We also explored introducing an auxiliary filtering model for post-processing candidates. Our proposed filtering model is able to refine the candidates generated by the NMT model, which improved the system's performance with respect to the weighted F1 score.

We share our results in Section 7. Our best result was a weighted F1 score of 27.56% on our own test set of 200 prompts randomly selected from the training data.

2 Corpora

2.1 Duolingo High-coverage Translations

Duolingo provided training, development and test sets (Mayhew et al., 2020). However, the development and test datasets were 'blind' and did not contain ground truth translations, so we did not use these for training or development.

The training set consists of 2,500 English prompts, each of which are paired with a variable number of Japanese translations (Table 1). Duolingo provides weights for each translation, which can be interpreted as a quality score. For our experiments, we randomly split the the 2,500 prompts into 2,100, 200 and 200-prompt training,

development and test sets respectively. For the shared task submission, we retrained a model over all 2,500 prompts with our best hyperparameters.

2.2 JParaCrawl

As our base model, we use a model pre-trained on the JParaCrawl corpus (Morishita et al., 2019). This corpus contains over 8.7 million sentence pairs which were crawled from the web and then automatically aligned, similar to European corpora in the ParaCrawl project[3]. Though noisy due to an imperfect alignment method, this is currently the largest publicly-available English-Japanese bitext corpus.

2.3 Japanese-English Subtitle Corpus

The Japanese-English Subtitle Corpus (JESC) (Pryzant et al., 2018), is a large parallel training corpus that contains 2.8 million pairs of TV and movie subtitles. With an average length of 8, the corpus mostly consists of short sentences, which is similar to the data present in the Duolingo training corpus. Even though JESC contains some noise, it captures sufficient information that is useful for downstream NMT tasks.

3 Related work

Machine Translation Machine translation (MT) involves finding a target sentence $\mathbf{y} = y_1, ... y_m$ with the maximum probability conditioned on a source sentence $\mathbf{x} = x_1, ... x_n$, i.e $\operatorname{argmax}_{\mathbf{y}} P(\mathbf{y}|\mathbf{x})$.

There are various neural approaches to tackle machine translation. These include utilizing recurrent neural networks (Cho et al., 2014b), convolutional neural networks (Kalchbrenner et al., 2016), attention-based models (Luong et al., 2014; Bahdanau et al., 2015) and transformer networks (Vaswani et al., 2017). Sequence to sequence models deal with the task of mapping an input sequence to an output sequence. These were first introduced by Sutskever et al. (2014) and typically use an RNN

---

[3]https://paracrawl.eu/

based encoder-decoder architecture, where the encoder outputs a fixed length representation of the input which is fed into the decoder to get a target translation. RNN and LSTM based approaches struggle to handle long sequences and long-range dependencies since the encoder network is tasked with encoding all relevant information in a fixed-length hidden state vector. Bahdanau et al. (2015) overcome this by utilizing attention, an alignment model that can attend to important parts of the input during translation. Luong et al. (2014) used the attention mechanism to great effect, observing gains of 5.0 BLEU over non-attention based techniques for NMT.

The Transformer Architecture   For our experiments, we used the the Transformer architecture proposed by Vaswani et al. (2017). It is a self-attention based model that produces superior results for machine translation tasks compared to CNN and LSTM based models. By stacking multiple layers of multi-head self-attention blocks, they demonstrate that the attention mechanism by itself is very powerful for sequence encoding and decoding. Recently, Transformer-based models that are pre-trained on large-scale datasets have produced superior performance on various Natural Language Processing (NLP) tasks (Rajpurkar et al., 2016; Talmor and Berant, 2019; Mayhew et al., 2019). In Section 4 we further describe the transformer architecture and our pretraining procedure.

Domain Adaptation   Domain adaptation involves making use of out-of-domain data in situations where high quality in-domain data are scarce. This fine tuning approach has been shown to be effective for NMT (Luong and Manning, 2015; Sennrich et al., 2015; Freitag and Al-Onaizan, 2016). Morishita et al. (2019) show that pre-training with JParaCrawl vastly improves in-domain performance for English-Japanese translations. We make use of these ideas in our multi-step fine-tuning experiments.

Inference with Beam Search   Beam Search is an approximate search algorithm used for finding high likelihood sequences from sequential decoders. At every time step, the top k outputs are traversed and the rest are discarded. A common issue with beam search is that it generates similar outputs that only differ by a few words or minor morphological variations (Li and Jurafsky, 2016). Vijayakumar et al. (2016) propose Diverse Beam Search, a

method that reduces redundancy during decoding in NMT models to generate a wider range of candidate outputs. This is achieved by splitting the beam width into evenly-sized groups and adding a penalty term for the presence of similar candidates across groups. The authors find most success with the Hamming Diversity penalty term, which penalizes the selection of tokens used in previous groups proportionally to the number of times it was selected before. We detail our experiments using both search strategies in Section 6.

Post-processing in NLP   For tasks that require sets of outputs rather than single outputs, post-processing or reranking methods are often used as a downstream step after a model generates an initial set. They have proven to be useful techniques for various NLP tasks, such as Question Answering (Kratzwald et al., 2019), Named Entity Recognition (Yang et al., 2017) and Neural Summarization (Cao et al., 2018). The basic methodology is to first generate an initial candidate set and rerank or prune these candidates to generate the final set. This set up reduces reliance on generators by introducing an auxiliary discriminator to refine the outputs of the generator. Section 6 describes our experiments with pruning or filtering Beam Search candidates during decoding.

4   Pretrained Base Model

As our base model, we used a model pretrained by Morishita et al. (2019) on the JParaCrawl data using the `fairseq` framework (Ott et al., 2019).

Data Preprocessing   Morishita et al. (2019) preprocessed the JParaCrawl English and Japanese text using `sentencepiece` (Kudo and Richardson, 2018) to obtain 32,000-token vocabularies on both the English and Japanese sides.

Architecture   The pretrained model follows the Transformer 'base' architecture (Vaswani et al., 2017), with a dropout probability of 0.3 (Srivastava et al., 2014).

Transformer is a multi-layer self-attention model. Both its encoder and its decoder contain multiple similar sub-modules which include a multi-head attention layer (MultiHead) and a position-wise feed-forward network (FFN).

$$\text{Attention}(Q, K, V) = \text{softmax}(\frac{QK^T}{\sqrt{d_k}})V \qquad (1)$$

$$\text{head}_i = \text{Attention}(QW_i^Q, KW_i^K, VW_i^V) \qquad (2)$$

$$\text{MultiHead}(Q, K, V)$$
$$= \text{Concat}(\text{head}_1, ..., \text{head}_h)W^O \qquad (3)$$

$$\text{FFN}(x) = \max(0, xW_1 + b_1)W_2 + b_2 \qquad (4)$$

Here, Q, K, V are the matrix representation of the query, key, and value separately. W and b denote the weights and biases of the linear layers. d_k denotes the dimension of the key matrix.

Optimizer The pretrained model was trained using the Adam optimizer (Kingma and Ba, 2014) with the hyperparameters $\beta_1 = 0.9$, $\beta_2 = 0.98$, $\alpha = 10^{-3}$ and $\epsilon = 10^{-9}$. The loss function used was cross entropy loss with $\epsilon_{ls} = 0.1$ loss smoothing (Szegedy et al., 2016). To improve update stability, gradients were clipped to a maximum norm of 1.0 (Pascanu et al., 2013).

Learning rate scheduling The learning rate schedule adopted for the pretrained model was the so-called 'Noam' schedule (Vaswani et al., 2017). This schedule linearly increases the learning rate for 4000 'warm-up' steps from a starting learning rate of 10^{-7} to the target learning rate of 10^{-3}, then decreases it from that point proportionally to the inverse square root of the step number.

5   Filtering Model

Apart from the NMT model, we additionally introduce a neural filtering model to post-process the NMT model's candidates. Instead of designing a model that will assign a real-value score to each of the candidates, we simplify the task by formulating it as a binary classification problem. Namely, the filtering model is trained to classify a given candidate sentence as a valid sample (in the gold-standard list) or an invalid sample. The intuition is that the gold-standard candidate list contains a small number of high-quality sentences (with larger weights) and a large number of lower-quality sentences. Thus it is more important to distinguish the hits from misses than high-quality hits from low-quality hits.

To construct the dataset for the filtering model, we augmented the Duolinguo dataset with the results of NMT model. Specifically, we labeled those result sentences that appear in the gold-standard list as *True* and labeled others as *False*.

As for the model architecture, we encode the source sentence and the candidate sentence separately with a one-layer bidirectional LSTM model. The encoding is the concatenation of the hidden vectors in both directions after complete traversal of the sequence, along with a (learned) positional embedding vector. This embedding encodes the position of the candidate sentence in the candidate list generated by the NMT model, which is sorted by descending score order.[4] Lastly, we use a multi-layer perception (MLP) to classify the concatenated vector.

$$v_s = \text{LSTM}_s(s) \qquad (5)$$
$$v_{c_i} = \text{LSTM}_c(c_i) \qquad (6)$$
$$p_i = \text{MLP}(\text{Dropout}([v_s : v_{c_i} : v_i])) \qquad (7)$$

Here, s denotes the source sentence, c_i denoted the i-th candidate, v_i denotes the positional encoding, and p_i denotes the predicted likelihood. The filtering model is optimized with binary cross-entropy loss.

6   Experiments

6.1   Multi-step Fine-tuning

We experiment with several different fine-tuning scenarios, each time evaluating the models using the Weighted F1 metric on our 200-prompt Duolingo test set. First as a baseline, we directly evaluate the JParaCrawl pretrained model without fine-tuning. Then we evaluate the performance of models fine-tuned on either JESC or on all English-Japanese pairs in our 2,100-prompt Duolingo training set.[5] Finally, we experiment with first fine-tuning on the JESC data and then on the Duolingo training set.

Before training, we preprocessed the JESC and Duolingo data using the same 32,000-token English and Japanese `sentencepiece` models as Morishita et al. (2019) used on the JParaCrawl data.

---

[4] In our experiments, we scored candidates using per token log likelihood (see Section 6.2 for further details.)

[5] The given English and Japanese sentences are unbalanced as there are multiple reference Japanese translations per English prompt. We balanced the training data by repeating the corresponding prompts over all reference translations to create English-Japanese pairs.

Training procedure We adopted the same optimizer settings as they used for the pretrained model, described in Section 4. Using mini-batches of up to 5,000 tokens, we made an update step every 16 mini-batches with mixed precision computation for increased training speed (Micikevicius et al., 2018). While the pretrained model was trained for 24,000 steps, each time we fine-tuned the model, we did so for 2,000 steps, continuing the inverse square root learning rate schedule from the pretraining. We saved the model parameters every 100 steps and for each fine-tuning experiment, we averaged the last eight parameter checkpoints to obtain our final model weights. For the model with two-step fine-tuning, we use the averaged checkpoint from the JESC fine-tuning experiment as the starting point for further fine-tuning on the Duolingo dataset.

6.2 Decoding Strategies

For producing multiple translations for each prompt, we output the entire beam width of candidates from the Beam Search or Diverse Beam Search (Vijayakumar et al., 2016) algorithms. Our motivation for experimenting with using Diverse Beam Search is to improve the coverage of our translation sets. In all our experiments, we capped the generated sequence length at 200 tokens.

Beam Search scoring Beam Search using sequence log likelihood (or likelihood) as scores results in a well-known length bias towards shorter sequences, with worsening bias for wider beams (Murray and Chiang, 2018). To address this, we scored beam candidates based on the mean log likelihood per token (Cho et al., 2014a). Further work could involve the use of more complex adjustments for length bias and including a coverage penalty over the source prompt (Wu et al., 2016).

6.3 Training Data Augmentation

Aligning data distributions The ground truth weights of the Duolingo reference translations invariably follow skewed distributions, with long tails of low weight translations (Figure 1). Consequently, one drawback of training with all English-Japanese pairs in the Duolingo data is that each pair is essentially provided to the model with equal weight. In other words, the distribution over reference translations at training time is uniform, whereas the distribution when evaluating weighted F1 score is skewed.

To address this, we sampled the training data

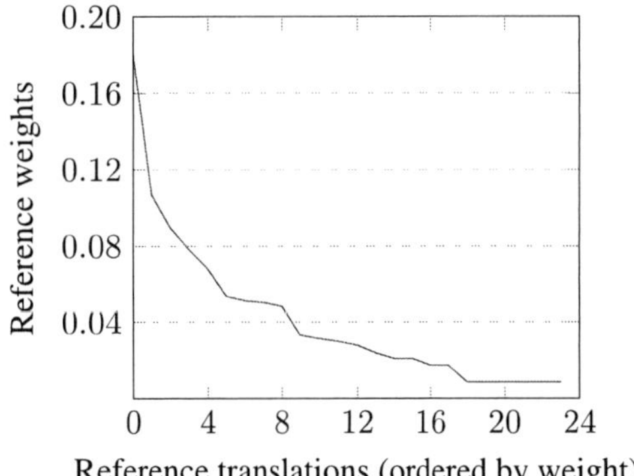

Figure 1: Typical distribution of ground truth weights

such that the model was trained on prompts with equal probability but for each prompt, reference translations were sampled according to the distribution given by the ground truth weights. In effect, this aligns the distribution over reference translations during training time and evaluation time.

Loss smoothing to improve coverage Aside from helping NMT models generalize, Müller et al. (2019) show that use of loss smoothing also better calibrates NMT models, preventing them from becoming over-confident. To encourage our NMT model to produce high-coverage translations, we hypothesize that increasing loss smoothing to decrease the model's confidence will improve its performance in producing a wider variety of correct translation candidates.

6.4 Filtering Model

Since our filtering model is trained with the results of the NMT model, we trained two filtering models with two different decoding strategies of the NMT model, namely, Regular and Diverse Beam Search with beam widths set such that approximately 100 unique candidates are output for each prompt. The NMT model is trained with the best hyper-parameters we found with the weighted sampling technique. We use the same train/dev/test splits as the NMT model and select the checkpoint with the best classification accuracy on the development set.

We used the Adam optimizer with initial learning rate 0.0001 and halved the learning rate when the validation accuracy plateaued for 2 epochs. The word embedding dimension, positional embedding dimension, the hidden dimension of the LSTM and MLP are all set to 128. The dropout rate was 0.2.

Fine-tuning	Precision	Recall	Weighted Recall	Weighted F1
None (JParaCrawl only)	18.57%	4.62%	16.97%	14.23%
JESC	13.37%	3.49%	13.12%	10.69%
Duolingo	34.59%	10.48%	26.90%	24.96%
JESC + Duolingo	35.98%	10.89%	27.85%	**25.92%**

Table 2: Results of different fine-tuning methods. Metrics evaluated on Beam Search beams of width 100 on our 200-prompt test set.

Beam	Mean # Cands	Precision	Recall	Weighted Recall	Weighted F1
50	49.6	46.27%	7.04%	21.29%	24.75%
100	98.6	35.98%	10.89%	27.85%	**25.92%**
150	147.1	29.98%	13.54%	31.33%	24.98%
200	195.4	26.01%	15.61%	33.92%	23.98%

Table 3: Results of tuning Beam (beam width). Mean # Cands refers to the mean number of unique candidates remaining after detokenizing subword tokens back into raw text and then removing duplicates. Metrics evaluated on our 200-prompt test set.

The post-processing procedure involved pruning all candidates with predicted likelihood less than 0.5.

7 Results

We conducted our experiments sequentially and generally used the best results so far as a baseline for subsequent experiments.

7.1 Multi-step Fine-tuning Results

Our best performing model was the one trained using multi-step fine-tuning, as shown in Table 2. The performance of this model was superior to the other fine-tuning settings on every metric, suggesting this result was not simply a matter of imbalance between precision and recall. This result provides strong evidence that the first fine-tuning step on the JESC data helped the model generalize to the Duolingo test set. In contrast, the model only fine-tuned on the Duolingo training set may not have generalized as well due to the training set's small size.

In order to balance precision and (weighted) recall appropriately to maximize the weighted F1 metric, we experimented with tuning the number of Beam Search candidates to output and found that 100 was optimal (Table 3). Note that the number of unique candidates returned can be fewer than the beam width as Beam Search searches over sequences of subword tokens and sometimes detokenization results in duplicates.

7.2 Diverse Beam Search Results

Our experiments with Diverse Beam Search show that using 3 beam groups with a very low Hamming diversity penalty can result in marginal performance improvement (Table 4). The algorithm evenly divides the total beam width between the groups and although the algorithm penalizes duplicate sequences, high scoring candidates are still often duplicated across groups. As such, we varied the total beam widths so that the mean number of unique candidates per prompt were approximately 100.[6] We conclude that encouraging a small amount diversity can allow the model to capture a wider range of variations without sacrificing too much precision.

We found that performance deteriorates when increasing the diversity penalty or the number of groups further. These results suggest that standard beam search by itself is relatively good at producing high-coverage translations and that acceptable variations of translations are rather homogeneous rather than diverse. To illustrate, Table 5 contains some examples of error candidates produced by Diverse Beam Search. Even though they would back-trackslate to the English prompt correctly, they nevertheless introduce a minor semantic variation that

---

[6]This duplication makes the number of outputs from Diverse Beam Search more variable. Our result with beam width 225 outputted 62-182 unique results per prompt with a standard deviation of 19.6, compared to 72-100 unique results with standard deviation of 4.0 from 100-width Regular Beam Search.

Groups	Penalty	Beam	Mean # Cands	Precision	Recall	Weighted Recall	Weighted F1
1	-	100	98.6	35.98%	10.89%	27.85%	**25.92%**
2	0.01	170	99.4	36.04%	11.00%	27.57%	26.18%
3	0.01	225	99.2	35.72%	10.88%	27.18%	**26.29%**
4	0.01	276	100.6	35.26%	10.90%	27.02%	26.23%
5	0.01	315	100.0	35.04%	10.76%	26.76%	26.21%
2	0.1	116	99.6	32.76%	10.03%	16.00%	24.42%
3	0.1	129	100.3	29.52%	9.10%	23.77%	22.59%

Table 4: Results of Diverse Beam Search on the test set. Beam refers to the beam width. Groups refers to the number of Diverse Groups (use of 1 group is equivalent to regular Beam Search). Penalty refers to the Hamming Diversity penalty in the Diverse Beam Search algorithm. Mean # Cands refers to the mean number of unique candidates remaining after detokenizing subword tokens back into raw text and then removing duplicates. Metrics evaluated on our 200-prompt test set.

Prompt	my parents have money
Incorrect	僕の両親はお金を持ってる
Diverse	僕の両親はお金を持ってます
Candidates	僕の両親には金があります

Table 5: Example incorrect candidates from Diverse Beam Search with 3 groups and 0.1 Hamming Diversity penalty. While the candidates would correctly back-translate to 'my parents have money', the first character of each candidate sentence indicates that the speaker / subject must be male (a restriction that is absent in the prompt).

Sampling	Smoothing	1-best BLEU	Precision	Recall	Weighted Recall	Weighted F1
Weighted	0	43.2	36.28%	10.95%	27.88%	26.88%
Weighted	0.05	42.5	37.41%	11.30%	28.31%	**27.43%**
Weighted	0.10	43.2	37.00%	11.27%	28.14%	**27.21%**
Unweighted	0.10	27.0	35.72%	10.88%	27.18%	**26.29%**
Weighted	0.15	41.8	36.84%	11.07%	28.01%	27.06%
Weighted	0.20	42.3	36.86%	11.09%	27.96%	27.04%

Table 6: Results of weighted sampling of input translation pairs and different loss smoothing rates on the test set. 1-best BLEU refers to corpus BLEU-4 score between the single highest-scoring Diverse Beam Search candidate and the single highest weighted reference translation for each prompt, smoothed with the NIST method (Chen and Cherry, 2014). The other metrics were evaluated over Diverse Beam Search with 225-width beams split across 3 groups and Hamming diversity penalty of 0.01. Metrics evaluated on our 200-prompt test set.

makes them unacceptable translations.

7.3 Training Data Augmentation Results

Sampling training data according to the ground truth weights meaningfully improves performance, as shown in Table 6. Our previous best weighted F1 score using Diverse Beam Search was 26.29%, and this improved to 27.21%. Moreover, evaluating the model on the standard machine translation metric of BLEU-4 score between the single best candidates and the single best ground truth translations, we observe a remarkable increase in BLEU score if weighted sampling is used during train-

ing. From this result, we conclude that unweighted sampling of training data overexposes the model to poorer translations, which significantly reduces the model's effectiveness as a general-purpose NMT model.

As for loss smoothing, contrary to our hypothesis, increasing the loss smoothing rate was detrimental. and, in fact, decreasing the rate from 0.1 to 0.05 even improved the weighted F1 score slightly from 27.21% to 27.43%. This suggests that the effect of loss smoothing on the high-coverage translation task is not necessarily different to the usual machine translation task.

Filtering	Decoding method	Precision	Recall	Weighted Recall	Weighted F1
None	Regular Beam Search	37.49%	**11.35%**	**28.93%**	27.00%
Filtered	Regular Beam Search	**38.89%**	10.87%	27.67%	**27.43%**
None	Diverse Beam Search	37.41%	**11.30%**	**28.31%**	27.43%
Filtered	Diverse Beam Search	**38.08%**	10.86%	26.94%	**27.56%**

Table 7: Results of filtering methods on our 200-prompt test set. Candidates were generated by the NMT models fine-tuned on JESC then Duolingo data with weighted sampling technique. Regular Beam Search used beam width 100 and Diverse Beam Search used beam width 225 over 3 groups with Hamming diversity penalty of 0.01 to yield approximately 100 candidates per prompt after deduplication. Candidates that have likelihoods greater than 0.5 assigned by the filtering model are selected as the results.

7.4 Beam Filtering Results

Table 7 shows the results of the filtering algorithm. The filtering model can improve the weighted F1 score with both the diverse beam search and regular beam search, especially with the regular beam search. This improvement results from a larger gain in precision from filtering than the loss in recall.

One thing to note is that our filtering model suffers from over-fitting. For example, with Regular Beam Search, our filtering model improves the weighted F1 score by 0.43% on the test set (Table 7). However, using the same technique on the training set results in an improvement of 6.25%.[7] This may result from the limited size of Duolinguo dataset, and the fact that over-fitting introduced by the NMT model would be amplified since the filtering model is trained on the results of the NMT model.

8 Conclusions and Future Work

Our machine translation system produces high-coverage sets of target language translations from single source language prompts.

We used multi-step fine-tuning to train a robust NMT model. This involved first training or fine-tuning a model on a large bitext dataset, then fine-tuning on the bitext dataset with high coverage sets of target language translations, which is likely to be small. In our experiments, we find that fine-tuning a pretrained model first on a corpus similar to our intended domain and then fine-tuning further on our smaller in-domain dataset produced the best results.

During training, we find that if the ground truth translations come with weights that indicate variations in their quality / likelihood, it is essential to expose the model to higher-quality translations more often during training. One way to do this is to to sample the training data with probabilities commensurate to the ground truth weights. Doing so will prevent overexposure to low-quality translations that ultimately harm the model's translation performance.

For decoding, we find that Beam Search scored on per token log likelihood finds very good translation candidates on its own. Nevertheless, instead using Diverse Beam Search with a very small penalty improves coverage.

We observed a further performance boost from post-processing the translation candidates. This was achieved by training an auxiliary filtering model on the results of the NMT model to prune unlikely candidates as a final step.

One idea for future work is to directly optimize the weighted F1 score during training using reinforcement learning. As the weighted F1 score is not a differentiable function, it is impossible to train directly on this metric using maximum likelihood estimation. Instead, one may use policy gradients under a reinforcement learning paradigm to do so.

References

Dzmitry Bahdanau, Kyunghyun Cho, and Yoshua Bengio. 2015. Neural machine translation by jointly learning to align and translate. In *3rd International Conference on Learning Representations, ICLR 2015, San Diego, CA, USA, May 7-9, 2015, Conference Track Proceedings*.

Ziqiang Cao, Wenjie Li, Sujian Li, and Furu Wei. 2018. Retrieve, rerank and rewrite: Soft template based neural summarization. In *Proceedings of the 56th Annual Meeting of the Association for Computational Linguistics (Volume 1: Long Papers)*, pages 152–161, Melbourne, Australia. Association for Computational Linguistics.

---

[7] On the training set, the filtering algorithm improves the weighted F1 score from 56.78% to 63.03%.

Boxing Chen and Colin Cherry. 2014. A systematic comparison of smoothing techniques for sentence-level bleu. In *WMT@ACL*.

Kyunghyun Cho, Bart van Merriënboer, Dzmitry Bahdanau, and Yoshua Bengio. 2014a. On the properties of neural machine translation: Encoder–decoder approaches. In *Proceedings of SSST-8, Eighth Workshop on Syntax, Semantics and Structure in Statistical Translation*, pages 103–111, Doha, Qatar. Association for Computational Linguistics.

Kyunghyun Cho, Bart van Merrienboer, Çaglar Gülçehre, Fethi Bougares, Holger Schwenk, and Yoshua Bengio. 2014b. Learning phrase representations using RNN encoder-decoder for statistical machine translation. *CoRR*, abs/1406.1078.

Markus Freitag and Yaser Al-Onaizan. 2016. Fast domain adaptation for neural machine translation. *CoRR*, abs/1612.06897.

Nal Kalchbrenner, Lasse Espeholt, Karen Simonyan, Aäron van den Oord, Alex Graves, and Koray Kavukcuoglu. 2016. Neural machine translation in linear time. *CoRR*, abs/1610.10099.

Diederik P. Kingma and Jimmy Ba. 2014. Adam: A method for stochastic optimization. *CoRR*, abs/1412.6980.

Bernhard Kratzwald, Anna Eigenmann, and Stefan Feuerriegel. 2019. Rankqa: Neural question answering with answer re-ranking. In *Proceedings of the 57th Annual Meeting of the Association for Computational Linguistics*, pages 6076–6085.

Taku Kudo and John Richardson. 2018. SentencePiece: A simple and language independent subword tokenizer and detokenizer for neural text processing. In *Proceedings of the 2018 Conference on Empirical Methods in Natural Language Processing: System Demonstrations*, pages 66–71, Brussels, Belgium. Association for Computational Linguistics.

Jiwei Li and Dan Jurafsky. 2016. Mutual information and diverse decoding improve neural machine translation. *CoRR*, abs/1601.00372.

Minh-Thang Luong and Christopher D. Manning. 2015. Stanford neural machine translation systems for spoken language domain. In *International Workshop on Spoken Language Translation*, Da Nang, Vietnam.

Minh-Thang Luong, Ilya Sutskever, Quoc V Le, Oriol Vinyals, and Wojciech Zaremba. 2014. Addressing the rare word problem in neural machine translation. *arXiv preprint arXiv:1410.8206*.

S. Mayhew, K. Bicknell, C. Brust, B. McDowell, W. Monroe, and B. Settles. 2020. Simultaneous translation and paraphrase for language education. In *Proceedings of the ACL Workshop on Neural Generation and Translation (WNGT)*. ACL.

Stephen Mayhew, Nitish Gupta, and Dan Roth. 2019. Robust named entity recognition with truecasing pretraining.

Paulius Micikevicius, Sharan Narang, Jonah Alben, Gregory Diamos, Erich Elsen, David Garcia, Boris Ginsburg, Michael Houston, Oleksii Kuchaiev, Ganesh Venkatesh, and Hao Wu. 2018. Mixed precision training. In *International Conference on Learning Representations*.

Makoto Morishita, Jun Suzuki, and Masaaki Nagata. 2019. JParaCrawl: A large scale web-based japanese-english parallel corpus. *arXiv preprint arXiv:1911.10668*.

Rafael Müller, Simon Kornblith, and Geoffrey E Hinton. 2019. When does label smoothing help? In H. Wallach, H. Larochelle, A. Beygelzimer, F. dAlché-Buc, E. Fox, and R. Garnett, editors, *Advances in Neural Information Processing Systems 32*, pages 4694–4703. Curran Associates, Inc.

Kenton Murray and David Chiang. 2018. Correcting length bias in neural machine translation. In *Proceedings of the Third Conference on Machine Translation: Research Papers*, pages 212–223, Brussels, Belgium. Association for Computational Linguistics.

Myle Ott, Sergey Edunov, Alexei Baevski, Angela Fan, Sam Gross, Nathan Ng, David Grangier, and Michael Auli. 2019. fairseq: A fast, extensible toolkit for sequence modeling. In *Proceedings of NAACL-HLT 2019: Demonstrations*.

Razvan Pascanu, Tomas Mikolov, and Yoshua Bengio. 2013. On the difficulty of training recurrent neural networks. In *Proceedings of the 30th International Conference on International Conference on Machine Learning - Volume 28*, ICML'13, page III–1310–III–1318. JMLR.org.

R. Pryzant, Y. Chung, D. Jurafsky, and D. Britz. 2018. JESC: Japanese-English Subtitle Corpus. *Language Resources and Evaluation Conference (LREC)*.

Pranav Rajpurkar, Jian Zhang, Konstantin Lopyrev, and Percy Liang. 2016. Squad: 100, 000+ questions for machine comprehension of text. *CoRR*, abs/1606.05250.

Rico Sennrich, Barry Haddow, and Alexandra Birch. 2015. Improving neural machine translation models with monolingual data.

Nitish Srivastava, Geoffrey E. Hinton, Alex Krizhevsky, Ilya Sutskever, and Ruslan Salakhutdinov. 2014. Dropout: a simple way to prevent neural networks from overfitting. *J. Mach. Learn. Res.*, 15:1929–1958.

Ilya Sutskever, Oriol Vinyals, and Quoc V. Le. 2014. Sequence to sequence learning with neural networks. *CoRR*, abs/1409.3215.

Christian Szegedy, Vincent Vanhoucke, Sergey Ioffe, Jon Shlens, and Zbigniew Wojna. 2016. Rethinking the inception architecture for computer vision. In *The IEEE Conference on Computer Vision and Pattern Recognition (CVPR)*.

Alon Talmor and Jonathan Berant. 2019. Multiqa: An empirical investigation of generalization and transfer in reading comprehension. *CoRR*, abs/1905.13453.

Ashish Vaswani, Noam Shazeer, Niki Parmar, Jakob Uszkoreit, Llion Jones, Aidan N Gomez, Ł ukasz Kaiser, and Illia Polosukhin. 2017. Attention is all you need. In *Advances in Neural Information Processing Systems 30*, pages 5998–6008. Curran Associates, Inc.

Ashwin K. Vijayakumar, Michael Cogswell, Ramprasaath R. Selvaraju, Qing Sun, Stefan Lee, David J. Crandall, and Dhruv Batra. 2016. Diverse beam search: Decoding diverse solutions from neural sequence models. *CoRR*, abs/1610.02424.

Yonghui Wu, Mike Schuster, Zhifeng Chen, Quoc V. Le, Mohammad Norouzi, Wolfgang Macherey, Maxim Krikun, Yuan Cao, Qin Gao, Klaus Macherey, Jeff Klingner, Apurva Shah, Melvin Johnson, Xiaobing Liu, Lukasz Kaiser, Stephan Gouws, Yoshikiyo Kato, Taku Kudo, Hideto Kazawa, Keith Stevens, George Kurian, Nishant Patil, Wei Wang, Cliff Young, Jason Smith, Jason Riesa, Alex Rudnick, Oriol Vinyals, Greg Corrado, Macduff Hughes, and Jeffrey Dean. 2016. Google's neural machine translation system: Bridging the gap between human and machine translation. *CoRR*, abs/1609.08144.

Jie Yang, Yue Zhang, and Fei Dong. 2017. Neural reranking for named entity recognition. In *Proceedings of the International Conference Recent Advances in Natural Language Processing, RANLP 2017*, pages 784–792, Varna, Bulgaria. INCOMA Ltd.

A   Appendices

To evaluate the result, the weighted macro F_1 (equation 8) with respect to the accepted translations is the metric of interest. This is the average weighted F_1 score (equation 12) over all prompts s in the corpus, where weighted F_1 is calculated with (unweighted) precision and weighted recall.

$$\textbf{Weighted Macro F}_1 = \sum_{s \in S} \frac{\textbf{Weighted F}_1(s)}{|S|} \tag{8}$$

Calculating the weighted recall requires the use of weights included in the dataset. These weights are associated with each human-curated acceptable translation, which represent the likelihood that an English learner would respond with that translation.

For each prompt s, the weighted true positives (WTP) and weighted false negatives (WFN) are:

$$\textbf{WTP}_s = \sum_{t \in \textbf{TP}_s} weight(t) \tag{9}$$

$$\textbf{WFN}_s = \sum_{t \in \textbf{FN}_s} weight(t) \tag{10}$$

With these, the weighted recall for each s can be calculated as follows

$$\textbf{Weighted Recall}(s) = \frac{\textbf{WTP}_s}{\textbf{WTP}_s + \textbf{WFN}_s} \tag{11}$$

Precision is calculated in the usual way, so the weighted F_1 score, $\textbf{Weighted F}_1(s)$, for a particular input s is given by

$$2 \cdot \frac{\textbf{Precision}(s) \cdot \textbf{WeightedRecall}(s)}{\textbf{Precision}(s) + \textbf{WeightedRecall}(s)} \tag{12}$$

Meeting the 2020 Duolingo Challenge on a Shoestring

Tadashi Nomoto
National Institute of Japanese Literature
10-3 Midori Tachikawa 190-0014 Japan
`nomoto@acm.org`

Abstract

What is given below is a brief description of the two systems, called gFCONV and c-VAE, which we built in a response to the 2020 Duolingo Challenge. Both are neural models that aim at disrupting a sentence representation the encoder generates with an eye on increasing the diversity of sentences that emerge out of the process. Importantly, we decided not to turn to external sources for extra ammunition, curious to know how far we can go while confining ourselves to the data released by Duolingo (Mayhew et al., 2020). gFCONV works by taking over a pre-trained sequence model, intercepting the output its encoder produces on its way to the decoder. c-VAE is a conditional variational auto-encoder, seeking the diversity by blurring the representation that the encoder derives. Experiments on a corpus constructed out of the public dataset from Duolingo, containing some 4 million pairs of sentences, found that gFCONV is a consistent winner over c-VAE though both suffered heavily from a low recall.

1 Introduction

A major driver for our participating in the challenge was the curiosity to see whether recent approaches to sentence encoding with the variational auto-encoder (VAE) have any relevance to the generation of diverse sentences. (Bowman et al., 2016) were the first to explore the use of VAE in language generation. The work demonstrated that VAE provides a continuous code space for sentences, where any randomly picked data point in the space can be decoded to yield a coherent sentence, which is significant given that the conventional RNNs do not provide such a capability. The problem with VAE however, is that it has no mechanism to ensure that the meaning of the source sentence is passed over to the output, which often causes a sentence to be altered, or deformed

beyond recognition. While VAE is a popular approach people turn to as a way to diversify sentences the model generates, no definitive answer has been found on how to control or tame what it spews out. A typical solution is to fuse a VAE code with the output of a regular sentence encoder, in order to encourage the decoder to output a sentence that retains some semantic features present in the source sentence (Gupta et al., 2017). Also noteworthy is a recent work by (Guu et al., 2018), who building on an idea similar to VAE, talk about modeling the distribution of cosine similarities between word vectors for the input and target. (Li et al., 2015) is something of an odd ball in the pursuit of the diversity in sentence generation. The authors argued that we could achieve the diversity by discouraging the decoder to select candidates that are similar to the input. A clear advantage they have over others is that their scheme does not involve any learning and is straightforward to implement.

The idea that one can view a latent representation as a sample drawn from some probabilistic distribution inspired people to explore its potential in a wide range of tasks and domains. (Miao et al., 2015), while working on document modeling, suggested that we use VAE as a way to get a compact representation for a document. (Fang et al., 2019) argued for using a sample based distribution over Gaussian distribution for a latent code to better express the holistic property of the source sentence.

In this work, we focus on two approaches, both based on VAE: one that attempts to achieve the diversity by generalizing the sentence representation produced by the encoder; and another which randomly perturbs the encoder's output during the sentence generation. We report here their respective performance on a test corpus we carved out of the official training data. For the final submission, we went along with the latter approach.

Proceedings of the 4th Workshop on Neural Generation and Translation (WNGT 2020), pages 129–133
Online, July 10, 2020. ©2020 Association for Computational Linguistics
www.aclweb.org/anthology/D19-56%2d

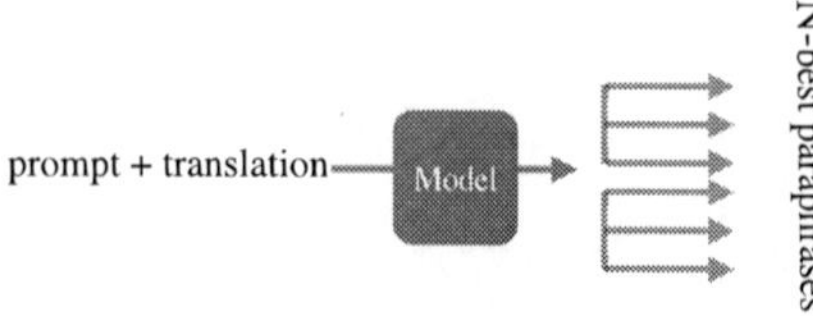

Figure 1: Translation as Paraphrase

2 Translation as Paraphrase

Our effort revolved around two questions: (1) how best to incorporate likelihood scores of target translations that were provided as part of the training data, and (2) how *not* to rely on an external resource while building a solution. We wanted to know how far we can go using only the data made available to us at the competition, and nothing more. Our answer to the first question takes advantage of the fact that a set of translations associated with each English prompt are considered an equivalence class in the sense that if we take any pair from the set, we can substitute one for the other without significantly affecting its meaning. We may take the likelihood that a human picks a particular sentence (call it X) as a good translation for some prompt (P) as the probability of its being a paraphrase of some other sentence (say Y) from a group of possible translations of which X is part. The intuition here is that if X is more typical as a translation of P, it is more likely to serve as a paraphrase of whatever other way we may have to express P in the target language. Following this idea, we created training data by randomly sampling a pair of sentences (both in the same language) that appear as alternate translations for a given prompt in accordance with their popular rating. For each prompt, we sampled 2,000 pairs of translations (which may include pairs consisting of identical sentences), resulting in 4,601,000 training instances (which amount to 2,300 prompts plus those provided in the development and test set) (Mayhew et al., 2020).[1] We set aside 100

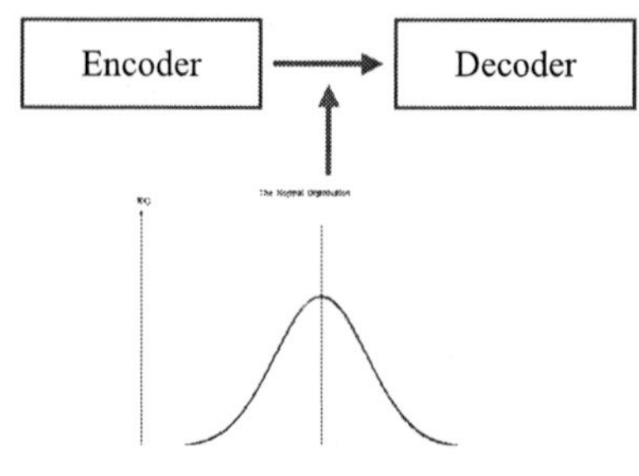

Figure 2: gFCONV

prompts as a private development set and another 100 for testing. We included in each training instance an English prompt as well as its translation in order to prevent paraphrases the algorithm generates from diverging from the meaning of the prompt (Table 1).

Figure 1 shows a schematic picture of how our approach works. We feed into the system a prompt and its translation which we assume to be given (via AWS, for example). Out comes its paraphrases (or translations in varied styles). The model we built is essentially one based on Fairseq's convolution to sequence architecture of the type called 'fconv_iwslt_de_en' (call it FCONV) which features 4 convolutional layers for the encoder and 3 for the decoder.[2] The embedding dimension for the input and output token was set to 256. We did not use pre-trained embeddings for either of the languages we dealt with. Neither did we make any architectural change to FCONV. We simply trained it as it was given. A departure comes in the testing phase. Following (Guu et al., 2018), we applied a Gaussian noise on the output of the encoder as it was sent to the decoder (Fig. 2).

$$u = E(x) + \epsilon, \quad \epsilon \sim \mathcal{N}(0, k) \tag{1}$$

where x is an input and $E(x)$ is an output from applying an encoder E on x. u denotes an input to a decoder. A larger noise means a greater disruption in the latent representation coming from the encoder, which we hoped would lead to an increase in the diversity of sentences being generated. We randomly sampled a noise from a normal distribution with the mean set to 0 and the variance rang-

---

[1] For this year's challenge, we worked only on the English-Japanese track. We included both test and development sets as part of training data, as a way to prevent the algorithm from stumbling upon unknown tokens in the test set. We don't see this as much of a problem because each prompt in development and test sets carries no more than one translation, i.e. a training pair we get from the development and test set has a same sentence for both source and target. We made use of MeCab for tokenizing sentences in Japanese.

[2] https://github.com/pytorch/fairseq

Table 1: Training Instances. The source part of each input consists of two sections: the first section contains a sentence in an original language, followed by a translation in a target language, demarcated by a separator '@@@@.'

SOURCE	that apple is very big . @@@@ その 林檎 は 非常 に でかい です 。 i like to work . @@@@ ボク は 仕事 は 好き です 。 he drinks milk . @@@@ 彼 は 牛乳 を 飲み ます 。 what are her strengths ? @@@@ 彼女 の 長所 は なん でしょう ？ what has she done ? @@@@ 彼女 は 何 を やり 終わった ん です か ？
TARGET	その りんご が とても でかい 。 私 は 働く の が 好き 。 かれ は ぎゅうにゅうを 飲み ます 。 何 が 彼女 の 強い 所 なの ？ 何 を 彼女 は 終わった の ？

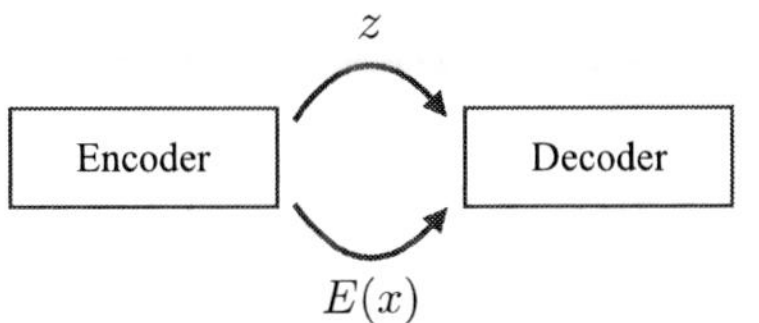

Figure 3: Conditional VAE

ing from 0 to 0.6. In what follows, we refer to the scheme as gFCONV.

We also looked at a conditional variational auto-encoder (c-VAE), a close cousin of gFCONV for the sake of comparison. While both aim at building a latent representation that embraces the notion of uncertainty, c-VAE differs from the variance based approach in that it seeks to find a probabilistic distribution that defines a range of representations that the encoder churns out. In terms of formulae, this comes to the following (also see Fig. 3 for a visual intuition).

$$u = E(x) + r * z, \qquad (2)$$

Here $z = \mu + \epsilon * v$ with $\epsilon \sim \text{Unif}[0, 1)$. μ and v are a mean and variance, defined as $\mu = g(x)$, and $v = f(x)$, respectively. x is an input, g and f are some arbitrary functions over x. $E(x)$ again denotes the output of an encoder. μ and v are learnable parameters, which means that they need to be trained to have them work. It is worth noting that gFCONV has no extra 'learnable' parameters. r is a hyper-parameter to be set manually, which determines the degree of contribution of z to a latent representation of x. We combine $E(x)$ and a representation sampled from a Gaussian distribution to build a final encoder output. Our decision to condition VAE on $E(x)$ is motivated by a frequent observation in the past literature that VAE is poor at preserving the meaning of the source sentence, often transforming it beyond recognition. Conditioning VAE on the input is a popular trick to discourage the algorithm from straying too far away from the source.

Implementation-wise, c-VAE was based on FCONV, from which we also built gFCONV. We kept all the hyper-parameter settings intact, e.g. the number of layers, the size and the number of filters, etc. We did not apply any scheduled annealing weight to the KL term in the loss function.

For gFCONV, we varied the variance parameter k (Eqn. 1) from 0.00 to 0.60 in increments of 0.05. For each value of k, we ran gFCONV on the test set 100 times, letting the model output 80 alternative translations for each prompt (Setting k to 0 reduces gFCONV to a vanilla FCONV). This had resulted in a pool of 8,000 candidates for a given prompt under a particular value of k. Out of which we retained only those that had a non zero similarity to gold translations by AWS.[3] We measured the similarity using LASER,[4] along with pre-trained word embeddings from FastText,[5] which LASER requires. We were interested to know how variance affected the performance, in particular how it contributed to improving the diversity.

---

[3]i.e. those found in the 'test.en_ja.aws_baseline.pred.txt' in the 'staple-2020-test-blind' directory.

[4]https://github.com/facebookresearch/LASER

[5]https://fasttext.cc/docs/en/crawl-vectors.html

Table 2: Variance vs. Performance. 'P' denotes precision, 'R' recall, and 'k' variance. Numbers in red represent the baseline and those in blue the best performing system where we have a minimum divergence between Micro and Macro F1.

		UNWEIGHTED			WEIGHTED		
k	P	R	Micro F1	Macro F1	R	Micro F1	Macro F1
0.00	39.16	3.83	6.97	11.37	13.62	20.21	16.35
0.05	33.24	5.09	8.83	12.77	15.60	21.23	17.13
0.10	28.10	6.18	10.14	13.46	17.47	21.54	17.38
0.15	23.41	7.45	11.30	13.66	19.34	21.18	16.92
0.20	20.08	8.62	12.06	13.73	21.10	20.58	16.48
0.25	16.93	9.57	12.22	13.18	22.37	19.27	15.40
0.30	14.17	10.24	11.89	12.27	23.36	17.64	14.13
0.35	12.02	10.69	11.31	11.22	24.16	16.05	12.74
0.40	10.92	11.49	11.20	10.70	24.70	15.14	12.03
0.45	9.15	11.23	10.08	9.67	24.38	13.30	10.73
0.50	8.21	10.81	9.33	8.72	23.24	12.14	9.72
0.55	7.24	9.99	8.40	7.90	22.84	11.00	8.78
0.60	6.92	9.30	7.94	7.54	22.25	10.56	8.38

Table 3: Conditional VAE

		UNWEIGHTED			WEIGHTED		
r	P	R	Micro F1	Macro F1	R	Micro F1	Macro F1
0.0	39.16	3.83	6.97	11.37	13.62	20.21	16.35
0.1	24.06	7.11	10.97	14.84	19.41	21.49	18.08
0.2	22.55	7.98	11.78	14.81	20.16	21.29	17.87
0.3	18.28	7.72	10.86	14.28	20.09	19.15	17.10
0.4	17.09	7.58	10.50	13.12	20.21	18.52	15.69
0.5	15.68	7.70	10.33	12.73	20.08	17.61	15.31

3 Results and Discussion

Results are provided in Table 2. The numbers shown were produced using the official scorer. In the following discussion, we concentrate on unweighted scores as our interest here is in knowing how much we improved the raw recall under the current setup. Note that weighted scores do not shed light on the true diversity of sentences we have garnered.

Looking at Table 2, we see gFCONV gaining on a vanilla FCONV, whose performance is represented by the numbers at $k = 0.00$. At $k = 0.25$, we see the raw recall jumping from 3.83 to 9.57, Micro F1 from 6.97 to 12.22, and Macro F1 from 11.37 to 13.18. Compare the difference between Micro and Macro F1 at $k = 0.00$ and that we have at $k = 0.25$. The difference for the latter is much smaller. This suggests that under gFCONV, the performance is more stable across test items compared to the vanilla FCONV. A large divergence at

$k = 0.00$ indicates wild ups and downs in performance, suggesting that the model is doing beautifully well on some but failing miserably on others. In contrast to Micro F1, Macro F1 is blind to how many candidate translations there are for each prompt, so may not give us an accurate picture of how the model is doing on each prompt.

As with gFCONV, we ran c-VAE on the test set 100 times, obtaining 100 distinct pools of candidate translations for each prompt.[6] We report in Table 3, figures that represent performance on all the results combined in the manner we described for gFCONV. We varied r (in Eqn. 2) from 0.1 to 0.5 in 0.1 increments. We observe that c-VAE is somewhat behind gFCONV (in terms of divergence between Micro and Macro F1), though performing well over the baseline (numbers in red). A large gap between (unweighted) Micro and Macro

---

[6] We generated 8,000 hypotheses for each prompt under a particular value of r, 80 at each round.

Table 4: Official Results. By W. Recall and W. F1, we mean Weighted Recall and F1.

Phase	Rank	Precision	W. Recall	W. F1
DEV	6/6	0.369	0.183	0.181
TEST	6/6	0.349	0.212	0.194

F1 again shows that the model suffers from a fluctuating performance, swinging wildly from one test item to another. The final submission for the official evaluation was prepared using gFCONV at $k = 0.10$, under the pseudonym 'darkside,' with the official results shown in Table 4.[7]

4 Conclusions

We discussed two approaches as a way to tackle the Duolingo Challenge. One is gFCONV, which takes over a pre-trained sequence model, intercepts and perturbs the output its encoder produces on its way to the decoder. Another is c-VAE, a conditional variational auto-encoder, which seeks the diversity by blurring the representation that the encoder derives. Either approach, it was found, outperformed the vanilla FCONV. We also noted a large discrepancy between Micro and Macro F1, suggesting that the models' performance is not even and fluctuates wildly from item to item. Moreover, there were some test prompts for which the models were not able to find any translations. We recognize that this is an area we need to scrutinize to further improve the performance. In the long run, it would be interesting to see if we can bring to the task recent developments in VAE such as (Bouchacourt et al., 2018).

References

Diane Bouchacourt, Ryota Tomioka, and Sebastian Nowozin. 2018. Multi-level variational autoencoder: Learning disentangled representations from grouped observations. In *AAAI 2018*.

Samuel R. Bowman, Luke Vilnis, Oriol Vinyals, Andrew Dai, Rafal Jozefowicz, and Samy Bengio. 2016. Generating sentences from a continuous space. In *Proceedings of The 20th SIGNLL Conference on Computational Natural Language Learning*, pages 10–21, Berlin, Germany. Association for Computational Linguistics.

Le Fang, Chunyuan Li, Jianfeng Gao, Wen Jun Dong, and Changyou Chen. 2019. Implicit deep latent variable models for text generation. In *EMNLP/IJCNLP*.

Ankush Gupta, Arvind Agarwal, Prawaan Singh, and Piyush Rai. 2017. A deep generative framework for paraphrase generation. *CoRR*, abs/1709.05074.

Kelvin Guu, Tatsunori B. Hashimoto, Yonatan Oren, and Percy Liang. 2018. Generating sentences by editing prototypes. *Transactions of the Association for Computational Linguistics*, 6:437–450.

Jiwei Li, Michel Galley, Chris Brockett, Jianfeng Gao, and Bill Dolan. 2015. A diversity-promoting objective function for neural conversation models. *CoRR*, abs/1510.03055.

S. Mayhew, K. Bicknell, C. Brust, B. McDowell, W. Monroe, and B. Settles. 2020. Simultaneous translation and paraphrase for language education. In *Proceedings of the ACL Workshop on Neural Generation and Translation (WNGT)*. ACL.

Yishu Miao, Lei Yu, and Phil Blunsom. 2015. Neural variational inference for text processing. *CoRR*, abs/1511.06038.

[7]We did not submit the version at 0.25 which turned out to be the best, due to its late discovery, which came well past the deadline.

English-to-Japanese Diverse Translation by Combining Forward and Backward Outputs

Masahiro Kaneko   Aizhan Imankulova   Tosho Hirasawa   Mamoru Komachi
Tokyo Metropolitan University
6-6 Asahigaoka, Hino, Tokyo 191-0065, Japan
`{kaneko-masahiro, imankulova-aizhan, hirasawa-tosho}@ed.tmu.ac.jp`
`komachi@tmu.ac.jp`

Abstract

We introduce our TMU system that is submitted to The 4th Workshop on Neural Generation and Translation (WNGT2020) to English-to-Japanese (En→Ja) track on Simultaneous Translation And Paraphrase for Language Education (STAPLE) shared task. In most cases machine translation systems generate a single output from the input sentence, however, in order to assist language learners in their journey with better and more diverse feedback, it is helpful to create a machine translation system that is able to produce diverse translations of each input sentence. However, creating such systems would require complex modifications in a model to ensure the diversity of outputs. In this paper, we investigated if it is possible to create such systems in a simple way and whether it can produce desired diverse outputs. In particular, we combined the outputs from forward and backward neural translation models (NMT). Our system achieved third place in En→Ja track, despite adopting only a simple approach.

1   Introduction

WNGT2020[1] on STAPLE[2] (Mayhew et al., 2020) addresses generating high-coverage sets of plausible translations which can be useful in machine translation (MT), MT evaluation, multilingual paraphrase, and language education technology fields. In Duolingo (the world's largest language learning platform), some learning takes place via translation-based exercises and assessment is done by comparing the learners' responses to a large set of acceptable human-generated translations. Therefore, retaining richer paraphrases of the translation results would help to generate more accurate feedback to the learners.

---

[1] `https://sharedtask.duolingo.cites.google.com/view/wngt20/home`
[2] `https://sharedtask.duolingo.com/`

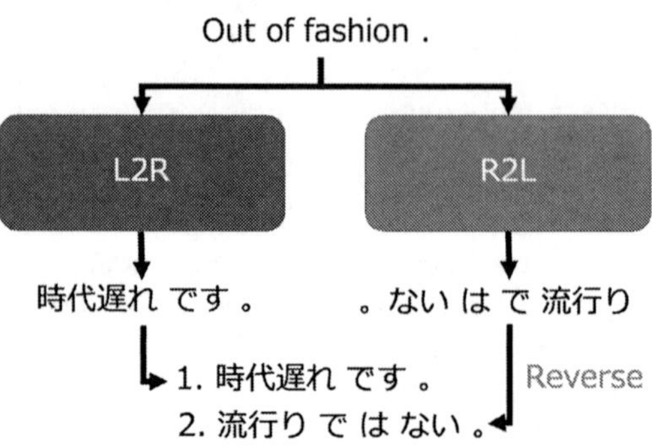

Figure 1: Architecture of TMU system.

Several studies have been conducted on the diversity of translation results (Vijayakumar et al., 2018; Xu et al., 2018; Shu et al., 2019; Ippolito et al., 2019). On the other hand, these methods rely on complex approaches. For example, modifying beam-search (Vijayakumar et al., 2018), introducing rewriting patterns or sentence codes (Xu et al., 2018; Shu et al., 2019) or using post-decoding clustering (Ippolito et al., 2019). However, we were curious if we can produce diverse outputs only using a simple approach.

Therefore, we aim to generate a variety of translations simply using generally adopted neural MT (NMT) methods. For that purpose, we use the models trained on the left-to-right (L2R) and right-to-left (R2L) directions, where L2R produces target sentences in a forward way and R2L will produce target sentences in a backward way as shown in Figure 1. We then combine the output of L2R and back-reversed output of R2L to produce diverse translations. We adopt this approach based on the following reasons:

- No need to modify the NMT model.

- Reversing only the target sentences is sufficient.

Proceedings of the 4th Workshop on Neural Generation and Translation (WNGT 2020), pages 134–138
Online, July 10, 2020. ©2020 Association for Computational Linguistics
www.aclweb.org/anthology/D19-56%2d

- It is known that L2R translates prefixes and R2L translates suffixes better (Liu et al., 2016). This indicates that L2R and R2L produce different translation results, which may have an impact on the diversity of generated translations.

In our experiments, we show that even the combination of L2R and R2L translation results can produce a sufficiently diverse set of translations. In addition, we demonstrate that even though we use a simple approach, it is possible to generate varied paraphrased transcriptions which do not simply replace one word with another, contrarily, it utilizes different styles, opposition, word order etc. Our TMU system achieved the third place using only the simple approach.

2 Related Work

Several models have been proposed to generate diverse decoding outputs for different tasks. For example, Xu et al. (2018) proposed diverse paraphrase generation by introducing rewriting patterns into the decoder of the encoder-decoder model. Vijayakumar et al. (2018) proposed diverse beam search algorithm for decoding diverse sequences. They describe beam search as an optimization problem and augment the objective with a diversity term. They encouraged diversity between beams at each step by rewarding each group for spending its beam budget to explore different parts of the output space rather than repeatedly chasing sub-optimal beams from prior groups. They report their results on image captioning, visual question generation, and MT tasks. Shu et al. (2019) generated diverse translations by conditioning sentence generation with the sentence codes. They explored two methods: (a) semantic coding model which extracted sentence codes from unsupervisedly learned semantic information and (b) syntactic coding model which derived the sentence codes from the parse trees produced by a constituency parser. Ippolito et al. (2019) proposed the use of over-sampling followed by post-decoding clustering to remove similar sequences. They evaluated several techniques on an open-ended dialog task and image captioning task.

These works introduce different complex modifications to the model in order to achieve diversity while generating the output. However, in this paper, we show how to simply generate diverse outputs.

Pre-train	
Model Architecture	Transformer-big
Number of epochs	20
Max tokens	4,096
Optimizer	Adam
	($\beta_1 = 0.9, \beta_2 = 0.98,$
	$\epsilon = 1 \times 10^{-8}$)
Learning rate	5×10^{-4}
Learning rate schedule	inverse sqrt
Warmup updates	4,000
Min learning rate	1×10^{-9}
Loss function	label smoothed cross-entropy
	($\epsilon_{ls} = 0.1$)
	(Szegedy et al., 2016)
Dropout	0.3
Gradient Clipping	0.1
Fine-tuning	
Number of epochs	10
Learning rate	3×10^{-5}
Learning rate schedule	fixed
Translation	
Beam size	64
Ensemble	4

Table 1: Hyperparameter values of NMT model.

3 Experiments

3.1 System

We used the open-source `fairseq`[3] (Ott et al., 2019) for training NMT models. We adopt the Transformer (Vaswani et al., 2017) as our translation model. We train two types of models, L2R and R2L for decoding. For L2R, we train a forward model in a traditional way. For R2L model, we first reverse the target sentences and train a model so it will produce the output from backward. Then the output of R2L is reversed again to forward direction. We exclude sentences from the translation results by normalizing the log probabilities of the hypothesis sentences by sentence length with less than -1.55 score. Then, the n-best translation results of each L2R and R2L are combined and if there is a duplication, one of the translations is removed.

In our preliminary experiments, we found that the NMT model cannot produce sufficient quality translations using only the official data set. Therefore, we pre-train the NMT models with additional datasets, followed by fine-tuning with the STAPLE dataset. Thus, we expect that a model learns

---

[3] `https://github.com/pytorch/fairseq`

Data	Size
Official STAPLE-train	2,500 / 855,941
Official STAPLE-dev	500 / 172,817
Official STAPLE-test	500 / 165,095
STAPLE-train	2,450 / 837,879
STAPLE-dev	50 / 18,062
OpenSubtitles	2,083,600
Tatoeba	202,167
TED-train	152,115
TED-dev	1,958
TED-test	1,982

Table 2: Statistics on official STAPLE data and data used in our experiments. For STAPLE data, the left side indicates the number of prompts and the right side indicates the total number of sentences contained in each prompt.

System	F1
jbrem	31.8
sweagraw	29.4
TMU	**28.3**
mzy	26.0
hzguo	23.9
jindra.helcl	21.3
darkside	19.4
STAPLE_aws_baseline	4.3
STAPLE_fairseq_baseline	3.3

Table 3: The official results on the test set for En→Ja in terms of weighted F1.

Model	F1
Single seed 1	23.7
Single seed 2	23.4
Multi seed	23.9
L2R	23.7
R2L	23.2
L2R & R2L	**24.7**

Table 4: The result for each model in terms of weighted F1 on the development set.

general translation ability during pre-training and further learns to produce more diverse translation during fine-tuning.

3.2 Hyperparameters

Table 1 lists some specific hyperparameters used in our experiments. For fine-tuning, we used the same values as we used for pre-training regarding the values that are not listed in the table. We trained four L2R models and four R2L models with different seeds on the same data, then ensembled all of them by taking the union of their outputs. We adjusted the hyperparameters using the development set, described in the next subsection.

3.3 Data

Table 2 summarizes the size of data used in our experiments for En→Ja track. The official dataset of STAPLE contains multiple translations for a single prompt. We did not use the official development and test data in our experiments because the correct data with answers were not available to the public. Therefore, we randomly divided the official training data into training data and development data in prompt units as shown in Table 2. We use OpenSubtitles[4] (Lison and Tiedemann, 2016), Tatoeba[5] (Tiedemann, 2012), TED[6] train and dev (Cettolo et al., 2012) corpora as additional dataset which are similar to the STAPLE data in

terms of sentence length and data domain. We used STAPLE-train, OpenSubtitles, Tatoeba and TED-train as training data and STAPLE-dev, TED-dev and TED-test as development data for the pre-training. In fine-tuning, we used STAPLE-train as training data and STAPLE-dev as development data.

We lowercased all the English data. English was tokenized using *tokenizer.perl* of Moses[7] (Koehn et al., 2007) and Japanese was tokenized using MeCab[8] with the IPA dictionary. After tokenization, we adopted sub-word segmentation mechanism (Sennrich et al., 2016)[9]. Note that, for the training of R2L, we first applied tokenization for the target sentences, then applied sub-word segmentation and then performed the reversing. The size of the sub-word vocabularies was set to 8,000. The sub-word vocabularies were constructed using pre-train training data.

---

[4] http://opus.nlpl.eu/OpenSubtitles-v2018.php
[5] http://opus.nlpl.eu/Tatoeba.php
[6] https://wit3.fbk.eu

[7] https://github.com/moses-smt/mosesdecoder
[8] http://taku910.github.io/mecab
[9] https://github.com/rsennrich/subword-nmt

Source	your skirt is out of fashion.	
Output 1	あなたのスカートは時代遅れである。	(Your skirt is outdated.)
Output 2	あなたのスカートは流行していない。	(Your skirt is not in fashion.)
Source	they give me water.	
Output 1	彼女らは私に水をくれる。	(They give me water.)
Output 2	私は彼らから水をもらいます。	(I get water from them.)
Source	she found another path.	
Output 1	彼女は違う道を見つけた。	(She found a different path.)
Output 2	彼女は別の道を見つけたわ	(She found another way)
Output 3	彼女は別の道を見つけたよ	(She found another way)

Table 5: Examples generated by the combination of four ensemble L2R and four ensemble R2L models' outputs using the development set. () indicate their English translation. The English translation of the third example can not fully represent the change of styles used in Japanese language output.

3.4 Results

We used weighted macro F1 as the main scoring metric (Mayhew et al., 2020). The system is scored based on its ability to return all acceptable human-made translations, weighted by the likelihood that the learner will respond to each translation. The weighted macro F1 calculates a weighted F1 for each prompt and takes the average of all the prompts in the corpus.

Table 3 lists the F1 scores of participating systems in En→Ja track. Our TMU system was ranked the third.

4 Discussion

4.1 Does translation in opposite directions contribute to a diverse translation?

We investigate whether decoding in opposite directions contribute to diversity in translation outputs. We compare the results for development set generated with beam size of 64 in one model (L2R, R2L, Single seed 1, Single seed 2) to those generated and combined two models (L2R & R2L, Multi seed) with beam size of 32. As a baseline, we also experiment with different seeds and examine their efficiency. This allows us to see how the direction or seed contribute to the diversity of translation.

Table 4 shows the results for top-2 single seeds models in terms of performance and multi seed model, and the best L2R, R2L, and L2R & R2L models. The results show that using multiple seeds leads to higher F1 scores, however, the improvement is not critical. On the other hand, L2R & R2L improved weighted F1 scores for 1.0 points. Therefore, we show that it is important to combine the outputs of the two directions.

4.2 Examples of Translations

Table 5 demonstrates the example of diverse translations generated by the combination of four ensemble L2R and four ensemble R2L models' outputs. Here we sampled the outputs from development set. The first example illustrates how our system uses negation to express the same meaning translations of the source sentence. The second example changed the syntax by using benefactive verbs for the output while preserving the same meaning and grammatical correctness. The third example uses different styles, which are specific for Japanese language, to introduce diversity.

Therefore, we can conclude that even using simple approach we can achieve diverse, grammatically correct translations without changing the meaning of the input sentence.

5 Conclusion

In this paper, we introduced our system submitted to WNGT2020 shared task to En→Ja track on STAPLE. We have shown that even a simple method which uses only forward and backward models' outputs can generate a variety of translations while maintaining original meaning and grammaticality.

In future, we plan to compare our system with existing systems that perform different types of language generation. In addition, we will investigate the impact of L2R and R2L models to the diverse output in depth.

References

Mauro Cettolo, Christian Girardi, and Marcello Federico. 2012. WIT^3: Web Inventory of Transcribed and Translated Talks. In *EAMT*.

Daphne Ippolito, Reno Kriz, Maria Kustikova, João Sedoc, and Chris Callison-Burch. 2019. Comparison of Diverse Decoding Methods from Conditional Language Models. In *ACL*.

Philipp Koehn, Hieu Hoang, Alexandra Birch, Chris Callison-Burch, Marcello Federico, Nicola Bertoldi, Brooke Cowan, Wade Shen, Christine Moran, Richard Zens, Chris Dyer, Ondrej Bojar, Alexandra Constantin, and Evan Herbst. 2007. Moses: Open Source Toolkit for Statistical Machine Translation. In *ACL*.

Pierre Lison and Jörg Tiedemann. 2016. OpenSubtitles2016: Extracting Large Parallel Corpora from Movie and TV Subtitles. In *LREC*.

Lemao Liu, Masao Utiyama, Andrew M. Finch, and Eiichiro Sumita. 2016. Agreement on Target-bidirectional Neural Machine Translation. In *HLT-NAACL*.

S. Mayhew, K. Bicknell, C. Brust, B. McDowell, W. Monroe, and B. Settles. 2020. Simultaneous Translation And Paraphrase for Language Education. In *WNGT@ACL*.

Myle Ott, Sergey Edunov, Alexei Baevski, Angela Fan, Sam Gross, Nathan Ng, David Grangier, and Michael Auli. 2019. fairseq: A Fast, Extensible Toolkit for Sequence Modeling. In *NAACL-HLT: Demonstrations*.

Rico Sennrich, Barry Haddow, and Alexandra Birch. 2016. Neural Machine Translation of Rare Words with Subword Units. In *ACL*.

Raphael Shu, Hideki Nakayama, and Kyunghyun Cho. 2019. Generating Diverse Translations with Sentence Codes. In *ACL*.

Christian Szegedy, Vincent Vanhoucke, Sergey Ioffe, Jon Shlens, and Zbigniew Wojna. 2016. Rethinking the Inception Architecture for Computer Vision. In *CVPR*.

Jorg Tiedemann. 2012. Parallel Data, Tools and Interfaces in OPUS. In *LREC*.

Ashish Vaswani, Noam Shazeer, Niki Parmar, Jakob Uszkoreit, Llion Jones, Aidan N. Gomez, Lukasz Kaiser, and Illia Polosukhin. 2017. Attention is All you Need. In *NeurIPS*.

Ashwin K. Vijayakumar, Michael Cogswell, Ramprasaath R. Selvaraju, Qing He Sun, Stefan Lee, David J. Crandall, and Dhruv Batra. 2018. Diverse beam search for improved description of complex scenes. In *AAAI*.

Qiongkai Xu, Juyan Zhang, Lizhen Qu, Lexing Xie, and Richard Nock. 2018. D-PAGE: Diverse Paraphrase Generation. *ArXiv*.

POSTECH Submission on Duolingo Shared Task

Junsu Park[1], Hongseok Kwon[1], Jong-Hyeok Lee[1,2]
Department of Computer Science and Engineering[1], Graduate School of Artificial Intelligence[2]
Pohang University of Science and Technology (POSTECH), Republic of Korea
`{jspak3, hkwon, jhlee}@postech.ac.kr`

Abstract

This paper describes POSTECH's submission to the 2020 Duolingo Shared Task on Simultaneous Translation And Paraphrase for Language Education (STAPLE) for the English-Korean language pair. In this paper, we propose a transfer learning based simultaneous translation model by extending BART. We pre-trained BART with Korean Wikipedia and a Korean news dataset, and fine-tuned it with an additional web-crawled parallel corpus and the 2020 Duolingo official training dataset. In our experiments on the 2020 Duolingo test dataset, our submission achieves 0.312 in weighted macro F1 score, and ranks second among the submitted En-Ko systems.

1 Introduction

Simultaneous Translation And Paraphrase for Language Education (STAPLE) is the task of automatically producing multiple translations from a single source sentence (Mayhew et al., 2020). Because STAPLE can be regarded as a mixture of the machine translation (MT) and paraphrasing problem, MT and paraphrasing techniques play an important role in this task. Unlike in a typical MT task, systems are demanded to generate high-coverage sets on a sentence-level, as opposed to word-level. Subsequently, systems require a deeper linguistic understanding of the target language to generate accurate target sentences.

Recent NLP studies have alleviated this problem by transfer learning (Ventura and Warnick, 2007) from pre-trained language models. Radford et al. (2018) proposed a generative pre-trained language model (GPT), which trains a Transformer decoder with large-scale monolingual data, to achieve significantly improved performance in nine out of the twelve datasets. Despite these improvements, GPT shows a limited ability to model bidirectional context due to using the classical generative model-

ing approach. On the other hand, Devlin et al. (2018) proposed bidirectional encoder representations from Transformers (BERT), trained for the reconstruction of natural language from sentences containing masked tokens, in order to obtain deeper representations for natural language. By training on an enormous amount of training data, they achieved state-of-the-art results on eleven NLP tasks. To take advantage of both pre-trained generative models and pre-trained bidirectional encoders, Lewis et al. (2019) introduced a denoising autoencoder for pre-training sequence-to-sequence models called BART. BART aims to learn linguistic knowledge in the process of first corrupting the text using various noise functions and then restoring it, and showed state-of-the-art performance in various tasks.

Given this background, we expected that using a transfer-learning-based approach could resolve two difficulties of the En-Ko track of STAPLE: data insufficiency and multiple sentence generation. Unlike recent MT models which used over 4.5 million sentence pair for training data, the STAPLE official dataset includes only 2500 En-Ko source sentences. With such small data, we predicted that recent NMT models would not be able to learn translation knowledge effectively. Also, we speculated that paraphrasing requires a deep understanding of the language. Based on this prediction, a well-trained language model and a generative model for target language were needed to achieve this task's objectives.

With these considerations, we concluded that BART, a sequence-to-sequence generative model pre-trained on a large amount of data, is most suitable for STAPLE and thus propose a transfer-learning-based simultaneous translation model by extending BART. Our model added a randomly initialized source-side encoder in place of the embedding layer of BART pre-trained by Korean monolingual data and predicts translation weights with

139

Proceedings of the 4th Workshop on Neural Generation and Translation (WNGT 2020), pages 139–143
Online, July 10, 2020. ©2020 Association for Computational Linguistics
www.aclweb.org/anthology/D19-56%2d

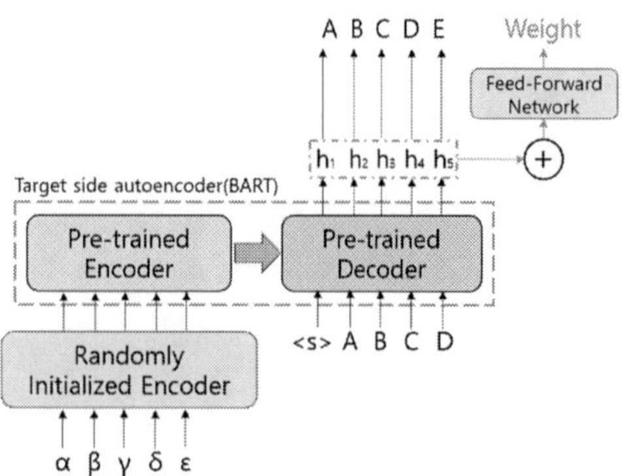

Figure 1: The overall architecture of the proposed model. The input vectors of feed-forward network are the sum of the pre-trained decoder's hidden vectors.

an additional feed-forward network using hidden vectors generated by the pre-trained decoder. The remainder of the paper is organized as follows: Section 2 describes our proposed method. Section 3 summarizes the experimental procedure and results, and Section 4 gives the conclusion.

2 Method

We adopt BART to the STAPLE problem, which takes source sentence to generate multiple target sentences. Our model consists of a pre-trained autoencoder with the source-side encoder that proposed in Lewis et al. (2019) and a feed-forward network to predict translation weights (Figure 1). In the following subsections, we describe our methods in detail.

2.1 Pre-trained autoencoder (BART)

We used BART as our pre-trained autoencoder structure. As was with BART, our autoencoder structure learns linguistic information of the target language by denoising various types of document corruptions. Among the five document corruption types proposed by BART, we applied Text Infilling and Sentence Permutation because they yielded the best results on Lewis et al. (2019).

2.2 Source-side Encoder

Pre-trained BART is a monolingual model, so the proposed model needs an additional encoder to function as translation model. After pre-training BART, we removed the embedding layer of the pre-trained encoder and added a randomly-initialized encoder instead (Lewis et al., 2019). In order to prevent corruption from the high loss in the randomly-

Dataset	Sentence	Word
Monolingual	31,654,593	447,754,804
Additional parallel	2,035,566	29,964,677
Official (1 to 1)	700,410	2,915,939

Table 1: **Dataset statistics** - number of target sentence and word.

initialized encoder during initial training, we freeze all pre-trained BART weights during the first fine-tuning step except for the self-attention input projection matrix of BART's first encoder layer. In the second step, we train all model parameters.

2.3 Feed-forward network for translation weight training

We added a feed-forward network to predict a translation weight on each generated sentence. The sum of hidden vectors which generated on the decoder is passed as the input of the feed-forward network. The output of the feed-forward network passed through a sigmoid layer becomes the final translation weight. During the generation step, the sentences with the high weights are selected.

3 Experiments

3.1 Dataset

Pre-training. For pre-training, we use text crawled from the Korean Wikipedia (5.8M words) and Korean online news sites (447M words). When crawling, we extracted only text passages and ignored headers, lists, and tables. To reduce training time, we filtered out any samples that exceed 100 tokens.

Fine-tuning. For fine-tuning, we used the STAPLE official training data (Duolingo, 2020) (700K sentences), setting aside 100 sentences each for the development set and test set. In addition, we adopted the web crawling parallel corpus (2M sentences) as additional training and development data for the source-side encoder. As with the pre-training corpus, we filtered out any training or development samples longer than 100 tokens.

3.2 Training Details

Settings. We modified the Fairseq (Ott et al., 2019) implementation of BART to build our model. Most hyperparameters of BART pre-training such as dropout ratio, hidden size, and etc. were copied from the base model described in Lewis et al.

	Decoding Option			Weighted Macro F1 ↑	Weighted Recall ↑	Precision ↑
	Beam Size	Diverse	Nbest (weight)			
Beam search	50	–	50	0.3192	0.3092	**0.5202**
	75	–	**75**	**0.3280**	0.3651	0.4628
	100	–	100	0.3234	0.4008	0.4214
	140	–	140	0.3108	0.4394	0.3680
	500	–	500	0.2218	**0.5817**	0.1865
Diverse beam search	100	5	100	0.1673	0.2069	0.2212
	100	10	100	0.1164	0.1474	0.1601
Beam search with weight	75	–	50	0.2695	0.2546	0.4630
	75	–	65	0.3064	0.3197	0.4615
	75	–	70	0.3163	0.3410	0.4596

Table 2: **Results of training variants** – each separated section corresponds to a different generation strategy (Beam search, Diverse beam search and Beam search with weight). Diverse is the number of group for diverse beam search and Nbest (weight) is the number of sentences selected by highest translation weight. The bold values indicate the best result in the metrics for each architecture.

(2019). For the document corruption scheme, we used the pre-training options of Lewis et al. (2019): Text Infilling and Sentence Shuffling. We set warm-up learning steps to 10K out of 250K total steps. For data preprocessing, we applied the sentence-piece (Kudo and Richardson, 2018) implementation of byte-pair encoding (Sennrich et al., 2016) with a 32k vocabulary on each language.

Pre-training. We trained target-side BART using Text Infilling and Sentence Shuffling as described in §2.1. We replaced 30% of tokens with single [MASK] symbols with span length distribution ($\lambda = 3$) on Text Infilling.

Fine-tuning. We divided fine-tuning step into four steps.

1. **Pre-train source-side encoder** After pre-training, we detached the embedding layer of BART encoder and attached a randomly initialized encoder as described in §2.2. We used only our web crawling parallel corpus for this step. During this step, we freeze the pre-trained model except the first encoder layer's projection weights to prevent the pre-trained weights being affected by the high loss while the encoder learns the source-side representation.

2. **Fine-tuning on MT** After pre-training the source-side encoder, we trained entire model on the same training data with a smaller learning rate. Because the size of the parallel data used for fine-tuning is much smaller than that of monolingual data used for pre-training, we expected pre-trained BART to generate the correct sentences even if the source-side encoder produced an incorrect expression.

3. **Fine-tuning on paraphrasing** After training on an additional parallel corpus, we trained the entire model on the official parallel corpus to reach the paraphrasing goal.

4. **Weight training** After learning all sentence representations, we trained a feed-forward network for translation weight prediction on the official target language weights. In order to train translation weights without corrupting the sentence generation model, we freeze all parts of the model excluding the feed forward network.

Experiment variations. We conduct multiple experiments on test set divided from official training set to determine the best generation strategy.

- **Beam search** with different beam size. We selected all generated sentences.

- **Diverse beam search** with different beam size and group size. We used the implementation of Vijayakumar et al. (2016).

- **Beam search w/ weight** with same beam size but different size of sentences selected by highest translation weight.

Systems	Weighted Macro F1 ↑	Weighted Recall ↑	Precision ↑
jbrem	**0.4035**	**0.4518**	0.4795
jspak3 (ours)	0.3116	0.3342	0.4701
sweagraw	0.2553	0.3168	0.3216
jindra.helcl	0.2058	0.1935	0.3894
STAPLE_fairseq_baseline	0.0486	0.0315	0.2204
STAPLE_aws_baseline	0.0412	0.0226	**0.6360**

Table 3: **Submission results** – the official results of 2020 Duolingo shared task in En-Ko language pair. The bold values indicate the best result in the metrics for the each architecture.

3.3 Results

We trained the model as described in §3.2 using various generation strategies. For evaluation, we used weighted macro F1 scores on our test set extracted from the 2020 Duolingo official dataset. Table 2 shows the scores of each generation strategy. In the case of beam size, results showed the highest weighted macro F1 score when the beam size was 75. We speculate this to be because of the trade-off between weighted recall and precision. Using diverse beam search with beam size 100 and beam search with translation weight showed ineffective results. We initially expected to attain a higher precision with similar weighted recall if the translation weights were predicted accurately, but it seems our feed-forward network was not able to learn the distribution of translation weights properly. Also, we had expected diverse beam decoding to help generate more diverse sentences, but it had an adverse effect on overall performance.

Submission results. The submission results on the official test set are reported in Table 3. We selected the decoding option obtained by applying beam search with beam size 75, Nbest 75 which showed the highest weighted macro F1 score in Table 2 as our final submission. Our submission achieves an improvement of +0.263 in weighted macro F1 score compared to the baseline. As a result, our system ranks second out of the four systems submitted this year.

4 Conclusion

In this paper, we present POSTECH's submissions to the 2020 Duolingo shared task. We propose a transfer-learning based simultaneous translation model by extending BART. The proposed model is first pre-trained by reconstructing large corrupted text using text infilling and sentence shuffling, and then fine-tuned with an additional parallel corpus and the official training dataset with a newly added randomly initialized encoder in place of the embedding layer. It has an additional feed-forward network to predict translation weight trained on the official dataset. Finally, our model outperforms the baseline by a large margin and ranks second out of the submitted systems.

References

Jacob Devlin, Ming-Wei Chang, Kenton Lee, and Kristina Toutanova. 2018. Bert: Pre-training of deep bidirectional transformers for language understanding.

Duolingo. 2020. Data for the 2020 Duolingo Shared Task on Simultaneous Translation And Paraphrase for Language Education (STAPLE).

Taku Kudo and John Richardson. 2018. Sentencepiece: A simple and language independent subword tokenizer and detokenizer for neural text processing.

Mike Lewis, Yinhan Liu, Naman Goyal, Marjan Ghazvininejad, Abdelrahman Mohamed, Omer Levy, Ves Stoyanov, and Luke Zettlemoyer. 2019. Bart: Denoising sequence-to-sequence pre-training for natural language generation, translation, and comprehension. *arXiv preprint arXiv:1910.13461*.

S. Mayhew, K. Bicknell, C. Brust, B. McDowell, W. Monroe, and B. Settles. 2020. Simultaneous translation and paraphrase for language education. In *Proceedings of the ACL Workshop on Neural Generation and Translation (WNGT)*. ACL.

Myle Ott, Sergey Edunov, Alexei Baevski, Angela Fan, Sam Gross, Nathan Ng, David Grangier, and Michael Auli. 2019. fairseq: A fast, extensible toolkit for sequence modeling. In *Proceedings of NAACL-HLT 2019: Demonstrations*.

Alec Radford, Karthik Narasimhan, Tim Salimans, and Ilya Sutskever. 2018. Improving language understanding by generative pre-training. *URL https://s3-us-west-2. amazonaws. com/openai-assets/researchcovers/languageunsupervised/language understanding paper. pdf.*

Rico Sennrich, Barry Haddow, and Alexandra Birch. 2016. Neural machine translation of rare words with subword units. In *Proceedings of the 54th Annual Meeting of the Association for Computational Linguistics (Volume 1: Long Papers)*, pages 1715–1725, Berlin, Germany. Association for Computational Linguistics.

Dan Ventura and Sean Warnick. 2007. A theoretical foundation for inductive transfer. *Brigham Young University, College of Physical and Mathematical Sciences.*

Ashwin K Vijayakumar, Michael Cogswell, Ramprasath R. Selvaraju, Qing Sun, Stefan Lee, David Crandall, and Dhruv Batra. 2016. Diverse beam search: Decoding diverse solutions from neural sequence models.

The ADAPT System Description for the STAPLE 2020
English-to-Portuguese Translation Task

Rejwanul Haque, Yasmin Moslem and Andy Way
ADAPT Centre
School of Computing
Dublin City University
Dublin, Ireland
`firstname.lastname@adaptcentre.ie`

Abstract

This paper describes the ADAPT Centre's submission to STAPLE (Simultaneous Translation and Paraphrase for Language Education) 2020, a shared task of the 4th Workshop on Neural Generation and Translation (WNGT), for the English-to-Portuguese translation task. In this shared task, the participants were asked to produce high-coverage sets of plausible translations given English prompts (input source sentences). We present our English-to-Portuguese machine translation (MT) models that were built applying various strategies, e.g. data and sentence selection, monolingual MT for generating alternative translations, and combining multiple n-best translations. Our experiments show that adding the aforementioned techniques to the baseline yields an excellent performance in the English-to-Portuguese translation task.

1 Introduction

The ADAPT Centre participated in STAPLE[1] (Mayhew et al., 2020), a shared task of the 4th WNGT which will be held at ACL 2020,[2] in the English-to-Portuguese language direction. The task focuses on a specific use case of MT, i.e. generating many possible translations for a given input text. Such situations are usually seen on language-learning platforms (e.g. Duolingo) where the learning process includes translation-based exercises, and evaluation is done by comparing learners' responses with a large set of human-curated acceptable translations. The shared task organisers (Duolingo) have released real language-learner data of Duolingo as training examples. We applied a number of strategies to our MT system building process, e.g. monolingual MT, extracting parallel sentences that are similar to the Duolingo's

real language-learner data from the freely available external parallel corpora, assembling n-best translations from multiple translation systems, which essentially led us to generate high-coverage sets of possible translations of the English prompts (input source sentences).

The remainder of the paper is organised as follows: Section 2 explains our approaches; Section 3 details of the datasets used, explains the experimental setups and presents the results with some discussions; and Section 4 concludes our work with avenues for future work.

2 Methodology

2.1 Selecting External Datasets

Since the shared task organisers released training data with a limited number of prompts (only 4,000 English prompts for English-to-Portuguese translation) and allowed participants to use external data, we made use of parallel corpora from a variety of existing sources, e.g. OPUS[3] (Tiedemann, 2012). First, we found out which corpora are similar to Duolingo's training dataset. For this, we measured perplexity of the source and target texts of the external datasets on the in-domain language models (LMs) (i.e. LMs were built on the Duolingo's data). We selected those corpora whose sentences are found to be more similar to those of Duolingo's language learning data.

2.2 Selecting 'Pseudo In-domain' Parallel Sentences from External Data

The state-of-the-art sentence selection method of Axelrod et al. (2011) is used to extract 'pseudo in-domain' data from large corpora using bilingual cross-entropy difference. The extracted data is usually used to train domain-specific MT systems or to fine-tune generic MT systems. We con-

---

[1] `https://sharedtask.duolingo.com/`
[2] `https://acl2020.org/`
[3] `http://opus.lingfil.uu.se/`

Proceedings of the 4th Workshop on Neural Generation and Translation (WNGT 2020), pages 144–152
Online, July 10, 2020. ©2020 Association for Computational Linguistics
www.aclweb.org/anthology/D19-56%2d

sider Duolingo's language learning data released in this shared task as the real in-domain data. In this task, we took each of the external parallel corpora (usually large in size) chosen following the approach described in Section 2.1, and selected top n sentence-pairs as per low cross-entropy differences over each side of the corpus (source and target) following Axelrod et al. (2011). This provided us with a 'pseudo in-domain' corpus (i.e. the extracted top n sentence-pairs) whose sentences are similar to the sentences of the Duolingo's data in terms of domain and style. We appended the extracted 'pseudo in-domain' data to the STAPLE's (Duolingo's) training data for building different MT systems which are described latter in the paper (cf. Section 3.5).

2.3 Same-language MT

Same-language MT has been successfully used in many NLP applications, e.g. text-to-speech synthesis for creating alternative target sequences (Cahill et al., 2009), translation between varieties of the same language (Brazilian Portuguese to European Portuguese) (Fancellu et al., 2014), paraphrase generation (Plachouras et al., 2018), and producing many alternative sequences of a given input question in question answering (Bhattacharjee et al., 2020). In our case, we developed Portuguese-to-Portuguese MT systems that were able to generate n-best (same-language) alternative sentences of an input Portuguese sentence. Using this monolingual MT systems, we could obtain a set of alternative sequences of a given Portuguese translation.

As mentioned earlier, the Duolingo training data includes a high-coverage set of Portuguese translations of the English prompts. We generated a set of source–target pairs (Portuguese-to-Portuguese) from each of the high-coverage sets of alternative Portuguese translations. This served as our training data for Portuguese-to-Portuguese MT system building. Additionally, we used an existing paraphrasing resource (Ganitkevitch and Callison-Burch, 2014) for Portuguese and appended that to the training data.

2.4 Combining multiple n-best Translations

In this work, we built a number of MT systems using the state-of-the-art phrase-based statistical MT (PB-SMT) (Koehn et al., 2003) and neural MT (NMT) (Vaswani et al., 2017) approaches. The n-best translations produced by the different MT systems (i.e. a PB-SMT and several NMT systems) are combined adopting a variety of approaches (e.g. majority voting) to produce the final sets of translations of the English prompts.

3 Experiments and Results

3.1 The MT system setups

As pointed out earlier, we chose the classical PB-SMT and emerging NMT paradigms for building our MT systems. To build our PB-SMT systems, we used the Moses toolkit (Koehn et al., 2007). We used a 5-gram LM trained with modified Kneser-Ney smoothing (Kneser and Ney, 1995) using the KenLM toolkit (Heafield et al., 2013). Our PB-SMT log-linear features include: (a) 4 translational features (forward and backward phrase and lexical probabilities), (b) 8 lexicalised reordering probabilities (*wbe-mslr-bidirectional-fe-allff*), (c) 5-gram LM probabilities, (d) 5 OSM features (Durrani et al., 2011), and (e) word-count and distortion penalties. In our experiments, word alignment models are trained using the GIZA++ toolkit[4] (Och and Ney, 2003), phrases are extracted following the *grow-diag-final-and* algorithm of Koehn et al. (2003), Kneser-Ney smoothing is applied at phrase scoring, and a smoothing constant (0.8u) is used for training lexicalised reordering models. The weights of the parameters are optimised using the margin-infused relaxed algorithm (Cherry and Foster, 2012) on the development set. For decoding, the cube-pruning algorithm (Huang and Chiang, 2007) is applied, with a distortion limit of 12.

To build our NMT systems, we used the Marian-NMT (Junczys-Dowmunt et al., 2018) toolkit. The NMT systems are Transformer models (Vaswani et al., 2017). In our experiments, we followed the recommended best set-up from Vaswani et al. (2017). The tokens of the training, evaluation and validation sets are segmented into sub-word units using the Byte-Pair Encoding (BPE) technique (Sennrich et al., 2016). We performed 32,000 join operations. Our training set-up is as follows.

We consider the size of the encoder and decoder layers to be 6. As in Vaswani et al. (2017), we employ residual connection around layers (He et al., 2015), followed by layer normalisation (Ba et al., 2016). The weight matrix between the embedding layers is shared, similar to Press and Wolf (2016). Dropout (Gal and Ghahramani, 2016) between layers is set to 0.10. We use mini-batches of

---

[4] `http://www.statmt.org/moses/giza/GIZA++.html`

size 64 for updating. The models are trained with the Adam optimizer (Kingma and Ba, 2014), with the learning-rate set to 0.0003 and reshuffling the training corpora for each epoch. As in Vaswani et al. (2017), we also use the learning rate warm-up strategy for Adam. Validation on the development set is performed using three cost functions: cross-entropy, perplexity and BLEU. The early-stopping criteria is based on cross-entropy while the final NMT system is selected as per the highest BLEU score on the validation set. The beam size for search is set to 12.

3.2 The Shared Task Data

The data released by STAPLE is compiled from Duolingo's language learning courses. The training data for English-to-Portuguese translation contains 4,000 English prompts, with multiple Portuguese translations, from which we obtained a total of 526,467 source–target segment-pairs. We randomly sampled 2,000 sentence-pairs from the training set, and considered them as development set. As for the development set, we chose the highest scoring Portuguese translations of the English prompts. The development set (blind) released by STAPLE contains 500 English prompts. They also provided a high-quality automatic reference translations of the development set sentences by Amazon Translate.[5] We considered the development set (with translations by Amazon translate as references) as our test set in order to evaluate our MT systems. We removed those entries from the training set (526,467 source–target segment-pairs) that overlap with entries (source or target counterparts) of the development and test sets. The training set is left with 258,306 source–target segment-pairs after discarding the overlapping entries. The statistics of training, development and test set sentences are shown in Table 1.

	sentences	words (en)	words (pt)
train set	258,306	2,063,108	2,128,044
dev set	2,000	14,557	14,196
test set	500	3,551	3,322

Table 1: The shared task data statistics.

3.3 The baseline MT systems

We first built MT systems with only the data provided by the shared task (cf. Table 1). We computed the BLEU (Papineni et al., 2002) score to

evaluate the MT systems on the test set, which are reported in Table 2. Note that we used translations by Amazon Translate provided by STAPLE as the reference translations, which are excellent in quality. Thus, the BLEU scores on the test set can provide indications how good or bad our MT systems are. Additionally, we have reported the MT systems' BLEU scores on the development set. As can be seen from Table 2, the BLEU scores of the MT systems are very low. These scores were expected given the (small) number of sentences used for training. Interestingly, PB-SMT outperforms NMT by a large margin in terms of BLEU, and this can happen in low-resource scenarios (Koehn and Knowles, 2017).

	BLEU	
	dev set	test set
PB-SMT	22.69	19.92
Transformer	9.57	9.23

Table 2: The BLEU scores of baseline MT systems.

3.4 The External Datasets Used

Since we (participants) are allowed to use external data, we decided to use freely available bilingual corpora whose sentences are similar to those of the Duolingo's English–Portuguese dataset. We took all bilingual corpora available in the OPUS repository, and measured perplexity of source and target texts on in-domain LMs (built on the Duolingo data only). We found that the most similar corpora to the English-side of the Duolingo's training corpus are OpenSubtitles[6] and Tatoeba[7] and to the Portuguese-side of that are Books[8] and Tatoeba. In addition to Tatoeba, Books and OpenSubtitles, we made use of ParaCrawl (parallel sentences crawled from Web)[9] and Wikipedia (parallel sentences extracted from Wikipedia)[10] which were found to be moderately similar to the task data according to the LM perplexity scores. Additionally, we also used several generic corpora for building an NMT

---

[5]https://aws.amazon.com/translate/

[6]http://opus.nlpl.eu/OpenSubtitles-v2018.php

[7]http://opus.nlpl.eu/Tatoeba-v20190709.php

[8]http://opus.nlpl.eu/Books-v1.php

[9]http://opus.nlpl.eu/ParaCrawl-v5.php

[10]http://opus.nlpl.eu/Wikipedia-v1.0.php

system, EUconst,[11] JRC-Acquis,[12] Europarl[13] and DGT.[14]

We manually looked at these datasets, and observed that the Tatoeba and Books corpora are good in quality. We directly used sentences of the Tatoeba and Books corpora for system building. In contrast, the OpenSubtitles corpus seems to have considerable noise intact in it. We also noticed that a corpus of one language (say, English) contains sentences of other languages, so we use a language identifier[15] in order to remove such noise. We applied a number of standard cleaning routines for removing noisy sentences, e.g. removing sentence-pairs that are too short, too long or which violate certain sentence-length ratios. The latter processing was applied to all corpora. In order to perform tokenisation for English and Portuguese, we used the standard tool[16] in the Moses toolkit.

As for the selection of "pseudo in-domain" sentence-pairs from the external bilingual corpora using bilingual cross-entropy difference measure (Axelrod et al., 2011) (cf. Section 2.2), we applied the strategy to every corpus except Tatoeba and Books. The so-called "pseudo in-domain" parallel sentences that were extracted from the out-of-domain data were appended to the in-domain (shared task) training data in order to build the MT systems.

3.5 The MT systems built using external datasets

3.5.1 The PB-SMT systems

This section presents the PB-SMT systems that were built on the training data augmented by appending external data (cf. Section 3.4) to the shared task data. As stated earlier, the performance of the PB-SMT systems on the development set and test sets in terms of BLEU are shown in Table 3. The second row of Table 3 represents the MT system built on the training data (Duo + Books + Tatoeba) that includes sentences of the Duolingo's training data and of two external corpora: Books and Tatoeba. We see that this MT system surpassed

the baseline PB-SMT system (cf. Table 2) by a large margin in terms of BLEU.

		dev set	test set
(a)	Baseline	22.69	19.92
(b)	Duo + Books + Tatoeba	53.18	49.42
(c)	(b) + 3M ParaWiki	57.80	55.27

Table 3: The BLEU scores of the PB-SMT systems. Duo: Duolingo's training data.

We merged the ParaCrawl and Wikipedia corpora, and from now on, we call the combined corpus ParaWiki. We took low-scoring (bilingual cross-entropy difference) (cf. Section 2.2) sentence-pairs from ParaWiki, added them to the training data (i.e. Duo + Books + Tatoeba) in various proportions, and built PB-SMT systems on them. The BLEU scores of the best system out of the PB-SMT systems that were built on these sets of training data on the development and test sets are shown in the last row of Table 2. As illustrated by the table, sentences of ParaWiki have a positive impact on the system's performance since we get further gains in terms of BLEU. In short, our best-performing PB-SMT system is the one that is built on training data compiled by three million sentences from ParaWiki, all sentences of the Books and Tatoeba corpora and the Duolingo's training data. From now on, this PB-SMT system is referred as PB-BEST. In this context, we also carried out a number of experiments and built many PB-SMT systems by adding sentences from other data sets (e.g. Open-Subtitles) to the training data in various proportions as above. None of the setups results in any other MT system that could outperform PB-BEST.

		dev set	test set
(a)	Baseline	9.57	9.23
(b)	Duo + Books + Tatoeba	62.19	58.17
(c)	(b) + 3M ParaWiki	60.77	62.61
(d)	(b) + 6M ParaWiki	**65.69**	**67.97**
(e)	(b) + 3M Generic	46.15	43.38
(f)	(b) + 8M Sub	50.83	57.82
(g)	(d) + 8M Sub	55.73	61.07

Table 4: The BLEU scores of the NMT systems. Duo: Duolingo's training data.

3.5.2 The NMT systems

This section presents our NMT systems that were built on the training data prepared by appending

---

[11] http://opus.nlpl.eu/EUconst-v1.php
[12] http://opus.nlpl.eu/JRC-Acquis-v3.0.php
[13] http://opus.nlpl.eu/Europarl-v8.php
[14] http://opus.nlpl.eu/DGT-v2019.php
[15] cld2: https://github.com/CLD2Owners/cld2
[16] https://github.com/moses-smt/mosesdecoder/blob/master/scripts/tokenizer/tokenizer.perl

external data (cf. Section 3.4) to the shared task data. We evaluate the NMT systems on the test set, and report BLEU scores in Table 4. As above, we also show their performance (i.e. BLEU scores) on the development set. When we compare the scores of Table 3 with those of Table 4 (rows (b) and (c)), we see that NMT outperforms PB-SMT with large margins. This time, our best setup is the one when we use training data compiled by six million sentences from ParaWiki, all sentences of the Books and Tatoeba corpora and the shared task training data (cf. row (d) of Table 4). From now on, we call this MT system NEURAL-BEST.

We also built MT systems using sentences from other datasets. We merged sentences of the generic corpora (EUconst, JRC-Acquis, Europarl, DGT), selected low-scoring 3M sentence-pairs from the combined corpus (i.e. the most similar sentences to those of the Duolingo's data), and added them to the baseline training set. We can see from Table 4 (row (e)) that the the MT system built on this training data does not perform well. We call this MT system NEURAL-Generic.

As mentioned above (cf. Section 3.4), sentences of the OpenSubtitles corpus are quite similar to those of Duolingo's training corpus. To this end, we carried out a series of experiments by selecting different sizes of sentences from this dataset following the approach described in Section 2.2. We found that this dataset does have much impact on our system building (cf. row (f) of Table 4). In fact, we see from the last row of Table 4 that inclusion of a part of the OpenSubtitles corpus to the training set of the best setup deteriorates the system's performance. We call this MT system (row (g)) NEURAL-OpenSub.

3.6 The Portuguese-to-Portuguese MT Systems

In Section 2.3, we explained the purpose of creating monolingual MT systems. This section describes our Portuguese-to-Portuguese MT systems. We prepare training data for the Portuguese-to-Portuguese MT system from the high-coverage set of Portuguese translations for the English prompts. Thus, the training data contains source–target pairs whose source and target counterparts are two variations of Portuguese translation. In Table 5, we show the number of training examples used for building monolingual Portuguese MT systems. The table also shows the maximum number of varia-

tions for a Portuguese translation used for forming the training set. Additionally, we used Portuguese paraphrases from the PPDB database[17] (Ganitkevitch and Callison-Burch, 2014) as the part of the training data for this task. We also used the target-side (Portuguese) sentences of the shared task training set (cf. Table 1), and add them (i.e. identical copy) to the both sides of the training set. The first 1,000 sentences of the development set (cf. Table 1) serves as our development set and the remaining sentences of the development set serves as our test set.

	Sentences	Variations
PB-SMT	3,091,264	30 (max.)
NMT	12,523,886	75 (max.)
Paraphrases	16,915,010	

Table 5: Number of training examples used for the monolingual MT training.

	BLEU
PB-SMT	72.30
NMT	40.73

Table 6: The BLEU scores of the monolingual MT systems.

We obtain the BLEU scores to evaluate the monolingual MT systems on the test set, and report them in Table 6. The learning objective of the monolingual MT models is to generate alternative sequences of a language given the sentences of the same language. Therefore, these scores, to a certain extent, show how likely an MT system can produce their own versions of the Portuguese sentences. We see from Table 6 that PB-SMT outperforms NMT with a large margin in terms of BLEU.

3.7 Generating Translations of English Prompts

This section presents our translation framework that is expected to generate high-coverage sets of plausible translations given the English prompts. In the translation framework, we made use of our best system NEURAL-BEST, and two more Transformer models, NEURAL-OpenSub and NEURAL-Generic (cf. Section 3.5.2), and best SMT system PB-BEST (cf. Section 3.5.1). Note that we make each of our final NMT models with ensembles of 4 models that are sampled from the

---

[17]http://paraphrase.org/#/download

training run, and one of them is selected as per highest BLEU score on the validation set.

The STAPLE development and test sets are blind, and participants were asked to submit the system's output via CodaLab[18] which displays system's scores upon submission. The main scoring metric for evaluation is weighted macro F_1. The precision and recall are calculated in unweighted and weighted fashions, respectively. In short, the systems are scored based on how well they can return all human-curated acceptable translations, weighted by the likelihood that an English learner would respond with each translation.

	R	P	F_1
NEURAL-BEST	0.4325	0.6564	0.4601
NEURAL-OpenSub	0.3922	0.5542	0.3922
NEURAL-Generic	0.3224	0.5541	0.3451
PB-BEST	0.2044	0.5643	0.2512
SysCom	0.4566	0.6019	0.4620
SysCom + MMT-B1	0.4551	0.6204	0.4669
SysCom + MMT-B5	0.4656	0.6138	0.4710

Table 7: Performance of our MT systems on dev set (submitted).

In Table 7, we present the performance of our submitted MT systems on the development set. The first row of Table 7 represents our best NMT system NEURAL-BEST which is competitive and produces an F_1 score of 0.4601 on the development set. As for this system, we generate 12-best ($n = 12$) translations for each English prompt. We tried higher values for n and the systems with different values of n are more or less comparable to the one reported in the table. Therefore, we keep the value of n 12 for generating alternative translations for all our MT systems. The system that represents the first row of the table can be seen as our baseline.

The next three rows of Table 7 show the scores of other two neural models, NEURAL-OpenSub and NEURAL-Generic, and the best PB-SMT system PB-BEST. We see from Table 7 that these MT systems perform much worse than NEURAL-BEST as far as the F_1 scores on the development set are concerned. Interestingly, precision of PB-BEST is relatively better than the other two MT systems despite its low recall which in fact is responsible for its low final F_1. We found that many 12-best translations produced by PB-BEST are identical.

[18]https://competitions.codalab.org/competitions/

This is the reason why its recall (and F_1) is too low.

The fifth row of Table 7 presents a system that combines n-best translations of different MT systems. We refer to this system as SysCom. The idea is to produce final sets of translations of the English prompts as exhaustive and precise as possible by combining 12-best translations produced by the different MT systems. We tried a number of ways for combining the translations produced by multiple systems, and the setup that worked best for us is described as follows. We took 12-best translations by NEURAL-BEST and 1-best translations by NEURAL-Generic, NEURAL-OpenSub and PB-BEST. Additionally, we also took translations from 12-best translations by NEURAL-Generic, NEURAL-OpenSub and PB-BEST with two out of three voting logic. The reason for using different MT methods and MT systems built on different data domains or styles in the system combination strategy is that such MT systems may produce some alternative translations that are to be different to each other. SysCom produces a 0.0019 F_1 point absolute (corresponding to 0.41% relative) gain over the baseline. Naturally, this approach increases the coverage of plausible translations of the English prompts, which causes a 0.0241 recall point absolute (corresponding to 5.57% relative) gain over the baseline however at the expense of precision.

The final two rows of Table 7 correspond to two system setups in which we used our monolingual Portuguese MT systems on top of the SysCom setup. In other words, we applied the monolingual Portuguese MT systems to the Portuguese translations of the English prompts in order to collect more viable alternative translations. We tried to avoid applying monolingual MT on the noisy translations generated in the previous stage (i.e. English-to-Portuguese MT). Accordingly, we adopted different setups in order to obtain translations that are to be as much error free as possible (i.e. a set of high precision n-best translations). The setup that worked best in our case is described as follows. We took 1-best (i.e. row 6 of Table 7; MMT-B1) or 5-best (i.e. row 7 of Table 7; MMT-B5) translations by both NEURAL-BEST and PB-BEST. We also took a set of translations which is an intersection of the sets of 12-best translations produced by NEURAL-BEST, NEURAL-Generic, NEURAL-OpenSub and PB-BEST. Let's call this set of translations *mono-set*.

We translated the sentences (i.e. Portuguese translations) of the mono-set using the monolingual Portuguese PB-SMT and NMT systems (cf. Section 3.6). For each sentence of mono-set we produce 12-best translations by the PB-SMT and NMT systems, take intersection of the two sets of 12-best translations, and consider the intersected set as the viable alternative translations. Nonetheless, this stage includes another screening that helps weed out as much noise as possible, which are described as follows. We used 12-best translations provided by the monolingual PB-SMT and NMT systems if and only if a certain portion of the translations by each system should appear in the output of SysCom. In other words, a ratio of the number of the overlapping translations by each of the monolingual MT systems with the translations provided by SysCom and the total number of the translations provided by SysCom should be greater than a threshold which we set to 0.2. The intersection operation on two sets of 12-best translations and the screening strategy, to a certain extent, ensures the translation variations generated by the monolingual MT systems of good quality. We see from the final two rows of Table 7 that the strategy of applying monolingual MT for generating alternative translations brings about moderate improvements in terms of F_1 over the baseline. The best setup (SysCom + MMT-B5) produces a 0.0109 F_1 point absolute (corresponding to 2.4% relative) gain over the baseline.

	R	P	F_1
SysCom + MMT-B1	0.4306	0.6379	0.4574
SysCom + MMT-B5	0.4377	0.6318	0.4597

Table 8: Performance of our MT systems on test set (submitted).

In Table 8, we show the performance of our submitted systems on the STAPLE 2020 test set. These systems in fact correspond to the two systems whose performance on the development set were presented in the last two rows of Table 7. The second row of Table 8 (SysCom + MMT-B5) represents the system whose submission earned us the fifth position in the competition.

4 Conclusion

This paper presents the ADAPT translation system for the STAPLE 2020 English-to-Portuguese Translation Task. We aimed to build a competitive translation system that can produce high-coverage sets of plausible translations given English prompts (input source sentences). For this, we applied various strategies, e.g. selecting data sources that are similar to STAPLE 2020 training data, selecting sentences from external corpora, applying monolingual MT for generating alternative translations, combining translations produced by multiple MT systems. We found that the systematic addition of these techniques to baseline yields moderate improvement over the baseline (0.0109 F_1 point absolute corresponding to 2.4% relative gain). The best experimental setup earned us the fifth position in the competition.

In the future, we aim to apply confusion network decoding in order to re-rank n-best translations generated by the multiple MT systems. We used monolingual MT for generating alternative sentences for the target (Portuguese) translations. We also aim to apply this strategy to the English prompts (i.e. source-side of the translation-pair) for generating alternative sequences of the input source sentences.

Acknowledgments

The ADAPT Centre for Digital Content Technology is funded under the Science Foundation Ireland (SFI) Research Centres Programme (Grant No. 13/RC/2106) and is co-funded under the European Regional Development Fund. This project has partially received funding from the European Union's Horizon 2020 research and innovation programme under the Marie Skłodowska-Curie grant agreement No. 713567, and the publication has emanated from research supported in part by a research grant from SFI under Grant Number 13/RC/2077.

References

Amittai Axelrod, Xiaodong He, and Jianfeng Gao. 2011. Domain adaptation via pseudo in-domain data selection. In *Proceedings of the 2011 Conference on Empirical Methods in Natural Language Processing*, pages 355–362, Edinburgh, Scotland, UK. Association for Computational Linguistics.

Jimmy Lei Ba, Jamie Ryan Kiros, and Geoffrey E Hinton. 2016. Layer normalization. *CoRR*, abs/1607.06450.

Santanu Bhattacharjee, Rejwanul Haque, Gideon Maillette de Buy Wenniger, and Andy Way. 2020. Investigating Query Expansion and Coreference Resolution in Question Answering on BERT. In *Proceedings of Natural Language Processing and Information Systems - 25th International Conference on Applications of Natural Language to Information Systems, NLDB 2020, page (to appear), Saarbrücken, Germany.

Peter Cahill, Jinhua Du, Andy Way, and Julie Carson-Berndsen. 2009. Using same-language machine translation to create alternative target sequences for text-to-speech synthesis. In *Proceedings of Interspeech 2009, the 10th Annual Conference of the International Speech Communication Association*, pages 1307–1310, Brighton, UK.

Colin Cherry and George Foster. 2012. Batch tuning strategies for statistical machine translation. In *Proceedings of the 2012 Conference of the North American Chapter of the Association for Computational Linguistics: Human Language Technologies*, pages 427–436, Montréal, Canada.

Nadir Durrani, Helmut Schmid, and Alexander Fraser. 2011. A joint sequence translation model with integrated reordering. In *Proceedings of the 49th Annual Meeting of the Association for Computational Linguistics: Human Language Technologies*, pages 1045–1054, Portland, Oregon, USA.

Federico Fancellu, Morgan O'Brien, and Andy Way. 2014. Standard language variety conversion using smt. In *Proceedings of the Seventeenth Annual Conference of the European Association for Machine Translation*, pages 143–149, Dubrovnik, Croatia.

Yarin Gal and Zoubin Ghahramani. 2016. A theoretically grounded application of dropout in recurrent neural networks. *CoRR*, abs/1512.05287.

Juri Ganitkevitch and Chris Callison-Burch. 2014. The multilingual paraphrase database. In *Proceedings of the Ninth International Conference on Language Resources and Evaluation (LREC'14)*, pages 4276–4283, Reykjavík, Iceland.

Kaiming He, Xiangyu Zhang, Shaoqing Ren, and Jian Sun. 2015. Deep residual learning for image recognition. *CoRR*, abs/1512.03385.

Kenneth Heafield, Ivan Pouzyrevsky, Jonathan H. Clark, and Philipp Koehn. 2013. Scalable modified kneser-ney language model estimation. In *Proceedings of the 51st Annual Meeting of the Association for Computational Linguistics (Volume 2: Short Papers)*, pages 690–696, Sofia, Bulgaria.

Liang Huang and David Chiang. 2007. Forest rescoring: Faster decoding with integrated language models. In *Proceedings of the 45th Annual Meeting of the Association of Computational Linguistics*, pages 144–151, Prague, Czech Republic.

Marcin Junczys-Dowmunt, Roman Grundkiewicz, Tomasz Dwojak, Hieu Hoang, Kenneth Heafield, Tom Neckermann, Frank Seide, Ulrich Germann, Alham Fikri Aji, Nikolay Bogoychev, André F. T. Martins, and Alexandra Birch. 2018. Marian: Fast neural machine translation in C++. In *Proceedings of ACL 2018, System Demonstrations*, pages 116–121, Melbourne, Australia. Association for Computational Linguistics.

Diederik P. Kingma and Jimmy Ba. 2014. Adam: A method for stochastic optimization. *CoRR*, abs/1412.6980.

R. Kneser and H. Ney. 1995. Improved backing-off for m-gram language modeling. In *1995 International Conference on Acoustics, Speech, and Signal Processing*, volume 1, pages 181–184 vol.1.

Philipp Koehn, Hieu Hoang, Alexandra Birch, Chris Callison-Burch, Marcello Federico, Nicola Bertoldi, Brooke Cowan, Wade Shen, Christine Moran, Richard Zens, Chris Dyer, Ondřej Bojar, Alexandra Constantin, Williams College, and Evan Herbst. 2007. Moses: Open source toolkit for statistical machine translation. In *ACL 2007, Proceedings of the Interactive Poster and Demonstration Sessions*, pages 177–180, Prague, Czech Republic.

Philipp Koehn and Rebecca Knowles. 2017. Six challenges for neural machine translation. In *Proceedings of the First Workshop on Neural Machine Translation*, pages 28–39, Vancouver. Association for Computational Linguistics.

Philipp Koehn, Franz Josef Och, and Daniel Marcu. 2003. Statistical phrase-based translation. In *HLT-NAACL 2003: conference combining Human Language Technology conference series and the North American Chapter of the Association for Computational Linguistics conference series*, pages 48–54, Edmonton, AB.

Stephen Mayhew, Klinton Bicknell, Chris Brust, Bill McDowell, Will Monroe, and Burr Settles. 2020. Simultaneous translation and paraphrase for language education. In *Proceedings of the ACL Workshop on Neural Generation and Translation (WNGT)*. ACL.

Franz Josef Och and Hermann Ney. 2003. A systematic comparison of various statistical alignment models. *Computational Linguistics*, 29(1):19–51.

Kishore Papineni, Salim Roukos, Todd Ward, and Wei-Jing Zhu. 2002. Bleu: a method for automatic evaluation of machine translation. In *Proceedings of the 40th Annual Meeting of the Association for Computational Linguistics*, pages 311–318, Philadelphia, Pennsylvania, USA. Association for Computational Linguistics.

Vassilis Plachouras, Fabio Petroni, Timothy Nugent, and Jochen L. Leidner. 2018. A comparison of two paraphrase models for taxonomy augmentation. In *Proceedings of the 2018 Conference of the North American Chapter of the Association for Computational Linguistics: Human Language Technologies, Volume 2 (Short Papers)*, pages 315–320, New Orleans, LA.

Ofir Press and Lior Wolf. 2016. Using the output embedding to improve language models. *CoRR*, abs/1608.05859.

Rico Sennrich, Barry Haddow, and Alexandra Birch. 2016. Neural machine translation of rare words with subword units. In *Proceedings of the 54th Annual Meeting of the Association for Computational Linguistics (Volume 1: Long Papers)*, pages 1715–1725, Berlin, Germany.

Jörg Tiedemann. 2012. Parallel data, tools and interfaces in OPUS. In *Proceedings of the 8th International Conference on Language Resources and Evaluation (LREC'2012)*, pages 2214–2218, Istanbul, Turkey.

Ashish Vaswani, Noam Shazeer, Niki Parmar, Jakob Uszkoreit, Llion Jones, Aidan N. Gomez, Lukasz Kaiser, and Illia Polosukhin. 2017. Attention is all you need. *CoRR*, abs/1706.03762.

Expand and Filter: CUNI and LMU Systems for the WNGT 2020 Duolingo Shared Task

Jindřich Libovický[1] and **Zdeněk Kasner**[2] and **Jindřich Helcl**[2] and **Ondřej Dušek**[2]

[1]Center for Information and Language Processing, LMU Munich, Germany
[2]Faculty of Mathematics and Physics, Charles University, Prague, Czech Republic
`libovicky@cis.lmu.de`, `{kasner,helcl,odusek}@ufal.mff.cuni.cz`

Abstract

We present our submission to the Simultaneous Translation And Paraphrase for Language Education (STAPLE) challenge. We used a standard Transformer model for translation, with a crosslingual classifier predicting correct translations on the output n-best list. To increase the diversity of the outputs, we used additional data to train the translation model, and we trained a paraphrasing model based on the Levenshtein Transformer architecture to generate further synonymous translations. The paraphrasing results were again filtered using our classifier. While the use of additional data and our classifier filter were able to improve results, the paraphrasing model produced too many invalid outputs to further improve the output quality. Our model without the paraphrasing component finished in the middle of the field for the shared task, improving over the best baseline by a margin of 10–22% weighted F1 absolute.

1 Introduction

The usual goal of machine translation (MT) is to generate a single correct translation of a source sentence. Neural machine translation (NMT; Bahdanau et al., 2015; Vaswani et al., 2017) models a conditional distribution over possible target sentences given a source sentence, and uses beam-search decoding as a heuristic to get one or more translations. However, the number of *possible* correct translations is often vast in comparison (Bojar et al., 2013).

The STAPLE challenge (Mayhew et al., 2020) poses the problem of MT slightly differently. Here, the goal is to generate as many correct translations as possible. Knowing many correct translations can be useful e.g. for automatic scoring in tools for language education, such as Duolingo.[1] On one hand, the learners should be guided to use the more common formulations, on the other hand, they should not be penalized for providing a correct but unusual answer.

We present a pipeline of two systems in our submission to the STAPLE challenge. As the first step, we use a standard NMT model trained with additional, carefully filtered data. The NMT output n-best lists are filtered using a classifier. Second, we use a Levenshtein Transformer model (Gu et al., 2019) to generate paraphrases of the outputs of the first model. Again, the outputs of the Levenshtein Transformer are filtered using another classifier.

The paper is structured as follows. Our training datasets are described in detail in Section 2. We describe the two models in Sections 3 and 4 respectively. We conduct experiments with all five target languages in the challenge, i.e. Hungarian, Japanese, Korean, Vietnamese and Portuguese. The source language is English in all setups. The experiment settings are shown in Section 5. The results (Section 6) show that the Levenshtein Transformer paraphrase generator cannot easily improve on the filtered NMT output n-best list.

2 Data

2.1 STAPLE Dataset

The data in the STAPLE shared task comes from the Duolingo language learning platform. This represents a specific domain with a limited number of mostly simple sentences targeted at learners, using a limited vocabulary.

Each source (English) sentence comes with a list of valid translations in the target language, ranging from a few up to hundreds of paraphrases. All of the valid translations are further annotated with a probability score indicating how frequent a given variant is. Statistics of the data are given in Table 1.

We held out 200 source sentences with all their

---

[1]`https://www.duolingo.com`

153

Proceedings of the 4th Workshop on Neural Generation and Translation (WNGT 2020), pages 153–160
Online, July 10, 2020. ©2020 Association for Computational Linguistics
www.aclweb.org/anthology/D19-56%2d

Language	Prompts	Trans.	Avg. P/S
Hungarian	3,800	238,467	62.75
Korean	2,300	646,410	281.05
Japanese	2,300	788,591	342.87
Portuguese	3,800	503,839	132.59
Vietnamese	3,300	183,339	55.57

Table 1: STAPLE training data statistics (target language set, number of source sentences (prompts), number of paraphrases (translations), average number of paraphrases per source).

translations as our internal validation dataset. We use this dataset for validating the translation models and for estimating the filtering thresholds.

2.2 Additional data for MT

For training the translation model, we obtained out-of-domain parallel corpora from the OPUS collection (Tiedemann, 2012) for all target languages, ParaCrawl (Esplà et al., 2019) for Portuguese and Hungarian, and JParaCrawl (Morishita et al., 2019) for Japanese. We applied FastText language identifier (Joulin et al., 2016b,a) to clean the corpora. Furthermore, we filtered out sentence pairs with a length ratio that differs from the estimated mean ratio by more than 2.5 times the standard deviation.

As in-domain training data, we mix data from the STAPLE training dataset and the Tatoeba[2] corpus (part of the OPUS collection). To balance the underrepresentation of the in-domain data in the training dataset, we oversample both the STAPLE dataset ($200\times$) and the Tatoeba dataset ($10\times$).

We use the combined mixed-domain parallel corpora for training backtranslation models (Sennrich et al., 2016) and an XLM-R-based domain classifier. The classifier is trained to predict whether a target sentence came from the STAPLE training dataset, conditioning on the source sentence.

The monolingual data consists of Wikipedia, WMT NewsCrawl (Barrault et al., 2019) for Hungarian, Japanese and Portuguese, Leipzig Corpora NewsCrawl (Goldhahn et al., 2012) for all languages and the jpWaC corpus for Japanese (Erjavec et al., 2008).

We filtered both the monolingual and parallel data using the domain classifier. The classifier has over 99% accuracy on balanced data. We set a permissive threshold for keeping the sentence pair to 10^{-5}.

Based on preliminary experiments, we include only a single correct translation from the STAPLE training set into the machine translation training data. This had a slightly positive effect on translation quality. Also, the n-best lists obtained by machine-translating the STAPLE dataset are more representative and thus more suitable for training the classifier for n-best list filtering than if we included all translations from the training set.

3 Translation and Filtering Model

3.1 Translation Model

Our pipeline starts with the Transformer model (Vaswani et al., 2017) trained on the provided dataset enriched with additional data (see Section 2). This provides initial translations of the source sentence on the output n-best list, which are further filtered.

3.2 Filtering Classifier

We train a crosslingual classifier which predicts whether a translation in the MT output n-best list is correct (given the source sentence). Using the trained translation model, we first generate large n-best lists for all English sentences in the original training data. Next, we label each generated sentence whether it is a positive or a negative sample (based on the reference data). Finally, we create a balanced mix of negative and positive samples. Since the n-best lists contained much more incorrect translations, we oversample the list of correct translations.

We use XLM-RoBERTa as our sentence classifier model (XLM-R; Conneau et al., 2020), specifically the pretrained variant available in the HuggingFace Transformers library[3] (Wolf et al., 2019). We finetune this model on the balanced mix of the correct and incorrect translations for a given sentence.

During inference, we generate an n-best list for a given source sentence, and we apply the classifier to filter out the sentences which are labeled as incorrect using a threshold value. The n-best list size and the threshold are hyperparameters of the method.

4 Paraphrasing Model

As an additional step to increase the number of valid translations produced, we train a target-

---

[2]https://tatoeba.org/

[3]https://github.com/huggingface/transformers

	All parallel	+ lang. & length filter	+ domain filtering	Monolingual	+ domain filtering	Total (unique)
Hungarian	56.1M	47.9 M	22.1M	54.3M	7.0M	27.1M
Japanese	14.7M	14.0 M	1.9M	44.2M	2.8M	4.7M
Korean	2.2M	2.0 M	0.6M	9.3M	0.8M	1.4M
Portuguese	63.5M	53.7 M	21.3M	30.0M	4.5M	25.8M
Vietnamese	3.9M	3.4 M	1.5M	9.7M	1.4M	2.8M

Table 2: Number of sentences in the parallel and monolingual data used for training the MT systems. The data in the second column were used for training the backtranslation systems, the last column corresponds to final translation systems.

language paraphrasing model. Rather than generating a translation directly from the source sentence, the model refines existing translations in order to produce new ones.

The model is based on the Levenshtein Transformer (LevT; Gu et al., 2019), which is a sequence generation model based on the Transformer (Vaswani et al., 2017) architecture. Instead of left-to-right autoregressive generation, LevT generates sequences in an arbitrary order using two basic operations – insertion and deletion. Using an initial sequence as a starting point, LevT is able to perform sequence refinement.

4.1 Training

LevT iteratively applies three policies represented by fully-connected neural network layers on top of the last layer of a Transformer decoder:

1. *Deletion* policy π^{del} removes tokens from the sequence;

2. *Placeholder* policy π^{plh} inserts placeholders into the sequence;

3. *Insertion* policy π^{ins} replaces placeholders with tokens from the vocabulary.

The policies are trained to follow oracle policies. Given a source sequence X and a target sequence Y, $L(X,Y)$ is a minimum sequence of edit operations (delete and insert) that transform X to Y. Its length is equal to the Levenshtein distance (Levenshtein, 1966) between X and Y. The operations in $L(X,Y)$ define oracle policies for π^{del}, π^{plh} and π^{ins}.

There are two other possible training strategies: Either training the insertion policy to repair a target sentence with randomly dropped tokens, or training the deletion policy to refine the output from the insertion policy. However, we do not use these strategies for our model. In the first case, we did not find it beneficial for the model performance. In the

second case, the option does not fit together with our inference scheme as described in Section 4.2.

To train the model to gradually produce more diverse, but still valid paraphrases, we provided the model with training paraphrase pairs with minimum edit distance. We represent the set of paraphrases as a complete graph with edges weighted by the Levenshtein distance (see Figure 1). We construct a minimum spanning tree of this graph and use the sentence pairs from the spanning tree edges as training examples.

Formally, a training example for LevT is a tuple (E,X_0,X,Y) where E is the original English sentence, X_0 is the gold translation, X is the source node and Y is the target node. (E,X_0) is processed by the encoder, X is used as the initial sequence for the decoder and Y acts as the ground truth. We do not use any additional data for LevT.

4.2 Inference

In the original LevT formulation, inference is done by applying the model over the initial sequence for several iterations. This approach aims to produce a single output translation and the intermediate translations are deemed to be incorrect. We redefine the generation process as *state-space search*, considering translations in each step as potentially correct and accepting the translations based on the classifier score. We also repurpose the deletion policy as *paraphrasing policy*, which gives us the possibility to generate multiple translations in each step. Similarly to the original LevT architecture, the encoder output is grounding the translations in the source sentence throughout the inference process.

The process can start from an arbitrary number of initial translations – in our case, the initial translations are the filtered outputs from the MT system. We put all the initial translations in a queue. In each step, we pop a translation from the queue, and we let the deletion policy mark all tokens suitable for paraphrasing. To expand our search space, we gen-

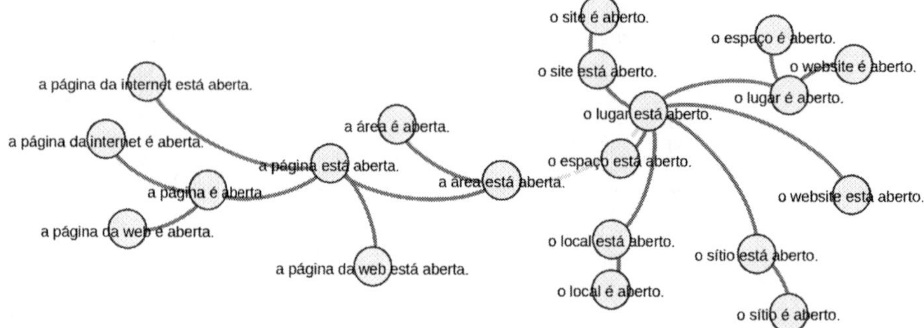

Figure 1: A minimum spanning tree of the graph of Portuguese translations for *"The site is open."*. Levenshtein distance (the sum of delete and insert operations) is 2 for solid green lines and 6 for the dashed yellow line.

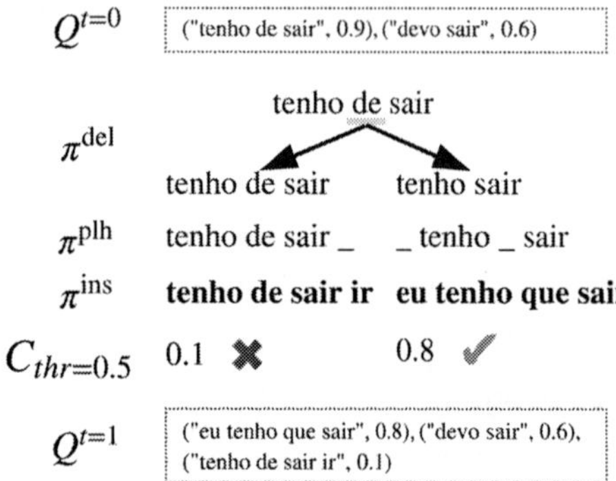

Figure 2: An example of a step of the inference algorithm of the paraphrasing model. A translation is taken from the queue $\mathcal{Q}$ and expanded using LevT policies. Results are scored by the classifier C; the translations scoring above the threshold $thr = 0.5$ are accepted. The translations are grounded in the source sentence by the encoder output.

erate multiple versions of the partially deleted sentence using all possible combinations of selected tokens, which are individually processed by the placeholder and insertion policies. We put the output translations in the queue and repeat the process until the queue is empty or we reach a preset limit on the number of generated sentences.

4.3 Filtering

Similarly to our NMT model, we filter relevant translations using a classifier built on top of XLM-R (see Section 3). In this case, the negative examples for the classifier are generated from LevT. We use the classifier's predictions to accept only translations passing a preset threshold. Moreover, we use the scores predicted by the classifier (probability of translation correctness) to define the priority of the translations in the queue, thus making it a pri-

ority queue. Figure 2 shows an example of a single step of the inference algorithm with filtering.

5 Experiments

5.1 Evaluation Metric

We use the official evaluation metric for the STA-PLE challenge, which is the *weighted macro F1 score*, computed by exact match with respect to the set of all valid translations for a given source sentence. The weighted F1 is a compound of unweighted precision and weighted recall, where the weight is determined based on each translation's probability (see Section 2.1).

5.2 Translation Model

We train the translation model using the Marian toolkit[4] (Junczys-Dowmunt et al., 2018). We use the Transformer Base hyperparameters, i.e., model dimension 512, feed-forward layer dimension 2048, 8 attention heads with a head dimension of 64. All models use SentencePiece-based (Kudo and Richardson, 2018) vocabulary of 32k units. Japanese was tokenized using UDPipe (Straka and Straková, 2017), other languages were processed with SentencePiece without tokenization.

The model is trained using the Adam optimizer (Kingma and Ba, 2015), with Noam learning schedule (Vaswani et al., 2017) with 8,000 warmup steps and initial learning rate $3 \cdot 10^{-4}$, dropout rate 0.1, label smoothing 0.1 and gradient clipping at 5.0. We set the training batch size to 4,096 tokens.

5.3 Paraphrasing Model

We base our paraphrasing model on the Levenshtein Transformer as implemented in fairseq[5] (Ott

---

[4] https://marian-nmt.github.io/
[5] https://github.com/pytorch/fairseq

et al., 2019). We replace the Transformer encoder with the pretrained XLM-R Base with 12 layers and 8 attention heads, keeping the vanilla Transformer decoder with 6 layers and 8 attention heads. We use the output layer of XLM-R as the decoder output layer and finetune it together with the last four layers of XLM-R (freezing the rest of XLM-R parameters). We train a separate decoder for each policy and employ the early exit as described by Gu et al. (2019) by using only the features from the third layer of the decoder for the deletion and placeholder policies.

The model is optimized using the Adam optimizer, with fixed learning rate 10^{-5}, batch size 1,500 tokens, dropout rate 0.5 and label smoothing 0.1. We set the maximum number of placeholders for each position at 3 instead of 256.

We experiment with various decoding strategies. For deletion and placeholder policies, we introduce a penalty parameter preventing the policy from producing the zero (unchanged) outcome. This proved beneficial in particular for the deletion policy, as it frequently did not mark any tokens for deletion, thus limiting the search process. Alternatively, we force the policy to produce an outcome by selecting top k results with the highest score. In both cases, we find that limiting the number of placeholders generated at the same position to 1 helps to prevent excessive sentence length.

For the insertion policy, we give up the non-autoregressivity and replace the placeholders in the left-to-right order, re-running the decoder in each step. This acts as a supplement for the fact that the insertion policy cannot repeatedly interact with the deletion policy in a single state-space search step.

Our experiments show that it is difficult to find a set of decoding parameters which would consistently produce meaningful output. For generating paraphrases, we find it useful to use the *penalty* strategy described above and tune the penalty separately for each language. Producing less paraphrases generally leads to better results, as it tends to limit the amount of incorrect output. On the contrary, we use the *top-k* strategy for generating the classifier training data, as it produces negative samples more robustly.

6   Results

The results on the blind development and test data are shown in Table 3. Our translation model was able to bring considerable improvements over the provided baseline models – 10–22% weighted F1 absolute due to increase in both precision and recall. We observed the highest improvements for Portuguese. Overall, our model tends to finish in the middle of the field.

Experiments with training data filtering showed that a smaller training set with better selected sentences leads to better trasnslation quality than using a larger general domain corpus (see Table 4), although the general corpus was double in the number of sentences (see Table 2). The optimal beam size for filtering only roughly corresponds to the average number of paraphrases in the data (see Table 1). Figure 3 shows the effect of beam size on the output quality. Without filtering, the precision quickly drops with increasing beam size. The filtering can partially compensate for the precision loss, however, at the expense of decreasing recall, too.

Despite our extensive efforts, the paraphrasing model did not bring substantial improvements over the translation model. Increase in recall typically came with lower precision and lower weighted F1 score. Even with the specific classifier training and its overall accuracy over 99%, the LevT output was too noisy to be precisely filtered. The only improvement was achieved for Portuguese, where the final paraphrasing and filtering setting resulted in slightly higher precision and similar recall. However, the improvement was mostly influenced by the second round of filtering (on the paraphrasing output). Therefore, we did not include the paraphrasing output in our primary submission.

We suppose that the inefficiency of the LevT model is caused by a mismatch between model training criteria and its application: the individual policies are trained separately, but need to complement each other to achieve good results. Moreover, the loss computed independently for each paraphrase may prevent the model from learning to generate multiple paraphrases. The shortage of useful paraphrases may be also caused by the lack of additional training data.

7   Conclusions

We presented our submission to the 2020 STAPLE translation and paraphrasing shared task. Our model is based on the Transformer architecture, used additional carefully selected training data, a XLM-R-based classifier to filter MT output beams, and an optional paraphrasing component based on the Levenshtein Transformer approach. The MT

Target	System	Development						Test					
		Rk	**Pre**	**W-R**	**W-F1**	**Δbase**	**Δbest**	**Rk**	**Pre**	**W-R**	**W-F1**	**Δbase**	**Δbest**
Hungarian	MT	4/9	50.65	50.66	46.25	+16.40	-13.58	4/7	51.04	45.77	43.49	+15.39	-11.91
	+Para	-	49.73	50.57	45.75	+15.90	-14.08	-	49.91	45.66	43.01	+14.91	-12.39
Japanese	MT	5/10	39.02	19.36	21.50	+17.25	-10.09	5/8	36.70	19.93	21.28	+16.97	-10.49
	+Para	-	38.27	19.32	21.34	+17.09	-10.25	-	35.76	19.87	21.08	+16.77	-10.69
Korean	MT	4/8	40.05	21.57	22.21	+16.76	-19.16	4/6	38.94	19.35	20.58	+15.71	-19.77
	+Para	-	39.65	21.06	21.87	+16.42	-19.50	-	38.42	18.92	20.29	+15.42	-20.06
Portuguese	MT	8/14	49.75	46.78	42.74	+21.59	-13.00	6/10	49.88	43.81	40.84	+19.54	-14.26
	+Para	-	50.72	46.60	43.22	+22.07	-12.52	-	50.94	43.44	41.18	+19.88	-13.92
Vietnamese	MT	3/6	52.27	37.36	38.26	+11.47	-16.47	3/5	51.59	36.84	37.71	+12.32	-17.85
	+Para	-	53.17	36.39	37.68	+10.89	-17.05	-	52.09	36.35	37.34	+11.95	-18.22

Table 3: Results for both system variants and all languages. "MT" denotes the variant without paraphrasing (final official result), "+Para" is the system with paraphrasing. Metrics: *Rk* = official competition rank (with the number of valid submissions), *Pre* = precision (%), *W-R* = weighted recall (%), *W-F1* = weighted F1 (%), *Δbase* = weighted F1 difference w. r. t. the best baseline model (% absolute), *Δbest* = w. r. t. the overall winner (% absolute).

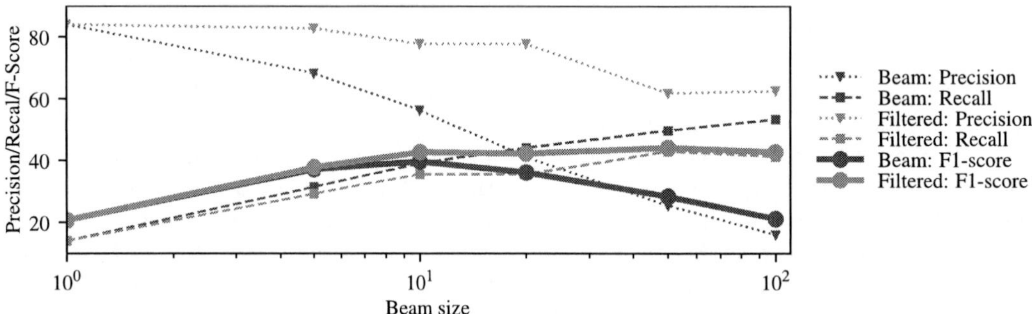

Figure 3: Precision, weighted recall and weighted F1 score for NMT decoding with different beam sizes and with and without beam filtering.

	AWS	**Gen.**	**Dom.**	**Best**	
Hungarian	29.2	27.4	40.2	49.1	100
Japanese	4.8	2.8	11.9	18.6	1000
Korean	4.9	6.5	11.5	22.0	1000
Portuguese	23.1	29.9	39.6	44.0	50
Vietnamese	20.3	33.0	38.5	42.1	5

Table 4: Translation quality measured by the weighted F1 score for general training (Gen.) data and domain-specific (Dom.) training data measured on our validation set with beam size 10 compared with the task baseline (AWS) and best filtered beam with beam size.

model with the filter was able to gain substantial increases over the baseline, but did not reach the top places in the challenge. The paraphrasing component's output proved too noisy to bring any substantial benefits – we only observed minor improvements in Portuguese. Therefore, the paraphrasing was not included in our primary submission.

Improving the paraphrasing model could be an interesting direction of future work. The amount of incorrect output could be reduced by better ac-counting for deletion and insertion policy interplay. However, computing the loss independently for each paraphrase may still hinder the ability of the model to generate multiple paraphrases for a single sentence. It may be thus necessary to rethink the training objective and tie it together with the inference process.

Acknowledgements

Work conducted at LMU was supported by the European Research Council (ERC) under the European Union's Horizon 2020 research and innovation programme (grant agreement No. 640550).

Work conducted at CUNI was supported by the Charles University grant No. 140320, the SVV project No. 260575, the European Union's Horizon 2020 research and innovation programme under grant agreement No. 825303 (Bergamot), Czech Science Foundation grant No. 19-26934X (NEUREM3), and the Charles University project PRIMUS/19/SCI/10.

References

Dzmitry Bahdanau, Kyunghyun Cho, and Yoshua Bengio. 2015. Neural machine translation by jointly learning to align and translate. In *3rd International Conference on Learning Representations (ICLR2015)*, San Diego, CA, USA.

Loïc Barrault, Ondřej Bojar, Marta R. Costa-jussà, Christian Federmann, Mark Fishel, Yvette Graham, Barry Haddow, Matthias Huck, Philipp Koehn, Shervin Malmasi, Christof Monz, Mathias Müller, Santanu Pal, Matt Post, and Marcos Zampieri. 2019. Findings of the 2019 conference on machine translation (WMT19). In *Proceedings of the Fourth Conference on Machine Translation (Volume 2: Shared Task Papers, Day 1)*, pages 1–61, Florence, Italy. Association for Computational Linguistics.

Ondřej Bojar, Matouš Macháček, Aleš Tamchyna, and Daniel Zeman. 2013. Scratching the surface of possible translations. In *Proc. of TSD 2013*, Lecture Notes in Artificial Intelligence, Berlin / Heidelberg. Západočeská univerzita v Plzni, Springer Verlag.

Alexis Conneau, Kartikay Khandelwal, Naman Goyal, Vishrav Chaudhary, Guillaume Wenzek, Francisco Guzmán, Edouard Grave, Myle Ott, Luke Zettlemoyer, and Veselin Stoyanov. 2020. Unsupervised cross-lingual representation learning at scale. In *Proceedings of ACL 2020*. ArXiv: 1911.02116.

Tomaž Erjavec, Kristina Hmeljak Sangawa, and Yoshiko Kawamura. 2008. Japanese web corpus with difficulty levels jpWaC-1 1.0. Slovenian language resource repository CLARIN.SI.

Miquel Esplà, Mikel Forcada, Gema Ramírez-Sánchez, and Hieu Hoang. 2019. ParaCrawl: Web-scale parallel corpora for the languages of the EU. In *Proceedings of Machine Translation Summit XVII Volume 2: Translator, Project and User Tracks*, pages 118–119, Dublin, Ireland. European Association for Machine Translation.

Dirk Goldhahn, Thomas Eckart, and Uwe Quasthoff. 2012. Building large monolingual dictionaries at the leipzig corpora collection: From 100 to 200 languages. In *Proceedings of the Eighth International Conference on Language Resources and Evaluation (LREC'12)*, pages 759–765, Istanbul, Turkey. European Language Resources Association (ELRA).

Jiatao Gu, Changhan Wang, and Junbo Zhao. 2019. Levenshtein transformer. In *Advances in Neural Information Processing Systems*, pages 11179–11189.

Armand Joulin, Edouard Grave, Piotr Bojanowski, Matthijs Douze, Hérve Jégou, and Tomas Mikolov. 2016a. Fasttext.zip: Compressing text classification models. *arXiv preprint arXiv:1612.03651*.

Armand Joulin, Edouard Grave, Piotr Bojanowski, and Tomas Mikolov. 2016b. Bag of tricks for efficient text classification. *arXiv preprint arXiv:1607.01759*.

Marcin Junczys-Dowmunt, Roman Grundkiewicz, Tomasz Dwojak, Hieu Hoang, Kenneth Heafield, Tom Neckermann, Frank Seide, Ulrich Germann, Alham Fikri Aji, Nikolay Bogoychev, André F. T. Martins, and Alexandra Birch. 2018. Marian: Fast neural machine translation in C++. In *Proceedings of ACL 2018, System Demonstrations*, pages 116–121, Melbourne, Australia. Association for Computational Linguistics.

Diederik P. Kingma and Jimmy Ba. 2015. Adam: A method for stochastic optimization. In *3rd International Conference on Learning Representations, ICLR 2015, San Diego, CA, USA, May 7-9, 2015, Conference Track Proceedings*.

Taku Kudo and John Richardson. 2018. SentencePiece: A simple and language independent subword tokenizer and detokenizer for neural text processing. In *Proceedings of the 2018 Conference on Empirical Methods in Natural Language Processing: System Demonstrations*, pages 66–71, Brussels, Belgium. Association for Computational Linguistics.

Vladimir I Levenshtein. 1966. Binary codes capable of correcting deletions, insertions, and reversals. In *Soviet physics doklady*, volume 10, pages 707–710.

Stephen Mayhew, Klinton Bicknell, Chris Brust, Bill McDowell, Will Monroe, and Burr Settles. 2020. Simultaneous translation and paraphrase for language education. In *Proceedings of the ACL Workshop on Neural Generation and Translation (WNGT)*. ACL.

Makoto Morishita, Jun Suzuki, and Masaaki Nagata. 2019. Jparacrawl: A large scale web-based english-japanese parallel corpus. *CoRR*, abs/1911.10668.

Myle Ott, Sergey Edunov, Alexei Baevski, Angela Fan, Sam Gross, Nathan Ng, David Grangier, and Michael Auli. 2019. fairseq: A fast, extensible toolkit for sequence modeling. In *Proceedings of NAACL-HLT 2019: Demonstrations*.

Rico Sennrich, Barry Haddow, and Alexandra Birch. 2016. Improving neural machine translation models with monolingual data. In *Proceedings of the 54th Annual Meeting of the Association for Computational Linguistics (Volume 1: Long Papers)*, pages 86–96, Berlin, Germany. Association for Computational Linguistics.

Milan Straka and Jana Straková. 2017. Tokenizing, POS tagging, lemmatizing and parsing UD 2.0 with UDPipe. In *Proceedings of the CoNLL 2017 Shared Task: Multilingual Parsing from Raw Text to Universal Dependencies*, pages 88–99, Vancouver, Canada. Association for Computational Linguistics.

Jörg Tiedemann. 2012. Parallel data, tools and interfaces in OPUS. In *Proceedings of the Eight International Conference on Language Resources and Evaluation (LREC'12)*, pages 2214–2218, Istanbul, Turkey. European Language Resources Association (ELRA).

Ashish Vaswani, Noam Shazeer, Niki Parmar, Jakob Uszkoreit, Llion Jones, Aidan N Gomez, Łukasz Kaiser, and Illia Polosukhin. 2017. Attention is all you need. In *Advances in Neural Information Processing Systems 30*, pages 6000–6010, Long Beach, CA, USA. Curran Associates, Inc.

Thomas Wolf, Lysandre Debut, Victor Sanh, Julien Chaumond, Clement Delangue, Anthony Moi, Pierric Cistac, Tim Rault, R'emi Louf, Morgan Funtowicz, and Jamie Brew. 2019. Huggingface's transformers: State-of-the-art natural language processing. *ArXiv preprint arXiv:1910.03771*.

Exploring Model Consensus to Generate Translation Paraphrases

Zhenhao Li[1], Marina Fomicheva[2], Lucia Specia[12]
[1] Department of Computing, Imperial College London
[2] Department of Computer Science, University of Sheffield
{zhenhao.li18, l.specia}@imperial.ac.uk
{m.fomicheva}@sheffield.ac.uk

Abstract

This paper describes our submission to the 2020 Duolingo Shared Task on Simultaneous Translation And Paraphrase for Language Education (STAPLE). This task focuses on improving the ability of neural MT systems to generate diverse translations. Our submission explores various methods, including N-best translation, Monte Carlo dropout, Diverse Beam Search, Mixture of Experts, Ensembling, and Lexical Substitution. Our main submission is based on the integration of multiple translations from multiple methods using Consensus Voting. Experiments show that the proposed approach achieves a considerable degree of diversity without introducing noisy translations. Our final submission[1] achieves 0.5510 weighted F1 score on the blind test set for the English-Portuguese track.

1 Introduction

Machine Translation (MT) systems are typically used to produce a single output for a given source sentence, whereas in human translation the same source sentence can often be translated in various different ways while still preserving its meaning.

In the 2020 Duolingo Shared Task on Simultaneous Translation And Paraphrase for Language Education (STAPLE) (Mayhew et al., 2020), participating MT systems are evaluated using multiple reference translations to measure their ability to generate diverse, yet high quality translations. For that, a new dataset with multiple human translations for each source sentence is provided. These human translations were produced by language learners as part of a translation exercise on the Duolingo platform[2] where they were asked to translate sentences from the language they were learning (e.g. English) to their native language. Each translation

in the dataset is assigned a weight based on the learner response frequency. Table 1 gives an example of the weighted translations in the dataset for English-Portuguese. The STAPLE dataset includes five language pairs: English to Portuguese, Hungarian, Japanese, Korean, and Vietnamese. In the shared task, we only participated in English-Portuguese (En-Pt) track.

Original	is my explanation clear?
Translation	minha explicação está clara? | 0.2673
	minha explicação é clara? | 0.1616
	a minha explicação está clara? | 0.1111
	a minha explicação é clara? | 0.0878
	minha explanação está clara? | 0.0572
	está clara minha explicação? | 0.0443
	minha explanação é clara? | 0.0392
	...

Table 1: An example of weighted translations in the STAPLE dataset for English-Portuguese.

In this paper, we experiment with various methods to improve the diversity of translations, while preserving their quality. We show that simply by generating N-best translations with larger beam size, we can already achieve a considerable degree of diversity. Our final submission is based on the integration of multiple translations from various methods, namely N-best translation, Monte Carlo dropout, Mixture of Experts, Ensembling, and Lexical Substitution, through a consensus voting mechanism. It achieves 0.5510 weighted F1 score on the official blind test set.

This paper is structured as follows: Section 2 describes the methods we used in our experiments. Section 3 introduces the experimental settings, including data preparation, model hyperparameters, and the evaluation procedure. Section 4 describes the results and analysis. Section 5 presents our three official submissions to STAPLE blind test set. Finally, Section 6 summarises our submission to the shared task and our contributions.

---

[1] https://github.com/Nickeilf/STAPLE20
[2] https://www.duolingo.com

Proceedings of the 4th Workshop on Neural Generation and Translation (WNGT 2020), pages 161–168
Online, July 10, 2020. ©2020 Association for Computational Linguistics
www.aclweb.org/anthology/D19-56%2d

2 Methods

In what follows we describe the methods used in our experiments, including N-best translation, Monte Carlo dropout, Diverse Beam Search, Mixture of Experts, Ensembling and Lexical Substitution. We combine all of these methods except the Diverse Beam Search in our official submissions through a consensus voting mechanism. Details about the submissions can be found in Section 5.

2.1 N-best

The simplest method to generate multiple translations for a given sentence is to use N-best translations with a large beam size during decoding. Larger beam size might lead to more translation options with similar meanings. We experimented with multiple sizes for N, and used the same value for N-best and beam size.

2.2 MC Dropout

Gal and Ghahramani (2016) proposed the Monte Carlo (MC) dropout method to estimate predictive NMT model uncertainty. The method consists in running several forward passes through the model (i.e., at inference time), each applying dropout before every weight layer and collecting posterior probabilities generated by the model with parameters perturbed by dropout. The mean and variance of the resulting distribution can then be used to represent model uncertainty. Instead of using this method for scoring translations, we use it as a way to generate alternative MT hypotheses for a given source sentence. Specifically, we run inference with dropout M times and collect the resulting translations. In our experiments, the dropout rate is set to 0.1 and $M = 10$.

2.3 Diverse Beam Search

Vijayakumar et al. (2016) proposed the Diverse Beam Search algorithm to improve the diversity of beam hypotheses. The algorithm proceeds by dividing the beam budget into groups and enforcing diversity between groups of beams. In our experiments we use the implementation of this algorithm in `fairseq` (Ott et al., 2019) with default parameters.

2.4 Mixture of Experts

Shen et al. (2019) introduced the Mixture of Experts (MoE) framework to capture the inherent uncertainty of the MT task where the same input sentence can have multiple correct translations. A mixture model introduces a multinomial latent variable to control generation and produce a diverse set of MT hypotheses. In our experiment we use hard mixture model with uniform prior and 5 mixture components.

2.5 Ensembling

Training an ensemble of various MT models initialized with different random seeds is a common strategy used to boost the output quality (Garmash and Monz, 2016). Unlike the typical ensembling method that combines prediction distributions from different models by averaging, we use each system in the ensemble to generate a separate set of translation hypotheses, and take the set of dictinct translations as the final output.

2.6 Lexical substitution

In the STAPLE dataset, we observed that many of the paraphrases in translations are simple variants with word substitutions in the target language. Therefore, we built a dictionary containing all lexical substitutions from the STAPLE training data. The substitutions are sorted according to two criteria: 1) number of occurrences 2) substitution probability. The substitution probability is calculated as follows:

$$P(sub) = \frac{\text{Count}(sub(w1, w2))}{\text{Count}(w1)} \qquad (1)$$

The top-5 lexical substitutions from frequency-sorted and probability-sorted dictionaries are listed in Table 2. We filtered the substitution dictionary with a stopword list[3] and a threshsold (which can be either frequency count or substitution probability), to avoid generating ungrammatical translations.

Frequency		Probability	
substitution	count	substitution	prob
neste-nesse	5091	baixar->descarregar	1.0
irá-vai	4920	descarregar->baixar	1.0
vou-irei	4645	situa-se->fica	1.0
local-lugar	2989	achasse->encontrasse	1.0
bem-bastante	2694	localizasse->achasse	1.0

Table 2: Top-5 lexical substitutions in frequency-sorted and probability-sorted dictionaries.

---

[3] `http://snowball.tartarus.org/algorithms/portuguese/stop.txt`

2.7 Consensus voting

To integrate translations from different models, we employed a consensus voting mechanism by counting the number of systems that predicted each translation. A threshold T_{con} is set, meaning that a translation must be predicted by at least $T_{con} + 1$ systems, otherwise it is removed. Considering the lexical translation might generate rare but correct translation, we assign the lexical-substituted translations a weight W_{sub} so that they can be seen as generated by W_{sub} systems. The consensus method guarantees a high precision by removing translations that are likely to be incorrect.

3 Experiments

3.1 Data

To build the NMT model, we used parallel corpora for En-Pt from OPUS (Tiedemann, 2012) as out-of-domain data, including ParaCrawl[4], EUbookshop[5], Europarl[6], Wikipedia[7], QED[8], and Tatoeba[9]. The combination of these corpora contains 22.42 million parallel sentence pairs. The STAPLE dataset, which contains 4000 source sentences with 526,466 translations, is used as in-domain data for fine-tuning.

Since in the STAPLE dataset a source sentence have an average number of 131 reference translations, we constructed parallel data by duplicating the source sentence to match the number of translations, as shown in Figure 1.

Figure 1: Constructing parallel fine-tuning data from the STAPLE dataset.

[4]http://opus.nlpl.eu/ParaCrawl-v5.php

[5]http://opus.nlpl.eu/EUbookshop-v2.php

[6]http://opus.nlpl.eu/Europarl-v8.php

[7]http://opus.nlpl.eu/Wikipedia-v1.0.php

[8]http://opus.nlpl.eu/QED-v2.0a.php

[9]http://opus.nlpl.eu/Tatoeba-v20190709.php

We also experimented with different data filtering strategies on the STAPLE dataset by only keeping the top-K translations with the highest weights (we refer to this as tune-K). Statistics regarding the corpus size after filtering are shown in Table 3.

Filtering	Source	Translations
tune-5	20,000	5.00
tune-10	40,000	10.00
tune-20	78,439	19.61
tune-all	526,466	131.62

Table 3: Size of parallel fine-tuning data after filtering the STAPLE dataset. **Source** indicates the number of source sentences and **Translations** indicates the average number of translations per source sentence

All sentences are tokenized with Moses (Koehn et al., 2007), and then processed via Byte-Pair-Encoding (BPE) (Sennrich et al., 2016). A shared vocabulary of 40,000 subwords is constructed for both English and Portuguese. The training data was then cleaned by removing sentence pairs with more than 250 subwords or with length ratio over 1.5, using the `clean-corpus-n.perl`[10] script in Moses.

3.2 Model and hyperparameters

We used the Transformer model (Vaswani et al., 2017) as our baseline model. The model is trained using `fairseq` toolkit (Ott et al., 2019) with the default hyperparameter settings using `transformer_wmt_en_de` architecture. The model was trained on 8 GPUs with a batch size of 4096 tokens on each GPU. We used mixed-precision training to accelerate the training. The model was pre-trained on OPUS data for 30 epochs and then fine-tuned on STAPLE data. We set 5 as the number of experts for training the MoE system. For ensembling, we pretrained with 3 random seeds and fine-tuned with 4 random seeds, resulting in 12 different MT systems.

3.3 Generation of Translations

When generating an integration of translations from multiple systems, we follows the procedure as described below:

1. Generate translations from N systems, resulting in N translation sets $s_1, s_2, s_3, ..., s_N$

[10]https://github.com/moses-smt/mosesdecoder/blob/master/scripts/training/clean-corpus-n.perl

2. Apply consensus voting to the N system translations with threshold T_{con}, resulting in one translation set $s_{consensus}$

3. Apply lexical substitution to $s_{consensus}$, resulting in a separate translation set $s_{lexical}$

4. Apply consensus voting to the N system translations and the lexical substitution translation $s_1, s_2, s_3, ..., s_N, s_{lexical}$ with threshold T_{con} and weight W_{sub}, resulting in the final translation set $s_{lexical\&consensus}$.

3.4 Evaluation

The shared task provides a blind dev set (blind-dev) and a blind test set (blind-test) for evaluation. Since the number of submissions is limited, we also take a small random split from the STAPLE training set for dev (heldout-dev) and test (heldout-test) sets with 500 source sentences.

The translations are evaluated at sentence-level as a classification problem where true positives (TP) occur when the system produces one of the translations in the given set of references, false positives (FP) when a translation out of this set is produced, and false negatives (FN) when translations in this set are missed by the system. The official evaluation metric is a weighted macro F1-score averaging over all source sentences. The weighted F1 score is calculated with weighted recall and unweighted precision:

$$recall = \sum_{t \in TP} \text{weight}(t)$$

$$precision = \frac{TP}{TP + FP}$$

$$weighted\, F_1 = \frac{2 * precision * recall}{precision + recall}$$

$$weighted\, macro\, F_1 = \sum_{s \in S} \frac{weighted\, F_1(s)}{|S|}$$

4   Results

N-best We present the F1 score with respect to n-best size (from 1 to 20) in Figure 2. The models fine-tuned with different filtered data are evaluated on our heldout test set. As shown in Figure 2, the pre-trained model (tune-0) shows a poorer performance than the other fine-tuned models. The tune-1 model shows a good performance when the N-best size is small, but experiences a degradation when N-best increases. Models

fine-tuned with 5, 10, and 20 reference translations show similar performances with F1 score around 0.49. However, the optimal n-best size is closely related to the number of translations used for fine-tuning, with N-best=3,10,12,18 for model tuned with 1, 5, 10 and 20 references respectively. The models fine-tuned with all translations in the STAPLE dataset show a growing trend in F1 score as n-best size increases, but the overall F1 score is still much lower than for the three fine-tuned models. We found that the upper bound for tune-all model is around 0.415 F1 score.

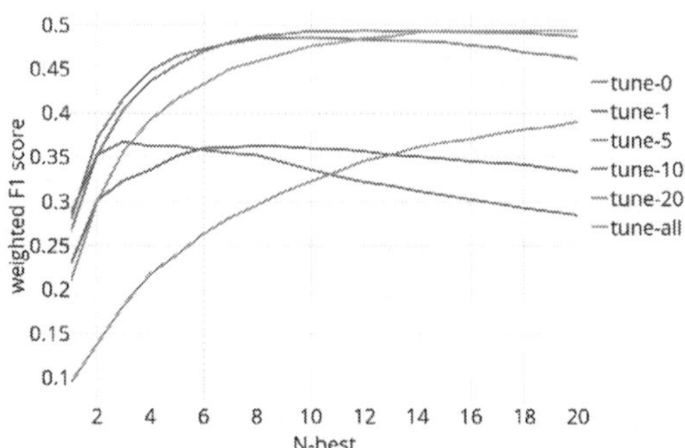

Figure 2: F1 score w.r.t N-best size for models fine-tuned with different number of reference translations.

MC dropout Table 4 shows a comparison on the heldout-test set between the N-best and N-best with MC dropout. It can be seen that the N-best12 achieves a higher recall than the N-best5, which leads to an increase of 0.038 in F1 score. When decoding with dropout, the N-best5 could match the performance of N-best12. Although noticing that MC Dropout could improve the performance for small N-best size, we found that when the N-best size gets larger the weighted F1 score does not improve further.

	Precision	Recall	F1
N-best12	0.717	0.452	0.494
N-best5	0.839	0.360	0.456
+dropout(H=10)	0.725	0.441	0.497

Table 4: A comparison between N-best and N-best with MC Dropout.

Diverse beam search When evaluating diverse beam search on the heldout-test set, we found that the model performance lags behind the N-best baseline to a large extent, with F1 score of only 0.292. We looked into some translation examples and noticed that although diverse beam search can lead to more diversity in translations, it sometimes adds an extra full stop at the end of translations. Considering that the evaluation is conducted at sentence-level, such a minor modification can lead to a large false positive number. In the final submission, we left this method out.

Mixture of experts Regarding the MoE method, we found that different experts show inconsistent performance. As shown in Table 5, with the same N-best size, experts 2, 3, and 5 show a good performance, achieving an F1 score over 0.4. However, the other two experts, especially expert 4, exhibit poorer performance. This might be caused by insufficient training for the experts that perform poorly. In the final submission, we removed translations from experts 1 and 4 to avoid incorrect predictions.

Expert	Precision	Recall	F1
1	0.425	0.320	0.312
2	0.708	0.426	0.475
3	0.647	0.374	0.415
4	0.276	0.217	0.193
5	0.640	0.404	0.437

Table 5: An illustration of the inconsistent performance from different experts in MoE (with N-best=12).

Ensemble & Consensus In Table 6, we present our ensembling submission and consensus submission (with threshold T_{con} set to 1) on the blind-dev set. Both ensembling and consensus voting improve over the N-best by increasing the recall and reducing the precision. However, since consensus voting removed translations with fewer votes from other systems, the precision score is higher than that of ensembling while the recall is similar. This leads to a higher F1 score with the consensus submission.

	Precision	Recall	F1
N-best	0.714	0.483	0.521
+Ensemble	0.617	0.549	0.523
+Consensus($T_{con} = 1$)	0.652	0.534	0.530

Table 6: A comparison between ensembling and consensus voting.

Ensembling can be seen as a special case of consensus voting, with the threshold T_{con} being zero. Ensembling maximizes the recall by taking translations from all the systems but sacrifices the precision. Increasing the value of the threshold T_{con} would compensate for the precision loss while maintaining the gain in recall.

Lexical substitution Table 7 shows the submissions on the blind-dev set after applying lexical substitution to a consensus output combining ensembled N-best, MC dropout, and MoE systems.We first generated a set of translations with all lexical substitutions, using the translations from an N-best system. The translations with lexical substitution achieve an F1 score of 0.127, which shows potential benefits of this method. However, as shown in Table 7, simply adding the substituted translations will harm performance, and this will happen for both frequency-based sorting and probability-based sorting. This is due to the fact that the translations after substitution are likely to be ungrammatical since the substituted word does not fit in the context. To alleviate this, we added the substituted translations to the consensus pool for higher precision. This only improves over the consensus system without lexical substitution by +0.002 F1 score.

	F1
Lexical only	0.127
Consensus($T_{con} = 5$)	0.542
+lexical (freq > 1000)	0.512
+lexical (prob > 0.85)	0.532
+lexical (prob > 0.85, consensus)	0.544

Table 7: An illustration of the benefit and harm from lexical substitution (evaluated on blind-dev set). The Consensus system combines the ensembled N-bset, MC-Dropout, and MoE systems.

In the experiment combining theses methods, we found that the N-best translations contributes the most score among all these methods. While an N-best system could achieve a weighted F1 score of nearly 0.5, other methods such as MC-Dropout, Ensembling and Consensus would only result in an extra improvement of less than 0.05 weighted F1 score. In our experiments, Diverse Beam Search and Mixture of Experts systems didn't contribute much.

5 Official submissions

Our official submissions combine translations from 12 tune-10 N-best systems (12 random seeds, finetuned with top-10 references, $N = 12$), 12 tune-20 N-best systems (12 random seeds, finetuned with top-20 references, $N = 20$), 2 MC Dropout systems ($n = 3$, $M = 50$; $n = 5$, $M = 10$), 3 experts from the MoE system, and lexical substitution (with a probability threshold of 0.7). The consensus voting threshold T_{con} is set to be 10, and the weight W_{sub} for lexical substitution is 9. Results for our three official submissions to the blind test set are shown in Table 8.

	Precision	Recall	F1
Consensus(T_{con}=10)+lexical	0.741	0.516	**0.551**
Consensus(T_{con}=10)	**0.757**	0.501	0.545
Consensus(T_{con}=1)+lexical	0.579	**0.580**	0.521

Table 8: Our three official submissions to STAPLE blind-test set.

The best submission, which achieves the best F1 score of 0.5510, applies both consensus voting and lexical substitution. As shown in the second submission, removing lexical substitution would reduce the F1 score by 0.006, although the precision is improved marginally. In the third submission, we set the consensus voting threshold T to be 1 to see the upper bound for recall. The recall increases from 0.516 to 0.580 while the precision drops significantly from 0.741 to 0.579.

Our best submission achieves the second position in the English-Portuguese track, with only 0.0006 weighted F1 score behind the winning submission. The official result on STAPLE test set is shown in Table 9.

Participant	Weighted F1
jbrem	0.5516
Ours	0.5510
rakchada	0.5440
aws_baseline	0.2130
fairseq_baseline	0.1357

Table 9: Official results on STAPLE test set in English-Portuguese translation (top-3 submissions and baselines).

6 Conclusions

This paper describes our submissions to the STAPLE shared task for English-Portuguese translation. We showed that simply generating N-best translations already achieves a considerable degree of diversity and quality. We experimented with various methods to improve the diversity in the MT output, including N-best translation, MC Dropout, Diverse Beam Search, Mixture of Experts, Ensembling, Consensus Voting, and Lexical Substitution. We showed the benefits and drawbacks of these methods in generating diverse, high quality translations. Our systems combining these methods further improve over the N-best translation and achieve 0.5510 weighted F1 score on STAPLE blind test set, which is only 0.0006 behind the winning submission.

References

Yarin Gal and Zoubin Ghahramani. 2016. Dropout as a Bayesian Approximation: Representing Model Uncertainty in Deep Learning. In *international conference on machine learning*, pages 1050–1059.

Ekaterina Garmash and Christof Monz. 2016. Ensemble learning for multi-source neural machine translation. In *Proceedings of COLING 2016, the 26th International Conference on Computational Linguistics: Technical Papers*, pages 1409–1418.

Philipp Koehn, Hieu Hoang, Alexandra Birch, Chris Callison-Burch, Marcello Federico, Nicola Bertoldi, Brooke Cowan, Wade Shen, Christine Moran, Richard Zens, Chris Dyer, Ondřej Bojar, Alexandra Constantin, and Evan Herbst. 2007. Moses: Open source toolkit for statistical machine translation. In *Proceedings of the 45th Annual Meeting of the Association for Computational Linguistics Companion Volume Proceedings of the Demo and Poster Sessions*, pages 177–180, Prague, Czech Republic. Association for Computational Linguistics.

Stephen Mayhew, Klinton Bicknell, Chris Brust, Bill McDowell, Will Monroe, and Burr Settles. 2020. Simultaneous translation and paraphrase for language education. In *Proceedings of the ACL Workshop on Neural Generation and Translation (WNGT)*. ACL.

Myle Ott, Sergey Edunov, Alexei Baevski, Angela Fan, Sam Gross, Nathan Ng, David Grangier, and Michael Auli. 2019. fairseq: A fast, extensible toolkit for sequence modeling. In *Proceedings of NAACL-HLT 2019: Demonstrations*.

Rico Sennrich, Barry Haddow, and Alexandra Birch. 2016. Neural machine translation of rare words with subword units. In *Proceedings of the 54th Annual Meeting of the Association for Computational Linguistics (Volume 1: Long Papers)*, pages 1715–1725, Berlin, Germany. Association for Computational Linguistics.

Tianxiao Shen, Myle Ott, Michael Auli, and Marc'Aurelio Ranzato. 2019. Mixture models for diverse machine translation: Tricks of the trade. *arXiv preprint arXiv:1902.07816.*

Jrg Tiedemann. 2012. Parallel data, tools and interfaces in opus. In *Proceedings of the Eight International Conference on Language Resources and Evaluation (LREC'12)*, Istanbul, Turkey. European Language Resources Association (ELRA).

Ashish Vaswani, Noam Shazeer, Niki Parmar, Jakob Uszkoreit, Llion Jones, Aidan N Gomez, Ł ukasz Kaiser, and Illia Polosukhin. 2017. Attention is all you need. In I. Guyon, U. V. Luxburg, S. Bengio, H. Wallach, R. Fergus, S. Vishwanathan, and R. Garnett, editors, *Advances in Neural Information Processing Systems 30*, pages 5998–6008. Curran Associates, Inc.

Ashwin K Vijayakumar, Michael Cogswell, Ramprasath R Selvaraju, Qing Sun, Stefan Lee, David Crandall, and Dhruv Batra. 2016. Diverse beam search: Decoding diverse solutions from neural sequence models. *arXiv preprint arXiv:1610.02424.*

A   Appendices

A.1   Checkpoiting vs tune-K

Table 10 presents the best finetuning checkpoint for models finetuned with different number of references. Models trained with more references might converge faster, and when the tuning number is larger than 40, only 1 epoch is used for finetuning.

Finetuning	Best checkpoint
tune-1	10
tune-5	10
tune-10	6
tune-20	4
tune-40	1
tune-all	1

Table 10: The best finetuning checkpoint vs the number of finetuning reference translations

A.2   Submission on blind-dev set

To provide a comprehensive understanding of the different methods, we selectively list our submissions to the blind-dev set in Table 11.

ID	System	Precision	Recall	F1	Hyperparameters
1	nbest	0.714	0.484	0.521	N=12, tune-10
2	ensemble	0.617	0.549	0.523	N=12, tune-10, 3 pretrain * 4 finetune seeds
3	nbest	0.645	0.522	0.518	N=18, tune-10
4	nbest	0.635	0.522	0.511	N=20, tune-20
5	MoE	0.368	0.527	0.385	N=12, tune-10, experts=5
6	MC Dropout	0.660	0.496	0.514	N=3, tune-10, M=50
7	MC Dropout	0.672	0.485	0.511	N=5, tune-10, M=10
8	Consensus	0.653	0.534	0.530	12*nbest systems(tune-10), $T_{con} = 1$
9	Consensus	0.641	0.541	0.529	12*nbest systems(tune-10), 2 MC Dropout systems(row 6 and 7), 5 experts, $T_{con} = 2$
10	Consensus	0.677	0.527	0.536	same as Row 9, $T_{con} = 3$
11	Lexical	0.443	0.538	0.428	same as Row 10, add lexical substitutions (frequency > 4000)
12	Lexical	0.612	0.534	0.509	same as Row 11, frequency > 5000
13	Consensus	0.633	0.565	0.538	24*nbest systems(tune-10, tune-20), 2 MC Dropout systems, 5 experts, $T_{con} = 4$
14	Consensus	0.652	0.558	0.542	same as Row 13, $T_{con} = 5$
15	Consensus	0.655	0.557	0.543	24*nbest systems(tune-10, tune-20), 2 MC Dropout systems, 3 experts, $T_{con} = 5$
16	Lexical	0.607	0.578	0.533	same as Row 15, add lexical substitution(probability > 0.85)
17	Lexical+Consensus	0.651	0.561	0.544	same as Row 15, add lexical substitution to consensus voting ($W_{sub} = 3$)
18	Lexical+Consensus	0.667	0.553	0.546	same as Row 17, $T_{con} = 6$
19	Lexical+Consensus	0.682	0.546	0.548	same as Row 17, $T_{con} = 7$
20	Lexical+Consensus	0.697	0.540	0.550	same as Row 17, $T_{con} = 8$
21	Consensus	0.710	0.530	0.550	same as Row 15, $T_{con} = 9$
22	Consensus	**0.721**	0.526	0.551	same as Row 15, $T_{con} = 10$
23	Lexical only	0.243	0.114	0.127	
24	Lexical+Consensus	0.720	0.526	0.550	same as Row 22, add lexical substitutions to consensus voting (frequency > 1000, $W_{sub} = 3$)
25	Consensus	0.564	**0.582**	0.506	36*nbest systems(tune-10, tune-20, tune-40), 2 MC Dropout systems, 3 experts, $T_{con} = 10$
26	Consensus	0.618	0.565	0.526	same as Row 25, $T_{con} = 11$
27	Lexical+Consensus	0.722	0.527	0.552	same as Row 22, add lexical substitutions to consensus voting (probability > 0.99, $W_{sub} = 3$)
28	Lexical+Consensus	0.720	0.529	0.552	same as Row 27, $W_{sub} = 7$
29	Lexical+Consensus	0.718	0.531	0.553	same as Row 27, $W_{sub} = 9$
30	Lexical+Consensus	0.715	0.535	0.554	same as Row 27, (probability > 0.90, $W_{sub} = 9$)
31	Lexical+Consensus	0.710	0.539	**0.555**	same as Row 27, (probability > 0.70, $W_{sub} = 9$)

Table 11: Submissions on the blind-dev set.

Growing Together: Modeling Human Language Learning With *n*-Best Multi-Checkpoint Machine Translation

El Moatez Billah Nagoudi[1]**, Muhammad Abdul-Mageed**[1]**, Hasan Cavusoglu** [2]

[1] Natural Language Processing Lab
[2] Sauder School of Business
[1,2] The University of British Columbia

[1] {muhammad.mageed,moatez.nagoudi}@ubc.ca, [2] cavusoglu@sauder.ubc.ca

Abstract

We describe our submission to the 2020 Duolingo Shared Task on Simultaneous Translation And Paraphrase for Language Education (STAPLE) (Mayhew et al., 2020). We view MT models at various training stages (i.e., checkpoints) as human learners at different levels. Hence, we employ an ensemble of multi-checkpoints from the same model to generate translation sequences with various levels of fluency. From each checkpoint, for our best model, we sample *n*-Best sequences ($n = 10$) with a beam width $= 100$. We achieve 37.57 *macro* F_1 with a 6 checkpoint model ensemble on the official English to Portuguese shared task test data, outperforming a baseline Amazon translation system of 21.30 *macro* F_1 and ultimately demonstrating the utility of our intuitive method.

1 Introduction

Machine Translation (MT) systems are usually trained to output a single translation. However, many possible translations of a given input text can be acceptable. This situation is common in online language learning applications such as *Duolingo*,[1] *Babbel*[2], and *Busuu*.[3] In applications of this type, learning happens via translation-based activities while evaluation is performed by comparing learners' responses to a large set of human acceptable translations. Figure 1 shows an example of a typical situation extracted from the Duolingo application.

The main set up of the 2020 Duolingo Shared Task on Simultaneous Translation And Paraphrase for Language Education (STAPLE 2020) (Mayhew et al., 2020) is such that one starts with a set of English sentences (prompts) and then generates high-coverage sets of plausible translations in the five

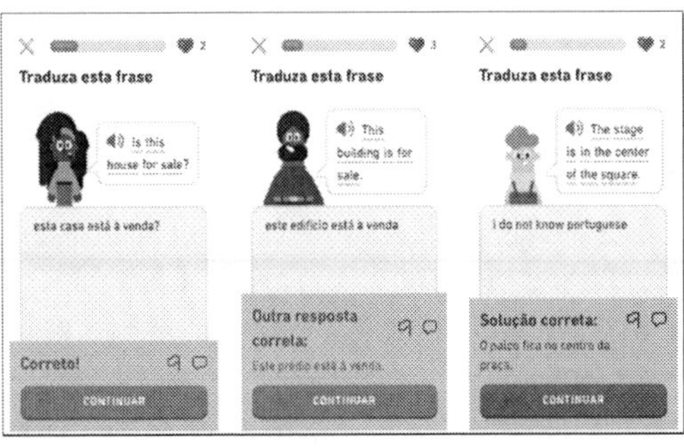

Figure 1: Translations proposed by English language learners at various levels of fluency, from diverse backgrounds. Our multi-checkpoint ensemble models mimic learner fluency.[4]

target languages: Portuguese, Hungarian, Japanese, Korean, and Vietnamese. For instance, if we want to translate the English (En) sentence *"is my explanation clear?"* to Portuguese (Pt), all the translated Portuguese sentences illustrated in Table 1 would be acceptable.[4]

Limited training data. One challenge for training a sufficiently effective model we faced is the limited size of the source training data released by organizers ($4,000$ source English sentences coupled with $226,466$ Portuguese target sentences). We circumvent this limitation by training a model on a large dataset acquired from the OPUS corpus (as described in Section 3), which gives us a powerful MT system that we build on (see Section 4.2). We then exploit the STAPLE-provided training data in multiple ways (see Sections 4.3 and 4.4) to extend this primary model as a way to nuance the model to the shared task domain.

Paraphrase via MT. In essence, the shared task is a mixture of MT and paraphrase. This poses a second challenge: there is no paraphrase dataset

---

[1] https://www.duolingo.com/
[2] https://www.babbel.com/
[3] https://www.busuu.com/

[4] Examples taken from shared task description at: https://sharedtask.duolingo.com/.

Proceedings of the 4th Workshop on Neural Generation and Translation (WNGT 2020), pages 169–177
Online, July 10, 2020. ©2020 Association for Computational Linguistics
www.aclweb.org/anthology/D19-56%2d

to train the system on. For this reason, we resort to using outputs from the MT system in place of paraphrases. This required generating multiple sentences for each source sentence. To meet this need, we generate multiple translation hypotheses (n-Best) using a wide beam search (Section 5.1), perform 'round-trip' translations exploiting these multiple outputs (Section 5.2), and employ ensembles of checkpoints (Section 5.3).

Diverse outputs. A third challenge is that the target Portuguese sentences provided for training by organizers are produced by learners of English at various levels of fluency. This makes some of these Portuguese translations inarticulate (i.e., not quite fluent). MT systems are not usually trained to produce inarticulate translations (part of the time), and hence we needed to offer a solution that matches the different levels of language learners who produced the translations. Intuitively, we view MT systems trained at various stages (i.e., checkpoint) as learners with various levels of fluency. As such, we employ an ensemble of checkpoints to generate translations matching the different levels of learner fluency (Section 5.3). Ultimately, ***our contributions lie in alleviating the 3 challenges listed above***.

The remainder of the paper is organized as follows: Section 2 is a brief overview of related work. In Section 3, we describe the data we use for both training and fine-tuning our models. Section 4 presents the proposed MT system. Section 5 describes our different methods. We discuss our results in Section 6, and conclude in Section 7.

2   Related Work

We focus our related work overview on the task of paraphrase generation and its intersection with machine translation. Paraphrasing is the task of expressing the same textual units (e.g. sentence) with alternative forms using different words while keeping the original meaning intact. [5] Over the last few years, MT has been the dominant approach for paraphrase generation. For instance, Barzilay and McKeown (2001); Pang et al. (2003) use multiple translations of the same text to train a paraphrase system. Similarly, Bannard and Callison-Burch (2005) use an MT phrase table to mapping an English sentences to various non-English sentences.

English sentence	is my explanation clear?
Accepted Portuguese Translations	- minha explicação está clara? - minha explicação é clara? - a minha explicação é clara? - está clara minha explicação? - minha explanação está clara? - é clara minha explicação?
English sentence	you look so pretty!
Accepted Portuguese Translations	- você está tão linda! - você está tão bonita! - você está muito linda! - você está muito bonita! - você parece tão linda! - você parece tão bonita!

Table 1: English sentences with their Portuguese translation samples from shared task training split.

More recently, advances in neural machine translation (NMT) have spurred interest in paraphrase generation (Sutskever et al., 2014; Luong and Manning, 2015; Aharoni et al., 2019). For example, Prakash et al. (2016) employ a stacked residual LSTM network to learn a sequence-to-sequence model on paraphrase data. A parpahrase model with adversarial training is presented by (Li et al., 2017). Wieting and Gimpel (2017); Iyyer et al. (2018) propose a translation-based paraphrasing system, which is based on NTM to translate one side of a parallel corpus. Paraphrase generation with pivot NMT is used by (Mallinson et al., 2017; Yu et al., 2018).

3   Data

3.1   Shared task data

As part of the STAPLE 2020 shared task, only `training` data were released. The target training split is a total of $526,466$ of learner translations of $4,000$ input (source) English sentences. We note that the number of translations of each English sentence varies, with an average of $\sim$ 132 Portuguese target sentences for each English source sentence. As shared task organizers point out, this training dataset can be used as a reference/anchor points, and also serves as a strong baseline. For `evaluation`, a sets of $60,294$ translations (learner-crafted sentences) of 500 input English sentences were available on Colab. `Test` data were also made available only via Colab and comprised 500 English sentences learner-translated

---

Corpus	Content	Documents	Sentences	En. Words	Pt. Words
ParaCrawl v5	Parallel corpora from Web Crawls collected in the ParaCrawl project	287	13.9M	341.4M	347.9M
TildeMODEL v2018	This is the Tilde MODEL Corpus – Multilingual Open Data for European Languages	6	3.6M	134.1M	100.4M
DGT	A collection of translation memories provided by the JRC	287	13.9M	341.4M	347.9M
SciELO	Parallel corpus of full-text articles in Portuguese, English and Spanish from SciELO	2	3.1M	92.8M	95.4M
OpenSubtitles	A new collection of translated movie subtitles	42,755	35.5M	283.4M	248.9M
Tanzil	A collection of Quran translations	15	0.1M	2.8M	2.4M
News Commentary	A parallel corpus of News Commentaries provided by WMT	7,185	0.6M	15.4M	15.5M
Europarl v8	A parallel corpus extracted from the European Parliament web site	10,344	2.0M	59.5M	6.1M
JW300 v1	JW300 is a parallel corpus of over 300 languages	26,991	2.2M	40.0M	40.8M
CAPES v1	Parallel corpus of theses and dissertation abstracts in Portuguese and English from CAPES	1	1.2M	38.4M	39.1M
EMEA v3	A parallel corpus from the European Medicines Agency	1,921	1.1M	12.0M	16.4M
QED v2.0a	Open multilingual collection of subtitles for educational videos and lectures	4,618	0.5M	8.7M	7.4M
JRC-Acquis v3.0	JRC-Acquis is a collection of legislative text of the European Union	20,507	1.7M	64.3M	64.8M
Wikipedia	A corpus of parallel sentences from Wikipedia	5	1.8M	47.0M	44.8M
TED2013	A parallel corpus of TED talk subtitles by CASMACAT	1	0.2M	3.1M	2.9M
GNOME.	A parallel corpus of GNOME localization files	1,307	0.6M	2.6M	3.7M
Tatoeba	A collection of translated sentences from Tatoeba	1	0.2M	11.0M	2.7M
ECB v1	Website and documentatuion from the European Central Bank	1	0.2M	5.8M	6.2M
bible-uedin v1	Multilingual parallel corpus created from translations of the Bible	2	62.2K	1.8M	1.7M
GlobalVoices	A parallel corpus of news from the Global Voices website	5,133	71.5k	2.3M	2.3M
KDE4	A parallel corpus of KDE4 system messages	2,136	0.2M	2.4M	2.7M
Ubuntu	A parallel corpus of the Ubuntu Dialogue Corpus	449	0.1M	0.7M	0.5M
EUconst v1	A parallel corpus collected from the European Constitution	47	10.9K	0.2M	0.2M
Books v1	A collection of copyright free book	1	1.4K	33.8K	32.3K
Total	All corpora extracted from OPUS	162,425	77.7M	1.5B	1.4B

Table 2: English-Portuguese datasets from Tiedemann (2012) used in our training.

into $67,865$ Portuguese sentences. For all training, development, and test data, these translations are ranked and weighted according to actual learner response frequency. We refer the reader to the shared task description for more information. [6]

3.2 OPUS data

In order to develop efficient English-Portuguese MT models that can possibly work across different text domains, we make use of a large dataset of parallel English-Portuguese sentences extracted from the Open Parallel Corpus Project (OPUS) (Tiedemann, 2012). OPUS[7] contains more than 2.7 billion parallel sentences in 90 languages. The specific corpus we extracted consists of data from multiple domains and sources including: ParaCrawl project (Esplà-Gomis et al., 2019), EUbookshop (Skadiņš et al., 2014), Tilde Model (Rozis and Skadinš, 2017), translation memories (DGT) (Steinberger et al., 2013), Open-Subtitles (Creutz, 2018), SciELO Parallel (Soares et al., 2018), JRC-Acquis Multilingual (Steinberger et al., 2006), Tanzil (Zarrabi-Zadeh, 2007), Eu-

roparl Parallel (Koehn, 2005), TED 2013 (Cettolo et al., 2012), Wikipedia (Wołk and Marasek, 2014), Tatoeba [8], QCRI Educational Domain (Abdelali et al., 2014), GNOME localization files, [9] Global Voices, [10] KDE4, [11] Ubuntu, [12] and Multilingual Bible (Christodouloupoulos and Steedman, 2015). To train our models, we extract more than $77.7M$ parallel (i.e., English-Portuguese) sentences from the whole collection. The extracted dataset comprises more than $1.5B$ English tokens and $1.4B$ Portuguese tokens. More details about the training dataset are given in Table 2.

3.3 Pre-Processing

Pre-processing is an important step in building any MT model as it can significantly affect the end results. We remove punctuation and tokenize all data with the Moses tokenizer (Koehn et al., 2007). We also use joint Byte-Pair Encoding (BPE) with 60K split operations for subword segmentation (Sennrich et al., 2016).

[6] https://sharedtask.duolingo.com/#data.
[7] http://opus.nlpl.eu/
[8] www.tatoeba.org
[9] www.10n.gnome.org
[10] www.globalvoices.org/
[11] www.i18n.kde.org
[12] www.translations.launchpad.net

4 Models

In this section, we first describe the architecture of our models. We then explain the different ways we train the models on various subsets of the data.

4.1 Architecture

Our models are mainly based on a Convolutional Neural Network (CNN) architecture (Kim, 2014; Gehring et al., 2017). This convolutional architecture exploits BPE (Sennrich et al., 2016). The architecture is as follows: 20 layers in the encoder and 20 layers in the decoder, a multiplicative attention (Luong et al., 2015) in every decoder layer, a kernel width of 3 for both the encoder and the decoder, a hidden size 512, and an embedding size of 512, and 256 for the encoder and decoder layers respectively. We use a Fairseq implementation (Ott et al., 2019).

4.2 Basic En↔Pt Models

We trained two MT models, English-to-Portuguese (En→Pt) and Portuguese-to-English (Pt→En), on 4 V100 GPUs, following the setup described in Ott et al. (2018). For both models, the learning rate was set to 0.25, a dropout of 0.2, and a maximum tokens of $4,000$ for each mini-batch. We train our models on the $77.7M$ parallel sentences of the OPUS dataset described in Section 3. Validation is performed on the development data from STAPLE 2020 (Mayhew et al., 2020).

4.3 En→Pt Extended Model

We use the training data of the STAPLE 2020 shared task[13] to create a new En-Pt parallel dataset. More specifically, at the *target* side, we use all the Portuguese gold translations while duplicating the same English source sentence at the *source* side. This results in a new training set of $251,442$ En-Pt parallel sentences. We refer to this training dataset as STAPLE-TRAIN, or simply *S-TRAIN*. We then merge OPUS and S-TRAIN to train an En→Pt model from scratch. We refer to this new model as the *extended model*.

4.4 En→Pt Fine-Tuned Model

Fine-tuning with domain-specific data, from a domain of interest, can be an effective strategy when it is desirable to develop systems for such a domain (Ott et al., 2019, 2018). Motivated by this,

we experiment with using the STAPLE-based S-TRAIN parallel dataset from the previous subsection to fine-tune our En→Pt *basic* model for 5 epochs. [14] We will refer to the model resulting from this fine-tuning process simply as the *fine-tuned model*.

5 Model Deployment Methods

In order to enhance the 1-to-n En-Pt translation, we propose three methods based on the previously discussed MT models (see section 4). These methods are n-*Best prediction*, *multi-checkpoint translation*, and *paraphrasing*.

5.1 *n*-Best Prediction

We first use our three MT models (*basic*, *extended*, and *fine-tuned*) with a beam search size of 100 to generate n-Best translation hypotheses. We then use the average log-likelihood to score each of these hypotheses. Finally, we select the hypothesis with the n highest score as our output.

5.2 Paraphrasing

Paraphrasing is an effective data augmentation method which is commonly used in MT tasks (Poliak et al., 2018; Iyyer et al., 2018). In order to extend the list of accepted Portuguese translations, we use both of our En→Pt and Pt→En models, as follows:

1. Translate the English sentences using the En→Pt model. For instance, we generate n-Best ($n = 10$) Portuguese sentences for each English source sentence.

2. Then, we use the Pt→En model to get n'-Best English translations (we experiment with $n' = 1$, 3, and 5) for each of the 10 Portuguese sentence. At this point, we would have $10 * n'$ new English sentences (oftentimes with duplicate generations that we remove). These new sentences represent paraphrases of the original English sentence.

3. After de-duplication, the new English sentences are fed to the En→Pt model to get the 1-Best Portuguese translation.

---

[13]http://sharedtask.duolingo.com/#data

[14]We choose the number of epochs arbitrarily, but note that it is a hyper-parameter that can be tuned.

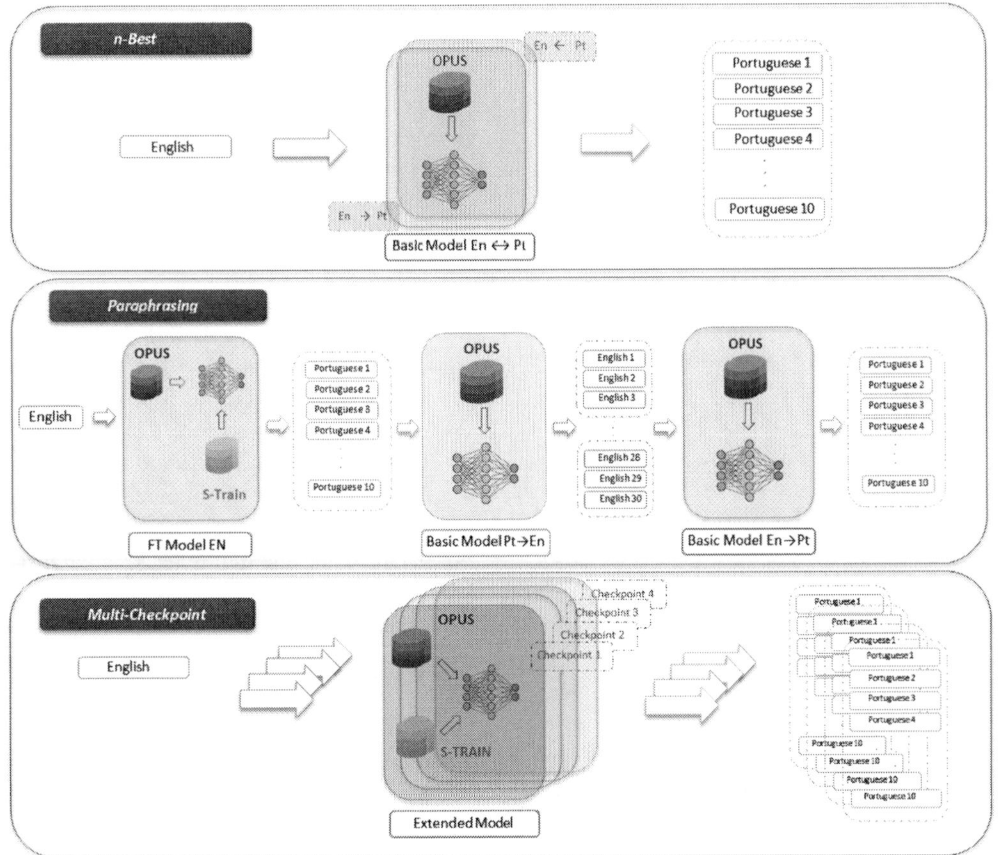

Figure 2: An illustration of our proposed models and methods: **(a) *n*-Best prediction method** with $n = 10$ resulting in the En→Pt *basic* model; **(b) paraphrasing method** with $n = 10$ and $n' = 3$ used in the En→Pt *fine-tuning* and the En↔Pt basic models, **(c) multi-checkpoint method** used with $n = 10$ and $m = 4$ for the En→Pt *extended* model.

5.3 Multi-Checkpoint Translation

Our third method is based on saving the models at given epochs (checkpoints) during training. We use the m last checkpoints (models) to generate the n-Best translation hypotheses (the same way as our n-Best prediction method). We then de-duplicate the outputs of all the m models and use them in evaluation. We now describe our evaluation.

6 Evaluation

In order to evaluate our methods, we carry out a number of experiments. First, we consider performance of each proposed method on the official `training` and `development` datasets of STA-PLE (Mayhew et al., 2020). Our models were ultimately evaluated on the shared task `test` data. We now describe STAPLE evaluation metrics and baselines as provided by organizers, before reporting on our results on training, development, and test.

6.1 Evaluation Metrics & Baselines

Weights of Translation. We note that each Portuguese translated sentence has a weight as provided in the gold dataset. The weights of translations correspond to user (learner) response rates. These weights are used primarily for scoring. The STAPLE 2020 shared task data takes the format illustrated in Table 3.

Metrics. Performance of MT systems in the shared task is quantified and scored based on how well a model can return all human-curated acceptable translations, weighted by the likelihood that an English learner would respond with each translation (Mayhew et al., 2020). As such, the main scoring metric is the *weighted macro* F_1, with respect to the accepted translations. To

English Sentence :	is my explanation clear?
Weights	**Portuguese Translation**
0.26739	- minha explicação está clara?
0.16168	- minha explicação é clara?
0.11109	- a minha explicação é clara?
0.08778	- está clara minha explicação?
0.05717	- minha explanação está clara?

English Sentence :	this is my fault.
Weights	**Portuguese translation**
0.17991	- isto é minha culpa.
0.10664	- isso é minha culpa.
0.08944	- esta é minha culpa.
0.07794	- isto é culpa minha.
0.06803	- é minha culpa.

Table 3: English sentences with their Portuguese translation and Weights samples from shared task train data.

compute *weighted macro* F_1 (see formula 6), the weighted F_1 for each English sentence (s) is calculated and the average over all the sentences in the corpus is computed. The weighted F_1 (see formula 5) is computed using the unweighted precision (see formula 1) and the weighted recall (see formulas 2, 3 and 4).

$$Precision\ (s) = \frac{TP_s}{TP_s + FN_s} \tag{1}$$

$$WTP_s = \sum_{s \in TP_s} weight(t) \tag{2}$$

$$WFN_s = \sum_{s \in FN_s} weight(t) \tag{3}$$

$$Weighted\ Recall\ (s) = \frac{WTP_s}{WTP_s + WFN_s} \tag{4}$$

$$Weighted\ F1(s) = \frac{2 \cdot Prec.\ (s) \cdot W.\ Recall\ (s)}{Prec.\ (s) + W.\ Recall\ (s)} \tag{5}$$

$$Weighted\ Macro\ F_1 = \sum_{s \in S} \frac{Weighted\ F1(s)}{|S|} \tag{6}$$

Baselines. We adopt the two baselines offered by the task organizers. These are based on Amazon and Fairseq translation systems and are at 21.30% and 13.57%, respectively. More information about these baselines can be reviewed at the shared task site listed earlier.

6.2 Evaluation on TRAIN and DEV

In this section, we report the results of our 3 proposed methods, *(a) n-Best prediction, (b) paraphrasing*, and *(c) multi-checkpoint translation* using the MT models presented in section 4.

Evaluation on TRAIN. For (a) the *n*-Best prediction method, we explore the 4 different values of n in the set {5, 10, 15, 20}. For (b) the paraphrase method, we set the number of Portuguese sentences to $n' = \{1, 3, 5\}$. Finally, (c) the multi-checkpoint method was tested with 4 different values for the number of checkpoints $m = \{2, 4, 6, 8\}$.

For paraphrasing and multi-checkpoint translation, we fix the number of *n*-best translations n to 10, varying the values of n' and m only when evaluating our *extended* model. This leads us to identifying the best evaluation values of $n' = 3$ and $m = 6$, which we then use when evaluating our *basic* and *fine-tuned* models.

Evaluation on DEV. For evaluation on the STAPLE development data, we adopt the same procedure followed for evaluation on the train split. Table 4 summarizes our experiments with different configurations (i.e., values of n, n', and m) on train and development task data, respectively.

Discussion. Results presented in Table 4 demonstrate that all the models with the different methods and configurations outperform the the official shared task baseline with *macro* F_1 scores between 27.41% and 40.78%. As expected, fine-tuning the En→Pt basic model with the S-TRAIN data-set improves the results with a mean of +1.46% on the training data. We also observe that training on the concatenated OPUS and S-TRAIN data-sets *from scratch* leads to better results compared to the *exclusive fine-tuning* method.

Based on these results, we can see that the best configuration is the multi-checkpoint method used with the *extended* MT model. This configuration obtains the best *macro* F_1 score of 40.78% and 39.21% on the training and development STAPLE data splits, respectively.

Train Data

Method	n	Prec.	W. Recall	W. F_1	Prec.	W. Recall	W. F_1	Prec.	W. Recall	W. F_1
		Basic Model			Extended Model			Fine-Tuned Model		
n-Best Prediction	5	55.44	23.87	27.41	45.51	28.24	29.43	44.68	26.91	28.38
	10	42.78	29.65	28.47	46.02	34.18	**33.51**	41.81	32.19	30.33
	15	37.42	27.09	29.17	39.25	35.50	31.80	45.51	28.24	29.43
	20	29.68	38.24	27.48	39.22	35.49	31.79	46.23	27.04	30.27

Method	n'	Prec.	W. Recall	W. F_1	Prec.	W. Recall	W. F_1	Prec.	W. Recall	W. F_1
Paraphrasing	1	-	-	-	40.24	35.01	31.68	-	-	-
	3	40.24	35.01	31.68	46.45	35.08	**34.39**	39.98	37.27	32.89
	5	-	-	-	40.44	39.20	34.16	-	-	-

Method	m	Prec.	W. Recall	W. F_1	Prec.	W. Recall	W. F_1	Prec.	W. Recall	W. F_1
Multi Checkpoint	2	-	-	-	58.81	31.57	36.57	-	-	-
	4	-	-	-	50.53	44.22	40.76	-	-	-
	6	44.44	45.52	39.46	49.58	44.92	**40.78**	36.77	52.73	38.54
	8	-	-	-	42.16	44.96	39.28	-	-	-

DEV Data

Method	n	Prec.	W. Recall	W. F_1	Prec.	W. Recall	W. F_1	Prec.	W. Recall	W. F_1
		Basic Model			Extended Model			Fine-Tuned Model		
n-Best Prediction	5	-	-	-	52.48	26.27	29.87	-	-	-
	10	32.56	36.83	29.33	36.52	41.09	**32.96**	35.39	37.84	31.30
	15	-	-	-	38.62	37.46	32.36	-	-	-
	20	-	-	-	36.03	37.44	31.33	-	-	-

Method	n'	Prec.	W. Recall	W. F_1	Prec.	W. Recall	W. F_1	Prec.	W. Recall	W. F_1
Paraphrasing	1	-	-	-	45.77	33.31	33.05	-	-	-
	3	48.66	31.17	32.43	46.34	33.85	33.17	39.98	37.27	32.89
	5	-	-		46.14	34.26	**33.40**	-	-	-

Method	m	Prec.	W. Recall	W. F_1	Prec.	W. Recall	W. F_1	Prec.	W. Recall	W. F_1
Multi Checkpoint	2	-	-	-	55.88	32.16	35.26	-	-	-
	4	-	-	-	52.27	37.35	38.25	-	-	-
	6	45.35	43.20	38.04	56.42	37.31	39.16	45.01	41.23	37.26
	8	-	-	-	53.83	38.85	**39.21**	-	-	-

Table 4: Performance on the STAPLE 2020 Train and Dev data splits.

		Extended Model		
Method	m	Prec.	W. Recall	W. F_1
Aws Baseline	-	87.80	13.98	21.29
Fairseq Baseline	-	28.25	11.70	13.57
Multi-Checkpoint	4	60.14	33.14	37.06
	6	53.83	36.50	**37.57**
	8	49.94	38.27	37.21

Table 5: Results on STAPLE 2020 Test Data.

6.3 Evaluation on TEST

In test phase, we submitted translations from 3 systems for the STAPLE English-Portuguese sub-task. The 3 systems are based on our *multi-checkpoint* translation with the *extended* model. The number of checkpoints used was $m = \{4, 6, 8\}$, and n is fixed to 10 (i.e., the best value of n identified on training data with our *extended* model). Table 5 shows the results of our 3 final submitted systems as returned by the shared task organizers.

Discussion. Our results indicate that when the multi-checkpoint method with the extended model and only two last checkpoints ($m = 4$) is used, the $macro\ F_1$ score reaches 37.07% (with a best precision of 60.14%). This method with $m = 6$ represents our best $macro\ F_1$ score 37.57% for the English-Portuguese translation sub-task. We note that with this configuration we outperform the Amazon and Fairseq translation baseline systems (at $+15.92\%$ and $+23.99\%$, respectively) provided by the task organizers. We also observe that when m is set to 8, the $macro\ F_1$ slightly decreases to 37.21%. Ultimately, our findings show the utility of using multiple checkpoint ensembles as a way to mimic the various levels of language learners. Simple as this approach is, we find it quite intuitive.

7 Conclusion

In this work, we described our contribution to the 2020 Duolingo Shared Task on Simultaneous Translation And Paraphrase for Language Education (STAPLE) (Mayhew et al., 2020). Our system targeted the English-Portuguese sub-task. Our models effectively make use of an approach based on n-Best prediction and multi-checkpoint translation. Our use of the OPUS dataset for training proved quite successful. In addition, based on our results, our intuitive deployment of a multi-checkpoint ensemble coupled with n-Best decoded translations seem to mirror leaner proficiency. As future work, we plan to explore other methods on new language pairs.

Acknowledgements

MAM gratefully acknowledge the support of the Natural Sciences and Engineering Research Council of Canada (NSERC), the Social Sciences Research Council of Canada (SSHRC), and Compute Canada (`www.computecanada.ca`).

References

Ahmed Abdelali, Francisco Guzman, Hassan Sajjad, and Stephan Vogel. 2014. The amara corpus: Building parallel language resources for the educational domain. In *LREC*, volume 14, pages 1044–1054.

Roee Aharoni, Melvin Johnson, and Orhan Firat. 2019. Massively multilingual neural machine translation. *arXiv preprint arXiv:1903.00089*.

Colin Bannard and Chris Callison-Burch. 2005. Paraphrasing with bilingual parallel corpora. In *Proceedings of the 43rd Annual Meeting on Association for Computational Linguistics*, pages 597–604. Association for Computational Linguistics.

Regina Barzilay and Kathleen McKeown. 2001. Extracting paraphrases from a parallel corpus. In *Proceedings of the 39th annual meeting of the Association for Computational Linguistics*, pages 50–57.

Mauro Cettolo, Christian Girardi, and Marcello Federico. 2012. Wit[3]: Web inventory of transcribed and translated talks. In *Proceedings of the 16th Conference of the European Association for Machine Translation (EAMT)*, pages 261–268, Trento, Italy.

Christos Christodouloupoulos and Mark Steedman. 2015. A massively parallel corpus: the bible in 100 languages. *Language resources and evaluation*, 49(2):375–395.

Mathias Creutz. 2018. Open subtitles paraphrase corpus for six languages. *arXiv preprint arXiv:1809.06142*.

Miquel Esplà-Gomis, Mikel L Forcada, Gema Ramírez-Sánchez, and Hieu Hoang. 2019. Paracrawl: Web-scale parallel corpora for the languages of the eu. In *Proceedings of Machine Translation Summit XVII Volume 2: Translator, Project and User Tracks*, pages 118–119.

Jonas Gehring, Michael Auli, David Grangier, Denis Yarats, and Yann N Dauphin. 2017. Convolutional sequence to sequence learning. In *Proceedings of the 34th International Conference on Machine Learning-Volume 70*, pages 1243–1252. JMLR. org.

Mohit Iyyer, John Wieting, Kevin Gimpel, and Luke Zettlemoyer. 2018. Adversarial example generation with syntactically controlled paraphrase networks. *arXiv preprint arXiv:1804.06059*.

Yoon Kim. 2014. Convolutional neural networks for sentence classification. *arXiv preprint arXiv:1408.5882*.

Philipp Koehn. 2005. Europarl: A parallel corpus for statistical machine translation. In *MT summit*, volume 5, pages 79–86. Citeseer.

Philipp Koehn, Marcello Federico, Wade Shen, Nicola Bertoldi, Ondrej Bojar, Chris Callison-Burch, Brooke Cowan, Chris Dyer, Hieu Hoang, Richard Zens, et al. 2007. Open source toolkit for statistical machine translation: Factored translation models and confusion network decoding. In *Final Report of the Johns Hopkins 2006 Summer Workshop*.

Zichao Li, Xin Jiang, Lifeng Shang, and Hang Li. 2017. Paraphrase generation with deep reinforcement learning. *arXiv preprint arXiv:1711.00279*.

Minh-Thang Luong and Christopher D Manning. 2015. Stanford neural machine translation systems for spoken language domains. In *Proceedings of the International Workshop on Spoken Language Translation*, pages 76–79.

Minh-Thang Luong, Hieu Pham, and Christopher D Manning. 2015. Effective approaches to attention-based neural machine translation. *arXiv preprint arXiv:1508.04025*.

Jonathan Mallinson, Rico Sennrich, and Mirella Lapata. 2017. Paraphrasing revisited with neural machine translation. In *Proceedings of the 15th Conference of the European Chapter of the Association for Computational Linguistics: Volume 1, Long Papers*, pages 881–893.

Stephen Mayhew, Klinton Bicknell, Chris Brust, Bill McDowell, Will Monroe, and Burr Settles. 2020. Simultaneous translation and paraphrase for language education. In *Proceedings of the ACL Workshop on Neural Generation and Translation (WNGT)*. ACL.

Myle Ott, Sergey Edunov, Alexei Baevski, Angela Fan, Sam Gross, Nathan Ng, David Grangier, and Michael Auli. 2019. fairseq: A fast, extensible toolkit for sequence modeling. *arXiv preprint arXiv:1904.01038*.

Myle Ott, Sergey Edunov, David Grangier, and Michael Auli. 2018. Scaling neural machine translation. *arXiv preprint arXiv:1806.00187*.

Bo Pang, Kevin Knight, and Daniel Marcu. 2003. Syntax-based alignment of multiple translations: Extracting paraphrases and generating new sentences. In *Proceedings of the 2003 Conference of the North American Chapter of the Association for Computational Linguistics on Human Language Technology-Volume 1*, pages 102–109. Association for Computational Linguistics.

Adam Poliak, Yonatan Belinkov, James Glass, and Benjamin Van Durme. 2018. On the evaluation of semantic phenomena in neural machine translation using natural language inference. *arXiv preprint arXiv:1804.09779*.

Aaditya Prakash, Sadid A Hasan, Kathy Lee, Vivek Datla, Ashequl Qadir, Joey Liu, and Oladimeji Farri. 2016. Neural paraphrase generation with stacked residual lstm networks. *arXiv preprint arXiv:1610.03098*.

Roberts Rozis and Raivis Skadiņš. 2017. Tilde model-multilingual open data for eu languages. In *Proceedings of the 21st Nordic Conference on Computational Linguistics, NoDaLiDa, 22-24 May 2017, Gothenburg, Sweden*, 131, pages 263–265. Linköping University Electronic Press.

Rico Sennrich, Barry Haddow, and Alexandra Birch. 2016. Neural machine translation of rare words with subword units. In *Proceedings of the 54th Annual Meeting of the Association for Computational Linguistics (Volume 1: Long Papers)*, pages 1715–1725, Berlin, Germany. Association for Computational Linguistics.

Raivis Skadiņš, Jörg Tiedemann, Roberts Rozis, and Daiga Deksne. 2014. Billions of parallel words for free: Building and using the eu bookshop corpus. In *Proceedings of LREC*.

Felipe Soares, Viviane Moreira, and Karin Becker. 2018. A large parallel corpus of full-text scientific articles. In *Proceedings of the Eleventh International Conference on Language Resources and Evaluation (LREC-2018)*.

Ralf Steinberger, Andreas Eisele, Szymon Klocek, Spyridon Pilos, and Patrick Schlüter. 2013. Dgt-tm: A freely available translation memory in 22 languages. *arXiv preprint arXiv:1309.5226*.

Ralf Steinberger, Bruno Pouliquen, Anna Widiger, Camelia Ignat, Tomaz Erjavec, Dan Tufis, and Dániel Varga. 2006. The jrc-acquis: A multilingual aligned parallel corpus with 20+ languages. *arXiv preprint cs/0609058*.

Ilya Sutskever, Oriol Vinyals, and Quoc V Le. 2014. Sequence to sequence learning with neural networks. In *Advances in neural information processing systems*, pages 3104–3112.

Jörg Tiedemann. 2012. Parallel data, tools and interfaces in opus. 2012:2214–2218.

John Wieting and Kevin Gimpel. 2017. Paranmt-50m: Pushing the limits of paraphrastic sentence embeddings with millions of machine translations. *arXiv preprint arXiv:1711.05732*.

Krzysztof Wołk and Krzysztof Marasek. 2014. Building subject-aligned comparable corpora and mining it for truly parallel sentence pairs. *Procedia Technology*, 18:126–132.

Adams Wei Yu, David Dohan, Minh-Thang Luong, Rui Zhao, Kai Chen, Mohammad Norouzi, and Quoc V Le. 2018. Qanet: Combining local convolution with global self-attention for reading comprehension. *arXiv preprint arXiv:1804.09541*.

Hamid Zarrabi-Zadeh. 2007. Tanzil project. *URL: http://tanzil. net/wiki/Tanzil_Project*.

Generating Diverse Translations via Weighted Fine-tuning and Hypotheses Filtering for the Duolingo STAPLE Task

Sweta Agrawal
Department of Computer Science
University of Maryland
sweagraw@cs.umd.edu

Marine Carpuat
Department of Computer Science
University of Maryland
marine@cs.umd.edu

Abstract

This paper describes the University of Maryland's submission to the Duolingo Shared Task on Simultaneous Translation And Paraphrase for Language Education (STAPLE). Unlike the standard machine translation task, STAPLE requires generating a set of outputs for a given input sequence, aiming to cover the space of translations produced by language learners. We adapt neural machine translation models to this requirement by (a) generating n-best translation hypotheses from a model fine-tuned on learner translations, oversampled to reflect the distribution of learner responses, and (b) filtering hypotheses using a feature-rich binary classifier that directly optimizes a close approximation of the official evaluation metric. Combination of systems that use these two strategies achieves F1 scores of 53.9% and 52.5% on Vietnamese and Portuguese, respectively ranking 2nd and 4th on the leaderboard.

1 Introduction

While machine translation (MT) typically produces a single output for each input, scoring and generation for second language learning applications might benefit from systems whose outputs better capture the diversity of translations produced by language learners. The Duolingo Simultaneous Translation And Paraphrase for Language Education (STAPLE) shared task (Mayhew et al., 2020) provides a framework for developing and testing such systems, grounded in real translations produced by English learners into five native languages (Portuguese, Vietnamese, Hungarian, Japanese, Korean). In this task, given an English sentence prompt, systems are asked to produce a set of translations for that prompt, and are scored based on how well their outputs cover human-curated acceptable translations, weighted by the likelihood that an English learner would respond with each translation (Table 1).

Prompt	is my explanation clear?	
	minha explicação está clara?	0.267
	minha explicação é clara?	0.161
	a minha explicação está clara?	0.111
Output	a minha explicação é clara?	0.088
	minha explanação está clara?	0.057
	está clara minha explicação?	0.044
	minha explanação é clara?	0.039

Table 1: STAPLE data: given a prompt in English, translation alternatives are weighted according to Learner Response Frequency (LRF)

While the multiple translations can be viewed as paraphrases, we propose to address the STAPLE task primarily as a MT task to better understand the strengths and weaknesses of neural MT architectures for generating multiple learner-relevant translations. Given a Transformer model for the language pair of interest, we use beam search to generate n-best translation candidates. However, since n-best lists are known to lack diversity, we propose to generate hypotheses that better match the requirements of the STAPLE task via:

1. **Frequency-Aware n-Best Lists**: We encourage hypotheses to reflect the diversity and frequency of learner responses by fine-tuning models on STAPLE data, oversampling translation options to reflect learner preferences.

2. **Hypothesis Filtering**: We filter the resulting n-best lists using a binary classifier which identifies good translations that are likely to be produced by a learner.

Controlled experiments and analysis show the benefits of both strategies. Our final submission which includes both techniques achieves F1 scores of 53.9% and 52.5% for en-vi and en-pt respec-

Proceedings of the 4th Workshop on Neural Generation and Translation (WNGT 2020), pages 178–187
Online, July 10, 2020. ©2020 Association for Computational Linguistics
www.aclweb.org/anthology/D19-56%2d

tively, reaching a rank of 2nd and 4th on the leaderboard, only 2 points below the top scoring system. For completeness, we also submitted systems for the remaining language pairs using Frequency-Aware n-best lists: our system ranked 2nd for Japanese and 3rd for Korean and Hungarian.

2   Background

Unlike in the STAPLE task, recent attempts at generating multiple translations for a single source have targeted output variability along specific stylistic dimensions (Sennrich et al., 2016b; Rabinovich et al., 2016; Niu et al., 2018; Agrawal and Carpuat, 2019) or produce diverse outputs without a specific use case (Kikuchi et al., 2016; Shu et al., 2019). The techniques used can be divided in three categories: (a) constrain the decoding process to generate diverse candidates (Li and Jurafsky, 2016; Li et al., 2015; Cho, 2016); (b) optimize via a diversity promoting loss function (Li et al., 2015); (c) expose the model to different translation candidates with side-constraints (Rabinovich et al., 2016; Sennrich et al., 2016a; Niu et al., 2018; Agrawal and Carpuat, 2019; Shu et al., 2019) or without (Shen et al., 2019). Since it is unclear what dimensions of variations are captured in the STAPLE translation, we focus instead on improving n-best lists generated by a standard neural MT model.

Source texts with multiple references have mostly been used to evaluate rather than train MT systems (Papineni et al., 2002; Banerjee and Lavie, 2005; Qin and Specia, 2015). Evaluation sets with 4 or 5 references have been converted to single-reference training samples (Zheng et al., 2018) to improve MT training, but reference translations vary in arbitrary ways and often exhibit poor diversity, mostly limited to translationese effects. The STAPLE data presents an opportunity to explore multiple translations generated in a more comprehensive fashion.

3   Approach

3.1   Frequency-Aware Hypotheses Generation

While neural MT systems can generate multiple translation candidates per source using beam search, the n-best translations often lack diversity. One issue is that systems are trained on single-translation training samples. We propose to tailor MT to the STAPLE task by fine-tuning models on LRF-weighted multi-reference samples to obtain more diverse translations and a ranking that better reflect learner preferences.

Given the STAPLE data for a language pair, where the i-th training example, $(\mathbf{e}_i, \mathbf{F}_i, \mathbf{W}_i)$ includes a source sentence in English, a reference set $\mathbf{F}_i = \{\mathbf{f}_i^1, \mathbf{f}_i^2, ..., \mathbf{f}_i^K\}$ of $\mathbf{K}$ translations and corresponding LRF weights $\mathbf{W}_i = \{\mathbf{w}_i^1, \mathbf{w}_i^2, ..., \mathbf{w}_i^K\}$, we create MT training samples by copying the translation pair $(\mathbf{e}_i, \mathbf{f}_i^j)$, $\mathbf{w}_i^j \times O$ times.[1] Given model parameters θ, this yields a weighted cross-entropy loss:

$$\mathcal{L}_{lrf}(\theta) = \sum_{i=1}^{M} \sum_{j=1}^{K} (w_i^j \times O) \log Pr(f_i^j | e_i; \theta) \quad (1)$$

3.2   Hypothesis Filtering as Binary Classification

Even when informed by STAPLE data and LRF scores, n-best lists might include translations that are not in the reference set, due to translation errors or selecting paraphrases that do not match language learners' preferences. We design a binary classifier that further filters the n-best lists by predicting for each hypothesis whether or not it should be included in the final set. This lets us define features based on the complete prompt and hypothesis sequence pairs, while the MT model generates the hypothesis incrementally.

Let $D = \{(\mathbf{e}_i, \hat{\mathbf{f}}_i^1, \hat{\mathbf{f}}_i^2, ..., \hat{\mathbf{f}}_i^N)\}_1^M$ represent the n-best list generated via beam search for all the source prompts in the training dataset: $\mathbf{e}_i$ corresponds to the i-th source prompt and $\hat{\mathbf{f}}_i^j$ corresponds to the j-th candidate hypothesis extracted via beam search. $\mathbf{x}_j^i$ represents the feature vector extracted from the source ($\mathbf{e}_i$) and j-th candidate hypothesis ($\hat{\mathbf{f}}_i^j$) and $\mathbf{y}_i^j$ is a binary label indicative of whether the candidate hypothesis, $\hat{\mathbf{f}}_i^j$, is found in the gold standard data. The classification model $f : X \to R$ maps the feature vector to a real value, where, f is a two-layer Neural Network (NN) to enable learning feature combinations.

Features   We aim to capture the quality of a source-hypothesis pair using multiple sentence-level features:

- Length features $|\hat{f}|$, $|e|$, $\frac{|\hat{f}|}{|e|}$, $\frac{|e|}{|\hat{f}|}$ might indicate mismatches between source and target content.

- Word alignment features have proved useful to identify semantic divergences in bitext

---

[1] We set $O = 1000$ in practice.

(Munteanu and Marcu, 2005; Vyas et al., 2018).
We use the Forward and Reverse Alignment
score, the count of unaligned words for source
and target, and the top three largest fertilities for
source and target.

- Scores from various MT models as often done
  when reranking n-best lists (Cherry and Foster,
  2012; Neubig et al., 2015; Hassan et al., 2018)
  including a left-to-right model, a right-to-left
  model, and a target-to-source model, which provide different views of the example and might
  better estimate the adequacy of the translation
  than the original MT model score.

- Target 5-gram language model score to estimate
  the fluency of the hypothesis.

Loss We optimize a Soft Macro-F1 objective
(Hsieh et al., 2018) function to approximate the
official evaluation metric.[2] The true positive (tp),
false positive(fp), and true negative (tn) rate for
each source prompt e_i are estimated as:

$$\text{tp}_{e_i} = \sum_{t=1}^{N} \hat{y}_i \times y_i$$

$$\text{fp}_{e_i} = \sum_{t=1}^{N} \hat{y}_i \times (1 - y_i)$$

$$\text{tn}_{e_i} = \sum_{t=1}^{N} (1 - \hat{y}_i) \times y_i$$

Then, the precision, recall, F1 for a source e_i, and
the loss are defined as:

$$P_{e_i} = \frac{\text{tp}_{e_i}}{\text{tp}_{e_i} + \text{fp}_{e_i} + \epsilon}$$

$$R_{e_i} = \frac{\text{tp}_{e_i}}{\text{tp}_{e_i} + \text{fn}_{e_i} + \epsilon}$$

$$F1_{\text{Macro}e_i} = \frac{2 \times P_{e_i} \times R_{e_i}}{P_{e_i} + R_{e_i} + \epsilon}$$

$$\text{Loss} = \sum_{i=1}^{M} (1 - F1_{\text{Macro}e_i})$$

4 Experiment Settings

4.1 Data

STAPLE Data The shared task provides English
source prompts, associated with high-coverage sets

---

[2] Preliminary experiments showed that a LRF-weighted
version of this loss resulted in unstable training and inconsistent results depending on initialization.

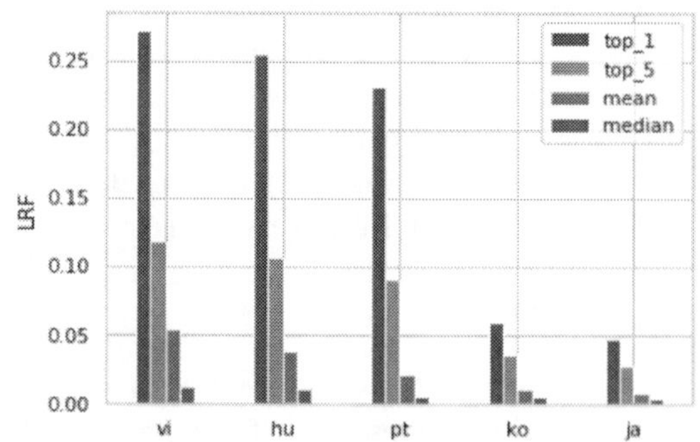

Figure 1: Average of the top-1, top-5, mean and median LRF values across source prompts: the LRF distribution is more uniform for languages with many more
references per prompt (e.g. en-ja).

of plausible translations in five other languages.
These translations are weighted and ranked according to LRF scores indicating which translations are
more likely. About 3000 prompts per language are
available (see Table 2 for details) and the number
of reference translations available per prompt vary
across languages (mean: 174.2, variance: 116). Figure 1 illustrates the differences in LRF distributions
across languages: for languages with many references per prompt (e.g. en-ja, en-ko), the gap between the top-1 and the mean LRF value is small,
indicating an almost uniform distribution. Average top-1 LRF scores also vary across languages
(e.g en-vi: 0.25, en-ja: 0.05) depending upon the
number of references available per prompt.

For system development, we divide the STAPLE
dataset into train, development and test datasets
using 72%, 8%, and 20% of source prompts respectively. We refer to these subsets as **STAPLE
train, internal dev** and **internal test**. Note that the
last two differ from the official blind development
and test sets available to participants on codalab.

Other Bitexts We use bitext from OpenSubtitles (Tiedemann, 2012) and Tatoeba (Tiedemann,
2012) as described in Table 3. The Tatoeba corpus
provides multiple reference translations for some
sources (with 2 translation per source on average),
but unlike in the STAPLE data, these translations
are not weighted by frequency of usage.

Preprocessing All datasets are pre-processed using Moses tools for normalization, tokenization
and lowercasing. We further segment tokens into
subwords using a joint source-target Byte Pair Encoding (Sennrich et al., 2016c) model with $32,000$

Language	Source					Target					T/S
	Train	Dev	Test	Types	Tokens	Train	Dev	Test	Types	Tokens	
en-pt	2.8K	300	800	2.3K	3.8M	380K	42K	104K	8.7K	4M	131
en-vi	2.5K	280	700	2.3K	950K	142K	14K	38K	1.7K	1.3M	56
en-ja	1.8K	200	500	1.3K	3.8M	600K	65K	166K	4K	6.8M	342
en-ko	1.8K	200	500	1.3K	3M	500K	57K	137K	17K	2.6M	280
en-hu	2.8K	320	800	1.5K	1.1M	182K	21K	47K	11K	1M	62

Table 2: STAPLE data statistics: segments in our train/dev/test split, overall vocabulary statistics and average translations per source prompt (T/S).

Language	OpenSubtitles	Tatoeba
en-pt	47.2M	196K
en-vi	3M	5.3K
en-ja	1.8M	200K
en-ko	1.2M	2.7K
en-hu	34.5M	102K

Table 3: Additional bitext used for training and fine-tuning MT models

operations. For Japanese, we use kytea [3] toolkit for word tokenization.

4.2 MT configurations

Model Architecture We use the Transformer model implemented in the Sockeye toolkit[4] as a baseline MT system. Both encoder and decoder are 6-layer Transformer models with model size of $1,024$, feed-forward network size of $4,096$, and 16 attention heads. We adopt label smoothing and weight tying. We tie the output weight matrix with the target embeddings. We use Adam optimizer with initial learning rate of 0.0002.

Experimental Conditions We train several models with the above configuration:

- **OpenSubs** a baseline model trained and validated on the OpenSubtitles bitext.

- **Unweighted** builds on the baseline by fine-tuning on multi-reference samples including the Tatoeba bitext and STAPLE train. We create one training sample per source-reference pair, and the resulting samples are not weighted. We use the internal dev set (1-best reference only) as a validation set.

- **Frequency-Aware** is fine-tuned as the unweighted model except that STAPLE train is oversampled as described in § 3.1.

We generate n-best list of translations for various models by running beam search with a beam size corresponding to the desired n.

4.3 Filtering configurations

Classifier The 2-layer feed-forward NN has 5 hidden units and 2 output units. It is trained with the Adam optimizer with an initial learning rate of 0.001 and runs for 2000 epochs on the internal dev set. The best model is selected based on internal test set performance. We consider two losses: the soft macro F1 loss which approximates the official evaluation metric (§ 3.2) and the standard cross-entropy loss as a baseline.

Reranking Baseline We compare our NN based classifer with a standard MT n-best list reranker trained on the internal dev set. We use the n-best batch MIRA ranker (Cherry and Foster, 2012) included in Moses. A threshold to filter candidates in the reranked list is selected by maximizing the Weighted Macro F1 on the internal dev dataset.

Features We use eflomal [5] trained on the Opensubtitles dataset to obtain word alignment between source and translation hypotheses. The language model is trained with the kenlm (Heafield, 2011) toolkit with default hyper-parameters[6] on the target side of the Opensubtitles and the STAPLE dataset. The Right-to-left and Target-to-source MT models were trained on OpenSubtitles (same configuration as in § 4.2).

[3] https://github.com/neubig/kytea
[4] https://github.com/awslabs/sockeye
[5] https://github.com/robertostling/eflomal
[6] https://github.com/kpu/kenlm

5   Evaluation

We evaluate the lowercased detokenized output of the systems on our internal test dataset using:

Weighted Macro F1   This is the official scoring metric which quantifies how the set of system outputs covers the human-curated acceptable translations, weighted by the LRF of each translation. It is defined as the harmonic mean of unweighted precision (P) and weighted recall (WR) calculated for each prompt e_i, and averaged over all the prompts in the corpus. Specifically, using the same notation as introduced in § 3.1, for each translation T_i generated by the MT model, we have:

$$\mathrm{WTP}_{e_i} = \sum_{t \in T_i} \sum_{f_i^j \in F_i} 1[t == f_i^j] w_i^j$$

$$\mathrm{WFN}_{e_i} = \sum_{f_i^j \notin T_i} w_i^j$$

$$\mathrm{WR}_{e_i} = \frac{\mathrm{WTP}_{e_i}}{\mathrm{WTP}_{e_i} + \mathrm{WFN}_{e_i}}$$

The weighted Macro F1 (WMF1) is then given by:

$$\mathrm{WMF1}_{e_i} = \frac{2 \times \mathrm{P}_{e_i} \times \mathrm{WR}_{e_i}}{\mathrm{P}_{e_i} + \mathrm{WR}_{e_i}}$$

$$\mathrm{WMF1} = \frac{1}{M} \sum_i^M \mathrm{WMF1}_{e_i}$$

BLEU@1   We also report the translation quality of the 1-best neural MT output compared against the highest LRF reference translation using the standard BLEU metric (Papineni et al., 2002).

6   Experiment Results

6.1   Impact of Frequency-Aware Fine-Tuning

Table 4 summarizes the evaluation of n-best lists obtained with our neural MT systems.

Baselines   We confirm that the neural MT configuration is sound by comparing our neural MT baseline to the provided AWS system. Our baseline ("OpenSubs") improves the BLEU@1 score by 2 points for en-pt, and remains 6 points lower for en-vi, as can be expected given the smaller size of the OpenSubtitles training set. However, the "Open-Subs" n-best lists improve over the AWS baseline according to the official task metric (WMF1), establishing that this system is a good starting point for fine-tuning.

Fine-Tuning   The Frequency-Aware n-best hypotheses consistently yield the best Weighted Recall and Weighted Macro-F1 scores for all languages. The improvement in recall and therefore F1 score is largest for en-ja and en-ko which have larger translation reference sets (Table 4). Frequency-Aware oversampling also improves precision over the Unweighted model for all but one language (en-pt). The impact on the auxiliary BLEU@1 metric is less consistent: the Frequency-Aware system achieves the best BLEU@1 in 3 out of 5 languages, but outperforms the OpenSubs baseline in 4 out of 5. BLEU@1 drops when fine-tuning on all the samples without weighting (Unweighted) which we attribute to the increased uncertainty during training as the model is exposed to many different translations for the same source English text.

Overall, these results show the benefits of fine-tuning on task-relevant data and shows that incorporating LRF weights via oversampling improves the ranking of n-best hypotheses. This is further illustrated in Table 5, which shows the top 10 Vietnamese translations for two randomly sampled source prompts: the Frequency-Aware n-best list yields Weighted Recall of 81% at a Precision of 60% and 76% at a Precision of 100% for the two source prompts respectively, illustrating that the model generates high-quality candidates that cover reference translations well, but not perfectly.

N-Best List Quality   How well do n-best translations cover the space of reference learner translations? Figure 2 shows the impact of increasing the decoding beam (and resulting n-best list size) from 10 to 500 for the Frequency-Aware model. For en-pt, while weighted recall increases up to 66%, the drop in precision hurts the weighted F1 score. The oracle F1 score, which represents the Weighted Macro F1 at a Precision of 100%, also increases gradually, reaching a score of 76%. This suggests that the raw n-best lists contain many useful translation candidates but need to be filtered down to better match translations preferred by language learners.

6.2   Impact of Hypothesis Filtering

Due to time constraints, we explore the impact of hypothesis filtering only for en-pt and en-vi.

Filtering   consistently improves Precision and Weighted Macro F1 (Table 6). The binary classifier that optimizes Soft Macro-F1 performs best,

Language	Method	BLEU@1	n-best size	P	WR	WMF1
en-pt	AWS	68.9	1	**86.67**	14.47	21.60
	OpenSubs	70.9	10	49.66	39.18	37.39
	Unweighted	61.5	10	72.69	40.58	46.11
	Frequency-Aware	**76.6**	10	67.31	**44.34**	**47.4**
en-vi	AWS	61.4	1	**65.09**	13.32	19.57
	OpenSubs	55.2	10	29.10	31.38	25.76
	Unweighted	49.8	10	56.43	42.91	41.00
	Frequency-Aware	**71.9**	10	61.61	**54.37**	**51.87**
en-ja	AWS	**50.6**	1	67.68	2.18	4.01
	OpenSubs	32.7	50	2.94	3.47	2.52
	Unweighted	30.1	50	45.71	21.21	24.88
	Frequency-Aware	42.4	50	47.29	**22.83**	**26.57**
en-hu	AWS	63.4	1	**83.70**	18.12	27.12
	OpenSubs	**64.4**	10	41.51	42.6	37.83
	Unweighted	26.2	10	47.11	29.7	31.62
	Frequency-Aware	51.4	10	52.22	**41.05**	**41.69**
en-ko	AWS	27.9	1	**60.68**	2.26	4.11
	OpenSubs	9.2	50	12.53	7.41	7.20
	Unweighted	14.8	50	33.82	18.8	19.78
	Frequency-Aware	**30.2**	50	35.31	**20.92**	**21.94**

Table 4: Frequency-Aware systems outperform both OpenSubs and Unweighted models for all languages. The size of the n-best list for each model was selected based on the WMF1 score on the internal test set.

as the loss leads to a better balance between Precision and Weighted Recall than cross-entropy. The classifier outperforms the MIRA reranker. Since the reranker is trained to maximize BLEU@1, it tends to prefer candidates that are lexically similar to the top reference translation and misses some of the more diverse learner translations. This confirms the benefits of framing the selection of candidate hypothesis as binary classification.

Ablation Experiments show that the MT scores are the most useful of the features used, as they capture not only the generation probability of a candidate hypothesis but estimate adequacy via the Target-to-source neural MT model (Table 8). Length features help precision but not recall, while the alignment and language model scores have little impact overall. This suggests that the classifier could benefit from improved feature design and selection in future work.

6.3 Analysis of Translation Diversity

How diverse are the translations returned by various system configurations? Following Zhang et al. (2018), we quantify diversity using the entropy of k-gram distributions within a translation set:

$$\text{Ent-k (V)} = -\frac{1}{\sum_w F(w)} \sum_{w \in V} F(w) \log \frac{F(w)}{\sum_w F(w)}$$

where V is the set of all k-grams that appear in the translation set, and $F(w)$ denotes the frequency of w in the translations. The higher the Ent-k score, the greater the diversity.

Fine-tuned models improve the diversity of 10-best lists compared to the "OpenSubs" baseline for both en-vi and en-pt (Table 9). Overall filtering bridges 40% and 25% of the gap between baseline and reference learner translations for en-pt and en-vi respectively.

6.4 System Combinations

A manual examination of translation sets returned by different models suggest that they make complementary errors. We therefore consider combining system outputs by taking the union of the set of translations they return. We evaluate the following combinations (Table 7):

C1 Frequency-aware (10-best) + Unweighted (10-best)

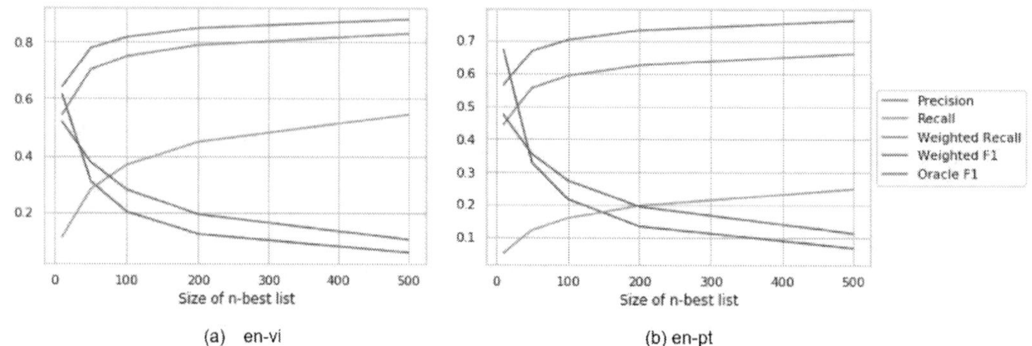

(a) en-vi   (b) en-pt

Figure 2: Increasing the size of n-best list with the Frequency-Aware system improves the coverage of learner translations for en-pt and en-vi. Oracle F1 is the Weighted Macro F1 at a Precision of 100% and represents the upper bound on WMF1 that can be achieved for a given n-best list.

Input: We live near the border.	LRF
chúng tôi sống gần biên giới.	0.250
chúng tôi sống ở gần biên giới.	0.053
chúng tôi sống gần đường biên giới.	0.267
chúng tôi sống bên cạnh biên giới.	0.018
chúng tôi sống ở cạnh biên giới.	0.013
chúng ta sống gần biên giới.	0.036
chúng tôi sống cạnh biên giới.	0.061
chúng tôi sống ở bên cạnh biên giới.	0.004
chúng tôi sống ở gần đường biên giới.	0.052
chúng ta sống ở gần biên giới.	0.004
Precision: 100%, Weighted Recall: 76%	

Input: My family lives in the south.	LRF
gia đình tôi sống ở miền nam.	0.285
gia đình của tôi sống ở miền nam.	0.134
gia đình tôi sống ở phương nam.	0.061
gia đình của tôi sống ở phương nam.	0.019
gia đình tôi sống ở phía nam.	0.208
gia đình của tôi sống ở phía nam.	0.099
nhà của tôi sống ở miền nam.	-
nhà tôi sống ở miền nam.	-
nhà của tôi sống ở phương nam.	-
gia đình tôi sống ở nam.	-
Precision: 60%, Weighted Recall: 81%	

Table 5: Frequency-Aware 10-best Vietnamese output for two randomly selected English prompts. LRF values are given for translations found in the reference set.

C2 Frequency-aware (10-best) + Frequency-aware (filtered 50-best)

C3 Unweighted (10-best) + Unweighted (filtered 50-best)

C4 Union of all of the above.

For en-pt and en-vi, it helps to combine higher precision unfiltered 10-best lists, and higher recall filtered 50-best lists. For en-pt, the union of all outputs (C4) performs best overall. Recall increases when combining the Frequency-Aware and the Unweighted model (C1) compared to individual lists (Unweighted: +1.6, Frequency-Aware: +2) without compromising Precision. Similar trends are observed when adding the filtered 50-best list to unfiltered 10-best lists (C2: +2.2, C3: +4.8). For en-vi, a different combination (C2) yields the best result, perhaps due to the smaller set of reference translations per source prompt (en-vi: 56, en-pt: 131) and high Precision of the "Unweighted" model for en-pt.

7 Submitted Systems

We tested our systems on the official blind development set to select the best performing models for final evaluation on the test set. For Portuguese and Vietnamese, our official submissions include frequency-aware hypothesis generation and hypothesis filtering:

en-vi C2: Frequency-aware (10-best) + Frequency-aware (filtered 50-best)

Method	en-vi				en-pt			
	P	WR	WMF1	K	P	WR	WMF1	K
No filtering	31.00	**70.31**	37.69	50	44.75	**57.21**	42.84	50
Reranker	**69.71**	46.85	50.67	9	67.44	41.82	45.51	14
Classifier with CE loss	69.70	47.74	48.77	12	69.26	42.70	46.60	10
Classifier with F1 loss	65.15	55.21	**53.69**	12	67.81	45.71	**48.68**	13
Oracle	100	70.31	77.90	15	100	70.31	66.9	16

Table 6: Filtering n-best lists consistently improves WMF1 and substantially reduces the size of the output set (K)

Method	en-pt				en-vi			
	P	R	WR	WMF1	P	R	WR	WMF1
Unweighted (10-best)	**72.69**	5.53	40.58	46.11	56.43	10.32	42.19	41.00
Unweighted (filtered 50-best)	67.81	9.68	45.71	48.17	63.14	15.23	54.35	51.48
Frequency-Aware (10-best)	67.31	5.07	44.34	47.40	61.61	11.28	54.37	51.87
Frequency-Aware (filtered 50-best)	64.33	6.40	36.94	41.44	**65.15**	15.33	55.21	53.69
C1	65.09	7.13	47.52	49.31	55.04	14.82	57.57	50.73
C2	64.33	7.30	48.67	48.81	60.41	16.07	60.19	**53.57**
C3	66.41	10.32	50.18	50.17	56.19	15.93	54.89	48.05
C4	59.76	**11.60**	**53.56**	**50.79**	53.75	**18.31**	61.04	50.78

Table 7: Combination of unfiltered 10-best lists (with better precision) and filtered 50-best lists (with better recall) improves Weighted Macro F1. See § 6.4 for details on combinations.

Features	P	R	WR	WMF1
All	63.71	15.97	55.91	**54.04**
- LM score	65.10	15.35	55.62	53.92
- Alignment	**65.21**	15.27	55.08	53.86
- Length	58.44	**16.49**	**55.98**	52.53
- MT Scores	43.77	10.88	31.02	28.06
Oracle	100	28.28	70.31	77.90

Table 8: Impact of dropping one feature type (§ 3.2) at a time from the "All" configuration for en-vi classifier.

Translations	en-pt		en-vi	
	Ent-4	n	Ent-4	n
OpenSubs	2.34	10	2.53	10
Unweighted	2.60	10	2.65	10
Frequency-Aware	2.59	10	2.67	10
Filtered	**2.95**	13	**2.71**	11
Reference	3.93	131	3.23	56

Table 9: Diversity in translation sets: Filtered sets are more diverse, bridging 40% of the gap between baseline and reference translations for en-pt.

en-pt C4: Frequency-aware (10-best) + Frequency-aware (filtered 50-best) + Unweighted (10-best) + Unweighted (filtered 50-best)

We did not build hypothesis filtering models for the other languages, and submitted systems based only on unfiltered models:

en-ja Frequency-aware (50-best) + Unweighted (50-best)

en-hu Frequency-aware (10-best) + Unweighted (10-best)

en-ko Frequency-aware (50-best) + Unweighted (50-best)

Table 10 and 11 compares our submissions to baselines, as well as top and median submissions across participants, for all the languages. On our focus languages (en-pt and en-vi), where systems benefitted from both frequency-aware generation and filtering models, our submissions obtain a Weighted Macro F1 score of 0.539 for en-vi and 0.525 for en-pt on the official test set, achieving a rank of 2nd and 4th on the leader-board, within 2% of the top performing submission. On the other language pairs, where our submissions did not use any filtering, Weighted Macro F1 outperform the baselines and median submission consistently. Interestingly on the en-ja task, our system ranks second amongst all the submissions despite not using any filtering.

Method	en-vi	en-pt	en-ja	en-hu	en-ko
AWS	0.210	0.211	0.042	0.298	0.040
Fairseq	0.267	0.151	0.031	0.130	0.054
Median	0.382	0.451	0.214	0.298	0.047
Top	0.547	0.557	0.316	0.598	0.413
Ours	0.537	0.538	0.283	0.492	0.254

Table 10: Excerpt from official results: weighted Macro F1 on the STAPLE dev set

Method	en-vi	en-pt	en-ja	en-hu	en-ko
AWS	0.198	0.213	0.043	0.281	0.041
Fairseq	0.254	0.136	0.033	0.124	0.049
Median	0.377	0.436	0.239	0.452	0.230
Top	0.558	0.552	0.318	0.555	0.404
Ours	0.539	0.525	0.294	0.469	0.255
Rank	2nd	4th	2nd	3rd	3rd

Table 11: Excerpt from official results: weighted Macro F1 on the STAPLE test set

8 Conclusion

We proposed two strategies to obtain multiple outputs that mimic translations by produced by language learners from a standard neural MT model. Our experiments showed that (1) finetuning MT models using all reference translations and their weight yields more diverse n-best hypotheses that better reflect learner preferences, and (2) filtering these n-best lists using a feature-rich classifier trained to maximize an approximation of the STAPLE evaluation metric yields further improvements. Combinations of systems that use these two strategies approach the top scoring submission in the official evaluation.

While these results suggest that some degree of output diversity can be achieved with little change to core neural MT models, oracle scores obtained with unfiltered n-best lists indicate that better modeling the space of learner translations might benefit both candidate generation and the filtering model in future work.

References

Sweta Agrawal and Marine Carpuat. 2019. Controlling text complexity in neural machine translation. In *Proceedings of the 2019 Conference on Empirical Methods in Natural Language Processing and the 9th International Joint Conference on Natural Language Processing (EMNLP-IJCNLP)*, pages 1549–1564, Hong Kong, China. Association for Computational Linguistics.

Satanjeev Banerjee and Alon Lavie. 2005. Meteor: An automatic metric for mt evaluation with improved correlation with human judgments. In *Proceedings of the acl workshop on intrinsic and extrinsic evaluation measures for machine translation and/or summarization*, pages 65–72.

Colin Cherry and George Foster. 2012. Batch tuning strategies for statistical machine translation. In *Proceedings of the 2012 Conference of the North American Chapter of the Association for Computational Linguistics: Human Language Technologies*, pages 427–436. Association for Computational Linguistics.

Kyunghyun Cho. 2016. Noisy parallel approximate decoding for conditional recurrent language model. *CoRR*, abs/1605.03835.

Hany Hassan, Anthony Aue, Chang Chen, Vishal Chowdhary, Jonathan Clark, Christian Federmann, Xuedong Huang, Marcin Junczys-Dowmunt, William Lewis, Mu Li, Shujie Liu, Tie-Yan Liu, Renqian Luo, Arul Menezes, Tao Qin, Frank Seide, Xu Tan, Fei Tian, Lijun Wu, Shuangzhi Wu, Yingce Xia, Dongdong Zhang, Zhirui Zhang, and Ming Zhou. 2018. Achieving human parity on automatic chinese to english news translation. *CoRR*, abs/1803.05567.

Kenneth Heafield. 2011. KenLM: Faster and smaller language model queries. In *Proceedings of the Sixth Workshop on Statistical Machine Translation*, pages 187–197, Edinburgh, Scotland. Association for Computational Linguistics.

Cheng-Yu Hsieh, Yi-An Lin, and Hsuan-Tien Lin. 2018. A deep model with local surrogate loss for general cost-sensitive multi-label learning. In *Thirty-Second AAAI Conference on Artificial Intelligence*.

Yuta Kikuchi, Graham Neubig, Ryohei Sasano, Hiroya Takamura, and Manabu Okumura. 2016. Controlling output length in neural encoder-decoders. In *Proceedings of the 2016 Conference on Empirical Methods in Natural Language Processing*, pages 1328–1338.

Jiwei Li, Michel Galley, Chris Brockett, Jianfeng Gao, and Bill Dolan. 2015. A diversity-promoting objective function for neural conversation models. *CoRR*, abs/1510.03055.

Jiwei Li and Dan Jurafsky. 2016. Mutual information and diverse decoding improve neural machine translation. *CoRR*, abs/1601.00372.

Stephen Mayhew, Klinton Bicknell, Chris Brust, Bill McDowell, Will Monroe, and Burr Settles. 2020. Simultaneous translation and paraphrase for language education. In *Proceedings of the ACL Workshop on Neural Generation and Translation (WNGT)*. ACL.

Dragos Stefan Munteanu and Daniel Marcu. 2005. Improving machine translation performance by exploiting non-parallel corpora. *Computational Linguistics*, 31(4):477–504.

Graham Neubig, Makoto Morishita, and Satoshi Nakamura. 2015. Neural reranking improves subjective quality of machine translation: Naist at wat2015. In *Proceedings of the 2nd Workshop on Asian Translation (WAT2015)*, pages 35–41.

Xing Niu, Sudha Rao, and Marine Carpuat. 2018. Multi-Task Neural Models for Translating Between Styles Within and Across Languages. In *27th International Conference on Computational Linguistics (COLING 2018)*.

Kishore Papineni, Salim Roukos, Todd Ward, and Wei-Jing Zhu. 2002. Bleu: a method for automatic evaluation of machine translation. In *Proceedings of the 40th Annual Meeting of the Association for Computational Linguistics*, pages 311–318, Philadelphia, Pennsylvania, USA. Association for Computational Linguistics.

Ying Qin and Lucia Specia. 2015. Truly exploring multiple references for machine translation evaluation. In *Proceedings of the 18th Annual Conference of the European Association for Machine Translation*, pages 113–120, Antalya, Turkey.

Ella Rabinovich, Shachar Mirkin, Raj Nath Patel, Lucia Specia, and Shuly Wintner. 2016. Personalized Machine Translation: Preserving Original Author Traits. *arXiv:1610.05461 [cs]*.

Rico Sennrich, Barry Haddow, and Alexandra Birch. 2016a. Controlling Politeness in Neural Machine Translation via Side Constraints. pages 35–40. Association for Computational Linguistics.

Rico Sennrich, Barry Haddow, and Alexandra Birch. 2016b. Neural Machine Translation of Rare Words with Subword Units. *Proceedings of the Meeting of the Association for Computational Linguistics (ACL)*.

Rico Sennrich, Barry Haddow, and Alexandra Birch. 2016c. Neural machine translation of rare words with subword units. In *Proceedings of the 54th Annual Meeting of the Association for Computational Linguistics (Volume 1: Long Papers)*, pages 1715–1725, Berlin, Germany. Association for Computational Linguistics.

Tianxiao Shen, Myle Ott, Michael Auli, and Marc'Aurelio Ranzato. 2019. Mixture models for diverse machine translation: Tricks of the trade. *CoRR*, abs/1902.07816.

Raphael Shu, Hideki Nakayama, and Kyunghyun Cho. 2019. Generating diverse translations with sentence codes. In *Proceedings of the 57th Annual Meeting of the Association for Computational Linguistics*, pages 1823–1827.

Jörg Tiedemann. 2012. Parallel data, tools and interfaces in opus. In *Lrec*, volume 2012, pages 2214–2218.

Yogarshi Vyas, Xing Niu, and Marine Carpuat. 2018. Identifying semantic divergences in parallel text without annotations. In *Proceedings of the 2018 Conference of the North American Chapter of the Association for Computational Linguistics: Human Language Technologies, Volume 1 (Long Papers)*, pages 1503–1515. Association for Computational Linguistics.

Yizhe Zhang, Michel Galley, Jianfeng Gao, Zhe Gan, Xiujun Li, Chris Brockett, and Bill Dolan. 2018. Generating informative and diverse conversational responses via adversarial information maximization. In *Advances in Neural Information Processing Systems*, pages 1810–1820.

Renjie Zheng, Mingbo Ma, and Liang Huang. 2018. Multi-reference training with pseudo-references for neural translation and text generation. In *Proceedings of the 2018 Conference on Empirical Methods in Natural Language Processing*, pages 3188–3197, Brussels, Belgium. Association for Computational Linguistics.

The JHU Submission to the 2020 Duolingo Shared Task on Simultaneous Translation and Paraphrase for Language Education

Huda Khayrallah[‡]   Jacob Bremerman[§]   Arya D. McCarthy[‡]
Kenton Murray[‡]   Winston Wu[‡] and Matt Post[‡,†]

[‡]Center for Language and Speech Processing, Johns Hopkins University
[†]Human Language Technology Center of Excellence, Johns Hopkins University
[§]University of Maryland, College Park

Abstract

This paper presents the Johns Hopkins University submission to the 2020 Duolingo Shared Task on Simultaneous Translation and Paraphrase for Language Education (STAPLE). We participated in all five language tasks, placing first in each. Our approach involved a language-agnostic pipeline of three components: (1) building strong machine translation systems on general-domain data, (2) fine-tuning on Duolingo-provided data, and (3) generating n-best lists which are then filtered with various score-based techniques. In addition to the language-agnostic pipeline, we attempted a number of linguistically-motivated approaches, with, unfortunately, little success. We also find that improving BLEU performance of the beam-search generated translation does not necessarily improve on the task metric—weighted macro F1 of an n-best list.

1 Introduction

The Duolingo 2020 STAPLE Shared Task (Mayhew et al., 2020) focuses on generating a comprehensive set of translations for a given sentence, translating from English into Hungarian, Japanese, Korean, Portuguese, and Vietnamese. The formulation of this task (§2) differs from the conventional machine translation setup: instead of the n-gram match (BLEU) against a single reference, sentence-level exact match is computed between a list of proposed candidates and a weighted list of references (as in Figure 1). The set of references is drawn from Duolingo's language-teaching app. Any auxiliary data is allowed for building systems, including existing very-large parallel corpora for translation.

Our approach begins with strong MT systems (§3) which are fine-tuned on Duolingo-provided data (§4). We then generate large n-best lists, from which we select our final candidate list (§5). Our

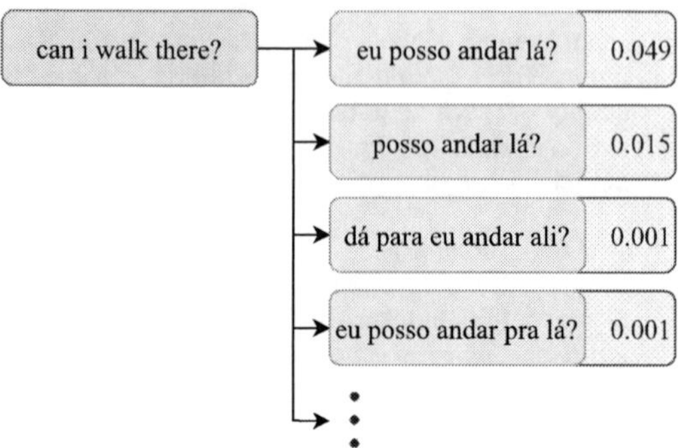

Figure 1: An example English source sentence with its weighted Portuguese target translations. The objective of the task is to recover the list of references, and performance is measured by a weighted F-score.

entries outperform baseline weighted F1 scores by a factor of 2 to 10 and are ranked first in the official evaluation for every language pair (§6.2).

In addition to our system description, we perform additional analysis (§7). We find that stronger BLEU performance of the beam-search generated translation is not indicative of improvements on the task metric—weighted macro F1 of a set of hypotheses—and suggest this should encourage further research on how to train NMT models when n-best lists are needed (§7.1). We perform detailed analysis on our output (§7.2), which led to additional development on English–Portuguese (§8.1). We also present additional linguistically-informed methods which we experimented with but which ultimately did not improve performance (§8).

2 Task Description

Data We use data provided by the STAPLE shared task (Mayhew et al., 2020). This data consists of a single English prompt sentence or phrase paired with multiple translations in the target lan-

Proceedings of the 4th Workshop on Neural Generation and Translation (WNGT 2020), pages 188–197
Online, July 10, 2020. ©2020 Association for Computational Linguistics
www.aclweb.org/anthology/D19-56%2d

	hu	ja	ko	pt	vi
total prompts	4,000	2,500	2,500	4,000	3,500
mean translations	63	342	280	132	56
median translations	36	192	154	68	30
STD. translations	66	362	311	150	62

Table 1: Statistics over the Duolingo-provided data.

guage. These translations come from courses intended to teach English to speakers of other languages; the references are initially generated by trained translators, and augmented by verified user translations. Each translation is associated with a relative frequency denoting how often it is selected by Duolingo users. Table 1 shows the total number of prompts provided as well as the mean, median, and standard deviation of the number of translations per training prompt. All of the provided task data is lower-cased.

For each language pair, we created an internal split of the Duolingo-provided training data: 100 training prompts for use in validating the MT system (JHU-VALID), another 100 intended for model selection (JHU-DEV),[1] and a 300-prompt test set for candidate selection (JHU-TEST). The remaining data (JHU-TRAIN) was used for training the MT models.

Evaluation metric The official metric is weighted macro F_1. This is defined as:

$$\text{Weighted Macro } F_1 = \sum_{s \in S} \frac{\text{Weighted } F_1(s)}{|S|},$$

where S is all prompts in the test corpus. The weighted F1 is computed with a weighted recall, where TP_s are the true positives for a prompt s, and FN_s are the false negatives for a prompt s:

$$\text{WTP}_s = \sum_{t \in TP_s} \text{weight}(t)$$

$$\text{WFN}_s = \sum_{t \in FN_s} \text{weight}(t)$$

$$\text{Weighted Recall}(s) = \frac{\text{WTP}_s}{\text{WTP}_s + \text{WFN}_s}.$$

Note that recall is weighted (according to weights provided with the gold data), but precision is not.

Evaluation is conducted on lowercased text with the punctuation removed.

---

[1] However, we discovered that BLEU did not correlate well enough with task performance to be used for this. See §7.1 for more analysis and discussion.

3 Machine Translation Systems

We began by building high-quality state-of-the-art machine translation systems.

Data and preprocessing Additional data for our systems was obtained from Opus (Tiedemann, 2012).[2] We removed duplicate bitext pairs, then reserved 3k random pairs from each dataset to create a validation, development, and test sets of 1k sentence each. The validation dataset is used as held-out data to determine when to stop training the MT system.[3] Table 2 shows the amount of training data used from each source.

The Duolingo data (including the evaluation data) is all lowercased. Since our approach is to overgenerate candidates and filter, we want to avoid glutting the decoder beam with spurious cased variants. For this reason, we lowercase all text on both the source and (where relevant) target sides prior to training. However, it is worth noting that this has a drawback, as source case can provide a signal towards meaning and word-sense disambiguation (e.g., *apple* versus *Apple*).

After lowercasing, we train separate Sentence-Piece models (Kudo and Richardson, 2018) on the source and target sides of the bitext, for each language. We train a regularized unigram model (Kudo, 2018) with a vocabulary size of 5,000 and a character coverage of 0.995. When applying the model, we set $\alpha = 0.5$. No other preprocessing was applied.

Translation models We used fairseq (Ott et al., 2019) to train standard Transformer (Vaswani et al., 2017) models with 6 encoder and decoder layers, a model size of 512, feed forward layer size of 2048, and 8 attention heads, and a dropout of 0.1. We used an effective batch size of 200k tokens.[4] We concatenated the development data across test sets, and quit training when validation perplexity had failed to improve for 10 consecutive checkpoints.

We trained two sets of models: MODEL1 was trained on just the data above the line in Table 2, while MODEL2 was trained on all the data.

---

[2] opus.nlpl.eu
[3] The other two were reserved for unanticipated use cases that never materialized.
[4] (batch size 4000) × (2 GPUs) × (update interval 25)

	hu	ja	ko	pt	vi
Europarl (Koehn, 2005)	2,351k	-	-	2,408k	-
GlobalVoices (opus.nlpl.eu/GlobalVoices.php)	194k	822k	37k	1,585k	-
OpenSubtitles (Lison and Tiedemann, 2016)	252,622k	13,097k	8,840k	196,960k	20,298k
Tatoeba (tatoeba.org)	580k	1,537k	-	1,215k	16k
WikiMatrix (Schwenk et al., 2019)	5,682k	9,013k	2,598k	45,147k	17,427k
JW300 (Agić and Vulić, 2019)	19,378k	34,325k	32,356k	39,023k	11,233k
QED (Abdelali et al., 2014)	5,693k	9,064k	9,992k	8,542k	5,482k

Table 2: Number of English word tokens for all datasets used to train the baseline MT models. Just the data above the line was used to train the MODEL1 baseline, all the data was used to train the MODEL2 baseline.

4 Fine-Tuning

After training general-domain machine translation models, we fine-tune them on the Duolingo data.[5] The Duolingo data pairs single prompts with up to hundreds of weighted translations; we turned this into bitext in three ways:

- **1-best:** the best translation per prompt.

- **all:** each translation paired with its prompt.

- **up-weighted:** all possible translations with an additional 1, 9, or 99 copies of the 1-best translation (giving the 1-best translation a weight of 2x, 10x, or 100x the others).[6]

We fine-tune with dropout of 0.1, and an effective batch size of 160k tokens. We sweep learning rates of 1×10^{-4} and 5×10^{-4}.

We withhold a relatively high percentage of the Duolingo training data for internal development (500 prompts total, which ranged from to 12.5 to 20% of the provided data), so we also train systems using all the released data (with none withheld), taking hyperparameters learned from our splits (number of fine-tuning epochs, candidate selection parameters, etc).

5 Candidate Generation and Selection

From the models trained on general-domain data (§3) and refined on in-domain data (§4), we generate 1,000-best translations. For each translation, fairseq provides word-level and length-normalized log-probability scores, which all serve as grist for the next stage of our pipeline: candidate selection.

5.1 Ensembling

For Portuguese only, we experimented with ensembling multiple fine-tuned models in two ways: (a) using models from different random seeds, and (b) using different types of systems.

5.2 Selecting top k hypotheses

As a baseline, we extract hypotheses from the n-best list using the provided `my_cands_extract.py` script.[7] which simply extracts the same number of hypotheses, k, per prompt. To determine how many hypotheses to retain from the model's n-best list, we conduct a sweep over k on JHU-TEST and select the best k per language pair based on weighted macro F1.

5.3 Probability score thresholding

We propose to use the log probability scores directly and choose a cutoff point based on the top score for each prompt.

We consider a multiplicative threshold on the probabilities of the hypothesis, relative to the best hypothesis. For example, if the threshold value is -0.40, for a prompt where the top hypothesis log-probability is -1.20, any hypothesis from the top 1000 with a log-probability greater than or equal to -1.60 will be selected.[8] As in §5.2, we sweep over this threshold value for each language pair and choose the value that results in the highest weighted macro F1 score from JHU-TEST.

---

[5] Training on the Duolingo data directly was less effective.

[6] A better method might be to train using the weights to weight the sentences in training as available in Marian (Junczys-Dowmunt et al., 2018) but that was not available in fairseq, so we improvised.

[7] github.com/duolingo/
duolingo-sharedtask-2020/blob/
626239b78621af96fbb324e678cca17b3dd4e470/
my_cands_extract.py

[8] In other words, we set a threshold of $\exp\{-0.40\}$ on the likelihood ratio.

en $\to x$		hu	ja	ko	pt	vi
MODEL1		44.8	11.8	4.0	32.6	27.2
fine-tune on:	JHU-TRAIN: 1-best	43.4	12.4	11.4	41.6	41.6
	JHU-TRAIN: all	52.1	23.1	23.1	49.3	52.0
	upweighted JHU-TRAIN: all + 1x 1-best	52.1	23.5	24.3	50.1	52.3
	upweighted JHU-TRAIN: all + 9x 1-best	**56.6**	**24.1**	**25.0**	**52.8**	**54.3**
	upweighted JHU-TRAIN: all + 99x 1-best	54.0	23.0	21.9	51.1	52.4

Table 3: The weighted macro F1 on JHU-TEST for MODEL1 and fine-tuned variants. Candidates are extracted from the n-best list using the proposed probability score thresholding (§5.3).

en $\to x$		ja	ko
MODEL2		16.8	12.5
fine-tune on:	JHU-TRAIN: 1-best	18.4	18.7
	JHU-TRAIN: all	31.5	38.0
	upweighted JHU-TRAIN: all + 1x 1-best	30.3	38.0
	upweighted JHU-TRAIN: all + 9x 1-best	**32.1**	**38.8**
	upweighted JHU-TRAIN: all + 99x 1-best	31.0	33.4

Table 4: The weighted macro F1 on JHU-TEST for MODEL2 and fine-tuned variants for Japanese and Korean. Candidates are extracted from the n-best list using the proposed probability score thresholding (§5.3).

6 Results

We present results of our different methods on our internal development set in §6.1 and present our official evaluation performance in §6.2.

6.1 Internal evaluation

Table 3 shows the weighted macro F1 performance on JHU-TEST for MODEL1 and fine-tuned variants. Candidates are extracted from the n-best list using the proposed probability score thresholding (§5.3). Fine-tuning improves performance (except for fine-tuning on just the 1-best translation in Hungarian). For all language pairs, the best fine-tuning performance came from training on the upweighted training data, where we trained on all possible translations with the 1-best up-weighted 10 times. For Japanese and Korean[9] MODEL2 (Table 4), all types of fine-tuning improve weighted F1, but for both language pairs, the best fine-tuning variant matches that of MODEL1.

Table 5 shows the weighted macro F1 on JHU-TEST for two methods of selecting candidates from the n-best list. The first line is the baseline top k hypothesis selection (§5.2), the second is our pro-posed probability score thresholding (§5.3). The best fine-tuned system is shown with each selection method for each language pair. The proposed probability score thresholding improves performance over the baseline top k candidate selection by 2–3.3 F1 points.

6.2 Official evaluation

In Table 6, we present the final results of our submission on the official test set (DUO-TEST). Our systems ranked first in all language pairs, with improvements of 0.1 to 9.2 over the next best teams. We denote in parenthesis the improvement over the next best team's system on DUO-TEST. We also report the score that our system achieved on our internal test set (JHU-TEST).

For Hungarian and Vietnamese, our winning submission was MODEL1 fine-tuned on the up-weighted Duolingo data (1-best repeated 10x) with a learning rate of 1×10^{-4}. For Japanese, our winning submission was MODEL2 fine-tuned on the up-weighted Duolingo data (1-best repeated 10x) with a learning rate of 5×10^{-4}. For Korean, our winning submission was MODEL2 fine-tuned on the up-weighted Duolingo data (1-best repeated 10x) with a learning rate of 1×10^{-4}, but without

---

[9]These were the two languages where MODEL2 improved fine-tuning performance compared to MODEL1.

en $\to x$	hu	ja	ko	pt	vi
top k hypothesis selection (§5.2)	54.6	29.5	35.6	50.0	51.0
Probability score thresholding (§5.3)	**56.6**	**32.1**	**38.8**	**52.8**	**54.3**

Table 5: The weighted macro F1 on JHU-TEST for two methods of selecting candidates from the n-best list: baseline top k hypothesis selected (discussed in §5.2), and our proposed probability score thresholding (§5.3). The best fine-tuned system is shown with each selection method for each language pair.

en $\to x$	DUO-TEST	JHU-TEST
hu	55.5 (+0.3)	56.6
ja	31.8 (+2.4)	32.1
ko	40.4 (+9.2)	38.9[10]
pt	55.2 (+0.1)	54.6
vi	55.8 (+1.9)	54.3

Table 6: The weighted macro F1 of our final submitted systems on the official shared task test set (DUO-TEST) on our internal test set (JHU-TEST). We denote in parenthesis the improvement over the next best team's system on DUO-TEST.

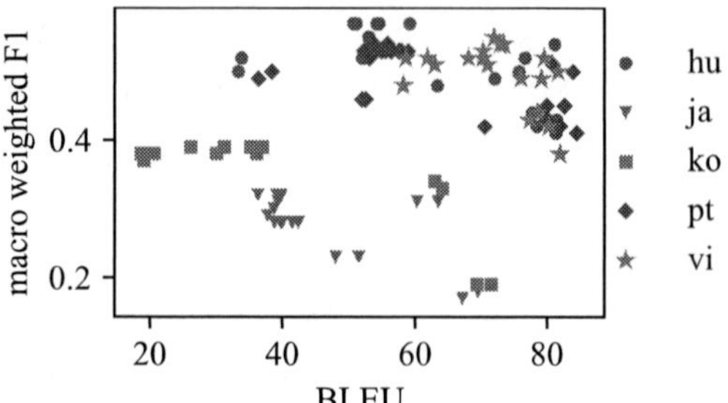

Figure 2: Macro Weighted F1 (JHU-TEST) vs. BLEU (JHU-DEV) for a variety of fine-tuned systems for each language pair. The two metrics are not well correlated within a language pair.

any internal development data withheld.[10]

For Portuguese, our winning submission was an ensemble of 3 systems. We began with MODEL1 fine-tuned on the up-weighted Duolingo data with a learning rate of 1×10^{-4}. We used fairseq's default ensembling to ensemble 3 systems trained on all the translations of each Duolingo prompt, with the 1-best data repeated a total of 2x, 10x, and 100x for each system.

While we submitted slightly different systems for each language pair, the following worked well overall: Fine-tuning on the Duolingo data was crucial. This is a domain adaptation task—the Duolingo data differs greatly from the standard MT bitext we pretrain on, such as Europarl proceedings, GlobalVoices news, Subtitles, or Wikipedia text.[11] Taking advantage of the relative weights of the training translations and up-weighting the best one was also helpful across the board. We suspect that using the weights in training directly (as opposed to our hack of upweight-

ing the best translation) would likely improve performance further.[12]

7 Analysis

We perform qualitative and quantitative analyses of our output, which informed our own work and will motivate future work.

7.1 BLEU vs. Macro Weighted F1

In Figure 2, we plot macro weighted F1 on JHU-TEST against BLEU score[13] on JHU-DEV for fine-tuned systems for each language. It is clear that this BLEU score did not identify the best performing system according to the macro weighted F1 metric. For example, performance on beam search BLEU could be improved by further fine-tuning systems that had already been fine-tuned on all translations of each prompt on just the 1-best translation of each prompt, but that degraded the task performance. In fact, the systems that performed best on macro weighted F1 in Hungarian and Korean were over 20 BLEU behind the highest BLEU score for those languages (and the top BLEU scoring systems did poorly on the task metric).

---

[10] As described in §4, we first fine-tune a system and use our internal splits for model selection from checkpoints and threshold selection. Then we apply all the same parameters to fine-tune a system with no data withheld. This was better than with holding data only for en-ko (on DUO-DEV). Since this en-ko system was trained on JHU-TEST, Table 6 reports the JHU-TEST results on the corresponding system that withheld that data.

[11] In addition to style differences, the Duolingo sentences are much shorter on average.

[12] This feature does exist in Marian (Junczys-Dowmunt et al., 2018) but not in Fairseq.

[13] Computed against the 1-best translation of each prompt.

While this phenomenon may be an artifact of these particular metrics, we suspect this is indicative of an interesting topic for further research. MT models trained with NLL are trained to match a 1-hot prediction, which may make their output distributions poorly calibrated (Ott et al., 2018; Kumar and Sarawagi, 2019; Desai and Durrett, 2020). More research is needed for strong conclusions, but our initial analysis suggests that training on the more diverse data improves quality of a deep n-best list of translations at the expense of the top beam search output. This may be important in cases where an n-best list of translations is being generated for a downstream NLP task.

The data for this task was unique in that it provided diverse translations for a given prompt. In most cases where this type of data is not available, training towards a distribution (rather than a single target word), as is done in word-level knowledge distillation (Buciluundefined et al., 2006; Hinton et al., 2015; Kim and Rush, 2016) may prove useful to introduce the diversity needed for a strong n-best list of translations. This can be done either towards a distribution of the base model when fine-tuning (Dakwale and Monz, 2017; Khayrallah et al., 2018) or towards the distribution of an auxiliary model, such as a paraphraser (Khayrallah et al., 2020).

7.2 Qualitative error analysis

In each language, we performed a qualitative error analysis by manually inspecting the difference between the gold and system translations for prompts with lowest weighted recall on JHU-TEST.

Our systems were often incapable of expressing target language *nuance* absent from the source language. For example, for the prompt "we have asked many times.", a gold translation was '私たちは何度も尋ねてしまった' whereas our system output '私たちは何度も尋ねました'. The gold translations often included the てしまった verb ending, which conveys a nuance similar to perfect aspect. The prompt's scenario would lead many Japanese users to use this nuanced ending when translating, but our system produces valid but less natural translations that do not appear in the references.

Another issue is *vocabulary choice* on a more general level. Often there are several ways to translate certain words or phrases, but our systems prefer the less common version. For example, a com-mon translation of 'please' in Portuguese is 'por favor', which appears in the high-weighted gold translations. Another possible translation, 'por obséquio', which our system seemed to prefer, appears in much lower-weighted translations. Another example is the translation of 'battery' in Korean. The high-weighted references include the common word for battery ('건전지') but only lower-weighted references include '배터리', which was preferred by our system.

Our system also struggled with *polysemous prompt words*. For example, for the prompt "cups are better than glasses.", our system output translations like '컵이 안경들보다 낫다', using 안경 (eyeglasses), instead of translations like '컵이 유리잔보다 낫다', using 유리잔 (drinking glasses). The systems seem to be incapable of considering the context, "cups" in this case, for the ambiguity resolution.

A final class of our system's errors is *grammatical errors*. For example, for the prompt "every night, the little sheep dreams about surfing.", the gold translations included sentences like 'toda noite a pequena ovelha sonha com surfe' whereas our system output sentences like 'toda noite as ovelhas pequenas sonham com surfe'. The error was that our output included 'ovelhas' (plural sheep), but the gold translations all used 'ovelha' (single sheep).

7.3 Missing paradigm slots in Duolingo data

We also find cases where our system produces valid translations but is penalized because these are not among the gold translations. We consider these cases as a result of an "incomplete" gold set with missing paradigms.[14]

For example, the Vietnamese pronouns for 'he' and 'she' can vary according to age (in relation to the speaker). From youngest to oldest, some pronouns for 'she' are 'chị ấy', 'cô ấy', and 'bà ấy'. For several of the prompts, the gold outputs only include some of these pronouns despite all being valid. In the prompt "she has bread", only the first two pronouns are present even though a translation representing the sentence as an older woman having bread should be equally valid. We also find this missing pronoun slot problem in Portuguese (references only using 'você' and not 'tu' for translations of 'you') and Japanese (only using 'あな

---

[14]The task website notes this phenomenon. It calls the set of targets 'comprehensive', though not 'exhaustive'.

た' and not '君' for translations of 'you').

We could not easily predict when slots would be missing. Because the data comes from Duolingo courses, we believe this may depend on the prompt's depth in the learning tree. As earlier lessons are studied by more users, we suspect they are also more likely to contain more complete gold translation sets due to more users submitting additional valid translations. This makes it difficult to assess the success of our models and distinguish "true errors" from valid hypotheses that are marked incorrect.

8 What Didn't Work

We explored additional methods both for selecting candidates from an n-best lists and for generating additional candidates based on an n-best list. While they did not improve performance and were not included in our final submission, we discuss the methods and the analyses learned from them.

8.1 Moore–Lewis filtering

Our error analysis revealed that our systems often output sentences that were not incorrect, but not optimized for the Duolingo task. For example, many of our top candidates for translations of "please" in Portuguese used *por obséquio*, which is a very formal version, instead of the more common *por favor*. While both versions were valid for the prompts, the gold translations with *por favor* were weighted higher, so we would desire models to prefer this translation. We interpret this as domain mismatch between the STAPLE data and our MT training data.

To filter out such bad candidates, we experimented with cross-entropy language model filtering (Moore and Lewis, 2010). This takes two language models: a (generally large) out-of-domain language model (OD), and a (typically small) in-domain language model (ID), and uses the difference in normalized cross-entropy from these two models to score sentences. Sentences with good OD scores and poor ID scores are likely out-of-domain and can be discarded based on a score threshold.

Experimenting on Portuguese, we used KenLM (Heafield, 2011) to train a Kneser–Ney-smoothed 5-gram model on the Portuguese side of the MT training data (Table 2) as the OD model and a 3-gram model on the Duolingo Portuguese data (ID). These were used to score all candidates t as

	JHU-TEST	DUO-TEST
Baseline	53.30	**55.16**
Baseline + Moore-Lewis	**53.70**	53.83

Table 7: Moore–Lewis filtering for Pt (macro F1).

$\mathrm{score}(t) = p_{\mathrm{ID}}(t) - p_{\mathrm{OD}}(t)$. We swept thresholds and minimum prompt lengths on our JHU-TEST data, and found with a threshold of -1.50 on 7-word prompts and longer performed the best.

Moore–Lewis filtering was originally designed for more coarse-grained selection of training data. We suspect (but did not have time to test) that a better idea is therefore to apply this upstream, using it to help select data used to train the general-domain MT system (Axelrod et al., 2011).

8.2 Dual conditional thresholding

Extending the probability score thresholding (§5.3), we consider incorporating a score from a reverse model that represents the probability that the original prompt was generated by the candidate. The reverse model score is also used in Dual Conditional Cross-Entropy Filtering when selecting clean data from noisy corpora (Junczys-Dowmunt, 2018), and for re-scoring n-best lists in MMI decoding (Li et al., 2016)

We train base and fine-tuned reverse systems for the five language pairs and use them to score the output translations. We compute the combined score of a hypothesis given a prompt as the arithmetic mean of the forward and backward log probability scores and use them in the probability score thresholding algorithm from §5.3. We find that after sweeping across threshold values, incorporating the reverse score performs slightly worse overall than the standard thresholding method for every language.

8.3 N-gram filtering

The Duolingo data generally consists of simple language, which means we did not expect to see novel phrases in the references that were not in our training corpora. We used this idea to filter hypotheses that had any n-grams that didn't appear in our training data. Our hope was that this would catch rare formulations or ungrammatical sentences, e.g. *cachorro preta*, which has the wrong gender on the adjective. However, even using bigrams caused this method to filter out too many hypotheses and hurt F1 performance.

None	elas	têm	cinco	meninas	?
Open	elas	V;3;PL	NUM	N;PL;FEM	?
Morph	PRO;3;PL;FEM	V;3;PL	NUM	N;PL;FEM	PUNCT
POS	PRO	V	NUM	N	PUNCT

Table 8: Preprocessing operations for filtering on one Portuguese gold output for the prompt *do they have five girls?*, organized from most specific to most general.

Part-of-speech filtering Although the language used in Duolingo is relatively simple, the number of unique types turned out to be quite large. However the number part-of-speech (POS) tags is small. Instead of filtering based on words, we count n-grams of POS tags, hoping to remove ungrammatical sentences with tags such as DET DET. In our experiments, this did not actually exclude any hypotheses.

Open class words and morphology In between the extremes of large number of types using raw lexical forms and few types using POS tags is to leverage open class words or additional morphological information. We morphologically tag the dataset with the Stanford NLP toolkit (Qi et al., 2018), then represent each sentence either by its words, its POS tags, its morphological tags, or words for closed-class items and tags for open-class items, as shown in Table 8. This too resulted in few hypotheses being filtered and did not impact F1 performance.

Filtering by difficulty level As the Duolingo data was generated by language learners, we also considered filtering sentences by the difficulty of the words within. Experimenting with Japanese, we examined the grade level of kanji[15] in each sentence. Ignoring non-kanji characters, the average grade level per sentence on the STAPLE training data was 3.77, indicating a 3rd–4th grade level. Future work could consider filtering by other measures such as the coreness of a word (Wu et al., 2020).

8.4   Generation via post-editing

Inspired by query expansion in information retrieval, we post-edit either by consider morphological variants in situations of underspecification, substituting forms in different scripts (for Japanese), or replacing long-form number names with numerals. We found these ineffective because

---

[15]Specified by the Japanese Ministry of Education and annotated in `edrdg.org/wiki/index.php/KANJIDIC_Project`

Strategy	P	RW	WF1macro
Baseline	26.91	69.70	34.49
Add 1;PL	26.62	69.84	34.27
Add 3;SG;MASC	23.97	70.19	33.42
Add 3;SG;FEM	24.69	70.49	33.51
Add 3;PL	22.28	69.75	31.89
Add most frequent 'she'	26.77	69.84	34.38
Swap most common 'he's	26.71	69.82	34.37
Swap 2nd most common 'he's	26.90	69.71	34.47
Swap 3rd most common 'he's	26.88	69.71	34.45

Table 9: Effect of pronoun-based augmentation on metrics in Vietnamese, computed on JHU-TEST. All strategies improve recall and weighted recall, but they cause precision and F1 to decrease.

several acceptable translations were not present in the ground truth dataset (see §7.3).

Morphological expansions English is morphologically poorer than 4 target languages. As an example, the English word 'you' may be translated into Portuguese as 'tu', 'você', 'vocês', or 'vós', to consider only nominative forms. We can thus generate three additional candidates by altering the morphosyntax (and maintaining grammatical concord) while keeping the meaning intact.

Evaluating in Portuguese and Vietnamese, we find that this is ineffective (see §7.3). Consider Vietnamese. It is a morphologically isolating and zero-marking language, so concord between constituents is not overtly marked. This leaves us fairly free to swap out morphological variants of pronouns: there may be difference in age, connotation, or register, but the overt semantics of the English prompt are preserved. All swapping transformations in Table 9 give poorer performance.

Hiragana replacement Japanese has three different writing systems—hiragana, katakana, and kanji—and sometimes a word written in kanji is considered an acceptable translation when written in hiragana. For example, the Japanese word for "child" is 子供 when written with kanji, but an acceptable alternative is the hiragana こども . We experiment with expanding translation candidates by replacing Japanese kanji with pronunciations from a furigana (hiragana pronunciation) dictionary but this method did not improve performance.

Numeral replacement For sentences containing numbers, the list of accepted translations often contains Arabic numbers, in addition to numbers in the native language. For example, 'o senhor smith virá no dia dez de julho' and 'o senhor smith virá no dia 10 de julho.' are both gold translations of "mr. smith will come on july tenth." We experiment with replacing native numbers with Arabic numerals in Japanese, Portuguese, and Vietnamese. This did not improve weighted F1.

9 Conclusion

Our approach was general, borrowing from best practices in machine translation. We built large, general-domain MT systems that were then fine-tuned on in-domain data. We then followed an "overgenerate and filter" approach that made effective use of the scores from the systems to find a per-prompt truncation of large n-best lists produced from these systems. These techniques performed very well, ranking first in all five language pairs. We expect that further refinement and exploration of standard MT techniques—as well as techniques that we were unsuccessful with (§8)—would bring further improvements that would accrue generally across languages.

At the same time, the Duolingo shared task is distinct from machine translation in subtle but important ways: presenting simpler, shorter sentences and a 0-1 objective. While we were not able to get additional gains from linguistic insights, we don't see these failures as conclusive indictments of those techniques, but instead as invitations to look deeper.

Acknowledgments

We thank Najoung Kim for remarks on Korean, An Nguyen for remarks on Vietnamese and Vinicius C. Costa for remarks on Portuguese, and Doug Oard for general advice.

References

Ahmed Abdelali, Francisco Guzman, Hassan Sajjad, and Stephan Vogel. 2014. The AMARA corpus: Building parallel language resources for the educational domain. In *Proceedings of the Ninth International Conference on Language Resources and Evaluation (LREC'14)*, pages 1856–1862, Reykjavik, Iceland. European Language Resources Association (ELRA).

Željko Agić and Ivan Vulić. 2019. JW300: A wide-coverage parallel corpus for low-resource languages. In *Proceedings of the 57th Annual Meeting of the Association for Computational Linguistics*, pages 3204–3210, Florence, Italy. Association for Computational Linguistics.

Amittai Axelrod, Xiaodong He, and Jianfeng Gao. 2011. Domain adaptation via pseudo in-domain data selection. In *Proceedings of the 2011 Conference on Empirical Methods in Natural Language Processing*, pages 355–362, Edinburgh, Scotland, UK. Association for Computational Linguistics.

Cristian Buciluundefined, Rich Caruana, and Alexandru Niculescu-Mizil. 2006. Model compression. In *Proceedings of the 12th ACM SIGKDD International Conference on Knowledge Discovery and Data Mining*, KDD '06, page 535–541, New York, NY, USA. Association for Computing Machinery.

Praveen Dakwale and Christof Monz. 2017. Fine-tuning for neural machine translation with limited degradation across in- and out-of-domain data. In *Proceedings of the 16th Machine Translation Summit (MT-Summit 2017)*, pages 156–169.

Shrey Desai and Greg Durrett. 2020. Calibration of pre-trained transformers.

Kenneth Heafield. 2011. KenLM: Faster and smaller language model queries. In *Proceedings of the Sixth Workshop on Statistical Machine Translation*, pages 187–197, Edinburgh, Scotland. Association for Computational Linguistics.

Geoffrey Hinton, Oriol Vinyals, and Jeff Dean. 2015. Distilling the knowledge in a neural network.

Marcin Junczys-Dowmunt. 2018. Dual conditional cross-entropy filtering of noisy parallel corpora. In *Proceedings of the Third Conference on Machine Translation: Shared Task Papers*, pages 888–895, Belgium, Brussels. Association for Computational Linguistics.

Marcin Junczys-Dowmunt, Roman Grundkiewicz, Tomasz Dwojak, Hieu Hoang, Kenneth Heafield, Tom Neckermann, Frank Seide, Ulrich Germann, Alham Fikri Aji, Nikolay Bogoychev, André F. T. Martins, and Alexandra Birch. 2018. Marian: Fast neural machine translation in C++. In *Proceedings of ACL 2018, System Demonstrations*, pages 116–121, Melbourne, Australia. Association for Computational Linguistics.

Huda Khayrallah, Brian Thompson, Kevin Duh, and Philipp Koehn. 2018. Regularized training objective for continued training for domain adaptation in neural machine translation. In *Proceedings of the 2nd Workshop on Neural Machine Translation and Generation*, pages 36–44, Melbourne, Australia. Association for Computational Linguistics.

Huda Khayrallah, Brian Thompson, Matt Post, and Philipp Koehn. 2020. Simulated multiple reference training improves low-resource machine translation. arXiv preprint arXiv:2004.14524.

Yoon Kim and Alexander M. Rush. 2016. Sequence-level knowledge distillation. In *Proceedings of the 2016 Conference on Empirical Methods in Natural Language Processing*, pages 1317–1327, Austin, Texas. Association for Computational Linguistics.

Philipp Koehn. 2005. Europarl: A parallel corpus for statistical machine translation. In *MT summit*, volume 5, pages 79–86. Citeseer.

Taku Kudo. 2018. Subword regularization: Improving neural network translation models with multiple subword candidates. In *Proceedings of the 56th Annual Meeting of the Association for Computational Linguistics (Volume 1: Long Papers)*, pages 66–75, Melbourne, Australia. Association for Computational Linguistics.

Taku Kudo and John Richardson. 2018. SentencePiece: A simple and language independent subword tokenizer and detokenizer for neural text processing. In *Proceedings of the 2018 Conference on Empirical Methods in Natural Language Processing: System Demonstrations*, pages 66–71, Brussels, Belgium. Association for Computational Linguistics.

Aviral Kumar and Sunita Sarawagi. 2019. Calibration of encoder decoder models for neural machine translation. *CoRR*, abs/1903.00802.

Jiwei Li, Michel Galley, Chris Brockett, Jianfeng Gao, and Bill Dolan. 2016. A diversity-promoting objective function for neural conversation models. In *Proceedings of the 2016 Conference of the North American Chapter of the Association for Computational Linguistics: Human Language Technologies*, pages 110–119, San Diego, California. Association for Computational Linguistics.

Pierre Lison and Jörg Tiedemann. 2016. OpenSubtitles2016: Extracting large parallel corpora from movie and TV subtitles. In *Proceedings of the Tenth International Conference on Language Resources and Evaluation (LREC'16)*, pages 923–929, Portorož, Slovenia. European Language Resources Association (ELRA).

Stephen Mayhew, Klinton Bicknell, Chris Brust, Bill McDowell, Will Monroe, and Burr Settles. 2020. Simultaneous translation and paraphrase for language education. In *Proceedings of the ACL Workshop on Neural Generation and Translation (WNGT)*. Association for Computational Linguistics.

Robert C. Moore and William Lewis. 2010. Intelligent selection of language model training data. In *Proceedings of the ACL 2010 Conference Short Papers*, pages 220–224, Uppsala, Sweden. Association for Computational Linguistics.

Myle Ott, Michael Auli, David Grangier, and Marc'Aurelio Ranzato. 2018. Analyzing uncertainty in neural machine translation. In *Proceedings of the 35th International Conference on Machine Learning*, volume 80 of *Proceedings of Machine Learning Research*, pages 3956–3965, Stockholmsmässan, Stockholm Sweden. PMLR.

Myle Ott, Sergey Edunov, Alexei Baevski, Angela Fan, Sam Gross, Nathan Ng, David Grangier, and Michael Auli. 2019. fairseq: A fast, extensible toolkit for sequence modeling. In *Proceedings of the 2019 Conference of the North American Chapter of the Association for Computational Linguistics (Demonstrations)*, pages 48–53, Minneapolis, Minnesota. Association for Computational Linguistics.

Peng Qi, Timothy Dozat, Yuhao Zhang, and Christopher D. Manning. 2018. Universal dependency parsing from scratch. In *Proceedings of the CoNLL 2018 Shared Task: Multilingual Parsing from Raw Text to Universal Dependencies*, pages 160–170, Brussels, Belgium. Association for Computational Linguistics.

Holger Schwenk, Vishrav Chaudhary, Shuo Sun, Hongyu Gong, and Francisco Guzmán. 2019. Wikimatrix: Mining 135m parallel sentences in 1620 language pairs from wikipedia. *CoRR*, abs/1907.05791.

Jörg Tiedemann. 2012. Parallel data, tools and interfaces in OPUS. In *Proceedings of the Eighth International Conference on Language Resources and Evaluation (LREC'12)*, pages 2214–2218, Istanbul, Turkey. European Language Resources Association (ELRA).

Ashish Vaswani, Noam Shazeer, Niki Parmar, Jakob Uszkoreit, Llion Jones, Aidan N Gomez, Ł ukasz Kaiser, and Illia Polosukhin. 2017. Attention is all you need. In I. Guyon, U. V. Luxburg, S. Bengio, H. Wallach, R. Fergus, S. Vishwanathan, and R. Garnett, editors, *Advances in Neural Information Processing Systems 30*, pages 5998–6008. Curran Associates, Inc.

Winston Wu, Garrett Nicolai, and David Yarowsky. 2020. Multilingual dictionary based construction of core vocabulary. In *Proceedings of The 12th Language Resources and Evaluation Conference*, pages 4204–4210, Marseille, France. European Language Resources Association.

Simultaneous paraphrasing and translation by fine-tuning Transformer models

Rakesh Chada
Amazon.com, Inc.,
rakchada@amazon.com

Abstract

This paper describes the third place submission to the shared task on simultaneous translation and paraphrasing for language education at the 4th workshop on Neural Generation and Translation (WNGT) for ACL 2020. The final system leverages pre-trained translation models and uses a Transformer architecture combined with an oversampling strategy to achieve a competitive performance. This system significantly outperforms the baseline on Hungarian (27% absolute improvement in Weighted Macro F1 score) and Portuguese (33% absolute improvement) languages.

1 Introduction

This paper describes the third place submission to the shared task Mayhew et al. (2020) on simultaneous translation and paraphrasing for language education at the 4th workshop on Neural Generation and Translation (WNGT) for ACL 2020. The shared task involves generating multiple translations for a given source text in English and a target language. The five target languages in the task are Hungarian (hu), Portuguese (pt), Japanese (ja), Korean (ko) and Vietnamese (vi). We competed in the Hungarian and Portuguese tracks. A goal of the shared task, hosted by Duolingo, is to enable development of automated grading processes and curation systems for language learners' responses. A high-coverage and precise multi-output translation and paraphrasing system would vastly help such automated efforts. For the task, participants were provided with hand-crafted and field-tested sets of several possible translations for each English sentence. Each of these translations were also ranked and weighted according to actual learner response frequency and these weights were provided as additional features. Along with these, translations from AWS were provided as a baseline and additional data. The challenges associated with

the shared task are two-fold: i) Translating from English to target languages and ii) Producing multiple valid translations (paraphrases) while balancing precision with the coverage. We conduct several experiments to address these two challenges and develop a simple system that leverages pre-trained transformer Vaswani et al. (2017) models and a wide beam search strategy. Furthermore, we leverage the provided translation scores and experiment with multiple training distribution strategies to develop a simple oversampling strategy that produces improvements over the vanilla method of using one translation one time.

2 Related work

Paraphrasing and machine translation are well-studied research areas in general but there's not much research specifically in the context of multi-output translation systems, especially for low resource languages. Tan et al. (2019) train a Transformer-based Neural Machine Translation model for Hungarian-English and Portugese-English translation. However, their goal was to assess the benefits of multilingual modeling by clustering languages and is different from that of a multi-output translation system. For English-Portuguese, Aires et al. (2016) build a phrase-based machine translation system to translate biomedical texts. For multilingual parahrasing, Ganitkevitch and Callison-Burch (2014) release a database consisting of paraphrases for several languages, including Hungarian and Portuguese, at lexical, phrasal and syntactic level. Guo et al. (2019) build a zero-shot multilingual paraphrase generation model to show mixed results. However, their end goal was to generate paraphrases in the same language (English) as opposed to our shared task which requires generating paraphrases in a different language.

Proceedings of the 4th Workshop on Neural Generation and Translation (WNGT 2020), pages 198–203
Online, July 10, 2020. ©2020 Association for Computational Linguistics
www.aclweb.org/anthology/D19-56%2d

Target Language	Train						Dev	Test
	Prompts	Pairs	MSL	MTL	99p SL	99p TL	Prompts	Pairs
Hungarian (hu)	4000	251442	21	21	11	14	500	500
Portuguese (pt)	4000	526466	33	21	25	15	500	500

Table 1: Dataset statistics. MSL=Maximum Source Length. MTL=Maximum Target Length. 99p SL=99th percentile Source Length. 99p TL=99th percentile Target Length.

Ippolito et al. (2019) study diverse decoding methods on conditional language models and show promising results on movie dialogue corpus and image captioning tasks.

3 Task

We describe dataset statistics and evaluation metrics in this section.

3.1 Data

There are two phases of the competition - Dev and Test. Table 1 shows data statistics for all phases. There were 4000 train prompts provided, in English, for both Hungarian and Portuguese languages. However, each of these prompts were accompanied with multiple translations leading to 251,442 English-Hungarian (en-hu) pairs and 526,466 English-Portuguese (en-pt) pairs. There were 500 prompts in both dev and test phases. After tokenization, for en-hu, most of the source sentences were shorter than 11 tokens and target sentences were shorter than 14 tokens. For en-pt, most of the source sentences were shorter than 25 tokens and target sentences were shorter than 15 tokens.

3.2 Evaluation Metrics

The main scoring metric for the competition is the weighted macro F1 score. This is a measure of how well the system returns all human-curated translations weighted by the likelihood that an English learner would respond with each translation. For each prompt p, weighted macro F1 is calculated as the harmonic mean of precision and weighted recall (note that the precision is unweighted). To calculated weighted recall for each example, we first calculate Weighted True Positives (WTP) and Weighted False Negatives (WFN) as:

$$WTP_p = \sum_{t \in TP_p} weight(t)$$

$$WFN_p = \sum_{t \in FN_p} weight(t)$$

Then, weighted recall (WR) is calculated as:

$$WR_p = \frac{WTP_p}{WTP_p + WFN_p}$$

The weighted Macro F1 (WF) over all prompts P is then calculated by averaging over all prompts in the corpus as:

$$WF = \sum_{p \in P} \frac{WF_p}{|P|}$$

4 System Design

We now describe the final submitted system design in detail. We have experimented with several other variants and describe these in a later section 5.

4.1 Data sampling

For the final system, we chose to use weighted sampling of the data where the weights correspond to the provided learner response frequency. Specifically, we multiply the frequency of the translation (a number between 0 and 1) with a heuristic value of 50 and duplicate the source-translation pair that many number of times. In effect, this would create repeated samples of certain pairs whose frequency is greater than 0.02 while eliminating pairs whose frequency is less than 0.02. With this sampling, we end up with 40,500 en-hu pairs and 42,000 en-pt pairs. We separate 15% of the provided prompts as a validation set. The performance on this validation set is used to pick the best model.

4.2 Preprocessing

For text pre-processing, we use sentencepiece tokenization Kudo and Richardson (2018) for en-hu and byte-pair encoding Sennrich et al. (2016) for en-pt data. We use pre-trained tokenization models provided in OPUS-MT.

4.3 Model Architecture

The final submitted model architecture, shown in Figure 1, uses the standard Transformer sequence-to-sequence model. This has 6 encoder and 6 decoder layers and an 8-headed attention mechanism

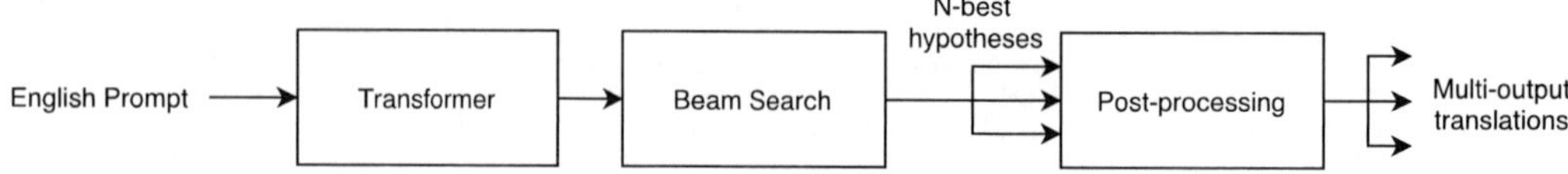

Figure 1: Architecture of the final system

in both encoder and decoder. We initialize the model with the pre-trained representations obtained from the OPUS-MT data. This model is then fine-tuned on the task data. We tie the encoder, decoder and output embedding weights and use a shared vocab size of 60,522. For position-wise feed-forward layers, the Swish activation function Ramachandran et al. (2018) is used. The whole model is fine-tuned, through an early stopping mechanism, on the dataset constructed as detailed in 4.1 .

For fine-tuning, we use the standard cross-entropy loss objective on the target sequence along with a label smoothing loss Szegedy et al. (2016).

For decoding, we use beam search with a beam size of 10 and select top 10 hypotheses for en-hu track. For en-pt track, we use a beam size of 28 and select top 28 hypotheses. We implement the model in Marian NMT Junczys-Dowmunt et al. (2018).

4.4 Postprocessing

The beam search outputs scores for each individual token. These scores represent the log likelihood of that token in the output sentence. As a post-processing step, we remove all translation predictions where the maximum of these token-level scores is less than -3.5. This value was determined by studying the impact of the maximum score thresholding on validation set performance.

4.5 Hyperparameters

We use the following hyperparameters. Batch size is set to 500. Dropout is set to 0.1. Label smoothing is set to 0.1. We use Adam optimizer with learning rate of 3e-4, β_1=0.9, β_2=0.98 and epsilon = 1e-9. We decay the learning rate by an inverse square root mechanism for 16000 steps. The gradient clip norm is set to 5. And patience for early stopping is set to 5.

5 Ablations

5.1 Ablations

We have performed several ablation studies on the en-hu task. The results of all these studies are listed in Table 3. We list the experiment methodologies below.

No fine-tuning: Here, we applied the pre-trained translation model directly on the task without any fine-tuning. The decoding was done using beam search beam size of 12 and by selecting top 12 hypotheses (determined based on validation performance).

No oversampling: Here, we use all provided translation pairs without any filtering based on the learner response frequency. We fine-tune the pre-trained model on this dataset and decode using beam search with a beam size of 15 and selecting top 15 hypotheses.

No post-processing: This is the same as the final submitted model without the post-processing (maximum score thresholding).

6 Other Modeling Variants

We experimented with different modeling alternatives for the shared task. We describe them in this section. The results of these variations are listed in Table 4.

6.1 Multi-output sequence formulation

Here, we re-formulate the task as a multi-output prediction task by taking the top 5 translation pairs (based on the learner response frequency) and concatenating them into a single target sequence. The pre-trained model is then fine-tuned on this dataset.

Nucleus sampling: Here, we use the above multi-output sequence model and add Nucleus sampling Holtzman et al. (2019) while decoding with p value set to 0.95.

6.2 Back Translation

Here, we start with a pre-trained hu-en translation model. We then construct a hu-en dataset from the provided en-hu translation pairs. The pre-trained model is fine-tuned on this dataset. We apply this fine-tuned hu-en model on the provided reference AWS translations of the target hu sentences. With a beam size of 15 and top-5 hypotheses selection,

Model	Validation			Dev			Test		
	P	**WR**	**WF**	**P**	**WR**	**WF**	**P**	**WR**	**WF**
Fairseq Baseline (en-hu)	-	-	-	19.35	12.47	13.02	18.3	11.8	12.17
AWS Baseline (en-hu)	-	-	-	**84.6**	19.9	29.85	**86.8**	18.9	28.1
Fine-tuned Transformer (en-hu)	75.14	50.34	56.72	75.2	**55.2**	**59.8**	75.5	**49.2**	**55.08**
Fairseq Baseline (en-pt)	-	-	-	29.86	13.3	15.14	28.2	11.7	13.57
AWS Baseline (en-pt)	-	-	-	**86.8**	14.09	21.15	**87.8**	13.9	21.3
Fine-tuned Transformer (en-pt)	72.14	49.22	54.25	69.96	**52.55**	**55.03**	72.06	**50.11**	**54.39**

Table 2: Final submission results. **Bold** indicates best performance. P=Precision. WR=Weighted Recall. WF=Weighted Macro F1.

Model	Validation						
	P	**R**	**WR**	**MiF**	**MaF**	**WMiF**	**WMaF**
No fine-tuning	52.41	6.32	41.18	11.28	19.21	46.12	41.31
No oversampling	58.40	13.26	46.70	**21.62**	**32.34**	51.90	45.98
No post-processing	74.04	9.28	49.71	16.49	28.81	59.49	54.93

Table 3: Performance of various en-hu ablations on validation dataset. **Bold** indicates best performance. R=Recall. MiF=Micro F1. MaF=Macro F1. WMiF=Weighted Micro F1. WMaF=Weighted Macro F1.

Model	Validation						
	P	**R**	**WR**	**MiF**	**MaF**	**WMiF**	**WMaF**
Multi-output sequence	**74.44**	7.33	44.35	13.35	23.58	55.59	52.29
Nucleus sampling	72.98	7.70	45.13	13.93	24.27	55.77	52.67
Back Translation	70.98	7.42	44.45	13.43	23.63	54.67	52.08
Model-based Prediction Filtering	72.71	**10.60**	**51.90**	18.51	31.01	**60.56**	**56.10**

Table 4: Performance of modeling variants on en-hu validation dataset. **Bold** indicates best performance.

we generate 5 English paraphrases for each given English prompt. Now, the en-hu fine-tuned model from the "Multi-output sequence formulation" ablation is made to predict separately for each of the generated English paraphrases and all the outputs are combined into the final prediction.

6.3 Model-based Prediction Filtering

Here, we start with the final submission model and build a binary XGBoost classifier on top of it to filter predictions (accept vs reject). The features of the XGBoost model are the token-level scores, as described in Section 4.4, that are obtained from the final submission model. As different sequences have different lengths, we build a fixed size feature vector by truncating or padding all sequences to a length of 11. This is the 99 percentile source length listed in Table 1. The binary labels for training are obtained by comparing output translation with the provided gold translations. We do a randomized search on "max_depth", "colsample_bytree", "colsample_bylevel" and "n_estimators" hyperparameters of the XGBoost model to find the best set of values. We then perform a 5-fold cross-validation to identify the best model. The F1 score of this model on the "accept" class is 0.81 and on the "reject" class is 0.48. The overall accuracy is about 72%.

7 Results & Discussion

Table 2 shows results of the final submission, for en-hu and en-pt tracks, along with a comparison to the baseline. As per the main evaluation metric (Weighted Macro F1 score), our model outperforms the strong AWS baseline by a significant margin on both en-hu and en-pt tracks. For en-hu, the improvement is about 30 absolute points on the dev dataset and 27 points on the test dataset. For en-pt, the improvement is about 34 absolute points on the dev dataset and 33 absolute points on the test dataset. This model ranked 1st on the dev leaderboard and 2nd on the test leaderboard for en-hu track. It ranked 2nd on the dev leaderboard and 3rd on the test leaderboard for en-pt track.

Table 3 shows the results for several ablations for en-hu model listed in section 5. And Table 4 shows results for several modeling variants listed in section 6. There are several interesting observations to be made from these ablations and variants. First, there's a clear improvement of about 15.4 points in Weighted Macro F1 from fine-tuning the pre-trained model on the provided dataset. The simple post-processing strategy of score thresholding yielded a gain of about 1.79 absolute points. Similarly, there's also a big improvement of about 10.7 absolute points from the oversampling strategy we used (as opposed to no oversampling). However, this gap seemed to have been closed by a big margin (about 7 absolute points) through the multi-output sequence formulation and slightly more by adding Nucleus sampling on top of it. A separate approach that uses back translation seemed to also have yielded similar gains upon the "No oversampling" approach. The model-based prediction filtering yielded an improvement of about 4 abso-lute points. Interestingly, all of these variants still ended up inferior (by varying levels) to the simple oversampling + fine-tuning + post-processing strategy that was used for the final submission.

8 Summary

We describe the system for our submission to the shared task on simultaneous translation and paraphrasing for language education at the 4th workshop on Neural Generation and Translation (WNGT) for ACL 2020. The final submitted system leverages pre-trained translation models, with Transformer architecture, and an oversampling strategy to achieve competitive performance. For future, it'd be interesting to see if initializing the model with latest state-of-the-art sequence-to-sequence pre-trained models such as BART Lewis et al. (2019) and T5 Raffel et al. (2019) and fine-tuning could help boost performance. It would also be a promising direction to explore the benefit of using cross-lingual models such as XLM-Roberta Conneau et al. (2019). One way to use them would be to initialize the encoder part of the architecture with pre-trained representations. Given the shared representations, it might be interesting to see if concatenating several language pairs' train datasets and training a joint model produces additional benefits.

Acknowledgments

We thank the Duolingo team for providing the dataset and organizing the competition and thank reviewers for providing valuable feedback.

References

José Aires, Gabriel Lopes, and Luís Gomes. 2016. English-Portuguese biomedical translation task using a genuine phrase-based statistical machine translation approach. In *Proceedings of the First Conference on Machine Translation: Volume 2, Shared Task Papers*, pages 456–462, Berlin, Germany. Association for Computational Linguistics.

Alexis Conneau, Kartikay Khandelwal, Naman Goyal, Vishrav Chaudhary, Guillaume Wenzek, Francisco Guzmán, Edouard Grave, Myle Ott, Luke Zettlemoyer, and Veselin Stoyanov. 2019. Unsupervised cross-lingual representation learning at scale.

Juri Ganitkevitch and Chris Callison-Burch. 2014. The multilingual paraphrase database. In *Proceedings of the Ninth International Conference on Language Resources and Evaluation (LREC-2014)*, pages 4276–

4283, Reykjavik, Iceland. European Languages Resources Association (ELRA).

Yinpeng Guo, Yi Liao, Xin Jiang, Qing Zhang, Yibo Zhang, and Qun Liu. 2019. Zero-shot paraphrase generation with multilingual language models.

Ari Holtzman, Jan Buys, Maxwell Forbes, and Yejin Choi. 2019. The curious case of neural text degeneration. *ArXiv*, abs/1904.09751.

Daphne Ippolito, Reno Kriz, Joao Sedoc, Maria Kustikova, and Chris Callison-Burch. 2019. Comparison of diverse decoding methods from conditional language models. In *Proceedings of the 57th Annual Meeting of the Association for Computational Linguistics*, pages 3752–3762, Florence, Italy. Association for Computational Linguistics.

Marcin Junczys-Dowmunt, Roman Grundkiewicz, Tomasz Dwojak, Hieu Hoang, Kenneth Heafield, Tom Neckermann, Frank Seide, Ulrich Germann, Alham Fikri Aji, Nikolay Bogoychev, André F. T. Martins, and Alexandra Birch. 2018. Marian: Fast neural machine translation in C++. In *Proceedings of ACL 2018, System Demonstrations*, pages 116–121, Melbourne, Australia. Association for Computational Linguistics.

Taku Kudo and John Richardson. 2018. SentencePiece: A simple and language independent subword tokenizer and detokenizer for neural text processing. In *Proceedings of the 2018 Conference on Empirical Methods in Natural Language Processing: System Demonstrations*, pages 66–71, Brussels, Belgium. Association for Computational Linguistics.

Mike Lewis, Yinhan Liu, Naman Goyal, Marjan Ghazvininejad, Abdelrahman Mohamed, Omer Levy, Ves Stoyanov, and Luke Zettlemoyer. 2019. Bart: Denoising sequence-to-sequence pre-training for natural language generation, translation, and comprehension.

Stephen Mayhew, Klinton Bicknell, Chris Brust, Bill McDowell, Will Monroe, and Burr Settles. 2020. Simultaneous translation and paraphrase for language education. In *Proceedings of the ACL Workshop on Neural Generation and Translation (WNGT)*. ACL.

Colin Raffel, Noam Shazeer, Adam Roberts, Katherine Lee, Sharan Narang, Michael Matena, Yanqi Zhou, Wei Li, and Peter J. Liu. 2019. Exploring the limits of transfer learning with a unified text-to-text transformer.

Prajit Ramachandran, Barret Zoph, and Quoc V. Le. 2018. Searching for activation functions.

Rico Sennrich, Barry Haddow, and Alexandra Birch. 2016. Neural machine translation of rare words with subword units. In *Proceedings of the 54th Annual Meeting of the Association for Computational Linguistics (Volume 1: Long Papers)*, pages 1715–1725, Berlin, Germany. Association for Computational Linguistics.

Christian Szegedy, Vincent Vanhoucke, Sergey Ioffe, Jon Shlens, and Zbigniew Wojna. 2016. Rethinking the inception architecture for computer vision. *2016 IEEE Conference on Computer Vision and Pattern Recognition (CVPR)*, pages 2818–2826.

Xu Tan, Jiale Chen, Di He, Yingce Xia, Tao Qin, and Tie-Yan Liu. 2019. Multilingual neural machine translation with language clustering.

Ashish Vaswani, Noam Shazeer, Niki Parmar, Jakob Uszkoreit, Llion Jones, Aidan N Gomez, Łukasz Kaiser, and Illia Polosukhin. 2017. Attention is all you need. In *Advances in neural information processing systems*, pages 5998–6008.

The NiuTrans System for WNGT 2020 Efficiency Task

Chi Hu[†] Bei Li[†] Ye Lin[†] Yinqiao Li[†]
Yanyang Li[†] Chenglong Wang[†]
Tong Xiao[†‡] Jingbo Zhu[†‡]
[†]NLP Lab, Northeastern University, Shenyang, China
[‡]NiuTrans Reasearch, Shenyang, China
huchinlp@gmail.com, libei_neu@outlook.com,
{xiaotong, zhujingbo}@mail.neu.edu.com,

Abstract

This paper describes the submissions of the NiuTrans Team to the WNGT 2020 Efficiency Shared Task. We focus on the efficient implementation of deep Transformer models (Wang et al., 2019; Li et al., 2019) using NiuTensor[1], a flexible toolkit for NLP tasks. We explored the combination of deep encoder and shallow decoder in Transformer models via model compression and knowledge distillation. The neural machine translation decoding also benefits from FP16 inference, attention caching, dynamic batching, and batch pruning. Our systems achieve promising results in both translation quality and efficiency, e.g., our fastest system can translate more than 40,000 tokens per second with an RTX 2080 Ti while maintaining 42.9 BLEU on *newstest2018*.

1 Introduction

In recent years, the Transformer model and its variants (Vaswani et al., 2017; Shaw et al., 2018; So et al., 2019; Wu et al., 2019; Wang et al., 2019) have established state-of-the-art results on machine translation (MT) tasks. However, achieving high performance requires an enormous amount of computations (Strubell et al., 2019), limiting the deployment of these models on devices with constrained hardware resources.

The efficiency task aims at developing MT systems to achieve not only translation accuracy but also memory efficiency or translation speed across different devices. This competition constraints systems to translate 1 million English sentences within 2 hours. Our goal is to improve the quality of translations while maintaining enough speed. We participated in both CPUs and GPUs tracks in the shared task.

Our system was built with NiuTensor, an open-source tensor toolkit written in C++ and CUDA

based on dynamic computational graphs. NiuTensor is developed for facilitating NLP research and industrial deployment. The system is lightweight, high-quality, production-ready, and incorporated with the latest research ideas.

We investigated with a different number of encoder/decoder layers to make trade-offs between translation performance and speed. We first trained several strong teacher models and then compressed teachers to compact student models via knowledge distillation (Hinton et al., 2015; Kim and Rush, 2016). We find that using a deep encoder (up to 35 layers) and a shallow decoder (1 layer) gives reasonable improvements in speed while maintaining high translation quality. We also optimized the Transformer model decoding in engineering, such as caching the decoder's attention results and using low precision data type.

We present teacher models and training details in Section 2, then in Section 3 we describe how to obtain lightweight student models for efficient decoding. Optimizations for the decoding across different devices are discussed in Section 4. We show the details of our submissions and the results in Section 5. Section 6 summarizes this paper and describes future work.

2 Deep Transformer Teachers

2.1 Deep Transformer Architectures

Recent years have witnessed the success of transformer-based models in MT tasks. Many works (Dehghani et al., 2019; Zhang et al., 2019; Li et al., 2020) focus on designing new attention mechanisms and Transformer architectures. Shaw et al. (2018) extended the self-attention to consider the relative position representations or distances between words. Wu et al. (2019) replaced the self-attention components with lightweight and dynamic convolutions. Deep Transformer mod-

---

[1]https://github.com/NiuTrans/NiuTensor

Proceedings of the 4th Workshop on Neural Generation and Translation (WNGT 2020), pages 204–210
Online, July 10, 2020. ©2020 Association for Computational Linguistics
www.aclweb.org/anthology/D19-56%2d

els also attracted a lot of attention. Wang et al. (2018) proposed a multi-layer representation fusion approach to learn a better representation from the stack. Wang et al. (2019) analyzed the high risk of gradient vanishing or exploring in the standard Transformer, which place the layer normalization (Ba et al., 2016) after the attention and feed-forward components. They showed that a deep Transformer model can surpass the big one by proper use of layer normalization and dynamic combinations of different layers. In their method, the input of layer $l + 1$ is defined by:

$$x_{l+1} = \mathcal{G}\left(y_0, \ldots, y_l\right) \tag{1}$$

$$\mathcal{G}\left(y_0, \ldots, y_l\right) = \sum_{k=0}^{l} W_k^{(l+1)} \mathrm{LN}\left(y_k\right) \tag{2}$$

where y_l is the output of the $l_t h$ layer and W is the weights of different layers.

We employed the dynamic linear combination of layers Transformer architecture incorporated with relative position representations as our teacher network, call it Transformer-DLCL-RPR.

2.2 Training Details

We followed the constrained condition of the WMT 2019 English-German news translation task and used the same data filtering method as (Li et al., 2019). We also normalized punctuation and tokenized all sentences with the Moses tokenizer (Koehn et al., 2007). The training set contains about 10M sentences pairs after processed. In our systems, the data was tokenized, and jointly byte pair encoded (Sennrich et al., 2016) with 32K merge operations using a shared vocabulary. After decoding, we removed the BPE separators and de-tokenize all tokens.

We trained four teacher models using *newstest2018* as the development set with fairseq (Ott et al., 2019). Table 1 shows the results of all teacher models and their ensemble, where we report SacreBLEU (Post, 2018) and the model size. The difference between teachers is the number of encoder layers and whether they contain a dynamic linear combination of layers. All teachers have 6 decoder layers, 512 hidden dimensions, and 8 attention heads. We shared the source-side and target-side embeddings with the decoder output weights. The maximum relative length was 8, and the maximum position for both source and target was 1024. We used the Adam optimizer (Kingma

Model	Param.	BLEU
Transformer-35-6	152M	43.3
Transformer-35-6+DLCL	152M	43.7
Transformer-40-6	168M	44.5
Transformer-40-6+DLCL	168M	43.9
Ensemble	640M	45.5

Table 1: Results on *newstest18* - Teacher Models. 35-6 means that the model contains 35 encoder layers and 6 decoder layers.

and Ba, 2015) with $\beta_1 = 0.9$, $\beta_2 = 0.997$ and $\epsilon = 10^{-8}$ as well as gradient accumulation due to the high GPU memory footprint. Each model was trained on 8 RTX 2080Ti GPUs for up to 21 epochs. We batched sentence pairs by approximate length and limited input/output tokens per batch to 2048/GPU. Following the method of (Wang et al., 2019), we accumulated every two steps for a better batching. This resulted in approximately 56000 tokens per training batch. The learning rate was decayed based on the inverse square root of the update number after 16000 warm-up steps, and maximum learning rate was 0.002. Furthermore, we averaged the last five checkpoints in the training process for all models.

As shown in Table 1, the best single teacher model achieves 44.5 BLEU (beam size 4) on *newstest2018*. Then we obtained an improvement of 1 BLEU via a simple ensemble strategy used in (Li et al., 2019).

3 Lightweight Student Models

After the training of deep Transformer teachers, we compressed the knowledge in an ensemble into a single model through knowledge distillation (Hinton et al., 2015; Kim and Rush, 2016). Then we analyzed the decoding time of each part in the deep Transformer. We further pruned the encoder and decoder layers to improve the decoding efficiency.

3.1 Knowledge Distillation

Knowledge distillation approaches (Hinton et al., 2015; Kim and Rush, 2016) have proven successful in reducing the size of neural networks. They learn a smaller student model to mimic the original teacher network by minimizing the loss between the student and teacher output. We applied the sequence-level knowledge distillation on the teacher ensemble described in Section 2. We used the ensemble to generate multiple translations of

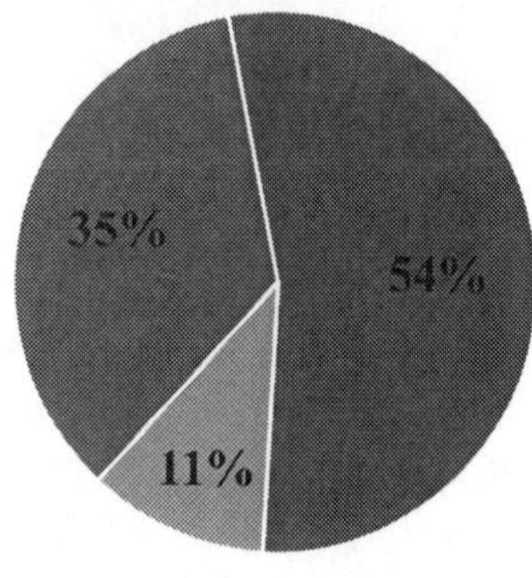

Figure 1: Profiling of the throughput during inference on *newstest2018* using a 35-6 model.

the raw English sentences. In particular, we collected the 4-best list for each sentence against the original target to create the synthetic training data. Our base student model consists of 35 encoder layers and six decoder layers (call it 35-6) with nearly 150M parameters. It achieves 44.6 BLEU on the test set.

3.2 Fast Student Models

Although the deep model can obtain high-quality translations, its speed is not satisfactory. For example, it costs 6.7 seconds to translate 2998 sentences on a 2080Ti GPU using a 35-6 model with the greedy search. Statistics show that the most time-consuming part of the decoding process is the decoder, as presented in Figure 1, so the most efficient optimization is to use a lightweight decoder. To make a comparison, we kept the 35 encoder layers and reduced the decoder layer to 1. In practice, we copied the bottom layers' parameters from big models to small models for initialization. Then we trained the small models as usual. Similar to (Wang et al., 2019), the encoder has a more significant influence on the translation quality than the decoder. Reducing the number of decoder layers brings us a speedup of more than 30% with a slight loss of 0.3 BLEU.

We further compressed the model by shrinking the encoder. Unless otherwise stated, the following student models have only one decoder layer. We copied the bottom layer parameters from big models to initialize small models to stabilize the training. We trained two small models with an 18-layer encoder and a 9-layer encoder, respectively. Table 2 shows the comparison of different teachers and students. Compared with the 35-1 model,

Model	Param.	Speedup	BLEU
Teacher-40-6	168M	1x	44.5
Student-35-6	152M	1.1x	44.6
Student-35-1	131M	1.6x	44.3
Student-18-1	77M	2.0x	43.4
Student-9-1	49M	2.4x	42.9
Student-tiny	25M	2.9x	37.2

Table 2: Results on *newstest18*. The students were trained by sequence-level knowledge distillation. The tiny setting keeps the 9-1 model's configurations except for using a model size of 256. We report the translation speed on a single 2080Ti.

cutting off half of the encoder layer reduces the parameters by nearly half and gives a speedup of 20% with a decrease of 0.2 BLEU. The 9-1 model is the fastest model we run on the GPU. It can translate *newstest2018* within 3 seconds on a 2080Ti GPU and obtain 42.9 BLEU.

All models mentioned above can translate 1 million sentences on the GPU in 2 hours. However, using a CPU to achieve this goal is not easy, so we need smaller models. We set the 9-1 model size to 256 for the CPU version, namely 9-1-tiny, which has only half the 9-1 model parameters. This model achieves 37.2 BLEU on *newstest2018* and reduces 90% parameters compared to the 35-6 model.

4 Optimizations for Decoding

4.1 General Optimizations

First, we discuss some device-independent optimization methods.

Caching   We can cache the output of the top layer of the encoder and each step of the decoder since we use an autoregressive model. More specifically, we cache the linear transformations for keys and values before the self-attention and cross-attention layers.

Faster Beam Search   Beam search is a common approach in sequence decoding. The standard beam search strategy generates the target sequence in a self-regression manner and keeps a fixed amount of active candidates during decoding. We adopt a basic strategy to accelerate beam search: the search ends when any candidate predicts the EOS symbol, and there are no candidates with higher scores. This strategy brings us up to a 20% speedup on the WMT test set. Other threshold-based pruning strategies (Freitag and Al-Onaizan, 2017) are not appropriate due to the complex hyper-parameters.

Batch Pruning　The length of target sequences may vary for different sentences in a batch, which makes the computation inefficient. We prune the finished hypotheses in a batch during decoding but only gain little accelerations on CPUs.

4.2　Optimizing for GPUs

For the GPU-based decoding, we mainly explored dynamic batching, FP16 inference, and profiling.

Dynamic Batching　Unlike the CPU version, the easiest way to reduce the translation time on GPUs is to increase the batch size within a specific range. We implemented a dynamic batching scheme that maximizes the number of sentences in the batch while limiting the number of tokens. This strategy significantly accelerates decoding compared to using a fixed batch size when the sequence length is short.

FP16 Inference　Since the Tesla T4 GPU supports calculations under FP16, our systems execute almost all operations in 16-bit floating-point. All model parameters are stored in FP16, which reduces the model size on disk by half. We tried to run all operations at a 16-bit floating-point. However, in our test, some particular inputs will cause numerical instability, such as large batch size or sequence length. To escape overflow, we convert the data type around some potentially problematic operations, i.e., all operations related to $reduce\_sum$.

4.3　Optimizing for CPUs

As mentioned above, the goal we set for the CPU version is to translate 1 million sentences in 2 hours. We used the same settings as the 9-1 model except that the model size is 256 and therefore sacrifice about 6 BLEU on the WMT test set. We employed two methods to speed up the decoding on CPUs.

Using of MKL　To make the full use of the Intel architecture and to extract the maximum performance, the NiuTensor framework is optimized using the Intel Math Kernel Library for basic operators. We can take advantage of this convenience with only minor changes to the configuration.

Decoding in Parallel　The target machine in this task has 96 logical processors (with hyper-threading) and 192 GB RAM so that we can run our multi-threading system. We split the input into several parts according to the number of lines and start multiple processes to translate simultaneously. Then we merge each part of translations to one file in the original order.

4.4　Other Optimizations

In addition to the methods above, we also tried to find the optimal settings for our system.

Greedy Search　In the practice of knowledge distillation, we find that our systems are insensitive to the beam size. It means that the translation quality is good enough even we use greedy search in all submissions.

Better decoding configurations　As mentioned earlier, our GPU versions use a large batch size, but the number on the CPU is much smaller. We use a fixed batch size (number of sentences) of 512 on the GPU and 64 on the CPU. We also set the number of processes on the CPU as 24 and use 2 MKL threads for each process. The maximum sequence length is 120 for the source and 200 for the target.

Profile-guided optimization　To further improve our systems' efficiency, we identified and optimized the performance bottlenecks in our implementation. There are many off-the-shelf tools for performance profiling such as the gprof[2] for C++ and the nvprof[3] for CUDA. We run our systems on the WMT test set for ten times and collect profile data for all functions. Figure 2(a) shows the profiling results for different operations on GPUs before optimizing. Before optimizing, the most time-consuming functions on CPUs is pre-processing and post-processing. We gain 2x speedup on CPUs by using multi-threads for Moses (4 threads) and replacing the Python subword tool with the C++ implementation[4].

For GPU-based decoding, the bottleneck is matrix multiplication and memory management. Therefore we use a memory pool to control allocation/deallocation, which dynamically allocates blocks during decoding and releases them after the translation finished. Compared with the on-the-fly mode, this strategy significantly improves the efficiency of our systems by up to 3x speedup and slightly increases the memory usage. We further remove the $log\_softmax$ in the output layer for greedy search and other data transfers with a slight acceleration of about 10%. Figure 2(b) shows the statistics of optimized operations. The data type conversion overhead takes about 12% of the decoding time.

---

[2]https://ftp.gnu.org/old-gnu/Manuals/gprof-2.9.1/html_node/gprof_toc.html
[3]http://docs.nvidia.com/cuda/profiler-users-guide/index.html
[4]https://github.com/glample/fastBPE

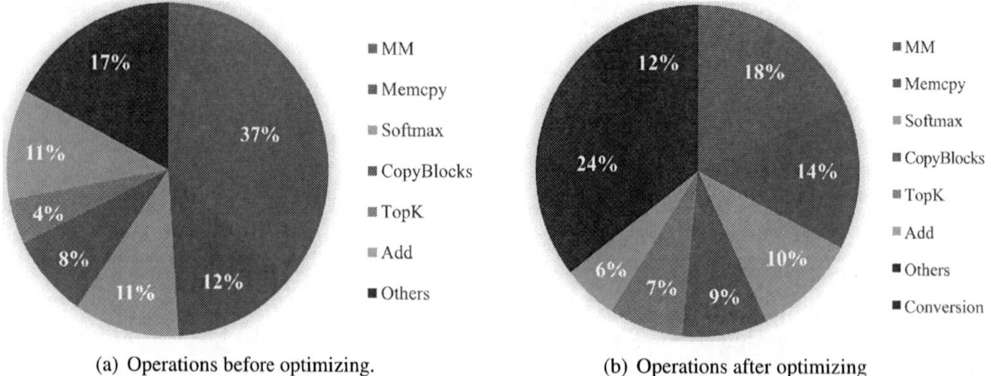

(a) Operations before optimizing.   (b) Operations after optimizing

Figure 2: Profiling results of all operations during inference before or after optimizing on *newstest2018* using a 9-1 model on a 2080Ti. We performed decoding for ten times to get more convincing results. Before optimizing, the decoding time is 76.9 seconds. The combination of different optimizations reduces the time to 24.9 seconds. MM is matrix multiplication, and CopyBlocks is used in the tensor copy.

5 Submissions and Results

We submitted five systems to this shared task, one for the CPU track and four for the GPU track, summarized as Table 3. We report file sizes, model architectures, configurations, metrics for translation, including BLEU on *newstest2018* and the real translation time on a combination of test sets. The BLEU and translation time were measured by the shared-task organizers on AWS c5.metal (CPU) and g4dn.xlarge (GPU) instances.

For the GPU tracks, our systems were measured on a Tesla T4 GPU. GPU versions were compiled with CUDA 10.1, and the executable file is about 96 MiB. Our models differ in encoder and decoder layers. The base model (35-6) has 35 encoder layers and six decoder layers and achieves 44.6 BLEU on the *newstest2018*. Then we see a speedup of more than one-third and a slight decrease of only 0.2 BLEU by reducing the decoder layer to 1 (35-1). We continue to reduce the number of encoder layers for more accelerations. The 18-1 system reduces the translation time by one-third with only half of the encoder layers compared to the 35-1 model. Our fastest system consists of 9 encoder layers and one decoder layer, which has one-third parameters of the 35-6 model, achieves 40 BLEU on the WMT 2019 test set, and speeds up the baseline by 3x.

For the CPU track, we used the entire machine, which has 96 virtual cores. Our CPU version is compiled with MKL static library, and the executable file is 22 MiB. We used a tiny model for the CPU with 256 hidden dimensions and kept other

hyper-parameters as the 9-1 model in the GPU version. Interestingly, using half of the hidden size significantly reduces the translation quality. The main reason is that the parameters of large models cannot be reused when using smaller dimensions. This also proves that reducing the number of encoder and decoder layers is a more effective compression method. The CPU system achieves 37.2 BLEU on the *newstest2018* and is 1.2x faster than the fastest GPU system.

We made fewer efforts to reduce the model size and memory footprint. Our systems use a global memory pool, and we sort the input sentences in descending order of length. Thus the memory consumption will reach a peak in the early stage of decoding and then decrease. Our base model contains 152 million parameters, and the file size is 291 MiB when stored in 16-bit floats. The docker image size ranges from 724 MiB to 930 MiB for our GPU systems, while the CPU version is 452 MiB. All systems running in docker are slightly slow down, and we plan to improve this in subsequent versions.

6 Conclusion

To maximize the decoding efficiency while ensuring sufficiently high translation quality, we explored different techniques, including knowledge distillation, model compression, and decoding algorithms. The deep encoder and shallow decoder networks achieve impressive performance in both translation quality and speed. We speed up the decoding by 3x with lightweight models and efficient

208

Model	MiB	Time	BLEU
Student-35-6	305	3166.4	44.6
Student-35-1	264	2023.3	44.3
Student-18-1	156	1355.0	43.4
Student-9-1	99	977.6	42.9
Student-9-1-tiny[†]	67	810.9	37.2

Table 3: Results of all submissions. [†] indicates the CPU system. All student systems were running with greedy search. The time was measured by the organizers on their test set and we only report the BLEU on the *newstest*2018.

implementations.

For the GPU system, we plan to optimize the FP16 inference by reducing the type conversion and applying kernel fusion (Wang et al., 2010) for Transformer models. For the CPU system, we will further speed up the inference by restricting the output vocabulary to a subset of likely candidates given the source (Shi and Knight, 2017; Senellart et al., 2018) and using low precision data type (Bhandare et al., 2019; Kim et al., 2019; Lin et al., 2020).

Acknowledgements

This work was supported in part by the National Science Foundation of China (Nos. 61876035 and 61732005) and the National Key R&D Program of China (No.2019QY1801). The authors would like to thank anonymous reviewers for their comments.

References

Jimmy Ba, Jamie Ryan Kiros, and Geoffrey E. Hinton. 2016. Layer normalization. *ArXiv*, abs/1607.06450.

Aishwarya Bhandare, Vamsi Sripathi, Deepthi Karkada, Vivek Menon, Sun Choi, Kushal Datta, and Vikram A. Saletore. 2019. Efficient 8-bit quantization of transformer neural machine language translation model. *ArXiv*, abs/1906.00532.

Mostafa Dehghani, Stephan Gouws, Oriol Vinyals, Jakob Uszkoreit, and Lukasz Kaiser. 2019. Universal transformers. *ArXiv*, abs/1807.03819.

Markus Freitag and Yaser Al-Onaizan. 2017. Beam search strategies for neural machine translation. In *Proceedings of the First Workshop on Neural Machine Translation*, pages 56–60, Vancouver. Association for Computational Linguistics.

Geoffrey E. Hinton, Oriol Vinyals, and Jeffrey Dean. 2015. Distilling the knowledge in a neural network. *ArXiv*, abs/1503.02531.

Yoon Kim and Alexander M. Rush. 2016. Sequence-level knowledge distillation. In *Proceedings of the 2016 Conference on Empirical Methods in Natural Language Processing*, pages 1317–1327, Austin, Texas. Association for Computational Linguistics.

Young Jin Kim, Marcin Junczys-Dowmunt, Hany Hassan, Alham Fikri Aji, Kenneth Heafield, Roman Grundkiewicz, and Nikolay Bogoychev. 2019. From research to production and back: Ludicrously fast neural machine translation. In *Proceedings of the 3rd Workshop on Neural Generation and Translation*, pages 280–288, Hong Kong. Association for Computational Linguistics.

Diederik P. Kingma and Jimmy Ba. 2015. Adam: A method for stochastic optimization. *CoRR*, abs/1412.6980.

Philipp Koehn, Hieu Hoang, Alexandra Birch, Chris Callison-Burch, Marcello Federico, Nicola Bertoldi, Brooke Cowan, Wade Shen, Christine Moran, Richard Zens, Chris Dyer, Ondřej Bojar, Alexandra Constantin, and Evan Herbst. 2007. Moses: Open source toolkit for statistical machine translation. In *Proceedings of the 45th Annual Meeting of the Association for Computational Linguistics Companion Volume Proceedings of the Demo and Poster Sessions*, pages 177–180, Prague, Czech Republic. Association for Computational Linguistics.

Bei Li, Yinqiao Li, Chen Xu, Ye Lin, Jiqiang Liu, Hui Liu, Ziyang Wang, Yuhao Zhang, Nuo Xu, Zeyang Wang, Kai Feng, Hexuan Chen, Tengbo Liu, Yanyang Li, Qiang Wang, Tong Xiao, and Jingbo Zhu. 2019. The NiuTrans machine translation systems for WMT19. In *Proceedings of the Fourth Conference on Machine Translation (Volume 2: Shared Task Papers, Day 1)*, pages 257–266, Florence, Italy. Association for Computational Linguistics.

Yanyang Li, Qiang Wang, Tong Xiao, T Liu, and Jingbo Zhu. 2020. Neural machine translation with joint representation. *ArXiv*, abs/2002.06546.

Ye Lin, Yanyang Li, Tengbo Liu, Tong Xiao, Tongran Liu, and Jingbo Zhu. 2020. Towards fully 8-bit integer inference for the transformer model. In *Proceedings of the Twenty-Ninth International Joint Conference on Artificial Intelligence*.

Myle Ott, Sergey Edunov, Alexei Baevski, Angela Fan, Sam Gross, Nathan Ng, David Grangier, and Michael Auli. 2019. fairseq: A fast, extensible toolkit for sequence modeling. In *Proceedings of the 2019 Conference of the North American Chapter of the Association for Computational Linguistics (Demonstrations)*, pages 48–53, Minneapolis, Minnesota. Association for Computational Linguistics.

Matt Post. 2018. A call for clarity in reporting BLEU scores. In *Proceedings of the Third Conference on Machine Translation: Research Papers*, pages 186–191, Brussels, Belgium. Association for Computational Linguistics.

Jean Senellart, Dakun Zhang, Bo Wang, Guillaume Klein, Jean-Pierre Ramatchandirin, Josep Crego, and Alexander Rush. 2018. OpenNMT system description for WNMT 2018: 800 words/sec on a single-core CPU. In *Proceedings of the 2nd Workshop on Neural Machine Translation and Generation*, pages 122–128, Melbourne, Australia. Association for Computational Linguistics.

Rico Sennrich, Barry Haddow, and Alexandra Birch. 2016. Neural machine translation of rare words with subword units. In *Proceedings of the 54th Annual Meeting of the Association for Computational Linguistics (Volume 1: Long Papers)*, pages 1715–1725, Berlin, Germany. Association for Computational Linguistics.

Peter Shaw, Jakob Uszkoreit, and Ashish Vaswani. 2018. Self-attention with relative position representations. In *Proceedings of the 2018 Conference of the North American Chapter of the Association for Computational Linguistics: Human Language Technologies, Volume 2 (Short Papers)*, pages 464–468, New Orleans, Louisiana. Association for Computational Linguistics.

Xing Shi and Kevin Knight. 2017. Speeding up neural machine translation decoding by shrinking runtime vocabulary. In *Proceedings of the 55th Annual Meeting of the Association for Computational Linguistics (Volume 2: Short Papers)*, pages 574–579, Vancouver, Canada. Association for Computational Linguistics.

David R. So, Chen Liang, and Quoc V. Le. 2019. The evolved transformer. *ArXiv*, abs/1901.11117.

Emma Strubell, Ananya Ganesh, and Andrew McCallum. 2019. Energy and policy considerations for deep learning in NLP. In *Proceedings of the 57th Annual Meeting of the Association for Computational Linguistics*, pages 3645–3650, Florence, Italy. Association for Computational Linguistics.

Ashish Vaswani, Noam Shazeer, Niki Parmar, Jakob Uszkoreit, Llion Jones, Aidan N. Gomez, Lukasz Kaiser, and Illia Polosukhin. 2017. Attention is all you need. *CoRR*, abs/1706.03762.

G. Wang, Y. Lin, and W. Yi. 2010. Kernel fusion: An effective method for better power efficiency on multithreaded gpu. In *2010 IEEE/ACM Int'l Conference on Green Computing and Communications Int'l Conference on Cyber, Physical and Social Computing*, pages 344–350.

Qiang Wang, Bei Li, Tong Xiao, Jingbo Zhu, Changliang Li, Derek F. Wong, and Lidia S. Chao. 2019. Learning deep transformer models for machine translation. In *Proceedings of the 57th Annual Meeting of the Association for Computational Linguistics*, pages 1810–1822, Florence, Italy. Association for Computational Linguistics.

Qiang Wang, Fuxue Li, Tong Xiao, Yanyang Li, Yinqiao Li, and Jingbo Zhu. 2018. Multi-layer representation fusion for neural machine translation. In *Proceedings of the 27th International Conference on Computational Linguistics*, pages 3015–3026, Santa Fe, New Mexico, USA. Association for Computational Linguistics.

Felix Wu, Angela Fan, Alexei Baevski, Yann Dauphin, and Michael Auli. 2019. Pay less attention with lightweight and dynamic convolutions. *ArXiv*, abs/1901.10430.

Biao Zhang, Ivan Titov, and Rico Sennrich. 2019. Improving deep transformer with depth-scaled initialization and merged attention. In *Proceedings of the 2019 Conference on Empirical Methods in Natural Language Processing and the 9th International Joint Conference on Natural Language Processing (EMNLP-IJCNLP)*, pages 898–909, Hong Kong, China. Association for Computational Linguistics.

Efficient and High-Quality Neural Machine Translation with OpenNMT

Guillaume Klein, Dakun Zhang, Clément Chouteau, Josep Crego, Jean Senellart

SYSTRAN, 5 rue Feydeau, 75002 Paris, France
`firstname.lastname@systrangroup.com`

Abstract

This paper describes the OpenNMT submissions to the WNGT 2020 efficiency shared task. We explore training and acceleration of Transformer models with various sizes that are trained in a teacher-student setup. We also present a custom and optimized C++ inference engine that enables fast CPU and GPU decoding with few dependencies. By combining additional optimizations and parallelization techniques, we create small, efficient, and high-quality neural machine translation models.

1   Introduction

This paper describes the OpenNMT (Klein et al., 2017) submissions to the Workshop on Neural Generation and Translation 2020 efficiency shared task. For WNMT 2018, we explored training and optimizations of small LSTM translation models combined with a customized runtime (Senellart et al., 2018). While this resulted in interesting decoding speed, there was still room for improvements in terms of quality, memory usage, and overall efficiency.

For this 2020 edition, we focus on the standard Transformer architecture (Vaswani et al., 2017) that is now commonly used in production machine translation systems. Similar to our first participation, we train smaller models using the teacher-student technique (Kim and Rush, 2016). We experiment with several encoder and decoder sizes following the work by Hongfei et al. (2020) which shows that reducing the number of decoder layers can improve decoding speed at a very limited accuracy cost.

We also keep the approach of running the models with a custom C++ runtime. This year we present CTranslate2[1], an optimized and production-grade

---

[1] `https://github.com/OpenNMT/CTranslate2`

inference engine for OpenNMT models that enables fast CPU and GPU decoding with few dependencies. This library implements several optimizations for decoding neural machine translation models such as 8-bit quantization, parallel translations, caching, and dynamic target vocabulary reduction.

Section 2 of this paper describes the data preparation and the training procedures we apply to train the candidate models. Section 3 presents the various optimizations we implemented to reduce model size and improve runtime efficiency. Finally, Section 4 details the accuracy and efficiency results achieved by the submitted models.

2   Teacher-student training

We train our systems using a teacher-student approach (Kim and Rush, 2016). First, a large model (the teacher) is trained on all available bilingual data, including synthetic data such as back-translations of monolingual target sentences (Sennrich et al., 2016; Edunov et al., 2018) and translations of monolingual source sentences (Zhang and Zong, 2016). Model ensembles are also typically used to build stronger teacher systems.

Then, a small model (the student) is trained by means of minimizing the loss between the student and teacher systems with the goal of distilling the knowledge of the teacher (Kim and Rush, 2016; Zhang et al., 2018) into a smaller model with comparable accuracy results. Crego and Senellart (2016) show that student models can even outperform to some extent their teacher counterparts.

Knowledge distillation is an effective approach to reduce the model size, thus lowering memory and computation requirements.

2.1   Teacher system

As suggested in the task description and given the limited amount of time available, we use Face-

Proceedings of the 4th Workshop on Neural Generation and Translation (WNGT 2020), pages 211–217
Online, July 10, 2020. ©2020 Association for Computational Linguistics
www.aclweb.org/anthology/D19-56%2d

book's WMT 2019 system as our teacher model (Ng et al., 2019). The system is trained as an ensemble of big Transformer models for both directions, English-German and German-English. Table 1 shows the BLEU (Papineni et al., 2002) evaluation results of this model over *newstest* public evaluation datasets.

	newstest2018	newstest2019
Facebook WMT 2019	49.1	42.1
Microsoft-Marian	48.3	44.9

Table 1: Evaluation of the teacher system on the English-German *newstest* files as reported by Sacre-BLEU (Post, 2018). The results for Microsoft-Marian are reported for comparison and retrieved from the WMT matrix[2].

2.2 Training data

We limit our training data to the WMT 2019 English-German translation task[3]. Table 2 summarizes the data provided by the task organizers which consist of more than 38M parallel sentences and 808M monolingual English sentences.

Corpora		# sents
	Europarl v9	1,838,568
	Common Crawl corpus	2,399,123
	News Commentary v14	338,285
Parallel	Wiki Titles v1	1,305,141
	Document-split Rapid	1,531,261
	ParaCrawl v3	31,358,551
	Total	38,770,929
	news-crawl 2007-2018	199,900,557
Mono	news-discuss 2011-2018	605,540,239
(Eng)	europarl-v9	2,295,044
	news-commentary-v14	545,919
	Total	808,281,759

Table 2: English-German parallel data and English monolingual data provided by the WMT 2019 translation task.

We use the following data to be translated by the Facebook's WMT 2019 teacher system: (a) English part of the bilingual data, (b) English part of ParaCrawl v3, and (c) English monolingual data.

Before translation, data is cleaned following several rules: sentences that are empty or longer than 100 tokens without considering tokenization are filtered out. We also use the language identification

[2]http://matrix.statmt.org/
[3]http://statmt.org/wmt19/
translation-task.html

(LID) toolkit `langid` (Lui and Baldwin, 2012) to further clean ParaCrawl and the English monolingual corpora which are known to contain a large number of noisy sentences. Nearly 5% of the sentences are discarded by the LID toolkit.

The cleaned data is then translated by the teacher model and the resulting synthesized parallel data is used to train the student systems[4].

2.3 Vocabulary

We build a joint subword segmentation model from the synthesized parallel data using SentencePiece (Kudo and Richardson, 2018). The vocabulary size is set to $32,000$ tokens. We removed the non-latin characters before building the vocabulary.

2.4 Student models

We train 4 different student systems based on the Transformer architecture (Vaswani et al., 2017). The candidate configurations are presented in Table 3. In addition to the base Transformer configuration, we train 3 model variants with different number of encoder layers N_{Enc}, decoder layers N_{Dec}, hidden size d_{model}, and feed-forward network size d_{ff}. We share both the source and target word embeddings and softmax weights in the 3 variants while the base configuration considers them as separate weights.

2.5 Student training

Since the amount of synthetic data is relatively large, we define an epoch as a random sampling of 5M sentences. We set the sampling weights of the selected data (a), (b), and (c) to 5, 2, and 2 respectively. That is, we consider a larger number of sentences synthesized from the English part of the bilingual data than from ParaCrawl or from the monolingual English data set.

We use the OpenNMT-tf[5] toolkit to train our student systems. Training is run on a single NVIDIA Tesla V100 GPU with an effective batch size of 25,000 tokens for the early epochs. Just before the final release, we train 10 additional epochs with a larger batch size by increasing the gradient update delay by a factor of 16 (Ott et al., 2018). Figure 1 shows the comparison with a larger batch size. We achieve an additional 0.1 to 0.2 BLEU using this

[4]Due to the long decoding time of the teacher system, the English monolingual data was partially translated. The final data pool used for training consists of: (a) 7.4M bilingual data, (b) 26.1M ParaCrawl data, and (c) 127M English monolingual data.
[5]https://github.com/OpenNMT/OpenNMT-tf

Transformer	N_{Enc}	N_{Dec}	h	d_{model}	d_{ff}	# params	newstest2018	newstest2019
Base	6	6	8	512	2048	93324544	46.7	43.0
(4:3 2xFFN)	4	3	8	256	2048	18221568	43.2	40.8
(6:3)	6	3	8	256	1024	16123904	43.0	40.3
(4:3)	4	3	8	256	1024	14544384	42.0	39.7

Table 3: Transformer configurations and their BLEU scores on *newstest2018* and *newstest2019*. Evaluation is performed without inference optimizations using OpenNMT-tf and a beam size of 4.

technique. Finally, we average the weights of the last 10 checkpoints to produce the final models.

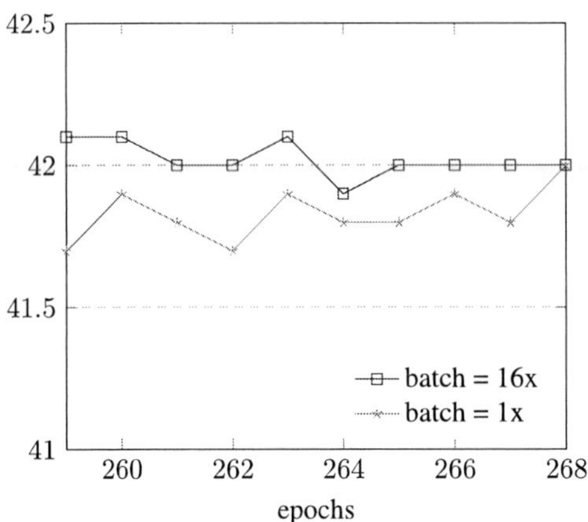

Figure 1: BLEU evaluations on larger batch size on *newstest2018*.

2.6 Evaluation

We list the number of parameters of the 4 trained models in Table 3 and their evaluation scores on the English-German *newstest2018* and *newstest2019* before any inference optimizations. The results correlate well with the expectation that more model parameters lead to better performance. The base Transformer model achieves better results on *newstest2019* than the Facebook's WMT 2019 model used as a teacher (43.0 vs. 42.1). This confirms the finding in Crego and Senellart (2016) that student systems can sometimes outperform their corresponding teacher networks.

3 Inference optimizations

All models are converted and executed with CTranslate2. We use the version 1.10.0 of the library.

3.1 CTranslate2 technical overview

CTranslate2 is a standalone C++ library that implements the complete logic of executing and decoding neural machine translation models with a focus on Transformer variants. This custom implementation supports CPU and GPU execution with the goal of being faster, lighter, and more customizable than a general-purpose deep learning framework. Key features of this project include model quantization, parallel translations, dynamic memory usage, and interactive decoding. Some of these features are difficult to implement effectively with standard deep learning frameworks and are the motivation for this project.

The CPU runtime is backed by Intel MKL, a popular math computation library optimized for Intel processors. We specialize operators with BLAS routines and Vector Mathematical functions whenever possible to benefit from vectorization. We also use the caching allocator provided by `mkl_malloc` and align allocated memory to 64 bytes. Other operations not available in Intel MKL are implemented in plain C++ using the STL and OpenMP.

The GPU runtime minimally requires the cuBLAS and Thrust libraries. Basic transformations are defined using Thrust while more complex layers such as layer normalization and softmax are using CUDA kernels ported from PyTorch (Paszke et al., 2019). We also integrate a caching allocator from the CUB library to reuse previously allocated buffers and minimize device synchronization.

3.2 8-bit quantization (CPU)

Quantization is a standard technique to reduce the model size in memory and accelerate its execution. We quantize the weights of linear and embedding layers to 8-bit signed integers after completing training. Experimental results show that model quantization can achieve high translation accuracy without making the training quantization-aware. We use the equation from Wu et al. (2016) to compute the quantized weight W^Q from the original weight W:

Quantization	Model size
None	373MB
16-bit	187MB
8-bit	94MB

Table 4: Effect of weight quantization on the model size on disk. The model is a base Transformer without shared embeddings.

$$s_i = \max_j |W_{i,j}|$$
$$W_{i,j}^Q = \left\lfloor \frac{127}{s_i} W_{i,j} \right\rfloor \tag{1}$$

Table 4 shows the effect of weight quantization on the final model size.

On CPU, we dynamically quantize the input of the linear layer using Equation 1, multiply the quantized input and weight with MKL's `cblas_gemm_s8u8s32` function, and dequantize the result before adding the bias term. In addition, we employ two notable techniques:

Weights pre-packing. On model load, we replace the quantized linear weights with the packed representation returned by MKL's packed GEMM API.

Unsigned compensation term. In row major mode, Intel MKL expects the input matrix a to be unsigned while the quantization Equation 1 produces signed values. To overcome this constraint, we shift a to the 8-bit unsigned domain and add a compensation term c to the output matrix. This compensation term only depends on the quantized weight matrix and can be computed once:

$$c_i = -128 \times \sum_{j=1}^{k} W_{i,j}^Q \tag{2}$$

On GPU, 8-bit computation is disabled as our implementation still requires some efficiency improvements regarding repetitive quantization and dequantization. In this case the weights are dequantized on load to single precision floating points.

3.3 Greedy decoding

To maximize speed and reduce memory usage, we use greedy search instead of beam search. During decoding, we also skip the final softmax layer and simply get the maximum from the output logits.

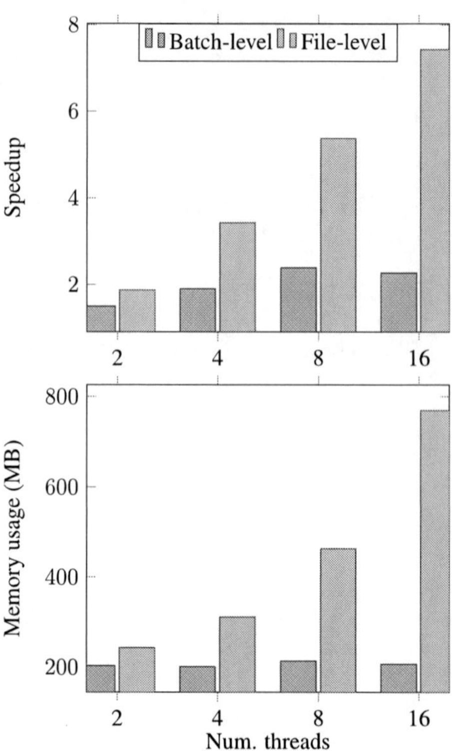

Figure 2: Speedup and memory usage for a base Transformer model when increasing the number of threads for batch translation, either at the batch level (left blue bars) or at the file level (right red bars).

3.4 Decoder projections caching

We apply the common technique of caching linear projections in the Transformer decoder layers. In particular, at step t the decoder self-attention layers compute $Attention(Q_t W^Q, Q_{1..t} W^K, Q_{1..t} W^V)$. As the matrix $Q_{1..t-1}$ is constant, we only compute $Q_t W^K$ and $Q_t W^V$ and concatenate the results to previous projections before calling the attention.

We also cache the encoder output projections KW^K and VW^V in the encoder-decoder attention layers as K and V remain constant during decoding.

For both cases, we transpose the matrices to delimit the attention heads before saving them in the cache.

3.5 File-level parallelism (CPU)

Figure 2 compares the observed speedup when increasing the number of threads at the batch level–the number of OpenMP threads–or at the file level–the number of batches processed in parallel. We use the same batch size in both cases.

As the number of threads increases, the first approach looses efficiency because not all operators within the model scale linearly and some of them are not parallelized at all. On the other hand, the second approach continues to improve as we add more threads because all batches are independent and the full decoding can be executed in parallel. However, the duplicated internal state of parallel translators increases memory usage. To mitigate this issue, we share the static model data among all parallel translators and read and write batches in a streaming manner while ensuring that the original order is preserved.

Given the large number of CPU cores available for this task, we chose to exploit parallelism at the file level to maximize the overall throughput. The number of parallel translators is set to the number of physical cores. Each translator is using a single thread so the decoding algorithm is executed sequentially and without OpenMP.

3.6 Sorted and dynamic batches

When setting the maximum batch size to N tokens, each consumer reads $8N$ contiguous tokens, sorts the sentences from the longest to the shortest, and then splits by batch of N tokens before running the model. The correct order is restored when returning the translation results. This local sorting makes the batches contain sentences of similar sizes which reduces the amount of padding and increases the computation efficiency.

We use $N = 6000$ for the GPU task, $N = 512$ for the single-core CPU task, and $N = 256$ for the multi-core CPU task.

During decoding we remove finished translations from the batch to avoid unnecessary computation. We also exploit the prior knowledge that short sentences finish early: by moving shorter sentences at then end of the batch, we reduce memory copies when updating the decoder cache in place.

3.7 Target vocabulary reduction

We generate a static source-target vocabulary mapping using the technique described in Senellart et al. (2018). We first train an alignment model with `fast_align` to align source and target words. To increase the coverage of this mapping, we build a phrase table from these alignments to extract the N-best translation hypotheses of 1-gram, 2-gram, ..., n-gram source sequences and include all target words in the mapping. We set $n = 3$ to generate

	Speed	BLEU
OpenNMT-tf	214.0	26.00
CTranslate2	242.5	26.00
+ int8	845.2	25.88
+ local sorting	1054.0	25.88
+ packed GEMM	1167.4	25.84
+ vocabulary reduction	1687.1	25.42

Table 5: Single-core greedy decoding speed (target tokens per second) for a base Transformer model. The BLEU scores are computed on an undisclosed test set and show the impact on quality (if any) of the enabled optimization.

the vocabulary mapping that are included in the models of this submission.

During decoding, we consider all 1-gram, 2-gram, and 3-gram sequences in the input batch and select the target tokens that are likely to appear in the translation according to the pretrained mapping as well as the 50 most frequent target tokens. These candidates are used to mask the weights of the final linear layer and effectively reduce its computational cost.

3.8 Docker images

The Docker images entrypoint is a small C++ main function that wraps the CTranslate2 and Sentence-Piece libraries and sets the decoding options that are relevant for this task.

We submit separate Docker images for CPU and GPU to only include the required dependencies. The images are based respectively on `ubuntu:18.04` and `nvidia/cuda:10.2-base-ubuntu18.04`. Without the model, the CPU image size is 104MB and the GPU image size is 210MB.

4 Optimization results

Table 5 shows the impact of selected optimizations when decoding a base Transformer model on a single CPU core. The CTranslate2 library combined with few optimizations can lead to a $8\times$ speedup with limited accuracy loss over a baseline Tensor-Flow program.

Finally, Table 6 summarizes the global impact of the optimizations described above that we compare against a baseline beam search decoding with OpenNMT-tf. For a base Transformer model, single-core CPU translation is $13\times$ faster while only loosing 0.8 BLEU points and GPU translation is $7\times$ faster for the same quality.

Transformer variant	Time (s)	BLEU
Baseline (single-core CPU)		
Base	522.1	43.0
(4:3 2xFFN)	251.5	40.8
(6:3)	238.7	40.3
(4:3)	238.0	39.7
Optimized (single-core CPU)		
Base	39.5	42.2
(4:3 2xFFN)	11.2	39.8
(6:3)	10.1	39.5
(4:3)	8.8	38.7
Optimized (multi-core CPU)[6]		
Base	5.2	42.0
(4:3 2xFFN)	2.5	39.7
(6:3)	2.5	39.3
(4:3)	2.3	38.5
Baseline (GPU)		
Base	57.6	43.0
(4:3 2xFFN)	40.7	40.8
(6:3)	41.6	40.3
(4:3)	42.1	39.7
Optimized (GPU)		
Base	7.7	43.0
(4:3 2xFFN)	4.0	40.1
(6:3)	3.9	39.9
(4:3)	3.8	39.0

Table 6: Time in seconds to translate *newstest2019* and BLEU scores as returned by SacreBLEU. The time includes model loading and tokenization. *Baseline* models are decoded with OpenNMT-tf using a beam of size 4; *Optimized* models are decoded with the final images submitted for this task. The runs were executed on a *c5.metal* AWS instance for CPU and a *g4dn.xlarge* instance for GPU.

5 Conclusion

We demonstrated that the OpenNMT ecosystem can be used to train efficient and high-quality neural machine translation models. The training frameworks–OpenNMT-tf and OpenNMT-py–include all features and procedures that are commonly applied to reach competitive translation scores. This year we presented CTranslate2, an optimized and production-grade inference engine for OpenNMT models that enables fast CPU and GPU decoding with few dependencies. By combining several optimizations and parallelization techniques, the library can drastically improve decoding speed and reduce memory usage over a general-purpose deep learning toolkit.

---

[6]The difference in BLEU score with the single-core runs comes from the smaller batch size which changes the candidates selected for reducing the target vocabulary.

References

Josep Maria Crego and Jean Senellart. 2016. Neural machine translation from simplified translations. *CoRR*, abs/1612.06139.

Sergey Edunov, Myle Ott, Michael Auli, and David Grangier. 2018. Understanding back-translation at scale. In *Proceedings of the 2018 Conference on Empirical Methods in Natural Language Processing*, pages 489–500, Brussels, Belgium. Association for Computational Linguistics.

Xy Hongfei, Deyi Xiong, Joseph van Genabith, and Liu Qiuhui. 2020. Analyzing word translation of transformer layers. *arXiv preprint arXiv:2003.09586v1*.

Yoon Kim and Alexander M. Rush. 2016. Sequence-level knowledge distillation. In *Proceedings of the 2016 Conference on Empirical Methods in Natural Language Processing*, pages 1317–1327, Austin, Texas. Association for Computational Linguistics.

Guillaume Klein, Yoon Kim, Yuntian Deng, Jean Senellart, and Alexander Rush. 2017. OpenNMT: Open-source toolkit for neural machine translation. In *Proceedings of ACL 2017, System Demonstrations*, pages 67–72, Vancouver, Canada. Association for Computational Linguistics.

Taku Kudo and John Richardson. 2018. SentencePiece: A simple and language independent subword tokenizer and detokenizer for neural text processing. In *Proceedings of the 2018 Conference on Empirical Methods in Natural Language Processing: System Demonstrations*, pages 66–71, Brussels, Belgium. Association for Computational Linguistics.

Marco Lui and Timothy Baldwin. 2012. langid.py: An off-the-shelf language identification tool. In *Proceedings of the ACL 2012 System Demonstrations*, pages 25–30, Jeju Island, Korea. Association for Computational Linguistics.

Nathan Ng, Kyra Yee, Alexei Baevski, Myle Ott, Michael Auli, and Sergey Edunov. 2019. Facebook fair wmt19 news translation task submission. In *Proceedings of the Fourth Conference on Machine Translation (Volume 2: Shared Task Papers, Day 1)*, pages 314–319, Florence, Italy. Association for Computational Linguistics.

Myle Ott, Sergey Edunov, David Grangier, and Michael Auli. 2018. Scaling neural machine translation. In *Proceedings of the Third Conference on Machine Translation: Research Papers*, pages 1–9, Brussels, Belgium. Association for Computational Linguistics.

Kishore Papineni, Salim Roukos, Todd Ward, and Wei-Jing Zhu. 2002. Bleu: a method for automatic evaluation of machine translation. In *Proceedings of the 40th Annual Meeting of the Association for Computational Linguistics*, pages 311–318, Philadelphia, Pennsylvania, USA. Association for Computational Linguistics.

Adam Paszke, Sam Gross, Francisco Massa, Adam Lerer, James Bradbury, Gregory Chanan, Trevor Killeen, Zeming Lin, Natalia Gimelshein, Luca Antiga, Alban Desmaison, Andreas Kopf, Edward Yang, Zachary DeVito, Martin Raison, Alykhan Tejani, Sasank Chilamkurthy, Benoit Steiner, Lu Fang, Junjie Bai, and Soumith Chintala. 2019. Pytorch: An imperative style, high-performance deep learning library. In H. Wallach, H. Larochelle, A. Beygelzimer, F. dAlché-Buc, E. Fox, and R. Garnett, editors, *Advances in Neural Information Processing Systems 32*, pages 8024–8035. Curran Associates, Inc.

Matt Post. 2018. A call for clarity in reporting BLEU scores. In *Proceedings of the Third Conference on Machine Translation: Research Papers*, pages 186–191, Belgium, Brussels. Association for Computational Linguistics.

Jean Senellart, Dakun Zhang, Bo Wang, Guillaume Klein, Jean-Pierre Ramatchandirin, Josep Crego, and Alexander Rush. 2018. OpenNMT system description for WNMT 2018: 800 words/sec on a single-core CPU. In *Proceedings of the 2nd Workshop on Neural Machine Translation and Generation*, pages 122–128, Melbourne, Australia. Association for Computational Linguistics.

Rico Sennrich, Barry Haddow, and Alexandra Birch. 2016. Improving neural machine translation models with monolingual data. In *Proceedings of the 54th Annual Meeting of the Association for Computational Linguistics (Volume 1: Long Papers)*, pages 86–96, Berlin, Germany. Association for Computational Linguistics.

Ashish Vaswani, Noam Shazeer, Niki Parmar, Jakob Uszkoreit, Llion Jones, Aidan N Gomez, Ł ukasz Kaiser, and Illia Polosukhin. 2017. Attention is all you need. In I. Guyon, U. V. Luxburg, S. Bengio, H. Wallach, R. Fergus, S. Vishwanathan, and R. Garnett, editors, *Advances in Neural Information Processing Systems 30*, pages 5998–6008. Curran Associates, Inc.

Yonghui Wu, Mike Schuster, Zhifeng Chen, Quoc V. Le, Mohammad Norouzi, Wolfgang Macherey, Maxim Krikun, Yuan Cao, Qin Gao, Klaus Macherey, Jeff Klingner, Apurva Shah, Melvin Johnson, Xiaobing Liu, Łukasz Kaiser, Stephan Gouws, Yoshikiyo Kato, Taku Kudo, Hideto Kazawa, Keith Stevens, George Kurian, Nishant Patil, Wei Wang, Cliff Young, Jason Smith, Jason Riesa, Alex Rudnick, Oriol Vinyals, Greg Corrado, Macduff Hughes, and Jeffrey Dean. 2016. Google's neural machine translation system: Bridging the gap between human and machine translation. *CoRR*, abs/1609.08144.

Dakun Zhang, Josep Crego, and Jean Senellart. 2018. Analyzing knowledge distillation in neural machine translation. In *15th International Workshop on Spoken Language Translation*.

Jiajun Zhang and Chengqing Zong. 2016. Exploiting source-side monolingual data in neural machine translation. In *Proceedings of the 2016 Conference on Empirical Methods in Natural Language Processing*, pages 1535–1545, Austin, Texas. Association for Computational Linguistics.

Edinburgh's Submissions to the 2020 Machine Translation Efficiency Task

Nikolay Bogoychev[†] Roman Grundkiewicz[†] Alham Fikri Aji[†] Maximiliana Behnke[†]

Kenneth Heafield[†] Sidharth Kashyap[‡] Emmanouil-Ioannis Farsarakis[‡] Mateusz Chudyk[††]

[†]University of Edinburgh
{n.bogoych,rgrundki,a.fikri,maximiliana.behnke,kenneth.heafield}@ed.ac.uk

[‡]Intel Corporation
{sidharth.n.kashyap,manos.farsarakis}@intel.com

[††]Samsung R&D Institute Poland
m.chudyk@samsung.com

Abstract

We participated in all tracks of the Workshop on Neural Generation and Translation 2020 Efficiency Shared Task: single-core CPU, multi-core CPU, and GPU. At the model level, we use teacher-student training with a variety of student sizes, tie embeddings and sometimes layers, use the Simpler Simple Recurrent Unit, and introduce head pruning. On GPUs, we used 16-bit floating-point tensor cores. On CPUs, we customized 8-bit quantization and multiple processes with affinity for the multi-core setting. To reduce model size, we experimented with 4-bit log quantization but use floats at runtime. In the shared task, most of our submissions were Pareto optimal with respect the trade-off between time and quality.

1 Introduction

This paper describes the University of Edinburgh's submissions to the Workshop on Neural Generation and Translation (WNGT) 2020 Efficiency Shared Task[1] using the Marian machine translation toolkit (Junczys-Dowmunt et al., 2018a). The task has GPU, single-core CPU, and multi-core CPU tracks. Our submissions focus on the trade-off between translation quality and speed; we also address model size after submission.

Starting from an ensemble of 4 transformer-big teacher models, we trained a variety of student configurations and on top of that sometimes pruned transformer heads. For the decoding process, we explored the use of lower precision GEMM for both our CPU and GPU submissions. Small models appear to be more sensitive to quantization than large models.

Most of our single-CPU submissions had a memory leak, which also impacted speed; we report results before and after fixing the leak.

2 Shared Task Summary

The task measures quality approximated by BLEU (Papineni et al., 2002), speed, model size, Docker image size, and memory consumption of a machine translation system from English to German for the WMT 2019 data condition (Barrault et al., 2019). We did not optimize Docker image size (using stock Ubuntu) or memory consumption (preferring large batches for speed).

The task intentionally did not specify a test set until after submissions were made. This was later revealed to be the average of BLEU from WMT test sets from 2010 through 2019, inclusive. However, the 2012 test set was excluded because it contains English sentences longer than 100 words and participants were promised input would be at most 100 words. We refer to the task's metric as WMT1*. All BLEU scores are reported using sacrebleu.[2]

The CPU tracks used an Intel Xeon Platinum 8275CL while the GPU track used an NVIDIA T4. For speed, the official input has 1 million lines of text with 15,048,961 space-separated words.

3 Teacher-student training

Following Junczys-Dowmunt et al. (2018b) and Kim et al. (2019), all our optimized models are students created using interpolated sequence-level knowledge distillation (Kim and Rush, 2016), and trained on data generated from a teacher system.

Teacher We used the sentence-level English-German system from Microsoft's constrained submission to the WMT'19 News Translation Task (Junczys-Dowmunt, 2019). It is an ensemble of four deep transformer-big models (Vaswani et al., 2017), each with 12 blocks of layers in encoder and decoder, model size of 1024, filter size of 4096,

---

[1] https://sites.google.com/view/wngt20/efficiency-task

[2] `BLEU+case.mixed+lang.en-de+numrefs.1+smooth.exp+test.wmt*+tok.13a+version.1.4.8` for various WMT test sets.

Proceedings of the 4th Workshop on Neural Generation and Translation (WNGT 2020), pages 218–224
Online, July 10, 2020. ©2020 Association for Computational Linguistics
www.aclweb.org/anthology/D19-56%2d

Model	Emb.	FFN	Enc./Dec. Depth	Voc.	Params.	Size	WMT16	BLEU WMT19	WMT1*
Teacher ×4	1024	4096	12/12	32k	385.5M	1.5GB	42.4	42.5	36.4
Large	1024	3072	6/6 tied	32k	108.4M	414MB	41.0	43.0	35.3
Base	512	2048	6/2 tied	32k	39.0M	149MB	40.0	42.7	34.6
Tiny.Untied	256	1536	6/2	32k	16.9M	65MB	39.0	42.1	33.4
Tiny	256	1536	6/2 tied	32k	15.7M	61MB	38.7	41.5	33.0
Tiny.8k	256	1536	6/2 tied	8k	9.6M	37MB	37.4	40.6	31.7
Micro.8k	256	1024	4/2 tied	8k	7.0M	27MB	35.7	38.8	30.0

Table 1: Architectures and reference BLEU scores (on a GPU) for the teacher and student models. Reported values are: size of embedding and filter layers, the number of encoder/decoder layers, vocabulary size, the total number of parameters, and model size on disk. WMT1* is defined in Section 2.

and 8 transformer heads.[3] The ensemble achieved 42.5 BLEU on the official WMT19 test set when decoded with beam size of 8. We refer the reader to the original paper for more details on how this system has been built.

Data and training Our student models were trained on pairs of original source and teacher-translated target sentences generated from parallel English-German datasets and English News Crawl data available for WMT19 (Barrault et al., 2019). For parallel data, we generated 8-best lists and selected translations with the highest sentence-level BLEU to reference sentences. Monolingual data was translated with beam size of 4. We filtered the data with language identification using Fast-Text[4] (Joulin et al., 2017), and then scored all sentence pairs with a German-English transformer-base model trained on a subset of original parallel data, about 7 million sentences. The obtained log probabilities were normalized with $\exp(0.1 \cdot p)$ and used for data weighting during training. We also removed ca. 5% of examples with worst scores from each dataset, except Paracrawl (Bañón et al., 2020), from which we used only 15M sentences with highest scores for processing. This procedure is similar to the single-direction step of the dual cross-entropy filtering method (Junczys-Dowmunt, 2018). The final training set consisted of 185M sentences, including 20M of originally parallel data.

All student models were trained using the concatenated English-German WMT test sets from 2016–2018 as a validation set[5] until BLEU has stopped improving for 20 consecutive validations, and select model checkpoints with highest BLEU scores. Since a student model should mimic the teacher as closely as possible, we did not use regularization like dropout and label smoothing. Other training hyperparameters were Marian defaults for training a transformer-base model.[6]

Student models All our students have standard transformer encoders (Vaswani et al., 2017) and light-weight RNN-based decoders with Simpler Simple Recurrent Unit (SSRU) (Kim et al., 2019), and differ in number of encoder and decoder blocks, and sizes of embedding and filter layers. Most models use shared vocabulary with 32,000 sub-word units created with SentencePiece (Kudo and Richardson, 2018), but we also experimented with a smaller vocabulary with only 8,000 units for model size optimized systems. Used student architectures are summarized in Table 1.

Interestingly, our student models do much better with originally English input, resulting in generally higher BLEU on the WMT19 test set w.r.t. the teacher's performance than on test sets from previous years, which consist of both translations and translationese. For example, the teacher achieves 42.4 and 42.2 BLEU on originally English and originally German subsets of the WMT16 test set, respectively, while the Base student model has 42.5 and only 35.6 BLEU. We think the reason for this is that student models were trained solely on teacher-translated data without back-translations.

4 Attention pruning

Attention is one of the most expensive operations in the transformer architecture, yet many of the heads can be pruned after training (Voita et al., 2019). Moreover, the lottery ticket hypothesis (Frankle

---

[3]This system refers to the (4×c) configuration in Table 2 from the original paper.

[4]`https://fasttext.cc/blog/2017/10/02/blog-post.html`

[5]The validation sentences were not teacher-translated.

[6]Available via `--task transformer-base`.

Model	Enc. heads	Params.	Size	BLEU WMT19	WMT1*	WPS
Tiny	8 8 8 8 8 8	15.7M	61MB	41.5	32.9	2050
Tiny.Steady.i12	2 0 1 2 3 4	14.5M	56MB	41.1	32.4	2282
Tiny.Steady.i14	0 0 1 1 1 3	14.3M	55MB	40.8	32.1	2350
Tiny.Pushy.i6	2 2 2 2 2 2	14.5M	56MB	41.4	32.4	2298
Tiny.Pushy.i7	1 1 1 1 1 1	14.3M	55MB	40.2	31.5	2346

Table 2: Students with pruned encoder attention. Words per second (WPS) is evaluated in *float32* with a single CPU core on the official input (Section 2).

and Carbin, 2018) and subsequent work on pruning optimisation (Frankle et al., 2019) suggests that pruning is less damaging during training rather than after training. Hence we combine these two ideas to prune attention heads during training.

Since we are starting from a relatively optimized model (Tiny in Table 1) whose decoder has one tied layer with SSRU self-attention, our pruning approach focuses on the 48 encoder heads. We apply a late resetting strategy that iteratively removes heads in short training loops (Frankle et al., 2019). This method starts by training the full model for 25k batches to create a checkpoint. Then we repeatedly train for 15k updates, remove N heads and revert the rest of the parameters to their value from the aforementioned checkpoint. Inspired by Voita et al. (2019), we calculate attention "confidence". Each time a head appears, we take the maximum of its attention weights. These maximums are then averaged across all appearances of the head to form a confidence score. Attention heads with high confidence are considered to contribute the most to the overall network performance. Thus, we remove the N least confident heads in each pruning iteration.

We try removing $N = 3$ or $N = 6$ heads per iteration, dubbing these Steady and Pushy in system names, respectively. Since the algorithm usually picks one head from each layer, the final architecture differs. For example, removing 6 heads per iteration results in a monotonic attention distribution across the 6 encoder layers. For submissions, we pruned 36 of the 48 heads; as an additional experiment we tried removing 42 of the 48 heads. The final attention distribution, size and BLEU scores for those models are presented in Table 2.

Considering that our students perform better on newer testsets, the pruning results show that it is possible to remove at least 75% of self-attention heads in an encoder with an average 0.4 BLEU loss. With harsher pruning, the model with even num-

bers of heads performs better than the one missing any from the first two layers. This indicates that, in extreme cases, it is better to have at least one head per layer than none. Since the dimension of each head was small (256 / 8 = 32), pruning has not reduced the overall size of the models drastically. The speed-up is about 10% on CPU with 75% encoder heads removed. In terms of on GPU, our best pruned model gains 15% speed-up w.r.t. words per second (WPS) losing 0.1 BLEU in comparison to an unpruned model (Tab. 4).

5 CPU optimizations

For our CPU optimization we build upon last year submission (Kim et al., 2019). We use the same lexical shortlist, but we extend the usage of 8bit integer quantized GEMM operations to also cover the shortlisted output layer in order to have faster computation and even smaller model size.

5.1 8-bit quantization

Quantization from 32-bit floats to 8-bit integers is well known (Kim et al., 2019; Bhandare et al., 2019; Rodriguez et al., 2018) and reportedly has minimal quality impact. For this year's submission, we used *intgemm*[7] instead of *FBGEMM*[8] as our 8bit GEMM backend. Vocabulary shortlisting entails selecting columns from the output matrix and *intgemm* can directly extract columns in its packed format. The packed format reduces memory accesses during multiplication. Users can also specify arbitrary postprocessing of the output matrix while it is still in registers before writing to RAM. Currently we use this to add the bias term in a streaming fashion, saving a memory roundtrip on the common $A * B + bias$ operation in neural network inference; in the future we plan to integrate activation functions.

---

[7] https://github.com/kpu/intgemm/
[8] https://github.com/pytorch/FBGEMM

Model	Size	*xzip* Size	BLEU			Words per second		
			WMT19	WMT1*		1 core Leak	1 core Fixed	Multi-core Fixed
Base + float32	149MB	135.0MB	42.6	34.53		843	843	19849
+ 8bit-untuned	38MB	25.4MB	42.5	34.29		Out of RAM	1648	39100
+ log-4bit	19MB	15.8MB	42.3	34.10			Run as *float32*	
Tiny + float32	65MB	58.9MB	41.5	32.91		2220	2220	47030
+ 8bit	17MB	11.2MB	41.6	32.89		1028	3135	70037
+ log-4bit	8MB	6.7MB	40.0	31.46			Run as *float32*	
Tiny.8k + float32	37MB	33.4MB	40.6	31.70		1956	1956	42085
+ 8bit	9MB	7.0MB	39.5	30.61		Not submitted	2664	60011
+ log-4bit	5MB	4.1MB	37.5	28.51			Run as *float32*	
Micro.8k + float32	27MB	21.6MB	38.8	30.03		2459	2459	53204
+ 8bit	7MB	4.4MB	37.5	29.01		2094	3229	79992

Table 3: Model sizes, average BLEU scores and speed for quantized models. For the official submission we only used the 8-bit quantized models. More information about the unquantized models can be found in Table 1. The suffix "-untuned" means the model was quantized without continued training. In the multi-core setting, fixing the memory leak had minor impact on speed so we only report fixed numbers. Here, size excludes a 315 KB sentence piece model and an optional (but useful for speed) 11 MB lexical shortlisting file.

Last year (Kim et al., 2019), parameters were quantized and packed offline from a fully trained model. This year, we noticed quality degradation when quantizing smaller models and therefore introduced continued training. Continued training ran for 5000–7000 mini-batches, emulating 8-bit GEMM by quantizing the activations and weights then restoring them to 32-bit values, borrowing from methods used for 4-bit quantization (Aji and Heafield, 2019).

Quantization entails computing a scaling factor to collapse the range of values to $[-127, 127]$. For parameters, this scaling factor is computed offline using the maximum absolute value[9] but activation tensors change at runtime. This year, we changed from computing a dynamic scaling factor on the fly for activations to computing a static scaling factor offline. We decoded the WMT16 dataset and recorded the scaling factor $\alpha(A_i) = 127/max(|A_i|)$ for each instance A_i of an activation tensor A. Then, for production, we fixed the scaling factor for activation tensor A to the mean scaling factor plus 1.1 standard deviation: $\alpha(A) = \mu(\{\alpha(A_i)\}) + 1.1 * \sigma(\{\alpha(A_i)\})$. These scaling factors were baked into the model file so that statistics were not computed at runtime.

All parameter matrices are prepared either offline, or when decoding the first word (in the case of the output layer) and later on they are reused for the GEMM operations (or in the case of the output layers, columns associated with vocabulary items are extracted from the prepared matrix).

For the GEMM operations at the attention layer, we used *cblas_sgemm_batched* from Intel's *MKL* Library. Model sizes, translation quality and speed are reported in Table 3.[10]

Memory leak Most of our CPU submissions had a memory leak due to failing to clear a cache of shortlisted output matrices. Hence our official CPU submissions using intgemm had unreasonable memory consumption after translating 1 million lines as specified in the shared task. In one case, this exceeded 192 GB RAM on the c5.metal instance and a submission was disqualified; in other cases the submissions ran but used too much RAM and likely more CPU time as a consequence. In practise, the negative effect on speed was only evident in the single core submissions because multi-core submissions divided work across processes.

5.2 Log 4-bit quantization

Model parameters follow normal distribution: most of them are near-zero. Therefore, a fixed-point quantization mechanism such as in Section 5.1 is not suitable when quantizing to lower precision. We can achieve a better model size compression by using a logarithmic 4-bit quantization (Aji and Heafield, 2019).

We start by quantizing a baseline model into 4-bit precision. We leave the biases unquantized as they do not follow the same distribution as the rest

---

[9]We tried a variety of statistics, including minimizing mean squared error, but none worked as well as continued training.

[10]Code for these models is at `https://github.com/marian-nmt/marian-dev/tree/intgemm_reintegrated_computestats`

of the parameters matrices and therefore quantize poorly. Moreover, the compression rate is practically unaffected since the biases are small in terms of number of parameters. Finally, the model must be fine tuned under 4-bit precision to restore the quality lost by quantization.

With 4-bit precision, we can achieve around 8x model size reduction. While 4-bit log quantization is in principle hardware-friendly since it uses only adds and shifts, current CPUs and GPUs do not natively support it (GPUs do support 4-bit fixed-point quantization, but this reduced quality compared to log quantization). The additional instructions required to implement 4-bit arithmetic made inference slower than with native 8-bit operations. Therefore, we focus on model size, useful for downloading, and dequantize before running the model in *float32*.

Model sizes and BLEU scores are reported in Table 3. Generally, quantizing the model is a better choice when aiming for lower model size, compared to reducing model parameters. For example, Base + log-4bit is as small as 19MB, while losing just 0.4 BLEU compared to the baseline. In contrast, the Tiny model is 65MB, but loses 1.5 BLEU compared to the *float32* and the *int8* settings.

We see that 4-bit log quantization achieves the best size and performance trade-off. For example, our Base + log-4bit (19MB) achieves the highest average BLEU of 34.1 among other models of similar size, such as Tiny + 8bit (17MB, 32.89 BLEU). Similarly, Our Tiny + log-4bit (8MB) achieves an average BLEU of 31.46, compared to others with similar range, for example Micro.8k + 8bit (9MB, 30.61 BLEU). However, larger models are more robust towards extreme quantization, compared to smaller models. Our Tiny.8k + log-4bit degrades significantly in terms of quality.

5.3 Multi-core configuration

For the multi-core track, we swept configurations of multiple processes and threads, settling on 24 processes with 2 threads each. The input text is simply split into 24 pieces and parallelized over processes. The mini-batch sizes did not impact performance substantially and 32 was chosen as the mini-batch size. The code profile under *VTune* revealed that the performance was limited by memory bandwidth, hence, the Hyperthreads available on the platform were not put into use and the 48 cores were saturated using 24 processes (Tange,

| Model | BLEU | | |
	WMT19	WMT1*	WPS
Large ($\star$)	43.0	35.27	2748
- w/o 16-bit	43.0	35.29	1764
- w/o shortlist	43.0	35.29	1775
Base ($\star$)	42.7	34.54	6138
Tiny.Untied ($\star$)	41.9	33.27	7602
Tiny	41.5	32.90	8210
Tiny.Steady.i12	41.4	32.36	9518
Tiny.Pushy.i6 ($\star$)	41.0	32.40	9508

Table 4: Performance of student models measured on an AWS *g4dn.xlarge* instance with one NVidia T4 GPU. BLEU scores, total translation times, and word per seconds (WPS). Models with ($\star$) have been submitted to the GPU track.

2011) running 2 threads each. Each process was bound to two cores assigned sequentially and to the memory domain corresponding to the socket with those cores using *numactl*. Output from the data-parallel run is then stitched together to produce the final translation.

6 GPU systems

This year, we did not implement any GPU-specific optimizations and focused on comparing the performance of student architectures, developed for CPU decoding, on the GPU. We made 4 submissions to the GPU track. The results for all student models, averaged across 3 runs are reported in Table 4. We decode on GPU using batched translation with mini-batch of 256 sentences, pervasive FP16 inference, and lexical shortlists (Kim et al., 2019). These are features already available in Marian 1.9.

The average speed-up from decoding in 16-bit floats is 21%, depending on the model architecture. The larger the model size, the larger speed improvement, with as high as 56% improvement for the Large student model, through 32% for Base, and only 13-18% for Tiny models. This is with barely any change in BLEU, lower than ±0.1. Models with pruned transformer heads are faster than the original Tiny model by 15% on GPU, but decrease the accuracy by 0.1-0.5 BLEU on the WMT19 test set. On this relatively small data set, we notice a small translation speed decrease of up to 2% from using lexical shortlists. Running concurrent streams on a single GPU did not yield significant improvements for us.

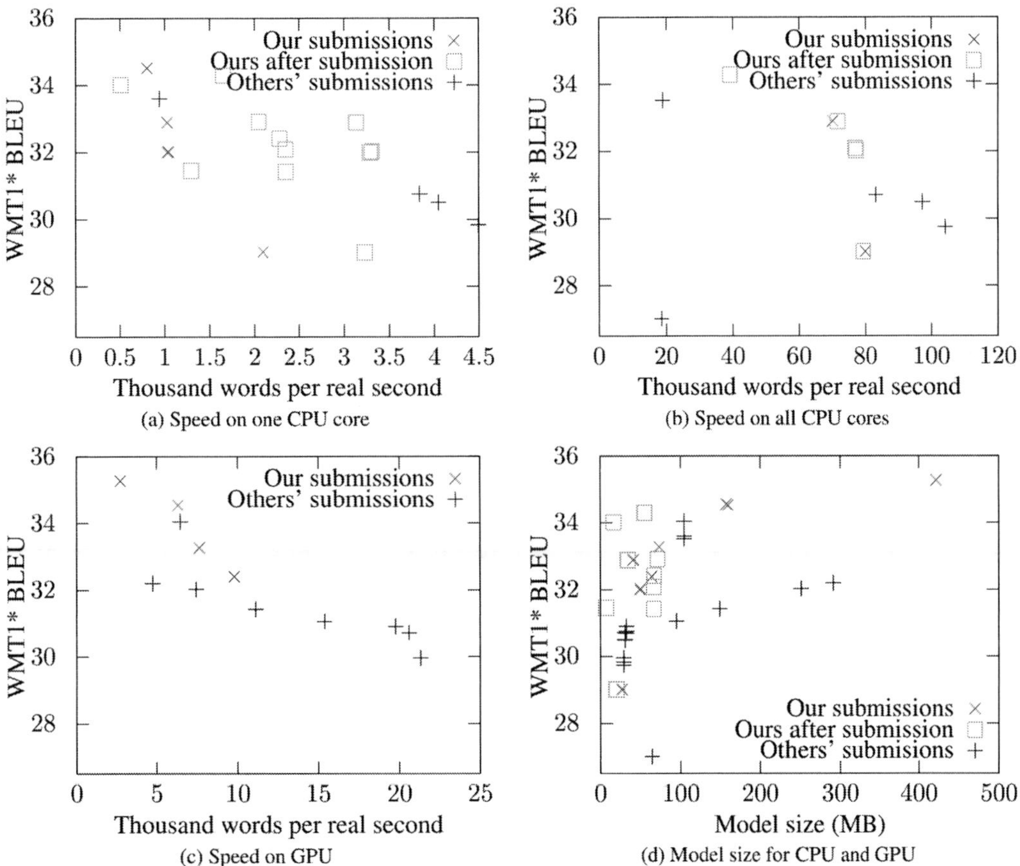

Figure 1: Performance of our models compared to other teams. Not all models sought to optimize both speed and space. For example, models stored in 4 bits ran with *float32*.

7 Results and discussion

All submissions and select experiments are depicted in Figure 1.

We explored a variety of ways to optimize the trade-off between quality, speed, and model size. We use an ensemble of 4 transformer-big teacher models to train a number of different student configurations. Smaller student models are faster to decode, but also further degrade the performance compared to the ensemble of teachers. Furthermore, we apply gradual transformer head pruning to the student models. While pruning the number of heads does not reduce the number of parameters significantly, it has a major impact on the computational cost and is beneficial for increasing translation speed, at a small penalty in BLEU score.

On the software side, we experiment with a number of methods that reduce the precision for the GEMM operations. For our GPU submissions, we decode using 16-bit floats and for CPU ones we use 8-bit integers. We note that the smaller (in terms of number of parameters) the model is, the more impacted quality is by quantization, and the bigger the model is, the larger the speed increase is. We found that fine tuning with a quantized GEMM can recover some of the quality loss from quantization.

We also experimented with logarithmic 4-bit model compression, which did not yield increased translation speed due to hardware, but produced the smallest model sizes.

Acknowledgements

We would like to thank Marcin Junczys-Dowmunt for sharing his English-German WMT'19 NMT system that we used as a teacher for our experiments.

This work was supported by funding from the European Union's Horizon 2020 research and innovation programme under grant agreement No 825303 (Bergamot) and by the Connecting Europe Facility (CEF) - Telecommunications from the project No 2019-EU-IA-0045 (User-focused Marian).

This work was performed using resources provided by the Cambridge Service for Data Driven Discovery (CSD3) operated by the University of Cambridge Research Computing Service (http://www.csd3.cam.ac.uk/), provided by Dell EMC and Intel using Tier-2 funding from the Engineering and Physical Sciences Research Council (capital grant EP/P020259/1), and DiRAC funding from the Science and Technology Facilities Council (www.dirac.ac.uk).

References

Alham Fikri Aji and Kenneth Heafield. 2019. Neural machine translation with 4-bit precision and beyond. arXiv preprint arXiv:1909.06091.

Loïc Barrault, Ondřej Bojar, Marta R. Costa-jussà, Christian Federmann, Mark Fishel, Yvette Graham, Barry Haddow, Matthias Huck, Philipp Koehn, Shervin Malmasi, Christof Monz, Mathias Müller, Santanu Pal, Matt Post, and Marcos Zampieri. 2019. Findings of the 2019 conference on machine translation (wmt19). In Proceedings of the Fourth Conference on Machine Translation (Volume 2: Shared Task Papers, Day 1), pages 1–61, Florence, Italy. Association for Computational Linguistics.

Marta Bañón, Pinzhen Chen, Barry Haddow, Kenneth Heafield, Hieu Hoang, Miquel Esplà-Gomis, Mikel L. Forcada, Amir Kamran, Faheem Kirefu, Philipp Koehn, Sergio Ortiz Rojas, Leopoldo Pla Sempere, Gema Ramírez-Sánchez, Elsa Sarrías, Marek Strelec, Brian Thompson, William Waites, Dion Wiggins, and Jaume Zaragoza. 2020. ParaCrawl: web-scale acquisition of parallel corpora. In Proceedings of the 2020 Annual Conference of the Association for Computational Linguistics, Seattle.

Aishwarya Bhandare, Vamsi Sripathi, Deepthi Karkada, Vivek Menon, Sun Choi, Kushal Datta, and Vikram Saletore. 2019. Efficient 8-bit quantization of transformer neural machine language translation model.

Jonathan Frankle and Michael Carbin. 2018. The lottery ticket hypothesis: Training pruned neural networks. CoRR, abs/1803.03635.

Jonathan Frankle, Gintare Karolina Dziugaite, Daniel M. Roy, and Michael Carbin. 2019. Stabilizing the lottery ticket hypothesis. CoRR, abs/1903.01611.

Armand Joulin, Edouard Grave, Piotr Bojanowski, and Tomas Mikolov. 2017. Bag of tricks for efficient text classification. In Proceedings of the 15th Conference of the European Chapter of the Association for Computational Linguistics: Volume 2, Short Papers, pages 427–431, Valencia, Spain. Association for Computational Linguistics.

Marcin Junczys-Dowmunt. 2018. Microsoft's submission to the WMT2018 news translation task: How I learned to stop worrying and love the data. In Proceedings of the Third Conference on Machine Translation: Shared Task Papers, pages 425–430, Belgium, Brussels. Association for Computational Linguistics.

Marcin Junczys-Dowmunt. 2019. Microsoft translator at WMT 2019: Towards large-scale document-level neural machine translation. In Proceedings of the Fourth Conference on Machine Translation (Volume 2: Shared Task Papers, Day 1), pages 225–233, Florence, Italy. Association for Computational Linguistics.

Marcin Junczys-Dowmunt, Roman Grundkiewicz, Tomasz Dwojak, Hieu Hoang, Kenneth Heafield, Tom Neckermann, Frank Seide, Ulrich Germann, Alham Fikri Aji, Nikolay

Bogoychev, et al. 2018a. Marian: Fast neural machine translation in C++. In Proceedings of ACL 2018, System Demonstrations, pages 116–121.

Marcin Junczys-Dowmunt, Kenneth Heafield, Hieu Hoang, Roman Grundkiewicz, and Anthony Aue. 2018b. Marian: Cost-effective high-quality neural machine translation in C++. In Proceedings of the 2nd Workshop on Neural Machine Translation and Generation, pages 129–135.

Yoon Kim and Alexander M Rush. 2016. Sequence-level knowledge distillation. In Proceedings of the 2016 Conference on Empirical Methods in Natural Language Processing, pages 1317–1327.

Young Jin Kim, Marcin Junczys-Dowmunt, Hany Hassan, Alham Fikri Aji, Kenneth Heafield, Roman Grundkiewicz, and Nikolay Bogoychev. 2019. From research to production and back: Ludicrously fast neural machine translation. In Proceedings of the 3rd Workshop on Neural Generation and Translation, pages 280–288, Hong Kong. Association for Computational Linguistics.

Taku Kudo and John Richardson. 2018. SentencePiece: A simple and language independent subword tokenizer and detokenizer for neural text processing. In Proceedings of the 2018 Conference on Empirical Methods in Natural Language Processing: System Demonstrations, pages 66–71.

Kishore Papineni, Salim Roukos, Todd Ward, and Wei-Jing Zhu. 2002. Bleu: a method for automatic evaluation of machine translation. In Proceedings of the 40th Annual Meeting of the Association for Computational Linguistics, pages 311–318, Philadelphia, Pennsylvania, USA. Association for Computational Linguistics.

Andres Rodriguez, Eden Segal, Etay Meiri, Evarist Fomenko, Young Jin Kim, Haihao Shen, and Barukh Ziv. 2018. Lower numerical precision deep learning inference and training.

O. Tange. 2011. Gnu parallel - the command-line power tool. ;login: The USENIX Magazine, 36(1):42–47.

Ashish Vaswani, Noam Shazeer, Niki Parmar, Jakob Uszkoreit, Llion Jones, Aidan N Gomez, Łukasz Kaiser, and Illia Polosukhin. 2017. Attention is all you need. In Advances in neural information processing systems, pages 5998–6008.

Elena Voita, David Talbot, Fedor Moiseev, Rico Sennrich, and Ivan Titov. 2019. Analyzing multi-head self-attention: Specialized heads do the heavy lifting, the rest can be pruned. In Proceedings of the 57th Annual Meeting of the Association for Computational Linguistics, pages 5797–5808, Florence, Italy. Association for Computational Linguistics.

Improving Document-Level Neural Machine Translation with Domain Adaptation

Sami Ul Haq[1], Sadaf Abdul Rauf[2,3], Arslan Shoukat[1] and Noor-e-Hira[2]
[1] National University of Sciences and Technology, Pakistan
[2] Fatima Jinnah Women University, Pakistan
[3] LIMSI-CNRS, France
`{sadaf.abdulrauf,noorehira94}@gmail.com`
`{sami.ulhaq,arslanshaukat}@ceme.nust.edu.pk`

Abstract

Recent studies have shown that translation quality of NMT systems can be improved by providing document-level contextual information. In general sentence-based NMT models are extended to capture contextual information from large-scale document-level corpora which are difficult to acquire. Domain adaptation on the other hand promises adapting components of already developed systems by exploiting limited in-domain data. This paper presents FJWU's system submission at WNGT, we specifically participated in Document level MT task for German-English translation. Our system is based on context-aware Transformer model developed on top of original NMT architecture by integrating contextual information using attention networks. Our experimental results show that providing previous sentences as context significantly improves the BLEU score as compared to a strong NMT baseline. We also studied the impact of domain adaptation on document level translation and were able to improve results by adapting the systems according to the testing domain.

1 Introduction

In past few years, machine translation systems have witnessed remarkable growth due to increasing amount of multilingual information. Neural Machine Translation (NMT) has become one of the powerful and de-facto approaches recognized for its generality and effectiveness (Li et al., 2018). Due to better accuracy of deep neural models, it has quickly achieved state of the art performance in machine translation (Shen et al., 2015).

Standard neural machine translation model works on individual sentences and focuses on short context windows for improving translation quality while ignoring cross-sentence links and dependencies (Xiong et al., 2019). Sentence-by-sentence translation of well-formed documents may generate an incoherent target text which is unable to span the entire document. This largely limits the success of NMT, as document context is totally ignored. Intuitively, to generate coherent translation of source document, machine learning models expect cross-sentence dependencies and linkages. To this end, several models (Voita et al., 2018; Wang et al., 2017; Tu et al., 2018; Maruf and Haffari, 2017; Bawden et al., 2017; Jean et al., 2017) have been proposed for document-wide translation.

Adapting NMT models for context-aware translations has the biggest challenge of limited availability of bilingual document-level corpora. Since, only few resources are available for training, the application domain of NMT may greatly vary from domain of training data. Consequently, the performance of NMT system may quickly degrade as soon as the testing conditions deviate from training conditions.

Domain adaptation has been an active research topic in the field of machine translation to improve translation performance often for low resource settings (Koehn and Schroeder, 2007). The quality of neural machine translation heavily depends upon domain-specificity of test data and the amount of parallel training data. The demand for high quality domain specific MT systems has significantly increased over the years but the bilingual corpora for relevant languages still lack in quantity (Chu and Wang, 2018).

In this work, we aim to demonstrate performance optimization in a particular domain by training document-level models on large out-of domain parallel corpus combined with small in-domain corpus using domain adaptation techniques. Our experiments on German-English data using document-level translation model (Miculicich et al., 2018) an extension of standard NMT Transformer (Vaswani et al., 2017) reveals the importance of contextual

225

Proceedings of the 4th Workshop on Neural Generation and Translation (WNGT 2020), pages 225–231
Online, July 10, 2020. ©2020 Association for Computational Linguistics
www.aclweb.org/anthology/D19-56%2d

information and domain adaptation on translation quality.

By comparing the performance with standard NMT baseline models trained on bilingual data, we show that NMT models exposed to random and actual contextual information are more sensitive to translation quality. We also demonstrate the impact of domain adaptation on translation quality by adapting document-level system to the testing domain.

2   Models

We use two types of models, sentence level and document-level context aware model, both built using Transformer architecture (Vaswani et al., 2017). For our primary submission we train document-level models on parallel corpus with document boundaries. The document level model consists of hierarchical attention encoder and decoder to capture both source and target side contextual information during training and testing.

2.1   Sentence-level Models

Our baseline for sentence-level models is OpenNMT-py (Klein et al., 2017) implementation of the Transformer architecture. To be able to establish comparison with document-level models, strong sentence-level baseline is defined with the same architecture (Vaswani et al., 2017) and training data as used for document-level models. Model configurations and training/evaluation data for sentence-level models are discussed in section 3.2.

2.2   Document-level Models

The motivation behind this research work is to test document-level NMT models on sports domain for WNGT20 shared task. The standard Transformer encoder and decoder are extended to take additional sentences as contextual input (Miculicich et al., 2018). Hierarchical attention networks (Yang et al., 2016) are employed on both sides of the NMT model to capture larger context. HAN encoder and decoder can be used jointly to provide dynamic access for selecting previous sentences or predicting most appropriate words.

3   Experimental Setup

The baseline and document-level models are trained on English-German parallel data of differ-

ent domains (i.e. news, press and sports) provided by WMT19[1] and WNGT20[2].

Corpus	Split	Sentences	Documents
Europarl v9	train	1.64M	109.9K
	valid	0.19M	12.93K
	test	0.09M	6.46K
Rapid	train	1.31M	42.9K
	valid	0.14M	5.04K
	test	0.07M	2.52K
News Commentary v14	train	0.28M	7.16K
	valid	0.03M	0.84K
	test	0.01M	0.42K
Rotowire	train	3.24K	242
	valid	3.32K	240
	test	3.24K	241

Table 1: Dataset statistics in terms of number of sentence pairs and documents and the corresponding train, test and development split.

3.1   Dataset

Document level models require parallel data with document boundaries for training and testing. Parallel data without document boundaries can not be directly used to train document level models, if it is imperative to use, then artificial document boundaries need to be generated. Our training corpus is also constrained to use only English-German data from the WMT19 shared task.

As mentioned earlier, one of the main constraints in training document-level models is limited availability of document-level corpora. WMT19 provides document split version of Europarl v9, New-Commentary v14 and Rapid corpus. Rotowire dataset, made available by WNGT20 DGT task also contains parallel data with document distinctions. For document-parallel data, we preserve the document boundaries during data filtering and concatenation as to get original documents back after translation. For DGT shared task submission, Rotowire test set is provided by WNGT20. Since, the models are trained on data from multiple domains, we create standard test set by selecting chunk of data from each domain to generate a more fair representation of each domain in standard test set. This was done by selecting multiple documents from a

---

[1] http://www.statmt.org/wmt19/
[2] https://sites.google.com/view/wngt20/

226

particular domain based on size of the dataset[3]. All datasets are tokenised using script provided by WNGT organizers[4]. Table 1 summarizes the corpus details.

3.1.1 In-domain data

RotoWire (Wiseman et al., 2017) is sports data consisting of article summaries about NBA basket ball games. RotoWire dataset is available in two formats, json and plain text. Both formats contain identical split for train/development and test sets. We used plain text format that contains separate files according to IDs of documents, each game summary is taken as a separate document.

3.1.2 Out-of-domain data

Major portion of training data includes out-of-domain parallel corpora taken from WMT19. We used English-German set of Rapid, News-commentary and Europarl with document boundaries. Document boundaries of Europarl v9 dataset resulted in very long documents, therefore we decided to redefine the document boundaries while keeping the same order of sentences[5]. For this, we take the average document size of Rotowire training data which gave us 14 sentences per document. After discarding original space split document boundaries from Europarl v9, we add new boundaries to keep a reasonable size of context.

3.2 Model Configuration and Training

Since our baseline and document-level MT systems use OpenNMT-py (Klein et al., 2017) implementation of Transformer model, we used similar configuration parameters are as reported in original transformer paper (Vaswani et al., 2017). Transformer model incorporates 6-hidden layers for encoder and decoder. All the hidden states have dropout of 0.1 and 512 dimensions. Model is trained with 8000 warm-up steps with a learning rate of 0.01. We checkpoint the model every 1000 steps for validation. Batch size is set to 2048 and modes are trained for 50K steps.

As in the original paper (Miculicich et al., 2018), two step process is followed for training the document-level models. In the first step, NMT

---

[3]For sentence based models, we can select sentences randomly but for document-level models entire document is considered for standard test set.

[4]`https://github.com/neulab/ie-eval`

[5]In the original approach for document-level NMT, they failed to obtain significant improvements when context increases beyond 3 sentences.

model is optimized without context-aware HAN. After that, we optimize the parameter's for HAN encoder, decoder and joint model. HAN Transformer models gave best performance for 1-3 previous sentences, we use k=3 previous sentences for both source and target side context.

4 Experimental Results

We present the results of experimentation from our models on German-English translation in Tables 2, 3 and 4.

4.1 Domain adaptation: Sentence level

In our initial experiments, we investigate the impact of domain adaptation on translation results at sentence-level. Since the NMT models are adapted for sports domain (RotoWire), so following (Hira et al., 2019) we gave more weightage to RotoWire corpus by replicating the corpus twice and thrice to study the impact.

Dataset	English	German	BLEU
rap	29.3M	30.0M	5.87
roto-rap	29.5M	30.2M	9.37
roto-rap-nc	35.2M	35.8M	7.90
roto2-rap-nc	35.4M	36.0M	**16.33**
roto3-rap-nc	35.6M	36.2M	**20.01**

Table 2: Table summarizing corpora size and BLEU scores for Transformer based NMT systems.

The results in Table 2 are reported on NMT model scores for Rotowire ($roto$), Rapid (rap) and News-Commentary (nc) corpus, here $roto$ is the in-domain corpus. Adding only 0.2M of in-domain $roto$ corpus to 30M rap German corpus yields a substantial improvement of around +4 BLEU points (Table 2: row 2). On the other hand, addition of 5.6M German nc corpus to previous systems, gives around +1.5 points improvement (row 3). This is an obvious demonstration of the positive effect of domain adaptation on translation quality.

We further explore this effect by replicating twice the $roto$ corpus, this gives a big improvement of 8.43 BLEU points on $roto2 - rap - nc$ (Table 2: row 4). Replicating $roto$ 3 times, however gives +3.68 points improvement from previous system and an overall improvements of +12.11 BLEU points from $roto - rap - nc$. Clearly, by adapting to the testing domain by updating the model weights, substantial improvements are achieved.

4.2 Document-level Adaptation with Context Aware Translation Experiments

For document-level models, taking a strong baseline of sentence level models, we achieved remarkable improvements by incorporating context as shown in Table 3. We report the results for 4 corpus combinations. The first column is a combination of four document segmented corpora. Starting with a baseline of 32.18 Bleu points on sentence level Transformer model on $Rotowire + Rapid + News - Commentary + Euro$ corpus, a gain of 3.79 points is achieved ($32.18 \Rightarrow 35.97$). This is achieved by incorporation of contextual information by HAN encoder. We have used a context of 3 sentences as this was reported to be the best for capturing context by (Miculicich et al., 2018). This shows a superiority of context based models on standard NMT models. With the joint model we get a score of 38.32 BLEU points.

In columns (3, 4) of Table 3, the effect of domain adaptation to test domain is reported on document-level systems. This years test data were the documents in the test folder provided by the organisers. We experimented by building systems by replicating the Rotowire training corpus, twice and thrice in an attempt to enable the translation model to learn parameter closer to the testing domain. We can clearly see that models with replicated in-domain corpus outperformed and achieved better score than previous document-level and sentence-based models. The best score of 43.08 is obtained when Rotowire is replicated thrice i.e. $RotoWire(*3) + Rapid + NC + Euro$.

All of our document-level models preformed better than sentence-level models but most importantly encoder models gave best scores which clearly indicates that source side provides correct contextual information as compared to target side. The highest score is achieved by combining HAN encoder and HAN decoder model for corpus in second and third two columns. Joint model for last column performed poorly, this can be attributed to the fact that HAN decoder is not contributing complementary information to further improve translations. Another reason can be our selection of decoder's context, as due to limited availability of time we only use decoded states of previous sentences for target side context while other configurations (Miculicich et al., 2018) are also available.

4.3 Other Context Integration Experiments

Table 4 presents results from our different context integration experiments. We have been interested to check how much improvement is due to additional contextual information, therefore we created a similar setup (Scherrer et al., 2019) for analysis of context. For this, we create three variants of our train and test set to evaluate context aware systems:

- **Regular context:** The order of sentences in train and test set is kept same as they appear in original documents to evaluate consistent contextual setting.

- **Random context:** The train and test set is shuffled such that the document boundaries now represent inconsistent contextual sentences.

- **No context:** Document boundaries of test set is modified such that one sentence now presents one document, which means no additional context is made available during translations. We are forcing document level model to avoid context by providing single sentence document during testing.

We report Blue score for context integration experiments in Table 4. Document-level models are expected to perform better when contextual information is available. The BLEU score decreases when we move from regular context to random and no context as indicated by row 1 and column 3-5 of Table 4. Context aware models when trained on inconsistent training data, it hardly effects their performance when actual context is random or missing during testing. Model in row 2 is trained on random or inconsistent document level data, column 3-5 represent scores for regular, random and non-contextual test data. Model trained on data with random context is insensitive to context during testing.

5 Related Work

5.1 Context-aware NMT

Improving machine translation systems by developing document-level models for SMT (Garcia et al., 2015; Hardmeier et al., 2013; Gong et al., 2011) and NMT(Maruf and Haffari, 2017; Tu et al., 2018; Voita et al., 2018; Kuang et al., 2017; Wang et al., 2017) has been an important research area. These contributions are briefly discussed in this section.

Models	BLEU Score		
	Roto+Rapid+NC+Euro	Roto(*2)+Rapid+NC+Euro	Roto(*3)+Rapid+NC+Euro
NMT Transformer	32.18	36.40	37.08
+ HAN encoder	35.97	39.31	43.08
+ HAN decoder	35.37	39.33	42.76
+ HAN encoder + HAN decoder	38.32	40.82	38.13

Table 3: Table summarizing HAN & NMT Transformer results (Rotowire official test) for adding document context and domain adaptation.

Models	Tokens		BLEU Score		
	EN	DE	Reg	Rand	None
HAN_reg	420M	489M	39.31	39.25	39.08
+HAN_rand	188M	224M	37.76	37.76	37.75

Table 4: BLEU for EN$\Rightarrow$DE translations using Regular, Random and None contextual settings of corpus.

(Miculicich et al., 2018) proposed document-level approach with Hierarchical Attention Network (HAN) to provide contextual information during translation. Two HANs are considered for integrating source and target context in NMT. HAN are believed to provide dynamic access to contextual information as compared to Hierarchical Recurrent Neural Networks (HRNN). However, the approach is restrictive for incorporating large contextual information by only considering a limited number of previous source/target sentences.

Cache-based memory approach is proposed by (Tu et al., 2018) to provide document context during translation. Memory networks keep the representation of a set of words in cache to provide contextual information to NMT in the form of words. However, the stored representations are considered irrespective of sentences in which they occur and do not provide actual context to NMT. Cache based memory models have been used in both SMT (Gong et al., 2011) and NMT to store rich representations of source and target text. (Kuang et al., 2017) use two caches, dynamic cache to capture dynamic context by storing words of translated sentence and topic cache which stores topical words of target side from entire document. Through a gating mechanism, the probability of NMT model and cache based neural model is combined to predict the next word.

Memory network-based approach presented by (Maruf and Haffari, 2017) is used to integrate global source and target context to sentence-based NMT. Keeping the source and target context in memory can be very time consuming and mem-

ory inefficient as the sentence pairs in document could be enormous. Another study by (Xiong et al., 2019) is based on deliberation networks to capture the cross-sentence context by improving the translation of baseline NMT system in the second pass. Generation of discourse coherent output is largely dependent upon the performance of the canonical NMT model.

The approach proposed by (Zhang et al., 2018) implemented with document-level context outperforms existing cache based RNN search model. Extending Transformer model has achieved better context awareness and a low computational overhead. (Voita et al., 2018) introduce a context aware NMT model in which they control and analyze the flow of information from the extended context to the translation model. They show that using the previous sentence as context their model is able to implicitly capture anaphora.

Both source and target side contextual information plays important role in document-level translation. Inspired from previous sentence-based context-aware approaches (Voita et al., 2018; Stojanovski and Fraser, 2019; Zhang et al., 2018), we are using extended Transformer model (Miculicich et al., 2018) with ability to use dynamic context for document-level experiments.

5.2 Domain Adaptation

The basic concept behind domain adaptation in NMT is utilizing large amount of available parallel data for training NMT models and adapting these to novel domains with small in-domain data (Freitag and Al-Onaizan, 2016). In the simplest approach, in-domain data can be used to fine-tune models trained on large-scale out-of-domain data. Training NMT models from scratch on combined data can take several weeks and may suffer from performance degradation on in-domain test data.

Fine-tuning is a fast and efficient method to integrate in-domain data, and does not need building systems from scratch. Fine tuning for NMT

(Dakwale and Monz, 2017; Freitag and Al-Onaizan, 2016; Luong and Manning, 2015) is achieved by further training a neural model on in-domain data which is already trained on large general domain training data. Adoption to new domain is achieved by (Sennrich et al., 2015) by using synthetic data through back-translation of target in-domain monolingual text and retraining on combined training corpus by adding new data.

For domain adaptation, we use data augmentation method similar to (Chu et al., 2017) by oversampling small in-domain corpus. This simple data augmentation approach does not require any modification in NMT architecture and forces NMT to pay equal/more attention to in-domain training data.

6   Conclusion

In this study, we present methods to improve document-level neural machine translation. Following recently reported results on the task, our experiments also reiterate the fact that incorporating context in translation helps considerably improve the quality. Taking a strong Transformer based baseline model trained on substantial corpus (a concatenation of four corpora RotoWire, Rapid, Euro and News Commentary), context aware document models result in significant improvement in BLEU points. We have also experimented with the effects of corpus replication to adapt to the domain of test corpus. We find it an effective method to improve translation quality and domain adaptation.

We have submitted results of our best model (HAN encoder) for German-English direction as reported in Table 3 , for official evaluation. Han encoder model with domain adaptation techniques achieved 43.08 BLEU score. We have computed BLEU scores using Moses $multi-blue.perl$ script.

Acknowledgments

This study is funded by Higher Education Commission of Pakistan's project: National Research Program for Universities (NRPU) (5469/Punjab/NRPU/R&D/HEC/2016).

References

Rachel Bawden, Rico Sennrich, Alexandra Birch, and Barry Haddow. 2017. Evaluating discourse phenomena in neural machine translation. *arXiv preprint arXiv:1711.00513*.

Chenhui Chu, Raj Dabre, and Sadao Kurohashi. 2017. An empirical comparison of domain adaptation methods for neural machine translation. In *Proceedings of the 55th Annual Meeting of the Association for Computational Linguistics (Volume 2: Short Papers)*, pages 385–391, Vancouver, Canada. Association for Computational Linguistics.

Chenhui Chu and Rui Wang. 2018. A survey of domain adaptation for neural machine translation. *arXiv preprint arXiv:1806.00258*.

Praveen Dakwale and Christof Monz. 2017. Fine-tuning for neural machine translation with limited degradation across in-and out-of-domain data. *Proceedings of the XVI Machine Translation Summit*, 117.

Markus Freitag and Yaser Al-Onaizan. 2016. Fast domain adaptation for neural machine translation. *CoRR*, abs/1612.06897.

Eva Martínez Garcia, Cristina España-Bonet, and Lluís Màrquez. 2015. Document-level machine translation with word vector models. In *Proceedings of the 18th Annual Conference of the European Association for Machine Translation*, pages 59–66.

Zhengxian Gong, Min Zhang, and Guodong Zhou. 2011. Cache-based document-level statistical machine translation. In *Proceedings of the Conference on Empirical Methods in Natural Language Processing*, pages 909–919. Association for Computational Linguistics.

Christian Hardmeier, Sara Stymne, Jörg Tiedemann, and Joakim Nivre. 2013. Docent: A document-level decoder for phrase-based statistical machine translation. In *ACL 2013 (51st Annual Meeting of the Association for Computational Linguistics); 4-9 August 2013; Sofia, Bulgaria*, pages 193–198. Association for Computational Linguistics.

Noor-e Hira, Sadaf Abdul Rauf, Kiran Kiani, Ammara Zafar, and Raheel Nawaz. 2019. Exploring transfer learning and domain data selection for the biomedical translation. In *Proceedings of the Fourth Conference on Machine Translation (Volume 3: Shared Task Papers, Day 2)*, pages 156–163, Florence, Italy. Association for Computational Linguistics.

Sebastien Jean, Stanislas Lauly, Orhan Firat, and Kyunghyun Cho. 2017. Does neural machine translation benefit from larger context? *arXiv preprint arXiv:1704.05135*.

Guillaume Klein, Yoon Kim, Yuntian Deng, Jean Senellart, and Alexander M Rush. 2017. Opennmt: Opensource toolkit for neural machine translation. *arXiv preprint arXiv:1701.02810*.

Philipp Koehn and Josh Schroeder. 2007. Experiments in domain adaptation for statistical machine translation. In *Proceedings of the Second Workshop on Statistical Machine Translation*, StatMT '07, pages 224–227, Stroudsburg, PA, USA. Association for Computational Linguistics.

Shaohui Kuang, Deyi Xiong, Weihua Luo, and Guodong Zhou. 2017. Modeling coherence for neural machine translation with dynamic and topic caches. *arXiv preprint arXiv:1711.11221*.

Qiang Li, Derek F Wong, Lidia S Chao, Muhua Zhu, Tong Xiao, Jingbo Zhu, and Min Zhang. 2018. Linguistic knowledge-aware neural machine translation. *IEEE/ACM Transactions on Audio, Speech and Language Processing (TASLP)*, 26(12):2341–2354.

Minh-Thang Luong and Christopher D Manning. 2015. Stanford neural machine translation systems for spoken language domains. In *Proceedings of the International Workshop on Spoken Language Translation*, pages 76–79.

Sameen Maruf and Gholamreza Haffari. 2017. Document context neural machine translation with memory networks. *arXiv preprint arXiv:1711.03688*.

Lesly Miculicich, Dhananjay Ram, Nikolaos Pappas, and James Henderson. 2018. Document-level neural machine translation with hierarchical attention networks. *arXiv preprint arXiv:1809.01576*.

Yves Scherrer, Jörg Tiedemann, and Sharid Loáiciga. 2019. Analysing concatenation approaches to document-level nmt in two different domains. In *Proceedings of the Fourth Workshop on Discourse in Machine Translation (DiscoMT 2019)*, pages 51–61.

Rico Sennrich, Barry Haddow, and Alexandra Birch. 2015. Improving neural machine translation models with monolingual data. *arXiv preprint arXiv:1511.06709*.

Shiqi Shen, Yong Cheng, Zhongjun He, Wei He, Hua Wu, Maosong Sun, and Yang Liu. 2015. Minimum risk training for neural machine translation. *arXiv preprint arXiv:1512.02433*.

Dario Stojanovski and Alexander Fraser. 2019. Combining local and document-level context: The lmu munich neural machine translation system at wmt19. In *Proceedings of the Fourth Conference on Machine Translation (Volume 2: Shared Task Papers, Day 1)*, pages 400–406.

Zhaopeng Tu, Yang Liu, Shuming Shi, and Tong Zhang. 2018. Learning to remember translation history with a continuous cache. *Transactions of the Association for Computational Linguistics*, 6:407–420.

Ashish Vaswani, Noam Shazeer, Niki Parmar, Jakob Uszkoreit, Llion Jones, Aidan N Gomez, Łukasz Kaiser, and Illia Polosukhin. 2017. Attention is all you need. In *Advances in neural information processing systems*, pages 5998–6008.

Elena Voita, Pavel Serdyukov, Rico Sennrich, and Ivan Titov. 2018. Context-aware neural machine translation learns anaphora resolution. *arXiv preprint arXiv:1805.10163*.

Longyue Wang, Zhaopeng Tu, Andy Way, and Qun Liu. 2017. Exploiting cross-sentence context for neural machine translation. *arXiv preprint arXiv:1704.04347*.

Sam Wiseman, Stuart M Shieber, and Alexander M Rush. 2017. Challenges in data-to-document generation. *arXiv preprint arXiv:1707.08052*.

Hao Xiong, Zhongjun He, Hua Wu, and Haifeng Wang. 2019. Modeling coherence for discourse neural machine translation. In *Proceedings of the AAAI Conference on Artificial Intelligence*, volume 33, pages 7338–7345.

Zichao Yang, Diyi Yang, Chris Dyer, Xiaodong He, Alex Smola, and Eduard Hovy. 2016. Hierarchical attention networks for document classification. In *Proceedings of the 2016 conference of the North American chapter of the association for computational linguistics: human language technologies*, pages 1480–1489.

Jiacheng Zhang, Huanbo Luan, Maosong Sun, Feifei Zhai, Jingfang Xu, Min Zhang, and Yang Liu. 2018. Improving the transformer translation model with document-level context. *arXiv preprint arXiv:1810.03581*.

Simultaneous Translation and Paraphrase for Language Education

Stephen Mayhew, Klinton Bicknell, Chris Brust,
Bill McDowell, Will Monroe, and **Burr Settles**
Duolingo
Pittsburgh, PA, USA
{stephen, klinton, chrisb, mcdowell, monroe, burr}@duolingo.com

Abstract

We present the task of *Simultaneous Translation and Paraphrasing for Language Education (STAPLE)*. Given a prompt in one language, the goal is to generate a diverse set of
correct translations that language learners are
likely to produce. This is motivated by the
need to create and maintain large, high-quality
sets of acceptable translations for exercises in
a language-learning application, and synthesizes work spanning machine translation, MT
evaluation, automatic paraphrasing, and language education technology.

We developed a novel corpus with unique properties for five languages (Hungarian, Japanese,
Korean, Portuguese, and Vietnamese), and report on the results of a shared task challenge
which attracted 20 teams to solve the task. In
our meta-analysis, we focus on three aspects
of the resulting systems: external training corpus selection, model architecture and training
decisions, and decoding and filtering strategies.
We find that strong systems start with a large
amount of generic training data, and then fine-
tune with in-domain data, sampled according
to our provided learner response frequencies.

1 Introduction

Machine translation systems are typically trained
to produce a single output, but in certain cases, it
is desirable to have many possible translations of
a given input text. For example, Duolingo—the
world's largest language-learning platform—uses
translation-based exercises for some of its lessons.
For any given translation prompt there may be hundreds or thousands of valid responses, so we use a
set of human-curated translations in order to grade
learner responses. The manual process of maintaining these sets is laborious, and we believe it
can be improved with the aid of rich multi-output
translation and paraphrase systems.

Prompt	
is my explanation clear?	
Reference Translation	
a minha explicação está clara?	
Accepted Translations	**Weight**
minha explicação está clara?	.267
minha explicação é clara?	.162
a minha explicação está clara?	.111
a minha explicação é clara?	.088
minha explanação está clara?	.057
está clara minha explicação?	.044
minha explanação é clara?	.039
a minha explanação está clara?	.036
...	...

Table 1: An example from the Portuguese dataset. In
this task, teams are given an English prompt and a
reference translation, and are required to produce as
many variants in the accepted translations as possible.
The evaluation favors translations with higher weight,
which is a measure of learner response frequency.

To this end, we introduce a new task called *Simultaneous Translation and Paraphrasing for Language Education (STAPLE)*. From the perspective
of the research community, we believe this poses an
interesting exercise that is similar to machine translation (MT), but also provides data with new and
unique properties that we expect to be of interest
to researchers in MT evaluation, multilingual paraphrasing, and even language education technology.
It is our hope that this new task can help synthesize
efforts from these various subfields to further the
state of the art, and broaden their applications.

2 Shared Task Description

For the STAPLE task, participants begin with English *prompts* and generate high-coverage sets of
plausible translations in five different languages.
For training and evaluation, each prompt is paired
with a relatively comprehensive set of handcrafted,

Proceedings of the 4th Workshop on Neural Generation and Translation (WNGT 2020), pages 232–243
Online, July 10, 2020. ©2020 Association for Computational Linguistics
www.aclweb.org/anthology/D19-56%2d

Figure 1: Screenshots from the Duolingo app (iOS, circa 2020), showing translation exercises for English prompts into Portuguese. The first two examples show correct student translations, with Duolingo suggesting an alternate, preferred translation in the second case. The third and fourth responses show incorrect translations.

field-tested *accepted translations*, each weighted and ranked according to their empirical frequency among Duolingo learners. We also provide a high-quality automatic *reference translation* of each prompt that may (optionally) be used as a reference or anchor point, in the event that researchers want to explore paraphrase-only approaches (this also serves as a strong baseline). See Table 1 for an example from the Portuguese dataset.

2.1 Corpus Collection

Data for the task are derived from Duolingo, a free, award-winning, online language-learning platform. Since launching in 2012, hundreds of millions of learners worldwide have enrolled in Duolingo's game-like courses via the website[1] or mobile apps. Learning happens through a variety of interactive exercise types, combining reading, writing, listening, and speaking activities.

One such format is a translation exercise— shown in Figure 1—in which the learner is shown a prompt in one language, and asked to translate it into the other. Since English is by far the most popular language to learn on Duolingo, we created a task corpus by sampling prompts from English courses, in which users are shown an English sentence, and then asked to translate it into a language they already know. For instance, the examples in Figure 1 come from the course for Portuguese speakers learning English.

Naturally, some prompts have more accepted translations (valid learner responses) than others, depending on such factors as polysemy, synonymy, or prompt length. We filtered out prompts for which the number of accepted translations was in the top or bottom deciles of a course, to avoid outliers. Although each accepted translation is technically correct, usually a small number of them are considered most fluent or idiomatic. To estimate this distribution empirically, we gathered learner response data from October–November 2019. For each translation, we counted the number of times that learners produced that translation (with some allowances for punctuation and capitalization).

This provided a count c_t for each translation t in the set of accepted translations A. Since many translations were never attested in learner data, we then smoothed and normalized these counts to produce a learner response frequency (LRF) weight w_t for each translation, such that they sum to 1 for each prompt:

$$w_t = \frac{\sqrt{c_t + 1}}{\sum_{t' \in A} \sqrt{c_{t'} + 1}}$$

These weights are a unique feature of the STAPLE corpus, and found in almost no other datasets.

Having gathered prompts from each course, we shuffled the prompt set and selected 500 prompts for development and 500 for test. Of the remaining prompts for each course, we created a training set by sampling according to course size, so smaller courses (e.g., Vietnamese) have fewer prompts. Statistics on the datasets can be found in Table 2.

	Train			**Dev**			**Test**		
Language	prompts	trans.	ratio	prompts	trans.	ratio	prompts	trans.	ratio
Hungarian	4,000	251,442	62.9	500	27,647	55.3	500	33,578	67.2
Japanese	2,500	855,941	342.4	500	172,817	345.6	500	165,095	330.2
Korean	2,500	700,410	280.2	500	140,353	280.7	500	150,477	301.0
Portuguese	4,000	526,466	131.6	500	60,294	120.6	500	67,865	135.7
Vietnamese	3,500	194,720	55.6	500	29,637	59.3	500	28,242	56.5

Table 2: Dataset sizes by number of prompt sentences, and total number of accepted translations.

2.2 Five Language Tracks

We provide data for translating English prompts into five languages: Hungarian, Japanese, Korean, Portuguese (Brazilian), and Vietnamese. These span five different language families, three different writing systems, and represent a wide variety of popular Duolingo courses. For example, as of this writing, English from Portuguese is the fourth-largest Duolingo course overall, whereas English from Korean is median-sized, with the others falling in between. As such, much effort has gone into developing their accepted translation sets, but there is probably still room for improvement. These five languages also vary widely in their status as high-to-low-resource languages in NLP research.

For the shared task, participants were allowed to submit results to any or all of these language tracks. Furthermore, there were no restrictions on the use of external data; teams were encouraged to use any available monolingual or parallel corpora.

2.3 Evaluation

The main scoring metric is (macro) weighted F1 with respect to the accepted translations. In short, systems are scored based on how well they can return all human-curated accepted translations, but with lower penalties on recall for failing to produce translations that learners rarely submit anyway.

For each prompt sentence s with accepted translation set $\mathcal{A}_s$ in the corpus, we evaluate the weighted recall of a system's predicted translation set $\mathcal{P}_s$ as follows:

$$\text{Weighted Recall}(\mathcal{P}_s) = \sum_{t \in |\mathcal{P}_s \cap \mathcal{A}_s|} w_t \Big/ \sum_{t \in |\mathcal{A}_s|} w_t$$

Precision is calculated in an unweighted fashion (as there is no weight for false positives), and weighted F1 for each $\mathcal{P}_s$ is simply the usual harmonic mean of precision and weighted recall. These weighted F1s for each prompt are then averaged over the entire evaluation dataset $\mathcal{D}$:

$$\text{(Macro) Weighted F1} = \sum_{s \in \mathcal{D}} \frac{\text{Weighted F1}(\mathcal{P}_s)}{|\mathcal{D}|}$$

Since evaluation is done by matching predictions with accepted translations, we ignore any differences due to punctuation, capitalization, or multiple whitespaces.

2.4 Challenge Timeline

We announced the shared task on December 20, 2019, with information about the task timeline, data, etc., published on a regular basis to a dedicated website[2]. We released the training data on January 15, blind dev data on March 2, and blind test data on March 30, 2020.

During the blind dev phase, participants were able to submit up to five submissions per day to an online evaluation leaderboard. Originally, we had planned on closing the dev phase at the start of the test phase, but upon request, we kept it open so that teams could continue to experiment and submit to the dev leaderboard even after the test phase opened, without counting against their final submission(s). We allowed up to three submissions in total to the test leaderboard (to account for technical problems, etc.).

3 Results

A total of 20 teams participated during the dev phase, 13 teams during the test phase, and 11 teams submitted system description papers. Of the teams with system descriptions, three of them (**jbrem, sweagraw, jindra.helcl**) participated in all five language tracks. One team (**rakchada**) submitted to two tracks, and the remaining teams only submitted to a single track, with Japanese and Portuguese being the most popular.

---

[2]https://sharedtask.duolingo.com

Team	Hungarian		Japanese		Korean		Portuguese		Vietnamese	
	Rank	F1	Rank	F1	Rank	F1	Rank	F1	Rank	F1
jbrem	1	.555	1	.318	1	.404	1	.552	1	.558
nickeilf		–		–		–	1	.551		–
rakchada	1	.552		–		–	1	.544		–
jspak3		–		–	2	.312		–		–
sweagraw	2	.469	2	.294	3	.255	2	.525	2	.539
masahiro		–	2	.283		–		–		–
mzy		–	3	.260		–		–		–
dcu		–		–		–	3	.460		–
jindra.helcl	3	.435	4	.213	4	.206	4	.412	3	.377
darkside		–	5	.194		–		–		–
nagoudi		–		–		–	5	.376		–
baseline_aws	4	.281	6	.043	5	.041	6	.213	4	.198
baseline_fairseq	5	.124	7	.033	5	.049	7	.136	5	.254

Table 3: F1 results for all systems, on all languages. Rank is assigned according to statistical significance (§3).

Official weighted F1 results are shown in Table 3. Ranks are determined using an approximate permutation test with 100,000 samples (Padó, 2006), and adjacent-scoring systems are considered significantly different at $p < .05$. Figure 3 provides additional detail on precision and weighted recall. Overall, teams outperformed our provided baselines by a wide margin, and submissions tended to score higher on precision than weighted recall.

3.1 Baselines

We prepared two very different baselines. For **baseline_aws**, we used Amazon Translate[3] to generate a single "best" machine translation from English into the target language. These were also provided as reference translations at each phase.

For **baseline_fairseq**, we used the fairseq framework (Ott et al., 2019) trained solely on the STAPLE task data. We created bitexts by pairing English prompts with each of their target language translations (making no use of the weights). The baseline employs a convolutional neural network (CNN) using byte-pair encoding (BPE) with a vocabulary size of 20,000, and simply outputs default n-best lists of size 10. While we ensured that the output BLEU scores of this model were sensible, we did not tune any parameters, instead treating this as a baseline that should be attainable by any team with minimal effort. Our baseline code was provided as a starting point for participants, and many chose to derive their systems from it.

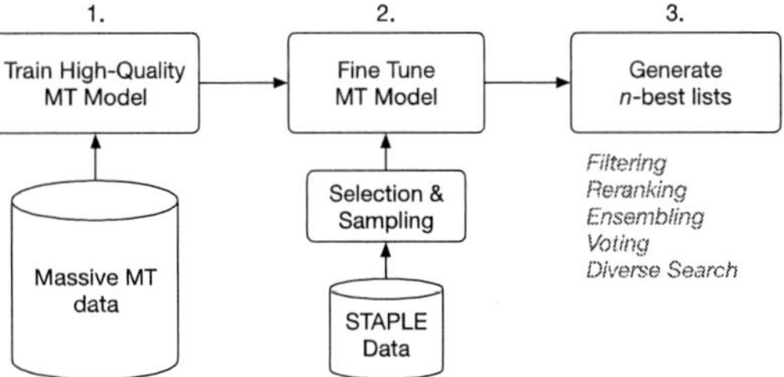

Figure 2: Generalized pipeline used by most systems.

3.2 Submitted Systems

With few exceptions, participating teams followed the generalized pipeline illustrated in Figure 2. This consists of (1) training a high-quality machine translation model using massive but mostly out-of-domain corpora, (2) fine-tuning the model using STAPLE task corpora (and sometimes others), and then (3) employing various tricks for diverse output generation and filtering.

jbrem (Khayrallah et al., 2020) took an approach involving score-based filtering of n-best lists, from a Transformer model pre-trained on large external corpora and then fine-tuned on the STAPLE data. The authors describe benefits from using various pre-training datasets, two different filtering methods, and various ways of upweighting of translations of high frequency (weight). The resulting system was among the strongest in the competition, ranking first in all five tracks.

nickeilf (Li et al., 2020) explored a family of diversification approaches including beam expansion, Monte Carlo random dropout, lexical substi-

---

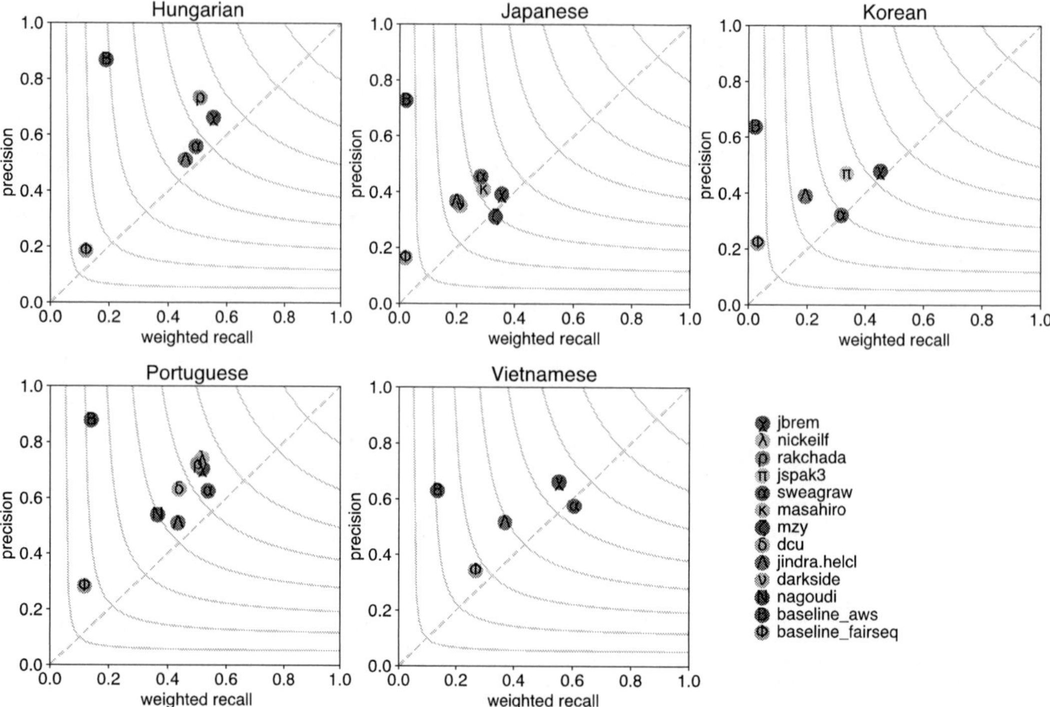

Figure 3: Precision and weighted recall for each system and language. The dashed line represents equal precision and weighted recall. Curved lines represent weighted F1 in increments of 0.1.

tution, and mixture of experts models, combined through ensemble-based consensus voting to generate a high quality set of translation suggestions. This tied for first place in the Portuguese track.

rakchada (Chada, 2020) used pre-trained Transformer models fine-tuned on the STAPLE data with an oversampling trick that afforded more weight to translations with higher frequency. They then used a classifier to filter the n-best lists based on predicted learner frequency. This tied for first place in the Hungarian and Portuguese tracks.

jspak3 (Park et al., 2020) took a similar approach to the original BART setup (Lewis et al., 2019), except they fine-tuned the model not only on larger parallel corpora, but also on the STAPLE data. This ranked second in the Korean track.

sweagraw (Agrawal and Carpuat, 2020) used a Transformer model pre-trained on the OpenSubtitles corpus, then fine-tuned on Tatoeba and the STAPLE data (§4.1), with the STAPLE translations oversampled to capture frequency. Resulting n-best lists were filtered with a two-layer neural classifier optimized for a soft-F1 objective. This ranked second or third in all five language tracks.

masahiro (Kaneko et al., 2020) took a simple ensemble approach that requires no modification to

an off-the-shelf NMT system (fairseq). The authors train multiple forward (L2R) and backward (R2L) models using different initial seeds, first by pre-training on general corpora and then fine-tuning on STAPLE data. Their experiments show that combining ensembling forward-backward models yields more diversity and higher F1 than simply using different seeds alone. This tied for second place in the Japanese track.

mzy (Yang et al., 2020) explored three particular strategies: pre-training on larger corpora before fine-tuning on in-domain corpora, using diverse beam search, and finally reranking candidate translations. The authors found that first fine-tuning on a similar intermediate corpus was better than fine-tuning on the STAPLE data alone. Diverse beam search provided modest further gains, although they report no improvement from beam re-ranking. This ranked third in the Japanese track.

dcu (Haque et al., 2020) compared both phrase-based and neural models by extending the STAPLE data with additional corpora (selected for similarity to the task data under a language model), with the neural model performing better. They generate sets of high-scoring predictions according to beam searches, majority voting, and other techniques,

236

and also run these initial translations through an additional paraphrasing model, placing third in the Portuguese track.

jindra.helcl (Libovický et al., 2020) trained a Transformer model by combining STAPLE data with additional parallel corpora and back-translated monolingual corpora. They also employed a filtering classifier that predicts whether their models' beam search outputs within accepted translations. This ranked third or fourth in all five tracks.

darkside (Nomoto, 2020) took a very different approach, treating the task as a paraphrase generation problem and using no data beyond what was provided for the shared task. They took two approaches, both based on autoencoders. The first is a sequence-to-sequence model with Gaussian noise added to the context vector, and the second is based on a conditional Variational Autoencoder, which has seen success in generating variations of input content in the literature (Bowman et al., 2015). This ranked fifth in the Japanese track.

nagoudi (Nagoudi et al., 2020) used a combination of data augmentation and ensembles. They combined STAPLE data with additional parallel corpora to train their models, finding (curiously) that this outperformed the fine-tuning approach employed by many others. They generated multiple translations by passing the source sentence through an ensemble of model training checkpoints, taking the n-best outputs from each and de-duplicating. This ranked fifth in the Portuguese track.

4 Meta-Analyses

In this section, we analyze different facets of the various approaches taken, in an effort to understand which design choices were most impactful on final results. We identified three major areas of variance: use of external training corpora (§4.1), model architecture and training procedures (§4.2), and decoding and filtering strategies (§4.3).

4.1 External Training Corpora

The STAPLE dataset is relatively small compared to many modern machine translation efforts. This is by design: it is challenging to develop a parallel corpus that is complete with many acceptable translations. One of our goals in organizing this task was to see how teams could effectively leverage existing corpora, with a modest amount of in-domain data, to bootstrap high-quality models for the task.

Corpus effects	Precision		W. Recall		W. F1	
(Intercept)	.418	***	.293	**	.283	**
Tatoeba	+.190		+.223	.	+.214	.
ParaCrawl	+.018		+.103		+.071	
Europarl	+.061		+.057		+.063	
QED	+.011		−.004		+.004	
OpenSubtitles	−.098		−.083		−.087	
Wikipedia	−.034		−.213		−.153	
Random effects	**St.Dev.**		**St.Dev.**		**St.Dev.**	
Prompt ID	±.183		±.210		±.173	
Track ID	±.085		±.106		±.103	
Team ID	±.082		±.080		±.075	

Table 4: Mixed-effects analysis of the most commonly-cited external corpora used for training.

Most teams began with a generic MT system pre-trained on massive but out-of-domain parallel corpora, either before or in tandem with the STAPLE task data. These were largely drawn from the Open Parallel Corpus (OPUS) project (Tiedemann, 2012). One natural question is whether the choice to train on a particular dataset from this collection had any meaningful impact on final results.

To answer this question, we coded each team with features variables indicating each corpus they reported using for their final submission, and used a regression analysis to see if these data choices significantly impacted precision, weighted recall, and weighted F1 scores for each prompt in the test set[4]. To analyze this properly, however, we need to distinguish between effects among data choices are actually meaningful versus those that can be explained by sampling error due to random variations among prompts, tracks, or teams. To do this, we use a *linear mixed-effects model* (cf., Baayen, 2008, Ch. 7). In addition to modeling the *fixed* effects of the various corpora, we can also model the *random* effects represented by the prompt ID (some sentences may be longer or harder), the track ID (the languages inherently vary), and the team ID (teams will differ in other aspects not captured by these corpus variables).

Table 4 presents a mixed-effects analysis for the most-cited corpora among participating teams, each used by at least four different systems. The intercepts can be interpreted as "average" metrics, which then go up or down according to fixed and random effects. Only the Tatoeba corpus appears to have a significant positive impact on metrics. In other words, we might expect that pre-training

---

[4]Thus, a team participating in all five tracks would yield $5 \times 500 = 2,500$ data points for this regression analysis.

	Feature \ Team	jbrem	nickeilf	rakchada	jspak3	sweagraw	masahiro	mzy	dcu	jindra.helcl	darkside	nagoudi
Model Architecture & Training	Transformer	✓	✓	✓	✓	✓	✓	✓	✓	✓		
	CNN										✓	✓
	LRF Weights	✓	✓	✓		✓					✓	
	Pre-train→Fine-tune	✓	✓	✓	✓	✓	✓	✓	✓			
	Train Combined									✓		✓
Decoding & Filtering	Diverse Beam Search		✓		✓			✓				
	Beam Reranking				✓	✓		✓				
	Beam Filtering	✓		✓		✓				✓	✓	
	Paraphrasing		✓						✓	✓		
	Ensembling	✓	✓				✓		✓			✓
	Backtranslation			✓						✓		✓

Table 5: Table of features used by team. Descriptions of features can be found in §4.2 and §4.3.

with Tatoeba would add $+.214$ to prompt-specific F1 scores ($p = .088$), all else being equal. Since Tatoeba is a collaborative online database[5] of sentences geared towards foreign language learners (some of which even have multiple translations, although no weights), it is extremely similar to the STAPLE task domain. Thus it makes sense that this corpus would be helpful; in fact, **sweagraw** and **jindra.helcl** included it alongside the STAPLE data in fine-tuning their models.

Other effects are smaller and statistically insignificant, suggesting that the particular choice of supplementary out-of-domain data may not matter as much as simply using a large amount. One notable exception is the parallel Wikipedia corpus (Wołk and Marasek, 2014), which exhibits a large negative trend on recall and F1, possibly due to its noisy, automatically-aligned provenance.

The volume of parallel training data may also impact performance. For example, for the Korean track **jbrem** report internal results using similar datasets to **sweagraw**, and achieving the same score. But further experiments extending the training set yielded improvements of about $+.1$ F1. However, simply using larger corpora in pre-training does not guarantee higher scores: **nagoudi** apparently trained on all of OPUS, yet had the lowest Portuguese scores among participants.

4.2 Model Architecture & Training

Decisions made on model architecture and training procedures seemed to have more impact on final system performance. We mapped many of these design decisions into high-level system features, summarized at the top of Table 5.

[5] https://tatoeba.org

***Transformer* vs. *CNN*.** The **baseline_fairseq** we provided is based on a convolutional neural network (CNN) architecture, and a few teams also went this route. However, top-ranking teams largely opted for a Transformer-based architecture (Vaswani et al., 2017) instead. **jspak3** notably used the BART architecture (Lewis et al., 2019) to pre-train a decoder in particular, and **dcu** also compared a phrase-based statistical MT approach (Koehn et al., 2007) to a Transformer-based neural MT system, with the latter performing better.

***LRF Weights*.** When training on STAPLE task data, teams had to decide how to convert the one-to-many relationship of prompts and accepted translations into standard bitext for more conventional MT training. Some teams simply repeated the English prompt for each target translation (as we did for **baseline_fairseq**), while others used only the highest-weighted translation. Some of the more successful teams took advantage of the weights associated with each accepted translation. In particular, **jbrem** included multiple copies of the highest-weighted translation, **nickeilf** used only the top k, and **sweagraw** and **rakchada** both sampled each translation in proportion to its weight.

***Pre-train→Fine-tune* vs. *Train Combined*.** Top-performing teams also tended to pre-train a generic MT model (e.g., trained on corpora from §4.1) and fine-tune it using STAPLE task data. This is opposed to pooling all data together for joint training. The latter approach certainly outperformed STAPLE-only baselines, but lagged behind fine-tuned pipeline approaches in most cases.

To measure the impact of these choices, we conducted a second mixed-effects regression analysis, coding each team with the model architecture and

Model effects	Precision		W. Recall		W. F1	
(Intercept)	.351	***	.232	**	.221	**
Transformer	+.107		+.098	.	+.107	.
LRF Weights	+.097	*	+.060	*	+.075	*
Pre-train→Fine-tune	+.050		+.080		+.065	
Random effects	**St.Dev.**		**St.Dev.**		**St.Dev.**	
Prompt ID	±.183		±.210		±.173	
Track ID	±.085		+.105		+.102	
Team ID	±.070		±.049		±.044	

Table 6: Mixed-effects analysis of various model architecture and training procedure choices.

training decisions that describe their final submissions. Results are presented in Table 6. Here we see empirical confirmation that Transformer-based systems tended to perform +.1 points better for all three metrics, although only marginally statistically significant (perhaps because it was also the most common choice).

Incorporating LRF weights in the fine-tuning strategy also appears to have a robust positive effect ($p < .05$ across all metrics). The importance of the weighting strategy can be further illustrated by comparing **jbrem** with **jindra.helcl**. Both systems submitted to all five tracks, and otherwise used similar approaches. However, **jbrem** reports on an ablation experiment using only the top-weighted translation, the results of which are similar to those of **jindra.helcl**, who used this very strategy.

Finally, there is also a positive trend favoring pre-training on external corpora before fine-tuning, as opposed to training on all data combined.

4.3 Decoding & Filtering

Since the STAPLE task requires multiple translations for each input prompt, all teams generated n-best lists, and employed various strategies for pruning them to contain only desirable translations. The feature group at the bottom of Table 5 represent these decoding and filtering steps.

Diverse Beam Search. Multiple teams attempted to use diverse beam search (Vijayakumar et al., 2016) to generate a more varied set of translation candidates. However, it proved either to be only marginally helpful (**nickeilf, mzy**) or unhelpful (**jspak3**) in various ablation experiments.

Beam Reranking. Two teams tried training an auxiliary model to rank output candidates by predicted learner response frequencies. In both cases, this approach performed poorly.

Beam Filtering. Several teams attempted to filter candidate translations, which were applied to candidate translations to decide if they should be removed from final predictions. Approaches to this varied significantly, from language-model probabilities (**jbrem**) to binary classifiers including gradient-boosted decision trees (**rakchada**), feed-forward neural networks (**sweagraw**), and multilingual transformers (**jindra.helcl**). **nickeilf** showed improvements using consensus voting among an ensemble of MT models, in which only sentences attested by multiple subsystems are retained. Most of these teams reported significant gains from filtering in ablation studies.

Paraphrasing. Three teams implemented monolingual paraphrasing models to increase the size of their n-best list of candidates. **jindra.helcl** reported experiments with a Levenshtein Transformer (Gu et al., 2019), a model that learns to create new paraphrases by editing candidate sentences. However, this produced output too noisy to be useful, and was omitted from their final submission.

Ensembling. A number of teams employed an ensemble of MT models, by combining either different training checkpoints, random initialization seeds, or other training regimes (such as training on reversed sequences, which was the main strategy used by **masahiro**, who tied for second in the Japanese track). Three teams also tried ***Backtranslation*** (Sennrich et al., 2016), with mixed results.

We conducted a mixed-effects analysis of decoding and filtering techniques, however, the effect sizes and p-values were much less significant than those from §4.1 and §4.2. These inconclusive results suggest that decoding and filtering play a smaller role in overall system performance than pre-training and model architecture decisions.

4.4 Scoring the Top-k Test Translations

The learner response frequency weights tend to have a tall head: a few common responses carry most of the weight, and many more responses carry much less weight (e.g., many human-curated accepted translations were not ever attested by learners during our data collection window). Since this distribution determines weighted recall, and therefore our overall evaluation metric, it is instructive to compare against a benchmark "oracle" that is able to return the top-k gold translations. Table 7 shows results of such an oracle for several values of k evaluated over the test set.

	Hun.	Jap.	Kor.	Por.	Vie.
$k = *$	1.0	<u>1.0</u>	<u>1.0</u>	1.0	1.0
$k = 10$	.735	.302	.350	.655	.789
$k = 5$	<u>.643</u>	.231	.266	<u>.578</u>	<u>.692</u>
$k = 1$	.372	.090	.101	.340	.387
jbrem	.555	.318	.404	.552	.558
sweagraw	.469	.294	.255	.525	539
jindra.helcl	.435	.213	.206	.412	.377
baseline_aws	.281	.043	.041	.213	.198

Table 7: Weighted F1 scores on the test set for an "oracle" that outputs the top k translations from gold data. All translations ($k = *$) gives a perfect score of 1.0. For comparison, we include teams who submitted to all tracks, and one baseline. <u>Underscores</u> show the smallest value of k to outperform **jbrem** (the top system).

At $k = 1$, macro weighted F1 is still relatively low, showing that systems need to return more than a single translation to do well. Comparing $k = 1$ to **baseline_aws** (both output a single translation) shows that this high-quality baseline still does not generally produce the translation favored by Duolingo learners. It is also worth noting that top-ranking systems output the $k = 1$ translation more often than that of **baseline_aws** (83% vs. 69%).

The top-ranking teams performed on par with or better than the $k = 5$ oracle, and much better for languages with a higher translation-to-prompt ratio (see Table 2). This suggests that high-performing models for this task are consistently producing output comparable to the five most commonly-attested translations, and often beyond (at some expense to precision, for which the oracle is perfect).

4.5 Error Analysis

So far we have discussed only quantitative outcomes for the STAPLE task. Here we present a qualitative analysis by inspecting the most common **recall errors** and **precision errors** among participating systems. These help us to get a sense for how important typical errors are for our educational use case, and shed light on what performance gaps need to be closed in future work.

Alternative word order or synonym variations were a challenge for all teams in all tracks. For example, here are the top four accepted translations for a prompt in the Portuguese test dataset:

1. *please don't smoke*
   por favor, não fume ($w_1 = .663$)
   não fume, **por favor** ($w_2 = .030$)
   por gentileza, não solte fumaça ($w_3 = .011$)
   não fume, **se faz favor** ($w_4 = .011$)

Most teams produced the top-weighted translation, several more identified other variants of *please*, but few systems generated reorderings that place it after the main clause (which, for this instance, accounts for $\approx .184$ of the total LRF weight). This can be partially explained by the use of fixed beam sizes. Since the number of translations grows exponentially with the number of lexical and structural variations, many correct combinations that the system could be capable of generating may still fall off the beam. One possible solution here would be to explore lattice-based decoding strategies that may avoid such bottlenecks.

Korean, Japanese, and Vietnamese have diverse sets of pronouns for use with different registers and relationships to the subject and the listener, as seen in this example from Japanese:

2. *i exercise*
   私は運動する (top translation)
   僕は運動する (not in accepted translations)

Here 私 (watashi) is the most common first person pronoun, but about half the submissions instead produced 僕 (boku) which carries with it more youthful or masculine connotations. While the latter is arguably correct, learners (especially beginners) are unlikely to use it, and it was also missing from the human-curated set of translations.

Pronouns were difficult in general, for multiple language tracks. All five languages allow some level of pronoun-dropping, as per these examples from Hungarian and Portuguese:

3. *we run to the garden*
   [mi] futunk a kertbe

4. *would **you** like to try on those shoes?*
   [você] gostaria de provar esses sapatos?

This resulted in both over- and under-use of pronouns, both in system outputs and occasionally gold data. While both variations (with or without the pronoun) may be correct, the rules governing which is more fluent or more appropriate for instruction are subtle, and remain challenging.

Systems often produced verb suffixes that convey discourse nuances or speaker attitudes not necessarily present in the English prompt or its accepted translations, as per these Korean and Japanese translations generated by multiple teams:

5. *the woman is pretty*
   그 여자는 예쁘네요
   ("**wow**, that woman is pretty")

6. *you are not a victim*
   あなたは被害者ではないよ
   ("you are not a victim, **you know**")

One likely explanation for this is the pervasive use of OpenSubtitles data in pre-training; such suffixes are especially common in on-screen dialogue.

Mistranslation of numbers was a common problem for multiple languages, which is unacceptable for education, or indeed most applications:

7. *i have **eighteen** horses*
   tizenhárom lovam van
   ("i have **thirteen** horses")

8. *she has **sixteen** cats*
   彼女は猫を六匹飼っています
   ("she has **six** cats")

Correct noun declension was also a struggle for all systems, particularly the allative case in Hungarian (-hoz/-hez/-höz); the following example was not produced by any system:

9. *we run **to the** garden*
   elrohanunk a kert**hez**

Similarly, noun cases and postpositions in Korean led some systems to alter the sentence meaning:

10. *who do **you love**?*
    누가 너를 사랑하니
    ("who **loves you**?")

For Japanese, many systems frequently used English loanwords in their translations:

11. *she makes me **happy***
    彼女は私をハッピーにしてくれる
    (uses phonetic English loan for **happy**)

These were generally missing from the gold data. Such loanwords are not especially rare, although one could also argue that using them is "cheating" in a language-learning context!

5   Related Work

The STAPLE task is similar to *machine translation* in that one takes input from one language, and produces output in another language. In fact, nearly all of the models used by participating teams were built using standard, off-the-shelf, modern machine translation software. But machine translation systems typically produce only a single output.

Ultimately our goal for Duolingo—a robust system for automatically grading learner translation submissions—is closer to the world of *machine translation evaluation*. Motivated by shortcomings of the BLEU metric (Papineni et al., 2002), some researchers have proposed alternative measures of evaluating MT systems against many references (Qin and Specia, 2015), or even exhaustive translation sets collected by human translators, as with HyTER (Dreyer and Marcu, 2012).

We even considered using these alternatives as official metrics for the STAPLE task. The main challenge is the difficulty of gathering *all* possible translations (the authors of HyTER estimate that creating all translation variants for a single sentence can take two hours or more), or the assumption that the translations are all equally important. To ease the burden of manually collecting references, there have been proposals for automatically generating them (Apidianaki et al., 2018) using paraphrase databases such as PPDB (Pavlick et al., 2015).

This brings us to other areas of research that are very related to our task: automatic *paraphrasing* (Wieting et al., 2015; Witteveen and Andrews, 2019), as well as research in diverse beam search methods (Vijayakumar et al., 2016; Li et al., 2016) for decoding multiple natural language outputs. We are happy that this shared task can serve as a forum for studying the intersection of these problems, and it is our hope that the STAPLE task data will continue to foster research in all of these areas.

6   Conclusion and Future Work

We have presented the STAPLE task, described a new and unique corpus for studying it, and reported on the results of a shared task challenge designed to explore this new domain. The task successfully drew participation from dozens of research teams from all over the world, synthesizing work in machine translation, MT evaluation, and automatic paraphrasing to name a few.

We learned that a pipeline of strong machine translation followed by fine-tuning on learner-weighted STAPLE data produces strong results. While the data for this task are geared toward language learners (and are therefore simpler than more commonly-studied domains such as newswire), it is our hope that the STAPLE task provides a blueprint for ongoing interdisciplinary work in this vein. All task data, including dev and test labels, will remain available at: https://doi.org/10.7910/DVN/380JR6

Acknowledgements

The authors would like to thank Colin Cherry for seeding the idea that ultimately became the STAPLE task. Thanks also to the organizers of the Workshop on Neural Generation and Translation (WNGT) for providing a forum for this work, as well as all the participating teams. Special thanks to Nathan Dalal and Andrew Runge for help reviewing and summarizing the system papers.

References

Sweta Agrawal and Marine Carpuat. 2020. Generating diverse translations via weighted fine-tuning and hypotheses filtering for the Duolingo STAPLE task. In *Proceedings of the ACL Workshop on Neural Generation and Translation (WNGT)*. ACL.

Marianna Apidianaki, Guillaume Wisniewski, Anne Cocos, and Chris Callison-Burch. 2018. Automated paraphrase lattice creation for HyTER machine translation evaluation. In *Proceedings of the 2018 Conference of the North American Chapter of the Association for Computational Linguistics: Human Language Technologies, Volume 2 (Short Papers)*, pages 480–485, New Orleans, Louisiana. Association for Computational Linguistics.

R.H. Baayen. 2008. *Analyzing Linguistic Data: A Practical Introduction to Statistics using R*. Cambridge University Press.

Samuel R Bowman, Luke Vilnis, Oriol Vinyals, Andrew M Dai, Rafal Jozefowicz, and Samy Bengio. 2015. Generating sentences from a continuous space. *arXiv preprint arXiv:1511.06349*.

Rakesh Chada. 2020. Simultaneous paraphrasing and translation by fine-tuning transformer models. In *Proceedings of the ACL Workshop on Neural Generation and Translation (WNGT)*. ACL.

Markus Dreyer and Daniel Marcu. 2012. HyTER: Meaning-equivalent semantics for translation evaluation. In *Proceedings of the 2012 Conference of the North American Chapter of the Association for Computational Linguistics: Human Language Technologies*, pages 162–171, Montréal, Canada. Association for Computational Linguistics.

Jiatao Gu, Changhan Wang, and Junbo Zhao. 2019. Levenshtein transformer. In *Advances in Neural Information Processing Systems*, pages 11179–11189.

Rejwanul Haque, Yasmin Moslem, and Andy Way. 2020. The ADAPT system description for the STAPLE 2020 English-to-Portuguese translation task. In *Proceedings of the ACL Workshop on Neural Generation and Translation (WNGT)*. ACL.

Masahiro Kaneko, Aizhan Imankulova, Tosho Hirasawa, and Mamoru Komachi. 2020. English-to-Japanese diverse translation by combining forward and backward outputs. In *Proceedings of the ACL Workshop on Neural Generation and Translation (WNGT)*. ACL.

Huda Khayrallah, Jacob Bremerman, Arya D. McCarthy, Kenton Murray, Winston Wu, and Matt Post. 2020. The JHU submission to the 2020 Duolingo shared task on simultaneous translation and paraphrase for language education. In *Proceedings of the ACL Workshop on Neural Generation and Translation (WNGT)*. ACL.

Philipp Koehn, Hieu Hoang, Alexandra Birch, Chris Callison-Burch, Marcello Federico, Nicola Bertoldi, Brooke Cowan, Wade Shen, Christine Moran, Richard Zens, Chris Dyer, Ondřej Bojar, Alexandra Constantin, and Evan Herbst. 2007. Moses: Open source toolkit for statistical machine translation. In *Proceedings of the 45th Annual Meeting of the Association for Computational Linguistics Companion Volume Proceedings of the Demo and Poster Sessions*, pages 177–180, Prague, Czech Republic. Association for Computational Linguistics.

Mike Lewis, Yinhan Liu, Naman Goyal, Marjan Ghazvininejad, Abdelrahman Mohamed, Omer Levy, Ves Stoyanov, and Luke Zettlemoyer. 2019. Bart: Denoising sequence-to-sequence pre-training for natural language generation, translation, and comprehension. *arXiv preprint arXiv:1910.13461*.

Jiwei Li, Will Monroe, and Dan Jurafsky. 2016. A simple, fast diverse decoding algorithm for neural generation. *arXiv preprint arXiv:1611.08562*.

Zhenhao Li, Marina Fomicheva, and Lucia Specia. 2020. Exploring model consensus to generate translation paraphrases. In *Proceedings of the ACL Workshop on Neural Generation and Translation (WNGT)*. ACL.

Jindřich Libovický, Zdeněk Kasner, Jindřich Helcl, and Ondřej Dušek. 2020. Expand and filter: CUNI and LMU systems for the WNGT 2020 Duolingo shared task. In *Proceedings of the ACL Workshop on Neural Generation and Translation (WNGT)*. ACL.

El Moatez Billah Nagoudi, Muhammad AbdulMageed, and Hasan Cavusoglu. 2020. Growing together: Modeling human language learning with n-best multi-checkpoint machine translation. In *Proceedings of the ACL Workshop on Neural Generation and Translation (WNGT)*. ACL.

Tadashi Nomoto. 2020. Meeting the 2020 Duolingo challenge on a shoestring. In *Proceedings of the ACL Workshop on Neural Generation and Translation (WNGT)*. ACL.

Myle Ott, Sergey Edunov, Alexei Baevski, Angela Fan, Sam Gross, Nathan Ng, David Grangier, and

Michael Auli. 2019. fairseq: A fast, extensible toolkit for sequence modeling. *arXiv preprint arXiv:1904.01038.*

Sebastian Padó. 2006. *User's guide to* sigf: *Significance testing by approximate randomisation.*

Kishore Papineni, Salim Roukos, Todd Ward, and Wei-Jing Zhu. 2002. Bleu: a method for automatic evaluation of machine translation. In *Proceedings of the 40th Annual Meeting of the Association for Computational Linguistics*, pages 311–318, Philadelphia, Pennsylvania, USA. Association for Computational Linguistics.

Junsu Park, Hongseok Kwon, and Jong-Hyeok Lee. 2020. POSTECH submission on Duolingo shared task. In *Proceedings of the ACL Workshop on Neural Generation and Translation (WNGT)*. ACL.

Ellie Pavlick, Pushpendre Rastogi, Juri Ganitkevitch, Benjamin Van Durme, and Chris Callison-Burch. 2015. PPDB 2.0: Better paraphrase ranking, fine-grained entailment relations, word embeddings, and style classification. In *Proceedings of the 53rd Annual Meeting of the Association for Computational Linguistics and the 7th International Joint Conference on Natural Language Processing (Volume 2: Short Papers)*, pages 425–430, Beijing, China. Association for Computational Linguistics.

Ying Qin and Lucia Specia. 2015. Truly exploring multiple references for machine translation evaluation. In *Proceedings of the 18th Annual Conference of the European Association for Machine Translation*, pages 113–120, Antalya, Turkey.

Rico Sennrich, Barry Haddow, and Alexandra Birch. 2016. Improving neural machine translation models with monolingual data. In *Proceedings of the 54th Annual Meeting of the Association for Computational Linguistics (Volume 1: Long Papers)*, pages 86–96, Berlin, Germany. Association for Computational Linguistics.

Jörg Tiedemann. 2012. Parallel data, tools and interfaces in opus. In *Proceedings of the Eight International Conference on Language Resources and Evaluation (LREC'12)*, Istanbul, Turkey. European Language Resources Association (ELRA).

Ashish Vaswani, Noam Shazeer, Niki Parmar, Jakob Uszkoreit, Llion Jones, Aidan N Gomez, Łukasz Kaiser, and Illia Polosukhin. 2017. Attention is all you need. In *Advances in neural information processing systems*, pages 5998–6008.

Ashwin K Vijayakumar, Michael Cogswell, Ramprasath R Selvaraju, Qing Sun, Stefan Lee, David Crandall, and Dhruv Batra. 2016. Diverse beam search: Decoding diverse solutions from neural sequence models. *arXiv preprint arXiv:1610.02424.*

John Wieting, Mohit Bansal, Kevin Gimpel, and Karen Livescu. 2015. Towards universal paraphrastic sentence embeddings. *CoRR*, abs/1511.08198.

Sam Witteveen and Martin Andrews. 2019. Paraphrasing with large language models. In *Proceedings of the 3rd Workshop on Neural Generation and Translation*, pages 215–220, Hong Kong. Association for Computational Linguistics.

Krzysztof Wołk and Krzysztof Marasek. 2014. Building subject-aligned comparable corpora and mining it for truly parallel sentence pairs. *Procedia Technology*, 18:126–132.

Michael Yang, Yixin Liu, and Rahul Mayuranath. 2020. Multi-step fine-tuning and encouraging diversity of high-coverage neural machine translation. In *Proceedings of the ACL Workshop on Neural Generation and Translation (WNGT)*. ACL.

Author Index